EUROPEAN MAGIC

READINGS IN MEDIEVAL CIVILIZATIONS AND CULTURES: XX
series editor: Paul Edward Dutton

EUROPEAN MAGIC AND WITCHCRAFT

A READER

edited by

MARTHA RAMPTON

UNIVERSITY OF TORONTO PRESS

Higher Education Division

utorontopress.com

LIBRARY AND ARCHIVES CANADA CATALOGUING IN PUBLICATION

European magic and witchcraft: a reader / edited by
Martha Rampton.

(Readings in medieval civilizations and cultures ; 20)
Includes bibliographical references and index.
Issued in print and electronic formats.

ISBN 978-1-4426-3420-6 (softcover).—ISBN 978-1-4426-3421-3
(hardcover).—ISBN 978-1-4426-3422-0 (EPUB).—ISBN 978-1-4426-3423-7 (PDF)

    1. Witchcraft—Europe—History—Sources. 2. Magic—Europe—
History—Sources. I. Rampton, Martha, 1952–, editor II. Series: Readings
in medieval civilizations and cultures ; 20

BF1584.E9E97 2018   133.4'3094   C2017-905336-1
                                                   C2017-905337-X

We welcome comments and suggestions regarding any aspect of our publications—please feel free to contact us at news@utphighereducation.com or visit our Internet site at utorontopress.com.

North America   UK, Ireland, and continental Europe
5201 Dufferin Street   NBN International
North York, Ontario, Canada, M3H 5T8   Estover Road, Plymouth, PL6 7PY, UK
                                           ORDERS PHONE: 44 (0) 1752 202301
2250 Military Road   ORDERS FAX: 44 (0) 1752 202333
Tonawanda, New York, USA, 14150   ORDERS E-MAIL: enquiries@nbninternational.com

ORDERS PHONE: 1-800-565-9523
ORDERS FAX: 1-800-221-9985
ORDERS E-MAIL: utpbooks@utpress.utoronto.ca

Every effort has been made to contact copyright holders; in the event of an error or omission, please notify the publisher.

The University of Toronto Press acknowledges the financial support for its publishing activities of the Government of Canada through the Canada Book Fund.

Printed in Canada

In memory of my parents
Byron Ray and Ruth Halliday Rampton

CONTENTS

ACKNOWLEDGEMENTS

A few years ago, Paul Dutton approached me at the International Congress on Medieval Studies in Kalamazoo, Michigan, and asked if I would like to produce an anthology on magic and witchcraft for the Readings in Medieval Civilizations and Cultures series. I was delighted and enthused. I said, "of course," but the project would have gone no further had it not been for Paul's unflagging encouragement and support, prodding, and patience. I wish to thank Paul for believing in me, reading the manuscript, sharing critical insights, and for his guidance through the process of producing *European Magic and Witchcraft*. I am also grateful to my students and colleagues who have, for years, joined me in conversation or read my papers on, medieval magic. My special thanks to Thomas F.X. Noble, Lynda Coon, Valerie Garver, Matthew Gillis, H.C. Erik Midelfort, Patrick Geary, and my husband, Steve Smith.

In a project such as this that depends on arcane texts and out-of-copyright editions, I cannot say enough about the service rendered by Virginia Adams of the Tran Library at Pacific University. She has been infinitely resourceful, pleasant, efficient, and patient as she ferreted out magic hidden in libraries across the world. The more obscure the book, the more pleasure she seemed to take in finding it. Thanks are also owed to the administrative assistants of the School of Social Sciences at Pacific University, and to Alina Button who served as my research assistant for a semester. Working with Natalie Fingerhut at the University of Toronto Press has been a delight. I am grateful to her and the production team for their professionalism, indulgence, and good counsel.

PREFACE

Those who have picked up this book are about to fly through a mirror, back through time, and look down upon an unfamiliar terrain. They will meet people who astound them, who understand cause and effect differently, and who inhabit a world animated by mysterious beings and creatures of all kinds, many of them invisible to the human eye. Reading *European Magic and Witchcraft* is best experienced by approaching these strangers with tolerance, charity, and imagination. It is always easy, even satisfying, to judge as "weird," "mad," and "cruel" that which is at odds with modern thought, and this is particularly tempting when dealing with a study of magic and witches. In the end, however, such assessments do not achieve that even more satisfying result of establishing empathetic relationships with people of the past. Those who populate this book are not unlike us in their desire to be safe, to see justice done, and to make sense of their existence.

There are a few managerial decisions that shape this book. First, the introduction to each reading is minimal, providing just enough information to establish context. That decision is pedagogical and intended to mute my editorial voice and give students the opportunity to hear the echoes of the past in primary documents (albeit through translations). I would rather readers discover the opinions of their medieval counterparts than my own. I would rather readers have the chance to understand the individuals whose lives they are, in a sense, sharing, however briefly, than to understand my interpretation of those lives. In this way, readers are less like voyeurs and more like witnesses: delighting in the ecstasy of the magician who masters cosmic forces within his magic circle, sharing the exasperation of a pastor who is unable to convince his parishioners that they ought not take their sick children to wise-women, suffering the indignities of a prisoner whose naked, shaved body is searched for the Devil's mark, and even grasping the logic of a magistrate who passes down death sentences on convicted witches.

A second guiding principle is that the selections are presented chronologically. Classifying the past by dividing it into eras is both a frustration and a blessing. Historical epochs come into being only after they have ended; people living at any given time rarely identify themselves as "medieval," "early modern," and so forth. History shows little respect for categories, yet without some principle of separation, we would not be able to talk about change over time. Despite its subjectivity, chopping the past up into bite-size pieces has some advantages, and that is what I have done. Each chapter begins with a short introduction to the historical period that places the readings in context.

I juxtapose materials from a variety of genres so that the reader sees the conflicting, complementary, and multifarious mélange of magical ideas that existed at any given time and comes to appreciate that the borders between one type of magic and another were unstable. The best chance we have of comprehending magic and witchcraft is to line up as many sources as possible and weave them together, letting the more vocal texts fill in the gaps created by the laconic ones. In this way, readers can see that thinking on magic was not monolithic; authors analyzed practices in different ways and did not use terms or embrace concepts with consistency. A church or secular body of authority might label a new practice "forbidden" and append it to the corpus of existing proscriptions without particular concern for standardization, redundancy, or contradiction.

There is no straight trajectory from primitive folkloric conjuring to the juridical burning of witches, but there are general trends in the story of magic and witchcraft. In each period the legal and the literary, the playful and the polemic exist side-by-side, and often each delivers quite a different take on the magic of the time. At the height of the witch trials in the seventeenth century, Shakespeare could stage a delightful play about fairies and hobgoblins, shape-shifting and magic spells, while outside the playhouse convicted witches were being hanged for similar conduct.

From reading to reading, I have tried to retain the tone of the original prose. That has not always been possible with material that was translated, in some cases, centuries ago; however, I have selected versions that feel true to the sources. Court cases retain a notarial format, treatises are polished, and poems are rhythmical. Some terminology is anachronistic. For example, the word "witch" is not, strictly speaking, an early-medieval concept, but the explication of nuances of that and other terms would take us far from the goal of the book. The distortion is slight. It has often been necessary to modernize syntax and word choice, but driven by my desire to make the readers' sojourn into the past as authentic as possible, I have kept such changes to a minimum.

European Magic and Witchcraft incorporates material from the ancient Hebrews to Renaissance humanists, from the erudition of the learned to peasants' gossip. Because medieval and early modern magic evolved from several historical and cultural milieus, I have included selections that draw on pre-Christian, Norse, Celtic, and Anglo-Saxon materials that portray pagan societies, albeit recorded by Christian clerics. I grant that beliefs about magic were transmitted overwhelmingly from the pens of the elite, but it is possible at least to glimpse the worldview of those who did not write; these texts describe, proscribe, or prescribe beliefs and behaviors of people across the social strata.

The scope of *European Magic and Witchcraft* is not haphazard; if it were, there are many additional quirky texts I would love to have included. Rather, this volume traces the evolution of European magic from its cradle in classical works and biblical motifs. Chapter One integrates select pagan and Hebrew texts with readings from the early Christian era that are foundational for grasping the development of the Christian understanding of magic as "trafficking with demons." A wide variety of types of material is represented here: running the gamut from ecclesiastical, to polemical, to pastoral, to Romance, to medical, to comical. I have gathered together a critical mass of evidence, without claiming that all of it contributed equally to contemporary perceptions of magic. Some sources were well known in their time, some not, but the viewpoint in any given text provides a piece of the puzzle, even if a particular work was not widely distributed. When discussing, for example, Justin Martyr's apologetic letters, a lead tablet found in a cemetery, and Marie de France's Celtic tales in the same voice, I am not confusing "real" practices (inasmuch as we can know what is real from any text) with literary imagination; rather, I am looking for cultural conceptions of magic and witchcraft that are manifest in the written record, fictional or otherwise.

I draw attention to particular themes that persist all the way from the pages of the Hebrew Bible to court records of the early modern witch trials so that the reader can watch them build and change: sometimes ever so slightly, and sometimes quite radically. Some motifs are stubborn in the extreme; some transmute nimbly over time. Particular readings have been selected that demonstrate the persistence of, for example, the association of women with the moon and night sky (the domain of Diana, who was first a goddess, later a demon); consternation over astrology; dependence on love magic; the phenomenon of the werewolf; and the piercing admonition from Exodus 22:18, "You shall not suffer a witch to live." In the end, the continuity is more striking than the change.

I leave the reader with a request, and it is the same plea with which I have begun my course on the history of magic and witchcraft for over twenty years. In this new world you are about to enter, try to sympathize with the people you meet, and if that is too hard, try to understand them—all of them, practitioners and persecutors, true believers and charlatans, the self-professed and the innocent. And examine as closely as you can the ideas that animated their lives.

CHAPTER ONE

LATE CLASSICAL AND EARLY
CHRISTIAN ARCHETYPES

Figure 1.1 Tales of the deeds of the desert father, Saint Antony (c. 251−356), became iconic in discussions of magic from Antony's own time throughout the period of the witch-hunts. Pictured here is *The Temptation of Saint Anthony* (1470s), an engraving by the German printmaker Martin Schongauer (c. 1448−1491). It draws from chapters 9 and 65 of Anthanasius's (c. 296−373) *Life of Anthony*, depicting the saint, assailed by demons but able to maintain his contemplative detachment. The pig staff and bound girdle book hanging from his belt are indicators of Antony's persona.

The archaic Greeks coined the word *mageia* to denote the ancient craft of the *magi* of the east (wise men and seers). Famous in Antiquity for divination, they read the stars and interpreted oracles from the natural world, such as numbers, the flight of birds, dreams, patterns in water, and the fall of lots. Because of the fame of the *magi*, the east was the hub of mystery and magic that conjured fantasies of Egypt, Chaldea, and wondrous lands beyond. In the ancient world, magic existed on a continuum with religion and was an amorphous constellation of undertakings that ranged from beneficial, to benign, to playful, to annoying, to dangerous. By the first century BCE, the term *mageia* had essentially become a term of abuse associated with impiety, pernicious curiosity, and possible criminality. Overtly harmful magic, or *maleficium*, was a matter of communal concern, not on religious or moral grounds but instead due to the threat it posed to public safety and common civility.

Theurgia came to replace *mageia* to denote mystical dealings with the gods. One of the central aspects of ancient pagan religions was divination. Although some classical writers criticized excesses in divinatory practice and drew a nebulous line between its legitimate and illicit uses, virtually no pagan rejected the possibility that the secrets of the gods, especially concerning the future, could be coaxed out of them if the proper procedures were followed. Humans could approach deity because of the interrelationship between the world and the sphere of translucent beings whose divine essence was diffused throughout the earthly plane. Late antique Neoplatonists distinguished common, vulgar sorcery from the sublime art of theurgy, the goal of which was to access divinity by transcending the profane. They disdained the crude use of cosmic "sympathy" to effect trivial and self-serving outcomes, like animating statues as though they were gods.

In the Christian writings of the first century, discussions of magic were embedded in the larger struggle to articulate the contours of the new faith and defend its theology. The effort to define and distinguish the infant religion compelled Christians to examine the entire fabric of pagan belief, and in that process demonology was a central focus. Pagan and Christian cosmologies were similar in that both consisted of a universe ordered in a continuous, pyramidal hierarchy arranged according to a "great chain of being." God was at the top and pure essence. Working down the chain, the beings that occupied each successive level were more corporeal than those on the rung above. After God were the angels and planets; then came the moon, which divided the upper and lower air. Demons (synonymous with "devils") were creatures of the lower air, and they were in no way supernatural but intrinsic to the inherent order of the universe. People, too, inhabited the realm of the lower air, but demons, having once been angels, had less physicality than human beings, which gave them powers of flight, invisibility, and myriad other capabilities that humans lacked. Magic amounted to traffic with these demons of the lower air.

Pagan competition and forms of opposition (although never unified) drove Christian discourse on magic and determined the shape that apologetics would take. One of the first and greatest concerns of the early church was idolatry; a second and related issue was the divinatory methods that pagans used to interact with what Christians held to be false gods and goddesses. Also, the nascent religion was assailed on all sides with charges of a variety of "misbehaviors" that compelled a response. Some of the most virulent of those indictments involved accusations of sorcery and magical "tricks." Pagan detractors cast Jesus' miracles as conjuring and cheap stunts—the kind any street magician could pull off. His revivification of Lazarus (John 11:43–44) was equated to the work of the most loathsome necromancers, a type well known in the ancient world. Apologists were obliged to counter these indictments, and in doing so they established the groundwork for the early Christian interpretation of many aspects of magic. Intellectuals drew from classical archetypes, the Hebrew Bible, and New Testament writings, to explain phenomena such as idols, omens, divination, false prophets, and female sorcery. Justin Martyr (c. 100–c. 165), advanced the position that worship of pagan deities constituted traffic with demons. He elucidated the kinds of deceits of which demons were capable in their ceaseless mission to ensnare humankind, and the scenario he developed came to be the standard Christian explanation of the true nature of pagan deities.

Whereas idolatry, divination, *maleficium*, and magical trickery demanded the attention of the pre-Constantinian church, once the religion was legalized in 313, the energy of ecclesiastics effectively shifted to organizational matters and core questions of Christology. In the doctrinal conflicts of the fourth and fifth centuries, magic and demonology were rarely addressed, not because Christian thinkers had reached consensus on magic; quite the opposite is true. Since magic was not a major interest during the era of the ecumenical councils, Christian positions on it were diverse, idiosyncratic, and largely unexamined by larger juridical church bodies. Justin Martyr's explanation of the pagan gods as fallen angels was unchallenged, but on other aspects of magic, opinions varied widely. There was little agreement, for example, on the efficacy of astrology or the ability of humans to shape-shift or copulate with demons in the form of *succubae* and *incubi*. Myriad methods of fortune-telling existed in the ancient world, and Christians held some of them to be genuine. The "craft" of bringing people back from the dead was highly controversial, given its role in the Old Testament episode of the raising of Samuel, the Gospels, and a multitude of saints' biographies.

Augustine (354–430) began the process of forging consensus (albeit a loose and fragile one) out of this confusion and ambiguity, at least for the learned and in the west. In his *City of God* and *On Christian Doctrine* he addressed questions of magic at length. The guiding principle behind Augustine's approach was that most of the putative powers of the fallen angels were fraudulent. He sought

4

always to preserve the omnipotence of God and argued that demons' seeming abilities to contravene natural law were delusionary. Demons could not really raise the dead, change shape, or know the future. That does not mean to say that magic—traffic with demons—did not trouble Augustine. Humans who sought the help of demons were no less culpable because demons were fakes; attempting to use demonic services constituted idolatry.

As imperial governmental policy came more and more to favor Christian interests in the 390s under the emperorship of Theodosius I (347–395), a major drive of the church was to tailor converts' daily behaviors and viewpoints to the new religion, focusing on the quotidian "superstitious" practices of Christians. As the project of proselytization unfolded, it became evident that there were layers upon layers of magical practices that would have to be peeled away: *maleficium*, divination, innumerable rites in honor of false deities, raising storms, spells manipulating love or birth, shape-shifting, and necromancy. Behaviors that seemed too similar to pagan forms of religion such as worship in the outdoors, dancing, singing, and juggling were also suspect. Even basic states of mind or internal dispositions of the soul, such as curiosity, pride, or covetousness, created fertile ground in which demonic magic might germinate.

Christianity grew from the soil of pagan thought; it was a product of the rich traditions of the Greco-Roman world. Yet, even though the church used the raw materials of pagan culture in forming religious practices, it consciously altered the signification of familiar objects and rites so as to inculcate new patterns of meaning through them. For example, Athanasius, bishop of Alexandria, recognized that the formalistic use of names could be demonic in some circumstances, but he insisted that ritualistically using the name of Jesus dispelled demons.

Throughout the late antique period, magic was gendered, although the division by gender was in no way absolute. Women were more inclined to personal, domestic sorcery and men to public magic. Rituals involving dramatic displays of thaumaturgy, spectacular public revivifications, and scholarly astrological prognostications were male activities. The earliest Christians understood female magic in the same way their pagan contemporaries did. Rituals of birth magic, healing, necromancy, frenzied forms of worship, and curious, nocturnal, clandestine activities were female proclivities. The craft of love magic was one of the most potent weapons in the woman's arsenal against men. Its goals were either to excite or to frustrate love and sexual desire, and it was as dreaded as it was common. Greek and Roman writers delighted in portraying both human and divine females, like Diana, Circe, Hecate, and Medea, in the role of the mystifying, enigmatic *femme fatale* and indulging their fantasy that "the woman" is a being, powerful—even lethal—if uncontrolled, whose essence lies in her alluring, sexually seductive otherness. Women's magic had that whiff of sexuality that was inherent in all female undertakings in the ancient world—a whiff that was ever on the verge of dangerous pungency.

In short, magic featured large in early Christian efforts to understand and define the religion. Most of what the pagans identified as sorcerous was interpreted in the same way by the new religionists; however, Christians added an important new dimension to the classical lexicon of "the magical" by insisting that at all levels it was demonic and that any implicit or explicit trafficking with demons was sinful.

The readings in Chapter One provide the foundation for the understanding of magic and witchcraft from the Hebrew tradition and Roman antiquity, including personages, texts, events, and seminal explanations of demons. Although over the millennium and a half covered in this book there were significant changes in the conceptualization of and responses to magic and demons, the continuity over these centuries is striking and, in the end, more impressive than the change.

1. MOSES AND AARON CHALLENGE PHARAOH'S MAGICIANS

According to the Hebrew Bible, God sent Moses and his brother Aaron to Pharaoh to demand that he release the Israelites from bondage in Egypt. The brothers engaged in a contest of skills with Pharaoh's priests (magi), Jannes and Jambres, that cast the two Israelites as magicians in the Jewish and Greco-Roman traditions of the ancient world. This characterization was so prevalent that for centuries Christian apologists were obliged to explain why God allowed Aaron and Moses to use magic in order to best the magi. The dramatic incident of the brothers' competition with the "wizards" in Exodus became a leitmotif in later writings about magic and provided a model for saints' "sacred biographies" (vitae) in which holy men and women compete with pagan priests to demonstrate the dominance of their God.

Source: Douay-Rheims Bible (Baltimore: John Murphy Co., 1914), pp. 65–66.

Exodus

Chapter 7:8. And the Lord said to Moses and Aaron,

9. "When Pharaoh shall say to you, 'Show signs;' you shall say to Aaron 'Take your rod and cast it down before Pharaoh, and it shall be turned into a serpent.'"

10. So Moses and Aaron went in unto Pharaoh and did as the Lord had commanded. And Aaron took the rod before Pharaoh and his servants, and it was turned into a serpent.

11. And Pharaoh called the wise men and the magicians, and they also, by Egyptian enchantments and certain secrets, did in like manner.

12. And they every one cast down their rods, and they were turned into serpents, but Aaron's rod devoured their rods.

13. And Pharaoh's heart was hardened, and he did not hearken to them as the Lord had commanded.

14. And the Lord said to Moses, "Pharaoh's heart is hardened, he will not let the people go.

15. Go to him in the morning, behold he will go out to the waters and you shall stand to meet him on the bank of the river, and you shall take in your hand the rod that was turned into a serpent.

16. And you shall say to him, 'The Lord God of the Hebrews sent me to you, saying, 'Let my people go to sacrifice to me in the desert, and hitherto you would not hear.

17. Thus therefore says the Lord, in this you shall know that I am the Lord; behold I will strike with the rod that is in my hand the water of the river, and it shall be turned into blood.

18. And the fishes that are in the river shall die, and the waters shall be corrupted, and the Egyptians shall be afflicted when they drink the water of the river.'"

19. The Lord also said to Moses, "Say to Aaron, 'Take your rod and stretch forth your hand upon the waters of Egypt, and upon their rivers, and streams and pools, and all the ponds of waters, that they may be turned into blood, and let blood be in all the land of Egypt, both in vessels of wood and of stone.'"

20. And Moses and Aaron did as the Lord had commanded, and lifting up the rod, he struck the water of the river before Pharaoh and his servants, and it was turned into blood.

21. And the fishes that were in the river died, and the river corrupted, and the Egyptians could not drink the water of the river, and there was blood in all the land of Egypt.

22. And the magicians of the Egyptians, with their enchantments, did in like manner, and Pharaoh's heart was hardened; neither did he hear them, as the Lord had commanded.

23. And he turned himself away, and went into his house; neither did he set his heart to it this time also.

24. And all the Egyptians dug round about the river for water to drink; for they could not drink of the water of the river.

25. And seven days were fully ended, after that the Lord struck the river.

Chapter 8:1. And the Lord said to Moses, "Go in to Pharaoh, and you shall say to him, 'Thus says the Lord, Let my people go to sacrifice to me'".

2. But if you will not let them go, behold I will strike all your coasts with frogs.

3. And the river shall bring forth an abundance of frogs, which shall come up and enter into your house, and your bedchamber, and upon your bed, and into the houses of your servants, and to your people, and into your ovens, and into the remains of your meats.

4. And the frogs shall come in to you, and to your people, and to all your servants.'"

5. And the Lord said to Moses, "Say to Aaron, 'Stretch forth your hand upon the streams, and upon the rivers and the pools, and bring forth frogs upon the land of Egypt.'"

6. And Aaron stretched forth his hand upon the waters of Egypt, and the frogs came up and covered the land of Egypt.

7. And the magicians also, by their enchantments, did in like manner, and they brought forth frogs upon the land of Egypt.

8. But Pharaoh called Moses and Aaron, and said to them, "Pray you to the Lord to take away the frogs from me and from my people, and I will let the people go to sacrifice to the Lord."

9. And Moses said to Pharaoh, "Set me a time when I shall pray for you, and for your servants, and for your people that the frogs may be driven away from you and from your house, and from your servants, and from your people and may remain only in the river."

10. And he answered, "Tomorrow." Then Moses said, "I will do according to your word that you may know that there is none like to the Lord our God.

11. And the frogs shall depart from you, and from your house, and from your servants, and from your people and shall remain only in the river."

12. And Moses and Aaron went forth from Pharaoh, and Moses cried to the Lord for the promise that he had made to Pharaoh concerning the frogs.

13. And the Lord did according to the word of Moses, and the frogs died out of the houses, and out of the villages, and out of the fields.

14. And they gathered them together into immense heaps, and the land was corrupted.

15. And Pharaoh seeing that relief was given, hardened his own heart and did not hear them, as the Lord had commanded.

16. And the Lord said to Moses, "Say to Aaron, 'Stretch forth your rod, and strike the dust of the earth, and may there be sciniphs [maggots] in all the land of Egypt.'"

17. And they did so. And Aaron stretched forth his hand, holding the rod, and he struck the dust of the earth, and there came sciniphs on men and on beasts; all the dust of the earth was turned into sciniphs through all the land of Egypt.

18. And the magicians with their enchantments practiced in like manner to bring forth sciniphs, and they could not, and there were sciniphs as well on men as on beasts.

19. And the magicians said to Pharaoh, "This is the finger of God." And Pharaoh's heart was hardened, and he hearkened not unto them as the Lord had commanded.

Questions: Why did God harden Pharaoh's heart, causing him to ignore Moses' entities, thus bringing hardships on the Israelites? Are Aaron's abilities characterized as magical? Why are Pharaoh's magi able to imitate Aaron's first three miracles but not able "to bring forth sciniphs"? What problems might this passage cause Christians in their campaigns against paganisms and superstitions?

2. THE PYTHONESS BRINGS THE DEAD TO LIFE: THE WITCH OF ENDOR

The Hebrew Bible's First Book of Kings (also Samuel) recounts the narrative of Samuel, beloved seer and king of ancient Israel, and his appearance to Saul in ghostly form. Saul, who succeeded Samuel as king, needs counsel as to the best course of action to defeat the assembled armies of the Philistines. Although Saul had recently decreed that all magicians be driven from the land, he resorts to asking advice from a local medium. In this dramatic story, the word "pythoness" is often translated as "witch," but the term literally denotes a woman who practices necromancy, meaning that she invokes the dead to predict the future. Some texts use the term "ventriloquist" rather than "witch" or "pythoness" because the woman of Endor draws words forth from the lifeless mouth of an inert body.

Both Catholic and Protestant theologians referenced the story of the Pythoness of Endor as a model of the female necromancer. This biblical text raised doctrinal questions as to whether ordinary humans had the power to compel souls to leave the spirit world. Most supported the opinion that the specter was not actually the ghost of Samuel, but a demon that assumed his shape or an illusion the pythoness created. This position, however, did not exonerate the pythoness, or those who emulated her, from the crime and sin of attempting to traffic with demons.

Source: Douay-Rheims Bible (Baltimore: John Murphy Co., 1914), pp. 289–91.

1 Kings 28: The Philistines go out to war against Israel. Saul being forsaken by God, has recourse to a witch. Samuel appears to him.

3. Now Samuel was dead, and all Israel mourned for him, and buried him in Ramatha, his city. And Saul had put away all the magicians and soothsayers out of the land.

4. And the Philistines were gathered together, and came and encamped in Sunam, and Saul also gathered together all Israel, and came to Gelboe.

5. And Saul saw the army of the Philistines, and was afraid, and his heart was very much dismayed.

6. And he consulted the Lord, and he answered him not, neither by dreams, nor by priests, nor by prophets.

7. And Saul said to his servants, "Seek me a woman who has a divining spirit, and I will go to her, and inquire by her." And his servants said to him, "There is a woman who has a divining spirit at Endor."

8. Then he disguised himself, and put on other clothes, and he went, and two men with him, and they came to the woman by night, and he said to her, "Divine to me by thy divining spirit, and bring me up him whom I shall tell you."

9. And the woman said to him, "Behold you know all that Saul has done, and how he has rooted out the magicians and soothsayers from the land, why then do you lay a snare for my life, to cause me to be put to death"?

10. And Saul swore unto her by the Lord, saying, "As the Lord lives, there shall no evil happen to you for this thing".

11. And the woman said to him, "Whom shall I bring up to you"? And he said, "Bring me up Samuel."

12. And when the woman saw Samuel, she cried out with a loud voice, and said to Saul, "Why have you deceived me? For you are Saul."

13. And the king said to her, "Fear not, what have you seen"? And the woman said to Saul, "I saw gods ascending out of the earth."

14. And he said to her, "What form is he of"? And she said, "An old man comes up, and he is covered with a mantle." And Saul understood that it was Samuel, and he bowed himself with his face to the ground, and adored.

15. And Samuel said to Saul, "Why have you disturbed my rest that I should be brought up"? And Saul said, "I am in great distress: for the Philistines fight against me, and God is departed from me and would not hear me, neither by the hand of prophets nor by dreams, therefore, I have called you that you may show me what I shall do."

16. And Samuel said, "Why ask you me, seeing the Lord has departed from you, and is gone over to your rival?

17. For the Lord will do to you as he spoke by me, and he will rend your kingdom out of your hand, and will give it to your neighbor, David.

18. Because you did not obey the voice of the Lord, neither did you execute the wrath of his indignation upon Amalec [Saul was to have completely destroyed all of Amalec, but he saved some of the livestock]. Therefore has the Lord done to you what you suffer this day.

19. And the Lord also will deliver Israel with you into the hands of the Philistines, and tomorrow you and your sons shall be with me, and the Lord will also deliver the army of Israel into the hands of the Philistines."

20. And forthwith Saul fell all along on the ground; for he was frightened with the words of Samuel, and there was no strength in him, for he had eaten no bread all that day.

21. And the woman came to Saul, (for he was very much troubled) and said to him, "Behold your handmaid has obeyed your voice, and I have put my life in my hand," and I hearkened unto the words that you spoke to me.

22. Now therefore, I pray you, hearken you also to the voice of your handmaid, and let me set before you a morsel of bread, that you may eat and recover strength, and be able to go on your journey.

23. But he refused, and said, "I will not eat." But his servants and the woman forced him, and at length hearkening to their voices, he arose from the ground, and sat upon the bed.

24. Now the woman had a fatted calf in the house, and she made haste and killed it, and taking meal, kneaded it, and baked some unleavened bread,

25. And set it before Saul, and before his servants. And when they had eaten they rose up, and walked all that night.

Questions: Do any of the characters in the reading evince skepticism about the ability of the pythoness to revivify Samuel? What substances or rituals did the pythoness use to bring Samuel from the dead? Is the woman of Endor a villain of the story because she uses magic? Why or why not? How might such a biblical story influence Christian thought about the validity of necromancy?

3. ODYSSEUS AND CIRCE THE SORCERESS

Circe, an enchantress from Homer's Odyssey *(c. 800 BCE), was one of the ancient world's archetypal sorceresses: beautiful, seductive, and dangerous. Her magical skill with wands and potions rendered men helpless and turned them into beasts. In classical literature Circe is a goddess of magic, and by some accounts daughter of Hecate, the triple-goddess of the underworld—herself a prominent and controversial figure throughout the history of magic and witchcraft.*

Several authors after Homer included Circe in their tales. In Virgil's (70–19 BCE) Aeneid, *Aeneas sails close enough to Circe's island to hear the cries of the men she has magically transformed into beasts. In his* Metamorphoses, *Ovid (43 BCE–c. 18 CE) tells the story of one of Circe's victims who was turned into a woodpecker. The demi-goddess also caught the imaginations of Christian writers, for whom she became the quintessential witch-temptress.*

Source: trans. Samuel Butler, *The Odyssey of Homer* (Toronto: D. Van Nostrand Company, 1944), pp. 120–27.

Book 10

Thus we [Odysseus and his crew] sailed sadly on, glad to have escaped death [at the hands of the Laestrygonians, a tribe of giant cannibals] though we had lost our comrades, and came to the Aegean island where Circe lives—a great and cunning goddess who is sister to the magician Aeetes, for they are both children of the sun by Peres, who is daughter to Oceanus. We brought our ship into a safe harbor without a word, for some god guided us thither, and having landed we lay there for two days and two nights, worn out in body and mind. When the morning of the third day came I took my spear and my sword and went away from the ship to reconnoiter and see if I could discover signs of human handiwork or hear the sound of voices. Climbing to the top of a high lookout, I espied the smoke of Circe's house rising upwards amid a dense forest of trees, and when I saw this I doubted whether, having seen the smoke, I should not go on at once and find out more, but in the end I deemed it best to go back to the ship, give the men their dinners, and send some of them instead of going myself. . . .

Thus through the livelong day to the going down of the sun we stayed there eating and drinking our fill, but when the sun went down and it came on dark, we camped upon the seashore. When the child of morning, rosy-fingered Dawn, appeared, I called a council and said, "My friends, we are in very great difficulties; listen therefore to me. We have no idea where the sun either sets or rises, so that we do not even know east from west. I see no way out of it; nevertheless, we must try and find one. We are certainly on an island, for I went as high as I could this morning and saw the sea reaching all round it to the horizon; it lies low, but towards the middle I saw smoke rising from out of a thick forest of trees."

Their hearts sank as they heard me, for they remembered how they had been treated by the Laestrygonian Antiphates and by the savage ogre Polyphemus. They wept bitterly in their dismay, but there was nothing to be got by crying, so I divided them into two companies and set a captain over each; I gave one company to Eurylochus, while I took command of the other myself. Then we cast lots in a helmet, and the lot fell upon Eurylochus; so he set out with his twenty-two men, and they wept, as also did we who were left behind.

When they reached Circe's house they found it built of cut stones on a site that could be seen from far, in the middle of the forest. There were wild mountain wolves and lions prowling all round it—poor bewitched creatures whom she had tamed by her enchantments and drugged into subjection. They did not attack my men, but wagged their great tails, fawned upon them, and rubbed their noses lovingly against them. As hounds crowd round their master when they see him coming from dinner—for they know he will bring them something—even so did these wolves and lions with their great claws fawn upon my men, but the men were terribly frightened at seeing such strange creatures. Presently they reached the gates of the goddess' house, and as they stood there they could hear Circe within, singing most beautifully as she worked at her loom making a web so fine, so soft, and of such dazzling colors as no one but a goddess could weave. On this Polites, whom I valued and trusted more than any other of my men, said, "There is someone inside working at a loom and singing most beautifully; the whole place resounds with it; let us call her and see whether she is woman or goddess."

They called her and she came down, unfastened the door, and bade them enter. They, thinking no evil, followed her, all except Eurylochus, who suspected mischief and stayed outside. When she had got them into her house, she set them upon benches and seats and mixed them a mess with cheese, honey, meal, and Pramnian wine, but she drugged it with wicked poisons to make them forget their homes, and when they had drunk she turned them into pigs by a stroke of her wand and shut them up in her pigsties. They were like pigs—head, hair, and all, and they grunted just as pigs do; but their senses were the same as before, and they remembered everything.

Thus then were they shut up squealing, and Circe threw them some acorns and beech masts [fruit of the beech tree] such as pigs eat, but Eurylochus hurried back to tell me about the sad fate of our comrades. He was so overcome with dismay that though he tried to speak, he could find no words to do so; his eyes filled with tears, and he could only sob and sigh until, at last, we forced his story out of him, and he told us what had happened to the others. . . .

With this I left the ship and went up inland. When I got through the charmed grove and was near the great house of the enchantress, Circe, I met Hermes [messenger of the gods] with his golden wand, disguised as a young man in the heyday of his youth and beauty with the down just coming upon his face. He came up to me and took my hand within his own, saying, "My poor unhappy man, whither are you going over this mountain top, alone and without knowing the way? Your men are shut up in Circe's pigsties like so many wild boars in their lairs. You surely do not fancy that you can set them free? I can tell you that you will never get back and will have to stay there with the rest of them. But never mind, I will protect you and get you out of your difficulty. Take this herb, which is one of great virtue, and keep it about you when you go to Circe's house; it will be a talisman to you against every kind of mischief.

And I will tell you of all the wicked witchcraft that Circe will try to practice upon you. She will mix a mess for you to drink, and she will drug the meal with which she makes it, but she will not be able to charm you, for the virtue of the herb that I shall give you will prevent her spells from working. I will tell you all about it.

When Circe strikes you with her wand, draw your sword and spring upon her as though you were going to kill her. She will then be frightened and will desire you to go to bed with her; on this you must not point blank refuse her, for you want her to set your companions free and to take good care also of yourself, but you must make her swear solemnly by all the blessed gods that she will plot no further mischief against you, or else when she has got you naked she will unman you and make you fit for nothing." As he spoke, he pulled the herb out of the ground and showed me what it was like. The root was black while the flower was as white as milk; the gods call it moly, and mortal men cannot uproot it, but the gods can do whatever they like.

Then Hermes went back to high Olympus passing over the wooded island; but I fared onward to the house of Circe, and my heart was clouded with care as I walked along. When I got to the gates I stood there and called the goddess, and as soon as she heard me she came down, opened the door, and asked me to come in; so I followed her—much troubled in my mind. She set me on a richly decorated seat inlaid with silver; there was a footstool also under my feet, and she mixed a mess in a golden goblet for me to drink, but she drugged it, for she meant me mischief. When she had given it me and I had drunk it without it charming me, she struck me with her wand. "There now," she cried, "be off to the pigsty, and make your lair with the rest of them." But I rushed at her with my sword drawn as though I would kill her, whereon she fell with a loud scream, clasped my knees, and spoke piteously, saying, "Who and whence are you? From what place and people have you come? How can it be that my drugs have no power to charm you? Never yet was any man able to stand so much as a taste of the herb I gave you; you must be spell-proof; surely you can be none other than the bold hero Odysseus, who Hermes always said would come here some day with his ship while on his way home from Troy. So be it then; sheathe your sword and let us go to bed that we may make friends and learn to trust each other."

And I answered, "Circe, how can you expect me to be friendly with you when you have just been turning all my men into pigs? And now that you have got me here myself, you mean me mischief when you ask me to go to bed with you and will unman me and make me fit for nothing. I shall certainly not consent to go to bed with you unless you will first take your solemn oath to plot no further harm against me." So she swore at once as I had told her, and when she had completed her oath then I went to bed with her.

Meanwhile her four servants, who are her housemaids, set about their work. They are the children of the groves and fountains and of the holy waters that run down into the sea. . . . [One of them] drew a clean table beside me; another servant brought me bread and offered me many things of what there was in the house, and then Circe bade me eat, but I would not and sat without heeding what was before me—still moody and suspicious.

When Circe saw me sitting there without eating and in great grief, she came to me and said, "Odysseus, why do you sit like that as though you were dumb, gnawing at your own heart, and refusing both meat and drink? Is it that you are still suspicious? You ought not to be, for I have already sworn solemnly that I will not hurt you." And I said, "Circe, no man with any sense of what is right can think of either eating or drinking in your house until you have set his friends free and let him see them. If you want me to eat and drink, you must free my men and bring them to me that I may see them with my own eyes."

When I had said this, she went straight through the court with her wand in her hand and opened the pigsty doors. My men came out like so many prime hogs and stood looking at her, but she went about among them and anointed each with a second drug, whereon the bristles that the bad drug had given them fell off, and they became men again, younger than they were before, and much taller and better looking. They knew me at once, seized me—each of them—by the hand, and wept for joy till the whole house was filled with the sound of their hullabalooing, and Circe herself was so sorry for them that she came up to me and said, "Odysseus, noble son of Laertes, go back at once to the sea where you have left your ship, and first draw it on to the land. Then, hide all your ship's gear and property in some cave, and come back here with your men."

Questions: How does the story of Circe comment on gender roles? Although in the text Circe is described as a minor goddess, in western literature she is often called a witch; what aspects of her behavior may account for this? What is the relationship between sorcery and sexuality? The Odyssey *counters one form of magic by another; what are the two types of magic?*

4. MEDEA: THE CLASSIC WITCH

Along with Circe, Medea is an archetypal witch in western literature. Granddaughter of the god Apollo and niece to Circe (see doc. 3), her name became a byword for the malign, unrestrained, and formidable female, who, by her immense force of will and skill with deadly magic, poisons, and prophecy, imposed her designs on a world created for and by men.

The story of Jason and Medea was a favorite among classical audiences. The Greek dramatist Euripides (c. 480–c. 406 BCE) wrote the most famous version of Medea in 431 BCE, and Seneca the Younger (c. 4 BCE–65 CE), a Roman statesman and playwright, produced his adaptation of the play around 50 CE. It was commonplace for Romans to borrow material from Greek artists, but Seneca's Medea differs from the character in Euripides' play in that from the beginning she is bent upon vengeance and blames Jason, not the gods, for the injustices done to her. She is all steel and fury—never the piteous, unwitting victim portrayed in the Greek original.

The background to the plot would have been well known to all who read Seneca's script (which most likely was never staged). Medea met Jason in her home of Colchis during his quest for the fleece of a winged ram, made all of gold, that belonged to King Aeëtes, Medea's father. She used her prodigious magic skills to help Jason acquire the "Golden Fleece," and as a result, the couple was forced to flee Colchis. In order to impede King Aeëtes' pursuit, Medea cut her brother, Apsyrtus, to pieces and threw these pieces into the sea. Once back in his home of Iolcus, King Pelias refused to give the crown to Jason, so Medea concocted a scheme that resulted in Pelias's own daughters dismembering their father and throwing him into a cauldron of boiling water. The couple escaped again, this time to Corinth, where they lived happily for ten years and bore two sons. But eventually the Corinthian king, Creon, pressured Jason, who was tempted by the prospect of political advancement, to abandon Medea and marry his daughter, Creusa.

Source: trans. Ella Isabel Harris, Seneca, *Medea*, in *Two Tragedies of Seneca: Medea and The Daughters of Troy* (Boston and New York: Houghton Mifflin and Company, 1899), pp. 8–9, 19–21, 23–24, 26–28, 31–33, 35–36, 38–43.

Act 2, Scene 1

MEDEA: Alas, the wedding chorus strikes my ears; now let me die. I could not hitherto believe—can hardly yet believe—such wrong. And this is Jason's deed? Of father, home, and kingdom bereft, can he desert me now, alone and in a foreign land? Can he despise my worth, who saw the flames and seas by my magic art conquered? Thinks he, perchance, all crime is exhausted. Tossed by every wave of doubt, I am distracted, seeking some revenge. Had he a brother's love [I would take my vengeance there], but ah, he has a bride; through her be thrust the sword. Is this enough? If Grecian or barbarian cities know a crime that this hand knows not, that crime be done. Your sins return to mind urging you on: the far-famed treasure [Golden Fleece] of a kingdom lost [your own dear brother, constant comrade,] destroyed, torn limb from limb and scattered on the sea, an offering to our father [who witnessed in terror the bloody deed]. Pelias, killed in the boiling cauldron. I have shed blood often basely, but alas, alas, t'was not in wrath; unhappy love did all.

Had Jason any choice, constrained by Corinth's foreign law and foreign power? He could have bared his breast to feel the sword. O bitter grief, speak milder, milder words. Let Jason live, mine as he was, if this be possible. But, if not mine, still let him live secure and keep unharmed the gift of life I gave him. The fault is Creon's; he abuses power to annul our marriage, sever strongest ties, and tear the children from their mother's breast. Let Creon pay the penalty he owes. I'll heap his home in ashes; the dark flame shall reach Malea's dreaded cape where ships find passage only after long delay. . . .

[Medea meets King Creon and requests a reprieve from banishment of one day to say goodbye to her children.]

Act 3, Scene 1

NURSE: Stay, foster child, why fly so swiftly hence? Restrain your wrath; curb your impetuous haste. Just as a Bacchante [priestess of Bacchus], frantic with the god and filled with rage divine, uncertain walks the top of snowy Pindus or the peak of Nyssa, so Medea wildly goes hither and thither, on her cheek the stain of bitter tears, her visage flushed, her breast shaken by sobs. She cries aloud; her eyes are drowned in scalding tears; again she laughs; all passions surge within her soul; she stays her steps; she threatens, makes complaint, weeps, groans. Where will she fling the burden of her soul? Where wreak her vengeance? Where will break this wave of fury? Passion overflows; she plans no easy crime, no ordinary deed. She conquers self; I recognize old signs of raging; something terrible she plans, some deed inhuman, devilish, and wild. You gods, avert the horrors I foresee.

MEDEA [ASKING HERSELF]: Do you seek how to show your hate, poor wretch? Imitate love. And must I then endure without revenge the royal marriage? Shall this day prove unfruitful, sought and gained only by earnest effort? While the earth hangs free within the heavens, while the vault of heaven sweeps round the earth with changeless change, while the sands lie unnumbered, while the day follows the sun, the night brings up the star, Arcturus, never wet in ocean's wave rolls round the pole while rivers seaward flow, my hate shall never cease to seek revenge. Did ever fierceness of a ravening beast or Scylla or Charybdis [mythical sea monsters] sucking down the waters of the wild Ausonian and the Sicilian seas; or Mount Ætna fierce, that holds imprisoned the great [giant] Enceladus breathing forth flame, so glow as I with threats? Not the swift rivers nor the force of flame fanned by storm-winds can imitate my wrath. I will o'erthrow and bring to naught the world.

Does Jason fear the king? Thessalian war? True love fears nothing. He was forced to yield; unwillingly he gave his hand. But still he might have sought his wife for one farewell. This too he feared to do. He might have gained from Creon some delay of [my] banishment. One day is granted for my two sons' sake. I do not make complaint of too short time; it is enough for much. This day shall see what none shall ever hide. I will attack the very gods and shake the universe. . . . Rest I can never find until I see all dragged with me to ruin; all shall fall when I do. So to share one's woe is joy.

NURSE: Think what you have to fear if you persist; no one can safely fight with princely power.

Scene 2

The Nurse withdraws; enter Jason.

JASON: . . . When angry Creon thought to have you slain, urged by my prayers, he gave you banishment.

MEDEA: I looked for a reward; the gift I see is exile.

JASON: While you can fly, fly in haste. The wrath of kings is ever hard to bear.

MEDEA: You give me such advice because you love Creusa and would divorce a hated wife.

JASON: And does Medea taunt me for my love?

MEDEA: More—treacheries and murders.

JASON: Can you charge such sins to me?

MEDEA: All I have ever done.

JASON: It only needs that I should share the guilt of these your crimes.

MEDEA: They are yours, yours alone; he who reaps the fruit is the criminal. Though all might brand your wife with infamy, you should defend and call her innocent; she who has sinned for you, toward you is pure. . . . My soul is strong enough to scorn the wealth of kings; this boon alone I crave, to take my children with me when I go; into their bosoms I would shed my tears; you will have new sons.

JASON: Would I might grant your prayer, but paternal love forbids me. Creon himself could not compel me to it. They alone lighten the sorrow of a grief-parched soul. For them I live; I sooner would resign breath, members, or light.

MEDEA (ASIDE): 'Tis well. He loves his sons. This, then, the place where he may feel a wound. [To Jason] Before I go, you will at least permit that I should give my sons a last farewell, a last embrace? But one thing more I ask, if in my grief I've poured forth threatening words, retain them not in mind; let memory hold only my softer speech, my words of wrath obliterate.

JASON: I have erased them all from my remembrance. I would counsel you be calm, act gently; calmness quiets pain.

Scene 3

MEDEA. He's gone! And can it be he leaves me so, forgetting me and all my guilt? Forgot? Nay, never shall Medea be forgot. Up! Act! Call all your power to aid you now; this fruit of crime is yours: to shun no crime. Deceit is useless as they fear my guile. Strike where they do not dream you can be feared. Medea, haste, be bold to undertake the possible—yea, and that which is not possible. You, faithful nurse, companion of my griefs and varying fortunes, aid my wretched plans. I have a robe, gift of the heavenly powers, an ornament of a king's palace given by Phœbus [the god Apollo] to my father as a pledge of fatherhood, and a necklace of wrought gold, and a bright diadem inlaid with gems, which used to bind my hair. These gifts, infused with poison by my magic arts, my sons shall carry for me to the bride. Pay vows to Hecate, bring the sacrifice, and set up the altars. Let the mounting flame envelop all the house.

Act 4, Scene 1

NURSE: I shrink with horror. Ruin threatens us. How terribly her wrath inflames itself. Her former force awakes; thus I have seen Medea raging and attacking god, compelling heaven. Greater crime than then she now prepares, for as with frantic step she sought the sanctuary of her crimes, she poured forth all her threats; and what before she feared she now brings forth. She lets loose a host of poisonous evils, arts mysterious, and with sad left hand outstretched, invokes all ills that Libyan sands with their fierce heat create or frost-bound Taurus encompassed by perpetual snow. Drawn by her magic spell the serpent drags his heavy length along, darts his forked tongue, and seeks his destined prey. Hearing her incantation, he draws back and knots his swelling body, coiling it.

"They are but feeble poisons earth brings forth and harmless darts," she says, "Heaven's ills I seek. Now is the time for deeper sorcery. The dragon like a torrent shall descend, whose mighty folds the Great and Lesser Bear [stellar constellations] know well; Ophiuchus [stellar constellation meaning 'serpent bearer'] shall loose his grasp and poison flow. Be present at my call, Python [serpent], who dared to fight twin deities. The [many-headed snake,] Hydra slain by Hercules shall come healed of his wound. Colchis, you dragon that guarded the Golden Fleece, be present with the rest—you, who first slept lulled by my incantations." When the brood of serpents has been called, she blends the juice of the poisonous herbs that all Mount Eryx's pathless heights bear or the open top of Caucasus, wet with Prometheus' blood [a god chained to a mountain peak for giving fire to humans] where winter reigns. She adds all that the rich Arabians use to tip their poisoned shafts, or the light Parthians, or warlike Medes, all that the brave Suabians cull in the Hyrcanian forests in the north, all poisons that the earth brings forth in spring when birds are nesting or when winter cold has torn away the beauty of the groves and bound the world in icy manacles. Whatever herb gives flower the cause of death or juice of twisted root, her hands have culled. These on Thessalian Athos grew, and those on mighty Pindus. On Pangæus' height she cut the tender herbs with bloody scythe. These River Tigris nurtured with its current deep, the Danube those; Hydaspes rich in gems flowing with current warm through levels dry, Bætis that gives its name to neighbouring lands and meets the western ocean languidly have nurtured these. Those have been cut at dawn; these other herbs at dead of night were reaped, and these were gathered with the enchanted hook.

Death-dealing plants she chooses, wrings the blood of serpents, and she takes ill-omened birds, the sad owl's heart, the quivering entrails cut from the horned owl living. In some the eager force of flame is found, in some the bitter cold of sluggish ice; to these she adds the venom of her words as greatly to be feared. She stamps her feet; she sings, and the world trembles at her song.

Scene 2
Medea, before the altar of Hecate [in this text, goddess of the moon]

Here I invoke you, silent company, infernal gods, blind Chaos [dark void of space], sunless home of shadowy Dis [Hades], and squalid caves of death bound by the banks of Tartarus [outer bounds of the ocean in the underworld]. Lost souls, for this new bridal leave your wonted toil; . . . I need your aid. . . . The altars find a voice; the tripod moves stirred by the favoring goddess [Hecate]. Her swift car I see approach—not the full-orbed that rolls all night through heaven; but as, with darkened light, troubled by the Thessalians [witches who draw down the moon] she comes, so her sad face upon my altars sheds a murky light. Terrify the men of earth with new dread. Costly Corinthian brass sounds in your honor, Hecate, and on ground made red with blood I pay these solemn rites to you; for you have stolen from the tomb this torch that gives its baleful funeral light. To you with bowed head I have made my prayer, and in accordance with my country's custom, my loose hair is bound up by a fillet like a corpse ready for burial. I have plucked for you this branch that grows beside hell's Stygian river. Like a wild Mænad [devotee of Bacchus] laying bare my breast, with sacred knife I cut for you my arm. My blood is on the altars. Hand, learn well to strike your dearest. See, my blood flows forth. Daughter of Perseus, have I asked too oft your aid? Recall no more my former prayers. Today as always I invoke your aid because of Jason. Infuse this robe with such a baleful power that the bride may feel at its first touch consuming fire of serpent's poison in her inmost veins. . . . I have bade all serve my secret sorcery; now, Hecate, add the sting of poison; aid the seeds of flame hid in my gift; let them deceive the sight but burn the touch; let the heat penetrate her very heart and veins, stiffen her limbs, consume her bones in smoke. Her burning hair shall glow more brightly than the nuptial torch. My vows are paid, and Hecate thrice has barked and shaken fire from her funeral torch. 'Tis finished. Call my sons. My precious gifts, you shall be borne by them to the new bride. Go, go, my sons, a hapless mother's sons. Placate with gifts and prayers your father's wife. But come again with speed, that I may have a last embrace.

Act 5, Scene 1

[A messenger reports that the king and his daughter are dead and a fire spreads through the city that water cannot quell—all conjured by Medea.]

Scene 2

NURSE: Up, up. Medea. Swiftly flee the land of Pelops [peninsula of southern Greece]; seek in haste a distant shore.

MEDEA: Shall I fly? I? Were I already gone I would return for this, that I might see these new betrothals. Do you pause, my soul? This joy's but the beginning of revenge. You do still love if you are satisfied to widow Jason. Seek new penalties; honor is gone and maiden modesty. It is a light revenge pure hands could yield. Strengthen your drooping spirit; stir up wrath; summon from your heart its former violence. Call your past deeds honor; now wake and act that all may see how light, of how little worth all former crimes are—just the prelude of revenge. What was there my novice hands could dare? What was the madness of my girlhood days?

I am Medea now, through sorrow strong. Rejoice, because through you your brother died; rejoice, because through you his limbs were torn. Through you your father lost the Golden Fleece; rejoice, that armed by you his daughters slew old Pelias. Seek revenge. No novice hand you bring to crime; what will you do; what dart let fly against your hated enemy? I know not what my maddened spirit plots nor yet dare I confess it to myself. In folly I made haste—I wish my foe had children by Creusa. Mine are his, but we'll say Creusa bore them. 'Tis enough; through them my heart at last finds full revenge. My soul must be prepared for this last crime. You who were once my children, mine no more. You pay the forfeit for your father's crimes. Awe strikes my spirit and benumbs my hand. My heart beats wildly; mother-love drives out hate of my husband. Shall I shed their blood—my children's blood? Demented one, rage not; let this crime be far from you. What guilt is theirs? Is Jason not their father; that is guilt enough. And worse, Medea claims them as her sons. They are not sons of mine, so let them die. Nay, rather let them perish because they are mine. They are innocent, as was my brother. Do you fear? Do tears already mar your cheek? Do wrath and love like adverse tides impel—now here, now there? As when the winds wage war and the wild waves against each other smite, my heart is beaten; duty drives out fear as wrath drives duty. Anger dies in love. Dear sons, sole solace of a storm-tossed house, come hither; he may have you safe if I may claim you too. But he has banished me; already from my bosom torn away they go lamenting—they must perish then to Jason as they will to me. My wrath again grows hot. Furies, I go wherever you may lead. Would that the children of the haughty child of Tantalus [killed his son and offered the meat to the gods] were mine, that I had borne twice seven sons. In bearing only two I have been cursed, and yet it is enough to avenge father and brother.

[Medea sees the Furies flying through the air—goddesses of justice and vengeance, who harry and drive wrongdoers mad, especially those who murder family members.]

Where does that horde of Furies haste, whom do they seek, for whom prepare their fires, or for whom intends the infernal band its bloody torch? Whom does Megaera [one of the Furies] seek with hostile brand? The mighty dragon lashes its fierce tail. What specter uncertain brings its scattered limbs? It is my brother, and he seeks revenge; I grant it; thrust the torches in my eyes; kill; burn; the Furies have me in their power. Brother, command the avenging goddesses to leave me and the shades to seek their place in the infernal regions without fear. Here leave me to myself, and use this hand that held the sword; your soul has found revenge. [Kills one of her sons). What is the sudden noise? They come in arms and think to drive me into banishment. I will go up on the high roof. Come you [Medea says to her living son]; I'll take the body [of my butchered son] with me. Now my soul, strike, hold not, hide your power but show the world what you are able to do. [Medea goes out with the nurse and the living boy and carries with her the body of her dead son.]

Scene 3
Jason in the foreground, Medea with the children appears upon the roof.

JASON: You faithful ones who share in the misfortunes of your harassed king, hasten to take the author of these deeds. Come hither, hither, cohorts of brave men; bring up your weapons; overthrow the house.

MEDEA: I have recaptured now my crown and throne, my brother and my father; Colchians hold the Golden Fleece; my kingdom is won back; my lost virginity returns to me. O gods appeased, marriage and happy days, go now; my vengeance is complete. Not yet; finish it while your hands are strong to strike. Why seek delay? Why hesitate, my soul? You are able. All your anger falls to naught. I do repent of that which I have done. Why did you do it, miserable one? Yea, miserable. 'Tis done, great joy fills my unwilling heart, and, lo, the joy increases. But one thing before was lacking: Jason did not see. All that he has not seen I count as lost.

JASON: She threatens from the roof; let fire be brought that she may perish, burned with her own flame.

MEDEA: Pile high the funeral pyre of your sons, and prepare their tomb. To Creon and your wife I have already paid the honors due. This son is dead, and the other soon shall be, and you shall see him perish.

JASON: By the gods, by our sad flight together and the bond I have not willingly forsaken, spare our son. If there is any crime, 'tis mine; put me to death; strike down the guilty one.

MEDEA: There where you ask mercy and can feel the sting, I thrust the sword. Go, Jason, seek your virgin bride; desert a mother's bed.

JASON: Let one [murdered son] suffice for vengeance.

MEDEA: Had it been that one could satisfy my hands with blood, I had slain none. But two is not enough.

JASON: Then go, fill up the measure of your crime; I ask for nothing but that you should make a speedy end.

MEDEA: Now, grief, take slow revenge; it is my day. Haste not; let me enjoy. [She kills the other child.]

JASON: Slay me, mine enemy.

MEDEA: Do you implore my pity? It is well; I am avenged. Grief, there is nothing more that you can slay. Look up, ungrateful Jason, recognize your wife; so I am wont to flee. The way lies open through the skies; two dragons bend their necks, submissive to the yoke. I go in my bright car through heaven. Take your sons. [She casts down to him the bodies of her children and is borne away in a chariot drawn by dragons.]

JASON: Go through the skies sublime, and going prove that no gods dwell in the heavens you seek.

Questions: Medea and Jason perpetrated some heinous crimes together; why is Medea considered bloodthirsty and not Jason? Is the type of magic Medea uses gendered? The author wants to communicate that Medea will go to any lengths to obtain revenge; what is the most shocking retribution that this woman (and the audience) can imagine?

5. ERICTHO: DIVINATION THROUGH THE DEAD

The Civil War (Pharsalia) *was written by the Roman poet Lucan (39–65 CE) about the conflict in 48 BCE between Julius Caesar (100–44 BCE) and the senatorial forces led by Pompey the Great (106–48 BCE). The title of the epic poem takes its name from the major battle of the war at Pharsalus in Thessaly, central Greece. In classical literature, stories of malevolent magic and exotic mystery are often set in Thessaly, thought to be a veritable hub of witchcraft and sorcery, so much so that Lucan refers to Erictho as Thessalis. In book six of* Pharsalia, *Pompey's son, Sextus Pompey (c. 67–35 BCE), seeks out this sinister prophetess amid the barren tombs of the dead, hoping she will revivify a corpse to predict the outcome of the impending battle. It was thought that when mortals die, they gain knowledge of the future. The chilling crimes and terrifying attributes of the insidious sorceress became leitmotifs of "the witch," both in western literature and in treatises on diabolical witchcraft through the early modern era.*

Source: trans. Edward Ridley, *The Pharsalia of Lucan*, 2nd ed. (New York, Longmans, Green, and Co., 1905), pp. 175–85, 187; rev. Martha Rampton.

Chapter 6

Deserted tombs were Erictho's dwelling-place, from which, darling of hell, / She dragged the dead. Nor life nor gods forbad / That she knew the secret homes of Styx [river separating earth and Hades] / And learned to hear the whispered voice of ghosts / At dread mysterious meetings. Never did the sun / Shed his pure light upon that haggard cheek, / Pale with the pallor of the shades, nor did the sun look / Upon those locks unkempt that crowned her brow.

In starless, stormy nights, the hag crept / Out from her tomb to seize the lightning bolt; / Treading the harvest with accursed foot / She burned the crops, and with her breath / Poisoned the air once pure. No prayer she breathed / Nor supplication to the gods for help, / Nor did she study entrails as priests who worship do. / Funeral pyres she loves to light / And snatch the incense from the flaming tomb. / The gods at her first utterance grant her prayer / For things unlawful, lest they hear again / her shrieking spell. Living men whose limbs were quick / With vital power she thrust within the grave, / Although the Fates [three deities who determined the length of a person's life] owned them more years to live. / Or she snatches from the center of the pyre / The smoking ashes and burning bones of the young / Along with the very torch from the hands of the grieving father. / She gathers up the remnants of the cremation through the black smoke / And grave-clothes and cinders that reek of the burned body. / When the dead are hidden in stone coffins / The internal moisture drains off and the rock absorbs the corruption of the marrow, and makes the corpse rigid. / Venting her rage, she tears the body limb by limb, she drags the bloodless eyes from their cavities, and mauls the nails / Upon the withered hands. She gnaws the noose / By which some wretch has died, and from the tree / Erictho drags down a hanging carcass, its members torn / Asunder to the winds. Forth from the palms she pries loose the nails that pierce the dead man's fist, / Hangs by her teeth on stubborn muscles, and with her hands collects / The slimy gore which drips upon the limbs. / Where lay a corpse upon the naked earth, / from ravening birds and beasts of prey the hag / Guards the corpse, nor mars her spoil by knife or hand / Till some nightly wolf seizes the victim; / Then she drags the morsel from his thirsty fangs. / Nor does she fear murder, if her rites demand / Fresh blood gushing from the gaping throat, or for her feast she wishes panting entrails. / By unnatural means pregnant wombs / Yield to her knife the infant to be placed / On flaming altars, and whene'er she needs / Some fierce undaunted ghost, he fails her not. / She has sway over all who die. / Her hand has chased / From smiling cheeks the rosy bloom of life, / And with sinister hand from dying youth / She has shorn the fatal lock. And holding oft / In foul embraces some departed friend's / Severed head, through the ghastly lips, she bites the tip of the tongue that lies motionless in the dry throat / then pours inarticulate sound into the cold lips and sends a message, / Dark with mysterious horror down to the shades of River Styx.

When rumor brought Erictho's name to Sextus, in the depth of night, / While the sun's chariot was beneath the earth / wheeling at full height, and here, / Night in mid-course, Sextus made his way / Through fields deserted while a faithful band, / His ministers in deeds of guilt, / Seeking the hag 'mid broken tombs and vaults, / Beheld her seated afar upon a lofty crag / Where Mount Haemus reaches Pharsalia's plain. / There was she uttering curses / Of magic, words unknown, and framing chants / Of dire and novel purpose, for she feared / Lest Mars might stray into another world / And spare Thessalian soil the blood soon / To flow in torrents after the battle; and she thus forbade / Pharsalia's field, polluted with her song, / Thick with her poisonous distilments sown, / To let the war pass by. Such deaths, she hopes, / Soon shall be hers; the blood of all the world / Shed for her use. To her it shall be given / To sever from their trunks the heads of kings, / Plunder the ashes of the noble dead, / Italy's bravest, and in triumph add / The mightiest warriors to her host of shades. / This was her sole desire, to snatch from Pompey's tombless corpse what she may / And grasp on which of Caesar's limbs she might fasten.

To her Sextus, the coward son / Of Pompey the Great said: "You greatest ornament / Of Thessaly's daughters, in whose power it lies / To reveal the Fates, or from its course / To turn the future, be it mine to know / By your sure utterance to what final end / Fortune now guides the issue. Not the least / Of all the Roman host on yonder plain / Am I, but Pompey's most illustrious son, / Lord of the world or heir to death and doom. Though the unknown affrights me, I can firmly face / The certain terror. Bid my destiny / Yield to your power the dark and hidden end, / And let me fall foreknowing. From the gods / Extort the truth, or, if not the gods, / Force it from hell itself. Fling back the gates / That bar the Elysian fields [abode of deceased heroes]; let death confess / Whom from our ranks he seeks. No humble task / I bring, but worthy of Erictho's skill / Of such a struggle fought for such a prize / To search and tell the issue."

Then the witch, / Pleased that her impious fame was noised abroad, / Thus made her answer, "If some lesser fates / Thy wish had been to change, against their wish / It had been easy to compel the gods / To its accomplishment. My spells have power to change the fate of one man and / The speedy death, to secure a delay. / And I am able by mystic herbs, though every star decrees the opposite, / To rob a man destined to a ripe old age and shear / The life midway. / But should some purpose be set from the beginning of the universe, such as the battle soon to be fought, / And all the laboring fortunes of mankind / Be brought in question, then Thessalian magic is useless. But if you be / Content to know the outcome pre-ordained, / Simple the task and plain; for earth and air / And sea and space and Rhodopaean crags [mountain range in southeastern Europe] / Shall speak the future. Yet it easiest seems / With so many dead here in these Thessalian fields / To raise a single corpse. From dead men's lips / Scarce cold, in fuller accents falls the voice; not from some mummied ghost in accents shrill / Uncertain to the ear."

Thus spoke the hag, / And through darkest night, a squalid veil / Swathing her pallid features, she stole among / Unburied carcasses. Fast fled the wolves, / The carrion birds with maw unsatisfied / Relaxed their talons, as with creeping step / She sought her ghostly prophet. Firm must be the flesh / As yet, though cold in death, and firm the lungs / Untouched by wound. . . . / At length the hag / Picks out her victim with pierced throat agape / Fit for her purpose. Gripped by pitiless hook / O'er rocks she drags him to the mountain cave, / Accursed by her fell rites, that shall restore / The dead man's life. . . . / Discordant hues / Flamed on her garb as by a fury worn; / Bare was her visage, and upon her brow / Dread vipers hissed, beneath her streaming locks / In sable coils entwined. But when she saw / The youth's companions trembling and Sextus himself / With eyes cast down, with visage as of death, / Thus spoke Erictho, "Forbid your craven souls / These fears to cherish. Soon returning life, / This frame shall quicken, and in tones which reach / Even the timorous ear shall speak the dead man. / If I have power the river Styx to show, / The bank that sounds with fire, the Furies, / And the chained bodies of the Giants the [children of Earth (Gaia)], and the hound [many-headed Cerberus that guards the gates to Hades] that shakes / Bristling with heads of snakes his triple head, / What fright is this that cringes at the sight / Of timid shivering shades who fear me?"

Then to her prayer. / First through his gaping bosom blood she pours / Still fervent, washing from his wounds the gore. / Then copious poisons from the moon distilled / Mixed with all monstrous things which nature's pangs / Bring to untimely birth; the froth from dogs / Stricken with madness, foaming at the stream; / A lynx's entrails, and the knot that grows / Upon the fell hyena; flesh of stags / Fed upon serpents; . . . / Nor Arabia's viper, nor the ocean snake, / Who in the Red Sea waters guards the shell, / Are wanting; nor the slough on Libyan sands / By horned reptile cast; nor ashes fail / Snatched from an altar where the Phoenix [immortal bird repeatedly reborn from its own ashes] died / And viler poisons many, which herself / Has made, / Pestiferous leaves pregnant with magic chants / And blades of grass which in their primal growth / Her cursed mouth had slimed. Last came her voice / More potent than all herbs to charm the gods / Who rule in Lethe [river whose waters induce forgetfulness] Dissonant murmurs first / And sounds discordant from the tongues of men / She utters, scarce articulate. The bay / Of wolves, and barking as of dogs, were mixed / With that fell chant; the screech of nightly owl / Raising her hoarse complaint; the howl of beast / And hissing sound of snake — all these were there; / And more — the wail of waters on the rock, / The sound of forests and the thunder peal. / Such was her voice; but soon in clearer tones / Reaching to Tartarus [dungeon where wicked deities are punished], she raised her song, / "You awful goddesses, avenging power / Of Hell upon the damned, and Chaos huge / Who striv'st to mix innumerable worlds, / And Pluto, king of earth, whose weary soul / Grieves at his godhead; Styx; and plains of bliss / We may not enter, and you, Proserpine [queen of Hades], / Hating thy mother and the skies above, / My patron goddess, last and lowest form / Of goddess, Hecate through whom the shades and I / Hold silent converse; warder of the gate / Who casts human offal to the dog. / You Fates who shall spin the threads again; / And you, O boatman of the burning wave of Styx, / Now wearied of the shades from hell to me / Returning, hear me if with voice I cry / Abhorred, polluted; if the flesh of man / Hath ne'er been absent from my proffered song, / Flesh washed with brains still quivering; if the child / who by this hand was killed whose severed head I placed upon / Your platter — a listening ear / Lend to my supplication. From the caves / Hid in the innermost recess of hell / I claim no soul long banished from the light. / For one but now departed, lingering still / Upon the brink of Orcus [the underworld] is my prayer. / Grant (for you may) that listening to the spell / Once more a fresh corpse seek, and let the shade / Of this our soldier perished (if the war / Well at your hands has merited), proclaim / The destiny of Pompey to his son."

Such prayers she uttered; then, upraised her head / And foaming lips, and present saw the ghost. / Hard by he stood, beside his own hated corpse / His ancient prison, and loathed to enter in. / There was the yawning chest where fell the blow / That was his death; and yet the gift supreme, / His right to die, was stolen (poor wretch) / Angered at death the witch, and at the pause / Conceded by the fates, with living snake / Scourges the moveless corpse, and on the dead / She barks through fissures gaping to her song, / Breaking the silence of their gloomy home . . . [The spirit reluctantly enters his mangled corpse.]

Then the blood / Grew warm and liquid, and with softening touch / Cherished the stiffened wounds and filled the veins, / Till throbbed once more the slow returning pulse / And every fiber trembled, as with death / Life was commingled. Then, not limb by limb, / With toil and strain, but rising at a bound / Leaped from the earth erect the living man. / Fierce glared his eyes uncovered, and the life / Was dim, and still upon his face remained / The pallid hues of hardly parted death. / Amazement seized upon him, to the earth / Brought back again, but from his lips tight drawn / No murmur issued; he only had the power to speak / When questioned to reply. "Speak," said the hag, / "As I shall bid you; great shall be your gain / If true your answers, freed for evermore / From all the magic arts. Such burial place / Shall now be yours, and on your funeral pyre / Such fatal woods shall burn, such chant shall sound, / That to your ghost no herb or magic song / Or spell shall reach, and your oblivious sleep / Shall never more be broken in a death / From me received anew; for such reward / Think not this second life enforced in vain. / Obscure may be the answers of the gods / By priestess spoken at the holy shrine; / But whoso braves the oracles of death / In search of truth, should gain a sure response. / Then speak, I pray you. Let the hidden fates / Tell through your voice the mysteries to come."

[The reanimated corpse foretells that Julius Caesar will win the battle the next day and Pompey will die soon thereafter.]

His task performed, / the shade of the soldier stands in mournful guise with silent look / Asking for death again; yet could not die / Till mystic herb and magic chant prevailed. / For nature's law, once used, had power no more / To slay the corpse and set the spirit free. / With plenteous wood she builds the funeral pyre / To which the dead man comes; then as the flames / Seized on his form outstretched, Sextus and Erictho / Together sought the military camp; and as the dawn / Now streaked the heavens, by the hag's command / The day was stayed till Sextus reached his tent, And mist and darkness veiled his safe return.

Questions: What does Erictho share in common with the Pythoness of Endor (see doc. 2)? What do you make of the fact that the two women come from literature of two very different cultures: Roman and Hebrew? Why is Erictho eager for the impending Battle of Pharsalus to take place? To make Erictho as repulsive as possible, what attributes does Lucan ascribe to her? Who is Hecate?

6. SIMON MAGUS: MONEY FOR MIRACLES

In the Acts of the Apostles, Simon Magus covets the apostles' ability to bestow the spirit of God by laying-on-of-hands and offers to pay money to learn their "tricks." Simon Magus is prominent in the study of European magic as the archetype of the deceptive, ambitious, and self-serving magician. The narrative was also instructive for early Christian thinkers who struggled to clarify the difference between magic and miracle. The derivation of the English word "simony," meaning trafficking in or buying ecclesiastical offices, is based on the biblical account of Simon Magus.

Source: Douay-Rheims Bible (Baltimore: John Murphy Co., 1914), pp. 130–31.

Acts of the Apostles

Chapter 8

5. And Philip, going down to the city of Samaria, preached Christ unto them.

6. And the people with one accord were attentive to those things which were said by Philip, hearing, and seeing the miracles which he did.

7. For many of them had unclean spirits, who, crying with a loud voice, went out.

8. And many, taken with the palsy, who were lame, were healed.

9. There was therefore great joy in that city. Now there was a certain man named Simon, who before had been a magician in that city, seducing the people of Samaria and giving out that he was some great personage.

10. To whom they all gave ear to him, from the least to the greatest, saying, "This man is the power of God, which is called great."

11. And they were attentive to him, because, for a long time, he had bewitched them with his magical practices.

12. But when they had believed Philip preaching of the kingdom of God in the name of Jesus Christ, they were baptized, both men and women.

13. Then Simon himself believed also, and, being baptized, he adhered to Philip. And being astonished, wondered to see the signs and exceeding great miracles that were done.

14. Now, when the apostles who were in Jerusalem had heard that Samaria had received the word of God, they sent unto them Peter and John.

15. Who, when they were come, prayed for them that they might receive the Holy Ghost.

16. For the Holy Ghost was not as yet come upon any of them: but they were only baptized in the name of the Lord Jesus.

17. Then Peter and John laid their hands upon them, and they received the Holy Ghost. The apostles administered the sacrament of confirmation by imposition of hands and prayer, and the faithful thereby received the Holy Ghost. They had received the grace of the Holy Ghost at their baptism but not that plenitude of grace and those spiritual gifts that they afterwards received from bishops in the sacrament of confirmation, which strengthened them to profess their faith publicly.

18. And when Simon saw that by the imposition of the hands of the apostles the Holy Ghost was given, he offered them money,

19. Saying, "Give me also this power that on whomsoever I shall lay my hands, he may receive the Holy Ghost." But Peter said to him,

20. "Keep your money to yourself to perish with you, because you have thought that the gift of God may be purchased with money.

21. You have no part nor lot in this matter. For your heart is not right in the sight of God.

22. Do penance therefore for this your wickedness, and pray to God that perhaps this thought of your heart may be forgiven you.

23. For I see you are in the gall of bitterness and in the bonds of iniquity."

24. Then Simon answering, said, "Pray you for me to the Lord that none of these things which you have spoken may come upon me."

25. And they indeed, having testified and preached the word of the Lord, returned to Jerusalem and preached the gospel to many countries of the Samaritans.

Questions: How is the word "simony" related to this selection from the New Testament? The relationship between Simon and Peter became a metaphor for the conflict between pagan religions and Christian missionaries; explain why.

7. GODDESS DIANA OF THE EPHESIANS BESTS THE APOSTLE PAUL

The Greek Temple of Artemis (similar to Diana in Latin), located in Ephesus in modern Turkey, was one of the seven wonders of the ancient world. At Ephesus, Diana's particular avatar was as goddess of fertility, symbolized by the multitude of breasts that covered her chest. Although herself a virgin, she was a patron of women in childbirth. The temple and city of Ephesus were magnificent and very wealthy. They enjoyed international renown and were the scene of large festivals and recipients of various emperors' donations, due in large part to the cult of Diana. The goddess posed a challenge to the Christian missionaries, a challenge to which they could not rise. Throughout the history of European magic, the personage of Diana continued to be synonymous with magic and unsubdued women.

Source: Douay-Rheims Bible (Baltimore: John Murphy Co., 1914), pp. 144–45.

Acts of the Apostles

Chapter 19

13. Now also some of the Jewish exorcists who went about attempted to invoke over them who had evil spirits, the name of the Lord Jesus, saying, "I conjure you by Jesus, whom Paul preaches."

14. And there were certain men, seven sons of Sceva, a Jew and a chief priest, who did this.

15. But the wicked spirit, answering, said to them, "Jesus I know, and Paul I know, but who are you?"

16. And the man in whom the wicked spirit dwelt, leaping upon them and mastering them both, prevailed against them, so that they fled out of that house naked and wounded.

17. And this became known to all the Jews and the Gentiles who dwelt at Ephesus, and fear fell on them all, and the name of the Lord Jesus was magnified.

18. And many of them who believed came confessing and declaring their deeds.

19. And many of them who had followed curious arts [magic], brought together their books and burnt them before all, and counting the price of them, they found the money to be fifty thousand pieces of silver.

20. So mightily grew the word of God which was confirmed.

21. And when these things were ended, Paul purposed in the spirit, when he had passed through Macedonia and Achaia, to go to Jerusalem, saying, "After I have been there, I must see Rome also."

22. And sending into Macedonia two of them who ministered to him, Timothy and Erastus, he himself remained for a time in Asia.

23. Now at that time there arose no small disturbance about the way of the Lord.

24. For a certain man named Demetrius, a silversmith who made silver temples for Diana, brought no small gain to the craftsmen;

25. And he, calling together the workmen of like occupation, said, "Sirs, you know that our gain is by this trade;

26. And you see and hear that this Paul, by persuasion, has drawn away a great multitude, not only of Ephesus, but almost of all Asia, saying, 'They are not gods which are made by hands.'

27. So that not only this, our craft, is in danger to be set at naught, but also the temple of great Diana shall be reputed for nothing; yea, and her majesty shall begin to be destroyed, whom all Asia and the world worships."

28. Having heard these things, they were full of anger and cried out, saying, "Great is Diana of the Ephesians."

29. And the whole city was filled with confusion, and having caught Gaius and Aristarchus, men of Macedonia, Paul's companions, they rushed with one accord into the theatre.

30. And when Paul would have entered into the theatre, the disciples stopped him.

31. And some also of the rulers of Asia, who were his friends, sent unto him, desiring that he would not go into the theatre.

32. Now some cried one thing, some another. For the assembly was confused, and the greater part knew not for what cause they were come together.

33. And they drew forth Alexander out of the multitude, the Jews thrusting him forward. And Alexander beckoning with his hand for silence, would have given the people satisfaction.

34. But as soon as they perceived him to be a Jew, all with one voice, for the space of about two hours, cried out, "Great is Diana of the Ephesians."

35. And when the town clerk had appeased the multitudes, he said, "You men of Ephesus, what man is there that knows not that the city of the Ephesians is a worshipper of the great Diana, and of Jupiter's offspring.

36. For as much therefore as these things cannot be contradicted, you ought to be quiet, and to do nothing rashly.

37. For you have brought hither these men, who are neither guilty of sacrilege nor of blasphemy against your goddess.

38. But if Demetrius and the craftsmen that are with him, have a matter against any man, the courts of justice are open, and there are proconsuls; let them accuse one another.

39. And if you inquire after any other matter, it may be decided in a lawful assembly.

40. For we are even in danger of being called into question for this day's uproar, there being no man guilty (of whom we may give account) of this concourse."

41. And when he had said these things, he dismissed the assembly.
Chapter 20

1. And after the tumult was ceased, Paul calling to him the disciples and exhorting them, took his leave and set forward to go into Macedonia.

Questions: What is the significance of the fact that the evil spirit would not exit the body of its victim at the insistence of the Jewish exorcists? Why does the silversmith of Ephesus oppose the religion of Paul? Who comes out ahead in the contest between the worshippers of Diana and the apostles?

8. HECATE AND THE CHALDEAN ORACLES

The Chaldean Oracles, as they exist today, are second-century fragments of commentaries on a mystic poem that allegedly originated in Chaldea (Babylon), revealed to and written by Julian the Theurgist and his father, Julian the Chaldean (both fl. late second century). The oracles are an amalgamation of Neoplatonic philosophy and eastern mystery religious belief that reveals a cosmology in which the universe derives from a primal, masculine, generative intellect, which is separated from the material world by a feminine "membrane" called Hecate, who mediates contact between the upper realm of intellect and the lower realm of matter.

Hecate is the World Soul from which nature emanates. Humans are separated from god (the highest intellect) because of their corporality, and they are subject to demonic powers that lurk between gods and mortals. Humans, however, can transcend their physicality and reconnect with the father-intellect through ascetic behavior and the proper execution of rituals. Hecate is a positive force in this view of the universe and protects humans from sub-lunar demons. Interestingly, in later European thought Hecate became the prototypical hag-like witch (see doc. 79). Early Christian writers dismissed the oracles as magic, but in the Renaissance, Neoplatonic theurgy, as captured in the Chaldean Oracles, *re-emerged among the educated European elite as a credible method of reaching beyond the mortal plane.*

Source: trans. Ruth Majercik, *The Chaldean Oracles: Text, Translation and Commentary,* Platonic Texts and Translations 8, 2nd ed. (Leiden: The Prometheus Trust, 2013), pp. 61, 69, 71, 77, 85, 101, 105, 109, 127, 135, 137.

35. Indeed, the First Once Transcendent communicates the *hebdomad* [seven days] to the gods themselves; but to others, it is communicated by him through participation, "For Implacable Thunders leap from him and the lightning-receiving womb of the shining ray of Hecate, who is generated from the father. From him leap the girdling flower of fire and the powerful breath (situated) beyond the fiery poles."

50. It is said by the gods that "the center of Hecate is borne in the midst of the Fathers."

51. It seems to me that the *Oracles* also speak about this light, when giving instructions concerning the principle of life by which the source of souls animates the All. It says, "Around the hollow of [Hecate's] right flank a great stream of the primordially-generated Soul gushes forth in abundance, totally ensouling light, fire, ether, worlds."

52. "In the left flank of Hecate exists the source of virtue, which remains entirely within and does not give up its virginity."

54. But even the theologians suppose that the source (of Nature) is in the generative goddess, "On the back of the goddess boundless Nature is suspended."

55. "For her hair appears dazzlingly in shimmering light," says one of the gods.

70. But the *Oracles* plainly state that Nature, advancing through all things, is suspended from the great Hecate. . . . "For untiring Nature rules both worlds and works, in order that the sky might turn round, pulling down its eternal course, and that the swift sun might come around the center, just as it is accustomed to do."

89. That (race of evil demons) draws down souls, (a race) which is also called ". . . bestial and shameless," since it is turned toward Nature.

90. ". . . from the hollows of the earth leap chthonian dogs, who never show a true sign to a mortal." The oracle is about demons involved in matter. These (demons) are called dogs because they are the avengers of souls.

91. Starting from the spirits of the air, irrational demons begin to come into existence. Therefore, the oracle says, "Driver (fem.) of dogs of the air, earth, and water."

92. Therefore, even the oracle calls these gods ". . . aquatic."

93. Thus, also, concerning the ". . . multiflowing tribes" of demons.

135. Therefore, even the gods exhort us not to gaze at (these demons) before-hand, until we have been strengthened by the powers from the initiation rites: "For you must not gaze at them until you have your body initiated. Being ter-restrial, these ill-tempered dogs are shameless." And for this reason, the *Oracles* add that "they enchant souls, forever turning them away from the rites."

149. "When you perceive an earthly demon approaching, offer the *mnizouris* stone while making an invocation. . . ."

157. " (For) earthly beasts will occupy your vessel." The "vessel" is the composite mixture of our life; the "earthly beasts" are those demons who roam about the earth. [In the following fragments, Hecate is drawn to earth and bound by the rituals of humans hoping to transcend their bodily essence.]

206. Magic Wheel. "Operate with the magic wheel of Hecate." . . . Therefore (the oracle) teaches how to operate the rite, truly the movement of such a magic wheel, since it has ineffable power.

208. Conjunction. For (Proclus) [Neoplatonic philosopher, 412–485] made use of the "conjunctions," prayers, and the divine, ineffable, magic wheels of the Chaldeans.

219. For all (the gods) say that they have come by Necessity, not simply so, but in a manner—so to speak—of persuasive Necessity. Earlier, we mentioned those (verses) of Hecate by which she is said to appear, "After daybreak, boundless, full of stars, I left the great, undefiled house of god and descended to life-nourishing earth at your request, and by the persuasion of ineffable words with which a mortal man delights in gladdening the hearts of immortals."

221. And still, more clearly, (Hecate says), "Why, from the eternally cours-ing ether, do you need to invoke me, the goddess Hecate, by constraints which bind the gods?"

222. And, again (Hecate says), "I have come, hearkening to your very eloquent prayer, which the nature of mortals has discovered at the suggestion of the gods."

223. And next (Hecate says), "Drawing them down from the ether by unspeak-able spells, you brought them easily to this earth against their will. But (the demons) in the middle—the ones who stand on the mid-most gales far from the divine fire— you treat (these) demons shamefully and send them to mortals as prophetic dreams."

224. That even (the gods) themselves have advised how their statues ought to be made and from what kind of material, will be clear from the statements of Hecate to this effect: "But execute my statue, purifying it as I shall instruct you. Make a form from wild rue and decorate it with small animals, such as lizards which live about the house. Rub a mixture of myrrh, gum, and frankincense with these animals, and out in the clear air under the waxing moon, complete this (statue) yourself while offering [a] prayer."

Questions: How does Hecate, as the female quintessence of mysteries, differ from Circe, Medea, and Erictho (see docs. 3, 4, 5)? Why might Augustine consider the oracle magic? How are demons characterized in the text?

9. MAGIC TRANSFORMS ONE INTO A BIRD, ANOTHER INTO AN ASS

Apuleius (c. 124–c. 170) was born in the city of Madaura on the North African coast in the Roman province of Numidia. He was from a locally renowned family, wealthy, well educated, and worldly. Apuleius's most famous work is The Golden Ass (Metamorphoses), *a collection of ribald and picaresque tales in which magic figures prominently as a plot device. Because of the intimate knowledge of magic that Apuleius reveals in* The Golden Ass, *he was brought to trial for sorcery, which leads us to believe that the text gives an accurate portrayal of magical beliefs in second-century Rome. Christian writers, such as Saint Augustine (354–430), knew Apuleius's work well and referred to him as a magician.*

Source: trans. William Adlington, Apuleius, *The Golden Ass: Being the Metamorphoses of Lucius Apuleius* (New York: Liveright Publishing Corp., 1927), pp. 75–78; rev. Martha Rampton.

Book 3

[Lucius is on a business trip in Thessaly and takes lodging at the home of a friend and his wife, Pamphile, where he has an affair with Fotis, a servant in the house.] One day Fotis came running to me in great trembling and said that in order to ensnare a man she desired, her mistress, Pamphile, intended the next night to transform herself into a bird and to fly to him. She said I should prepare myself to witness the transformation. About the first watch of night, she led me, walking a-tiptoe softly, into a high chamber and bid me look through the chink of a door. I first saw how Pamphile stripped off all her garments and took out of a certain coffer various kinds of boxes. She opened one of them and warmed the ointment with her fingers and then rubbed it on her body from the sole of the foot to the crown of the head. After she had whispered [a spell] to the candle she held in her hand, she shook all the parts of her body, and as they gently moved, behold, I perceived a plume of feathers burgeon out upon them. Strong wings grew, her nose became crooked and hard, her nails turned into claws, and so Pamphile became an owl. Then she cried and screeched like a bird of that kind, and testing herself, hopped up and down on the ground little by little, until at last she leaped up and flew away. Thus by her sorcery she transformed her body into whatever shape she wished. . . .

I took Fotis by the hand and moved it to my eyes and said, "I pray you, since the opportunity has presented itself that I may have the benefits of your love towards me and grant me some of this ointment. O Fotis, my honey, I pray you, by your sweet breasts, that I will ever hereafter be bound to you by a mighty gift and obedient to your commandment, if you will help me turn into a bird and stand like Cupid with his wings beside you, my Venus. . . . "But I pray you, Fotis, (which I had almost forgotten) tell me by what means, when I am an owl, I shall return to my pristine shape and become Lucius again?"

"Fear not," she said, "for my mistress has taught me the way to bring that to pass and to turn those transformed back into human shape. She did not tell me for any good will or favor to me, but to the end that I might minister this remedy to her when she returns home. Consider I pray you, with what frivolous trifles and herbs so marvelous a thing is wrought; for I give her nothing save a little dill and laurel leaves in well water which she drinks and uses to wash herself."

When Fotis had spoken she went all trembling into the chamber and took a box out of the coffer, which I first kissed and embraced, and then prayed that I might have success in my flight. And then I put off all my garments and greedily thrust my hand into the box and took out a good deal of ointment, and after I had well rubbed every part and member of my body, I hovered with my arms and hopped around, waiting to be changed into a bird as Pamphile had been. But behold neither did feathers burgeon out nor the appearance of wings, but my hair did turn into rugged bristles, and my tender skin became tough and hard, my fingers and toes losing the number of five, grew together into hooves, and from the end of my back grew a great tail. And now, my face became monstrous and my mouth long and my nostrils wide, my lips hanging down and my ears exceedingly increased with bristles. I could find no comfort in my transformation, save that the nature of my members was increasing likewise, to the great discomfiture of Fotis. And so without all help (viewing every part of my poor body) I perceived that I was no bird but a plain ass. Then I thought to blame Fotis, but being deprived of both language and human gestures, all I could do is look at her with hanging lips and watery eyes.

Questions: What comment does the tale of Pamphile make about magic and gender? Is magic a highly specialized skill?

10. JUSTIN MARTYR AND THE FALLEN ANGELS

Justin Martyr (c. 100–c. 165), a philosopher and apologist for the early church, was beheaded for his religious beliefs along with several of his students. In his two treatises, The First Apology *and* The Second Apology, *Justin defends Christianity and explains the basic precepts, rituals, and emerging theology of the fledgling church in an attempt to convince the Roman emperor Antonius Pius (86–161) and his sons (First Apology) and the Senate (Second Apology) to end the persecution of Christians. In The Second Apology, Justin lays out the seminal explanation of the role of demons in Christian thought. Unlike most other ancient cults where demons could be agents for good or ill, in the Christian scheme demons were, by definition, evil.*

Source: trans. Marcus Dods, George Reith, and B.P. Pratton. *The Writings of Justin Martyr and Athenagoras*, Ante-Nicene Christian Library, vol. 2 (Edinburgh: T. and T. Clark, 1874), pp. 75–76, 13, 17–18.

The Second Apology

Chapter 5. If some think that since we Christians acknowledge God as our helper, we should not, as we say, be oppressed and persecuted by the wicked; this I will explain. God made the whole world and subjected things earthly to man and arranged the heavenly elements for the increase of fruits and rotation of the seasons, and he appointed this divine law—for these things also he evidently made for man. At that time he committed the care of men and of all things under heaven to angels [Nephilim] whom he appointed over them. But the angels transgressed this appointment and were captivated by love of women and begat children who are called demons [Genesis 6:1–4]. They, afterward, subdued the human race to themselves, partly by magical writings, partly by fears and the punishments they occasioned, and partly by teaching them to offer sacrifices, incense, and libations, of which things the demons stood in need after they were enslaved by lustful passions. Among men the demons sowed murders, wars, adulteries, intemperate deeds, and all wickedness. Whence the poets and mythologists, not knowing that it was the fallen angels and those demons who had been begotten by them that did these things to men, women, cities, and nations, ascribed them to the god Zeus himself, and to those who were accounted to be his very offspring, and to the offspring of those who were called his brothers, Neptune and Pluto, and to the children again of these their offspring. For whatever name each of the fallen angels had given to himself and his children, by that name the pagans have called them.

The First Apology

9. And neither do we honor with many sacrifices and garlands of flowers such deities as men have formed and set in shrines and called gods, since we see that these are soulless and dead and have not the form of God (for we do not consider that God has such a form as some say that they imitate to his honor), but have the

names and forms of those wicked demons which have appeared. For why need we tell you, who already know into what forms the craftsmen—carving and cutting, casting and hammering—fashion the materials? And often out of vessels of dishonor, by merely changing the form and making an image of the requisite shape, they make what they call a god, which we consider not only senseless, but to be even insulting to God, who, having ineffable glory and form, thus gets his name attached to things that are corruptible and require constant service. And that the artificers of these are both intemperate and, not to enter into particulars, are practiced in every vice. You very well know that even their own girls who work along with them they corrupt. What infatuation that dissolute men should be said to fashion and make gods for your worship, and that you should appoint such men the guardians of the temples where they are enshrined, not recognizing that it is unlawful even to think or say that men are the guardians of gods.

14. For we forewarn you to be on your guard, lest those demons whom we have been accusing should deceive you and quite divert you from reading and understanding what we say. For they strive to hold you their slaves and servants, and sometimes by appearances in dreams and sometimes by magical impositions, they subdue all who make no strong opposing effort for their own salvation. And thus do we also, since our conversion to Christ, stand aloof from them (the demons) and follow the only unbegotten God through his son—we who formerly delighted in fornication but now embrace chastity alone; we who formerly used magical arts, dedicate ourselves to the good and unbegotten God; we who valued above all things the acquisition of wealth and possessions, now bring what we have into a common stock and communicate to everyone in need; we who hated and destroyed one another, and on account of their different manners would not live with men of a different tribe, now, since the coming of Christ, live familiarly with them, pray for our enemies, and endeavor to persuade those who hate us unjustly to live conformably to the good precepts of Christ, to the end that they may become partakers with us of the same joyful hope of a reward from God the ruler of all. But lest we should seem to be reasoning sophistically [confusing or partially incorrect], we consider it right, before giving you the promised explanation, to cite a few precepts given by Christ himself. And be it yours, as powerful rulers, to inquire whether we have been taught and do teach these things truly. Brief and concise utterances fell from him, for he was no sophist, but his word was the power of God.

Questions: For Justin, what form do the demons take on earth? If demons' abilities are efficacious, why should Christians, nevertheless, avoid them? On what grounds is Justin asking for leniency for Christians?

11. THE APOSTLE PETER TRIUMPHS OVER SIMON MAGUS

The Recognitions of Pseudo-Clement, also called Clementina, *is a fictional account in the form of a letter from Clement, perhaps a reference to Clement I, bishop of Rome (c. 35–c. 100), to the apostle James the Just, the first bishop of Jerusalem (d. c. 65). The author relates the story of how he met the apostle Peter, became his traveling companion, and converted to Christianity. A large portion of the work is devoted to Clement's theological discussions with Peter and Peter's public debates with Simon Magus, the infamous magician of Acts 8:9–24. The text is considered a novel (or romance) because of the lengthy sections that recount the dramatic story of Clement's separation from and reunification with his family.*

The basic outline of the narrative exists in two versions. One is the Clementine Homilies, *the other is* The Recognitions. *The two are very much alike, and although each has a different textual tradition, most historians conclude that both come from an earlier prototype, now lost. Scholars have debated for two centuries about the authorship, date of composition, doctrinal status, provenance, and relationship between the two texts. The original story was probably written after 325, and the* Recognitions, *represented in this reading, was composed in Greek in the second half of the fourth century. The Greek original is lost, but a monk named Tyrannius Rufinus (c. 345–410/411) condensed and translated the work into Latin about 400. It was a well-known, much cited, and often-copied story. The Recognitions contains a full range of motifs drawn from biblical sorcery, and it foreshadows elements of magic that became common throughout medieval and early modern Europe.*

Source: trans. B.P. Pratten, Marcus Dods, and Thomas Smith, "The Clementine Recognitions," in *The Writings of Tatian and Theophilus and The Clementine Recognitions,* Ante-Nicene Christian Library, vol. 3 (Edinburgh: T. and T. Clark, 1871), pp. 151, 196–202, 264, 268, 280, 289–94, 296–97, 300, 302, 322–23, 408–9, 434, 459–61, 464–65, 469.

Book 1

[Clement, concerned about his mortality, explores all possible avenues in the quest for truth. When he finally hears of Jesus of Nazareth, who worked miracles and spoke of an afterlife, Clement travels to Caesarea in Judea to consult the apostle Peter about the Christian faith.]

12. . . . When I had landed and was seeking for an inn, I learned from the conversation of the people that one Peter, a most approved disciple of him who appeared in Judaea and showed many signs and miracles divinely performed among men, was going to hold a discussion of words and questions the next day with one Simon [Magus], a Samaritan. Having heard this, I asked to be shown his lodging, and having found it and standing before the door, I informed the

doorkeeper who I was and whence I came, and behold, Barnabas [a Christian Clement had met in Rome] came out. As soon as he saw me, he rushed into my arms, weeping for joy and seizing me by the hand, he led me into Peter, having pointed him out to me at a distance. . . .

Book 2

[Niceta and Aquila of the Christian faction take Clement under their wings, warning him of Simon Magus.]

7. [Aquila begins to speak,] "This Simon's father was Antonius and his mother, Rachel. By nationality he is a Samaritan from a village of the Gettones; by profession he is a magician yet exceedingly well trained in Greek literature. He is desirous of glory and boastful above all the human race, so that he wishes himself to be believed to be an exalted power above God the creator and to be thought to be the Christ and to be called the Standing One. And he uses this name as implying that he can never be dissolved, asserting that his flesh is so compacted by the power of his divinity, that it can endure to eternity. Hence, therefore, he is called the Standing One, as though he cannot fall by any corruption."

9. . . . . "And Simon promised that, as a reward of our service, he would cause us to be invested with the highest honors, and we would be believed by men to be gods. 'Only, however, on condition,' says he, 'that you confer the chief place upon me, Simon, who by magic art am able to show many signs and prodigies, by means of which either my glory or our sect may be established. For I am able to render myself invisible to those who wish to lay hold of me, and again to be visible when I am willing to be seen. If I wish to flee, I can dig through the mountains and pass through rocks as if they were clay. If I should throw myself headlong from a lofty mountain, I should be born unhurt to the earth, as if I were held up. When bound, I can lose myself and bind those who had bound me; being shut up in prison, I can make the barriers open of their own accord; I can render statues animated, so that those who see suppose that they are men. I can make new trees suddenly spring up and produce sprouts at once. I can throw myself into the fire, and not be burnt; I can change my countenance so that I cannot be recognized; and I can show people that I have two faces. I shall change myself into a sheep or a goat; I shall make a beard to grow upon little boys; I shall ascend by flight into the air; I shall exhibit abundance of gold and shall make and unmake kings. I shall be worshipped as God; I shall have divine honors publicly assigned to me so that an image of me shall be set up; and I shall be worshipped and adored as God. And what need of more words? Whatever I wish, that I shall be able to do. For already I have achieved many things by way of experiment. In short,' says he, 'once when my mother Rachel ordered me to

go to the field to reap, and I saw a sickle lying, I ordered it to go and reap, and it reaped ten times more than the others. Lately, I produced many new sprouts from the earth, and made them bear leaves and produce fruit in a moment, and the nearest mountain I successfully bored through.'"

12. . . . "Simon took a woman called Luna to himself, and with her he still goes about, as you see, deceiving multitudes, and asserting that he himself is a certain power which is above God the creator, while Luna, who is with him, has been brought down from the higher heavens, and that she is Wisdom, the mother of all things. He says that the Greeks and barbarians were able in some measure to see an image of her, but of herself, as she is—as the dweller with the first and only God—they were wholly ignorant. Propounding these and other things of the same sort, he has deceived many. But I ought also to state this, which I remember that I myself saw. Once, when this Luna of his was in a certain tower, a great multitude had assembled to see her and were standing around the tower on all sides, and she was seen by all the people to lean forward, and to look out at the same time through all the windows of that tower. Many other wonderful things he did and does, so that men, being astonished at them, think that he himself is the great God."

13. "Now Niceta and I once asked him to explain to us how these things could be affected by the magic art . . . 'I have,' said Simon, 'made the soul of a boy, unsullied and violently slain, and invoked by unutterable adjurations, to assist me, and all is done that I command.' 'But,' said I, 'is it possible for a soul to do these things' He answered, 'I would have you know this, that the soul of man holds the next place after God, when once it is set free from the darkness of his body. And immediately it acquires prescience, wherefore it is invoked for necromancy.' Then I answered, 'Why, then, do not the souls of persons who are slain take vengeance on their slayers?' 'Do you not remember,' said he, 'that I told you, that when it goes out of the body the soul acquires knowledge of the future?' 'I remember,' said I. 'Well, then,' said he, 'as soon as it goes out of the body, it immediately knows that there is a judgment to come, and that everyone shall suffer punishment for those evils that he has done; and therefore they are unwilling to take vengeance on their slayers because they themselves are enduring torments for their own evil deeds which they had done here, and they know that severer punishments await them in the judgment. Moreover, they are not permitted by the angels who preside over them to go out, or to do anything.' 'Then,' I replied, 'if the angels do not permit them to come hither, or to do what they please, how can the souls obey the magician who invokes them?' 'It is not,' said he, 'that they grant indulgence to the souls that are willing to come, but when the presiding angels are adjured by one greater than themselves [such as myself], they have the excuse of our violence who adjure them, to permit the souls which we invoke to go out. . . .'"

14. [Niceta asks Simon if he fears the day of judgement, and] Simon grew pale; but after a little, recollecting himself, he thus answered, "Do not think that I am a man of your race. . . . For before my mother Rachel and [my father] came together, she, still a virgin, conceived me, while it was in my power to be either small or great and to appear as a man among men. Therefore I have chosen you first as my friends, for the purpose of trying you, that I may place you first in my heavenly and unspeakable places when I shall have convinced you. Therefore I have pretended to be a man, that I might more clearly ascertain if you cherish entire affection toward me." . . .

15. . . . "Now, then, I shall begin to unfold to you what is true. Once, I, by my power, turning air into water, and water again into blood, and solidifying it into flesh, formed a new human creature—a boy—and produced a much nobler work than God the Creator. For he created a man from the earth, but I from air—a far more difficult matter; and again, I unmade him and restored him to air, but not until I had placed his picture and image in my bed-chamber, as a proof and memorial of my work." Then we understood that he spoke concerning that boy, whose soul, after he had been slain by violence, he made use of for those services which he required.

Book 3

[Peter and Simon engage in a public debate.]

47. . . [Simon responds to Peter,] "Your words are all vain, nor can you perform any real works (such as I have earlier mentioned), as he also who sent you [Jesus] is a magician, who yet could not deliver himself from the suffering of the cross."

55. [Peter answers,] "On account of those, therefore, who by neglect of their own salvation please the evil one and those, who by study of their own profit seek to please the good one, ten things have been prescribed as a test to this present age according to the number of the ten plagues which were brought upon Egypt. For when Moses, according to the commandment of God, demanded of Pharaoh that he should let the people go and in token of his heavenly commission showed signs; his rod being thrown upon the ground, was turned into a serpent. And when Pharaoh could not by these means be brought to consent, as having freedom of will, again the magicians seemed to do similar signs by permission of God so that the purpose of the king might be proved from the freedom of his will, whether he would rather believe the signs wrought by Moses, who was sent by God, or those which the magicians seemed to work rather than actually wrought." [see doc. 1] . . .

[Simon Magus goes to Rome in an attempt to garner followers.]

73. A letter was received from the brethren who had gone before in which were detailed the crimes of Simon: how going from city to city he was deceiving multitudes and everywhere maligning Peter so that when he should come, no one might afford him a hearing. For he asserted that Peter was a magician, a godless man, injurious, cunning, ignorant, and professing impossible things. "For," says Simon, "Peter asserts that the dead shall rise again, which is impossible. But if any one attempts to confute him, he is cut off by secret snares through means of his attendants. Wherefore," says Simon, "when I had vanquished him and triumphed over him, I also fled for fear of his snares, lest he should destroy me by incantations or cause my death by plots." They intimated also that he mainly stayed at Tripoli.

[Peter, Clement, and their companions travel to Rome; Peter preaches and heals the sick along the way.]

Book 4

13. [Peter expounds,] "But when [Noah was saved from the flood], men turned again to impiety, and on this account a law was given by God to instruct them in the manner of living. But in process of time, the worship of God and righteousness were corrupted by the unbelieving and the wicked, as we shall show more fully by and by. Moreover, perverse and erratic religions were introduced in which the greater part of men gave themselves up to holidays and solemnities, instituting drinking and banquets, following pipes and flutes and harps and diverse kinds of musical instruments, and indulging themselves in all kinds of drunkenness and luxury. Hence every kind of error arose; they invented groves and altars, fillets [animal sacrifices], and victims; and after drunkenness they were agitated as if with mad emotions. By this means power was given to the demons to enter into minds of this sort so that they seemed to lead insane dances and to rave like Bacchanalians [participants in frenzied rituals dedicated to the god Bacchus]; hence were invented the gnashing of teeth and bellowing from the depth of their bowels. So a terrible countenance and a fierce aspect in men, whom drunkenness had subverted and a demon had instigated, was believed by the deceived and the erring to be filled with the deity."

15. "Therefore demons, as we have just said, when once they have been able, by means of opportunities afforded them, to convey themselves through base and evil actions into the bodies of men, if they remain in them a long time through their own negligence, because they do not seek after what is profitable to their souls, they necessarily compel them for the future to fulfill the desires of the demons who dwell in them. But what is worst of all, at the end of the world when that demon shall be consigned to eternal fire, of necessity, the soul

also which obeyed him shall, with him, be tortured in eternal fires together with its body which it has polluted."

16. "Now that the demons are desirous of occupying the bodies of men, this is the reason. They are spirits baring their purpose turned to wickedness. Therefore by immoderate eating and drinking and lust, they urge men on to sin, but only those who entertain the purpose of sinning, who, while they seem simply desirous of satisfying the necessary cravings of nature, give opportunity to the demons to enter into them because through excess they do not maintain moderation. For as long as the measure of nature is kept and legitimate moderation is preserved, the mercy of God does not give them liberty to enter into men. But when either the mind falls into impiety, or the body is filled with immoderate meat or drink, then, as if invited by the will and purpose of those who thus neglect themselves, they receive power as against those who have broken the law imposed by God."

17. "You see, then, how important is the acknowledgment of God and the observance of the divine religion, which not only protects those who believe from the assaults of the demon, but also gives them command over those who rule over others. And therefore it is necessary for you, who are of the gentiles, to betake yourselves to God and to keep yourselves from all uncleanness that the demons may be expelled and God may dwell in you. And at the same time, by prayers, commit yourselves to God, and call for his aid against the impudence of the demons; for 'whatever things ye ask, believing, ye shall receive' [Matthew 21:22]. But even the demons themselves, in proportion as they see faith grow in a man, in that proportion they depart from him, residing only in that part in which something of infidelity still remains, but from those who believe with full faith, they depart without any delay. For when a soul has come to the faith of God, it obtains the virtue of heavenly water by which it extinguishes the demon like a spark of fire."

19. "There is also another error of the demons, which they suggest to the senses of men such that they think that those things which they suffer, they suffer from such as are called gods, in order that thereby, offering sacrifices and gifts, as if to propitiate them, they may strengthen the worship of false religion and avoid us who are interested in their salvation that they may be freed from error. But this they do, as I have said, not knowing that these things are suggested to them by demons, for fear that they should be saved.

It is, therefore, in the power of everyone, since man has been given possession of free will, whether he shall follow us to life or the demons to destruction. Also to some the demons, appearing visibly under various figures, sometimes throw out threats, sometimes promise relief from sufferings so that they themselves may instill in those whom they deceive the opinion that they are gods so that it may not be known that they are demons. But they are not concealed from us who know the mysteries of the creation, and for what reason it is permitted to the demons to do those things in the present world? How it is allowed them to transform themselves into what figures they please, and to suggest evil thoughts, and to convey themselves by means of meats and of drink consecrated to them into the minds or bodies of those who partake of it, and to concoct vain dreams to further the worship of some idol?"

21. "Whence it is evident that they, since they are demoniac spirits, know some things both more quickly and more perfectly (than men), for they are not retarded in their learning by the heaviness of a body. And therefore they, as being spirits, know without delay and without difficulty what physicians attain after a long time and by much labor. It is no wonder, therefore, if they know somewhat more than men do. But this is to be observed, that what they know they do not employ for the salvation of souls but for the deception of them that by means of it they may indoctrinate them in the worship of false religion.

But God, that the error of so great deception might not be concealed, and that he himself might not seem to be a cause of error in permitting them so great license to deceive men by divinations, and cures, and dreams, has of his mercy furnished men with a remedy and has made the distinction of falsehood and truth obvious to those who desire to know.

This, therefore, is that distinction: what the true God speaks, whether by prophets or by diverse visions, is always true, but what is foretold by demons is not always true. It is, therefore, an evident sign that those things are not spoken by the true God if at any time there is falsehood; for in truth there is never falsehood. But in the case of those who speak falsehoods, there may occasionally be a slight mixture of truth to give, as it were, seasoning to the falsehoods."

26. "Now therefore, since you do not yet understand how great the darkness of ignorance surrounds you, meantime I wish to explain to you whence the worship of idols began in this world. And by idols I mean those lifeless images, which you worship, whether made of wood, or earthenware, or stone, or brass, or any other metals. Of these the beginning was in this way. Certain angels, having left the course of their proper order, began to favor the vices of men and in some measure to lend unworthy aid to their lust in order that by these means they might indulge their own pleasures the more, then, that they might not seem to be inclined of their own accord to unworthy services, they taught men that demons could, by certain arts—that is, by magical invocations—be made to obey men, and so, as from a furnace and workshop of wickedness, they filled the whole world with the smoke of impiety, the light of piety being withdrawn."

27. "For these and some other causes, a flood was brought upon the world, as we have said already, and shall say again, and all who were upon the earth were destroyed, except the family of Noah, who survived with his three sons and their wives. One of these, named Ham, unhappily discovered the magical

act and handed down the instruction of it to one of his sons, who was called Mesraim, from whom the race of the Egyptians and Babylonians and Persians are descended. The nations that then existed called Mesraim by the name of Zoroaster, admiring him as the first author of the magic art—under whose name also many books on this subject exist. He therefore, being much and frequently intent upon the stars and wishing to be esteemed a god among them, began to draw forth, as it were, certain sparks from the stars and to show them to men in order that the rude and ignorant might be astonished, as with a miracle, and desiring to increase this estimation of himself. He attempted these things again and again until he was set on fire and consumed by the demon himself, whom he accosted with too great importunity."

32. . . . "For the demons themselves know and acknowledge those who have given themselves up to God, and sometimes they are driven out by the mere presence of such, as you saw a little while ago, how, when we had only addressed to you the word of salutation, straightway the demons, on account of their respect for our religion, began to cry out and could not bear our presence even for a little?"

36. "But the ways in which the garment of baptism may be spotted are these: if anyone withdraw from God, the father and creator of all, receiving another teacher besides Christ, who alone is the faithful and true prophet and who has sent us twelve apostles to preach the word, or if anyone think otherwise than worthily of the substance of the godhead, which excels all things; these are the things which even fatally pollute the garment of baptism. But the things, which pollute it in actions, are these: murders, adulteries, hatreds, avarice, and evil ambition. And the things which pollute at once the soul and the body are these: to partake of the table of demons, that is, to taste things sacrificed, or blood, or a carcass that is strangled, and if there be aught else which has been offered to demons. Be this therefore the first step to you of three; which step brings forth thirty commands, and the second sixty, and the third a hundred, as we shall expound more fully to you at another time."

Book 5

[The travelers retire for the night and the next morning Peter continues teaching.]

31. "But some say, 'These things [holidays and celebrations] are instituted for the sake of joy and for refreshing our minds, and they have been devised for this end, that the human mind may be relaxed for a little from cares and sorrows.' See now what a charge you yourselves bring upon the things that you practice. If these things have been invented for the purpose of lightening sorrow and affording enjoyment, how is it that the invocations of demons are performed in groves and woods? What is the meaning of the insane whirling, and the slashing of limbs, and the cutting off of members? How is it that mad

rage is produced in them? How is insanity produced? How is it that women are driven violently, raging with disheveled hair? Whence the shrieking and gnashing of teeth? Whence the bellowing of the heart and the bowels, and all those things which, whether they are pretended or are contrived by the ministration of demons, are exhibited to the terror of the foolish and ignorant? Are these things done for the sake of easing the mind or rather for the sake of oppressing it? Do you not yet perceive nor understand that these are the counsels of the serpent lurking within you, which draws you away from the apprehension of truth by irrational suggestions of errors that he may hold you as slaves and servants of lust and concupiscence and every disgraceful thing?"

[Peter continues to travel and spread the word of God for three months, converting multitudes, and Clement accepts baptism from Peter. Clement tells Peter his life story and is reunited with his two brothers and his mother, from whom he had been separated since childhood.]

Book 9

[Clement explains God's plan to an old man, who turns out to be his father, Faustinianus, and points out the illogic of astrology and the errors of other religious traditions.]

12. "Therefore the astrologers, being ignorant of such mysteries, think that things happen by the courses of the heavenly bodies; hence also, in their answers to those who go to them to consult them as to future things, they are deceived in very many instances. Nor is it to be wondered at, for they are not prophets, but, by long practice, the authors of errors find a sort of refuge in those things by which they were deceived and introduce certain climacteric [critical, precarious] periods so that they may pretend a knowledge of uncertain things. For they represent these climacterics as times of danger in which one sometimes is destroyed, sometimes is not destroyed, but not knowing that it is not the course of the stars but the operation of demons that regulates these things. And those demons, being anxious to confirm the error of astrology, deceive men to sin by mathematical calculations so that when they suffer the punishment of sin, either by the permission of God or by legal sentence, the astrologer may seem to have spoken truth. And yet they are deceived even in this; for if men be quickly turned to repentance and remember and fear the future judgment, the punishment of death is remitted to those who are converted to God by the grace of baptism."

Book 10

12. [Clement continues,] "For, as usually happens when men see unfavorable dreams and can make nothing certain out of them, when any event

occurs, then they adapt what they saw in the dream to what has occurred; so also is mathematics. For before anything happens, nothing is declared with certainty; but after something has happened, astrologers gather the causes of the event. And thus often, when they have been at fault and the thing has fallen out otherwise then they predicted, they take the blame to themselves, saying that it was such and such a star which opposed and that they did not see it, not knowing that their error does not proceed from their unskillfulness in their art, but from the inconsistency of the whole system. . . ."

[Clement's father has gone off to visit some friends in the city of Laodicea where a group of missionaries is staying.]

53. But we, sitting with Peter the whole night, asking questions and learning from him on many subjects, remained awake through a deep delight in his teaching and the sweetness of his words. And when it was daybreak, Peter, looking at me and my brothers, said: "I wonder what has befallen your father." And while he was speaking my father came in and found Peter speaking to us about him. And when he had saluted he began to apologize, and to explain the reason why he had remained abroad. But we, looking at him, were horrified, for we saw on him the face of Simon, yet we heard the voice of our father. And when we shrank from him and cursed him, my father was astonished at our treating him so harshly and barbarously. Yet Peter was the only one who saw his natural countenance, and he said to us, "Why do you curse your father?"

And we, along with our mother, answered him, "He appears to us to be Simon, though he has our father's voice."

Then Peter said, "You indeed know only his voice, which has not been changed by the sorceries, but to me also his face, which to others appears changed by Simon's art, is known to be that of your father, Faustinianus." And looking at my father, he said, "The cause of the dismay of your wife and your sons is that the appearance of your countenance does not seem to be as it was, but the face of the detestable Simon appears in you."

54. And while [Peter] was thus speaking, one of those returned who had gone before to Antioch, and said to Peter, "I wish you to know, my lord Peter, that Simon at Antioch, doing many signs and prodigies in public, has inculcated upon the people nothing but what tends to excite hatred against you, calling you a magician, a sorcerer, a murderer; and to such an extent has he stirred up such hatred against you that they greatly desire, if they can find you anywhere, even to devour your flesh. And therefore we who were sent before, seeing the city greatly moved against you, met together in secret and considered what ought to be done."

55. And when we saw no way of getting out of the difficulty, there came Cornelius the centurion, being sent by Caesar to the president of Caesarea on public business. Him we sent with for alone and told him the reason why we were sorrowful and entreated him that, if he could do anything, he should help us. Then he most readily promised that he would straightway put Simon to flight, if only we would aid his plans. And when we promised that we would be active in doing everything, he said, "Caesar has ordered sorcerers to be sought out and destroyed in the city of Rome and through the provinces, and a great number of them have been already destroyed." . . .

56. . . . Peter, looking to our father, said, "Faustinianus, your countenance has been transformed by Simon Magus, as is evident, for he, thinking that he was being sought by Caesar for punishment, has fled in terror and has placed his own countenance upon you, if haply you might be apprehended instead of him and put to death so he might cause sorrow to your sons." . . .

60. Then Peter, moved with compassion, promised that he would restore the face of our father, saying to him, "Listen, Faustinianus, as soon as the error of your transformed countenance shall have conferred some advantage on us and shall have served the designs which we have in view, then I shall restore to you the true form of your countenance, on condition, however, that you first dispatch what I shall command you." . . .

[Peter asks Faustinianus to go to Antioch and, in the guise of Simon, extol Peter, admit Simon's error and renounce magic for Christianity.]

62. . . . And Peter gave him further instruction, saying: "When therefore you come to the place, and see the people turned by your discourse and laying aside their hatred and returning to their longing for me, send and tell me, and I shall come immediately. And when I come, I shall without delay set you free from this strange countenance and restore to you your own face, which is known to all your friends." . . .

[The plot works, the people of Antioch embrace the teachings of Peter, Peter restores Faustinianus's face, and Simon is driven from the city.]

68. . . . And the whole city began to hear, through Niceta and Aquila, that Peter was coming. Then all the people of the city of Antioch, hearing of Peter's arrival, went to meet him, and almost all the old men and the nobles came with ashes sprinkled on their heads, in this way testifying to their repentance, because they had listened to the magician Simon, in opposition to Peter's preaching.

Questions: Why does Simon Magus claim himself superior to the Christians, especially Peter? How does the author use instances of biblical magic in his defense? How do demons take control of humans? How can humans defend themselves? What is the essential difference in the methods and circumstances under which Peter and Simon use power?

12. ANTONY OF THE DESERT COMBATS DEMONS

Antony the Great (c. 251–356) has been called the "father of monasticism," and although he was not the first to seek solitude and an ascetic life of prayer in the deserts of the east, Athanasius's (c. 296–373) biography of Antony made him the most famous of the early desert fathers. Athanasius composed this paradigmatic text in Greek around 360; it reached the west through Latin translations, and it was among the best-known literary works throughout the Middle Ages. The vita *("life," i.e., biography) introduces* topoi *that became standard in hagiography, and primary among them is that holy men and women are tested by demons. Faith and the sign of the cross always triumph over the somewhat ineffectual devils, but not without a fight.*

Hagiography is a genre of literature about the saints: their lives, suffering, deaths, deeds, post-mortem miracles, cults, and the "translation" of their relics from place to place. Biographies of the holy ones were written to inspire emulation and perpetuate the memory of the saints. Hagiography is a rich source for the study of magic because the saints formed the front line against paganism and unbelief.

The text begins with a young, wealthy man from Egypt who comes across a verse in Matthew (19:21): "If you want to be perfect, go, sell what you have and give to the poor, and you will have treasures in heaven; and come, follow me." Antony, taking these words to heart, sells his goods and retreats to the desert west of Alexandria, where he lives the rest of his life as an eremitic monk. Antony faces several challenges living the life of a hermit; one is combating devils in their attempts to break his resolve and keep Christians out of the wilderness, which demons claim as their own abode. A second challenge Antony faces is coping with his own renown. Hundreds of devout imitators seek him out so that he might instruct them in the practice of monastic life. Realizing that solitary asceticism has become a movement and he its leader, Antony accepts the responsibility and schools his acolytes in all aspects of the discipline, including how to deal with the temptations and assaults of demons.

Source: trans. H. Ellershaw, Athanasius of Alexandria, *Life of Saint Antony* from *Nicene and Post-Nicene Fathers*, second series, vol. 4, St. Athanasius: Select Works and Letters (Grand Rapids, MI: Wm. B. Eerdmans Publishing Company, 1891), pp. 196–99, 201–3, 205, 207, 210, 213.

The Life of Antony

5. The Devil, who hates and envies what is good, could not endure to see such a resolution in a youth and endeavored to carry out against him what he had been wont to effect against others. First of all, he tried to lead him away from the discipline, whispering to him the remembrance of his wealth, care for his sister, claims of kindred, love of money, love of glory, the various pleasures of the table and the other relaxations of life, and at last the difficulty of virtue and

the labor of it; he suggested also the infirmity of the body and the length of time. In a word he raised in his mind a great dust of debate, wishing to debar him from his settled purpose. But the enemy saw himself to be too weak for Antony's determination, and that he rather was conquered by the other's firmness, overthrown by his great faith, and falling through his constant prayers. Then at length, putting his trust in the weapons which are "in the navel of his belly" [Job 40:16] and boasting in them, for they are his first snare for the young, he attacked the young man, disturbing him by night and harassing him by day, so that even onlookers saw the struggle which was going on between them. The one [the Devil] would suggest foul thoughts and the other [Antony] counter them with prayers, the one fire him with lust, the other, as one who seemed to blush, fortify his body with faith, prayers, and fasting. And the Devil, unhappy wight, one night even took upon him the shape of a woman and imitated all her acts simply to beguile Antony. But he, his mind filled with Christ and the nobility inspired by him, and considering the spirituality of the soul, quenched the coal of the other's deceit. Again the enemy suggested the ease of pleasure. But he like a man filled with rage and grief turned his thoughts to the threatened fire and the gnawing worm, and setting these in array against his adversary, passed through the temptation unscathed. All this was a source of shame to his foe. For he, deeming himself like God, was now mocked by a young man, and he who boasted himself against flesh and blood was being put to flight by a man in the flesh. For the Lord was working with Antony—the Lord who, for our sake, took flesh and gave the body victory over the Devil, so that all who truly fight can say, "Not I but the grace of God which was with me" [1 Corinthians 15:10].

6. At last when the dragon could not even thus overthrow Antony but saw himself thrust out of his heart, gnashing his teeth as it is written, and as it were beside himself, he appeared to Antony like a black boy, taking a visible shape in accordance with the color of his mind. And cringing to him, as it were, he plied him with thoughts no longer, for guileful as he was, he had been worsted, but at last spoke in human voice and said, "Many I deceived, many I cast down; but now attacking you and your labors as I had many others, I proved weak." When Antony asked, "Who are you who speaks thus with me?" he answered with a lamentable voice, "I am the friend of whoredom, and have taken upon me incitements which lead to it against the young. I am called the spirit of lust. How many have I deceived who wished to live soberly, how many are the chaste whom, by my incitements, I have over-persuaded? I am he on account of whom also the prophet reproves those who have fallen, saying, 'You have been caused to err by the spirit of whoredom' [Hosiah 4:12]. For by me they have been tripped up. I am he who have so often troubled you and have so often been overthrown by you." But Antony, having given thanks to the Lord, with good courage said to him, "You are very despicable then, for you are black-hearted

and weak as a child. Henceforth I shall have no trouble from you, for the Lord is my helper, and I shall look down on my enemies. Having heard this, the black one straightway fled, shuddering at the words and dreading any longer even to come near the man.

8. Thus tightening his hold upon himself, Antony departed to the tombs, which happened to be at a distance from the village, and having bid one of his acquaintances to bring him bread at intervals of many days, he entered one of the tombs, and his friend having shut the door on him, he remained within alone. And when the enemy could not endure it, but was even fearful that in a short time Antony would fill the desert with the discipline [ascetic hermits], coming one night with a multitude of demons, he so cut Anthony with stripes that he lay on the ground speechless from the excessive pain. For he affirmed that the torture had been so excessive that no blows inflicted by man could ever have caused him such torment. But by the providence of God—for the Lord never overlooks them that hope in him—the next day his acquaintance came bringing him the loaves. And having opened the door and seeing him lying on the ground as though dead, he lifted him up, and carried him to the church in the village, and laid him upon the ground. And many of his kinsfolk and the villagers sat around Antony as round a corpse. But about midnight he came to himself and arose, and when he saw them all asleep and his comrade alone watching, he motioned with his head for him to approach and asked him to carry him again to the tombs without waking anybody.

9. He was carried therefore by the man, and as he was wont, when the door was shut he was within alone. And he could not stand up on account of the blows, but he prayed as he lay. And after he had prayed, he said with a shout, "Here am I, Antony; I flee not from your stripes; for even if you inflict more, nothing shall separate me from the love of Christ" [Romans 8:35]. And then he sang, "Though a camp be set against me, my heart shall not be afraid" [Psalm 27:3]. These were the thoughts and words of this ascetic. But the enemy, who hates good, marveling that after the blows he dared to return, called together his hounds and burst forth, "You see," said he, "that neither by the spirit of lust nor by blows did we stay the man, but that he braves us; let us attack him in another fashion." But changes of form for evil are easy for the Devil, so in the night they made such a din that the whole of that place seemed to be shaken by an earthquake, and the demons, as if breaking the four walls of the dwelling, seemed to enter through them, coming in the likeness of beasts and creeping things. And the place was on a sudden filled with the forms of lions, bears, leopards, bulls, serpents, asps, scorpions, and wolves, and each of them was moving according to his nature. The lion was roaring, wishing to attack, the bull seeming to toss with its horns, the serpent writhing but unable to approach, and the wolf as it rushed on was restrained; altogether the noises of the apparitions,

with their angry raging, were dreadful. But Antony, stricken and goaded by them, felt bodily pains severer still. He lay watching, however, with unshaken soul, groaning from bodily anguish; but his mind was clear, and as in mockery he said, "If there had been any power in you, it would have sufficed had one of you come, but since the Lord has made you weak, you attempt to terrify me by numbers, and a proof of your weakness is that you take the shapes of brute beasts." And again with boldness he said, "If you are able and have received power against me, delay not to attack; but if you are unable, why trouble me in vain? For faith in our Lord is a seal and a wall of safety to us." So after many attempts they gnashed their teeth before him, because they were mocking themselves rather than him.

10. Nor was the Lord then forgetful of Antony's wrestling but was at hand to help him. So looking up he saw the roof as it were opened and a ray of light descending to him. The demons suddenly vanished, the pain of his body straightway ceased, and the building was again whole. But Antony feeling the help, and getting his breath again, and being freed from pain, besought the vision which had appeared to him, saying, "Where were you? Why did you not appear at the beginning to make my pains to cease?" And a voice came to him, "Antony, I was here, but I waited to see your fight; wherefore since you have endured and have not been worsted, I will ever be a succor to you and will make your name known everywhere." Having heard this, Antony arose and prayed and received such strength that he perceived that he had more power in his body than formerly. And he was then about thirty-five years old.

11. And on the day following he went forth still more eagerly bent on the service of God, and having fallen in with [an] old man he had met previously, he asked him to dwell with him in the desert. But when the other declined on account of his great age and because as yet there was no such custom, Antony himself set off immediately to the mountain. And yet again the enemy, seeing his zeal and wishing to hinder it, cast in his way what seemed to be a great silver dish. But Antony, seeing the guile of the evil one, stood, and having looked on the dish, he put the Devil in it to shame, saying, "Whence comes a dish in the desert? This road is not well-worn, nor is there here a trace of any wayfarer; it could not have fallen without being missed on account of its size, and he who had lost it having turned back to seek it, would have found it, for it is a desert place. This is some wile of the Devil. O you evil one, not with this shall you hinder my purpose; let it go with you to destruction." And when Antony had said this, it vanished like smoke from the face of fire.

12. Then again as he went on he saw what was this time not visionary, but real gold scattered in the way. But whether the Devil showed it, or some better power to try the athlete and show the evil one that Antony truly cared not for money, neither he told nor do we know, but it is certain that that which

appeared was gold. And Antony marveled at the quantity, but passed it by as though he were going over fire; so he did not even turn, but hurried on at a run to lose sight of the place. More and more confirmed in his purpose, he hurried to the mountain, and on the other side of the river, and having found a fort so long deserted that it was full of creeping things, he crossed over to it and dwelt there. The reptiles, as though some one were chasing them, immediately left the place. But he built up the entrance completely, having stored up loaves for six months—this is a custom of the Thebans, and the loaves often remain fresh a whole year—and as he found water within, he descended as into a shrine and abode within by himself, never going forth nor looking at any one who came. Thus he employed a long time training himself, and received loaves, let down from above, twice in the year.

13. But those of his acquaintances who came, since he did not permit them to enter, often used to spend days and nights outside, and heard as it were crowds within clamoring, dinning, sending forth piteous voices and crying, "Go from what is ours. Why are you even in the desert? You cannot abide our attack." So at first those outside thought there were some men fighting with him and that they had entered by ladders, but when stooping down they saw through a hole there was nobody; they were afraid, accounting them to be demons, and they called on Antony. Them he quickly heard, though he had not given a thought to the demons, and coming to the door he besought them to depart and not to be afraid. "For thus," said he, "the demons make their seeming onslaughts against those who are cowardly. Sign yourselves therefore with the cross and depart boldly, and let these make sport for themselves." So they departed fortified with the sign of the cross. But he remained in no wise harmed by the evil spirits, nor was he wearied with the contest, for there came to his aid visions from above, and the weakness of the foe relieved him of much trouble and armed him with greater zeal. For his acquaintances used often to come expecting to find him dead and would hear him singing, "Let God arise and let his enemies be scattered, let them also that hate him flee before his face [Psalm 68.1]. As smoke vanishes, let them vanish, as wax melts before the face of fire, so let the sinners perish from the face of God." And again, "All nations compassed me about, and in the name of the Lord I requited them" [Psalm 118:10].

[Despite his desire to be alone with God, Christians fled to the desert to hear and emulate Antony, and as a result, he began to instruct would-be ascetics on monastic discipline.]

21. "And let us strive that wrath rule us not nor lust overcome us, for it is written, 'The wrath of man works not the righteousness of God. And lust, when it has conceived, bears sin, and the sin when it is full-grown brings forth death' [James 1:20]. Thus living, let us keep guard carefully, and as it is written, 'keep our hearts with all watchfulness [Proverbs 4:23].' For we have terrible and

crafty foes—the evil spirits—and against them we wrestle, as the apostle [Paul] said, 'Not against flesh and blood, but against the principalities and against the powers, against the world rulers of this darkness, against the spiritual hosts of wickedness in the heavenly places' [Ephesians 6:12]. Great is their number in the air around us, and they are not far from us. Now there are great distinctions among them, and concerning their nature and distinctions much could be said, but such a description is for others of greater powers than we possess. But at this time it is pressing and necessary for us only to know their wiles against ourselves.

22. First, therefore, we must know this: that the demons have not been created like what we mean when we call them by that name; for God made nothing evil, but even they have been made good. Having fallen, however, from the heavenly wisdom, since then they have been groveling on earth. On the one hand they deceived the Greeks with their displays [the Greeks thought the demons were deities], while out of envy of us Christians they move all things in their desire to hinder us from entry into the heavens in order that we should not ascend up there from whence they fell. Thus there is need of much prayer and of discipline so that when a man has received, through the spirit, the gift of discerning spirits, he may have power to recognize their characteristics: which of them are less and which more evil, of what nature is the special pursuit of each, and how each of them is overthrown and cast out. For their villainies and the changes in their plots are many. The blessed Apostle and his followers knew such things when they said, 'For we are not ignorant of his devices' [2 Corinthians 2:11]. And we, from the temptations we have suffered at their hands, ought to correct one another under them. Wherefore I, having had proof of them, speak as to children.

25. Again they are treacherous and are ready to change themselves into all forms and assume all appearances. Very often also, without appearing, they imitate the music of harp and voice and recall the words of Scripture. Sometimes, too, while we are reading, they immediately repeat many times, like an echo, what is read. They arouse us from our sleep to prayers; and this constantly, hardly allowing us to sleep at all. At another time they assume the appearance of monks and feign the speech of holy men, that by their similarity they may deceive and thus drag their victims where they will. But no heed must be paid them even if they arouse to prayer, even if they counsel us not to eat at all, even though they seem to accuse and cast shame upon us for those things which once they allowed. For they do this not for the sake of piety or truth, but that they may carry off the simple to despair and that they may say the discipline is useless, and make men loathe the solitary life as a trouble and burden and hinder those who, in spite of them, walk in it.

35. When, therefore, they come by night to you and wish to tell the future, or say, 'We are the angels,' give no heed; for they lie. Yea even if they praise your

discipline and call you blessed; hear them not and have no dealings with them, but rather sign yourselves and your houses, and pray, and you shall see them vanish. For they are cowards and greatly fear the sign of the Lord's cross, since of a truth in it, the savior stripped them and made an example of them [Colossians 2:15]. But if they shamelessly stand their ground, capering and changing their forms of appearance, fear them not, nor shrink, nor heed them as though they were good spirits. For the presence either of the good or evil, by the help of God, can easily be distinguished. The vision of the holy ones is not fraught with distraction. 'For they will not strive, nor cry, nor shall anyone hear their voice [Matthew 12:19],' but it comes so quietly and gently that immediately joy, gladness and courage arise in the soul. . . .

41. And since I have become a fool in detailing these things, receive this also as an aid to your safety and fearlessness; and believe me for I do not lie. Once someone knocked at the door of my cell, and going forth I saw one who seemed of great size and tall. Then when I enquired, 'Who are you?' he said, 'I am Satan.' Then when I said, 'Why are you here?' He answered, 'Why do the monks and all other Christians blame me undeservedly? Why do they curse me hourly?' Then I answered, 'Wherefore do you trouble them?' He said, 'I am not he who troubles them, but they trouble themselves, for I have become weak. Have they not read, 'The swords of the enemy have come to an end, and you have destroyed the cities?' [Psalm 9:6]. I have no longer a place, a weapon, a city. The Christians are spread everywhere, and at length even the desert is filled with monks. Let them take heed to themselves, and let them not curse me undeservedly.' Then I marveled at the grace of the Lord and said to him, 'You who are ever a liar and never speak the truth, this at length, even against your will, you have truly spoken. For the coming of Christ has made you weak, and he has cast you down and stripped you.' But he, having heard the savior's name and not being able to bear the burning from it, vanished."

53. A few days after, as he was working (for he was careful to work hard), someone stood at the door and pulled the plait which he was working, for he used to weave baskets that he gave to those who came in return for what they brought him. And rising up he saw a beast: like a man to the thighs but having legs and feet like those of an ass. And Antony only signed himself and said, "I am a servant of Christ. If you are sent against me, behold I am here." But the beast together with his evil spirits fled, so that, through his speed, he fell and died. And the death of the beast was the fall of the demons. For they strove in all manner of ways to lead Antony from the desert and were not able.

64. And another, a person of rank, came to him, possessed by a demon, and the demon was so terrible that the man possessed did not know that he was coming to Antony. But he even ate the excreta from his body. So those who brought him besought Antony to pray for him. And Antony pitying the young

man, prayed and kept watch with him all the night. And about dawn the young man suddenly attacked Antony and gave him a push. But when those who came with him were angry, Antony said, "Be not angry with the young man, for it is not he, but the demon which is in him." And being rebuked and commanded to go into dry places, the demon became raging mad, and he has done this. "Wherefore give thanks to the Lord, for his attack on me thus is a sign of the departure of the evil spirit." When Antony had said this, straightway the young man had become whole, and having come at last to his right mind, knew where he was, and saluted the old man and gave thanks to God.

Questions: How does Antony advise his acolytes to protect themselves from demons? Why does God allow Antony to suffer? Assaults of the Devil and demons are never life-threatening in this text; how, then, is Athanasius using them as a rhetorical device? How does the desert act as the ideal terrain to promote the author's spiritual message?

13. CURSE TABLETS AND BINDING SPELLS

In the classical world there was a brisk market in the sale of ritual curses and spells inscribed on thin sheets of lead or other materials. These tablets were folded, fixed closed with nails, and deposited near the person targeted wherever the tablet would be most efficacious, such as under a threshold or in a well. Tablets were also put into graves when the agent of the curse was the spirit of the deceased person in whose tomb the tablet was placed. Sometimes the curse took the form of pictures of the victim bound with ropes or of figurines stuck with nails. Spells were generally purchased from professional scribes, and the production of binding tablets became a veritable cottage industry. Curses were regularly employed for centuries and across the social spectrum for a variety of purposes, such as success in business, winning a sporting event or a court case, to attract lovers or punish unfaithful spouses, and as counter spells. A given charm often constrained the spirits of people who died before their time and always invoked gods or goddesses to "bind" the intended victims of the spell in order to control their behaviors, for example, to appear befuddled in court or become frigid with anyone but the author of the spell. The eclectic littering of incomprehensible words and names of foreign or unknown deities throughout the spells gave the curses a potent mystical power.

Source: trans. John G. Gager, *Curse Tablets and Binding Spells from the Ancient World* (New York: Oxford University Press, 1992), pp. 57–58, 72, 103–6, 261.

[The scene in Figure 1.2 comes from a lead tablet measuring 9 x 10 centimeters fashioned in late-fourth-century Rome. The spell concerns competition in a chariot race between two teams, the Blues and the Greens. The target of the curse is members of the Blues. The square at the top left is a coffin.]

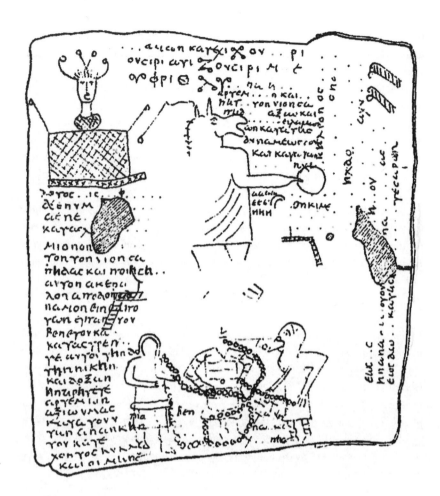

Figure 1.2: Curse tablet

Life of Saint Hilarion the Hermit

[Jerome's (c. 347–420) *Life of Saint Hilarion the Hermit* (291–371), written in the late fourth or early fifth century, demonstrates that the use of magic tablets was common enough to be a plot element in the saint's biography. In the *Life of Saint Hilarion*, a young man from Gaza unsuccessfully seeks the affection of a Christian virgin. He travels to Egypt to study the making of binding spells from a pagan healer and inscribes a magic charm on a metal tablet designed to excite the woman's desire.]

After a year of instruction with the prophets of Asclepius [god of healing], who are trained not to heal souls but to destroy them, he returned home, excited by his dreams of debauchery; at the home of the young women, under the threshold, he buried a metal tablet, made of bronze from Cyprus, engraved with various portentous words and potent figures. Immediately the young virgin went crazy [with desire for the young man].

[The following fifth-century binding spell is written on papyrus sheets measuring 22.5 x 55 centimeters and was found with two wax figures wrapped in an embrace, simulating the relationship the spell is designed to bring about. The papyrus and effigies were placed in a clay pot deposited in a cemetery, perhaps in Egypt, but the exact location is unknown.]

I bind you with the unbreakable bonds of the Fates in the underworld and powerful Necessity. For I invoke you *daimones* who lie here, who are continually nourished here and who reside here and also you young ones who have died prematurely. I invoke you by the unconquerable god IAÔ BARBATHIAÔ BRIMIAÔ [epithet for Hecate] CHERMARI. Rouse yourselves, you *daimones* who lie here and seek out Euphêmia, to whom Dôrothea gave birth, for Theôn, to whom Proechia gave birth. Let her not be able to sleep for the entire night, but lead her until she comes to his feet, loving him with a frenzied love, with affection, and with sexual intercourse. For I have bound her brain and hands and viscera and genitals and heart for the love of me, Theôn. If you ignore me and fail to carry out quickly what I tell you, the sun will not sink below the earth, nor will Hades and Earth continue to exist. But if you bring Euphêmia, to whom Dôrothea gave birth, to me, Theôn, to whom Proechia gave birth, I will give you Osiris NOPHRIÔTH, the brother of Isis [Egyptian goddess of protection], who brings cool water and will give rest to your soul. But if you fail to do what I tell you, EÔNEBUÔTH will burn you up. I invoke you, *daimones* who lie here: IEÔ IIIAIA ÊIA IAÔ IAÊ IAÔ ALILAMPS. I hand over (this spell) to you in the land of the dogs [grave yard]. Bind Euphêmia for love of me, Theôn. *Daimones*, I place an oath on you in/by the stele of the gods. I place an oath on you by those (gods) in the inner sanctuary. I place an oath on you by the names of the all-seeing god: IA IA IA IÔ IÔ IÔ IE IE IE OUÔA ADÔNAI. I invoke you who are content in the temple and (are content with) the blood seized/drunk by the great god IÔTHATH (in the temple). I invoke you by the one who sits upon the four points of the winds. Do not ignore me, but act very quickly, for I have commanded you— AKRAMMACHAMARI, BOULOMENTHOREB, GENIOMOUTHIG, DÊMOGENÊD, ENKUK-LIE, ZÊNOBIÔTHIZ, ÊSKÔTHÔRÊ, THÔTHOUTHÔTH, IAEOUÔI, KORKOUNOÔK, LOULOENÊL, MOROTHOÊPNAM, NERXIARXIN,

XONOPHOÊNAX, ORNEOPHAO, PUROBORUP, REROUTOÊR, SES-
ENMENOURES, TAUROPOLIT [epithet of Artemis], UPERPHENOUPU,
PHIMEMAMEPH, CHENNEOPHEOCH, PSUCHOPOMPOIAPS, Orion
the true! Let me not be forced to say the same things again. . . . Cause her
[Euphêmia's] limbs, her liver, and her genitals to burn until she comes to me,
loving me and not ignoring me . . . and by the implacable god CHMOUÔR
ABRASAX IPSENTHANCHOUCHAINCHOUCHEÔCH. Grab Euphêmia
and lead her to me, Theôn, loving me with a frenzied love, and bind her with
bonds that are unbreakable, strong and adamantine, so that she loves me,
Theôn; and do not allow her to eat, drink, sleep, or joke or laugh but make
(her) rush out of every place and dwelling, abandon father, mother, brothers,
and sisters, until she comes to me, Theôn, loving me, wanting me (with a)
divine, unceasing, and a wild love. And if she holds someone else to her bosom,
let her put him out, forget him, and hate him, but love, desire, and want me;
may she give herself to me freely and do nothing contrary to my will. You
holy names and powers, be strong and carry out this perfect spell. Now, now.
Quickly, quickly.

[The following spell was incised on a lead tablet of 11.8 x 5.2 centimeters in the
late fifth century and found in Apamea, a Greek city in Syria. The curse was
occasioned by a chariot competition between the Blues and the Greens.]

Most holy Lord *Charaktêres* [higher powers] tie up, bind the feet, the hands,
the sinews, the eyes, the knees, the courage, the leaps, the whip (?), the victory and the crowning of Porphuras and Hapsicratês, who are in the middle
left, as well as his co-drivers of the Blue colors in the stable of Eugenius.
From this very hour, from today, may they not eat or drink or sleep; instead,
from the (starting) gates may they see *daimones* (of those) who have died
prematurely, spirits (of those) who have died violently, and the fire of Hep-
haestus [Greek god of the forge] . . . in the hippodrome at the moment when
they are about to compete may they not squeeze over, may they not collide,
may they not extend, may they not force (us) out, may they not overtake, may
they not break off (in a new direction?) for the entire day when they are
about to race. May they be broken, may they be dragged (on the ground),
may they be destroyed; by Topos [deity] and by Zablas [angel]. Now, now,
quickly, quickly!

*Question: Interpret the elements in the image of the binding spell. Does Jerome hold
that spells are efficacious? What are the various forces Theôn enlists and techniques
he employs to achieve his ends? What beings are expected to carry out the spell from
Apamea, Greece?*

14. SAINT MARTIN BATTLES WITH PAGANS AND DEMONS

Martin, the bishop of Tours from 371/372 to 397, began his career in the Roman army, but he found war incompatible with his newly acquired Christian faith. Just before a major battle near Amiens, France, he said, "I am the soldier of Christ; it is not lawful for me to fight" (p. 6). Martin left the military and eventually settled in France, where he established the first monastery in Europe at Ligugé near Poitiers, which became a center for missionary work and preaching.

His friend and biographer, Sulpicius Severus (c. 363–c. 425), recorded Martin's deeds in one of the west's earliest and most influential hagiographical texts. Consistent with sacred biographies, Martin's vita incorporates plot elements involving contests between competing forms of spiritual expression, featuring Martin destroying outdoor pagan shrines and replacing them with churches. A sacred space purified of demons replaces an outdoor area polluted by them. In addition to converting pagans, Martin is ever vigilant against the deceits of the Devil and other demons as they battle for dominance over humankind.

Source: trans. Alexander Roberts, "Sulpitius Severus on the Life of St. Martin," in *The Works of Sulpicius Severus*, A Select Library of Nicene and Post-Nicene Fathers of the Christian Church, second series, vol. 11 (New York: The Christian Literature Company; Oxford and London: Parker & Company, 1894), pp. 10–12, 14–16.

Life of Saint Martin of Tours

[Martin destroys pagan holy places.]

13. [When in a certain village Martin] had demolished a very ancient temple and had set about cutting down a pine-tree which stood close to the temple, the chief priest of that place and a crowd of other heathens began to oppose him. And these people, under the influence of the Lord, had been quiet while the temple was being overthrown, but could not patiently allow the tree to be cut down. Martin carefully instructed them that there was nothing sacred in the trunk of a tree and urged them rather to honor God whom he himself served. He added that there was a moral necessity why that tree should be cut down, because it had been dedicated to a demon. Then one of them who was bolder than the others said, "If you have any trust in your God, whom you say you worship, we ourselves will cut down this tree, and you will stand under it as it falls; for if, as you declare, your Lord is with you, you will escape all injury." Then Martin, courageously trusting in the Lord, promised that he would do what had been asked. Upon this, all that crowd of heathens agreed to the condition named; for they held the loss of their tree a small matter if only they got the enemy of their religion buried beneath its fall. Accordingly, since

that pine tree was hanging over in one direction so that there was no doubt as to what side it would fall after being cut, Martin, having been bound, was, in accordance with the decision of these pagans, placed in that spot where, as no one doubted, the tree was about to fall. They began, therefore, to cut down their own tree with great glee and joyfulness, while there was at some distance a great multitude of wondering spectators. And now the pine tree began to totter and to threaten its own ruin by falling. The monks, at a distance grew pale and terrified by the danger coming ever nearer, and had lost all hope and confidence, expecting only the death of Martin. But he, trusting in the Lord and waiting courageously, when now the falling pine had uttered its expiring crash, while it was now falling, while it was just rushing upon him, simply holding up his hand against it, he put in its way the sign of salvation [by crossing himself]. Then, indeed, after the manner of a spinning-top (one might have thought it driven back), it swept round to the opposite side to such a degree that it almost crushed the rustics, who had taken their places there in what was deemed a safe spot. Then truly, a shout being raised to heaven, the heathen were amazed by the miracle while the monks wept for joy, and the name of Christ was in common extolled by all. The well-known result was that on that day salvation came to that region. For there was hardly one of that immense multitude of heathens who did not express a desire for the imposition of hands, and abandoning his impious errors, made a profession of faith in the Lord Jesus. Certainly, before the times of Martin, very few, nay, almost none, in those regions had received the name of Christ, but through his virtues and example, that name has prevailed to such an extent that now there is no place thereabouts which is not filled either with very crowded churches or monasteries. For wherever he destroyed heathen temples, there he used immediately to build either churches or monasteries.

14. . . . In a village which was named Leprosum, Martin wished to overthrow a temple which had acquired great wealth through the superstitious ideas the villagers held of its sanctity, and a multitude of the heathen resisted him to such a degree that he was driven back, not without bodily injury. He, therefore, withdrew to a place in the vicinity, and there for three days, clothed in sackcloth and ashes fasting and praying the whole time, he besought the Lord, that, as he had not been able to overthrow that temple by human effort, divine power might be exerted to destroy it. Then two angels with spears and shields, after the manner of heavenly warriors, suddenly presented themselves to him saying that they were sent by the Lord to put to flight the rustic multitude and to furnish protection to Martin, in case, while the temple was being destroyed, anyone should offer resistance. They told him, therefore, to return and complete the blessed work, which he had begun. Accordingly Martin returned to the village, and while the crowds of heathen looked on in

perfect quiet as he razed the pagan temple, even to the foundations, he also reduced all the altars and images to dust. At this sight the rustics, being so astounded and terrified by an intervention of the divine will and not wanting to be found fighting against the bishop, almost all believed in the Lord Jesus. They then began to cry out openly and to confess that the God of Martin ought to be worshiped and that the idols, which were not able to help them, should be despised.

15. Not unlike this was that other event which happened to Martin when a certain man had resolved to wound him with a knife as he was destroying some idols; at the very moment of fetching the blow, the weapon was struck out of his hands and disappeared. Very frequently, too, when the pagans were addressing him to the effect that he would not overthrow their temples, he so soothed and conciliated the minds of the heathen by his holy discourse that the light of truth, having been revealed to them, they themselves overthrew their own temples.

[Martin emulates Jesus by casting out devils.]

17. At the same time, the servant of one Tetradius, a man of pro-consular [governmental] rank, having been laid hold of by a demon, was tormented with the most miserable results. Martin, therefore, having been asked to lay his hands on him, ordered the servant to be brought to him, but the evil spirit could, in no way, be brought forth from the cell in which he was; he showed himself so fearful, with ferocious teeth, to those who attempted to draw near. Then Tetradius threw himself at the feet of the saintly man, imploring that he himself would go down to the house in which the possessed of the Devil was kept. But Martin then declared that he could not visit the house of an unconverted heathen. For Tetradius, at that time, was still involved in the errors of heathenism. He, therefore, pledged his word that if the demon were driven out of the boy, he would become a Christian. Martin, then, laying his hand upon the boy, cast the evil spirit out of him. On seeing this, Tetradius believed in the Lord Jesus and immediately became a catechumen and, not long after, he was baptized, and he always regarded Martin with extraordinary affection, as having been the author of his salvation.

About the same time, having entered the dwelling of a certain householder in the same town, he stopped short at the very threshold and said that he perceived a horrible demon in the courtyard of the house. When Martin ordered it to depart, it laid hold of a certain member of the family who was staying in the inner part of the house, and the poor wretch began at once to rage with his teeth and to lacerate whomsoever he met. The house was thrown into disorder, the family was in confusion, and the people present took to flight. Martin threw himself in the way of the frenzied creature and first of all commanded him to stand still. But when he continued to gnash with his teeth and, with gaping mouth, was threatening to bite, Martin inserted his fingers into his mouth and said, "If you possess any power, devour these." But then, as if red-hot iron had entered his jaws, drawing his teeth far away he took care not to touch the fingers of the saintly man, and when he was compelled by punishments and tortures to flee out of the possessed body, while he had no power of escaping by the mouth, he was cast out by means of a defluxion of the belly [excrement], leaving disgusting traces behind him.

18. In the meanwhile, as a sudden report had troubled the city as to the movement and inroad of the barbarians, Martin ordered a possessed person to be set before him, and commanded him to declare whether this message was true or not. Then he confessed that there were sixteen demons who had spread this report among the people in order that, by the fear thus excited, Martin might have to flee from the city, but that, in fact, nothing was less in the minds of the barbarians than to make any inroad. When the unclean spirit thus acknowledged these things in the midst of the church, the city was set free from the fear and tumult which had at the time been felt.

At Paris, again, when Martin was entering the gate of the city with large crowds attending him, he gave a kiss to a leper of miserable appearance, while all shuddered at seeing him do so, and Martin blessed him with the result that he was instantly cleansed from all his misery. On the following day, the man appearing in the church with a healthy skin gave thanks for the soundness of body, which he had recovered. This fact, too, ought not to be passed over in silence, that threads from Martin's garment, or such as had been plucked from the sackcloth which he wore, wrought frequent miracles upon those who were sick. For, by either being tied round the fingers or placed about the neck, they very often drove away diseases from the afflicted.

[Martin bests the Devil at every turn.]

21. It is also well known that angels were very often seen by him so that they spoke in turns with him in set speech. As to the Devil, Martin held him so visible and ever under the power of his eyes, that whether he kept himself in his proper form, or changed himself into different shapes of spiritual wickedness, he was perceived by Martin under whatever guise he appeared. The Devil knew well that he could not escape discovery and therefore frequently heaped insults upon Martin, being unable to beguile him by trickery. On one occasion the Devil, holding in his hand the bloody horn of an ox, rushed into Martin's [monastic] cell with great noise, and holding out to him his bloody right hand, while at the same time he exulted in the crime he had committed, said, "Where, O Martin, is your power? I have just slain one of your people." Then Martin assembled the brethren and related to them what the Devil had disclosed; then he ordered them carefully to search the several cells in order to discover who had been visited with this calamity. They reported that no one of the monks was missing but that one peasant, hired by them, had gone to the

forest to bring home wood in his wagon. Upon hearing this, Martin instructed some of them to go and meet him. On their doing so, the man was found almost dead at no great distance from the monastery. Although just drawing his last breath, he made known to the brethren the cause of his wound and death. He said that while he was drawing tighter the thongs, which had got loose on the oxen yoked together, one of the oxen, throwing his head free, had wounded him with his horn in the groin, and not long after the man expired. You see with what judgment of the Lord this power was given to the Devil. This was a marvelous feature in Martin that not only on this occasion to which I have specially referred, but on many occasions of the same kind, in fact as often as such things occurred, he perceived them long beforehand and disclosed the things which had been revealed to him to the brethren.

22. Now, the Devil, while he tried to impose upon the holy man by a thousand injurious arts, often thrust himself upon him in a visible form but in very various shapes. For sometimes he presented himself to his view changed into the person of Jupiter, often into that of Mercury and Minerva. Often, too, were heard words of reproach, in which the crowd of demons assailed Martin with scurrilous expressions. But knowing that all were false and groundless, he was not affected by the charges brought against him. Moreover, some of the brethren bore witness that they had heard a demon reproaching Martin in abusive terms, asking why he had taken back, on their subsequent repentance, certain of the brethren who had, some time previously, lost their baptism by falling into various errors. The demon set forth the crimes of each of them, but they added that Martin, resisting the Devil firmly, answered him that past sins are cleansed away by leading a better life and that through the mercy of God, those are to be absolved from their sins who have given up their evil ways. The Devil saying in opposition to this that such guilty men as those referred to did not come within the pale of pardon and that no mercy was extended by the Lord to those who had once fallen away. Martin is said to have cried out in words to the following effect, "If you, yourself, wretched being, would but desist from attacking mankind and even, at this period, when the day of judgment is at hand, would only repent of your deeds, I, with a true confidence in the Lord, would promise you the mercy of Christ." O what a holy boldness with respect to the loving kindness of the Lord, in which, although he could not assert authority, he nevertheless showed the feelings dwelling within him! And since our discourse has here sprung up concerning the Devil and his devices, it does not seem far from the point, although the matter does not bear immediately upon Martin, to relate what took place, both because the virtues of Martin do, to some extent, appear in the transaction, and the incident, which was worthy of a miracle, will properly be put on record with the view of furnishing a caution, should anything of a similar character subsequently occur.

24. It was found, again, that about the same time there was a young man in Spain, who, having by many signs obtained for himself authority among the people, was puffed up to such a pitch that he gave himself out as being Elias [a Hebrew prophet]. And when multitudes had too readily believed this, he went on to say that he was actually Christ, and he succeeded so well even in this delusion that a certain bishop named Rufus worshiped him as being the Lord. For so doing, we have seen this bishop at a later date deprived of his office. Many of the brethren have also informed me that at the same time one arose in the east who boasted that he was John [a disciple of Jesus]. We may infer from this, since false prophets of such a kind have appeared, that the coming of Antichrist is at hand, for he is already practicing in these persons the mystery of iniquity. And truly I think this point should not be passed over, with what arts the Devil about this very time tempted Martin. For, on a certain day, prayer having been previously offered, the fiend himself stood by the side of Martin as he was praying in his cell. He was surrounded by a purple light in order that he might the more easily deceive people by the brilliance of the splendor assumed, clothed also in a royal robe and with a crown of precious stones and gold encircling his head, his shoes too being inlaid with gold, while he presented a tranquil countenance and a generally rejoicing aspect so that no such thought as that he was the Devil might be entertained. The saint being dazzled by his first appearance, preserved a long and deep silence. This was first broken by the Devil, who said, "Acknowledge, Martin, who it is that you behold. I am Christ, and being just about to descend to earth, I wished first to manifest myself to you." When Martin kept silence on hearing these words and gave no answer whatever, the Devil dared to repeat his audacious declaration. "Martin, why do you hesitate to believe when you see? I am Christ." Then Martin, the Holy Spirit revealing the truth to him that he might understand it was the Devil, and not God, replied as follows, "The Lord Jesus did not predict that he would come clothed in purple and with a glittering crown upon his head. I will not believe that Christ has come unless he appears with that appearance and form in which he suffered and openly displaying the marks of his wounds upon the cross." On hearing these words, the Devil vanished like smoke and filled the cell with such a disgusting smell that he left unmistakable evidences of his real character. This event, as I have just related, took place in the way which I have stated, and my information regarding it was derived from the lips of Martin himself; therefore, let no one regard it as fabulous.

Questions: How are the miracles of Martin distinguishable from magic? What influences do you see on the text from the story of Aaron and the Pharaoh (doc. 1)? What role do demons and the Devil play in this text?

15. AUGUSTINE: DEMONS AND MAGIC IN THE CITY OF GOD

Saint Augustine (354–430) was the bishop of Hippo Regius (modern Annaba, Algeria). He was pre-eminent among the most influential theologians of the early church, and his articulation of numerous aspects of belief and practice was determinative in the development of Christian doctrine. In On Christian Doctrine *and* The City of God, *Augustine articulates an explanation of demons that incorporated earlier thinking and formed the basis for the Christian understanding of magic. He makes clear that the essence of magic is trafficking with demons and that it encompasses all exceptional phenomena that do not originate with God and are beyond the limits of human power. Following Augustine's lead, from Late Antiquity through the early modern era, many intellectuals held that magic involved traffic with demons and proscribed it on that basis.*

Augustine's goal in On Christian Doctrine *is to help readers teach, defend, and interpret the obscurity of Scripture. In this process, he exposes demons' putative powers as fraudulent and warns that empirical knowledge pursued for its own sake and not from or relevant to the understanding of Scripture constitutes, at best, idle curiosity and vainglory, and, at worst, hazardous traffic with demons.*

Augustine wrote The City of God *late in his life to refute charges that the Visigoths were able to sack the city of Rome in 410 because Romans had abandoned their ancestral deities for the Christian God. The book is an* opus magnum *on the great thinker's theology as it had ripened over several decades, and Augustine's synthesis became a cornerstone of Christian thought. The bishop defends the Christian religion by taking on superstitions and other belief systems of his day, but he is particularly eager to expose the errors of the Neoplatonists and their concept of the human being's relationship and access to the divine.*

Sources: trans. J.F. Shaw, *On Christian Doctrine*, in *Augustine's* City of God *and* Christian Doctrine, Nicene and Post-Nicene Fathers, vol. 2 (Buffalo: Christian Literature Company, 1887), pp. 545–47, 549–50, 553; trans. Marcus Dods, *The Works of Aurelius Augustine, Bishop*, *The City of God*, 2 vols. (Edinburgh: T & T Clark, 1872), vol. 1, pp. 186–88, 393–400, 404–7; vol. 2, pp. 235–38, 424–25.

On Christian Doctrine

Book 2

CHAPTER 20

30. All the arrangements made by men to the making and worshipping of idols are superstitious, pertaining as they do either to the worship of what is created or of some part of it as God, or to consultations and arrangements about signs and pacts with demons such, for example, as are employed in the magical arts

and which the poets are accustomed, not so much to teach, as to celebrate. And to this class belong, but with a bolder reach of deception, the books of the haruspices and augurs [religious specialists who tell the future by reading the livers of animals or the flight of birds]. In this class we must place also all amulets and cures which the medical art condemns, whether these consist in incantations or in marks, which they call characters, or in hanging or tying on or in any way wearing certain articles, not with reference to the condition of the body, but on account of certain signs hidden or manifest, and these remedies they call by the less offensive name of *physica* [medicine] so as to appear not to be engaged in superstitious observances but to be taking advantage of the forces of nature. Examples of these are the ear-rings on the top of each ear, or the rings of ostrich bone on the fingers, or telling you when you hiccup to hold your left thumb in your right hand.

31. To these we may add thousands of the most frivolous practices that are to be observed if any part of the body should jump or if, when friends are walking arm-in-arm, a stone, or a dog, or a boy should come between them. However, kicking a stone, for fear it could destroy a friendship, does less harm than to cuff an innocent boy if he happens to run between men who are walking side by side. But it is delightful that the boys are sometimes avenged by the dogs; for frequently men are so superstitious as to strike a dog who has run between them, (not with impunity however) for instead of a superstitious remedy, the dog sometimes makes his assailant run in hot haste for a real surgeon. To this class, too, belong the following rules: to tread upon the threshold when you go out in front of the house, to go back to bed if anyone should sneeze when you are putting on your slippers, to return home if you stumble when going to a place, when your clothes are eaten by mice, to be more frightened at the prospect of coming misfortune than grieved by your present loss. Whence that witty saying of Cato [Roman statesman, 234–149 BCE], who when consulted by a man who told him that the mice had eaten his boots replied, "That is not strange, but it would have been very strange indeed if the boots had eaten the mice."

CHAPTER 21

32. Nor can we exclude from this kind of superstition those who were called *genethliaci* [astrologers], on account of their attention to birthdays, but are now commonly called *mathematici*. For these, too, although they may seek with pains for the true position of the stars at the time of our birth and may sometimes even find it out, yet in so far as they attempt to predict our actions or the con-sequences of our actions, they grievously err and sell inexperienced men into a miserable bondage. For when any free man goes to an astrologer of this kind, he gives money and comes away the slave either of Mars or of Venus. Or he is a slave to all of the stars which those who first fell into this error and handed it on

to posterity have given the names either of beasts, on account of their likeness to beasts, or of men, with a view to confer honor on those men. [Augustine is referring to constellations of stars.] And this is not to be wondered at when we consider that even in times more recent and nearer our own, the Romans made an attempt to dedicate the star, which we call Lucifer, to the name and honor of [Julius] Caesar. . . .

But whatever they may be called by men, still there are stars that God has made and set in order after his own pleasure, and they have a fixed movement by which the seasons are distinguished and varied. And when anyone is born, it is easy to observe this movement by use of the rules discovered and laid down by those whom Scripture condemns in these terms, "For if they were able to know so much that they could weigh the world, how did they not more easily find out the Lord thereof?" [Wisdom 13:9].

CHAPTER 22

33. But to desire to predict the characters, the acts, and the fate of those who are born from such an observation is a great delusion and great madness. And among those at least who have any sort of acquaintance with matters of this kind (which, indeed, are only fit to be unlearnt again), this superstition is refuted beyond the reach of doubt. For the observation is of the position of the stars, which they call constellations, at the time when the person was born about whom these wretched men are consulted by their still more wretched dupes. Now it may happen that, in the case of twins, one follows the other out of the womb so closely that there is no interval of time between them that can be apprehended and marked in the position of the constellations. Whence it necessarily follows that twins are in many cases born under the same stars, but they do not meet with equal fortune either in what they do or what they suffer, but they often meet with fates so different that one of them has a most fortunate life, the other a most unfortunate. As, for example, we are told that Esau and Jacob were born twins and in such close succession that Jacob, who was born last, was found to have laid hold with his hand upon the heel of his brother who preceded him [Genesis 25:26]. Now, assuredly, the day and hour of the birth of these two could not be marked in any way that would not give both the same constellation. But what a difference there was between the characters, the actions, the labors, and the fortunes of these two. The Scriptures bear witness, which are now so widely spread as to be in the mouth of all nations.

34. Nor is it to the point to say that the very smallest and briefest moment of time that separates the birth of twins produces great effects in nature and in the extremely rapid motion of the heavenly bodies. For, although I may grant that it does produce the greatest effects, yet the astrologer cannot discover this in the constellations, and it is by looking into these that he professes to read the fates. If,

then, he does not discover the difference when he examines the constellations, which must, of course, be the same whether he is consulted about Jacob or his brother, what does it profit him that there is a difference in the heavens, which he rashly and carelessly brings into disrepute, when there is no difference in his chart, which he looks into anxiously but in vain? And so these notions also, which have their origin in certain signs of things being arbitrarily fixed upon by the presumption of men, are to be referred to the same class as if they were pacts and covenants with devils.

CHAPTER 23

35. For in this way it comes to pass that men who lust after evil things are, by a secret judgment of God, delivered over to be mocked and deceived as the just reward of their evil desires. For they are deluded and imposed on by the false angels to whom the lowest part of the world has been put in subjection by the law of God's providence and in accordance with his most admirable arrangement of things. And the result of these delusions and deceptions is that, through these superstitious and baneful modes of divination, many things in the past and future are made known and turn out just as they are foretold, and in the case of those who practice superstitious observances, many things turn out agreeably to their observances, and, ensnared by these successes, they become more eagerly inquisitive and involve themselves further and further in a labyrinth of most pernicious error. And to our advantage, the word of God is not silent about this species of fornication of the soul, and it does not warn the soul against following such practices on the ground that those who profess them speak lies, rather it says, "Even if what they tell you should come to pass, hearken not unto them" [see Deuteronomy 13:1–3]. For though the ghost of the dead Samuel foretold the truth to King Saul [see doc. 2], that does not make such sacrilegious observances as those by which his ghost was brought up the less detestable; and though the ventriloquist woman in the Acts of the Apostles bore true testimony to the apostles of the Lord, the apostle, Paul, did not spare the evil spirit on that account, but rebuked and cast it out, and so made the woman clean [Acts 16:16–18].

36. All arts of this sort, therefore, are either vacuous or are part of a guilty superstition springing out of a baleful fellowship between men and devils and are to be utterly repudiated and avoided by Christians as the covenants of a false and treacherous friendship. Not as if the idol were anything, says the Apostle [Paul], "but because the things which they sacrifice they sacrifice to devils and not to God, and I would not that you should have fellowship with devils" [1 Corinthians 10:19–20]. What the Apostle has said about idols and the sacrifices offered in their honor we ought to feel in regard to all fancied signs which lead either to the worship of idols or to worshipping creation or its parts instead of God or

which are connected with attention to medicinal charms and other observances. For these are not appointed by God as the public means of promoting love towards God and our neighbor, but they waste the hearts of wretched men in private and selfish strivings after temporal things. Accordingly, in regard to all these branches of knowledge, we must fear and shun the fellowship of demons who, with the Devil their prince, strive only to shut and bar the door against our return. Just as from the stars, which God created and ordained, men have drawn lying omens of their own fancy, so also from things that are born or in any other way come into existence under the government of God's providence. If there is something unusual in the occurrence—as when a mule brings forth young or an object is struck by lightning—men have frequently drawn omens by conjecture of their own and have committed them to writing as if they had drawn them by rule.

CHAPTER 29

45. . . . For it is one thing to say, "If you drink the juice of this herb, it will remove the pain from your stomach," and another to say, "If you hang this herb round your neck, it will remove the pain from your stomach." In the former case the wholesome mixture is approved of, in the latter the superstitious charm is condemned. Even if no incantations, invocations, and marks are used, the question is whether the thing that is tied or fixed in any way to the body to heal it acts as a natural cure; in that case, it may be freely used. But if it acts as a sort of charm, it behooves the Christian to avoid it all the more carefully the more effective it may seem to be, because when the reason for the efficacy of the thing is unclear, the intention with which it is used is of great importance, at least in healing or in tempering bodies, whether in medicine or in agriculture.

The knowledge of the stars, again, is not a matter of narration, but of description. Very few of these, however, are mentioned in Scripture. And as the course of the moon, which is regularly employed in reference to celebrating the anniversary of our Lord's passion, is known to most people, but the rising and setting and other movements of the rest of the heavenly bodies are thoroughly known to very few. And this knowledge, although in itself it involves no superstition, renders very little, indeed almost no, assistance in the interpretation of holy Scripture, and is, in fact, a hindrance. It is more convenient and becoming to neglect it because it is closely related to the very pernicious error of astrologers. It involves, moreover, in addition to a description of the present state of things, something like a narrative of the past, because one may go back from the present position and motion of the stars and trace their past movements. It involves also regular anticipations of the future, not in the way of portents and omens, but by way of sure calculation, not with the design of drawing any information from them as to our own acts and fates in the absurd fashion of the *genethliaci*, but only as to the motions of the heavenly bodies themselves. For, as the man who computes the moon's age can tell, when he has found out her age today, what her age was any number of years ago, or what will be her age any number of years hence, in just the same way men who are skilled in such computations are accustomed to answer like questions about every one of the heavenly bodies. And I have stated what my views are about all this knowledge so far as regards its utility.

CHAPTER 39

58. Accordingly, I think that it is well to warn studious and able young men, who fear God and are seeking for happiness of life, not to venture heedlessly upon the pursuit of the branches of learning that are in vogue beyond the pale of the church of Christ, as if these could secure for them the happiness they seek. Rather they should soberly and carefully choose among them. And if they find any of those which have been instituted by men varying by reason of the diverse motives of their founders and tainted by erroneous conjectures, especially if they involve entering into fellowship with devils by means of pacts and covenants about signs, let these be utterly rejected and held in detestation. Let the young men also withdraw their attention from such institutions of men as are unnecessary and luxurious. But for the sake of the necessities of this life we must not neglect the arrangements of men that enable us to carry on intercourse with those around us. I think, however, there is nothing useful in the other branches of learning that are found among the heathen except information about objects, either past or present, that relate to the bodily senses, in which are included also the experiments and conclusions of the useful mechanical arts, except also the sciences of reasoning and of number. And in regard to all these we must hold by the maxim, "Nothing in excess," especially in the case of those which, pertaining as they do to the senses, are subject to the relations of space and time.

The City of God

Volume 1

BOOK 5

7. Now, will any one bring forward this, that in choosing certain particular days for particular actions, men bring about certain new destinies for their actions? That man, for instance, according to this doctrine, was not born to have an illustrious son, but rather a contemptible one, and therefore, being a man of learning, he chose an hour in which to lie with his wife. He made, therefore, a destiny which he did not have before, and from that destiny of his own making something began to be fatal which was not contained in the destiny of his natal hour.

Oh, singular stupidity! A day is chosen on which to marry, and for this reason, I believe, that unless a day be chosen, the marriage may fall on an unlucky day, and turn out an unhappy one. What then becomes of what the stars have already decreed at the hour of birth? Can a man be said to change by an act of choice that which has already been determined for him, while that which he himself has determined in the choosing of a day cannot be changed by another power? Thus, if men alone, and not all things under heaven, are subject to the influence of the stars, why do they choose some days as suitable for planting vines or trees or for sowing grain, other days as suitable for taming beasts on or for putting the males to the females that the cows and mares may be impregnated and for such-like things? If it be said that certain chosen days have an influence on these things, because the constellations rule over all terrestrial bodies—animate and inanimate—according to differences in moments of time, let it be considered what innumerable multitudes of beings are born or arise, or take their origin at the very same instant of time, which come to ends so different, that they may persuade any little boy that these observations about days are ridiculous.

For who is so mad as to dare affirm that all trees, all herbs, all beasts, serpents, birds, fishes, worms, have each separately their own moments of birth or commencement? Nevertheless, men are wont, in order to try the skill of the *mathematici*, to bring before them the constellations of dumb animals, the constellations of whose birth they diligently observe at home with a view to this discovery, and they prefer those *mathematici* to all others, who say from the inspection of the constellations that they indicate the birth of a beast and not of a man. They also dare tell what kind of beast it is, whether it is a wool-bearing beast, or a beast suited for carrying burdens, or one fit for the plough, or for watching a house; for the astrologers are also tried with respect to the fates of dogs, and their answers concerning these are followed by shouts of admiration on the part of those who consult them. They so deceive men as to make them think that during the birth of a man the births of all other beings are suspended, so that not even a fly comes to life at the same time that he is being born, under the same region of the heavens. And if this be admitted with respect to the fly, the reasoning cannot stop there but must ascend from flies till it lead them up to camels and elephants. Nor are they willing to attend to this, that when a day has been chosen whereon to sow a field, so many grains fall into the ground simultaneously, germinate simultaneously, spring up, come to perfection, and ripen simultaneously; and yet, of all the ears which are coeval [same date of origin], and, so to speak, con-germinal, some are destroyed by mildew, some are devoured by the birds, and some are pulled by men. How can they say that all these had their different constellations, which they see coming to so different ends? Will they confess that it is folly to choose days for such things and to affirm that they do not come within the sphere of the celestial decree, while they subject men alone to the stars, on whom alone in the world God has bestowed free wills? All these things being considered, we have good reason to believe that, when the astrologers give very many wonderful answers, it is to be attributed to the occult inspiration of spirits not of the best kind, whose care it is to insinuate into the minds of men, and to confirm in them, those false and noxious opinions concerning the fatal influence of the stars, and not to their marking and inspecting of horoscopes, according to some kind of art which in reality has no existence.

BOOK 10

8. . . . How striking also were the wonders done by Moses to rescue God's people from the yoke of slavery in Egypt, when the *magi* of the pharaoh, that is, the king of Egypt, who tyrannized over this people, were suffered to do some wonderful things that they might be vanquished all the more signally! They did these things by the magical arts and incantations to which the evil spirits or demons are addicted; while Moses, having as much greater power as he had right on his side, and having the aid of angels, easily conquered them in the name of the Lord who made heaven and earth. And, in fact, the magicians failed at the third plague; whereas Moses, dealing out the miracles delegated to him, brought ten plagues upon the land. . . .

9. These miracles, and many others of the same nature, which it is tedious to mention, were wrought for the purpose of commending the worship of the one true God and prohibiting the worship of a multitude of false gods. Moreover, they were wrought by simple faith and godly confidence, not by the incantations and charms composed under the influence of a criminal tampering with the unseen world, of an art which they call either "magic," or by the more abominable title "necromancy," or the more honorable designation "theurgy"; for they wish to discriminate between those whom the people call magicians, who practice necromancy, and are addicted to illicit arts and condemned, and those others who seem to them to be worthy of praise for their practice of theurgy—the truth, however, being that both classes are the slaves of the deceitful rites of the demons whom they invoke under the names of angels. . . .

One time [Porphyry, philosopher, c. 233–c. 305 CE], warns us to avoid [theurgy] as deceitful, and prohibited by law, and dangerous to those who practice it; then again, as if in deference to its advocates, he declares it useful for cleansing one part of the soul, not, indeed, the intellectual part, by which the truth of things intelligible, which have no sensible images, is recognized, but the spiritual part, which takes cognizance of the images of things material. This part, he says, is prepared and fitted for intercourse with spirits and angels and for the vision of the gods, by the help of certain theurgic consecrations, or, as they call them, mysteries. . . . And therefore, although he distinguishes angels from demons, asserting that the habitation of the latter is in the air, while the former dwell in the ether and empyrean [the highest heaven], and although he advises us to cultivate the friendship of some demons, who may be able after our death to assist us and elevate us at least a little above the earth—for he owns that it is by another way we must reach the heavenly society of the angels—he at the same time distinctly warns us to avoid the society of demons, saying that the soul, expiating its sin after death, execrates the worship of demons by whom it was entangled. And of theurgy itself, though he recommends it as reconciling angels and demons, he cannot deny that it treats with powers, which either themselves envy the soul its purity or serve the arts of those who do envy it. He complains of this through the mouth of some Chaldean or other, "A good man in Chaldea complains," he says, "that his most strenuous efforts to cleanse his soul were frustrated because another man, who had influence in these matters and who envied his purity, had prayed to the powers, and bound them by his conjuring not to listen to his request. Therefore," adds Porphyry, "What the one man bound, the other could not loose."

10. . . . O excellent theurgy! O admirable purification of the soul!—a theurgy in which the violence of an impure envy has more influence than the entreaty of purity and holiness. Rather let us abominate and avoid the deceit of such wicked spirits and listen to sound doctrine. As to those who perform these filthy cleansings by sacrilegious rites and see in their initiated state (as [Porphyry] further tells us, though we may question this vision) certain wonderfully lovely appearances of angels or gods; this is what the Apostle refers to when he speaks of "Satan transforming himself into an angel of light" [2 Corinthians 11:14]. For these are the delusive appearances of that spirit who longs to entangle wretched souls in the deceptive worship of many and false gods and to turn them aside from the true worship of the true God, by whom alone they are cleansed and healed, and who, as was said of Proteus, "turns himself into all shapes" [Virgil, 70–19 BCE, *Georgics*, iv.411], equally hurtful, whether he assaults us as an enemy, or assumes the disguise of a friend.

11. [Porphyry] inquires further, and still as one in doubt, whether diviners and wonderworkers are men of unusually powerful souls, or whether the power to do these things is communicated by spirits from without. He inclines to the latter opinion, on the ground that it is by the use of stones and herbs that they lay spells on people, and open closed doors, and do similar wonders. And on this account, he says that some suppose that there is a race of beings whose property it is to listen to men—a race deceitful, full of contrivances, capable of assuming all forms, simulating gods, demons, and dead men—and that it is this race which brings about all these things which have the appearance of good or evil, but that what is really good they never help us in, and are indeed unacquainted with, for they make wickedness easy but throw obstacles in the path of those who eagerly

follow virtue. And that they are filled with pride and rashness, delight in sacrificial odors, are taken with flattery. These and the other characteristics of this race of deceitful and malicious spirits, who come into the souls of men and delude their senses, both in sleep and waking, . . . [are] commonly received opinions. . . .

As to his idea that by means of herbs, and stones, and animals, and certain incantations and noises, and drawings—sometimes fanciful, and sometimes copied from the motions of the heavenly bodies—men create upon earth powers capable of bringing about various results; all that is only the mystification which these demons practice on those who are subject to them, for the sake of furnishing themselves with merriment at the expense of their dupes. . . .

16. What angels, then, are we to believe in this matter of blessed and eternal life?—those who wish to be worshipped with religious rites and observances and require that men sacrifice to them, or those who say that all this worship is due to one God, the creator, and teach us to render it with true piety to him. . . . Prodigies, which at intervals happen from some unknown physical causes and which are arranged and appointed by divine providence, such as monstrous births and unusual meteorological phenomena, whether startling only, or also injurious, are said to be brought about and removed by communication with demons, and by their most deceitful craft. . . . If, therefore, any angels demand sacrifice for themselves, we must prefer those who demand it, not for themselves, but for God, the creator of all, whom they serve. For thus they prove how sincerely they love us, since they wish by sacrifice to subject us, not to themselves, but to him by the contemplation of whom they themselves are blessed, and to bring us to him from whom they themselves have never strayed. If, on the other hand, any angels wish us to sacrifice, not to one, but to many, not, indeed, to themselves, but to the gods whose angels they are, we must in this case also prefer those who are the angels of the one God of gods, and who so bid us to worship him as to preclude our worshipping any other. But, further, if it be the case, as their pride and deceitfulness rather indicate, that they are neither good angels nor the angels of good gods, but wicked demons, who wish sacrifice to be paid, not to the one only and supreme God, but to themselves, what better protection against them can we choose than that of the one God whom the good angels serve, the angels who bid us sacrifice, not to themselves, but to him whose sacrifice we ourselves ought to be?

Volume 2

BOOK 18

18. Perhaps our readers expect us to say something about this so great delusion wrought by the demons, and what shall we say but that men must fly out of the

midst of Babylon? [Isaiah 48:20]. For this prophetic precept is to be understood spiritually in this sense, that by going forward in the living God, by the steps of faith, which work by love, we must flee out of the city of this world, which is altogether a society of ungodly angels and men. Yea, the greater we see the power of the demons to be in these depths, so much the more tenaciously must we cleave to the mediator through whom we ascend from these lowest to the highest places. For if we should say these things are not to be credited, there are not wanting even now some who would affirm that they had either heard on the best authority, or even themselves experienced, something of that kind. Indeed, we ourselves, when in Italy, heard such things about a certain region there, where landladies of inns, imbued with these wicked arts, were said to be in the habit of giving to such travelers as they chose, or could manage, something in a piece of cheese by which they were changed on the spot into beasts of burden, and carried whatever was necessary, and were restored to their own form when the work was done. Yet their mind did not become bestial, but remained rational and human, just as Apuleius, in the books he wrote with the title of *The Golden Ass* [see doc. 9] has told, or feigned, that it happened to his own self that, on taking poison, he became an ass, while retaining his human mind.

These things are either false, or so extraordinary as to be with good reason disbelieved. But it is to be most firmly believed that almighty God can do whatever he pleases, whether in punishing or favoring, and that the demons can accomplish nothing by their natural power (for their created being is itself angelic, although made malign by their own fault), except what he may permit, whose judgments are often hidden but never unrighteous. And indeed the demons, if they really do such things as these on which this discussion turns, do not create real substances, but only change the appearance of things created by the true God so as to make them seem to be what they are not. I cannot therefore believe that even the body, much less the mind, can really be changed into bestial forms and lineaments by any reason, art, or power of the demons, but the phantasm of a man, which even in thought or dreams goes through innumerable changes, may, when the man's senses are laid asleep or overpowered, be presented to the senses of others in a corporeal form, in some indescribable way unknown to me, so that men's bodies themselves may lie somewhere, alive, indeed, yet with their senses locked up much more heavily and firmly than by sleep, while that phantasm, as it were embodied in the shape of some animal, may appear to the senses of others and may even seem to the man himself to be changed, just as he may seem to himself in sleep to be so changed, and to bear burdens. And these burdens, if they are real substances, are borne by the demons, that men may be deceived by beholding at the same time the real substance of the burdens and the simulated bodies of the beasts of burden.

For a certain man called Præstantius used to tell that it had happened to his father in his own house, that he took that poison in a piece of cheese and lay in his bed as if sleeping, yet could by no means be aroused. But he said that after a few days he, as it were, woke up and related the things he had suffered as if they had been dreams, namely, that he had been made a sumpter horse, and, along with other beasts of burden, had carried provisions for the soldiers of what is called the Rhœtian Legion, because it was sent to Rhœtia. And all this was found to have taken place just as he told; yet it had seemed to him to be his own dream. And another man declared that in his own house at night, before he slept, he saw a certain philosopher, whom he knew very well, come to him and explain to him some things in the Platonic philosophy, which he had previously declined to explain when asked. And when he had asked this philosopher why he did in his house what he had refused to do at home, he said, "I did not do it, but I dreamed I had done it." And thus what the one saw when sleeping was shown to the other when awake by a phantasmal image.

These things have not come to us from persons we might deem unworthy of credit, but from informants we could not imagine to be deceiving us. Therefore, what men say and have committed to writing about the Arcadians being often changed into wolves by the Arcadian gods, or demons rather, and what is told in song about Circe transforming the companions of Ulysses, if they were really done, may, in my opinion, have been done in the way I have said. . . .

Book 21

6. . . . Now devils are attracted to dwell in certain temples by means of the creatures (God's creatures, not theirs), who present to them what suits their various tastes. They are attracted, not by food like animals, but, like spirits, by such symbols as suit their taste: various kinds of stones, woods, plants, animals, songs, rites. And that men may provide these attractions, the devils first of all cunningly seduce them, either by imbuing their hearts with a secret poison or by revealing themselves under a friendly guise, and thus make a few of them their disciples, who become the instructors of the multitude. For unless they first instructed men, it were impossible to know what each of them desires, what they shrink from, by what name they should be invoked or constrained to be present. Hence the origin of magic and magicians. But, above all, they possess the hearts of men and are chiefly proud of this possession when they transform themselves into angels of light. Very many things that occur, therefore, are their doing, and these deeds of theirs we ought all the more carefully to shun as we acknowledge them to be very surprising. And yet these very deeds forward my present arguments. For if such marvels are wrought by unclean devils, how much mightier are the holy angels! And what cannot that God do who made the angels themselves capable of working miracles?

Questions: To what does Augustine refer when he speaks of the Chaldean? There is evidence of a binding spell in the reading; how does it operate? What form of magic does Augustine spend the most effort refuting? What is the nature of the demons in the readings? How powerful are they? How does Augustine distinguish when medical cures are legitimate and when they are not? Why does Augustine object to what he considers silly superstitions? Under what circumstances is it acceptable to wear amulets around the neck? What is Augustine's objection to amulets when used inappropriately? Why is Augustine opposed to astrology? Is astrology magical? What is Augustine's understanding of the Pythoness of Endor's revivification of Samuel? For Augustine, how does one learn truths about the physical world?

CHAPTER TWO

POST-ROMAN KINGDOMS OF EUROPE: TRAFFIC WITH DEMONS (500–750)

Figure 2.1 Merovingian chatelaine. A chatelaine is a tinned copper-alloy plate that was attached to a woman's belt suspended from a chain designed for carrying items such as keys. The girdle-hanger, found in Amiens, Somme in Northern France and held at the British Museum, captures the syncretism between pagan and Christian iconography in the Merovingian period. The eagle has pagan connotations of Jupiter for the Romans and Woden for the Franks. The fact, however, that similar plates with incised crosses have been found at other sites suggests that a Christian interpretation may overlay the pagan scene, with the eagle representing Christ, and the fish a redeemed human soul.

Christianity was legalized in 313, and by the late fourth century the imperial government's patronage of the church had significantly undermined pagan cults in the urban centers, but the struggle to convert the diverse peoples of the vast Roman Empire had barely begun. If the denizens of the east and cities bordering the Mediterranean were essentially proselytized by 500, that was not the case with the country-dwellers or *pagani* of northern and western Europe. The project of indoctrinating into the faith nominal Christians across the continent and British Isles was one of the major undertakings of European post-Roman institutions and would continue for centuries.

The efforts of the church to penetrate the continent and bring people to a deep and full understanding of Christianity were bedeviled by the shortage of personnel. There simply were not enough bishops, priests, nuns and monks to do the job, and given this, ritual became an important tactic of evangelization. Without the resources to impart a sound and thorough grasp of doctrine, the church sought to exact a program of rites that would keep the *rustici* (not to mention the urbanites) on the path to salvation. Whereas it was impractical to educate the average person on subtle theological doctrine, it seemed possible to convince all Christians that power inhered in the sign of the cross or the water of the baptismal font.

The basic theological assessment of magic in Europe and Anglo-Saxon England was similar to that of the early church. The understanding of magic as traffic with the evil spirits that fell from heaven stayed consistent, and the teachings of church fathers such as Justin Martyr (c. 100–c. 165) and Augustine (354–430) were authoritative (see docs. 10, 15). Overt idolatry remained a concern for the church, but the challenge lay not so much in the ancient cities of the Fertile Crescent and Levant as it did in the forests and farms of the northwest. Pagan religions continued to flourish, and their eradication is a persistent theme in the literature of the period, particularly in hagiography. Even trickier than suppressing organized cults, however, was the problem of persistent pagan/ demonic "superstitions" thoroughly ingrained in the daily lives of the people. As ecclesiastics refined and more carefully sculpted the contours of the religion, they found ever more superstitions to weed out, so new practices were continually added to the catalogue of forbidden rites. Forms of cult worship, once thought of as sacred by the people who inherited them, were condemned as demonic.

In the late Roman state, magic was most strenuously opposed when it entered the political arena because magicians had the ability to manipulate public events, but by the sixth century that was no longer the major concern. Sorcery still had a significant political dimension (for example, fortune-telling could affect the elevation of bishops), but the real threat lay in *maleficium* and other forms of day-to-day magic, which were practiced covertly in the homes, fields, and forests of all classes, from the powerful to the less enfranchised.

The demonology that Augustine articulated as to the limitations of evils spirits' capabilities would hold for centuries, but by the sixth century there was still no consistent understanding as to which of the symbols, signs, and ritual objects inherited from classical paganism were acceptable for Christian devotion and which were so tainted by their pagan origins that they were, in fact, demonic. Added to this was the complicating fact that other paganisms—Germanic and Celtic—with their own vocabularies of magic had to be scrutinized once they were encountered by those structuring the expanding church.

The many pagan rituals in the home for health, harvests, and the like, and domestic magical customs persisted and looked eerily similar to orthodox Christian practice because pagan and Christian religious systems constructed meaning from a common storehouse of signs and symbols. This, in part, accounts for people's continued use of Christian verbal formulas, symbols, and rituals in what elites considered atavistic pagan worship. The clergy's frustration expressed in the sources is palpable over the seeming inability of the Christian flock to distinguish the work of God from the deceits of demons and their refusal to abandon ancient cults. So while stamping out pagan, demonic, and superstitious practices, the early medieval church was tasked with the additional challenge of clarifying and re-clarifying acceptable rites that employed long-established language, symbols, and substances and separating them from their old pagan connotations.

Early medieval devils, including Satan himself, had little chance of success in any given contest with Christians who properly used prophylactic rituals such as crossing themselves. Humans, who appropriately solicited divine help, could always prevail. Generally demons were bunglers and so pathetically outdone that they appeared despondent and childlike, almost pitiable in their ineptitude in the face of simple Christian formulas. The motif commonly contrived in early medieval hagiography, whereby a saint is tempted by and easily subdues demons, rendered demons familiar and manageable. In contests between the power of saints and demonic pagan deities, the saints always prevailed, and rather handily. For this reason, although medieval people recognized the reality of demons and magic, they were in no sense preoccupied with or terrified by them. This is even the case in clerical writings where magic is taken very seriously, but it is put in the same class as many other sins. Sorcerous magic was commonplace, natural—one more effort on the part of the forces of evil to tempt humankind.

In short, in post-Roman Europe, magic and magical ritual, especially in the form of *maleficium* and superstition, were components of men's and women's everyday reality. Largely for this reason, magic was a persistent thorn in the side of religious and secular authorities who labored to identify and eradicate it, often by introducing Christian rituals in place of those that summoned the demons of the lower air.

16. THREE POST-ROMAN LAW CODES AGAINST MALICIOUS MAGIC

Secular law codes of the early medieval kingdoms cast light on early medieval magic. They do not aim to regulate morals or even to comment on fitting Christian behavior; rather, their focus is on property rights, injury, marriage, slander, and compliance with authority. They seek to obviate feuds and secure the peace by ensuring that aggrieved families or individuals are duly compensated based on an index of fines calibrated on the social class of the offended party. Magic is rarely mentioned, and when it is, the laws deal with personal injury and slander. The moral dimension of causing harm by sorcery was essentially a church matter and is addressed in other types of sources, such as penitentials and ecclesiastical council records.

Salic Law Code

The Salic law code commissioned by King Clovis (c. 466– c. 511), founder of the Frankish Merovingian dynasty, was the first written compilation of civil law in the post-Roman west. The code was used in Francia throughout the early Middle Ages. Eighty copies of the manuscript from the sixth to the ninth centuries and four redactions are extant. The Salic law code was reissued several times, but whether or not the laws were enforced as written is not certain.

Source: trans. Martha Rampton, *Pactus legis Salicae*, ed. K.A. Eckhardt, Monumenta Germaniae Historica, *Leges* 4.1 (Hanover: Brepols, 1962), pp. 81–82, 230–31.

19. About Magic or Herbs

1. If anyone enchants another person by giving him an herbal potion to drink and that person dies and it can be proven, let him be judged liable for 8000 *denarii* [silver coins], which make 200 *solidi* [gold coins], or he will surely be burned.

2. If anyone gives another person an herbal potion to drink in order to enchant him and the person who drank the potion survives, let the doer of these evil deeds, who has been proven to be guilty and is convicted, be judged liable for 2500 *denarii*, which make 62 and a half *solidi*.

3. If anyone throws a magic spell on another wherever he goes, let him be judged liable for 2500 *denarii*, which make 62 and a half *solidi*.

4. If any woman works magic on another woman such that she is not able to have children, let her be judged liable for 2500 *denarii*, which make 62 and a half *solidi*.

64. About Sorcerers

1. If anyone calls another person a sorcerer, meaning a maker of magic potions, or claims that the accused person carries a kettle to the place where sorceresses cook, and none of this can be proven let him be judged liable for 2500 *denarii*, which make 62 and a half *solidi*.

2. If, with intent, anyone calls a free woman a witch or a prostitute, and it cannot be proven, let him be judged liable for 2500 *denarii* which make 87 [sic] and a half *solidi*.

3. If a female witch eats a man and it is proven, let her be judged liable for 8000 *denarii*, which make 200 *solidi*.

The Visigoth Code

The Visigoths were Germanic peoples who entered the Roman Empire from the east in the late fourth century as federates. After a period of warfare with Rome, the Visigoths settled in southern Gaul and Spain, where they adapted to Roman culture and accepted Catholic Christianity. King Chindasuinth (c. 563–653) promulgated the law code of the Visigoths in 643, and subsequent kings added to and amended the original. The entries below fall under Title Two, *which also includes abortion, injuries, wounds, mutilations, and homicide, thus indicating how magic was categorized. The code contains twelve "books," each with multiple "titles," so proscriptions of magic represent a minor proportion of the whole.*

Source: trans. S.P. Scott, *The Visigothic Code (Forum Judicum)* (Boston: The Boston Book Company, 1910), pp. 203–5.

Book 6: Concerning Crimes and Tortures

TITLE 2: CONCERNING MALEFACTORS AND THEIR ADVISERS AND POISONERS

1. Whoever plots the death of the king or any of his subjects, and, with a view to the execution of such a crime, consults diviners, augurs, or soothsayers, should he be freeborn, he shall be scourged and be condemned to perpetual slavery in the public service, after the confiscation of all his property, or he shall be delivered up as a slave to anyone whom the king may select, and those who have given him advice shall undergo the same penalty. And if any children should be implicated in the crime of their parents, they shall be punished in like manner. But if said children should be innocent, they shall not be degraded in rank and shall enjoy full and undisturbed possession of all the property which their parents have lost. Slaves who are implicated in such offences shall be tortured in various

ways, sold, and transported beyond the sea; as the vengeance of the law does not excuse those who have voluntarily participated in such infamous proceedings.

3. Enchanters and invokers of tempests, who, by their incantations, bring hailstorms upon vineyards and fields of grain, or those who disturb the minds of men by the invocation of demons or celebrate nocturnal sacrifices to devils, summoning them to their presence by infamous rites; all such persons detected, or found guilty of such offences by any judge, agent, or superintendent of the locality where these acts were committed, shall be publicly scourged with two hundred lashes, shall be scalped, and shall be dragged by force through ten villages of the neighborhood, as a warning to others. And the judge, lest, hereafter, the aforesaid persons may again indulge in such practices, shall place them in confinement and see that they are provided with clothing and food, to deprive them of any opportunity of inflicting further injury; or he may lay the matter before the king, to be disposed of at his royal pleasure. Those who are convicted of having given advice to such persons, shall each receive two hundred lashes in the assembly of the people, in order that all who have aided in the commission of such a crime may not go unpunished.

4. We decree, by the present law, that if any freeman or slave, of either sex, should attempt to employ, or should employ witchcraft, charms, or incantations of any kind with intent to strike dumb, maim, or kill, either men or animals, or injure anything movable, or should practice said arts to the detriment of crops, vineyards, or trees; he shall suffer in person and property the same damage he endeavored to inflict upon others.

Law of the Lombards

The Lombards migrated from Germany into Italy in the mid-sixth century. In 643, King Rothair (c. 606–652) instigated the first written law code, and between 713 and 744, King Luitprand (c. 690–744) expanded on Rothair's collection by adding 153 titles.

Source: trans. Martha Rampton, *Die Gesetze der Langobarden*, ed. Franz Beyerle (Weimar: H. Böhlaus Nachf, 1947), pp. 76, 148, 152, 248–50.

Rothair's Edicts

197. On the abominable crime [of *maleficium*]. If anyone who has the *mundium* [legal guardianship] of a free girl or a woman, other than her father or brother, calls her a witch, (that is a sorceress) he will lose her *mundium*. She then has the right to choose whether she wishes to return to her relatives or commend herself and her own property to the court of the king, who will then control her *mundium*. If the accuser denies the charge, he may purify himself [by oath], and if he clears himself, he will have her *mundium*, just as before.

198. On the crime of accusing a girl. If someone accuses a girl or free woman who is in the *mundium* of another of being a harlot or a witch, and he seems clearly to have blurted out this accusation due to intense fury, then he can offer an oath with his twelve oath helpers [character witnesses] confirming that he accused her of this abominable crime in anger and not with sure knowledge. For these idle and thoughtless words that he should not have spoken, he will pay twelve *solidi* and be exonerated. But if he perseveres and says that he is able to prove the accusation, then the case will be determined by a duel according to the judgment of God. And if he proves that she is guilty, she will be judged according to this code. . . .

368. On Duelers. When fighting a duel, a man may not carry on himself herbs prepared by witches or any other such things except the agreed upon weapons. If it is suspected that he secretly carries these things, the judge will search him and the objects will be pulled out and thrown away. . . . He will swear that he does not have on himself anything that belongs to witches. Then he can proceed to the contest.

376. No one may presume to kill another person's *aldia*, or female servant, on the grounds that she is a witch (which people call sorceress), because it is in no way believable to Christian minds that it is possible for a woman to eat a living man from the inside. If anyone presumes to perpetuate such an unlawful and abominable affair, that is if he kills an *aldia* for this reason, he shall pay compensation. . . .

Laws of Luitprand, fifteenth year (727) 84.1. If anyone, ignoring the fear of God, goes to male or female fortune-tellers for receiving from them divination or information of any such kind, he shall pay compensation to the royal fisc [treasury], and in addition he shall do penance according to the established canon. Similarly, if he prays to a tree that the peasants consider sacred, worships springs, or makes sacrilegious incantations, he shall also pay compensation to the royal fisc. If he knows of fortune-tellers but does not expose them or conceals those who go to fortune-tellers and does not report them, he shall be subjected to the punishment indicated above. Further, he who sends his male or female servants to these fortune-tellers for information and it is proven, he shall be subjected to the punishment noted above. If servants visit fortune-tellers for the purpose of acquiring knowledge without the will, much less the authority, of their lord, then their lord ought to sell them outside the region. And if the lord neglects to do this he shall be subject to the punishment indicated above.

Questions: Which of the crimes above is the most serious? How do we know? What protections do the codes provide against false accusation? Why is the punishment for those using magic carried out publicly in the Visigoth Code? Do the Lombard laws explain why people should not go to or tolerate fortune-tellers? What protection do the laws provide for women?

17. CAESARIUS OF ARLES PREACHES AGAINST MAGIC AND PAGANISM

Among the most valuable collections for the study of magic in Merovingian Gaul are the sermons of Caesarius (c. 470–542). He was the bishop of Arles for forty years and a man renowned and respected for his intellectual acumen and statesmanship. He dedicated himself to fostering a deeper understanding of the faith in Christian communities. Caesarius was solicitous of the laity and composed over 250 sermons dedicated, in part, to helping his parishioners understand the perilous dimensions of demonism and to dissuading them from illicit popular practices. Many of his orations are deeply indebted to the works of Augustine (see doc. 15), and he quoted the Bishop of Hippo frequently. The sermons were widely distributed and reproduced throughout the early Middle Ages. Caesarius sent his divine readings to several bishops, urging that they be used in monasteries and read out in local churches. The impact of the bishop's works endured in western Europe for centuries.

The sermons are particularly articulate about how magic worked on a day-to-day basis. Because they were so widely known, Caesarius's descriptions of sorcery, superstition, and pagan practices are especially helpful in understanding broad societal perceptions of the magic arts of the time.

Source: trans. Mary M. Mueller, *Saint Caesarius of Arles, Sermons*, vol. 1 (New York: Fathers of the Church, 1956), pp. 253–54, 256–70.

Sermon 50

1. You know, dearly beloved, that all men seek bodily health, but this we should acknowledge, that, although health of body is good, health of the heart is much better. Consequently, all Christians should always pray especially that God will deign to grant them health of soul because of their devout life. . . . If only they would run to the church even when they are sick in body and ask for healing from the mercy of Christ. What is deplorable is that there are some who seek soothsayers in every kind of infirmity. They consult seers and divines, summon enchanters, and hang diabolical phylacteries and magic letters on themselves. Often enough they receive charms even from priests and monks, who, however, are not really religious or clerics but the Devil's helpers. See, brethren, how I plead with you not to consent to accept these wicked objects, even if they are offered by clerics. There is no remedy of Christ in them, but the poison of the Devil, which will not cure your body but will kill your poor soul with the sword of infidelity. Even if you are told that the phylacteries contain holy facts and divine lessons, let no one believe it or expect health to come to him from them. If some people have recovered their health by these charms, it was the Devil's cunning that did it. Sometimes he has taken away bodily infirmity

because he has already killed the soul. The Devil, indeed, does not want to kill the body as much as the soul. To try us he sometimes is permitted to strike our bodies with some infirmity; then, when we later agree to enchanters and phylacteries, he may kill our soul. For this reason, the phylacteries sometimes seem to have power and beneficial effects; when the Devil has affected the soul with its consent, then he ceases to trouble the body. Anyone who makes these phylacteries or asks to have them made, as well as all those who consent to it have become pagans, and unless they perform sufficient penance they cannot escape punishment. However, brethren, ask health from Christ who is the true light. Hurry to church, be anointed with holy oil, and receive the Eucharistic Christ. If you do this, you will receive health of soul as well as of body.

Sermon 51

1. Some men and women, dearly beloved, when they see that they have no children in their married life, often become too sad. To make matters worse, they often are prevailed upon to believe that they can have children like the sap of trees, not from God but from some kind of impious drug. If anyone, deceived by a friend of the Devil, has done this, he should do penance with great compunction of heart; whoever with the Lord's help has not done so should see to it that he never does. Not only should a man refrain from it himself, but to the best of his ability by his salutary advice he should not allow others to do it either. If God does not want to give them children, devout Christians should not suffer too much mental anxiety. When God grants children we should thank him, and if he does not give them we should nevertheless thank him, because he knows best what is good for us.

4. Therefore, those to whom God is unwilling to give children should not try to have them by means of herbs or magic signs or evil charms. It is becoming and proper for Christians especially not to seem to fight against the dispensation of Christ by cruel, wicked boldness. Just as women whom God wants to bear more children should not take medicines to prevent their conception, so those whom God wishes to remain sterile should desire and seek this gift from God alone. They should always leave it to divine providence, asking in their prayers that God in his goodness may deign to grant what is best for them. Those women whom God wants to bear children should take care of all that are conceived, or give them to someone else to rear. As many as they kill after they are already conceived or born, before the tribunal of the eternal judge they will be held guilty of so many murders. If women attempt to kill the children within them by evil medicines, and themselves die in the act, they become guilty of three crimes on their own: suicide, spiritual adultery, and murder of the unborn child. Therefore, women do wrong when they seek to have children by means of evil drugs. They sin still more grievously when they kill the children who are already

conceived or born, and when by taking impious drugs to prevent conception they condemn in themselves the nature which God wanted to be fruitful. Let them not doubt that they have committed as many murders as the number of the children they might have begotten.

Sermon 52

1. I repeat again as I have frequently admonished you, dearly beloved, that no one of you should think that martyrs cannot live in our times. Martyr is a Greek word, which in Latin means a witness. As we have often said, anyone who bears witness to Christ for the sake of justice is without doubt a martyr. Likewise, anyone who resists the champions of dissipation and persecutors of chastity out of love for God will receive the crown of martyrdom. Therefore, there are martyrs even in our day. If a man reproves evil-doers with justice and charity, or warns against the indiscriminate taking of oaths, perjury, calumny, and slander, he will be Christ's martyr by giving testimony to the things which please God. Moreover, one who restrains men from observing omens, wearing phylacteries, or consulting magicians and seers is known to bear testimony to Christ when he speaks against these temptations of the Devil.

2. Besides, dearly beloved, the temptation of our adversary is not slight when foolish men think that days and months, the sun and the moon, should be worshiped. What is worse, so true is what we are talking about that not only in other places but in this very city there are said to be some unfortunate women who refuse to spin or weave on Thursday in honor of Jove. In such people baptism is violated and the sacraments of Christ suffer injury.

3. How is it that foolish men think they should, as it were, help the moon in its eclipse? When its shining orb is covered at certain times by a natural condition of the air or is suffused with the nearby heat of the setting sun, they think that there is some conflict of incantations against heaven. This they imagine they can overcome by the sound of a trumpet or the ridiculous tinkling of bells that are violently shaken, through the vain persuasion of pagans believing they make the moon friendly to themselves by their wicked shouting. Now, since at God's bidding it renders service to rational man, why does man render foolish obedience to it, to the insult of God? Let every wise and pious man, we beg you, avoid and detest these errors, or, rather, this madness, this shameful mockery. If the substance of this heavenly body is inferior to you, why do you fear to offend it by your silence? If it is superior to you, why do you think it needs your help?

5. Dearly beloved, it is also due to the deadly cleverness of the hidden persecutor [Devil], as we have said before, that mothers in grief and terror hasten when their sons are troubled with various trials or infirmities. What is worse, they do not entreat the church's remedy, the author of salvation and the

eucharistic Christ. Nor, as it is written that they should, do they ask the priests to anoint them with blessed oil, or place all their hopes in God. They act in the opposite manner, so that while they seek bodily health they effect the death of souls. If only they would seek that health from the simple skill of doctors! However, they say to themselves, "Let us consult that soothsayer, seer, oracle, or witch. Let us sacrifice a garment of the sick person, a girdle that can be seen and measured. Let us offer some magic letters, let us hang some charms on his neck." In all this the Devil has one aim: either to cruelly kill the children by abortion, or to heal them still more cruelly by the charms.

Sermon 53

1. It is a source of pleasure to us, dearly beloved, to see you faithfully coming to church, and for this we give the greatest thanks to God. Truly, this is becoming and proper for Christians, to hasten like good sons to their mother, the church, with the greatest longing and true piety. But, although we rejoice at this, dearly beloved, to see you hasten faithfully to church, we are sad and we grieve because we know that some of you rather frequently go over to the ancient worship of idols, like the pagans who have no God or grace of baptism. We have heard that some of you make vows to trees, pray to fountains, and practice diabolical augury. Because of this there is such sorrow in our hearts that we cannot receive any consolation. What is worse, there are some unfortunate and miserable people who not only are unwilling to destroy the shrines of the pagans, but even are not afraid or ashamed to build up those which have been destroyed. Moreover, if anyone with a thought of God wants to burn the wood of those shrines or to tear to pieces and destroy the diabolical altars, they become angry, rave with fury, and are excited with excessive frenzy. They even go so far as to dare to strike those who, out of love for God, are trying to overthrow the wicked idols; perhaps they do not even hesitate to plan their death. What are these unfortunate, miserable people doing? They are deserting the light and running to darkness; they reject God and embrace the Devil. They desert life while they follow after death; by repudiating Christ they proceed to impiety. Why, then, did these miserable people come to church? Why did they receive the sacrament of baptism, afterwards they intended to return to the profanation of idols? Truly in them is fulfilled what was written, "The dog is returned to his vomit and the pig to his wallowing in the mire" [2 Peter 2:22]. They do not fear what the Lord said through his Prophet, "He that sacrifices to gods shall be put to death, save only to the Lord" [Exodus 22:20], moreover, in the Psalms, "All the gods of the gentiles are devils, but the Lord made the heavens"; and again, "Let them be all confounded that adore graven things, and that glory in their idols" [Psalms 96:5, Vulgate].

2. Therefore, brethren, whoever you are who have not done such wrong to the loving Christ, see to it that you never do so. Be careful lest those desperate, wicked men overwhelm you, and lest after Christ's sacraments you return to the poison of the Devil. Rather, rebuke whomever you recognize as such, admonish them quite harshly, chide them quite severely. If they are not corrected, strike them if you can; if they are not corrected thus, pull their hair. If they still continue, tie them with bonds of iron, so that a chain may hold those whom Christ's grace does not hold. Then, do not permit them to restore the shrine, but endeavor to tear to pieces and destroy them wherever they are. Cut the impious wood down to the roots, break up the altars of the Devil. Moreover, know this, dearly beloved, that when he is baptized every man is separated from the following and army of the Devil. However, if later on there is a return to the practice of that impiety which we mentioned before, Christ is immediately deserted and the Devil again takes hold. It would have been a less serious matter not to come to Christ than afterwards to desert him, according to what the apostle, Peter, says about the matter, "It were better for them not to have known the way of justice than, having known it, to turn back" [2 Peter 2:21].

Sermon 54

1. You well know, dearly beloved, that I have frequently exhorted you with paternal solicitude, advising and proclaiming that you should by no means observe those wicked practices of the pagans. However, as I hear reported of many, our admonition has not profited some individuals. If I do not speak about it, I will have to render an evil account on judgment day for both of us, and I, together with you, will have to endure eternal punishments. Therefore, I acquit myself before God if I admonish you repeatedly and assert that none of you should consult sorcerers, seers, or soothsayers, questioning them for any reason or infirmity. No one should summon charmers, for if a man does this evil, he immediately loses the sacrament of baptism, becoming at once impious and pagan. Unless generous almsgiving together with hard, prolonged penance saves him, such a man will perish forever. Likewise, do not observe omens or pay attention to singing birds when you are on the road, nor dare to announce devilish prophecies as a result of their song. No one should set any store on certain days for leaving home and certain days for returning again, because God made all the days. As Scripture says, "And there was made the first day" [Genesis 1:5], also a second and third in like manner, then a fourth, a fifth, a sixth, and a sabbath; and "God made all very good" [Genesis 1:31]. And do not pin any faith on or pay any attention to the both impious and ridiculous (interpretation of) sneezes. As often as there is need for you to hurry, sign yourself in

the name of Christ, devoutly recite the Creed or Lord's Prayer, and go on your way secure in God's help.

2. If under God's inspiration you scorn and despise all those impious practices, the Devil will not accept this willingly. When he sees you leave his friendship and society, despising the evil with which he deceived you, he is going to do other villainy to you, perhaps cause some infirmity or take away one of your animals through disease or wandering. God allows this to happen to find out whether you are coming to him with devotion, wholeheartedly despising the Devil's inventions, and whether his love or the loss of an animal has more weight with you. If with your whole strength and complete fidelity you despise the wickedness which the Devil inspires, God will deign to keep the Devil himself from attacking you, and he will never be able to deceive you with his cleverness. However, even if men who are careless and easily swayed, with weak wills and a tepid faith, begin, they do not persevere in the works of God. When they refrain from the evil practices that have been indicated and allow even one of the Devil's tricks, they immediately repent of their conversion to God and abandonment of the Devil's inventions. Such men return again to the observance of omens, as dogs to their vomit. You, however, to whom God has given wisdom and true faith, should despise with all your heart the illusions of the Devil, and faithfully be converted to God. Then you will patiently and courageously endure whatever the Devil wishes to send you, saying with blessed Job [in the Hebrew Bible, a righteous man whom God punished] that the Lord gave, and the Lord has taken away; as it has "pleased the Lord, so is it done" [Job 1:21]. With the Apostle [Paul], too, you may say with a firm and generous heart, "Who shall separate us from the love of Christ? Shall tribulation, or persecution, or distress, or hunger, or nakedness, or the sword, or danger?" [Romans 8:35]. Good Christians are not separated from Christ even by torture. Tepid and careless ones, however, are sometimes separated from him by idle tales; if they suffer even a slight loss they are immediately scandalized, dare to murmur against God, and return to their impious, detestable omens.

3. Perhaps someone says, "What are we to do, for the magicians and seers often announce true omens to us?" Concerning this the Scriptures warn and advise us: even if they tell you the truth, do not believe them, "For the Lord your God tries you, whether you fear him, or not" [Deuteronomy 13:3]. Again you say, "Sometimes many would run the risk even of death from the bite of a snake or some infirmity if there were no magicians." It is true, dearly beloved, that God permits this to the Devil, as I already mentioned above, to try Christian people. Thus, when they sometimes are able to recover from sickness by these impious remedies, men see some truth in them and afterwards more readily believe the Devil. However, if a man wants to practice the Christian religion with all his heart, he should despise all these things with all the strength of his soul, fearing the Apostle's rebuke, "You are observing

days and seasons; I fear for you, lest perhaps I have labored among you in vain" [Galatians 4:10–11]. Behold, the Apostle says that one who observes omens receives his teaching to no purpose. Therefore, avoid the Devil's tricks as much as you can.

4. Above all, brethren, know that the Devil cannot injure you, those who belong to you, your animals, or the rest of your earthly substance even in small matters, unless he receives his power from God. Just as he did not dare to destroy the wealth of holy Job without the Lord's permission, so we read in the Gospel that when the demons were driven out of men they asked to be allowed to enter swine. I beseech you to consider this, brethren. If the demons did not dare to enter swine without receiving the Lord's permission, who would be so perfidious as to believe they can harm good Christians in any way unless God allows it in his providence? God permits this for two reasons: either to try us, if we are good, or to punish us, if we are sinners. However, if a man patiently endures the dispensation of the Lord—and, as I already said, when he loses something says, "The Lord gave, and the Lord has taken away. As it has pleased the Lord, so is it done; blessed be the name of the Lord" [Job 1:21]—he will receive a crown for his patience that is pleasing to God if he is just, and forgiveness if he is a sinner. Notice, brethren, that when the Devil had destroyed all the earthly substance of blessed Job, Job did not say that the Lord gave, the Devil has taken away, but "The Lord gave, and the Lord has taken away." That holy man was unwilling to give the Devil the glory of being able to take away anything that the Lord had not permitted him to remove. Since the Devil could not have injured the children, youths, camels, asses, or sheep of blessed Job before the Lord gave his permission, why do we think that he can do to Christians more than the divine power allows in its just and secret judgment?

5. Therefore, since we believe most certainly that we can lose nothing but what God allows to be taken away, let us cling to his mercy with all our heart, and after faithfully abandoning impious observances let us always presume upon his help. If a man believes in the aforementioned evils—magicians, seers, soothsayers, phylacteries, and other omens—it profits him nothing even if he fasts, prays, continually runs to church, gives generous alms, and afflicts his body with every sort of mortification, as long as he does not abandon those impious practices. That impious, wicked observance ruins and destroys all those good actions to such an extent that they cannot profit men when they wish to exercise good works along with those evils. What the Apostle says is true: "A little leaven ferments the whole lump," and "You cannot drink the cup of the Lord and the cup of devils; you cannot be partakers of the table of the Lord and of the table of devils" [1 Corinthians 10:20, 21]. Moreover, the Lord says in the Gospel, "No man can serve two masters" [Matthew 6:24]. Therefore,

Christians should not fulfill vows to trees or adore fountains, if by God's grace they desire to be free from eternal punishment. So, if a man has any kind of shrines on his land or in his country house, trees or altars near his estate where miserable men are wont to fulfill such vows, if he does not destroy them and cut them down, he will doubtless be a participant in those impious practices which are carried on there. How is it that when those trees where vows were fulfilled are cut down no one takes the wood of them for his hearth? See the misery and foolishness of men; they pay honor to a dead tree, but despise the commands of the living God. They do not dare to throw the branches of a tree into the hearth, but by their wickedness they cast themselves into hell. If anyone does not practice this evil, he should rejoice and thank God, faithfully striving to persevere in good works. However, if anyone has surrendered himself as the Devil's captive by these devilish practices, he should do penance with all his heart. He should flee and despise those aforementioned evils in all horror so that God may grant him pardon and make him arrive at eternal bliss for the glory of his name.

6. It further occurs to me that some people, through either simplicity or ignorance or, what is certainly more likely, gluttony, do not fear or blush to eat of that impious food and those wicked sacrifices which are still offered according to the custom of the pagans. For this reason, I exhort you, and before God and his angels I proclaim, that you should not come to those devilish banquets which are held at a shrine or fountains or trees. Moreover, if anything from them comes to you, shudder and reject it as if you saw the Devil himself; refuse it in such a way that you do not permit anything from such an impious feast to be brought into your home. As the Apostle says, "You cannot drink the cup of the Lord and the cup of devils; you cannot be partakers of the table of the Lord and of the table of devils" [1 Corinthians 10:20–21]. Although some are accustomed to say, "I sign myself and then eat," no one should presume to do this. If a man signs himself on the lips and puts a sword into his heart, then, just as the body is slain with a sword, so the soul is killed by that evil food. However, we trust in God's mercy that he will deign to inspire you to do what is right so that the wickedness of the Devil may never overtake you in omens or the other impious practices and prophecies which were mentioned above. Thus, you will place all your hope in God, seeing that you never return to those abominable evils which are included above—with the help of our Lord Jesus Christ, to whom is honor and might for ever and ever. Amen.

Questions: What is Caesarius's position on the efficacy of magic? Why does he insist that his parishioners avoid the practices he proscribes? Why does Caesarius refer to various passages of the Bible? How does Caesarius view poison?

18. CONTINUITY IN MAGIC SPELLS

The curse tablets and binding spells used on a routine basis in the Roman world persisted well into the sixth century when Christianity was the dominant religion in Europe, despite the clergy's unrelenting insistence that Christian rituals such as prayer and making the sign of the cross replace pagan magical formulas. Whether references to the magic tablets reflected contemporary practice or constituted standard formulas copied from text to text over the centuries is not always clear. Below are two examples of magic tablets appearing in the storylines of saints' biographies.

Source: trans. John G. Gager, *Curse Tablets and Binding Spells from the Ancient World* (New York: Oxford University Press, 1992), pp. 262–63.

164. Cyril of Scythopolis c. 525–c. 558,
Life of Saint Euthymius 377–473

. . . The brother of a certain presbyter, Achthabios, falls seriously ill after an enemy persuades a local wizard (*goês*) to kill him through a spell. The ill man, Romanos, prays to Euthymius for help. The saint appears in response to the pious prayer. . . .

"I am Euthymius, summoned here in faith [in spirit form]. There is no need to be afraid. Show me where your pain is." When he pointed to his stomach, the apparition (the saint) straightened out his fingers, cut open the spot as if with a sword and withdrew from his stomach a tin strip which had certain *charaktêres* [in a mysterious script] on it and placed it on the table in front of him. He then wiped clean the spot with his hand and closed the incision.

165. Sophronius (c. 560–638),
Account of the Miracles of Saints Cyrus and John . . . (d. 304 or 311)

[Sophronius was a patriarch of Jerusalem. His life of two Alexandrian saints, Cyrus and John, narrates several episodes relating to spells and charms in which the saints show their superior power by overcoming curses invoked by pagan practitioners.]

How Theophilos Was Bound Hand and Foot by Magic.

Certain people wanted him (the devil) to do him (Theophilos) harm and enlisted him on their side. He was persuaded by their foul petitions and caused no slight harm to the poor man by binding him hand and foot and afflicting him with terrible pains. . . . (Local doctors fail to heal Theophilos and he appeals to the saint) . . . They appeared to him in a dream and gave him the following instructions: "Ask the *philoponoi* [medical assistants] to carry you and go to the sea early in the morning. There you will come upon one of the fishermen casting his net into the water. Agree on a fee with him to toss the net into the water for you. Whatever he catches will be the source of your cure." . . . After a short time he tossed the net and pulled out a very small box, secured not just with locks but muzzled with lead seals. . . . (There followed a dispute about ownership) . . . With much effort they opened the box before everyone's eyes and discovered a terrible and disturbing sight . . . a carved image in human form, made of bronze and resembling Theophilos, with four nails driven into its hands and feet, one nail for each limb. When the bystanders beheld this, they were astonished and did not know what to make of it. . . . One of them gave the command to pull the nails out, if it could be done. He took the statue and grabbled the nail stuck into the right hand, and with much effort, succeeded in drawing it out. Once it was out, Theophilos' right hand was immediately restored, and he ceased suffering the great pain and the related condition of paralysis. And it became clear to all what abominable magic the charlatans had used against him in cooperation with those most evil demons by throwing it (the box) into the deep waters so that it would not be recovered. . . . They hastened to remove the remaining nails. . . . As they removed them, the ill man was released from his bonds and suffering, until all of them were drawn out. Thus the sick man was relieved of the entire diabolical business. When they removed the nail on the left hand of the statue, the suffering man was able immediately to stretch out. And when they pulled out the nails driven into its feet, the sick man was able to move with no pain at all.

Questions: A new element appears in the binding spells in the stories of Euthymius and Theophilos that is missing in some earlier charms (see doc. 13); what is that element? Why were local doctors ineffective in curing Theophilos?

19. A WARNING TO PEASANTS ABOUT THE EVILS OF TRAFFICKING WITH DEMONS

Saint Martin (c. 520–580) was an archbishop of Braga (in modern Portugal), the founder of several monasteries, and a leading ecclesiastical figure in the Spanish church. A prolific writer, he authored a collection of the sayings of Egyptian monks, wrote poetry, and composed two works adapted from the essays of the Roman writer Seneca (c. 4 BCE–65 CE, see doc. 4). The sermon composed in letter form to his fellow bishop, Polemius of Astorga (in modern Spain, fl. 570), is written in a rustic style, seemingly with the expectation that it would be read out in church. It is a valuable source of information on peasant mentality—or rather the elite view of peasant mentality. Much of On the Correction of the Peasants echoes standard beliefs of the intelligentsia and clerical injunctions against rural paganism and superstitious practices reminiscent of the early period of Christian history. The letter evinces acquaintance with Caesarius of Arles's sermons (see doc. 17). Although the population in and surrounding Braga was nominally converted, the bishop explains once more, with a sense of frustration, the rudiments of what it meant to be a Christian in good standing.

Source: trans. Martha Rampton, Martin of Braga, *On the Correction of the Peasants, Opera Omnia*, ed. C.W. Barlow (New Haven, CT: Yale University Press, 1950), pp. 183–88, 191–92, 194–95, 197–200.

Bishop Martin to the most blessed lord and brother in Christ, Bishop Polemius, whom I very greatly miss.

1. I have received the letter of your holy charity, in which you write to me in order that I might send to you some writings on the origin of idols and on their crimes for the correction of the peasants, who, held captive in their former superstition of the pagans, pay more attention to demons than to God. . . . And therefore, with God aiding you, this shall be the beginning of your sermon.

3. When in the beginning God made heaven and earth, he created in that heavenly dwelling spiritual creatures, that is to say, angels, who stood in his presence and praised him. One of them, who was the first created of all the archangels, seeing himself shining in such glory, did not give honor to God his creator, but said that he was equal to him. And due to this pride, he and many other angels who conspired with him, were flung from the celestial seat into the air which is under heaven. And he who had previously been an archangel, lost the light of his glory and became a dark and horrible devil. The angels who were in league with him were also banished from heaven, and they lost their splendor and became demons. There remained, however, angels who were subject to God and remained in glorious splendor in the sight of the Lord. And they are called the holy angels. Now those who with their prince Satan were hurled from heaven because of their pride, are called the renegade angels and demons.

4. After this angelic ruin it pleased God to fashion humans from the slime of the earth, whom he put in paradise and said to them that if they obey the commandments of the Lord, they will advance without death to that celestial place from whence the renegade angels fell. If, however, they should disregard the commands of God, they will perish in death. The Devil seeing that man had been made for that reason and would replace him in the kingdom of God from which, due to envy, he had fallen, he persuaded man to ignore the commands of God. . . .

7. Then the Devil who was thrown out of heaven along with his ministers, the demons, saw that ignorant humans were ignoring God their creator and were led astray by these creatures. They began to show themselves to humans in various forms and to talk to them and ask them for sacrifices in the highest

mountains and in the leafy forests and to worship them instead of God. They took for themselves the names of evil people [from the past], who had lived their lives in crime and villainy. Thus, one said that he was Jupiter and a magician; he was so unchaste in adulteries that he took his own sister as his wife. She was called Juno. Jupiter defiled his own daughters, Minerva and Venus, and vilely debauched his nieces and all his family. Another demon called himself Mars, who had been a perpetrator of arguments and discord. And then another demon wanted to call himself Mercury, and he was the cunning inventor of all theft and fraud whom greedy men honored as if he were the god of profit. They made a place to render sacrifice to him by heaping stones together into a pile of rocks where four roads crossed. Also, another demon gave himself the name of Saturn, who lived in all cruelty and even devoured the sons born to him. Another demon fashioned herself as Venus, who was a prostitute. Not only did she prostitute herself with many adulterers, but also with her own father, Jove and her own brother Mars.

8. Behold what kind of desolate, lost people there were at that time, who ignorant peasants, because of their delusions, most wickedly honored. And so the demons took on the names of [Jupiter, Venus and the like] and imitated the deeds of those whose names they had assumed in order that humans might worship them as gods and offer them sacrifices. These demons also persuaded people to make temples for them and to put pictures and statues there of accursed men and to construct altars to them at which they poured out, in their honor, not only the blood of animals but even that of humans. Furthermore, many demons among those who were expelled from heaven presided over the sea, or rivers, or springs, or forests. The people of the time, ignoring God, worshipped demons as though they were gods, and sacrificed to them. In the sea the demon is called Neptune; in the rivers, Lamia; in the springs, Nymphs; and in the forests, Diana, and all of them are malignant demons and vile spirits, who injure and harass faithless humans who do not know how to defend themselves by the sign of the cross. . . .

11. . . . Behold, you [the peasants] carry out your silly superstitions in secret or openly and never cease from sacrificing to these demons. And why do they not provide for you so that you are always full and secure and happy? Why, when God is angered, do these vane sacrifices not defend you from the locust, the mouse and many other tribulations that an angry God visits upon you?

12. Do you not clearly understand that the demons are lying to you in these, your beliefs that you hold in vain, and they fool you in your auguries that you attend frequently? For as the most wise Solomon said, "Divinations and auguries are vanities" [Ecclesiasticus 34:5], and the more a man fears these things, the more his heart is deceived. "Do not set your heart upon [dreams], for they have betrayed many" [cf. Ecclesiasticus 34:6–7]. Behold, sacred Scripture says, and it

is most certainly true, that so long as demons persuade unhappy men through the call of birds, for the sake of frivolous and empty things, they lose their faith in Christ. Unexpectedly, they will encounter ruin through their own deaths. God has not ordained that people should know future things, but has ordered them always to live in fear of him and to seek from him direction and aid in their lives. It is for God alone to know something before it happens. However, demons trick foolish men through various arguments until they are led to offend God, and then the demons drag human souls with them into hell. From the beginning demons have done this due to envy, lest a man should enter the kingdom of heaven from which they were evicted.

14. . . . For the unbelievers, or those who have not been baptized, or if by chance they were baptized but after baptism returned again to idols and murders or adulteries or perjuries and all kinds of evil deeds and died without penance, all these are damned with the Devil, and with all the demons that they adored and whose work they have done, they are bodily sent into the eternal fire of hell. . . .

16. Behold, by what kind of command and confession you are held before God! And how is it that some of you, who renounced the Devil, and his angels, and his cult, and his works of evil again revert to the cult of the Devil? For to burn candles at rocks and trees and springs and at crossroads, is this anything except the worship of the devil ?. To heed divinations and auguries and observe the days of the idols, what is that except worship of the Devil? To observe the *Vulcanalia* [festivals for Vulcan] and the *kalends* [feasts on the first day of the months], to adorn tables with laurel wreaths, and watch your step or scatter wine and fruit on the hearth or the trunk of a tree or to put bread into a spring, what is this if not worship of the Devil? When women call on Minerva at their looms and plan their weddings on the day of Venus, to pay attention as to which day to leave for a journey, is this anything but the worship of the Devil? To sing spells over herbs and invoke the name of demons, is this anything other than worship of the Devil? And many other things like this you do that are too numerous to mention. Behold, all these things after renouncing the Devil, after you have been baptized! You return to the worship of demons and to the evil works of idols; you break your faith and ignore the pact you made with God. You dismiss the sign of the cross that you accepted in baptism and honor other signs of the Devil through little birds, and sneezings, and many other things like this. How are you or I or any proper Christian not hurt by augury? Because where the sign of the cross excels, the sign of the Devil is nothing. Why does this injure you? Because you scorn the sign of the cross, and yet you fear the power that you yourselves have attached to the sign. Likewise, you dismiss holy incantations, that is the words that you accepted in baptism, "I believe in God the all-powerful father," and the Lord's Prayer, that is "Our Father who art in heaven." You hold onto diabolical incantations and songs. Therefore, whoever scorns the sign of the

cross of Christ and recognizes other signs loses the sign of the cross which he accepted in baptism. Similarly, he who holds fast to other incantations invented by magicians and evil-doers loses the incantation of the holy creed and of the Lord's prayer, which he received in the faith of Christ. He tramples the faith of Christ; because it is not possible to honor both God and the Devil.

Questions: What elements of the theology contained in the sermons are consistent with early Christian literature, and what might the inclusion of these elements lead you to conclude about the source? To what motive does Martin seem to attribute the recidivism of peasants? What does the sermon suggest about Martin's approach to persistent paganism and superstitious practices?

20. SORCERY IN GREGORY OF TOURS'S SIXTH-CENTURY GAUL

Gregory of Tours (c. 538–594) was a Gallo-Roman bishop whose works are critical to scholars of the sixth century, because sources are relatively scant for the Merovingian period. Ten Books of History *is a panorama of Gregory's world. Tours was the site of the cult of Saint Martin (see doc. 14) and a major pilgrimage destination. It banks the Loire River and was a key route between the Frankish north, Aquitaine in the south, and Visigoth Spain. The cultures of the Franks and the Gallo-Romans converged in Tours, so as prelate of this important city, Gregory was well placed to take part in the major events of his period, both in Tours and beyond. Magic appears in Gregory's history when it disrupts public life.*

Source: trans. Ernest Brehaut, Gregory of Tours, *History of the Franks*, Records of Civilization: Sources and Studies (New York: Columbia University Press, 1916), pp. 162–63, 244–45.

Ten Books of History

Book 6

35. In the meantime, the queen [Fredegund, c. 545–597] was told that [her son], who had died, had been taken away by evil arts and enchantments and that Mummolus the prefect, whom the queen had long hated, had a share in the death of her son Theodoric [584]. And it happened that while Mummolus was dining at home, one from the king's court complained that a boy whom he loved had been attacked by dysentery. And the prefect said to him, "I have an herb at hand, a draught of which will soon cure a sufferer from dysentery no matter how desperate the case." This was reported to the queen, and she was the more enraged. Meantime she apprehended some women of Paris and plied them with tortures and strove to force them by blows to confess what they knew. And they

admitted that they practiced magic and testified that they had caused many to die, adding what I do not allow anyone to believe, "We gave your son, O Queen, in exchange for Mummolus the prefect's life."

Then the queen used severer torture on the women and caused some to be drowned, and delivered others over to fire, and tied others to wheels where their bones were broken. And then she retired with the king to the villa of Compiègne and there disclosed to him what she had heard of the prefect. The king sent his men and ordered him summoned, and after examining him they loaded him with chains and subjected him to torture. He was hung to a beam with his hands tied behind his back and there asked what he knew of the evil arts, but he confessed nothing of what we have told above. Nevertheless he told how he had often received from these women ointments and potions to secure for him the favor of the king and queen. Now when released from torture, he called a reader and said to him, "Tell my master the king that I feel no ill effect of the tortures inflicted on me." Hearing this the king said, "Is it not true that he practices evil arts if he has not been harmed by these tortures?" Then he was stretched on the wheel and beaten with triple thongs until his torturers were wearied out. Then they put splinters under his finger and toenails. And when it had come to this, that the sword hung over him to cut his head off, the queen obtained his life, but a disgrace not less than death followed. Everything was taken from him, and he was put on a rough wagon and sent to his birthplace, the city of Bordeaux. But on the way he had a stroke of apoplexy and was scarcely able to reach his destination. And not long after he died. . . .

Book 10

25. Now in Gaul the disease I have mentioned attacked the province of Marseilles, and a great famine oppressed Angers, Nantes, and Mans. These are the beginning of sorrows according to what the Lord says in the Gospel: "There shall be pestilence and famines and earthquakes in different places and false Christs and false prophets shall arise and give signs and prodigies in the heavens so as to put the elect astray" [cf. Mark 13:22], as is true at the present time.

For a certain man of Bourges, as he himself told later, went into the deep woods to cut logs which he needed for a certain work, and a swarm of flies surrounded him, as a result of which he was considered crazy for two years; whence it may be believed that they were a wickedness sent by the Devil. Then he passed through the neighboring cities and went to the province of Arles and there wore skins and prayed like one of the devout, and to make a fool of him, the enemy gave him the power of divination. After this he rose from his place and left the province mentioned in order to become more expert in wickedness, and entered the territory of Gévaudan, conducting himself as a great man and not afraid to say that he was Christ. He took with him a woman who passed as his sister to whom he gave the name of Mary. A multitude of people flocked to him bringing the sick, whom he touched and restored to health. They who came to him brought him also gold, and silver, and garments. These he distributed among the poor to deceive them the more easily, and throwing himself on the ground and praying with the woman I have mentioned and rising, he would give orders to the bystanders to worship him in turn. He foretold the future and announced that disease would come to some, to others losses, and to others health. But all this he did by some arts and trickeries of the Devil.

A great multitude of people was led astray by him, not only the common folk but bishops of the church. More than three thousand people followed him. Meantime he began to spoil and plunder those whom he met on the road; the booty, however, he gave to those who had nothing. He threatened with death bishops and citizens, because they disdained to worship him. He entered La Velay and went to the place called Le Puy and halted with all his host at the churches near there, marshaling his line of battle to make war on Aurelius, who was then bishop, and sending messengers forward, naked men who danced and played and announced his coming. The bishop was amazed at this and sent strong men to ask what his doings meant. One of these, the leader, bent down as if to embrace his knees and [stop him passing] and (the impostor) ordered him to be seized and [stripped]. But the other at once drew his sword and cut him into bits and that "Christ" who ought rather to be named anti-Christ fell dead, and all who were with him dispersed. Mary was tortured and revealed all his impostures and deceits. But the men whom he had excited to a belief in him by the trickery of the Devil never returned to their sound senses, but they always said that this man was Christ, in a sense, and that Mary had a share in his divine nature. . . .

Questions: Based on the story of Fredegund, how common was sorcery in Merovingian Gaul? Why does Bishop Gregory consider the man from Bourges and Mary a problem? How were they a threat?

21. SAINT PATRICK BATTLES PAGAN MAGICIANS

Saint Patrick (c. 387–c. 460) known as the "Apostle of Ireland," was a British missionary and the first bishop of Armagh. Muirchú moccu Machtheni (fl. 700), a monk from Leinster, wrote The Life of Saint Patrick, *and it was produced in its present form in 807. The text survives in four fragmented copies, one of which was written in Ireland—precious because it is in rare Old Irish script. Although Muirchú composed his hagiographical text long after Patrick died, it is of historical value in understanding both the fifth century, when the famous saint lived, and the seventh century, when the* vita *was composed.*

Muirchú portrays the saint as a firebrand who duels with magicians and proves the superiority of the Christian God through spectacular displays of miraculous power. The vita *mixes seventh-century perceptions of pagan sorcery with allusions to biblical magicians. Models for Muirchú's Patrick are Aaron and Moses from the Book of Exodus, who outdo Pharaoh's magicians and free the Hebrews from their enslavement in a pagan land (see doc. 1). Also notable is the reference to Simon Magus (see doc. 6), who, according to apocryphal texts, used magic to fly and was dashed to the ground by Saint Peter's prayers.*

Source: trans. Newport D.J. White, in *St. Patrick: His Writings and Life*, Translations of Christian Literature, series 5, Lives of the Celtic Saints, Society for Promoting Christian Knowledge (London: Richard Clay & Sons; New York: The McMillian Company, 1920), pp. 78–79, 82–91.

The Life of Saint Patrick

10. Now in the days in which these things happened, there was in the aforesaid country a certain great king, a fierce and heathen high-king of barbarians, reigning in Temoria, which was the capital of the kingdom of the Irish, Loiguire by name, the son of Neill, who is the ancestor of the royal stock of almost the whole of this island.

Now he had about him wise men and magicians and augurs and enchanters and inventors of every evil art, who, through their heathenish and idolatrous religion, had skill to know and foresee all things before they came to pass. And of these there were two who were preferred beyond the others, whose names were Lothroch, otherwise Lochru, and Lucetmael, otherwise Ronal. And these two by their magical arts frequently foretold the coming of a certain foreign religion, in the manner of a kingdom, with a certain strange and harmful doctrine brought from a long distance across the seas, which would be proclaimed by a few, accepted by the many, and honored by all: one that would overturn kingdoms, slay kings who resist it, lead away multitudes, destroy all their gods, and, having cast down all the resources of their art, reign for ever and ever.

Moreover they indicated him who should bear and advocate this religion. And they prophesied in the following words cast into poetical form, words frequently uttered by them more especially in the two or three years which preceded the coming of Patrick. . . . "When therefore all these things come to pass, our kingdom, which is a heathen one, will not stand." And so it afterwards came to pass. For the worship of idols having been overturned on the coming of Patrick, the faith of Christ—our Catholic faith—filled the whole land. But let this suffice on this matter. Let us return to our subject.

13. Now in those days the Passover drew near, which was the first Passover celebrated for God in the Egypt of this island, as once it was (celebrated) in Goshen. And they took counsel as to where they should celebrate the first Passover

among the nations to whom God had sent them. And when many suggestions had been thrown out on this subject, at last it seemed good to Saint Patrick, inspired by God as he was, that this great feast of the Lord, which is the chief of all feasts, should be celebrated in the great plain where was the chief kingdom of those tribes, which was the head of all heathenism and idolatry, so that this unconquered wedge should be driven at the outset into the head of all idolatry by the mallet of a mighty work joined with faith, (wielded) by the spiritual hands of Saint Patrick and his companions, so that it should never more be able to rise against the faith of Christ. And so it came to pass.

15. Now it happened that in that year the heathen were wont to celebrate an idolatrous feast with many incantations and magical devices and other superstitions of idolatry. And there were also gathered together kings, satraps, leaders, princes, and chief men of the people, and moreover, magicians and enchanters and augurs and those who sought out and taught every art and every wile were called to King Loiguire, as once upon a time to King Nebuchadnezzar, to Temoria, their Babylon. [Nebuchadnezzar II was a Babylonian king, d. c. 562 BCE, who trained Hebrew youths in the magical arts.]

And it was on the same night that Saint Patrick was observing the Paschal feast [Easter] that they were celebrating their heathen festival. Moreover there was a custom among them, made known to all by an edict, that whoever in the whole district, whether far off or near, should in that night kindle a fire before one should have been lighted in the royal house, that is, in the palace of Temoria, his soul should be cut off from among his people.

Accordingly Saint Patrick, in his celebration of the holy Paschal feast, kindled a divine fire, very bright and blessed, which as it shone forth at night was seen by almost all the dwellers in the plain. Accordingly it happened that it was seen from Temoria, and when it was seen, all beheld it and were amazed. And when all the nobles and elders and magicians had been gathered together, the king said to them, "What is this? Who is it that has dared to do this impiety in my kingdom? Let him die the death!" And all the nobles and elders made answer, "We know not who has done this thing." Then the magicians answered and said, "O king, live forever. As for this fire which we behold and which has been lighted up this night before one was lighted in your house, that is, in the palace of Temoria, unless it be put out on this night on which it has been lighted up, it will not be put out forever. Moreover it will overcome all the fires of our religion. And he who kindled it and the kingdom that will follow from which it is kindled this night will overcome all of us and you too, and it will draw away all the men of your kingdom, and all kingdoms will yield to it, and he will fill all things, and will reign forever and ever."

16. When King Loiguire had heard these things, he was like Herod of old, very troubled along with all the city of Temoria [Matthew 2:3.] And he answered

and said, "It shall not be so, but now we will go that we may see the issue of the matter, and we shall take and slay those who do such an impiety against our kingdom."

And so, having yoked nine chariots, in accordance with the tradition of the gods, and taking with him for the conflict those two magicians who excelled all others, that is to say, Lucetmael and Lochru, Loiguire proceeded at the close of that night from Temoria to The Graves of the Men of Fecc, turning the faces of the men and of the horses to the left, in accordance with their notion of what is fitting (in such a case).

And as they went on their way, the magicians said to the king, "O king, you must not go into the place in which the fire is, lest afterwards perchance you worship him who kindled it, but you must be outside it, near at hand, and he will be summoned to you that he may worship you and you have dominion over him (or be owned as lord). And we and he shall parley with one another in your presence, O king, and in this way you will test us." And the king answered and said, "You have advised well; I will do as you have said." And when they arrived at the appointed place, they alighted from their chariots and horses, and they entered not into the enclosure of the place where the fire had been kindled, but took their seats close by.

17. And Saint Patrick was called to the king outside the place where the fire had been kindled. And the magicians said to their people, "Let us not rise up at the approach of this fellow, for whosoever rises up at the approach of this fellow will afterwards believe in him and worship him." At last Saint Patrick rose, and when he saw their many chariots and horses, he came to them, singing with voice and heart, very appropriately, the following verse of the Psalmist: "Some put their trust in chariots and some in horses, but we will walk in the name of the Lord our God" [Psalm 20:7]. They, however, did not rise at his approach. But only one, helped by the Lord, who willed not to obey the words of the magicians, rose up. This was Ercc the son of Daig, whose relics are now venerated in the city called Slane. And Patrick blessed him, and he believed in the everlasting God.

And when they began to parley with one another, the second magician, named Lochru, was insolent in the saint's presence and had the audacity with swelling words to disparage the Catholic faith. As he uttered such things, Saint Patrick regarded him with a stern glance, as Peter once looked on Simon, and powerfully, with a loud voice, he confidently addressed the Lord and said, "O Lord, who can do all things, and in whose power all things hold together, and who hast sent me here—as for this impious man who blasphemes your name, let him now be taken up and die speedily." And when he had thus spoken, the magician was caught up into the air, and then let fall from above, and, his skull striking on a rock, he was dashed to pieces and killed before their faces, and the heathen folk were dismayed.

18. Now the king with his people, enraged with Patrick on account of this thing, were minded to slay him and said, "Lay hands on this fellow who is destroying us." Then Saint Patrick, seeing that the ungodly heathen folk were about to rush upon him, rose up, and with a clear voice said, "Let God arise, and let his enemies be scattered; let them also that hate him flee before him." And straightway darkness came down, and a certain horrible commotion arose, and the ungodly men fought among themselves, one rising up against another, and there was a great earthquake, "and he bound the axles of their chariots and drove them with violence" [referencing the Egyptians pursuing the Hebrews when God parted the Red Sea: Exodus 14:25], and they rushed in headlong flight—both chariots and horses—over the level ground of the great plain, till at last only a few of them escaped half alive to the mountain of Monduirn, and, at the curse of Patrick, seven times seven men were laid low by this stroke in the presence of the king and his elders, until there remained only himself and his wife and two others of his companions, and they were sore afraid. So the queen approached Patrick and said to him, "O man, righteous and mighty, do not destroy the king; for the king will come and kneel and worship your Lord." And the king, compelled by fear, came and knelt before the saint, and feigned to worship him whom he did not wish to worship.

And when they had parted from one another, the king went a little way, and called Saint Patrick with feigned words, minding to slay him by some means. But Saint Patrick, knowing the thoughts of the villainous king, blessed his companions (eight men and a lad) in the name of Jesus Christ, and came to the king. The king counted them as they came, and straightway they were nowhere to be seen, taken away from the king's sight, but the heathen folk saw nothing but eight stags and a fawn going, as it were, to the wilderness. And King Loiguire, with the few that had escaped, returned at dawn to Temoria sad, cowed, and humiliated.

19. Now on the next day, that is, the day of the Paschal feast, the kings and princes and magicians of all Ireland were sitting at meat in Loiguire's house, for it was the chief of their festivals. And as they were eating and drinking wine in the palace of Temoria, and some were talking and others thinking of the things which had come to pass, Saint Patrick came with five men only—the doors being shut, as we read about Christ—to contend for the holy faith, and preach the word of God in Temoria before all the tribes of the Irish people there gathered together. . . . So when Patrick appeared, he was invited by the heathen to partake of food that they might prove him in respect of things that should come to pass. He, however, knowing the things that should come to pass, did not refuse to eat.

20. Now while all were feasting, the magician Lucetmael, who had taken part in the contest at night, was eager, even that day when his comrade was

dead, to contend with Saint Patrick. And to make a beginning of the matter, he put, while the others were looking, some liquor from his own vessel into Patrick's cup to see what he would do. Saint Patrick, perceiving the kind of trial intended, blessed his cup in the sight of all, and, lo, the liquor was turned into ice. And when he had turned the vessel upside down, that drop only fell out which the magician had put into it. And he blessed his cup again, and the liquor was restored to its own nature, and all marveled.

And after (the trial of) the cup, the magician said, "Let us work miracles on this great plain." And Patrick answered and said, "What miracles?" And the magician said, "Let us bring snow upon the earth." Then said Patrick, "I do not wish to bring things that are contrary to the will of God." And the magician said, "I shall bring it in the sight of all." Then he began his magical incantations and brought down snow over the whole plain to the depth of a man's waist, and all saw it and marveled. And Saint Patrick said, "Lo, we see this thing; now take it away." And he said, "I cannot take it away till this time to-morrow." And the saint said, "You are able to do evil, but not good; I am not of that sort." Then he blessed the whole plain round about, and the snow vanished quicker than a word could be uttered without any rain or cloud or wind. And the multitude shouted aloud and marveled greatly. And a little after this, the magician invoked his demons and brought upon the earth a very thick darkness, as a miracle, and all murmured at it. And the saint said, "Drive away the darkness." But he could not in this case either. St. Patrick however prayed and uttered a blessing, and suddenly the darkness was driven away, and the sun shone forth. And all shouted aloud and gave thanks.

Now when all these things had been done by the magician and Patrick in the sight of the king, the king said to them, "Throw your books into water, and we shall worship him whose books come out unharmed. Patrick replied, "I will do it." But the magician said, "I do not wish to enter into a trial by water with this fellow, for water is his God." He had evidently heard of baptism by water given by Patrick. And the king answered and said, "Throw them into fire." And Patrick said, "I am ready." But the magician, being unwilling, said, "This man worships as his God water and fire every alternate year." . . .

[Then] a house was built for Patrick and the magician, whereof one half was built of green wood and the other half of dry. And the magician was put into the part of the house made of green wood, and one of Saint Patrick's lads, named Benineus, was put with a magician's robe into the part that was made of dry wood. The house was then shut up from the outside and set on fire before the whole multitude. And it came to pass in that hour that as Patrick prayed, the flame of the fire burnt up the magician with the half of the house that was made of green wood, the cloak of Saint Patrick only remaining whole, inasmuch as the fire did not touch it. Benineus, on the other hand, was fortunate with the half of the house that was made of dry wood, for, as it is told about the "three children" [Daniel 3:23–25] the fire did not touch him at all, nor was he alarmed, nor did it do him any harm; only the cloak of the magician, which was around him, was, by the will of God, burnt up.

And the king was greatly enraged against Patrick because of the death of his magician, and he almost rushed upon him, minding to slay him, but God hindered him. For at the prayer of Patrick and at his cry, the wrath of God fell upon the ungodly people, and many of them perished. And Saint Patrick said to the king, "Unless you believe now, you shall die speedily, because the wrath of God will fall upon your head." And the king feared exceedingly, "and his heart was moved" [Isaiah 7:2], and his whole city with him.

21. And so when the elders and all his senate were gathered together, King Loiguire said to them, "It is better for me to believe than to die." And after taking counsel, he believed on that day, by the advice of his friends, and turned to the everlasting Lord God of Israel, and there many others believed as well. And Saint Patrick said to the king, "Because you did withstand my teaching, and were a stumbling-block to me, although the days of your reign shall be prolonged, nevertheless none of your seed shall be king forever."

Questions: What is Patrick's approach to conversion? How are the miracles of Patrick and the magic of the priests distinguishable?

22. EARLY MEDIEVAL SAINTHOOD AND DEMONS: SAINT RADEGUND

Radegund (c. 520–587) was a princess of Thuringia until King Lothar I (c. 497–561) conquered her native land and carried her (still a child) from the battlefield, having won her in a gambling match. When Radegund came of age, she married the Frankish king, but her biographers make it clear that by temperament and inclination Radegund was better suited to the life of a nun than that of a queen. Yet even after she founded and joined the Abbey of the Holy Cross in Poitiers, Radegund maintained ties to the world outside the monastery and continued to be a significant player in contemporary politics. Through her machinations, she obtained from Jerusalem a fragment of the "true cross," on which Jesus was crucified, to be housed in her monastery. Radegund's life was thoroughly documented, and her sanctity was broadly celebrated. The saint's friend and confessor, Venantius Fortunatus (c. 530–c. 609) wrote her biography, to which was appended a second vita *by Baudonivia, her spiritual sister.*

As in the vita *of Saint Martin (see doc. 14), Saint Radegund's story is peppered with demonic beings that she easily brings to heel. Unlike Martin, who traversed Gaul to battle demons and convert pagans to Christ, Radegund's dominance over "the adversary" took place in an enclosed monastery, but* vitae *of both draw parallels between Jesus and the saint. Both heal the sick, raise the dead, and cast out demons.*

Source: trans. JoAnn McNamara and John E. Halborg, *Sainted Women of the Dark Ages*, ed. Gordon E. Whatley (Durham, NC: Duke University Press, 1992), pp. 70, 82–85, 98–99, 104–5.

The Life of the Holy Radegund by Venantius Fortunatus

1. Our Redeemer is so richly and abundantly generous that he wins mighty victories through the female sex, and despite their frail physique, he confers glory and greatness on women through strength of mind. By faith, Christ makes them strong who were born weak so that, when those who appeared to be imbeciles are crowned with their merits by him who made them; they garner praise for their creator, who hid heavenly treasure in earthen vessels. For Christ the king dwells with his riches in their bowels. Mortifying themselves in the world, despising earthly consort, purified of worldly contamination, trusting not in the transitory, dwelling not in error but seeking to live with God, they are united with the Redeemer's glory in paradise. One of that company is she whose earthly life we are attempting to present to the public, though in homely style, so that the glorious memory that she, who lives with Christ, has left us, will be celebrated in this world. So ends the prologue.

[Radegund's early life is laid out and her merits praised; then the text turns to her miracles.]

28. Similarly, a girl named Fraifled, whom the enemy vexed, was violently contorted and most wretched. Without delay, she was found worthy of a cure at the saint's hands at Saix. Nor should we omit to mention the following miracle, revealed through the blessed woman at this time. The next day a woman named Leubela, who was gravely vexed in the back by the adversary, was publicly restored to health when the saint prayed for her and Christ worked a new miracle of healing. For a rustling sound came from under the skin of her shoulder blades and a worm emerged. Treading it underfoot, she went home liberated.

30. Let us increase her praise by recounting another miracle that has rightly not been forgotten. A certain woman labored so heavily under an invasion of the enemy that the struggling foe could scarcely be brought to the saint. She commanded the adversary to lie prostrate on the pavement and show her some respect. The moment the blessed woman spoke, he threw himself down, for she frightened him who was feared. When the saint, full of faith, trod on the nape of her neck, [the adversary] left her in a flux [of excrement] that poured from her belly. Also from small things great glory may accrue to the creator. Once, a ball of thread which the saint had spun was hanging from the vault when a shrewmouse came to nibble it. But, before he could break the thread, he hung there dead in the very act of biting.

33. The more we omit for brevity's sake, the greater grows our guilt. Therefore, as we dispose quickly of the remainder, our relief is slowed. A carpenter's wife had been tormented by diabolic possession for many days. Jokingly, the

venerable abbess said of her to the holy woman, "Believe me, mother, I will excommunicate you if the woman is not purged of the enemy and restored in three days." She said this publicly, but she made the holy woman secretly sorry that she had been so slow to heal the afflicted. To be brief, at the saint's prayer on the next day, the adversary went roaring out of her ear and abandoned the little vessel he had violently seized. Unhurt, the woman returned to the hospice with her husband. Nor should we neglect a similar deed. The most blessed one asked that a flourishing laurel tree be uprooted and transferred to her cell so she could enjoy it there. But when this was done all the leaves withered because the transplanted tree did not take root. The abbess jokingly remarked that she had better pray for the tree to take root in the ground or she herself would be separated from her food. She did not speak in vain for, through the saint's intercession, the laurel with the withered root grew green again in leaf and branch.

37. In praise of Christ, let us proclaim a miracle from our own time patterned after an ancient model in the tradition of the blessed Martin. When the most blessed female was secluded in her cell, she heard a nun crying. At the signal, she entered and asked what was the matter. She answered that her infant sister was dead, and though still warm she was laid out and ready to be washed in cold water. Condoling with her, the saint bade her bring the corpse to her in her cell. There she took it into her own hands, closing the door behind her and ordering the other to withdraw to a distance lest she sense what she was doing. But what she did secretly could not be concealed for long. By time the services for the dead were prepared, she had handled the corpse of the dead little girl for seven hours. But seeing a faith he could not deny, Christ utterly restored her health. When the saint rose from prayer, the infant rose from the dead. The old woman got up when the infant revived. When the signal was repeated, she joyfully restored alive the one who was dead when she had tearfully received her.

Book 2

16. . . . Thus, though she would always be able to help them when she was in glory with the king of heaven, this best provider, this good shepherdess, would not leave her sheep in disarray. She bequeathed a heavenly gift, the ransom of the world from Christ's relics [a sliver of the cross], which she had searched out from faraway places for the honor of the place and the salvation of the people in her monastery. Thus, with the aid of God's might and heaven's power, the blind receive light for their eyes, the ears of the deaf open, the tongues of the mute resume their office, the lame walk, and demons are put to flight in that place. What more? Anyone who comes in faith, whatever the infirmity that binds them, goes away healed by the virtue of the Holy Cross. Who could attempt to tell the greatness and richness of the gift the blessed woman conferred on this city? For this, all who live by faith do bless her name. . . .

27. It is the custom here for all the nearby monasteries to celebrate vigils together for the feast of Saint Hilary [14 January] until the middle of the night. Then each abbot returns with his brethren to his own monastery to celebrate the office. While they were keeping vigil in the basilica of the blessed primate (Saint Hilary) [c. 310–c. 368], those possessed by demons clamored all night among whom were two women gravely infested by the enemy. Indeed, one raved so violently that she shook the whole basilica with her roaring. After the venerable Arnegiselus, abbot of the blessed queen's basilica, went with his monks to their own basilica, which Radegund had loved so well, to complete the office they heard the clamoring women coming after them. Vociferously, they entered the basilica and prayed that the Lady Radegund would spare them. One of them was gravely troubled indeed; her evil spirit had flagellated her for fifteen years. But while Matins was being sung, the raging enemy abandoned the vessel he had invaded. The other was freed at Terce before the gates of the same basilica. That most evil adversary never again had power to harm them afterwards. Oh, how bountiful and rich is the mercy of God that makes his own folk stand in awe of him and seeks out the places where he may show his power to the faithful as the giver and dispenser of virtues. Some were liberated at the holy man's basilica while others were brought to Lady Radegund's basilica for, as they were equal in grace, so were they both shown equal in virtue.

Questions: How does Radegund show herself to be Christ-like? Is magic per se a factor in the above sections of Radegund's vita? *What is the nature of "the adversary" or "enemy" in the biography?*

23. ISIDORE OF SEVILLE DEFINES MAGIC: *THE ETYMOLOGIES*

Isidore, an archbishop of Seville (c. 560–636), was revered in his own time for erudition and tireless service to church, and he was one of the most influential scholars of the Middle Ages. Isidore lived in Spain during the rule of the Visigoths and was intensely involved in regnal politics. Working with the newly Christianized Visigoth kings, he was instrumental in suppressing the Arian heresy in Spain.

The Etymologies *(also called* Origins) *is Isidore's most influential work. It was the archbishop's ambitious attempt to gather all the knowledge of his day and lay it out in a systematic summa of twenty volumes. The format consists of short abridgments and summaries laced with countless etymologies, often fanciful, and is indebted to the many ancient texts that Isidore consulted. The work was purported to contain all secular knowledge worth knowing. It was one of the books most likely to have been in any medieval library, and between 1470 and 1530* Etymologies *was printed in ten editions. Given its fame, it is*

not surprising that for hundreds of years Isidore's catalogue of classical, early Christian, and con-
temporary learning acted as a textbook for theologians who echoed his dicta on demons and magic.

Source: trans. Martha Rampton, Isidore of Seville, *Etymologiarum sive originum libri XX*, ed. W.M. Lindsay, Scriptorum Classicorum Biblioteca Oxoniensis, vol. 1 (Oxford: Clarendon Press, 1911), 8.9–11.

Book 8

9. The first of the magicians was Zoroaster, king of the Bactrians whom Ninus, king of the Assyrians killed in battle. About Zoroaster, Aristotle [384–322 BCE] writes that the two million verses he composed are listed in the index of his volumes. Democritus [c. 460–c. 370 BCE] developed the art of magic after many centuries when the discipline of medicine flourished under Hippocrates [Greek physician, c. 460–c. 370 BCE]. Among the Assyrians, the magic arts were copious as noted by Lucan, "Who can know fate from entrails, who explain the birds, who watches lightning-flashes in the sky and with Assyrian skill examines stars?" (*Civil Wars* 6.427). So this folly of the magic arts has been handed down for many centuries and spread throughout the entire earth by the teachings of the evil angels. Through a certain knowledge of the future and the summoning of hellish things there developed, divination, auguries, and those things which are called oracles and necromancy. Nothing is surprising about the tricks of magicians because they were so advanced in their skills with the arts of magic that they even countered Moses by marvels very similar to his—transforming staffs into snakes and water into blood [see doc. 1]. It is also reported that a certain very famous magician named Circe changed Ulysses' friends into beasts [see doc. 3]. We also read about the sacrificial burnt offerings that the Arcadians made to their god Lycaeus and that anyone who consumed [the meat] was changed into the form of a beast. Therefore, what the noble poet [Virgil, 70–19 BCE] wrote about a certain woman who excelled in the magic arts does not appear to be completely improbable. "She promises by her spells to soothe the minds of those whom she wishes but sends hard cares to others; she stills river waters, turns back the stars, and arouses night ghosts; you will see the earth groan under her feet and the ash trees descend from the hills (*Aeneid* 4.487).

Further, if it can be believed, the Pythoness (1 Kings 28:3–25) evoked the spirit of the prophet Samuel from the recesses of hell and made him visible to the living—at least if we believe that this was the spirit of the prophet and not just a fantastical illusion created by the deceits of Satan [see doc. 2]. Prudentius [Christian poet, 348–c. 413] also said of Mercury, "It is said that he recalled [from Hades] perished spirits into the light by wielding his wand, but damned others to death." And shortly after he adds, "For with a magic murmur you know how to summon shady forms and bewitch sepulchral ashes. Likewise, the black art knows how to rob others of life." (*Against the Oration of Symmachus* 1.90). . . .

Necromancers are those who bring the dead back to life and, by their incantations, the revivified spirits seem to prophesy and to respond to questions. In Greek, "ηεκρὸς" [nekros] means "dead," and divination is called "μαντεια" [panteia]. The blood of the corpse is used for the interrogation, for demons are lured by the blood attached to the corpse, for demons are said to love blood. Therefore, whenever necromancy is practiced, gore is mixed with water so demons are called more easily by the gore of the blood.

Those called hydromaners get their name from water, for hydromancy is staring into water to evoke the shades of demons and to see their images and illusions and to hear something from them when they question those from the lower regions by offering blood. This kind of divination is reported to have been brought from Persia. Varro [Roman scholar, 116–27 BCE] says that there are four types of divination: earth, water, air and fire. That is geomancy, hydromancy, aeromancy, and pyromancy. Diviners are so called as though they were imbued with godhood, for they pretend to be full of divine inspiration, and by a certain crafty deceit, predict the future for people. However, there are two types of divination: artful and mad. Those who execute their art with words are called enchanters. *Arioli* are so called because they utter abominable prayers around the altars of idols and offer disgraceful sacrifices, and in these rituals they receive the answers of the demons. *Haruspices* are labeled as "observers of the hours." They watch after the days and the hours for doing business and other works, and they attend to what a person ought to pay attention to at any given time. They also inspect the entrails of large animals and from them predict the future. Augurs are those who pay attention to the flight and calls of birds and to other signs of things or unexpected observations that influence people. They are the same as those who observe auspices. For favorable signs are those to which people making a journey pay attention. Some observe birds and bird calls, meaning the songs and language of birds, which are called "auspicious signs" to the extent that *augurium* seems to amount to *avigerium* or "what the birds communicate." There are two kinds of auspicious signs, however, one pertaining to the eyes and another to the ears. That is, to the eyes: flight, and to the ears: the voices of birds.

The pythonesses are so called after Pythian Apollo, who was the author of divination. Those who make predications from the stars are called astrologers. *Genethliaci* are so called because of their inspection of [nativities] the day of a person's birth. They describe the nativities of people according to the twelve signs of the heavens, and they attempt to predict the conduct, circumstances, and actions of people by the course of the stars at their birth by noting who was born under what sign and predicting what form of life the person who is born will have. In Latin they are commonly called *mathematici*, and this type of superstition is called "constellations," that is, charting the stars as to how they relate to each other when someone is born. At first, interpreters of the stars were called Magi, as we read in the Gospels, who announced the birth of Christ. Later they had simply the name of *mathematici*. The knowledge of this art was allowed only until the time of the Gospel, so once Christ was born no one from that time further could interpret the birth of anyone from the heavens. *Horoscopi* are so called because they observe the hours of people's births in order to determine what is dissimilar and diverse in their destinies. *Sortilegi* are those who, under the name of false religion, profess to know the science of divination through what are called "sacred lots." They claim to know the future by examining passages from Scripture. *Salisatores* are so called because when any of their limbs jerk or palpitate they proclaim that this portends something either favorable or unfortunate for themselves thereafter. Pertinent to all these things are amulets, or anything suspended from or tied to a person which are filled with execrable remedies involving things such as incantations and magic writings called "characters" that medical science condemns. In all this is the craft of demons that comes from a certain pestilential alliance of humans and evil angels. Hence, all these things ought to be shunned and thoroughly repudiated and condemned by Christians with every curse [see doc. 15].

Although the Phrygians were the first to discover the auguries of birds, Mercury is said to have first invented magical illusions. They are called illusions because they dull the sharpness of the eyes. A certain Tages is said to have first given the craft of *aruspicina* [divination by reading animal entrails] orally to the Etruscans and then he disappeared. It is fabled that when a certain farmer was ploughing, suddenly Tages leapt from the clods and dictated the art of *aruspicina*, and on that same day he died. The Romans translated these books from the Etruscan language into their own.

10. Pagans are so called after the regions [*pagas*] of Athens where they originated. There in the countryside and rural districts the gentiles [pagans] established groves and erected idols, from such a beginning, the pagans received their name. . . .

11. Those whom the pagans claim to be gods were discovered once to have been humans, and after death they began to be worshipped among their people because of the life and merits of each of them, Isis is worshipped among the Egyptians, Jove among the Cretans, Iuba among the Moors, among the Latins is Faunus, and among the Romans is Quiriuns. And in the same way, among the Athenians is Minerva, in Samos is Juno, in Paphos is Venus, in Lemnos-Vulcan, Liber in Naxos, and, Apollo is thus honored in Delos. In their songs, poets joined in praise of these luminaries and elevated them to the skies. In their cults they are said to have given birth to the invention of certain arts, such as medicine by Aesculapius and forging by Vulcan. They are named based on their activities, for example, Mercury because he has command of commerce, Liber from liberty. Indeed, there were certain powerful men, founders of cities,

of whom the people who loved them made likenesses after they died in order that they might have some solace by contemplating these images. However, by the persuasion of demons, an error gradually crept into later generations in such a way that those whom people had once honored only for the memory of their names, their successors considered gods and worshipped them.

The use of likenesses appeared when, out of grief for the dead, images or effigies were erected that looked just like those heroes who had been received in heaven, and demons insinuated themselves into the statues to be worshiped among men, and by deception persuaded the forlorn people to make sacrifices to themselves. And images are named from "semblance" because by the hands of artisans, the faces of those in whose honor the likenesses are shaped are imitated in stone or some other material. Therefore, they are likenesses either because they are similar or because they are fabricated; in which case, they are false. And it should be noted that the Latin term also exists among the Hebrews, for among them an idol or likeness is called "Semel." The Jews say that Ishmael first made a likeness from clay. The pagans, however, assert that Prometheus first made a likeness of humans from clay and that from him the art of shaping likenesses and statues was born. Whence the poets surmised that humans first assumed their form from Prometheus because of these effigies. The city the Athenians was named after Minerva, and the Greeks believe that it was Cecrops under whom the first olive tree sprung up on the Capitoline Hill. He was the first to call on Jupiter, craft images, erect altars, and make sacrificial offerings, such things by no means having at any time been seen in Greece.

Idolatry is interpreted as service to idols or their cults, for "λατρεία" [latreia] in Greek is rendered in Latin as "servitude." Servitude, according to the true religion, is strictly and exclusively owed to the one and only God. Just as, due to the impious pride or wishes of demons that servitude be conferred on themselves, but pious humility in humans and the holy angels compels them to refuse servitude if offered, and they show to whom worship is owed. According to the interpretation of the word, an idol is a likeness made as an effigy of a human that is consecrated. The Greek expression is "ειδος" [eidos] and means "shape," and derived from this term it is the word "idol" which gives us the equivalent diminutive form. Therefore every effigy and form should be called an idol. Thence, all idolatry is servitude and slavery to any idol. Certain Latin speakers, unfamiliar with Greek, ignorantly say that "idol" assumes its name from "deception," because the Devil brought worship of a divine name to creation.

They say that the Greeks call demons "δαημωυ" [daimon] as if the word meant clever and experienced in matters. . . . [Demons] operate according to the nature of aerial bodies. Indeed, before their transgression [and fall from heaven] they had celestial bodies. Once fallen, they assumed an aerial quality, and they are not permitted to attain to the purer spaces of the air, but only the murky regions, and this is to them like a prison until the day of judgment. They are the prevaricating angels of whom the Devil is the prince. Devil in Hebrew means "sinking downwards," because he distained to remain quiet in the height of the heavens, but, due to the weight of his pride, tottering, he fell.

In fact, in Greek a slanderer is called "devil," either because he puts before God the crimes into which he himself seduces others, or because he accuses the innocence of the chosen with fictitious crimes, whence in the Apocalypse (12:10) the voice of an angel says, "The accuser of our brothers is cast out, he who accused them in the sight of our God day and night."

In Latin Satan means "adversary" or "transgressor." He is indeed an adversary who is an enemy to the truth and always strives against the virtue of the holy. He is a transgressor because he is an apostate and did not remain steadfast in the truth in which he was created. Similarly, he is a tempter because he demands that the innocence of the just be tested, just as it is written in [the Book of] Job. He is called the Antichrist because he will fight against Christ [in the last days]. Some foolish people think he is called Antichrist because he will come before Christ, that is Christ is to come after him. That is not the case; he is called Antichrist in Greek, which means "against Christ" in Latin. Indeed, "*avrì*" in Greek means "against." He will pretend that he is Christ when he comes and will fight against him and oppose Christ's sacraments in order to destroy the gospel of his truth. For he will attempt to restore the temple in Jerusalem and to reestablish the rituals of the old [Jewish] laws. But this Antichrist is one who denies that Christ is God; he is indeed against Christ. All who leave the church and are cut off from the unity of faith are themselves Antichrists. . . .

Beelzebub was the idol of Accaron and the word is translated as "man of flies," for "zebub" means fly. The most impure of idols, therefore, was called man of flies because of the filth of idolatry or for its foulness. . . . Behemoth, from the Hebrew language is called "animal" in the Latin tongue because he fell from the skies to the earth, and, according to his merit, was caused to be a beastly animal. He is also Leviathan, that is a serpent of the sea, because in the whirling sea of the world, he makes his way with cunning. Leviathan means "thing that increases." Indeed, was it not "the thing that increases" in human beings, to whom he once introduced the sin of deceit into paradise and, by persuasion, extends this deceit daily up to the point of eternal death? . . .

They also say that Diana [Apollo's] twin is the moon and protector of roads; hence, they deem her a virgin because a road gives birth to nothing. Both [Apollo and Diana] are fancied to have arrows because both heavenly bodies cast rays of light from the heavens to the earth. Diana is called *Duana* [from "duo"] because the moon can appear both day and night. People also claim that she is Lucina because she gives light. At the same time, she is Trivia because she assumes three forms. About her Virgil says, "Three faces of the virgin Diana"

(*Aeneid* 4.511) because this same goddess is called Luna, Diana, and Proserpina. But when Luna is imagined "She shines with a shimmering cloak. When fitted up, she shoots her arrows. She is the virgin Latonia. When seated resting on her throne, she is Pluto's wife" (Prudentius, *Against the Oration of Symmachus* 1.365). And Diana is also Latonia, because she was the daughter of Latona.

Questions: On what sources does Isidore principally rely to make his argument? Why? Which of the forms of magic are efficacious in Isidore's opinion and which are deceits of demons? The term "necromancy" changes substantially over the centuries; what does it mean for Isidore? How does Isidore account for the fact that honored personages of the Old and New Testaments used magic?

24. PENANCE FOR SINS OF MAGIC

Penitentials are lists of sins and their concomitant penances that guided clergy in taking confessions; they also served as juridical and canonical reference books. Manuals of penance address both public and domestic realms and are exhaustive in their endeavor to provide confessors with as much detail as possible about parishioners' transgressions. This makes them an invaluable source for bringing into focus the personal and family lives of all classes of Europeans and shedding light on the whole spectrum of magic and ritual.

Penitential handbooks were at times resistant to modernization because ecclesiastical compilers, who readily borrowed both ideas and exact phraseology from extant documents, were apt to be reverential when dealing with authoritative texts and hesitant to make changes. As a result, the penitentials contain material cut-and-pasted from generation to generation. Nevertheless, significant differences in penitential materials compiled over the early medieval centuries can be identified, and these changes allow a glimpse beyond the formulas of the manuals into society at a given time. The sections below illustrate the way in which sins of magic were blended with other offences, which is informative as to how magic was perceived in the early Middle Ages.

The Penitential of Theodore is based on rulings of Theodore, archbishop of Canterbury (c. 602–690), which "the Disciple of the Northumbrians" compiled one or two decades after Theodore's death. The handbook incorporates elements of Irish, Greek, and indigenous Anglo-Saxon practices, and it became a model for subsequent English and European penitentials. The penitential attributed to Bede (c. 673–735) is of uncertain authorship and provenance. Parts of it were almost certainly written in England, but versions of the text also circulated on the continent. The Burgundian Penitential, produced in the early eighth century, is one of the first books of penance to originate in Frankish lands.

Source: trans. John T. McNeill and Helena M. Gamer, *Medieval Handbooks of Penance* (New York: Columbia University Press, 1938), pp. 198, 207, 226–29, 274–77.

Penitential of Theodore

Book 1

15: OF THE WORSHIP OF IDOLS

1. He who sacrifices to demons in trivial matters shall do penance for one year, but he who (does so) in serious matters shall do penance for ten years.

2. If any woman puts her daughter upon a roof or into an oven for the cure of a fever, she shall do penance for seven years.

3. He who causes grains to be burned where a man has died, for the health of the living and of the house, shall do penance for five years.

4. If a woman performs diabolical incantations or divinations, she shall do penance for one year or the three forty-day periods, or forty days, according to the nature of the offense. Of this matter it is said in the canon [that] he who celebrates auguries, omens from birds, or dreams, or any divinations according to the custom of the heathen, or introduces such people into his houses, in seeking out any trick of the magicians—when these become penitents, if they belong to the clergy they shall be cast out, but if they are secular persons they shall do penance for five years.

Book 2

10. OF THOSE WHO ARE VEXED BY THE DEVIL

1. If a man is vexed by the Devil and can do nothing but run about everywhere, and (if he) slays himself, there may be some reason to pray for him if he was formerly religious.

2. If it was on account of despair, or of some fear, or for unknown reasons, we ought to leave to God the decision of this matter, and we dare not pray for him.

3. In the case of one who of his own will slay himself, masses may not be said for him; but we may only pray and dispense alms.

4. If any Christian goes insane through a sudden seizure, or as a result of insanity slays himself—there are some who celebrate masses for such a one.

5. One who is possessed of a demon may have stones and herbs, without (the use of) incantation.

Penitential Attributed to Bede

5. Of the Capital Sins

1. Now therefore I shall explain the capital offenses according to the canons. First pride, envy, fornication, vainglory, anger of long standing, worldly sadness,

avarice, gluttony, and Augustine adds sacrilege, that is, the theft of sacred things (and this is a very great theft) or else a serving of things offered to idols, that is, for auspices and so forth; then adultery, false witness, theft, robbery, continual drunkenness, idolatry, effeminacy, sodomy, evil speaking, perjury. These are capital offenses as Saints Paul and Augustine and other saints have reckoned them. For these, liberal alms are to be given and protracted fasting is to be kept; that is, as some judge for the capital (offenses), namely, adulteries, murders, perjuries, acts of fornication, and the like: laymen, three years; clerics, five years; sub-deacons, six years; deacons, seven years; presbyters, ten years; bishops, twelve years. If it was habitual: bishops, fourteen years; presbyters, twelve years; deacons, ten years; sub-deacons, nine years; clerics, seven years; laymen, five.

6. Of Greed and Other Vices

12. Those who sacrifice to demons in great matters, if it is habitual, shall do penance for ten years, in small matters, one year.

13. Auguries and divinations, five years

14. Those who conjure up storms shall do penance for seven years.

10. Of Auguries or Divinations

1. He who observes auguries or the oracles which are falsely called *sortes sanctorum* [divination by opening the Bible at random], or divinations, or other things to come by looking at some sort of writings, or takes a vow on a tree or on anything, except at a church, if clerics or laymen do this they shall be excommunicated from the church; or else, a cleric shall do penance for three years, laymen two, or one and one-half.

2. If a woman places her child upon a roof or in an oven in order to cure a fever, she shall do penance for five years.

3 and 4. Do not employ adroit jugglers and chanting diviners when the moon is eclipsed, since by sacrilegious custom they trust they can protect themselves by their outcries and magical arts, even (by) the attaching of diabolical amulets whether of grass or of amber to their people or to themselves; nor celebrate Thursday in honor of Jupiter or the Kalends of January [1 January] according to pagan tradition. Offenders, if clerics, shall do penance for five years, laymen, for three or five years.

The Burgundian Penitential

9. If by his magic anyone destroys anybody, he shall do penance for seven years, three of these on bread and water.

10. If anyone is a magician for love and destroys nobody, if he is a cleric, he shall do penance for an entire year on bread and water; if a deacon, three (years), one of these on bread and water; if a priest, five, two of these on bread and water. Especially if by this anyone deceives a woman with respect to her child, each one shall increase (the penance) by five forty-day periods on bread and water, lest he be charged with homicide.

20. If, indeed, anyone is a wizard, that is, a conjurer-up of storms, he shall do penance for seven years, three of these on bread and water.

24. If anyone commits sacrilege (that is, they call augurs those who pay respect to omens) whether he, takes auguries by birds or by whatever evil device (he does it), he shall do penance for three years on bread and water.

25. If any soothsayer (those whom they call diviners) makes any divinations, since this is also of the demons, he shall do penance for five years, three of these on bread and water.

28. If anyone has what is called without reason the *sortes sanctorum*, or other oracles, or draws lots by any evil device or regards such practices with awe, he shall do penance for three years.

29. If anyone takes a vow or absolves from one by trees or springs or lattices or anywhere except in a church, he shall do penance for three years on bread and water; for this also is sacrilege or of the demons. He who eats or drinks in these places shall do penance for a year on bread and water.

34. If anyone (does) what many do on the Kalends of January as was done hitherto among the pagans, seats himself on a stag, as it is called, or goes about in (the guise of) a calf, he shall do penance for three years, for this is demoniacal.

35. If any woman intentionally brings about abortion, she shall do penance for three years on bread and water.

36. If anyone is a wizard, that is, takes away the minds of men by the invocation of demons or renders them mad, he shall do penance for five years, three of these on bread and water.

Questions: Looking at sins of magic in context with other sins, what is the relative gravity of magic? What is the relationship between demon possession and madness? How do the authors of the penitentials signal when a particular behavior is magical? Why does the severity of the assigned penance vary for the same transgression?

25. A DEMONIAC IN EARLY MEDIEVAL ENGLAND: BEDE

The Venerable Bede (c. 673–735) was a monk at the monastery of St. Peter's at Wearmouth and St. Paul's at Jarrow in northern England. His Ecclesiastical History of the English People, *which documents the checkered process of the Anglo-Saxons' conversion* to Christianity, is among the most important sources for the history of England. Bede has little to say about magic per se, but demons play a role in the text at some points, such as when the author describes how Saint Oswald's (c. 604–642) hallowed remains are able to cast devils out of the body of a man possessed. One of the most common types of interaction between humans and demons throughout the medieval and early modern eras came in the guise of possession, but humans possessed by devils were not themselves considered sorcerous; rather, they were innocent and hapless victims.

Source: trans. A.M. Sellar, *Bede's Ecclesiastical History of England* (London: George Bell and Sons, 1906), pp. 157–59.

Book 3

11. . . . . There is a famous monastery in the province of Lindsey, called Beardaneu, which Queen Osthryth [d. 697] and her husband, King Ethelred [c. 654-c. 709], greatly loved and venerated, conferring upon it many honors. It was here that Osthryth was desirous to lay the revered bones of her uncle. When the wagon in which those bones were carried arrived toward evening at the monastery, the inhabitants were unwilling to admit them because, though they knew him to be a holy man, yet, as he was a native of another province and had obtained the sovereignty over them, they retained their ancient aversion to him even after his death. Thus it came to pass that the relics were left in the open air all that night with only a large tent spread over the wagon which contained them. But it was revealed by a sign from heaven with how much reverence they ought to be received by all the faithful, for all that night a pillar of light, reaching from the wagon up to heaven, was visible in almost every part of the province of Lindsey. Hereupon, in the morning the brethren of that monastery, who had refused it the day before, began to pray earnestly that those holy relics, beloved of God, might be laid among them. Accordingly, the bones, being washed, were put into a shrine which they had made for that purpose and placed in the church with due honor. And that there might be a perpetual memorial of the royal character of this holy man, they hung his banner of gold and purple over the monument. Then they poured out in the corner of the cemetery the water in which they had washed the bones. From that time, the very earth which received that holy water had the power of saving grace in casting out devils from the bodies of persons possessed.

When the queen afterwards dwelt some time in that monastery, there came to visit her a certain venerable abbess, who is still living, called Ethelhild. . . . [I]n a conversation between her and the queen, the discourse, among other things, turning upon Oswald, she said that she also had that night seen the light over his relics reaching up to heaven. The queen thereupon added that the very dust of the pavement on which the water that washed the bones had been poured, had already healed many sick persons. The abbess thereupon desired that some of that health-bringing dust might be given her, and, receiving it, she tied it up in a cloth, and, putting it into a casket, returned home. Sometime after when she was in her monastery, there came a guest, who was wont often in the night to be suddenly grievously tormented with an unclean spirit. Being hospitably entertained, when he had gone to bed after supper, he was suddenly seized by a devil and began to cry out, to gnash his teeth, to foam at the mouth, and to writhe and distort his limbs. None being able to hold or bind him, the servant ran, and knocking at the door, told the abbess. She, opening the monastery door, went out herself with one of the nuns to the men's apartment, and calling a priest, desired that he would go with her to the sufferer. They arrived, and seeing many present who had not been able, by their efforts, to hold the tormented person and restrain his convulsive movements, the priest used exorcisms and did all that he could to assuage the madness of the unfortunate man, but, though he took many pains, he could not prevail. When no hope appeared of easing him in his ravings, the abbess thought of the dust and immediately bade her handmaiden go and fetch her the casket in which it was kept. As soon as she came with it, as she had been bidden, and was entering the hall of the house in the inner part where the possessed person was writhing in torment, he suddenly became silent and laid down his head as if he had been falling asleep, stretching out all his limbs to rest. "Silence fell upon all and intent they gazed" [Virgil, *Aeneid*, 2.1], anxiously waiting to see the end of the matter. And after about the space of an hour, the man who had been tormented sat up and fetching a deep sigh, said, "Now I am whole, for I am restored to my senses." They earnestly inquired how that came to pass, and he answered, "As soon as that maiden drew near the hall of this house with the casket she brought, all the evil spirits that vexed me departed and left me and were no more to be seen." Then the abbess gave him a little of that dust, and the priest having prayed, passed that night in great peace; nor was he, from that time forward, alarmed by night, or in any way troubled by his old enemy.

Questions: In this story of the demoniac, what is more important to Bede: the danger of demons or the power of Saint Oswald? How difficult was it for the protagonists of the story to accomplish the exorcism? How powerful was the demon?

CHAPTER THREE

THE CAROLINGIAN DYNASTY: DEMONS CUT DOWN TO SIZE (750–1000)

Figure 3.1 The Utrecht Psalter (c. 850), a masterpiece of Carolingian art, is a book composed of pen drawings depicting the psalms. The illustration accompanying Psalm 37 shows demons attacking a sinner and tearing at his cloak: "3 For your arrows are fastened in me, and your hand has been strong upon me. 4 There is no health in my flesh because of your wrath; there is no peace for my bones because of my sins. 6 My sores are putrefied and corrupted because of my foolishness." In this representation, inequities and illness are portrayed as arrows and equated with demons.

Because the Carolingian era was a period of codification and cultural self-examination and definition, it is reasonable to expect a re-evaluation of traditional assumptions about magic to emerge from it. Exercise of the holy through popular religious practices, monastic behavior, and ecclesiastical customs and rituals came under scrutiny, yet in the sources from the eighth through eleventh centuries, magic seldom emerges as a central reform issue in and of itself. This is the case despite the fact that throughout the period, due to missionaries expanding Christianity outside the empire, the church and Frankish kings were still combating paganism, rationalizing foreign mythologies to steer their adherents from the "worship of demons," and equating cultic worship with idolatry and superstition. This was also the case in Anglo-Saxon England.

Still, in this process of regularization, some of the greatest thinkers of the Carolingian era did turn their attention to questions of demonology and magic, which, in their varied forms, were entwined with virtually every societal institution and assumption about the workings of the universe. Most intellectuals were skeptical of the supposed abilities of both demons and magicians and tended to be more troubled about errors of belief than the commission of what they considered futile and fraudulent magical acts. When magic was discussed, anxiety was centered on the disruption to the Christian community caused by sins of intention rather than on the harm such actions might cause. Authorities were primarily interested in, first, stamping out persisting superstitious practices and the beliefs that generated them, and second, bringing irregular behaviors in line with the design of the increasingly centralized church and Carolingian rule. In other words, the efforts to subdue paganism and superstition were indexed on two interrelated factors: the escalating power of the state, and the drive to shape proper Christian worship upon which the well-being of governing structures were contingent.

Almost invariably, historians writing about medieval magic and the demons that facilitated it treat them as supernatural phenomena, but this does not accurately characterize the Carolingian intellectual perspective. Demons were a preternatural and superhuman feature of creation, but they were not supernatural. Magic was akin to a marvel, an extraordinary but explicable element within the natural order. It operated through the work of demons that possessed abilities both mystifying and remarkable to humans but integral to the make-up of the demonic creature itself. To think otherwise was to call into question the uniqueness of God. Only the Lord, the creator of natural law, was thought capable of meddling with that law, and he was willing to do so through miracles in order to guide humankind. Demons were not able to effect miracles; they could only approximate them and, in the process, mock and damn the human beings who collaborated with them. This assessment of demons was not new to Carolingian thinkers, whose scholarship drew readily on patristic works, but it undergirded their disdain for and intolerance of those who presumed to traffic with demons and use the magic arts to disrupt the natural order of the divine cosmos and the new vision that the Carolingian reformers propagated.

Whereas the primitive church eschewed excessive religious ceremonials, by 750, Christians were no longer uncomfortable with highly stylized observances and had developed a deep and rich program of ritual. The ceremonial aspect of many forms of magic was no longer a factor in its condemnation, as had been the case in Late Antiquity, but the fact that many pagan, demonic, and counter-culture beliefs were sustained in traditional ritual forms continued to be a grave concern for both church and secular governments.

There was a significant change in the mid-ninth century in terms of the way in which women's magic was perceived, which is related to women's exercise of sacred power generally. In the Merovingian period (c. 500–751), the monastic movement gave women an opportunity to exercise leadership and exert influence within their societies, but by the beginning of the eighth century there was a decline in the number of new religious communities, both male and female. As legitimate miracle working was generally perceived to be the prerogative of monks, nuns, and secular clergy, such as bishops and priests (men only), one result of the changes in ninth-century monastic patterns was that fewer women than men were in a position to perform miracles under the auspices of the church.

The same impulse that relegated women to supporting or informal roles in most areas of the organizational church structure affected perceptions about their magical effectiveness. The decline in the perception that women's magic was potent and powerful—capable of causing serious harm—is related to a broader understanding by Carolingian thinkers of the ideal sphere for women in spiritual matters. In magic and miracle, they had become tamed and docile. This was, in any case, the assessment of the literate. Although there was no significant change in the Carolingian period in the perceptions of what constituted "women's magic," there was a shift in how writers viewed it and in the frequency with which they targeted for censure activities specific to women. Carolingian intellectuals acknowledged that women practiced magic, but they dismissed it as ineffectual and the women as deluded.

In short, the Carolingian period witnessed both continuity and some significant changes in the understanding of magic. The magic arts were peripheral to larger reform efforts, never central to them. With the notable exception of Hrabanus Maurus's (c. 780–856) short treatise (see doc. 31), discussions of magic were embedded in writings about other subjects, such as marriage and political upheaval. The particular acts that constituted magic did not change so much as the response to them. Leaders' efforts to corral authority and eradicate illicit spiritual charisma were driven by a desire for authentication and standardization of every facet of social behavior; it was essential that all rites reinforced the goals of societal renovation.

Alongside the rhetoric of the elite there were voices in the early Middle Ages that differed in tone and enunciated an approach to the demonic that was out of alignment with clerical discourse. Among the best examples of this sort of source are literary texts such as the epic poem *Beowulf.* Also, as thorough as the Carolingian reforms were, the medical literature of the period was essentially ignored by reformers of the eighth and ninth centuries. There was virtually no discussion or revision of healing manuals, such as herbals (collections of botanical medical cures), and clerics continued to copy them from generation to generation. The herbals are syncretic, blending an undercurrent of old pagan sensitivities with traditional Christian accouterments and rituals, which presents interpretative challenges. They are practical, not didactic; they are manuals, not treatises. Magic per se is virtually never mentioned, but demons abound and are both the cause of disease and disease itself. Although, according to Christian belief, ultimately all sickness was thought to be punishment for sin inflicted by disease-infesting demons, on a practical day-to-day basis the herbals leave the theology and etiology of illness in the background and concentrate on treating symptoms. They are purely descriptive, not polemical or moralizing, and their purpose is pragmatic: to cure disorders. But in the case of certain ailments whose causes do not seem clearly somatic, the demonic theory of disease comes to the foreground.

26. AN EIGHTH-CENTURY LIST OF PAGAN PRACTICES

This list of superstitions and pagan customs (Indiculus superstitionum et paganiarum) *appears to be an index of practices that may have been appended to a now-lost manuscript that explained the behaviors in more detail. The author and purpose of the list are uncertain, but Boniface (c. 675–754), a missionary in Germany and counselor to early Carolingian rulers, or one of his companions, may have composed it in 742 or 743 in conjunction with a church council* (Concilium Germanicum). *The document is important because it provides insight into the traditions of pagan and nominally Christian peoples in Saxony and northeastern Gaul. Many of the activities listed are recognizable from other writings of the period, but some are quite obscure, and it is these that are particularly interesting. Behaviors that are proscribed in similar language from text to text over the centuries may be obsolescent survivals from the past, but because the* Indiculus *hints at unfamiliar magical rituals, we can assume they may have been practices current in the eighth century.*

Source: trans. John T. McNeill and Helena M. Gamer, *Medieval Handbooks of Penance* (New York: Columbia University Press, 1938), pp. 419–21.

1. Of sacrilege at the graves of the dead.

    2. Of sacrilege over the departed, that is, "*dadsias*" [dirges].

    3. Of the swinish feasts in February.

    4. Of the little houses, that is, sanctuaries.

    5. Of sacrilegious acts in connection with churches.

    6. Of the sacred rites of the woods which they call "*nimidas*" [of groves].

    7. Of those things which they do upon stones.

    8. Of the sacred rites of Mercury and of Jupiter.

    9. Of the sacrifice which is offered to any of the saints.

    10. Of amulets and knots.

    11. Of the fountains of sacrifices.

    12. Of incantations.

    13. Of auguries, the dung or sneezing of birds or of horses or of cattle.

    14. Of diviners or sorcerers.

    15. Of fire made by friction from wood, that is, the "*nodfyr.*"

    16. Of the brains of animals.

    17. Of the observance of the pagans on the hearth or in the inception of any business.

    18. Of undetermined places which they celebrate as holy.

    19. Of the bed-straw which good folk call Holy Mary's [Our Lady's Bedstraw, a plant].

    20. Of the days which they make for Jupiter and Mercury.

    21. Of the eclipse of the moon—what they call, "Triumph, Moon!"

    22. Of storms, and horns, and snail shells.

    23. Of furrows around villas.

    24. Of the pagan course which [they] call "yrias," with torn garments of footwear.

    25. Of this, that they feign for themselves that dead persons of whatever sort are saints.

    26. Of an idol made of dough.

    27. Of idols made of rags.

    28. Of an idol which they carry through the fields.

    29. Of wooden feet or hands in a pagan rite.

    30. Of this: that they believe that women command the moon [or "swallow up the moon"] that they may be able to take way the hearts of men, according to the pagans.

Questions: Which of the titles are recognizable from classical magical traditions, and which titles suggest magical practices that are new to this source? To what natural phenomenon might item 30 refer?

27. PAGANISM OF THE SAXONS

Capitularies are legislative and administrative decrees by which Carolingian royal authorities and the nobility established regulations for the governance of the kingdom (later, the empire). The First Saxon Capitulary was drafted c. 782 in order to deal with what was, for Carolingian leaders, the persistent problem of the disloyalty and paganism of the Saxons, which in many ways were two sides of the same coin: obedience to the king and adherence to Christianity went hand in hand. From 775 to 790, the nominally Christianized Saxons of northern Germany vacillated between the new religion and the pagan cults of their ancestors, and warfare between the Saxons and Carolingians was endemic during this period. The severity of the First Saxon Capitulary is evidence of Charlemagne's frustration with the Saxons' tenacious "perfidy." The capitulary consists of thirty-four chapters, nearly half of which deal with religious practices.

Source: trans. D.C. Munro, *Translations and Reprints from the Original Sources of European History*, vol. 6.5, Laws of Charles the Great (Philadelphia: The University of Pennsylvania, 1900), pp. 2–5.

First Saxon Capitulary

1. It was pleasing to all that the churches of Christ, which are now being built in Saxony and consecrated to God, should not have less, but greater and more illustrious honor, than the temples of the idols had.

2. If anyone shall have fled to a church for refuge, let no one presume to expel him from the church by violence, but he shall be left in peace until he shall be brought to the judicial assemblage; and on account of the honor due to God and the saints, and the reverence due to the church itself, let his life and all his members be granted to him. Moreover, let him plead his cause as best he can, and he shall be judged; and so let him be led into the presence of the lord king, and the latter shall send him where it shall have seemed fitting according to his clemency.

4. If anyone, out of contempt for Christianity, shall have despised the holy Lenten fast and shall have eaten flesh, let him be punished by death. But, nevertheless, let it be taken into consideration by a priest, lest perchance anyone from necessity has been led to eat flesh.

5. If anyone shall have killed a bishop or priest or deacon, let him likewise be punished capitally.

6. If anyone deceived by the Devil shall have believed, after the manner of the pagans, that any man or woman is a witch and eats men, and on this account shall have burned the person or shall have given the person's flesh to others to eat, or shall have eaten it himself, let him be punished by a capital sentence.

7. If anyone, in accordance with pagan rites, shall have caused the body of a dead man to be burned and shall have reduced his bones to ashes, let him be punished capitally.

8. If anyone of the race of the Saxons, hereafter concealed among them, shall have wished to hide himself unbaptized, and shall have scorned to come to baptism and shall have wished to remain a pagan, let him be punished by death.

9. If anyone shall have sacrificed a man to a devil, and after the manner of the pagans shall have presented him as a victim to the demons, let him be punished by death.

10. If anyone shall have formed a conspiracy with the pagans against the Christians, or shall have wished to join with them in opposition to the Christians, let him be punished by death. And whosoever shall have consented to this same, fraudulently against the king and the Christian people, let him be punished by death.

18. That on the Lord's day no meetings and public judicial assemblages shall be held, unless perchance in a case of great necessity or when war compels it, but all shall go to the church to hear the word of God, and shall be free for prayers or good works. Likewise, also, on special festivals they shall devote themselves to God and to the services of the church, and shall refrain from secular assemblies.

19. Likewise, it has been pleasing to insert in these decrees that all infants shall be baptized within a year, and we have decreed this, that if anyone shall have despised to bring his infant to baptism within the course of a year, without the advice or permission of the priest, if he is a noble he shall pay 120 *solidi* to the treasury, if a freeman 60, if a servant 30.

21. If anyone shall have made a vow at springs or trees or groves, or shall have made any offering after the manner of the heathen and shall have partaken of a repast in honor of the demons, if he shall be a noble, 60 *solidi*, if a freeman 30, if a servant 30.

22. We command that the bodies of Saxon Christians shall be carried to the church cemeteries and not the mounds of the pagans.

23. We have ordered that diviners and soothsayers shall be handed over to the churches and priests.

32. If anyone owes an oath to any man whatsoever, let him duly make his oaths to that one at the church on the day appointed; and if he shall have despised to take the oath, let him give a pledge, and let him who was contumacious pay fifteen *solidi*, and afterwards let him fully compound for his act.

Questions: What does it suggest that the language of some charges of paganism is familiar from sources written centuries earlier? What role does magic play in the capitulary? The church building itself serves an important purpose other than providing a place for people to worship; what is that purpose? What offences of the Saxons seem to be the most egregious in the text?

28. BEOWULF FIGHTS THE DEMONS: GRENDEL, AND GRENDEL'S MOTHER

Beowulf *is an alliterative Old English epic poem whose authorship is unknown. The provenance of the work is certainly Anglo-Saxon England, but the date of its composition has been a topic of intense research and much debate, partially revolving around the question of whether or not the work was orally composed and transmitted. Various scholars have placed the poem somewhere between the eighth and early eleventh centuries, but the earlier date is more likely. The setting of the story is Scandinavia, Beowulf is from Geatland (now Götaland in Sweden), and he goes to the rescue of the Scylding clan in Denmark. Several of the references and events are historical, reaching back to the sixth century.*

Although written in an era of Anglo-Saxon church reform and government rationalization, Beowulf *seems far removed from the intellectual tenor of the time. Although the author was undoubtedly a cleric, the story is grounded in a pre-Christian worldview with only a patina of Christian elements superficially applied. The bulk of the narrative is driven by a monster, an aquatic she-demon, and a dragon. A question that warrants pondering is whether or not a selection such as* Beowulf *belongs in a collection of readings on magic and witchcraft. Is magic evident in the text?*

Source: trans. Lesslie Hall, *Beowulf, An Anglo-Saxon Epic Poem* (Boston, New York, Chicago: D.C. Heath & Co., 1892), pp. 3–7, 24–29, 44–45.

2. Scyld's Successors. Hrothgar's Great Mead-Hall

To adorn the great folk-hall. In due time it happened
Early 'mong men, that 'twas finished entirely,
The greatest of hall-buildings; Heorot [King Hrothgar] named it. . . .
[The monster, Grendel, who lived in a lair near the hall]
Bore it bitterly, he who bided in darkness,
That light-hearted laughter loud in the building
Greeted him daily; there was dulcet harp-music,
Clear song of the singer. . . .
So blessed with abundance, brimming with joy,
The warriors abided, till a certain one began to
Dog them with deeds of the most dire malice,
A foe in the hall building: this horrible demon
Was Grendel named, the march-stepper famous
Who dwelt in the moor-fens, the marsh and the fastness;
The wan-mooded being abode for a season
In the land of the giants, when the Lord and creator

Had banned him and branded. For that bitter murder,
The killing of Abel, all-ruling Father
The kindred of Cain crushed with his vengeance;
In the feud he rejoiced not, but far away drove him
From kindred and kind, that crime to atone for,
Dispenser of justice. Thence ill-favored creatures,
Elves and giants, monsters of ocean,
Came into being, and the giants that longtime
Grappled with God; he gave them requital.

3. Grendel the Murderer

When the sun was sunken, he set out to visit
The lofty hall-building, how the Ring-Danes had used it
For beds and benches when the banquet was over.
Then he found there reposing many a noble
Asleep after supper; sorrow the heroes,
Misery knew not. The monster of evil
Greedy and cruel tarried but little,
Fell and frantic, and forced from their slumbers
Thirty of thane men; thence he departed
Leaping and laughing, his lair to return to,
With surfeit of slaughter sallying homeward.
In the dusk of the dawning, as the day was just breaking,
Was Grendel's prowess revealed to the warriors:
Then, his meal-taking finished, a moan was uplifted,
Morning-cry mighty. The man-ruler famous,
The long-worthy atheling [prince], sat very woeful,
Suffered great sorrow, sighed for his liegemen,
When they had seen the track of the hateful pursuer,
The spirit accursed: too crushing that sorrow,
Too loathsome and lasting. Not longer he tarried,
But one night after continued his slaughter
Shameless and shocking, shrinking but little
From malice and murder; they mastered him fully. . . .
So ruled he and strongly strove against justice
Lone against all men, till empty uptowered
The choicest of houses. Long was the season:
Twelve-winters' time torture suffered
The friend of the Scyldings, every affliction,

Endless agony; hence it after became
Certainly known to the children of men
Sadly in measures, that long against Hrothgar
Grendel struggled:—his grudges he cherished,
Murderous malice, many a winter,
Strife unremitting, . . .
The monster of evil fiercely did harass,
The ill-planning death-shade, both elder and younger,
Trapping and tricking them. He trod every night then
The mist-covered moor-fens; men do not know where
Witches and wizards wander and ramble.
So the foe of mankind many of evils
Grievous injuries, often accomplished,
Horrible hermit; Heorot he frequented,
Gem-bedecked palace, when night-shades had fallen . . .
At the shrines of their idols often they promised
Gifts and offerings, earnestly prayed they
The Devil from hell would help them to lighten
Their people's oppression. Such practice they used then,
Hope of the heathen; hell they remembered
In innermost spirit, God they knew not,
Judge of their actions, All-wielding Ruler,
No praise could they give the Guardian of Heaven,
The Wielder of Glory. . . .
[Beowulf, a brave and renowned warrior of the Geats heard of Hrothgar's troubles. He sailed to the land of the Scyldings and offered his assistance against Grendel. All were relieved at Beowulf's arrival, seeing deliverance in sight. The king and his retainers feasted at Heorot, and after dinner, retired for the night. Beowulf lay in the hall and took off his armor, planning to fight Grendel barehanded. When night fell, Grendel came to Heorot.]

11. All Sleep Save One

. . . The trav'ler-at-twilight came tramping and striding.
The warriors were sleeping who should watch the horned-building,
One only excepted. 'Mid earthmen 'twas 'stablished,
Th' implacable foeman [adversary] was powerless to hurl them
To the land of shadows, if the Lord were unwilling;
But serving as warder, in terror to foemen,
He angrily bided the issue of battle.

12. Grendel and Beowulf

'Neath the cloudy cliffs came from the moor then
Grendel going, God's anger bare he.
The monster intended some one of earthmen
In the hall-building grand to entrap and make way with:
He went under welkin [sky] where well he knew of
The wine-joyous building, brilliant with plating,
Gold-hall of earthmen. Not the [first] occasion
He the home and manor of Hrothgar had sought:
Ne'er found he in life-days later nor earlier
Hardier hero, hall-thanes more sturdy!
Then came to the building the warrior marching,
Bereft of his joyance. The door quickly opened
On fire-hinges fastened, when his fingers had touched it;
The fell one had flung then—his fury so bitter—
Open the entrance. Early thereafter
The foeman trod the shining hall-pavement,
He strides furiously into the hall.
Strode he angrily; from the eyes of him glimmered
A lustre unlovely likest to fire.
He beheld in the hall the heroes in numbers,
A circle of kinsmen sleeping together,
A throng of thane men [king's warriors]: then his thoughts were exultant,
He minded to sunder from each of the thanemen
The life from his body, horrible demon,
Ere morning came, since fate had allowed him
The prospect of plenty. Providence willed not
To permit him any more of men under heaven
To eat in the nighttime. Hygelac's [king of Geatland] kinsman
Great sorrow endured how the dire-mooded creature
In unlooked-for assaults were likely to bear him.
No thought had the monster of deferring the matter,
But on earliest occasion he quickly laid hold of
A soldier asleep, suddenly tore him,
Bit his bone-prison, the blood drank in currents,
Swallowed in mouthfuls: he soon had the dead man's
Feet and hands, too, eaten entirely.
Nearer he strode then, the stout-hearted warrior
Snatched as he slumbered, seizing with hand-grip,
Forward the foeman joined with his hand;

Caught he quickly the cunning deviser,
On his elbow he rested. This early discovered
The master of malice, that in middle-earth's regions,
'Neath the whole of the heavens, no hand-grapple greater
In any man else had he ever encountered:
Fearful in spirit, faint-mooded waxed he,
Not off could betake him; death he was pondering,
Would fly to his covert, seek the devils' assembly:
His calling no more was the same he had followed
Long in his lifetime. The liege-kinsman worthy
Of Hygelac minded his speech of the evening,
Stood he up straight and stoutly did seize him.
His fingers crackled; the giant was outward,
The earl stepped farther. The famous one minded
To flee away farther, if he found an occasion,
And off and away, avoiding delay,
To fly to the fen-moors; he fully was ware of
The strength of his grapple in the grip of the foeman.
'Twas an ill-taken journey that the injury-bringing,
Harrying harmer to Heorot wandered:
The palace re-echoed; to all of the Danemen, . . .
Novel enough; on the North Danes fastened
A terror of anguish, on all of the men there
Who heard from the wall the weeping and plaining,
The song of defeat from the foeman of heaven,
Heard him hymns of horror howl, and his sorrow
Hell-bound bewailing. He held him too firmly
Who was strongest of main-strength of men of that era.

13. Grendel Is Vanquished

. . . The direful demon, damage incurable
Was seen on his shoulder, his sinews were shivered,
His body did burst. To Beowulf was given
Glory in battle; Grendel from thence ward
Must flee and hide him in the fen-cliffs and marshes,
Sick unto death, his dwelling must look for
Unwinsome and woeful; he wished the more fully
The end of his earthly existence was nearing,
His life-days' limits. At last for the Danemen,
When the slaughter was over, their wish was accomplished.

The comer-from-far-land [Beowulf] had cleansed then of evil,
Wise and valiant, the war-hall of Hrothgar,
Saved it from violence. He joyed in the night-work,
In repute for prowess; the prince of the Geatmen
For the East-Danish people his boast had accomplished,
Bettered their burdensome bale-sorrows fully,
The craft-begot evil they erstwhile had suffered
And were forced to endure from crushing oppression,
Their manifold misery. 'Twas a manifest token,
When the hero-in-battle the hand suspended,
The arm and the shoulder (there was all of the claw
Of Grendel together) 'neath great-stretching hall-roof. . . .
[His arm having been ripped off by Beowulf, Grendel—called "the worm"—
slinked back to his lair and died there.]

20. The Mother of Grendel

. . . Known unto earth-folk, that still an avenger
Outlived the loathed one, long since the sorrow
Caused by the struggle; the mother of Grendel,
Devil-shaped woman, her woe ever minded,
Who was held to inhabit the horrible waters,
The cold-flowing currents, after Cain had become a
Slayer-with-edges to his one only brother,
The son of his sire; he set out then banished,
Marked as a murderer, man-joys avoiding,
Lived in the desert. Thence demons unnumbered
Fate-sent awoke; one of them Grendel,
Sword-cursèd, hateful, who at Heorot met with
A man that was watching, waiting the struggle, . . .
Eager and gloomy was anxious to go on
Her mournful mission, mindful of vengeance
For the death of her son. She came then to Heorot
[to retrieve Grendel's severed arm] . . .
She went then hastily, outward would get her
Her life for to save, when someone did spy her;
Soon she had grappled one of the warriors
Fast and firmly, when fenward she hied her;
That one to Hrothgar was liefest of heroes
In rank of retainer where waters encircle,
A mighty shield-warrior, whom she murdered at slumber,

A broadly famed battle-knight. Beowulf was absent,
But another apartment was erstwhile devoted
To the glory-decked Geatman when gold was distributed.
There was hubbub in Heorot. The hand that was famous
She grasped in its gore, . . .
[Grendel's mother returned to the marshes with her son's arm, and there she
lived out her life.]

*Questions: What evil creatures seem to be from the continental Christian tradition?
Beowulf's author paints the outdoors as dangerous and foreboding, as opposed to the
warmth and good cheer of Heorot; why? Is the author's perception of the natural world a
consistent feature of works dealing with magic in the western tradition? Explain.*

29. AGOBARD OF LYONS AND WEATHER MAGIC

*Agobard (c. 779–d. 840) was the archbishop of Lyons and active in Carolingian politics
and the reform movement during the reigns of Charlemagne (742–814) and his son, Louis
the Pious (778–840). He is known for his theological treatises and role in the civil wars
of the 830s. When Agobard was the suffragan bishop of Lyons, he wrote a short piece on
a problem that had developed in his diocese due to a widespread belief in weather magic.
The bishop was exasperated by the credulity of people in the region and by what, for
him, amounted to an affront to God. The text is a treasure because, at the time, so little
was written describing the viewpoints and behaviors of common people. Most of what we
know of sub-literate culture comes from proscriptive texts such as laws, penitentials, and
canons prohibiting particular behaviors and beliefs concomitant to them.*

Source: trans. P.E. Dutton, "Agobard of Lyons and the Popular Belief in Weather Magic," in *Carolingian Civilization: A Reader*, 2nd ed., ed. P.E. Dutton (Toronto: University of Toronto Press, 2009),
pp. 220–23.

1. In these regions, almost everyone—nobles and common people, city folk
and country folk, the old and young—believe that hail and thunder can be
caused by the will of humans. For as soon as they have heard thunder or seen
lightning, they say, "The wind has been raised." When asked why it is (called)
a raised wind, some with shame, their consciences troubling them a little, others boldly, as is the way of the ignorant, answer that the wind was raised by
the incantations of people who are called storm-makers (*tempestarii*). Hence it
is called a raised wind.

Whether that is true, as is popularly believed, should be verified by the
authority of holy Scripture. If, however, it is false, as we believe without doubt,
it ought to be emphasized just how great the crime is of him who attributes to
humans the work of God. . . .

2. We have seen and heard of many overcome by such great madness and deranged by such great foolishness that they believe and claim that there is a certain region called Magonia (Magic Land) from which ships travel in the clouds. These ships, (so they believe), carry crops that were knocked down by hail and perished in storms back to that same region. Those cloud-sailors (are thought to) give a fee to the storm-makers and to take back grain and other crops. So blinded are some by this great and foolish belief that they believe that these things can (actually) be done.

We (once) saw many people gathered together in a crowd who were showing off four captives, three men and a woman, as though they had fallen out of some such ships. These people had been held for some time in chains. But at last, as I said, they were exhibited to that crowd of people in our presence as (criminals) fit to be stoned to death. Nevertheless the truth did come out. After much argument, those who exhibited those captives were, as the Prophet [Isaiah] says, "confused, just as the thief is confused when apprehended."

3. Because this error, which in this area possesses the minds of almost everyone, ought to be judged by reason, let us offer up the witness of Scripture through which the matter can be judged. After inspecting those witnesses, it will not be us, but truth itself that will overcome that stupid error, and everyone who recognizes the truth will denounce the instruments of error and say with the Apostle [Paul], "No lie is of the truth." What is not from the truth is especially not from God, and because it is not from God, he hears not its words. . . .

7. If therefore the almighty God through the power of his arm whips the wicked with new waters, hail, and rains and whose hand it is impossible to flee, then those people are entirely ignorant of God who believe that humans can do these things. For if people can send hail, then they can make it rain anywhere, for no one ever sees hail without rain. They could also protect themselves from their enemies, not only by the theft of crops, but also by taking away a life. For when it happens that the enemies of the storm-makers are in a road or a field, they could kill them; they could send an entire hail-storm down upon them in one mass and bury them. Some claim that they themselves know some storm-makers who can make a diffuse pattern of hail that is falling throughout a region fall instead in a heap upon a river or a useless forest or upon a tub under which the storm-maker himself is hiding. Often we have heard it said by many, that they knew that such things were certainly done in (specific) places, but we have never yet heard anyone claim that they themselves had seen these things. Once it was reported to me that someone said that he himself had seen such things. With great interest I myself set out to see him, and I did. But when I was speaking with him and encouraging him, with many prayers and entreaties, to say whether he had seen such things, I (nevertheless) pressed him with divine threats not to say anything unless it were true. Then he declared that what he said was indeed

true and he named the person, the time, and place, but nevertheless confessed that he himself had not been present at that time. . . .

13. Also in our times we sometimes see that, with the crops and grapes harvested, farmers cannot sow (the next crop) on account of the dryness of the land. Why do you not ask your storm-makers to send their raised winds to wet the land so that you might sow them then? But because you do not do that, nor did you ever see or hear of anyone doing it, listen to what the Lord himself, the creator of all things, the ruler, governor, arranger, and provider says to his blessed servant Job about things of this sort. . . .

14. Look at the great works of God, the existence of which the blessed Job himself was not able to admire fully and loftily. If the Lord has a treasure-trove of hail that he alone sees, and which even the blessed Job never saw, where do the storm-makers discover what the blessed Job never found? . . .

15. This stupidity is not the least part of this unfaithfulness, for it has now grown into such a great evil, that in many places there are wretched people who say indeed that they do not know how to send storms, but nevertheless know how to defend the inhabitants of a place against storms. They have determined how much of a crop they should be given and call this a regular tribute (*canonicum*). There are many people who never freely give tithes to priests, nor give alms to widows, orphans, and other poor people. Though the importance of almsgiving is preached to them, is repeatedly read out, and encouraged, they still do not give any. They pay the *canonicum*, however, voluntarily to their defenders, by whom they believe they are protected from storms. And all of this is accomplished without any preaching, any admonishment, any exhortation, except the seduction of the Devil. . . .

16. A few years ago (that is, in 810) a certain foolish story spread. Since at that time cattle were dying off, people said that Duke Grimoald of Benevento [r. 806–817] had sent people with a dust which they were to spread on the fields, mountains, meadows, and wells and that it was because of the dust they spread that the cattle died. He did this (they say) because he was an enemy of our most Christian Emperor Charles. For this reason we heard and saw that many people were captured and some were killed. Most of them, with plaques attached, were cast into the river and drowned. And, what is truly remarkable, those captured gave testimony against themselves, admitting that they had such dust and had spread it. For so the Devil, by the secret and just judgment of God, having received power over them, was able to succeed over them that they gave false witness against themselves and died. Neither learning, nor torture, nor death itself deterred them from daring to give false witness against themselves. This story was so widely believed that there were very few to whom it seemed absurd. They did not rationally consider how such dust could be made, how it could kill only cattle and not other animals, how it could be carried and spread over such

a vast territory by humans. Nor did they consider whether there were enough Beneventan men and women, old and young, to go out from their region in wheeled carts loaded down with dust. Such is the great foolishness that oppresses the wretched world. . . .

Questions: What are both the theological and practical concerns Agobard has with his parishioners' belief in weather-makers? As an investigator, does he make the case, to your satisfaction, that people actually believed in the existence of weather magic, in reference both to magicians (the tempestarii)*, and those who defended against storms? Why or why not? What did he discover in the case of those caught and about to be stoned?*

30. CAROLINGIAN CATALOGUE OF MAGICAL ACTS: COUNCIL OF PARIS

The Council of Paris took place when Louis the Pious (778–840) was emperor. The assembly was a comprehensive reform council, and the record of it shows a full range of magical activities that occurred when human beings were complicit in trusting, supporting, assisting, or colluding with demons. In the early Middle Ages there was some inconsistency on the specifics of what particular conduct constituted traffic with demons. While acknowledging the fluidity of the parameters of magic in the period and variation over time, a clear pattern emerged by the ninth century. Some of the practices captured in the council record were ossified hold-overs from earlier eras, but that does not make the list any less valuable as a summary of acts that were identified as magic in the Carolingian era. Chapter Two, which amounts to an official inventory of magic, is perfunctory and places magical acts among a variety of unrelated misbehaviors. Because the council was all-inclusive, magic was naturally addressed, but given the demands on the reformers' attention, it was a low priority.

Source: trans. Martha Rampton, from *Monumenta Germaniae Historica. Concilia Aevi Karolini* 1.2, ed. Albert Werminghoff (Hannover: Hahnsche Buchhandlung, 1979), p. 669.

2. Perpetrators of Various Evils

There are without doubt those guilty of various evils whom divine law both rejects and condemns, and through their many evils and scandals, the people are beaten down by famine and pestilence, the condition of the church weakened, and the kingdom put in jeopardy . . . [Denunciation in the harshest terms of same-sex intercourse and bestiality follows.]

There exist other most insidious evils, which, no doubt, remain with us from heathen rites, such as sorcery, soothsaying, drawing lots, poisonings, divination, incantations, and interpreting dreams, for which divine law unhesitatingly stipulates punishment, about which it is said in the Scriptures, "The person who will turn to magicians and soothsayers and prostitute himself to them, I will set my face against that person, and I will [cut him off] from among his people. Sanctify yourselves and be holy, because I your Lord God am holy. Keep my commandments and carry them out, because I am the Lord who sanctifies you" [Leviticus 20:6–8]. And elsewhere it says, "You shall not suffer magicians and diviners and evil doers of the land to live" [cf. Exodus 22:18]. Doubtless there are many who, by the same deceptions and diabolical illusions, infect the minds of others by love potions, drugged food, or charms, so that they become insane and are not aware of the abuses they suffer. It is said that they can, by their sorcery, disturb the air, send hailstorms, predict the future, move fruit and milk from one person to another, and innumerable other such things. If someone of this sort should be found, whether men or women, they should be very sternly corrected because, in their crimes and temerity, they do not fear to serve the Devil nor do they renounce him publically. Of these things it is also written in the Council of Ancyra [314], title 23 [or 24], "Those who practice divination, and follow the customs of the pagans, or take people into their houses to introduce the evil arts for the invention of sorceries, or for lustrations, fall under the canon of five years [penance], according to the prescribed degrees; that is, three years as prostrators, and two of prayer without oblation."

Questions: Why does the council object to magic? Whom does it affect? Why does the scribe refer to the New Testament and the Council of Ancyra?

31. TREATISE ON MAGIC: HRABANUS MAURUS

Hrabanus Maurus (c. 780–856) was the archbishop of Mainz, Germany. He was one of the keenest minds and prolific writers of the Carolingian era, which won him the appellation "Teacher of Germany." Hrabanus's short treatise on magic is one of his lesser-known works. Little is original in the text; it is heavily reliant on biblical passages and works of the church fathers.

Source: trans. Martha Rampton, Hrabanus Maurus, On the Magic Arts, in Patrologiae cursus completus, Latin series, vol. 100, ed. Jacques-Paul Migne (1844–55), cols. 1095–97.

On the Magic Arts

It is clearly established by the authority of the Old and New Testaments what divine law ordains regarding the magic arts, both incantations and various superstitions that pagans and false Christians, in their divinations and perverse observations, follow. Indeed, divine law curses them where in the book of

Exodus [22:18] it says, "Do not allow sorcerers to live in your land." And it also says, "Anyone who sacrifices to gods other than the only God must be killed" [22:20]. And in Leviticus [19:26] it says, "You shall not eat meat [contaminated] with blood, practice auguries or observe dreams, and you shall not cut your flesh for the sake of the dead nor make any figures or signs on your skin. I am the Lord." And moreover it says, "Do not pollute yourself by resorting to magicians or inquiring of fortune-tellers" [19:31]. And again, "A man or a woman who is a spirit medium or a necromancer shall be put to death. They shall be pelted with stones, and (the guilt of) their blood shall be upon themselves" [20:27]. In Deuteronomy [18:9–14] it also states, "When you enter the land that your God will give to you, take care not to imitate the detestable abominations of the gentiles. There shall not be found among you who sacrifices his son or his daughter by passing them through the fire, one who inquires of fortunetellers, or observes auguries and dreams. You shall not be a sorcerer or enchanter or consult spirit mediums or diviners who seek information from the dead. Anyone who does these evil things is abominable to the Lord; because of these same evil practices the Lord will annihilate those who were there before you. You must be perfect and without stain before the Lord your God. The peoples of the land you will possess listen to augurs and diviners, but you are instructed by the Lord your God to do otherwise." And following this the text says, "In my stead, your Lord God will raise up for you a prophet from among you, of your own people, and you must listen to him. This is what you asked of your Lord God when you met together at Horeb, and you said, 'We no longer want to hear the voice of our Lord God or to see the great flame, or we will die.' And the Lord said to me, 'All that they said is good. I will raise up a prophet for them, like you, from among your fellow Israelites and put my words in his mouth, and he will convey to them all that I command. Anyone who does not listen to him who speaks in my name, I will judge. But a prophet who has the presumption to distort the words that he speaks in my name or that I did not command of him, or in the name of other gods, is to be killed" [18:15–20]. And this will be a prophet whose words you must hear and who must be obeyed with all the effort of will.

This is clear when the Evangelist [John] writes that a crowd of the faithful seeing miracles and signs that Jesus performed said, clamoring, "Truly this is a prophet who has come into the world" [John 6:14]. And elsewhere of him it is written, "They were all filled with wonder and exalted God saying, 'A great prophet has risen up among us. God has come to his people'" [Luke 7:16]. Here indeed is a prophet and the lord of all prophets, who is the way, the truth, and the life, the creator in both testaments, not just in the old but also in the new, who rejects and condemns all errors and divinations and the noxious arts. Not from anyone other than from [God] should you want to look for truth or health which comes from the father and the holy spirit who is the one true and omnipotent

God, who alone makes great miracles. Hence, in the Gospel he beckons all to come to him saying, "Come to me all who labor and are burdened and I will rescue you. Take my yoke upon yourselves and learn from me, because I am gentle and humble of heart, and you will find rest for your spirits, indeed, my yoke is comfortable and my burden is light" [Matthew 11:28–30]. And again, "I am the light of the world, he who follows me will not walk in shadows but will have the light of life" [John 8:12]. Likewise, according to Paul, [Jesus] is the savior of all people of great faith about whom Peter said, "There is no other name on earth given to humans by which we might be saved" [Acts 4:12]. Through the church, daily there will be great miracles and healing because of the prayers of the faithful, for in the Gospels [Jesus] himself said this to his disciples, "Behold I give you the power to trample serpents and scorpions and all the strength of the enemy. Preach the gospel, cure the sick, revive the dead, and cast out demons" [Luke 10:19]. And Mark testifies to this saying, "For he cured so many of those sick or with wounds of all kinds that many more crushed in on him in order to touch him. When the unclean spirits saw him, they fell down before him and cried out saying, 'You are the Son of God.' But he ordered them sternly not to make him known to others. And ascending the mountain, he called to those he wanted and they went to him. He appointed twelve as his apostles to preach the gospel, and he gave them the power to heal the sick and cast out demons" [Mark 3:11–14].

What else then is necessary for health other than to consult a competent doctor? And why seek knowledge or wisdom anywhere than from the font of all knowledge and wisdom? Of this is written, all wisdom is from the Lord God, and was always with him, even before time. Who counted the grains of sand on the seashores, the drops of rain, and the days of the world. Who measured the height of the sky, the width of the land, and the depth of the abyss? Who comprehended the all-surpassing wisdom of God? Wisdom came into being before everything else, and knowledge is eternal. The fountain of wisdom is the word of God in the highest, and the beginning of these eternal commandments.

Who indeed wants to have health without the savior, and who considers himself clever without true wisdom? That is not health but disease, that is not wisdom but stupidity. Who would persist in constant affliction, who would endure in blind, stupid and senseless wrongdoing? It is preferable always to seek cures from God than to persist in idolatry by desiring them from demons themselves. That is not life but death, and those who seek cures from demons, if they will not reform, are headed for eternal damnation.

As the Psalmist says, "All gods of the pagans are demons" [Psalm 95]. Those people who hold these beliefs are happy to be deceived daily, and thus, they bring about their own ruin. Therefore, the falsehood of the magic arts, from the teaching of the evil angels, has prevailed throughout the world for virtually all time. Through knowledge of the future and of the dead, and through their strategies, aruspices, auguries, and that which is called prophecy and necromancy, were invented.

Questions: Does Hrabanus's treatise shed light on sorcery of his own time? Explain. On what grounds does Hrabanus object to sorcery? The author's position on health is consistent with other thinkers in the early Middle Ages; what is that position?

32. MAGIC AT THE COURT OF LOUIS THE PIOUS: PASCHASIUS RADBERTUS

Louis the Pious (778–840) inherited the governance of Carolingian Europe from Charlemagne (742–814). He and his wife, Ermengarde (c. 788–818), had an exceptionally stable marriage for about twenty-four years and bore three sons and two daughters. Emperor Louis was widowed in 818, and less than a year later he married the young, beautiful Judith (c. 797–843), who bore a child in 823. The birth of Charles (823–877) meant that the arrangements Louis had made for the division of his kingdom would have to be altered to allow Charles his patrimony. In 829, plans for a redistribution of the empire were drawn up, and in the following years, Louis's older sons rebelled against him twice, throwing Francia into a state of civil and fratricidal war.

There is a scholarly tradition that puts Empress Judith at the center of the rebellion of the emperor's sons. According to this scenario, by manipulating her aging husband, Judith destabilized the status quo to her stepsons' disadvantage in order to ensure Charles's inheritance. Although that portrait of events has been revised, there were some writers of the period who clearly judged Judith's influence to be prodigious and dangerous; Paschasius Radbertus, abbot of Corbie (c. 785–c. 865), was one of them. He wrote the Life of Wala *[c. 755-836], the former abbot of Corbie, in the form of a discussion among a group of monks. The* vita *was meant to honor and defend Wala, and in the text Paschasius pours forth his frustration and chagrin at the dominance of Empress Judith, who, he bemoans, undermined the purity of the palace where the old, lax, befuddled emperor was cuckolded by Judith and the chamberlain, Bernard of Septimania (c. 795–844). Paschasius attributes the cancer festering in the body politic to Bernard and the empress. He accuses the two of numerous transgressions, sorcery being among that complex of denunciations. Although the* Life of Wala *survives in only one manuscript dating from the period shortly after its completion, it nevertheless provides important insights about perceived court magic of the time.*

Paschasius uses pseudonyms for the characters in his text, but they are omitted below for the sake of clarity.

Source: Allen Cabaniss, *Charlemagne's Cousins: Contemporary Lives of Adalard and Wala* (Syracuse, NY: Syracuse University Press, 1967), pp. 158–62, 164, 166–67.

Life of Wala

Book 2

CHAPTER 7

2. Paschasius: Alas, [the negligence of Emperor Louis] which almost brought eternal darkness and peril to this orb; which split to pieces and divided this empire formerly at peace and united; which violated, broke off close blood relationships, begot enmities everywhere, and scattered fellow citizens, destroyed faith, erased charity, churches, and corrupted everything! Civil wars—more than civil wars—occur daily.

Hither and thither the army of the whole country almost perishes. Far and wide, provinces, the countryside, and cities are depopulated. If any are left, they flee everywhere without strength or they are hewn down with swords. On all sides are invasions by pagan enemies. All the people perish. Villas and cities without number are burned. Alas, wretched day which a more unhappy night follows!

3. But no more unhappy day there was than that when the accursed Bernard was summoned from the Spains, that Amisarius [i.e. Bernard] who had abandoned everything honorable in which he had been reared.

Vain he plunged into the hog wallows of filth. . . .

CHAPTER 8

2. Paschasius: It is true, brother, that [Wala] saw the ills which daily arose without number and without measure. But he could not foreknow the future.

As much as he could, Wala wished to meet and resist them for loyalty to realm and king, for devotion to country and people, for the religion of churches and safety of the citizens. All these were dearer to him than his own life. But since such matters had not been checked and repressed initially, since faults were compelling, they had superior power with impunity toward the mischief of everyone. There was no one already strong and wise enough to prevent [them]. When he recovered from his infirmity, the same one began to hear from all sides infamous and obscene, shameful and foul reports, not of ordinary kind, but of such kind as had never been heard in this our age. Because of this, his heart, so fond of religion, was soon disturbed.

3. The palace became a theater, formerly of honor, in which such great recurring illusions of soothsayers were welling up as were believed not to exist in the whole world. He could not restrain himself from tears of grief and love when these matters were reported to him day and night by good men, most eminent and most truthful. The more Wala loved Christ's church and emperor with his people and offspring, the more he was afflicted with grief. Chiefs of the palace of both orders were coming and declaring all such things to be true or rather worse than popularly reported.

He thereupon decided to come and try by his reproof, persuasion, and counsel to help, so that the scourge might be averted before it disturbed and overturned everything. Thus he did what he could. He spoke with the emperor and leaders concerning what he had heard. He forewarned what he felt in those matters that were happening.

4. The seditious monster himself [Bernard] he even addressed with every expression of loyalty and friendship, since the latter's father and he had been close friends. For once upon a time Wala had taken as his wife the latter's sister, daughter of a most noble and high-minded man. From the cradle he had, like a father, displayed a holy care, and solicitude toward him in all respects, more even than if he were his father. But when he saw that he was already blind and mad in mind and that he was already rushing headlong, he said whatever he could. But Bernard would not listen, for he was already abandoned in morals and drunk with venom of desire. When Wala realized that he was making no progress, he returned without result to his monastery, grieving and mourning over what he had observed. After a brief lapse of time, the rulers and chiefs of the palace, banished and deposed, soon followed him, weeping and bemoaning.

6. When such facts had been ascertained, they related to Wala evils of the age which have scarcely ever been heard of before, how in so glorious an empire everything had thus been suddenly and completely altered. The palace had become a brothel where adultery is queen and an adulterer reigns. Crimes are heaped up, all unmentionable kinds of soothsaying and sorcery are demanded, such as I never believed to have still remained in the world. Of all evils nothing has been omitted, and everything is gossiped about by everyone. Nonetheless the sober and wary man was moved only to tears until a plot was disclosed and indeed strengthened by the very ones who were fully aware of such perverse plans. The tyrant [Bernard] sought by some means secretly to slay the emperor so it would appear that he died of his own infirmity. Thereafter his sons and the best princes of the realm were to be murdered by whatever guile he could plan. These matters were reported by the most sober and truthful men and there could be no doubt about them.

CHAPTER 9

1. Paschasius: You urge us well [not to falter], brother, unless things should be so great that we are not adequate to recall nor to contemplate them. I am not speaking of what happened once upon a time, but only of what happened when that infamous and impious enemy of all religion confounded, disturbed, perverted, commingled honorable matters with indecent ones and religious matters with vain ones. There is no mind nor tongue nor voice which can relate the endeavors of that mad man who was protected "by the dregs of all crimes" [Cicero, *Pro Sestio* 7.15]. He thought to seize everything in advance with diabolical sorceries,

to overcome not by counsel but by omens, to grasp in advance by divinations. He so held the most sacred emperor by his misleading delusions that those whom the latter or his great imperial father had cherished he drove away away from intimacy, from conference, from secret counsel, from faithful trust, from honors, and from every fellowship of earlier life. When this scourge and author of crime had been secured by royal power, he shone in preference because he was the punishment for past crimes and the increment of evil.

4. [Louis's son, Pepin, c. 797–838] . . . related everything that he had learned while under detention [by his father's opponents]. No doubt had remained in anyone about adultery and about sorceries and divinations, but from him it was learned how many from every part of the world had been assembled in the palace and what kinds, such as no one believed to be still practiced. It was as if Antichrist had appeared with his sorceries.

Lastly he spoke concerning the proposed murder of his father and overthrow of the empire. He told how it had been projected in advance by omens, forebodings, plots and stratagems, as well as with every malign craft. Thereupon all the nobles and the two sons who were present, Pepin and Louis [the German, c. 804–876], decided that they ought to die rather than agree to such proceedings. They decided that only one [Bernard] was infamous to them, shameful, and the author of every malice destined for violence, ruin, and everlasting reproach to all.

5. Although grieving and lamenting with divine fear, Wala acquiesced in this plan and explanation, because he could at that time find no other opportunity to evade it. But he did not want the emperor to be deprived of empire nor, as far as the result of the affair would allow, to be treated dishonorably in any respect by anyone. He wanted simply for the enemy and his accomplices to be driven away and for adultery, which was already common fame, to be no longer concealed to the confusion of everyone. He sought that soothsayers there assembled, diviners, seers, and mutes, as well as dream-interpreters and those who consult entrails, and indeed all those skilled in malign crafts to be expelled from the sacred place. So many and so great were the forebodings of the unmentionable art as to drag a vast number of people into error. All the figments of devilish art seemed to have again sprung up in the world, so that when everything about the emperor was done by fraud and guile; it was possible for no one to be deeply aware of what was happening daily. Evidence that he was deluded by malicious crafts lies in the fact that he refused to heed the most faithful consuls and the most holy prelates and that he believed evil things about him whose counsel he had always employed in the past. He refused to receive anyone into his confidence except those whom Judith approved.

6. As long as this condition prevailed, he was unable to listen to any other or love any other or agree with any other than those whom she commended to his confidence. But even more ominously as they say, he could not will anything

other than what she willed. There was, for instance, a certain bishop at that meeting with all the prelates of Christ and senate of the whole empire. They were denouncing the emperor with insistent confidence for such things. The aforesaid bishop, however, observed, "I know about the kind and the enormity of the matters mentioned, and I know that you [Emperor Louis], being badly misled by these arts, still approve. Yet when you have been divested of those regalia with which you have been clothed, you will receive yourself again and you will be, as you were the best of emperors."

7. Adeodatus: In our age, so far as I am aware, an occurrence like this has never been known before, that a people would act thus for prince against prince. It was, I believe, either extreme love of our senators and prelates toward the emperor and his offspring that they, when the reasons had been made clear, raised him again to the realm so respectfully; or blind foolhardiness that they dared such things without any evidence of adultery, sorcery, and other offenses, except in the opinion of the masses.

Consequently it does not seem to me that the entire ecclesiastical establishment and the whole ruling class should for such reasons rise in revolt or should be incited to rebellion against Louis, unless perhaps something lay hidden in the background which may be more serious. . . .

Questions: How do the denunciations lodged against Judith follow a predictable pattern where women are concerned? What particular kinds of sorcery are at issue in the text? Accusations against Bernard are made within a complex of charges; how does sorcery function within this grouping? The emperor himself is not spared in the text; although he is held innocent of overt crimes, Paschasius implies that Louis has failed as a king. Why?

33. THE DEVIL OF KEMPTEN AND THE VILLAGER

Although magic, by definition, depended on the cooperation of demons, demons did not require the complicity of human beings in order to cause mischief. The Annals of Fulda is a chronicle of events that took place in ninth-century east Francia. The authors and the provenance of the work are unclear, but based on the topics of interest in The Annals, it was likely written by members of court circles. Under the entry for 858 an unusual incident is reported from the Bavarian village of Kempten in Germany, where a rogue demon acts independently and performs many of the functions for which sorcerers were reproved.

Source: trans. Timothy Reuter, *The Annals of Fulda* (Manchester: Manchester University Press, 1992), pp. 44–45.

There is a certain *villa* (Kempten) not far from the town of Bingen [in modern Germany], called "Caput Montium" [Head of the Mountains] because the mountains along the valley of the Rhine begin here (though the common people corrupt the name to "Chamund"). Here an evil spirit gave an open sign of his wickedness. First, by throwing stones and banging on the walls as if with a hammer, he made a nuisance of himself to the people living there. Then he spoke openly and revealed what had been stolen from certain people, and then caused disputes among the inhabitants of the place. Finally he stirred up everyone's hatred against one man, as if it were for his sins that everyone had to suffer such things; and so that he might be the more hated, the evil spirit caused every house which the man entered to catch fire.

As a result the man was forced to live outside the *villa* in the fields with his wife and children, as all his kin feared to take him in. But he was not even allowed to remain there in safety, for when he had gathered in and stacked his crops, the evil spirit came unexpectedly and burnt them. To try to appease the feelings of the inhabitants, who wished to kill him, he took the ordeal of hot iron and proved himself innocent of the crimes which were alleged against him. Priests and deacons were therefore sent from the town of Mainz with relics and crosses to expel the wicked spirit from that place. As they were saying the litany and sprinkling holy water in a house where he had been particularly active, the old enemy threw stones at men coming there from the *villa* and wounded them. After the clerics who had been sent there had departed, the same devil made lamentable speeches in the hearing of many. He named a certain priest and said that he had stood underneath his cope [liturgical cloak] at the time when the holy water was being spread around the building. Then, as men crossed themselves in fear, he said of the same priest, "He is my servant. For anyone who is conquered by someone is his servant; and lately at my persuasion he slept with the daughter of the bailiff of this *villa*." This crime had not before been known to anyone except those who had committed it. It is clear that as the word of truth says, "Nothing is hidden which will not be revealed" (Matthew 10:26). With these and similar deeds the apostate spirit was a burden to the above-mentioned place for the course of three whole years, and he did not desist until he had destroyed almost all the buildings with fire.

Question: Other than working without the aid of a human agent, how is this demon different from demons of the early medieval period?

34. MARRIAGE AND MAGIC: THE DIVORCE OF LOTHAR

Bishop Hincmar of Rheims (c. 806–822) authored two treatises on the efforts of King Lothar II of Lotharingia (835–869) to divorce his wife, Theutberga (d. 875). This cause célèbre carried political, ecclesiastical, and theological ramifications for all of Europe and came at a point in the development of canon law [church law] when the subject of marriage and the legitimacy of divorce were undergoing scrutiny and revision by Carolingian reformers.

Hincmar, who evinced relatively scant interest in sorcery across his writings, addressed magic in his lengthy treatises to counter Lothar's claim that his marriage was not binding because there was magic involved. Most of Hincmar's material comes from earlier authorities, such as Isidore of Seville (see doc. 23).

Source: trans. Rachel Stone and Charles West, *The Divorce of King Lothar and Queen Theutberga: Hincmar of Rheims'* De divortio (Manchester: Manchester University Press, 2016), pp. 235–37.

Question 15. About that which was asked, "And if it might be true, as many people say, that there are women who by their sorcery (*maleficium*) are able to provoke irreconcilable hatred between man and wife and to sow an indescribable love between a man and woman," and all the rest which the questioners wanted to bring into investigation.

Response 15. Let them reread the history of the Book of Kings [also Samuel], how after David's sin with Bathsheba, the wife of Uriah, Amnon, the son of the same David, by the Devil's prompting fell passionately in love with his sister Tamar, and how on the advice of Jonadab, representing the Devil who slew Adam through Eve's encouragement to sin, he slept with this sister. And how before that sleeping together he (Amnon) loved her so much that he was wholly lost in her and fell sick for her love. But after their sleeping together, "He hated exceedingly, so that the hatred wherewith he now hated her was greater than the love wherewith he had loved her" [2 Samuel 13:1–16]. And this devilish work ran on through fratricide to other evils, which readers will find there. . . .

And in a certain diocese of ours, what we shall explain took place. A certain young man of noble birth fell passionately in love with a woman of not ignoble ancestry. And seeking her legally from her parents, he won assent from her father, but the girl's mother totally refused his request. But, what rarely happens, the father prevailed in agreeing to the young man's demands. After betrothal, the giving of a dowry and a marriage celebration, the young man led her to a private room, but he was in no way able to sleep with her as is customary. After they had led a life made wearisome by irremediable hatred for two years, the young man went to the bishop, forced by necessity for he could not find advice anywhere else, with words of persuasion, requests and threats: that unless he (the bishop) allowed the marriage to be dissolved, he would take out his sword, through which murder would occur if the marriage could not be dissolved in any other way. But this bishop, sifting through many other such things often done by the Devil, brought back to mind what the Lord said through the prophet, "Son of man, dig now in the wall, and behold the wicked abominations that they do here. And when I had digged in the wall, behold a door" [Ezekiel 8:7–10] and the rest which is read there. And he went from meeting to meeting, and through many discussions of this sort took the matter from dispute to settlement, until the works of the Devil were dissolved by the grace of God, and sexual relations, which had been possible with enjoyment with a concubine before but impossible with his legally acquired wife, were made possible for the young man with her, after penance and church medicine. And the devilish hatred was driven off, and the restored conjugal love amongst the spouses has persisted up till now with due affection, and the married couple rejoice in numerous children.

It is shameful to repeat the stories known to us, and it takes a long time to reckon the sacrilege which we learn takes place in this sort of matter, with the bones of the dead, ashes and burned coal, and with hairs from the head and from men's and women's genital areas together with threads of many colors, and with various herbs and small snails and snakes, all put together while songs are chanted. Freed and healed from these things, thanks to the blessing of the church, people have full enjoyment of conjugal favor and the natural debt. Some men were dressed up or covered over by enchanted clothing, others were found to be driven mad by sorcerers by a drink, some by food, some mesmerized by witches by chants alone, and made almost enfeebled. Some men were debilitated by witches or weaving women, some women are even found to have suffered sleeping with demons in the shape of the men for whom they were burning in love. Divine power has restored these men and women alike to health, with devilish fantasies suppressed and cast off by exorcisms and catholic remedies. There are other things which necessity compels us to investigate and to judge, which we do not want to talk about because of the abominable shamefulness.

Questions: Does Hincmar think that marriage should be dissolved in cases where magic was used to make the partners distasteful to each other? Explain. How does Hincmar understand the role of gender in terms of love magic?

35. LOOSED WOMEN AND NIGHT FLIGHT: *CANON EPISCOPI*

In the ancient world, Diana (see doc. 7) had many attributes; she was the virgin goddess of nature, fertility, and the hunt, but most significantly for the history of magic and witchcraft, Diana was mistress of the moon and one of the most powerful deities of the classical pagan pantheon. All the pagan gods and goddesses were demonized by Christians, but Diana had primacy of place as perhaps the most formidable and enduring of them all. The fact that she was unmarried—an intrepid female on her own—contributed to her later reputation as the goddess who enticed crowds of women to leave their husbands' beds at night and follow her in a fantastic flight across the moonlit sky.

Around 906, Bishop Regino of Prüm (d. 915) compiled a collection of canonical and penitential regulations called On Synodal Cases and Church Discipline. *One of the entries in the text came to be known as the* Canon episcopi *(so-called after the first two words of the canon). It was mistakenly believed to have originated in the prestigious Council of Ancyra (314), which gave it special legitimacy. The canon lays out a prohibition that would have a long history in European magic and witchcraft. It proscribes the belief that hordes of unloosed women customarily fly across the night sky in the company of demons led by Diana.*

A century after Regino wrote, Bishop Burchard of Worms (c. 950–1025) included three versions of the Canon episcopi *in his* Decretum, *a compendium of church law that borrows liberally from Regino's text. In one rendition of the canon, Burchard replaces Diana with Hulda, a German goddess, and in another adaptation he introduces Herodias as one of the leaders of the flying horde of women. Herodias was the infamous lover of Herod Antipas (c. 20 BCE–c. 39 CE) and the epitome of female seduction responsible for the arrest and decapitation of John the Baptist. Other possibilities for her inclusion are that Herodias was a Teutonic goddess of fertility, or because her name is similar to Hecate, pagan goddess of birth, death, and the underworld, who was often conflated with Diana.*

A redaction of the canon found its way into an authoritative corpus of church law, also called the Decretum *(c. 1140), compiled by Gratian, an obscure Bolognese canon lawyer. As such it was a touchstone for the understanding of Diana and night flight throughout the medieval and early modern periods. The interpretation of Regino's and Burchard's canons mutated over the centuries, and later European witchcraft theorists read the texts differently than the authors intended.*

Sources: trans. Martha Rampton from Regino of Prüm, *De synodalibus causis et disciplinis ecclesiasticis* 2.371, ed. F.G.A. Wasserschleben (Leipzig: Engelmann, 1840; rpt. Graz: Akademische Druck- u. Verlagsanstalt, 1964), pp. 354–56; and Burchard of Worms, *Decretum* 10.1 and 19.5.170, ed. J.P. Migne, *Patrologiae cursus complectus. Series Latina*, vol. 140 (Paris, 1841–65), cols. 831–32, 973.

Regino of Prüm, *On Synodal Cases and Church Discipline*

Book 2

Canon 371. On Women who are said to Ride with Demons in the Hours of the Night.

Bishops and all those men who assist them should strenuously labor in order that the pernicious arts of drawing lots and sorcery, which were invented by the Devil, are completely eradicated from their parishes, and if they find any man or woman of this evil sect, they should be ejected with disgrace from the decent people of their parishes. For as the Apostle [Paul] says, "Avoid a heretic after the first and second warning, knowing that such a man is subverted" [Timothy 3:10–11]. Those who leave their creator to seek the aid of the Devil have been subverted and are held captive by the Devil, and therefore the holy church ought to be cleansed of such a pest.

It is also not to be omitted that some wicked women, turning back to Satan, seduced by illusions and phantasms of demons, believe and claim that in the hours of night they ride on certain beasts with Diana, goddess of the pagans, and an innumerable multitude of women; they are called to her service on particular nights, and in the dismal silence of the night, traverse great spaces of earth and obey her commands as mistress. But if only they alone would perish in their deceitfulness and did not drag many others with them into this destruction of infidelity. For an innumerable multitude, deceived by this false opinion, believe it to be true, and believing, deviate from the right faith and return to the error of the pagans when they think there is anything of divinity or divine power beyond the one God.

For this reason, priests, through churches entrusted to them, should preach urgently to all the people so they know that this belief is unconditionally false and that such phantoms are impressed on the minds of the unfaithful, not from a divine source, but from a malignant spirit. For it is Satan, who transforms himself into an angel of light, and when he has captured the mind of some little woman and subjugated her to himself through infidelity and incredulity, he immediately transforms himself into the species and likeness of various personages, and deluding her mind which he holds captive, showing things in dreams, whether joyous or sad, and persons, whether known or unknown, and leads [her mind] through devious paths. And although it is only her spirit that endures this, the faithless mind thinks that it happens not in the spirit but in the body. Who indeed has not been led out of himself in dreams and nocturnal visions and sees many things while sleeping which he had never seen while awake? Who indeed is so stupid and dull that they think that these things occur in the body that happen in the spirit only, since the prophet Ezekiel saw visions of the Lord in the spirit, not in the body [Ezekiel 8:3], and the Apostle [Paul], who John saw and heard the mysteries of the Apocalypse, said as much himself, "At once I was in spirit" [Revelation 4:2], and Paul does not dare to say that [a particular man he knew] was carried up [to the third heaven] in the body [2 Corinthians 12:1–4]. Therefore, it is to be announced publicly to all, that he who believes such things or things like them loses the faith, and he who does not have the right faith in God is not of God but is of that in which he believes, and that is the Devil. For it is written of our Lord, "All things were made through him" [John 1:3]. Anyone, therefore, who believes that something can be made or any creature can be changed or transformed for the better or the worse into another species or likeness except by the creator himself, who made all things and through whom all things were made, is without doubt an infidel.

Burchard of Worms, *Decretum*

Book 10

Chapter 1. It ought not be overlooked that some wicked women, turning back to Satan, seduced by illusions and fantasies of demons, believe that in the hours of the night they ride out on certain beasts with Diana, goddess of the pagans, or with Herodias, and an enormous multitude of women. They claim that they are called to serve Diana on particular nights, and in the gloomy silence of the nighttime, they cross great expanses of earth and obey her commands as if she were their mistress. . . .

Book 19 (Corrector sive Medicus)

Chapter 5

Canon 70. Have you believed that it is possible, as those deceived by the Devil affirm, that a woman, claiming that what she does is out of necessity on the Devil's command, rides on certain beasts on special nights with a multitude of demons transformed into the likeness of women and (led by a witch who is foolishly called Hulda) allows herself to be numbered with their band? If you have participated in this faithlessness, you should do penance for one year on the appointed fast days.

Canon 170 [This canon is not considered a version of the *Canon episcopi*, but it shares elements with it.] Have you believed what many women who have turned back to Satan believe and affirm to be true, namely, that in the quiet of the night when you go in bed with your husband laying next to you, and while still in your body, you are able to go through closed doors and traverse vast spaces of the earth with many others who are deceived by a similar error, and without visible arms can kill people who have been baptized and redeemed by the blood of Christ in order to eat their cooked flesh, and in place of their heart to put something like straw or wood, and once they are eaten you can make them live again for another interval of life. If you have believed this you must do penance for 40 days, that is a carina, on bread and water for seven successive years.

Questions: What is the significance of Burchard replacing the classical goddess Diana with a Germanic deity, Hulda? Based on the versions of the Canon episcopi, *are those in the wild ride demons or women? Both canons canons 70 and 170 are listed with sins employing the magic arts, yet yet Burchard insists that the night rides are illusionary; given this, what is "magical" about them? Is the association of Diana, the moon, and magic new with Regino's text?*

36. ANGLO-SAXON HEALING CURES AND CHARMS

The compilation of mid-tenth-century texts called the Leechbook of Bald *("leech" means "medic") is enigmatic, and the genesis of the text is uncertain. Most likely written at Winchester in Old English, the* Leechbook *was the first European medical treatise in a vernacular language and is the oldest English herbal to survive in complete form. A metrical colophon at the end of the second book reads: "This book belongs to Bald, which he ordered Cild to compile (or transcribe)"; scholars, however, have not been able to identify Bald or Cild. The manuscript is composed of three discrete books, and the first two are referred to as Bald's leechbook, proper. The third is a mélange of medical recipes and charms that was not originally assembled with the other two. The compiler of the* Leechbook of Bald, *obviously a physician learned in classical medical literature, borrowed and discarded information from his Mediterranean sources and made substitutions of indigenous plants for herbs unavailable in England. He was not simply copying venerated texts; rather, he composed a medical manual for use in the British Isles.*

There has been considerable debate as to whether the medical recipes in Bald's leechbook are magical/superstitious in nature, and, if so, by what definition that is the case. Although most of the recipes in the Leechbook *require simple preparation of herbs for ailments that moderns would recognize as commonplace, a handful of cures rely on ritualistic formulas and curious rites. The agents of illness are devils, the fiend, elves, serpents, and worms, and although the remedies for fiend-like diseases are laced with Christian imagery and involve prayers, masses, and the paraphernalia of the church for their efficacy, they also employ measures such as hanging amulets around the neck, talismans, and timing the collection of herbs and their application to the stages of the moon. According to venerated authorities such as Augustine and Caesarius of Arles (see docs. 15, 17), cures reliant on such procedures were effective only with the cooperation of demons, even if those cures were facilitated by priests, monks, or nuns.*

Source: trans. Oswald Cockayne, *Leechdoms, Wortcunning, and Starcraft of Early England*, vol. 2, Roll Series 35, in *Chronicles and Memorials of Great Britain and Ireland during the Middle Ages* (London: Longman, Green, Longman, Roberts, and Green, 1865), pp. 105, 137–41, 343–53.

Book 1

39.3. For fellon [infection], catch a fox, strike off from him (while) quick, (that is alive), the tusk, (or canine tooth), let (the fox) run away, bind it in a fawn's skin, and wear it upon you.

63. For a fiend sick man (or demoniac), when a devil possesses the man or controls him from within with disease: a spew drink (or emetic), lupin, bishopwort, henbane, cropleek; pound (these together), add ale for a liquid, let (it) stand for a night, add fifty libcorns (or cathartic grains), and holy water. A drink for a fiend sick man to be drunk out of a church bell: githrife, cynoglossum, yarrow, lupin, betony, attorlothe, cassock, flower de luce, fennel, church lichen, lichen of Christ's mark (or cross), lovage; work up the drink of clear ale, sing seven masses over the worts [herbs], add garlic and holy water, and drip the

drink into every drink which he will subsequently drink, and let him sing the psalms, *Beati immaculati* [Psalm 118], and *Exurgat* [Psalm 67], and *Salvum me fac, deus* [Psalm 68], and then let him drink the drink out of a church bell, and let the mass priest after the drink sing this over him, *Domine, sancte pater omnipotens* [O holy lord, father almighty] . . .

64. Against every evil rune-lay [curse], and one full of elfish tricks, write (for the bewitched man) this writing in Greek letters: *alfa, omega* [first and the last], *IESVUM* (?) *BERONIKH* [reference to the miraculous image of Jesus that appeared on Veronica's handkerchief at the crucifixion]. Again another dust (or powder) and drink against a rune-lay; take a bramble apple, and lupins, and pulegium, pound them, then sift them, put them in a pouch, lay them under the altar, sing nine masses over them, put the dust into milk, drip thrice some holy water upon, administer (this) to drink at three hours, at *undern* (or nine in the morning) at midday, at noon (*hora nana*—or three in the afternoon). . . . If a nightmare (or hag) ride a man, take lupins, and garlic, and betony, and frankincense, bind them in a fawn's skin, let a man have the worts on him, and let him go in (to his home).

Book 3

54. Work a salve against nocturnal (goblin) visitors; boil in butter lupins, hedger-ife, bishopwort, red maythe, cropleek, salt; smear (the man) therewith, it will soon be well with him.

58. Against temptation of the fiend, a wort bright red niolin (red stalk); it grows by running water; if you have it on you, and under your head bolster, and over your house doors, the Devil may not injure you, within nor without.

61. Work thus a salve against the elfin race and nocturnal (goblin) visitors, and for the women with whom the Devil has carnal relations; take [a long list of herbs follows] . . . put these worts into a vessel, set (them) under the altar, sing over them nine masses, boil them in butter and sheep's grease, add much holy salt, strain through a cloth, throw the worts into running water. If any ill tempting [sexual urgings?] occur to a man by the visitation of an elf or (goblin) night visitors (come), smear his forehead with this salve, and put it on his eyes, and where his body is sore, and cense him with incense, and sign him frequently with the sign of the cross; his condition will soon be better.

62. Against elf disease, take bishopwort, fennel, lupin, the lower part of enchanters nightshade, and moss or lichen from the hallowed sign of Christ, and incense take a handful of each; bind all the worts in a cloth, dip it thrice in hallowed font water, have sung over it three masses, one "Omnibus sanctis," another "Contra tribulationem," a third "Pro infirmis." Then put gledes [hot coals]

in a glede pan, and lay the worts on; smoke the man with the worts before nine in the morning, and at night, and sing a litany, and the Credo [statement of doctrine], and the [Lord's Prayer], and write Christ's mark on each of his limbs, and take a little handful of worts of the same kind, similarly hallowed, and boil in milk, drop thrice some hallowed water into it, and let him sip of it before he eats his meat; it will soon be well with him. For that ilk, go on Thursday evening, when the sun is set, where you know that helenium stands, then sing the "Benedicite," and Paternoster, and a litany, and stick your knife into the wort, make it stick fast, and go away. Go again, when day and night just divide; at the same period; go first to church and cross yourself, and commend yourself to God; then go in silence, and even if you are threatened by a man of an awful sort, say nothing to him, before you come to the wort, which you marked the evening before; then sing the "Benedicite", and the Paternoster, and a litany; delve up the wort, let the knife stick in it; go again as quick as you are able to church, and lay it under the altar with the knife; let it lie till the sun is up, wash it afterwards, and make into a drink, add bishopwort, and lichen off a crucifix; boil in milk thrice, thrice pour holy water upon it, and sing over it the Paternoster, the Credo, and the "Gloria in Excelsis Deo" [hymn], and sing upon it a litany, and score with a sword a cross round about it on three sides, and then after that let the man drink the wort; soon will it be well with him. . . .

If a man has elf-hicket [disease], his eyes are yellow, where they should be red. If you have a will to cure the man, observe his gestures, and consider of what sex he be; if it be a man and he looks up when you first see him, and the countenance is yellowish black, you may cure the man thoroughly if he is not too long in the disease; if it is a woman and she looks down when you first see her, and her countenance is livid red, you may also cure that. If it has been upon (the man) longer than a twelvemonth and a day, and the aspect be such as this, then you may amend it for a while, and notwithstanding [you] still may not entirely cure it. [The leech is instructed to write a designated message in Latin, to concoct a drink of font water and various herbs, and to sing a particular verse in Latin over the drink and the writing]. Write a cross three times with the oil of unction, and say, "Pax tibi" [Peace to you]. Then take the writing, make the sign of the cross with it over the drink, and sing this over it, "Dominus omnipotens, pater domini nostri Iesu Christi, per impositionem huius scripturae et per gustum huius expelle diabolum a famulo tuo" [Almighty lord, father of our lord Jesus Chris, through the laying-on and tasting of these writings, expel the devil from your servant]; (here insert the name), and the Credo, and Paternoster. Wet the writing in the drink, and write a cross with it on every limb, and say, "Signum crucis Christi conservet te in vitam aeternam. Amen" [May the sign of the cross of Christ preserve you in eternal life]. If you wish not (to take this trouble), bid (the man) himself, or whomsoever may be his nearest relation (to do it), and let him cross him as well as he can. This craft is powerful against every temptation of the fiend.

63. If a man has the water-elf disease, then are the nails of his hand livid, and the eyes tearful, and he will look downwards. Give him this [a collection of herbs] for a leechdom; pour them over with ale, add holy water, sing this charm over them thrice:

I have wreathed round the wounds / the best of healing wreaths, / that the baneful sores may / neither burn nor burst, / nor find their way further, / nor turn foul and fallow, / nor thump and throb on, / nor be wicked wounds, / nor dig deeply down; / but he himself / may hold / in a way to health. / Let it ache you no more, / than ear in earth [grave] aches.

Sing (also) this many times, "May earth bear on you [the elf] with all her might and main." These charms a man may sing over a wound.

Questions: Are any of the procedures listed in the Leechbook *magical, and if so, by what definition? What is the significance of the use of Christian references, prayers, masses, and rites in the cures? Entry 39 is different from the rest of the cures listed as it does not refer to elves or devils, yet Augustine would likely have considered this cure "magical." Why? Is it probable that the remedies listed above were actually used? Why or why not? What are the symptoms of elf-sickness or devil-sickness?*

37. ANGLO-SAXON SERMON AGAINST AUGURY: AELFRIC OF EYNSHAM

Aelfric of Eynsham (c. 955–c. 1010) was an Anglo-Saxon abbot remembered for his contributions to Old English literature, particularly homilies, saints' lives and biblical commentaries. The Lives of the Saints is a collection of homilies that includes "On Auguries," which relies heavily on New Testament theology to discount magical practices. The homily is in keeping with the pan-Christian rhetoric on magic and witchcraft. Appended to The Lives of the Saints is a treatise called On False Gods, in which Aelfric draws from biblical and classical sources to illustrate that the worship of demons as gods continues in his own time under the pagan Danish (Viking) invaders. The abbot often uses staid, conventional language and antiquated categories to discuss the threat of demonism; for instance, he equates Jove with the Germanic god, Thor. But these archaisms do not mask Aelfric's immediate unease about the influx of a vigorous paganism from Scandinavia.

Like On False Gods, "On Auguries" relies heavily on New Testament theology to discount magical practices. The homily is in keeping with the pan-Christian rhetoric on magic and witchcraft. It is interesting to note the other transgressions with which Aelfric categorizes magic.

Source: trans. Elizabeth Gunning and Ms. Wilkinson, *Ælfric's Lives of Saints, Being a Set of Sermons on Saints' Days Formerly Observed by the English Church,* Early English Text Society 57, ed. Walter W. Skeat, 2 vols. (London: Trübner & Company, 1881), pp. 364–83.

"On Auguries"

The Apostle [Paul], the teacher of all nations, exhorted those Christians whom he had formerly converted to the faith, in an epistle, that is a letter, thus saying, "My brethren, walk in the spirit, that is in spiritual conversation, and you shall not fulfill the lusts of your flesh. The flesh verily wars against the spirit and the spirit against the flesh" [Galatians 5:16]. These things verily, that is the body and the soul, fight between themselves. But the soul is the flesh's mistress, and it befits her that she should ever rule the bondmaid, that is the flesh, according to her behest. Ill fares it with the house where the bondmaid is the ruler of the mistress and the mistress is in subjection to the bondmaid. So also will the life of man be ordered backward if the flesh, which is corruptible and mortal, shall subdue the spirit, which is eternal and imperishable, to its base lusts, which will destroy them both and bring them to everlasting torments.

The Apostle [Paul] said, "If you be led by the spirit, then are you not under the law" [Galatians 5:18]. He said in another place, "There is no law set for righteous men, but for unrighteous and disobedient, for the profane and the guilty" [cf. 1 Timothy 1:9], because the law, that is the righteous rule, will not greet the righteous man with any evil, but it will punish the unrighteous according to their works. The righteous verily need not fear the strict rule which God's law teaches if he restrains himself from all foolishness. Paul said, "Manifest are the works of the flesh, adultery and uncleanness, lasciviousness or lust, idolatry or witchcraft, enmity and strife, spite and anger, contention and sedition, heresy and envy, murder and drunkenness, surfeiting and other such like, the which I tell you beforehand, even as I told you formerly; for those who do such works shall not attain to God's kingdom" [Galatians 5:19–21]. Everyone may cease from evil and amend, but if he continues in wickedness and despises his creator's commands and pleases the Devil's, then shall he, against his will, suffer in eternity in the unquenchable fire amidst the worst serpent-kind which shall never be destroyed, but shall ever chew the bodies of the wicked in the fire of hell. Again, said the Apostle in another epistle, "My brethren, be you not deceived, neither fornicators, nor those who serve idols, nor those who have other men's wives, nor the effeminate or weak-minded—these are they who have no sternness against sins—nor thieves, nor covetous, nor drinkers—these are they who love drunkenness—nor revilers, whose mouths are ever filled with poisoned cursing, nor robbers, shall ever possess God's kingdom" [1 Corinthians 6:9–10]. He said yet again to the people thus, "Such you were, but now are you cleansed, but you are sanctified, but you are justified in the name of the Lord our savior Christ, and in the spirit of our God" [1 Corinthians 6:11].

Idolatry is that a man forsakes his lord and his Christianity and yields to diabolical heathenism, dishonoring his creator. There is another idolatry, hurtful to the soul, when the man despises his creator's commands and practices the shameful sins that the Devil teaches him. . . . Augustine, the wise bishop, said likewise in a certain book, "My brethren most beloved, often I have warned you, and with fatherly carefulness I lovingly exhorted you that, as for the odious witchcraft which unwise men observe, you should altogether renounce (it) like faithful men. For [if I do not warn] you and forbid you that mischief, I shall have to give an account to the righteous judge for my carelessness and shall be condemned with you" [*Sermon on Auguries*]. Now I deliver myself as regards God, and with love forbid that any of you should inquire through any witchcraft concerning anything, or concerning any sickness, or seek enchanters to anger his creator. For him that does this lets go his Christianity and is like the heathen who cast lots concerning themselves by means of the Devil's art, which will destroy them forever, and unless he offers alms and much penance to his creator, he shall be lost eternally. Nevertheless a man may cast lots, in faith, in worldly things, without witchcraft, that he may allot himself pastures, if men wish to divide anything (land) this is no sorcery, but is very often a direction. So likewise, he who trusts in auguries, either from birds or from sneezings, either from horses or from dogs, he is no Christian, but is an infamous apostate. Neither may any man give heed to days, on which day he shall journey or on which he shall return, because God created all the seven days which succeed in the week, until this world's ending. But he who wishes to journey anywhere, let him sing his Paternoster [Lord's Prayer] and Credo [statement of doctrine], if he knows (them), and cry to his Lord, and cross himself, and travel without care through God's protection, without the Devil's sorceries.

It shames us to tell all the shameful sorceries, which you foolish men practice through the Devil's lore, whether in wiving [marriage], or in traveling, or in brewing, or if a man prays for anything when they begin anything, or anything is born to them. But know truly that the Devil teaches you such delusions that he may have your souls when you believe his lying deceits. Now a certain sorcerer says that witches often declare what will happen with a true result. Now we speak the truth, that the invisible Devil, who flies through these worlds and sees many things, reveals to the witch what she shall say to men that they may be destroyed who seek this sorcery. Pharaoh's magicians, Jannes and Jambres, said many things through the Devil's art, even as Moses wrote, and they seduced Pharaoh with their deceits, until he was drowned in the deep sea [see doc. 1]. So likewise Simon Magus [see doc. 6], the wily sorcerer, strove so long with Saint Peter, until he was cast down, when he desired to fly to heaven, so that he burst into four parts, and so that impious man departed in torment to hell. Many others have perished who followed sorcery, even as we read in books, but their stories are tedious.

Neither shall the Christian inquire of the foul witch concerning his health, though she may be able to tell something through the Devil, for it will be harmful, and all will be poisonous which comes from him, and all his followers shall perish in the end. Some men are so blinded that they bring their offerings to an earth-fast stone and speak to trees and to well-springs, even as witches teach, and will not understand how foolishly they act or how the dead stone or the dumb tree can help them or give them health when they themselves never stir from the place. The Christian man must cry to his Lord with mind and with mouth and beseech his protection, that [God] may shield him against the Devil's snares and set his hope in the true God, who alone rules over all creatures, that [God] may provide for his safety, even lo! as he will [provide], because he is the all-ruling God. We should on every occasion and in every trouble cross ourselves with true faith and, by the sign of the cross, put to fight the wicked ones, because the wicked Devil was vanquished by the cross, and it is ever our beacon of victory against the fiend.

Likewise some witless women go to crossroads and draw their children through the earth and thus commit themselves and their children to the Devil. Some of them kill their children before they are born or after birth so that they may not be discovered nor their wicked adultery be betrayed, but their wickedness is awful, and everlasting their perdition. Then the child perishes, a loathsome heathen, and the wicked mother [likewise perishes], unless she does penance for it. Some of them devise drinks (philters) for their wooers or some mischief that they may have them in marriage [love magic]. But such shameful ones shall go to hell, where they shall ever suffer in the tormenting fire and in awful punishments for their witlessness. But Christian men must fight against devils by strong faith, like trained champions, and shun those hags and such heathendom and the Devil's delusions, and worship their Lord. Then will the Devil see that you despise him, and it will be grievous to him, in his accursed mind, that you are so steadfast, and he will be indignant against you and will vex you with some sickness or suddenly kill some of your cattle, because he must try every man, in many ways, to see whether his mind will swerve through persecution from the almighty God.

But know you for certain that the cruel Devil cannot hurt men by any sickness, neither destroy their cattle, without the Lord's permission. God is all goodness, and he always wills well. But the minds of men may be excited to evil; then God permits the Devil very often to punish men for their misdeeds. We ought to seek, if we be afflicted, restoration from God, not from the cruel witches, and with all our hearts please our savior, because nothing can withstand his might. He says in his Gospel that without God's command, not even a bird falls in death. It is to be expected that he will ever watch over his servants both in life and in death, since the little bird falls not into a snare without God's will. Our savior drove devils out of a possessed man. There was nearby a herd of swine, and [the devils] straightway prayed that they might go into the swine, and thereupon the lord granted it to the devils. Then they (entered) into the swine, and they all became mad and ran to the sea and forthwith were drowned. The Devil cannot hurt men without God's permission nor mar their property, since he could not go even into the swine, unless the savior permitted him. If the Devil vexes us or destroys our property, this happens for (one of) two reasons. Either God so punishes our perverse deeds, or he [allows us to prove ourselves] through the peril, and the fiend shall vanish away from us if we are steadfast in our faith, and Christ shall drive him away so that he shall not harm us if we humbly endure the persecution and ever thank God without murmuring. Nevertheless, it will all happen to us for good if we are patient, and thank our Lord, and in the trial pray for his assistance, who can always easily deliver us from all perils of fiendish temptations.

Medicine is granted for bodily infirmity and holy prayers, with God's blessing, and all other aids are hateful to God, even as Paul wrote, saying these words, "You cannot drink both our Lord's chalice and the Devil's cup to the death of your souls" [1 Corinthians 10:21]. And our Lord said, "A man cannot please two masters at once, lest he should despise one" [Matthew 6:24]; neither can we please both Christ and the Devil.

Now some men say that it must happen to them even as it was determined for them and ordained from the beginning and that they cannot avoid acting amiss. Now say we of a truth, if it is to be so (that it is a useless command) which God commanded through David, "Turn from evil and do good" [Psalm 34:14], and again the Apostle says, "How much more a man labor for God, so much better reward shall he have" [cf. 1 Cor 3:8]. If each man's life can ever take such a course that he cannot turn aside from shameful deeds, then it is unjust for the unrighteous to receive any punishment for their wickedness. Likewise the good are unjustly honored if it can be true that it was so determined for them, and we labor in vain in our service, either in alms, or in other deeds, if we have no reward from our Lord for it than those reckless men who live without consideration, and go in all things by their own will, and spend their lives in their own pleasures. God almighty formed many creatures and gave to none of them their own freedom or reason, except to the shining angels and to men— the creatures he formed by his hands. These two creations possess reason, and every man has his own freedom so that he knows [what he should and should not do], but nevertheless, God does not compel us to do good; neither does he bar us from working evil, because he has given us our own choice. He gave a most steadfast gift and a most steadfast law together with that gift to every man until his end, both to poor and rich. This is the gift, that a man may do what he will, and this is the law, that God recompenses to every man according to his works, both in this world and in that which is to come, whether good or evil, whichever he practices.

Now if any man should wonder why God willed to give to evil men their own freedom when he knows beforehand that they will do evil, then say we that it is not befitting any rich king that they all should be slaves who have to serve him and that there should not be one free man in his dominion. So likewise it does not befit the almighty Lord that in all his kingdom there should not be any creature who should not be strictly compelled in doing [good] service. Now our freedom ever needs God's assistance, because we can do no good thing without God's help. May he ever guide us in this world and bring us through himself to the eternal life, even as he promised to all of them who love him. To him be praise and glory forever and ever. Amen.

Questions: With what sins does Aelfric classify witchcraft (or sorcery), and what does this reveal about his conception of sorcery? How does Aelfric distinguish between acceptable and unacceptable casting of lots? What are the gender dynamics at play in the reading? What are Aelfric's sources for the sermon—both those he quotes directly and others implicit in his thinking? Explain why God allows humans to sin.

38. A PRAYER TO MOTHER EARTH AND OTHER CHARMS

"A Prayer to Mother Earth" was found bound with herbal recipes compiled in the late tenth or early eleventh century. Little is known of the document, but the compiler identifies the prayer as one that pagans spoke when gathering herbs. The referent in the charm is clearly a medical practitioner.

Lacnunga, meaning "remedies," is a collection of about 200 Anglo-Saxon herbal cures, prayers, and charms written in Old English, Latin, and Irish, which was discovered along with eleventh-century herbal texts. It is not a single manuscript but a collection of discrete writings. Medical writers envisioned disease as airborne, flying, and dart-like. Demons and elves, the agents of ailments, were thought to bolt through the vapor and infiltrate the lower air. Hence the notion that sickness came at people through the atmosphere like darts, spears, and arrows is fitting. Also notable in the prayers, charms, and medical recipes is the role of mighty female forces.

The contents of Lacnunga vary. Some of the recipes, charms, and prayers are clearly from a Christian milieu, some are superficially Christian but deeply informed by the pagan religion of the northern high gods or Æsir, and some venerate pagan deities and are completely lacking a Christian orientation.

Sources: "Prayer to Mother Earth": trans. G.G. Coulton, *Life in the Middle Ages*, vol. 1, Cambridge Anthologies (New York: The Macmillan Company, 1928), pp. 41–42; rev. Martha Rampton; *Lacnunga*: trans. Karen Louise Jolly, in *Popular Religion in Late Saxon England: Elf Charms in Context* (Chapel Hill: University of North Carolina Press, 1996), pp. 125–27, 139.

"Prayer to Mother Earth"

Holy Goddess Earth, mother of nature, who generates all things and brings forth anew the sun which you alone show to the folk on earth. You guardian of heaven and sea and arbiter of all the gods, by whose influence nature is wrapped in silence and slumber, you are she who restores day and puts the darkness to flight. You govern the shades of night and wrap us in security. You restrain at your will the mighty chaos, winds, rain and storms and let them loose again. You churn the deep to foam and put the sun to flight. You arouse the tempests, and, again at your pleasure, you send forth the glad daylight. You give us food in safety by a perpetual covenant, and when our souls flee away, it is in your bosom that we find our haven of rest.

By their loving kindness the gods also call you Great Mother. You conquer by your mighty name. You are the force of the nations and the mother of the gods without whom nothing can be born or come to maturity. Mighty are you, queen of the gods! O Goddess, I adore you as divine, and on your name do I call. Vouchsafe now to fulfil my prayer, and I will give you thanks, O Goddess, with the faith that you deserve. I beseech you to hear and favor my prayers. Vouchsafe to me, O Goddess, that for which I now pray. Grant freely to all nations upon earth all herbs that your majesty brings to life and allow me to gather your medicines [herbs]. Come to me with your healing powers; grant success to whatsoever I shall make from these herbs, and may those to whom I administer them thrive. May all your gifts to us prosper. To you all things return. Let men take these herbs from my hand, I beseech you now, O Goddess, and may your gift make the sick whole. I beseech you as a suppliant that by your majesty you grant me this boon.

Lacnunga

"Lay of the Nine Herbs"

Be mindful, Mugwort, / what you revealed, / What you established / at the great proclamation / Una you are called, / oldest of herbs, you are strong against three / and against thirty, / you are strong against poison / and against onfliers (flying venoms) you are strong against the foe / who goes through the land. / And you, Waybroad (Plantain), / mother of herbs, / open from the east, / mighty within. / Over you chariots creaked, / over you queens rode, / over you brides cried out, / over you bulls snorted. / All this you withstood, / and confounded. / So you withstand / poison and flying venom, / and the foe / who goes through the land. / Stune this herb is called, / she grew on a stone, / she stands against poison, / she attacks pain. / Stithe (hard) she is called, / she confounds poison, / she drives out evils, / she casts out poison. / This is the herb / that fought against the worm, / this is strong against poison, / she is strong against flying venoms, / she is strong against the foe / who goes through the land. / Rout you now, Attorlathe (Venomloather), / the less the more / the more the less / until there be a remedy for him against both. / Remember you, May-the (Camomile), / what you revealed, /what you accomplished / at Alorford, / that never for flying venom / did he yield life / since for him a man prepared / Maythe for food. / This is the herb / this is called Wergule. / This is a seal sent / over the sea ridges, / as a remedy / against the harm of another poison.

"Lay of the Nine Twigs of Woden"

These nine go / against nine poisons. / A worm came crawling, / he wounded nothing. Then Woden took / nine glory-twigs (wuldor tanas) / smote then the adder / that it flew apart into nine (parts). / There apple and poison / brought it about / that she never would / dwell in the house. / Chervil and Fennel, / very mighty two, / these herbs he created, / the wise Lord / holy in heaven / when he hung; / he established and sent them / into the seven worlds, / to the poor and the rich, / for all a remedy. / She stands against pain; / she assaults poison, / who has power against three / and against thirty, / against enemy's hand / and against great terror / against the bewitching of little / vile wights [men]. / Now these nine herbs have power / against nine evil spirits / fugitives from glory / against nine poisons / and against nine flying venoms: / Against the red poison, / against the foul poison / against the white poison, / against the purple poison, / against the yellow poison, / against the green poison, / against the dark poison, / against the blue poison, / against the brown poison, / against the crimson poison. / Against worm-blister, / against water-blister, / against thorn-blister, / against thistle-blister, / against ice-blister, / against poison-blister. / If any poison / flying from the east, / or any from the north / . . . come / or any from the west / over humanity. / Christ stood over the old ones, / the malignant ones (?). / I alone know / running streams / and the nine adders / now they behold (?). / All weeds must now / give way to herbs / the seas slip apart, / all salt water, / when I this poison / blow from you.

"For a Sudden Stitch [Stabbing Pain]"

Feverfew and the red nettle that grows into a house [or "in the grain"] / and waybroad; boil in butter. / Loud were they, lo loud, / when they rode over the mound, / they were fierce / when they rode over the land. / Shield yourself now / that you may escape this evil. / Out, little spear, / if herein you be! / Stood under linden, / under a light shield, / where the mighty women / readied their power, / and they screaming / spears sent. / I back to them / again will send another, / a flying dart / against them in return. / Out, little spear, / if herein it be! / Sat a smith, / forged he a knife, / little iron / strong wound. / Out, little spear, / if herein it be! / Six smiths sat, / war-spears they made. / Out, spear, / not in, spear! / If herein be / a bit of iron, / hag's work, / it shall melt. / If you were in the skin shot, / or were in flesh shot, / or were in the blood shot, / or were in bone shot, / or were in limb shot, / may your life never be torn apart. / If it were Æsir shot, / or it were Elves' shot, / or it were hag's shot, / now I will help you. / This your remedy for Æsir shot, / this your remedy for Elves' shot; / This remedy for hag's shot; / I will help you. / It fled there into the mountains . . . no rest had it. / Whole be you now! / Lord help you! / Then take the knife; / dip into liquid.

Questions: The selections from Lacnunga *are cures for disease; what does "flying venom" likely refer to? What do the "Prayer to Mother Earth" and the "Lay of Nine Herbs" have in common? How do the "Lay of Nine Herbs" and the "Lay of the Nine Twigs of Woden" differ? What might be an explanation for the fact that the prayer and medical texts were written in Christian regions and yet extol pagan deities?*

39. AN ELEVENTH-CENTURY PENITENTIAL: BURCHARD OF WORMS

The Decretum *of Bishop Burchard of Worms (c. 950–1025) is a thorough regrouping and (in many cases) reinterpretation of earlier canon-law texts. Although he edited this compilation of documents on church governance and law for the purpose of aiding the clergy under his direction, the impact of his opus went far beyond Burchard's own diocese in southwest Germany. It was regarded as an authoritative work on canon law in the west for more than a century.*

The Decretum *is divided into twenty books. Book 19, called* Corrector sive Medicus, *is penitential in nature, and many of the* Decretum's *dicta about magical ritual are found in it (including the* Canon episcopi; *see doc. 35). Several of the canons in the* Corrector *target female practices, and this has led some historians to deduce, incorrectly, that for Burchard magic was largely the woman's craft. Women were, however, associated with particular types of magic, as reflected in the selections below, and many of them involved stealth and secrecy.*

In composing his Corrector, *Burchard borrowed liberally from a variety of earlier manuals of penance, and, as is true for virtually all penitential literature, much of the material in Burchard's text is copied from earlier works. As a rule, it is difficult to know whether the prohibited behaviors described in penitentials were taking place at the time of the composition of the penitential or whether the condemned activities were vestiges of earlier practices copied from text to text over time. In the* Corrector, *however, several of the canons regarding sorcery and superstition are new with Burchard and very likely describe contemporary magic and ritual.*

Source: trans. John T. McNeill and Helena M. Gamer, *Medieval Handbooks of Penance* (New York: Columbia University Press, 1938), pp. 329–31, 333–35, 337–41.

Book 19 (*Corrector sive Medicus*)

Chapter 5

60. Have you consulted magicians and led them into your house in order to seek out any magical trick, or to avert it; or have you invited to yourself, according to pagan custom, diviners who would divine for you, to demand of them the things to come as from a prophet, and those who practice lots or expect by lots to foreknow the future, or those who are devoted to auguries or incantations? If you have, you will do penance for two years in the appointed feast days.

61. Have you observed the traditions of the pagans, which, as if by hereditary right, with the assistance of the Devil, fathers have ever left to their sons, even to these days, that is, that you should worship the elements, the moon or the sun or the course of the stars, the new moon, or the eclipse of the moon, that you should be able by your shouts or by your aid to restore her splendor, or these elements (be able) to succor yourself, or that you should have power with them? Or have you observed the new moon for building a house or making marriages? If you have, you will do penance for two years in the appointed fast days; for it is written, "All, whatsoever you do in word and in work, do all in the name of our Lord Jesus Christ" [Colossians 3:17].

63. Have you made knots, and incantations, and those various enchantments which evil men, swineherds, plowmen, and sometimes hunters make, while they say diabolical formulas over bread or grass and over certain nefarious bandages, and either hide these in a tree or throw them where two roads, or three roads, meet, that they may set free their animals or dogs from pestilence or destruction and destroy those of another? If you have, you will do penance for two years on the appointed days.

64. Have you been present at or consented to the vanities which women practice in their woolen work, in their webs, who, when they begin their webs, hope to be able to bring it about that with incantations and with the beginning of these the threads of the warp and of the woof become so mingled together that unless they supplement these in turn by other counter-incantations of the

Devil, the whole will perish? If you have been present or consented, you will do penance for thirty days on bread and water.

65. Have you collected medicinal herbs with evil incantations, not with the creed and the Lord's Prayer, that is, with the singing of the *credo in Deum* and the Paternoster? If you have done it otherwise (than with the Christian formula mentioned) you will do penance for ten days on bread and water.

66. Have you come to any place to pray other than a church or other religious place which your bishop or your priest showed you, that is, either to springs or to stones or to trees or to crossroads, and there in reverence for the place lighted a candle or a torch or carried there bread or any offering or eaten there or sought there any healing of body or mind? If you have done or consented to such things, you will do penance for three years on the appointed fast days.

68. Have you ever believed or participated in this perfidy, that enchanters and those who say that they can let loose tempests should be able, through incantation of demons, to arouse tempests or to change the minds of men? If you have believed or participated in this, you will do penance for one year on the appointed fast days.

69. Have you believed or participated in this infidelity, that there is any woman who through certain spells and incantations can turn about the minds of men, either from hatred to love or from love to hatred, or by her bewitchments can snatch away men's goods? If you have believed or participated in such acts, you will do penance for one year in the appointed fast days.

91. Have you observed funeral wakes, that is, been present at the watch over the corpses of the dead when the bodies of Christians are guarded by a ritual of the pagans; and have you sung diabolical songs there and performed dances which the pagans have invented by the teaching of the Devil, and have you drunk there and relaxed your countenance with laughter, and, setting aside all compassion and emotion of charity, have you appeared as if rejoicing over a brother's death? If you have, you will do penance for thirty days on bread and water.

92. Have you made diabolical phylacteries or diabolical characters, which some are accustomed to make at the persuasion of the Devil, of grass or of amber; or have you observed Thursday in honor of Jupiter? If you have done or consented to such (deeds), you will do penance for forty days on bread and water.

96. Have you done or consented to those vanities which foolish women are accustomed to enact, (who) while the corpse of a dead person still lies in the house, run to the water and silently bring a jar of water, and when the dead body is raised up, pour this water under the bier, and as the body is being carried from the house, watch that it be not raised higher than to the knees, and do this as a kind of means of healing? If you have done or consented to this, you will do penance for ten days on bread and water.

99. Have you done anything like what the pagans did, and still do, on the first of January in (the guise of) a stag or a calf? If you have you will do penance for thirty days on bread and water.

101. Have you done what many do? They scrape the place where they are accustomed to make the fire in their house and put grains of barley there in the warm spot, and if the grains jump (they believe) there will be danger, but if they remain, things will go well. If you have, you will do penance for ten days on bread and water.

102. Have you done what some do when they are visiting any sick person? When they approach the house where the sick person lies, if they find a stone lying nearby, they turn the stone over and look in the place where the stone was lying (to see) if there is anything living under it, and if they find there a worm or a fly or an ant or anything that moves, then they aver that the sick person will recover. But if they find there nothing that moves, they say he will die. If you have done or believed in this, you will do penance for twenty days on bread and water.

103. Have you made little boys' size bows and boys' shoes and cast them into your storeroom or your barn so that satyrs or goblins might sport with them in order that they might bring to you the goods of others so that you will become richer? If you have, you will do penance for ten days on bread and water.

104. Have you done what some do on the first of January (that is on the eighth day after the Lord's Nativity)—who on that holy night wind magic skeins, spin, sew: all at the prompting of the Devil beginning whatever task they can begin on account of the new year? If you have, you will do penance for forty days on bread and water.

149. Have you believed what some are wont to believe? When they make any journey, if a crow croaks from their left side to their right, they hope on this account to have a prosperous journey. And when they are worried about a lodging place, if then that bird which is called the mouse-catcher, for the reason that it catches mice and is named from what it feeds on, flies in front of them, across the road on which they go, they trust more to this augury and omen than to God. If you have done or believed these things, you should do penance for five days on bread and water.

151. Have you believed what some are wont to believe, either that those who are commonly called the Fates exist, or that they can do that which they are believed to do? That is, that while any person is being born, they are able even then to determine his life to what they wish, so that no matter what the person wants, he can be transformed into a wolf, that which vulgar folly calls a werewolf, or into any other shape. If you believe what never took place or could take place, that the divine image can be changed into any form or appearance by anyone except almighty God, you should do penance for ten days on bread and water.

152. Have you believed what some are wont to believe, that there are women of the wilds, called "the sylvan ones" who they say are in bodily form, and when they wish, show themselves to their lovers and, they say, have taken delight with these, and then when they wish they depart and vanish? If you so believe, you will do penance for ten days on bread and water.

153. Have you done as some women are wont to do at certain times of the year? That is, have you prepared the table in your house and set on the table your food and drink, with three knives, that if those three sisters whom past generations and old-time foolishness called the Fates should come they may take refreshment there; and have you taken away the power and name of the Divine Piety and handed it over to the Devil, so, I say, as to believe that those whom you called "the sisters" can do or avail aught for you either now or in the future? If you have done or consented to this, you will do penance for one year on the appointed days.

167. Have you drunk the holy oil in order to annul a judgment of God or made or taken counsel with others in making anything in grass or in words or in wood or in stone or in anything foolishly believed in, or held them in your mouth, or had them sewn in your clothing or tied about you, or performed any kind of trick that you did believe could annul the divine judgment? If you have, you should do penance for seven years on the appointed days.

175. Have you done what some women, filled with the discipline of Satan are wont to do, who watch the footprints and traces of Christians and remove a turf from their footprint and watch it and hope thereby to take away their health or life? If you have done or consented to this, you should do penance for five years on the appointed days.

180. Have you done what some women do at the instigation of the Devil? When any child has died without baptism, they take the corpse of the little one and place it in some secret place and transfix its little body with a stake, saying that if they did not do so the little child would arise and would injure many? If you have done, or consented to, or believed this, you should do penance for two years on the appointed days.

181. Have you done what some women, filled with the boldness of the Devil are wont to do? When some woman is to bear a child and is not able, if when she cannot bear it she dies in her pangs, they transfix the mother and the child in the same grave with a stake (driven) into the earth. If you have done or consented to this, you should do penance for two years on the appointed days.

185. Have you done what some women are wont to do? When a child is newly born and immediately baptized and then dies, when they bury him they put in his right hand a paten of wax with the host and in his left hand put a chalice also of wax, with wine, and so they bury him. If you have, you should do penance for ten days on bread and water.

186. Have you done what some adulteresses are wont to do? When first they learn that their lovers wish to take legitimate wives, they thereupon by some trick of magic extinguish the male desire, so that they are impotent and cannot consummate their union with their legitimate wives. If you have done or taught others to do this, you should do penance for forty days on bread and water.

193. Have you done what some women are wont to do? They take off their clothes and anoint their whole naked body with honey, and laying down their honey-smeared body upon wheat on some linen on the earth, roll to and fro often, then carefully gather all the grains of wheat which stick to the moist body, place it in a mill, and make the mill go round backwards against the sun and so grind it to flour; and they make bread from that flour and then give it to their husbands to eat, that on eating the bread they may become feeble and pine away. If you have (done this), you shall do penance for forty days on bread and water.

194. Have you done what some women are wont to do? When they have no rain and need it, then they assemble a number of girls, and they put forward one little maiden as a leader, and strip her, and bring her thus stripped outside the village, where they find the herb henbane, which is called in German "belisa," and they make this nude maiden dig up the plant with the little finger of her right hand, and when it is dug up they make her tie it with a string to the little toe of her right foot. Then while each girl holds a twig in her hands, they bring the aforesaid maiden, dragging the plant behind her, to a nearby river and with these twigs sprinkle her with the water and thus they hope that by their charms they shall have rain. Afterwards they bring back the nude maiden from the river to the village between their hands, her footsteps being turned about and changed into the manner of a crab. If you have done or consented to this, you should do penance for twenty days on bread and water.

Questions: What kinds of magic, generally speaking, does Burchard attribute specifically to women? Does Burchard credit the reality of the activities he describes in the canons above, and if yes, which ones? If magic in this period equates to traffic with demons, are the behaviors described in the Corrector *magical? Which of the activities discussed above are traditional in that they appear in earlier materials on magic?*

CHAPTER FOUR

THE HIGH MIDDLE AGES:
MANY THREADS (1000–1300)

Figure 4.1 Portrayal of episodes from the story of the Volsung clan carved in the twelfth century on a wood panel from the portal of Hylestad stave church in Setesdal, Norway, which is on display at the Museum of Cultural History in Oslo. Among the scenes are Sigurd slaying Fafnir the dragon, roasting Fafnir's heart, and sucking the dragon's blood off his thumb.

The eleventh century was the entry point to the development of a new Europe. The political, ecclesiastical, and intellectual concerns that occupied the Carolingian world were changing. Political units became smaller as Carolingian rulers sub-divided patrimonies among their heirs, castles rose for regional defense, economies became localized, Cluniac monastic reformers expanded the authority of the pope, and the crusades inspired a warrior elite to take up the cross and transverse Europe to seize the Holy Land from the Muslims who occupied it. The twelfth century was one of remarkable cultural creativity and economic growth—so much so that it has been labelled the Twelfth-Century Renaissance. Europeans at every social level were caught up in the transformation of their world. There was new enthusiasm for a triumphant Christendom unified by the papacy.

In the optimistic environment of a dynamic re-envisioning of the Christian world, paganism was a thing of the past, or at least dealt with in the west and on the defensive in eastern Europe. The clergy understood that some cultural customs and ritualistic practices smacked of paganism, but such vestiges of days gone by were well under control. The commitment and values of the three orders of high medieval clerical, knightly, and peasant society lay elsewhere—or rather that was the reality for the literate elite.

Magic, in fact, seemed so tamed that it appeared with positive connotations as a plot element in several literary genres. Chivalry and courtly love came to life in romance verse literature with themes drawn from Celtic legends, and many of these narratives were laced with tales of magic. Shape-shifting, fortune-telling, magic potions, ships, rings, letters, ethereal fairies, and the like are central to the novels and short stories of writers such as Marie de France (fl. twelfth century) and Chrétien de Troyes (c. 1160–c. 1191). Romance literature and courtly love were enormously popular phenomena in aristocratic courts. Novelists portrayed the "magical" and "fantastic" sympathetically—not as demonic, but as marvel-ous prodigies, inexplicable but natural occurrences in a fascinating universe. It is important not to ignore, however, that the rigid conventions of chivalric behavior, the excesses of frivolity, adulterous relationships, and dalliance with magic of various forms still drew criticism from some quarters.

Courtly literature was not the only genre of the period in which magic plays a benign or even beneficial role. In the frontier societies of Scandinavia, quasi-mythical/quasi-historical lore was preserved orally, and beginning in the thir-teenth century, authors turned those tales into narrative prose sagas. Norse deities, giants, Valkyries, dwarves, and dragons are important characters to the plots, and the boundaries separating humans, nature, and the supernatural are permeable. The blatantly pagan worldview of the literature did not deter Christians from carving scenes from their legends on stone crosses, baptismal fonts, and church portals. Especially frequent are depictions of dragon-slaying because of the natu-ral assimilation of Satan, the serpent in the Garden of Eden, to the dragon.

A form of proto-science referred to as "natural magic" (or "natural philosophy") also found fertile ground in the secular and ecclesiastical courts of Europe. Natural philosophy was informed by Hermeticism, a philosophical and religious system based on esoteric writings attributed to the illusive late-antique Hermes Trismegistus (meaning "Thrice Great"), which held that God gave humans a single and universal truth discoverable in the natural world through "sciences" such as astrology and alchemy. For progressive thinkers, the crude interactions with demons that characterized simple sorcery were ignoble pursuits of the lower classes. Natural magic, informed by Neoplatonic philosophy and works by Islamic and Jewish thinkers, offered a method of accessing the occult through forces innate in the physical world by exploiting the vast knowledge demons gained from long experience, they having dwelt in sub-lunar space since their expulsion from heaven. Demons' power could be harnessed, but only in very controlled, highly ritualistic environments. Those clerics who dabbled in the arts of natural philosophy were well aware that their activities could be misconstrued as necromancy, a word formerly meaning prophesy through the dead that had become synonymous with learned magic.

In short, the fact that superstitious practices were—to a great extent—unmoored from their pagan origins allowed magic to emerge in romance and heroic literature and among the courtiers of Europe, and although some churchmen and churchwomen still characterized peasant customs as "pagan," it was the credulity of the peasants that clerics sought to curb more than any real fear of the harm that spells and sorceries could inflict. This is evident in sermons, where magic is one of many misdemeanors for which parishioners are chastised, but seeking out magic practitioners for punishment was of no great import. Magicians' feats were often entertainment at courts, marvels, and evidence of the incomprehensively mystifying universe. For some, natural magic was a path to enlightenment.

The seeds of change, however, were germinating at the great universities in the minds of scholastic theologians. Scholasticism is an approach to examining concepts by juxtaposing contrary points of view in order to resolve contradictions. The scholastic method is based on Aristotelian logic, Neoplatonic mysticism, the Christian philosophical tradition, and dialectical reasoning. Scholars applied it to venerated theological texts and Christian dogma with the aim of harmonizing all knowledge through the application of human reason and ordinary experience in the natural world. The most famous architect of scholasticism was Thomas Aquinas (1225–1274), so much so that the term "Thomism" is a reference to Aquinas's system of determining truth. This great scholar was not particularly interested in magic, although he was a key figure in the transition from magic as "marvel" or cautionary tale to the concept of witchcraft.

In his comprehensive works, Aquinas analyzes the origins and nature of evil, and in this process he imposes order on earlier concepts of the fallen angels.

For Aquinas, the Devil becomes more than one of several pestilential demons that plague humankind; he is the adversary of God. Satan is menacing and brilliant in his ability to deceive. He is the magnificent prince of multitudes of demons inferior to himself that are compelled to do his bidding. This commander of all malign forces lures humans into heinous sin for the purpose of damning their souls and, ultimately, destroying all Christendom. In order for the Devil and his human accomplices to cement their collation, they make a pact. This is important to Aquinas because it safeguards the concept of free will; humans who contract with Satan do so of their own volition. The notion of Satan as a challenger to God is potentially incongruent within a cosmic scheme in which God is omnipotent, but Aquinas and other scholastics put stress on the notion, articulated in patristic and early medieval writings, that Satan is able to snare individuals only with God's permission. Aquinas held that the experience of wickedness helps humans more fully comprehend the good because evil is the inverse of godly. The great university scholars did not speak of witches, but they set the stage for those who would.

40. EVIL ANGELS: LOMBARD'S *SENTENCES*

Peter Lombard (c. 1100–c. 1160) was born in Italy. He taught at the cathedral school of Notre Dame and became the bishop of Paris in 1159, the year before he died. He is best known for his Four Books of Sentences, *arguably the most influential reference collection on Catholic theology in the high and late Middle Ages. Even Protestant reformers such as Martin Luther (1483–1546) and John Calvin (1509–1564) quoted Lombard's work. In the* Sentences, *Lombard codified virtually all writings on Christian doctrine, relying heavily on Scripture and the works of the church fathers. The* Sentences *was instrumental in developing the basic principles of scholastic dogma in European universities as it unfolded over the four centuries after Lombard's life. Because of its centrality, Lombard's work ensured that educated, elite discourse on magic and demonology remained moored to conservative patristic thought throughout the Middle Ages. Note the familiarity of the evidence Lombard brings to the service of his arguments on magic and his defense of God's omnipotence.*

Source: trans. Robert O'Brien, *The Sentences of Peter Lombard*, vol. 2 (Toronto: Pontifical Institute of Medieval Studies, 2007–10), pp. 355–58; rev. Martha Rampton.

Book 2, Distinction 7

Chapter 5. And although the evil angels, through malice, have been made obstinate; nevertheless, they have not been deprived of the natural vigor of sense. Now as Isidore Seville [c. 560–636] says, "Demons thrive by reason of three forms of trickery in their knowledge: by the subtlety of their nature, by the experience of time, and by the revelation due to their character as superior spirits. [*Sentences* 1.10].

Concerning this, furthermore, Augustine says "Certain evil spirits are permitted to become acquainted with truths concerning temporal things partly by reason of the subtlety of sense, partly because of the length of their lives, partly because the holy angels, by God's command, teach them that which they themselves have learned from the omnipotent God. Sometimes these same disgusting spirits foretell what they are about to do, as though they have predicted it" [*On the Literal Meaning of Genesis* 2.17].

Chapter 6. By means of knowledge and strength, furthermore, are the magical arts employed, which have been given to evil spirits as power from God, either to cheat by deceitfulness, or as punishment for the faithful, or according to exercising and testing the patience of the righteous.

Along these lines, Augustine in book three, *On the Trinity* says, "I see that it may possibly occur to those with weak minds that miracles can be made by arts of magic inasmuch as, by magic, Pharaoh's magicians made snakes and other effects. But that is to be admired more because of the method and power of the magic by which the magicians were able to make serpents, yet they could not make the most minute flies. As a result of the flies having wholly failed, the third plague of Egypt was ineffectual. At that point, certainly the magicians failed, saying, 'This is worthy of God' [Exodus 8:19]. So it is understood that these transgressing angels—who were the potentates of the lower air, having been thrust down into the bottommost darkness when their generation was incarcerated after being thrust out of the sublime purity of the ethereal habitation—through those arts of magic, do have power and can, to some extent, do some things, but only as a gift of power from God above. The power to do magic is given, (a) either as the most deceptive of fallacies, just as in the case of the Egyptians—for it had been given to the magicians so that in themselves, that is to say their own minds, they considered their operations admirable, when really they were damnable—; (b) as a warning to the faithful that they should not yearn for anything that is made from magic just because in the Scriptures there are magical prodigies; (c) for the testing and the manifesting of patience for the upright.

Chapter 8. It is not sensible to say that these evil angels are creators just because through their magic they made frogs and snakes; in fact these creatures themselves are not created. Certainly all things that are corporeal and visible are born. God inserted some certain hidden seeds of these elements which are latent in the body of the world. He, himself, therefore, is the creator of all things in that he is the creator of the invisible seeds, since whatsoever is born before our eyes, comes from the hidden seeds and has taken its upward growth—from the beginning through increments to the destined magnitude—and assumes its form from the rules of its origins, taken from the original.

Just as we do not say that parents are the creators of the man, nor the farmers of the fruits—though they are called into being from the outside motion of these—rather the act of creating operates from the inside through the power of God; thus, neither the evil nor the good angles have knowledge to the decree that is the agent of creation. . . . Now the iniquitous have their own desire for unrighteousness as the result of malice; however, they do not have the power to do evil, unless they have received it justly from God. . . ." [Augustine, *On Christian Doctrine* 3.7–8].

Questions: What is the major theological point that Lombard is making in the excerpts above, and why is it important to him? What is the relationship between good and evil spirits? Does Lombard credit the power of magic, and does he consider demons (evil spirits) dangerous?

41. DIVINATION AND THE COURT: THE *POLICRATICUS*

John of Salisbury (c. 1120–1180), an Englishman of modest background, was fully involved in the momentous events of his day. He studied scholasticism under the most renowned teachers of Europe and became a friend and secretary to the controversial Thomas Becket, archbishop of Canterbury (c. 1120–1170), whose biography he wrote after the archbishop's murder. John knew the palace environment well, having lived his adult life in secular and ecclesiastical courts across Europe.

The Policraticus *comprises eight books. The first three differ from the other five, which lay out a philosophy of ethical politics. In books 1 through 3, John reflects on the frivolities of courtiers and discusses the magic most practiced at court. The organization of the work is random at points and moves from topic to topic with bewildering speed. This style results in some confusion concerning John's attitudes toward various kinds of magic. For a person who was held to be one of the best educated men of Europe, his analysis of divination, augury, and popular superstition is surprisingly unsystematic.*

Source: trans. Joseph B. Pike, John of Salisbury, *Frivolities of Courtiers and Footprints of Philosophers: Being a Translation of the First, Second, and Third Books and Selections from the Seventh and Eighth Books of the* Policraticus *of John of Salisbury* (Minneapolis: University of Minnesota Press, 1938), pp. 39–45, 56, 59–60, 87, 93–94, 144–47.

Book 1

9. Long ago the Christian fathers condemned those who practiced the more demoralizing forms of legerdemain, the art of magic and astrology, because they realized that all these arts, or rather artifices, derive from unholy commerce between men and demons. Very frequently their practitioners cite truth with

the sole intent to deceive, and of these our Lord warns the souls of his faithful: if they shall tell you and so it come to pass, believe them not [Matthew 24:36]. The word *praestigium* is said to have been invented by Mercury for the reason that he blinds the eyes. He was the most adept of magicians and could make invisible whatever he desired or, as it appears, change it into other forms. Indeed, all manifestations of *mathesis*, if the penultimate syllable be pronounced long, may be referred to magic, and of this there are many different forms.

10. Magicians do indeed exist and are so called because of the magnitude of their incantations; for they, by God's grace, cause the elements to shudder, destroy the identity of things, often predict the future, cloud the minds of men, send dreams, and, so far as that goes, by the violence of their charms, slay [people]. . . . You are aware that James and Jambres, magicians of Pharaoh (for Egypt is the mother of such kinds of superstition and sorcery), not only withstood Moses but vied in signs and miracles with him, though afterward, quite reluctantly, they were forced to acknowledge that the hand of God was in the signs of Moses.

12. Enchanters are they who practice their art by means of words. Wizards are they who, on altars, make their unholy prayers and accursed sacrifices. On their necks the hand of the Lord weighs, for his prophet says, "You do not permit wizards and magicians to live" [Exodus 22:18]. Soothsayers are they who consider the hours and prescribe the expedient time for action. Their error the apostle damns in [these] words: "I am afraid of you lest perhaps I have labored in vain among you for you observe days and months and seasons and years" [Galatians 4:10–11]. Success should be attained not from [omens] but from the name of God.

Auspice taking also has to do with the inspection of vitals . . . [which] is meant all that is covered by the outer skin, as a consequence of which it is clear that those who base their prophecies on the dry bones of animals without blood, whether they expound the present or the past, are classed as soothsayers. For prophecy is the art by which, as the result of knowledge of the truth, the hidden is revealed, since it is conceded that the art deals not only with the future but also with the present, the future, and the past. If, however, use is made of blood we enter the domain of the black art, which is so called because it depends entirely upon investigation of the dead. Its essential character is that of being able to raise the dead for the purpose of ascertaining truth. It is indeed a trick of demons who mock and play with human frailty.

Prophets are those who are filled with the prophetic spirit. This works more frequently in [virgins] that it may delude all the more, as if the unclean spirit were attracted by a mind and body undefiled. *Vultivoli* are they who, for the purpose of working upon the feelings of men, fashion in a somewhat soft substance (as wax or clay) images of those whose natures they are striving to distort. . . .

Their sorcery, although they do much harm, may be easily counteracted; for example, if the persons suspected, being confronted by someone, deny their crime or, having confessed, are compelled to revoke their incantation. *Imaginarii* are they who send, as it were, the figures they fashion to the presiding spirits that by them they may be informed on matters of doubt. Holy Scripture assures that such are idolaters are condemned by the judgment of divine majesty. Dream interpreters are they who, by some art, claim they have the power of interpreting dreams. Palmists are they who, by inspecting the hands, prophesy concerning things unknown. Crystal seers are they who, by gazing into smooth and polished surfaces, such as shining sword blades, basins, cups, and mirrors of various types, satisfy the curiosity of their clients. . . . Astrologers [sometimes called *horoscopi*] are they (though this word has a wider application as well) who, from the position of the stars, the situation of the firmament, and the movement of the planets, foretell the future . . . as if it were an established fact that the courses of the stars and their connection—the one with the other—fix, so to speak, a kind of fated course for things, which in reality results from the free action of the will. The error of the astrologist is repeated in the calculator of nativities who specializes upon the hour of birth. . . . This science flourished and doubtless was lawfully practiced to a certain extent until after the star in the heavens announced the birth of Christ and with its strange, marvelous guidance, led the magi, then men of worth, to offer their adoration, the first fruits of piety. Thereafter, however, astrology was absolutely banned. *Salisatores* are they who, as a result of palpitation in the limbs or unexpected movements of the body, pronounce a future event favorable or unfavorable. . . .

13. A Roman consul, having been sent on a military expedition and being unable to secure favorable auspices, directed that pigeons which had been starved for some time, be sent on ahead and that kernels of wheat be spread on the road where he was to pass in order that by their omen, at least, he might offset, to some extent, the unfavorable auspices. However, when they persisted in refusing food he ordered them hurled into the river that they at any rate might drink. Drowned in the swift current they served as a premonition that the consul and his army would perish in like manner. Such in fact was their fate. . . .

If you place credence to the nonsense of the Spaniards and notice on beginning a task, that your clothing has been gnawed by mice, desist from your undertaking. If as you go out of the house and trip on the threshold, stop. If on the point of transacting business you suffer some loss, defer what you have begun lest you be entirely thwarted or what you do accomplish prove ineffectual. Wait until such time as you may begin again under better auspices. Everything has some significance. When you sally forth, birds which are named prophetic will indicate to you the secrets of the future. What are those birds, you ask? Why, those which the poets assert have been changed from human beings into the form of birds. Listen with attention to what the crow says. Be sure not to disregard its position when perched or flying. It is indeed significant whether it be on the right or left; in what position it be as it turns its eye upon your elbow as you walk along; whether it chatter, caw, or be quite silent; whether it go on ahead or follow; whether it await your coming as you pass, or fly away; and in what direction it goes. . . .

Book 2

1 . . . . I, for my part, whatever may be the nature of these things, firmly believe that only those things should be accepted which are the product of faith and are attributed to the glory of an omnipotent God; for I know that it has been written, "And whatever you do in word or deed, do all in the name of the Lord" [Colossians 3:17], in whom alone the way of man prospers. . . . One Cuthbert [Celtic saint of Northern England, c. 634–687], the standard-bearer of our people in the law of God, placed the Gospel of Saint John upon the bodies of the afflicted, and they were made well. A tunic of Saint Stephen [martyr of the early church, c. 5–c. 34 CE] was placed upon the body of a dead man, and he arose. One possessed by devils has been cured by the Apostles' Creed which he was carrying. The Lord's Prayer repeated in perfect faith while herbs are being gathered or administered, has frequently produced the medicinal effect required. . . .

3. The signs which occur in accordance with nature's laws in the case of the sun and the moon are quite definite and attested by many authors. . . . As often therefore as the sun appears double in the heaven, the earth beneath may expect floods. This rare and seemingly miraculous appearance is nonetheless a phenomenon of nature, there being in reality not two suns but a reflection in the clouds of the one. This is called "parelion," which means a cloud of the semblance of the sun, a sign of considerable but not of general application, for some signs are specific and others general—specific when they affect individuals; general when they affect many, or all. Each type is thought to originate sometimes in the will of a kind creator, sometimes in nature's laws, and again in malicious spirits whom God permits to torment men. . . .

17. . . . [When spirits appear in dreams] the devout soul should reject every image except that which leaves its innocence unimpaired. For should the dream add fuel to vice, perchance by inducing lust and avarice or by inspiring greed for dominion or anything of the sort to destroy the soul, undoubtedly it is the flesh or the evil spirit that sends it. This spirit, with the permission of the Lord because of their sins, wreaks its unbridled wickedness upon some men so violently that what they suffer in the spirit they wretchedly but falsely believe comes to pass in the flesh. For example, it is said that some Moon [Diana] or

Herodias or Mistress of the Night calls together councils and assemblies, that banquets are held, that different kinds of rites are performed, and that some are dragged to punishment for their deeds and others raised to glory. Moreover, babes are exposed to witches and at one time their mangled limbs are eagerly devoured, at another they are flung back and restored to their cradles if the pity of her who presides is aroused.

Cannot even the blind see that this is but the wickedness of mocking demons? This is quite apparent from the fact that it is for the weaker sex and for men of little strength or sense that they disport themselves in such a cult. If, in fact, anyone who suffers from such illusion is firmly censured by someone or by some sign, the malign influence is either overcome or yields, and, as the saying is, as soon as one is censured in the light, the works of darkness cease. The most effective cure however for this bane is for one to embrace the true faith, refuse to listen to such lies, and never to give thought to follies and inanities of the sort.

19. Because it is plausible that there is some potency in the phenomena of the heavens, since on earth also it is believed that nothing is done which does not bestow from the hand of the creator some beneficial result, inquisitive minds investigate the powers of celestial phenomena and endeavor to explain, by the rules of their type of astronomy, everything which comes to pass on this world below. Now astronomy is a noble and glorious science if it confines its disciples within the bounds of moderation, but if it be presumptuous enough to transgress these it is rather a deception of impiety than a phase of philosophy.

There is indeed much that is common to astronomy and astrology, but the latter tends to exceed the bounds of reason and, differing in its entire aim, does not enlighten its exponent but misleads him. The following is common to each: dividing into zones, drawing parallels, turning the zodiac and its signs obliquely, encircling almost the whole celestial globe with the colures [two circles of the celestial sphere, intersecting at the poles], measuring the eclipse of planets, making the outer celestial sphere independent of motion, drawing lines from the north to the south pole, dividing the signs of the zodiac by grades and points, maintaining the balance of the rising and setting constellations. Each agrees with physicians in that they do not consider that fine, tenuous bodies are distributed along fixed paths, as it were, and segments of circles. . . . But astrology, deriving its origin in the principles of philosophy, as stated above, goes too far, and with rash pride infringes upon the prerogative of [God], "who counts the stars, whose names and signs and power, courses, places, and times, are known to him alone" [Sedulius, *Carmen Paschale* 1, 66–67], since the astrologer, thanks to his art, claims this power for himself. They wander farther from the knowledge of the truth in proportion to the arrogance with which they strive to force their way to it. Pondering therefore on the nature of the signs as they had perchance come to know it, they say that some of them as they roved aimlessly among the companion stars, are of masculine—others of feminine—gender, and that perhaps they would have multiplied by offspring were it not for the fact that, being separated in space, they were unable to embrace each other. They explore diligently the intentions of the planets, which they regard as governing the twelve constellations. And this is something easy to ascertain from their relation, motion, and attraction, the one for the other, and for the hosts of stars. Saturn, therefore, [for example] because old and cold, is stern and harmful, malicious by nature and morose because of age. Hence, inimical to all, he scarcely spares his own disciples.

28. Crystal seers falsely flatter themselves that they offer no sacrifices, that they harm no one, that often they are helpful in detecting theft and purging the world of malefactors, and that they seek only truth that is helpful and practical. The wicked are not so. "He that gathers not with me," [Jesus] said, "scatters, and he who is not with me is against me" [Matthew 12:30]. In practicing such arts, despite the prohibition of God, what else are the wicked doing than lifting up the heel against him who prohibits them? . . . But that which influences the minds of the simple, to wit, that the secrets of the future can be made manifest only by the hand of him in whose power are times and seasons, does not touch the crux of the matter. For although there is but one arbiter of the future, who is the Lord God of all, nonetheless the future at times becomes known to men through signs. . . . Moreover, propitious powers, which with affection and devoted obedience zealously serve the Lord, are indeed able to reveal secrets to seers and are at times supposed to do so. Yet it is not forthwith true that discredited seers perceive and predict; rather on occasion they hasten to announce what they suspect or fear, with the result that they appear to be aware of secrets.

. . . During my boyhood, I was placed under the direction of a priest to teach me psalms. As he practiced the art of crystal gazing, it chanced that he, after preliminary magical rites, made use of me and a boy somewhat older as we sat at his feet for his sacrilegious art in order that what he was seeking by means of finger nails moistened with some sort of sacred oil or chrism or of the smooth polished surface of a basin, might be made manifest to him by information imparted by us. And so, after pronouncing names which by the horror they inspired seemed to me, child though I was, to belong to demons, and after administering oaths of which, at God's instance, I know nothing, my companion asserted that he saw certain misty figures, but dimly, while I was so blind to all this that nothing appeared to me except the nails or basin and the other objects I had seen there before.

As a consequence, I was adjudged useless for such purposes, and, as though I impeded the sacrilegious practices, I was condemned to have nothing to do with such things, and as often as they decided to practice their art I was banished as if an obstacle to the whole procedure, so propitious was God to me even at that early age. But as I grew older, more and more did I abominate this wickedness, and my horror of it was strengthened because, though at the time I made the acquaintance of many practitioners of the art, all of them before they died were deprived of their sight, either as the result of physical defect or by the hand of God, not to mention other miseries with, which in my plain view, they were afflicted. There were two exceptions—the priest whom I have mentioned and a certain deacon; for they, seeing the affliction of the crystal gazers, fled (the one to the bosom of the collegiate church—the other to the refuge of the monastery of Cluny) and adopted holy garb. Nonetheless I am sorry to say that even they, in comparison to others in their congregations, suffered many afflictions afterward.

Questions: How does John of Salisbury differentiate various kinds of omens? What consistencies are there in his analysis of the efficacy of omens? What is John's assessment of the tales of the cult of Diana/Herodias? What elements of the cult differ from the description of the followers of Diana/Herodias in the Canon episcopi *(see doc. 35)? According to the* Policraticus, *what is the difference between astrology and astronomy? Why did the priest require that the young boys gaze into the crystals rather than doing it himself?*

42. LANVAL AND THE FAIRY QUEEN: MARIE DE FRANCE

Marie de France (fl. twelfth century), an otherwise enigmatic historical figure, is well known for her writings, particularly twelve short narrative lais *that survive in five manuscripts. Although Marie identifies herself as French in the prologue to one of her* lais, *she lived in England and was familiar with the court of Henry II (r. 1154–89). She may have been the king's half-sister, or others suggest that she was the abbess of Shaftesbury, Reading, or Barking. Marie was one of the first authors of the romance genre and developed some of its distinguishing tropes. She borrowed themes and motifs from the Celtic oral traditions of Brittany, featuring the fabled land of King Arthur and his coterie. Courtly love and adultery figure in Marie's work, which she champions under certain circumstances. In her stories, genuine affection between a man and a woman is more prized than marriage bonds when one of the partners is unhappy or unwilling. Marie's literary technique was innovative, and her* lais *had immediate appeal. The tales are replete with elements that in an earlier era were seen as magical, but in the cultural context of the time, they were considered marvelous. These marvels often drive the plot and make it possible for the lovers to find fulfillment.*

Source: trans. Eugene Mason, *French Medieval Romances from the Lays of Marie de France*, Everyman's Library (London: J.M. Dent & Sons, 1911), pp. 61–76.

"Lanval"

At the time of Pentecost, [King Arthur] announced a great feast where he gave many rich gifts to his counts and barons and to the Knights of the Round Table. Never were such worship and bounty shown before at any feast, for Arthur bestowed honors and lands on all his servants—save only on one. This lord, who was forgotten and the king disliked was named Lanval. However, he was beloved by many of the court because of his beauty and prowess, for he was a worthy knight, open of heart and a skilled warrior. These lords, to whom their comrade was dear, felt little joy to see so stout a knight misjudged. . . .

Now one day Sir Lanval got on his horse to get away and find some pleasure for a while. He came forth from the city alone, attended by neither servant nor squire. He wandered through a green meadow until he stood by a river of clear running water. Sir Lanval would have crossed this stream without thought of pass or ford, but he could not do so because his horse was all fearful and trembling. Seeing that he was hindered in this fashion, Lanval unbridled his steed and let him pasture in that fair meadow where they had come. Then he folded his cloak to serve him as a pillow and lay upon the ground. Lanval lay in great unease because of his heavy thoughts and the discomfort of his bed. He turned from side to side and could not sleep. Now as the knight looked towards the river he saw two damsels coming towards him; fairer maidens Lanval had never seen. These two maidens were richly dressed in kirtles [loose gowns] closely laced and shaped to their persons and wore mantles of a goodly purple hue. Sweet and dainty were the damsels, alike in raiment and in face. The elder of these ladies carried in her hands a basin of pure gold, cunningly wrought by some crafty smith; very fair and precious was the cup, and the younger bore a towel of soft white linen. These maidens turned neither to the right hand nor to the left, but went directly to the place where Lanval lay. When Lanval saw that their business was with him, he stood upon his feet like a discreet and courteous gentleman. After they had greeted the knight, one of the maidens delivered the message with which she was charged.

"Sir Lanval, my mistress, as gracious as she is fair, prays that you will follow us, her messengers, as she has a certain word to speak with you. We will lead you swiftly to her pavilion, for our lady is very near at hand. If you but lift your eyes you may see where her tent is spread."

Right glad was the knight to do the bidding of the maidens. He gave no heed to his horse, but left him to graze in the meadow. All his desire was to go with the damsels to that pavilion of silk and many colors pitched in so fair a place. Certainly, neither Semiramis [mythical queen of Babylon] in the days of her most wanton power, nor Octavian [63 BCE–14 CE], the emperor of all the west, had so gracious a covering from sun and rain. Above the tent was set an eagle of gold, so rich and precious that none might count the cost. The cords and fringes thereof were of silken thread, and the lances, which bore aloft the pavilion, were of refined gold. No king on earth might have so sweet a shelter, not though he gave in fee the value of his realm. Within this pavilion Lanval came upon the maiden. Whiter she was than any altar lily and more sweetly flushed than the new born rose in time of summer heat. She lay upon a bed with napery [linen] and coverlet of richer worth than could be furnished by a castle's riches. Very fresh and slender showed the lady in her vesture of spotless linen. About her person she had drawn a mantle of ermine edged with purple dye from the vats of Alexandria. By reason of the heat her raiment was unfastened for a little, and her throat and the hint of her bosom showed whiter and more untouched than hawthorn in May. The knight came before the bed and stood gazing on so sweet a sight. The maiden beckoned him to draw near, and when he had seated himself at the foot of her couch spoke her mind.

"Lanval," she said, "fair friend, it is for you that I have come from my own far land. I bring you my love. If you are prudent and discreet as you are handsome, there is no emperor, nor count, nor king whose day shall be so filled with riches and with mirth as yours."

When Lanval heard these words, he rejoiced greatly, for his heart was lit by another's torch.

"Fair lady," he answered, "since it pleases you to be so gracious, and to honor so graceless a knight with your love, there is naught that you may bid me do—right or wrong, evil or good—that I will not do to the utmost of my power. I will observe your commandment and serve in your quarrels. For you I renounce my father and my father's house. This only I pray, that I may dwell with you in your lodging and that you will never send me from your side."

When the maiden heard the words of him whom so fondly she desired to love, she was altogether moved and granted him forthwith her heart and her tenderness. To her bounty she added another gift besides. Never might Lanval be desirous of aught, but he would have according to his wish. He might waste and spend at will, but his purse would always be full. No more was Lanval sad. Right merry was the pilgrim, since one had set him on the way with such a gift that the more pennies he bestowed, the more silver and gold were in his pouch.

But the maiden had yet a word to say. "Friend," she said, "hearken to my counsel. I lay this charge upon you and pray you urgently that you tell not to any person the secret of our love. If you reveal this matter, you will lose your friend forever and a day. Never again may you see my face. Never again will you have the pleasure of that body which is now so tender in your eyes."

Lanval made a promise that right strictly he would observe this commandment. So, the maiden granted him her kiss and her embrace and very sweetly in that fair lodging passed the day till evensong was come. Right loath was Lanval to depart from the pavilion at the vesper hour, and gladly would he have stayed had he been able and his lady wished.

"Fair friend," said she, "rise up, for no longer may you tarry. The hour is come that we must part. But one thing I have to say before you go. When you would speak with me I shall hasten to come before your wish. Well I deem that you will only call your friend where she may be found without reproach or shame of men. You may see me at your pleasure; my voice shall speak softly in your ear at will, but your comrades must never know me, nor must they ever hear my voice."

Right joyous was Lanval to hear this thing. He sealed the covenant with a kiss and stood upon his feet. Then there entered the two maidens who had led him to the pavilion bringing with them rich raiment, fitting for a knight's apparel. When Lanval had clothed himself therewith there seemed no goodlier knight under heaven, for certainly he was fair and true. After these maidens had refreshed him with clear water and dried his hands upon the napkin, Lanval sat down to eat. His friend sat at table with him, and he had no desire to refuse her courtesy. Very serviceably the damsels bore the meats, and Lanval and the maiden ate and drank with mirth and content. But one dish was more to the knight's relish than any other. Sweeter than the dainties within his mouth was the lady's kiss upon his lips.

When supper was ended, Lanval rose from table, for his horse stood waiting without the pavilion. The warhorse was newly saddled and bridled and showed proudly in his rich gay trappings. So Lanval kissed, and bade farewell, and went his way. He rode back towards the city at a slow pace. Often he checked his steed and looked behind him, for he was filled with amazement and all bemused concerning this adventure. In his heart he wondered if it was but a dream. He was altogether astonished and knew not what to do. He feared that pavilion and maiden alike were from the realm of the fairies. Lanval returned to his lodging, clad no longer in ragged raiment, and he was greeted by attendants. He fared richly, lay softly, and spent largely, but never knew how his purse was filled. There was no lord who had need of a lodging in the town, but Lanval brought him to his hall for refreshment and delight. Lanval bestowed rich gifts. Lanval redeemed the poor captive. Lanval clothed in scarlet the minstrel. Lanval gave honor where honor was due. Stranger and friend alike he comforted at need. So, whether by night or by day, Lanval lived greatly at his ease. His lady, she came at will and pleasure, and for the rest, all was granted unto him.

Now it chanced the same year about the feast of Saint John, a company of knights came for their solace to an orchard beneath that tower where dwelt the queen. . . . When the queen noticed that Lanval went aside, she went his way, and seating herself upon the grass, called the knight before her. Then she opened out her heart.

"Lanval, I have honored you for long as a worthy knight and have praised and cherished you very dearly. You may receive a queen's whole love, if such be your wish. Be content; he to whom my heart is given has small reason to complain."

"Lady," answered the knight, "grant me leave to go, for this grace is not for me. I am the king's man, and dare not break my troth. Not for the highest lady in the world, not even for her love, will I set this reproach upon my lord."

When the Queen heard this, she was full of wrath, and spoke many hot and bitter words.

"Lanval," she cried, "well I know that you think little of woman and her love. These are black sins that a man may have upon his soul. Traitor you are and false. Right evil counsel they gave to my lord who convinced him to invite you to his court. That you remain is a disgrace to the king."

Lanval was very sorrowful to hear this thing. He was not slow to take up the queen's glove [her challenge], and in his haste spoke words that he repented long and with tears.

"Lady," said he, "I am not the kind of man of which you speak. Neither am I a despiser of woman since I love and am loved of one who would bear the prize for beauty from all the ladies in the land. Dame, know now and be persuaded that she, whom I serve, is so rich in state that the very meanest of her maidens excels you, Lady Queen, as much in skill and goodness as in sweetness of body and face and in every virtue."

The queen rose straightway to her feet and fled to her chamber, weeping. Right wrathful and heavy was she because of the words that had besmirched her. She lay sick upon her bed from which, she said, she would never rise until the king had done her justice and righted this bitter wrong. Now the king that day had taken his pleasure within the woods. He returned from the chase towards evening and sought the chamber of the queen. When the lady saw him, she sprang from her bed, and kneeling at his feet, pleaded for grace and pity. She said that Lanval had shamed her by demanding her love. When she firmly refused her advanced, he insulted her by boasting that his love was already set on a lady so proud and noble that her meanest wench went more richly and smiled more sweetly than the queen. Thereat the king became marvelously wrathful and swore a great oath that he would set Lanval within a fire or hang him from a tree if he could not deny this thing before his peers.

Arthur came forth from the queen's chamber and called to him three of his lords. These he sent to seek the knight who so evilly tried to seduce the queen. Lanval, for his part, had returned to his lodging in a sad and sorrowful case. He saw very clearly that he had lost his friend since he had declared their love to the queen. Lanval sat within his chamber, sick and heavy of thought. Often he called upon his friend, but the lady would not hear his voice. He bewailed his evil lot with tears; for grief he nearly swooned; a hundred times he implored the maiden that she would deign to speak with her knight. Then, since the lady yet refrained from speech, Lanval cursed his hot and unruly tongue. Very near he came to ending all this trouble with his knife. He could do nothing but to wring his hands and call upon the maiden, begging her to forgive his trespass and to talk with him again as friend to friend. But little peace is there for him who is harassed by a king. . . .

[King Arthur summoned Lanval.] "Vassal," said he, harshly, "you have done me a bitter wrong. It was a foul deed to seek to shame me in this ugly fashion and to smirch the honor of the queen. Is it folly or lightness which leads you to boast of that lady, the least of whose maidens is fairer and goes more richly than the queen?"

Lanval protested that never had he set such shame upon his lord. Word by word he told the tale of how he denied the queen within the orchard. But concerning that which he had spoken of the lady, he owned up to the truth and his folly, the love of whom he bragged was now lost to him by his own exceeding fault. He cared little for his life, and was content to obey the judgment of the court.

Right wrathful was the king at Lanval's words. He conjured his barons to give him such wise counsel so that wrong might be done to none. The lords did the king's bidding—whether good came of the matter, or evil. They gathered themselves together and appointed a certain day that Lanval should abide the judgment of his peers. . . . They blamed him greatly because of his foolish love and chastened him grievously for the sorrow he made for them all. Every day they came to his chamber to make sure he was eating and drinking, for they greatly feared that soon he would become mad.

The lords of the household came together on the day appointed for this judgment. The king was on his chair with the queen sitting at his side. . . .

[The duke of Cornwall rose and said,] "Now, if it be according to Arthur's will, let us take oath of Lanval that he seeks this lady, who has put such strife between him and the queen. If her beauty be such as he has told us, the queen will have no cause for wrath. She must pardon Lanval for his rudeness, since it will be plain that he did not speak out of a malicious heart. Should Lanval fail his word and not return with the lady, or should her fairness fall beneath his boast, then let him be cast off from our fellowship and be sent forth from the service of the king."

This counsel seemed good to the lords of the household. They sent certain of his friends to Lanval to acquaint him with their judgment, bidding him to summon his damsel to the court that he might be acquitted of this blame. The knight made answer that in no wise could he do this thing. So those who pledged returned before the judges saying that Lanval hoped neither for refuge nor for succor from the lady, and Arthur urged them to a speedy ending because of the prompting of the queen.

The judges were about to give sentence upon Lanval when . . . there came two other damsels riding to the hall on two Spanish mules. Very richly arrayed were these damsels in raiment of fine needlework, and their gowns were covered by fresh fair mantles embroidered with gold. Great joy had Lanval's comrades when they marked these ladies. They said between themselves that doubtless they came for the succor of the good knight.

Gawain and certain of his company made haste to Lanval and said, "Sir, be not cast down. Two ladies are near at hand, right dainty of dress and gracious of person. Tell us truly, for the love of God, is one of these your friend?"

But Lanval answered very simply that never before had he seen these damsels with his eyes nor known and loved them in his heart. The maidens dismounted from their mules and stood before Arthur in the sight of all. Greatly were they praised by many because of their beauty and the color of their faces and hair. Some there were who deemed already that the queen was overborne. The elder of the damsels carried herself modestly and well and sweetly told over the message wherewith she was charged.

"Sire, make ready for us chambers, where we may abide with our lady, for even now she comes to speak with you."

The king commanded that the ladies should be led to their companions [other damsels who had arrived from the maiden's court] and bestowed in the same honorable fashion as they. Then he bade the lords of his household to consider their judgment, since he would endure no further delays. The court already had given too much time to the business and the queen was growing wrathful because of the blame that was hers. Now the judges were about to proclaim their sentence, when, amidst the tumult of the town, there came riding to the palace the flower of all the ladies of the world. She came mounted upon a palfrey, white as snow, which carried her softly as though she loved her burden. Beneath the sky was no better steed nor one more gentle to the hand. The harness of the palfrey was so rich that no king on earth might hope to buy trappings so precious unless he sold his kingdom. The maiden herself showed such as I will tell you. Passing slim was the lady, sweet of bodice and slender of girdle. Her throat was whiter than snow on a branch, and her eyes were like flowers in the pallor of her face. She had a witching mouth, a dainty nose, and an open brow. Her eyebrows were brown, and her golden hair parted in two soft waves upon her head. She was clad in a shift of spotless linen, and above her snowy gown was set a mantle of royal purple clasped upon her breast. She carried a hooded falcon upon her glove and a greyhound followed closely after. As the maiden rode at a slow pace through the streets of the city, there was none—neither great nor small, youth nor sergeant—but ran forth from his house that he might content his heart with so great beauty. Every man that saw her with his eyes marveled at a fairness beyond that of any earthly woman.

Little he cared for any mortal maiden after he had seen this sight. The friends of Sir Lanval hastened to the knight, to tell him of his lady's succor, if so it were according to God's will.

"Sir comrade, truly is not this your friend? This lady is neither black nor golden, mean nor tall. She is only the most lovely thing in all the world."

When Lanval heard this, he sighed, for by their words he knew again his friend. He raised his head, and as the blood rushed to his face, speech flowed from his lips.

"By my faith," cried he, "yes, she is indeed my friend. It is a small matter now whether men slay me or set me free; for I am made whole of my hurt just by looking on her face."

The maiden entered in the palace, where none so fair had come before, and stood before the king in the presence of his household. She loosed the clasp of her mantle so that men might the more easily perceive the grace of her person. The courteous king advanced to meet her, and all the court got on their feet and offered themselves in her service. When the lords had gazed upon her for a space and praised the sum of her beauty, the lady spoke to Arthur in this fashion, for she was anxious to be gone.

"Sire, I have loved one of your vassals: the knight who stands in bonds, Sir Lanval. He was always unappreciated in your court and his every action turned to blame. You know what he said; his tongue was over hasty before the queen. But he never craved her in love, however loud his boasting. I cannot permit that he should come to hurt or harm because of me. In the hope of freeing Lanval from his bonds, I have obeyed your summons. Let now your barons look boldly upon my face, and deal justly in this quarrel between the queen and me."

The king commanded that this should be done, and looking upon her eyes, not one of the judges but was persuaded that her favor exceeded that of the queen. Since Lanval had not spoken in malice against his lady, the lords of the household gave him again his sword. When the trial had come thus to an end the maiden took her leave of the king, and made herself ready to depart. Gladly would Arthur have had her lodge with him for a little, and many a lord would have rejoiced to serve her, but she would not tarry. Now outside the hall stood a great stone of dull marble where it was the wont of lords departing from the court to climb into the saddle, and Lanval was [waiting on her horse] by the stone. The maiden came forth from the doors of the palace, and mounting on the stone, seated herself on the palfrey, behind her friend. Then they rode across the plain together, and were no more seen. The Bretons tell that the knight was transported by his lady to an island, very dim and very fair, known as Avalon. But none has had speech with Lanval and his fairy love since then, and for my part I can tell you no more of the matter.

Questions: Is there a sub-text of the demonic in "Lanval"? What is the source of power that allows Lanval's love to appear and disappear? In what way is Lanval's mistress similar and in what way is she different from the classical Circe (see doc. 3)? Describe the gendered power relationships in the story.

43. THE GENTLE WEREWOLF: MARIE DE FRANCE

Marie's lais *incorporate many fantastic, seemingly magical, plot elements, including the topos of the werewolf, which is one of the most enduring motifs of folk literature. Early Christian writers such as Augustine (354–430) debated whether human beings are able to change shape. Augustine was skeptical, and following his lead, most ecclesiastics through the medieval period were very clear that shape-shifting was an illusion that demons produced. However, all of that scholarly disputation was irrelevant in the world of Marie's* lais.

Source: trans. Eugene Mason, *Medieval Romances from the Lays of Marie de France* (London: J.M. Dent & Sons, 1911), pp. 83–90.

"The Lay of the Werewolf" ["Bisclavaret"]

In Brittany there dwelt a baron who was marvelously esteemed by all his fellows. He was a stout knight, and comely, and a man of office and repute. He was a devoted confidant of his lord and dear to his neighbors. This baron was wedded to a very worthy dame—right fair to see and sweet of countenance. All his love was set on her, and all her love was given again to him. One only grief had this lady. For three whole days in every week her lord was absent from her side. She knew not where he went nor on what errand. Neither did any of his house know the business which called him forth.

On a day when this lord was come again to his house, altogether joyous and content, the lady took him to task, right sweetly, in this fashion, . . . "Husband, right long and wearisome are the days that you spend away from your home. I rise from my bed in the morning, sick at heart, I know not why. So fearful am I, lest you fall into danger, that I may not find any comfort. Very quickly shall I die for reason of my dread. Tell me now, where you go and on what business! How may the knowledge of one who loves so closely, bring you to harm?" . . .

"Wife, I become the werewolf, Bisclavaret. I enter in the forest and live on prey and roots within the thickest of the wood."

After she had learned his secret, she prayed and entreated the more as to whether he ran in his raiment, or went without clothing.

"Wife," said he, "I go naked as a beast."

"Tell me, for hope of grace, what you do with your clothing?"

"Fair wife, that will I never. If I should lose my raiment, or even be seen as I undress, then a werewolf I must go for all the days of my life. Never again should I become man, save in that hour my clothing was given back to me. For this reason never will I show my lair."

"Husband," replied the lady to him, "I love you better than all the world. The less cause have you for doubting my faith or hiding any confidence from me. What distrust is there of friendship? How have I made forfeit of your love; for what sin do you mistrust my honor? Open now your heart, and tell what is good to be known."

So at the end, wearied and overborne by her importunity, [he revealed that he hid his clothes in a hollow stone near an ancient chapel]. . . . On hearing this marvel the lady blushed, because of her exceeding fear. She dared no longer to lie at his side and turned over in her mind, this way and that, how best she could get away from him. Now there was a certain knight of those parts, who, for a great while, had sought this lady for her love. This knight had spent long years in her service, but little enough had he got thereby, not even fair words, or a promise. To him the dame wrote a letter, and on meeting him, made her purpose plain.

"Fair friend," said she, "be happy. That which you have coveted so long a time, I will grant without delay. Never again will I deny your suit. My heart, and all I have to give, are yours, so take me now as love and dame."

Right sweetly the knight thanked her for her grace, and pledged his faith and fealty. When she had confirmed him by an oath, then she told him all this business of her lord—why he went, and what he became, and of his ravening within the wood. So she showed him the chapel, and the hollow stone, and how to despoil the werewolf of his clothes. Thus, by the kiss of his wife was Bisclavaret betrayed. Often enough had he ravished his prey in desolate places, but from this journey he never returned. His kinsfolk and acquaintance came together to ask of his tidings when this absence was noised abroad. Many a man, on many a day, searched the woodland, but none could find him, nor learn where Bisclavaret was gone.

The lady was wedded to the knight who had cherished her for so long a space. More than a year had passed since Bisclavaret disappeared. Then it chanced that the king would hunt in that same wood where the werewolf lurked. When the hounds were unleashed they ran this way and that and swiftly came upon his scent. At the view, the huntsman blew on his horn, and the whole pack were at his heels. They followed him from morn to eve, till he was torn and bleeding, and dreaded that they would pull him down. Now the king was very close to the quarry, and when Bisclavaret looked upon his master, he ran to him for pity and for grace. He took the stirrup within his paws and fawned upon the prince's foot. The king was very fearful at this sight, but presently he called his courtiers to his aid.

"Lords," cried he, "hasten hither, and see this marvelous thing. Here is a beast who has the sense of man. He abases himself before his foe and cries for mercy, although he cannot speak. Beat off the hounds, and let no man do him harm. We will hunt no more today but return to our own place with the wonderful quarry we have taken."

The king turned himself about and rode to his hall—Bisclavaret follow-ing at his side. Very near to his master the werewolf went, like any dog, and had no care to seek again the wood. When the king had brought him safely to his own castle, he rejoiced greatly, for the beast was fair and strong, no mightier had any man seen. Much pride had the king in his marvelous beast. He held him so dear that he bade all those who wished for his love to cross the wolf in nothing, neither to strike him with a rod, but ever to see that he was richly fed and kenneled warm. This commandment the court observed willingly. So all the day the wolf sported with the lords, and at night he lay within the chamber of the king. There was not a man who did not make much of the beast, so frank was he and debonair. None had reason to do him wrong; forever was he about his master, and for his part did evil to none. Every day were these two companions together, and all perceived that the king loved him as his friend.

Hearken now to that which chanced. The king held a high court and bade his great vassals and barons and all the lords he hunted with to the feast. Never was there a goodlier feast nor one set forth with sweeter show and pomp. Among those who were bidden, came that same knight who had the wife of Bisclavaret for dame. He came to the castle, richly gowned, with a fair company, but little he knew whom he would find so near. Bisclavaret marked his foe the moment he stood within the hall. He ran towards him and seized him with his fangs in the king's very presence and to the view of all. Doubtless he would have done him much harm, had not the king called and scolded him and threatened him with a rod. . . .

Not long after the feast, it came to pass that the courteous king went hunt-ing in that forest where Bisclavaret was found. With the prince came his wolf and a fair company. Now at nightfall the king abode within a certain lodge of that country, and this was known to that dame who before was the wife of Bisclavaret. In the morning the lady clothed herself in her most dainty apparel and hastened to the lodge, since she desired to speak with the king, and to offer him a rich present. When the lady entered in the chamber, neither man nor leash could restrain the fury of the wolf. He became as a mad dog in his hatred and malice. Breaking from his bonds he sprang at the lady's face and bit the nose from her visage. From every side, men ran to the succor of the dame. They beat off the wolf from his prey, and for a little would have cut him in pieces with their swords.

But a certain wise counselor said to the king, "Sire, hearken now to me. This beast is always with you, and there is not one of us all who has not known him for long. He goes in and out among us nor has molested any man neither done wrong or felony to any, save only to this dame—one only time as we have seen. He has done evil to this lady and to that knight, who is now the husband of the dame. Sire, she was once the wife of that lord who was so close and dear to your heart, but who went, and none could find where he had gone. Now, therefore, put the dame in a sure place, and question her directly so that she may tell—if perchance she knows thereof—for what reason this beast holds her in such mortal hate. For many a strange deed has chanced, as well we know, in this marvelous land of Brittany."

The king listened to these words and deemed the counsel good. He laid hands upon the knight and put the dame in surety in another place. He caused them to be questioned right straightly so that their torment was very grievous. At the end, partly because of her distress, and partly by reason of her exceeding fear, the lady's lips were loosed, and she told her tale. She told them of the betrayal of her lord and how his raiment was stolen from the hollow stone. Since then she knew not where he went nor what had befallen him, for he had never come again to his own land. Only, in her heart, well she deemed and was persuaded, that he was Bisclavaret.

Straightway the king demanded the clothing of his baron, whether this was the wish of the lady or whether it was against her wish. When the raiment was brought him, he caused it to be spread before Bisclavaret, but the wolf made as though he had not seen. Then that cunning and crafty counselor took the king apart, that he might give him a fresh advice. "Sire," said he, "you do not wisely, nor well, to set this raiment before Bisclavaret, in the sight of all. In shame and much tribulation must he lay aside the beast, and again become man. Carry your wolf within your most secret chamber, and put his clothing therein. Then close the door upon him, and leave him alone for a space, so we shall see presently whether the ravening beast may indeed return to human shape."

The king carried the wolf to his chamber and shut the doors upon him fast. He delayed for a brief while, and taking two lords of his fellowship with him, came again to the room. Entering therein, all three, softly together, they found the knight sleeping in the king's bed, like a little child. The king ran swiftly to the bed and taking his friend in his arms, embraced and kissed him fondly, above a hundred times. When man's speech returned once more, he told him of his adventure. Then the king restored to his friend the fief [land] that was stolen from him and gave such rich gifts, moreover, as I cannot tell. As for the wife who had betrayed Bisclavaret, he bade her avoid his country and chased her from the realm. So she went forth, she and her second lord together, to seek a more abiding city, and were no more seen. . . .

Questions: It is not clear what source of power compels Bisclavaret to become a werewolf. Why might Marie have omitted that information? Why did Bisclavaret require clothing in order to assume his human shape?

44. GUIDE FOR THE PERPLEXED: JEWISH MAGIC AND MAIMONIDES

Moses Maimonides (1135–1204) was a Sephardic Jew born in Muslim-controlled Spain and one of the most prolific and famous Torah scholars of the medieval period. After the Almohads, a Berber dynasty, conquered Córdoba in 1148, Maimonides chose to flee Spain due to persecution against Jews, and he spent the rest of his life in Palestine and Egypt, where he became the leader of the Jewish community in Fustat. Although some of his works on theology and ethics were controversial, especially in Spain, he was given the honorific "The Great Eagle," and Jewish, Muslim, and Christian intellectuals acknowledged him as one of the best thinkers of his time.

Maimonides wrote Guide for the Perplexed *about 1190 for his student Rabbi Joseph ben Judah of Ceuta (c. 1150–1226). Through the text the scholar's goal is to reconcile Aristotelian philosophy with the Hebrew Scriptures and their commentaries. Throughout his copious works, including the* Guide, *the Jewish thinker touched on virtually every topic of interest in his day, but, like Thomas Aquinas (see doc. 53), he was not particularly interested in sorcery, except inasmuch as he considered it a form of idolatry.*

Source: trans. Michael Friedländer, Moses Maimonides, *Guide for the Perplexed*, 2nd ed. (New York: Dover Publications, 1961), pp. 332–38.

Part 3

37. The precepts of the second class are those which we have enumerated in the section "On idolatry." It is doubtless that they all tend to save man from the error of idolatry and the evil practices connected with it; for example, observing the times, enchantment, sorcery, incantation, consulting with familiar spirits, and the like. When you read the books which I mentioned to you, you will find that sorcery, which will be described to you, is part of the customs of the Sabeans, Kasdim, Chaldeans, and to a higher degree, of the Egyptians and Canaanites. They caused others to believe, or they themselves believed, that by means of these arts they would perform wonderful things in reference to an individual person or to the inhabitants of a whole country; although no analogy and no reasoning can discover any relation between these performances of the witches and the promised result. Thus they are careful to collect certain plants at a particular time, and to take a definite number of certain objects. There are many things comprised by sorcery; they may be divided into three classes: first,

sorcery connected with objects in nature—such as plants, animals, or minerals. Secondly, sorcery dependent for its performance on a certain time; and thirdly, sorcery dependent on the performance of certain acts of man, such as dancing, clapping, laughing, jumping with one leg, lying on the ground with the face upward, burning a thing, fumigating with a certain material, or speaking intelligible or unintelligible words.

These are the various kinds of sorcery. In some cases all these various performances are required. Thus the witches sometimes order [one to] take a leaf of a certain plant when the moon is seen in a certain degree (of the zodiac) in the east point or in one of the other cardinal points (of the horizon), also a certain quantity of the horn, the sweat, the hair and the blood of a certain animal when the sun is, for example, in the middle of the sky or in some other definite place and a portion of a certain mineral or minerals, melted at a certain conjunction of sun and moon, and at a definite position of the stars. [They] speak then, and say certain words and fumigate with those leaves, or similar ones, to that molten image, and such and such a thing will happen. In other instances of sorcery it is assumed that one of the above performances suffices. In most cases the condition is added that women must perform these actions. Thus it is stated in reference to the means of obtaining rain, that ten virgins dressed with diadems and red garments should dance, push each other, moving backwards and forwards, and make signs to the sun. The result of this long process was believed (by the idolaters) to be a downpour of rain.

It is further stated that if four women lay on their backs, with their feet spread and lifted up, said certain words and did certain things while in this disgraceful position, hail would discontinue coming down in that place. The number of these stupid and mad things is great; in all of them without exception women are required to be the agent. Sorcery is intimately connected with astrology; those that practice it assign each plant, animal, or mineral to a certain star and believe that the above processes of sorcery are different forms of worship offered to that star, which is pleased with that act, word, or offering of incense, and fulfills their wishes.

After this remark, which you will understand when you have read such of their works as are at present extant and have been mentioned by me, hear what I will tell you. It is the object and center of the whole Law [Jewish religious law] to abolish idolatry and utterly uproot it and to overthrow the opinion that any of the stars could interfere for good or evil in human matters, because it leads to the worship of stars. It was therefore necessary to slay all witches as being undoubtedly idolaters, because every witch is an idolater: they only have their own strange ways of worship, which are different from the common mode of worship offered to those deities. But in all performances of sorcery it is laid down as a rule that women should be employed in the chief operation; and therefore the Law says, "You shall not suffer a witch to live" (Exodus 22:18). Another reason is the natural reluctance of people to slay women. This is also the cause why in the law of idolatry it is said "man or woman" (Deuteronomy 17:2), and again repeated a second time, "the man or the woman" (Deuteronomy 17:5)—a phrase which does not occur in the Law about the breaking of Sabbath, or in any other law; for great sympathy is naturally shown to women.

Now the witches believed that they produced a certain result by their sorcery; that they were able through the above-mentioned actions to drive such dangerous animals as lions, serpents, and the like out of the cities and to remove various kinds of damage from the products of the earth. Thus they imagine that they are able by certain acts to prevent hail from coming down, and by certain other acts to kill the worms in the vineyards, whereby the latter are protected from injury. In fact, the killing of the worms in vineyards, and other superstitions mentioned in the *Nabatean Agriculture*, are fully described by the Sabeans. They [witches] likewise imagine that they know certain acts by which they can prevent the dropping of leaves from the trees and the untimely falling of their fruit. On account of these ideas, which were general in those days, the Law declares in "the words of the covenant" as follows, The same idolatry and superstitious performances which, in your belief, keep certain misfortunes far from you, will cause those very misfortunes to befall you. . . .

In order that we may keep far from all kinds of sorcery, we are warned not to adopt any of the practices of the idolaters, even such as are connected with agriculture, the keeping of cattle, and similar work. (The Law prohibits) everything that the idolaters, according to their doctrine, and contrary to reason, consider as being useful and acting in the manner of certain mysterious forces. Compare: "Neither shall you walk in their ordinances" (Leviticus 18:3). "And you shall not walk in the manners of the nation which I cast out before you" (Leviticus 20:23). Our sages call such acts "the ways of the Amorite"; they are kinds of sorcery, because they are not arrived at by reason but are similar to the performances of sorcery, which is necessarily connected with the influences of the stars; thus ("the manners of the nations") lead people to extol, worship, and praise the stars. Our sages say distinctly, "Whatever is used as medicine" does not come under the law of "the ways of the Amorite"; for they hold that only such cures as are recommended by reason are permitted, and other cures are prohibited. . . . For the same reason our sages said, "The uterus of animals which have been selected for the sanctuary must be buried; it must not be suspended from a tree, and not buried in the crossroad [a location with particular magical potency], because this is one of 'the ways of the Amorite.'" Hence you may learn how to treat similar cases.

It is not inconsistent that a nail of the gallows and the tooth of a fox have been permitted to be used as cures; for these things have been considered in those days as facts established by experiment. They served as cures, in the same manner as the hanging of the peony over a person subject to epileptic fits or the application of a dog's refuse to the swellings of the throat, and of the vapors of vinegar and marcasite [a mineral] to the swelling of hard tumors. For the Law permits as medicine everything that has been verified by experiment, although it cannot be explained by analogy. The above-named cures are permitted in the same way as the application of purgatives. Learn, reader, these noteworthy lessons from this my work, and keep them; "For they are a diadem of grace for your head" (Proverbs 4:9).

We have explained in our large work that it is prohibited to round the corners of the head and to mar the corners of the beard, because it was the custom of idolatrous priests. For the same reason, the wearing of garments made of linen and wool is prohibited. The heathen priests adorned themselves with garments containing vegetable and animal material, while they held in their hand a seal made of a mineral. This you find written in their books. The same is also the reason of the precept, "The woman shall not wear that which pertains unto a man" (Deuteronomy 22:5). You find it in the book *Tomtom* that a male person should wear colored woman's dress when he stands before Venus, and a female, when standing before Mars, should wear a buckler and other armor. I think that this precept has also another reason; namely, that the interchange of dress creates lust and leads to immorality. . . .

We must also point out that originators of false, baseless, and useless principles scheme and plan for the firm establishment of their faith, and tell their fellow men that a certain plague will befall those who will not perform the act by which that faith is supported and confirmed forever; this plague may one day accidentally befall a person, who will then direct his attention to the performance of that act, and adopt idolatry. It being well known that people are naturally most in fear and dread of the loss of their property and their children, the worshippers of fire spread the tale, that if any one did not pass his son and daughter through the fire, he will lose his children by death. There is no doubt that on account of this absurd menace everyone at once obeyed, out of pity and sympathy for the child; especially as it was a trifling and a light thing that was demanded, in passing the child over the fire.

We must further take into account that the care of young children is entrusted to women, who are generally weak-minded, and ready to believe everything, as is well known. The Law makes, therefore, an earnest stand against this practice, and uses in reference to it stronger terms than in any other kind of idolatry; namely, "He defiles my sanctuary, and profanes my holy name" (Leviticus 20:3). The true prophet then declares in the name of God that the very act which is performed for the purpose of keeping the child alive will bring death upon him who performs it, and destruction upon his seed. . . . "And I will set my face against that man and against his family," and so forth (Leviticus 20:5). Know that traces of this practice have survived even to the present day, because it was widespread in the world. You can see how midwives take a young child wrapped in its swaddling clothes, and after having placed incense of a disagreeable smell on the fire, swing the child in the smoke over that fire. This is certainly a kind of passing children through the fire, and we must not do it. Reflect on the evil cunning of the author of this doctrine, how people continued to adhere to this doctrine, and how, in spite of the opposition of the Law during thousands of years, its name is not blotted out, and its traces are still in existence.

Idolaters have acted similarly in reference to property. They made it a law that a certain tree, the asherah, should be worshipped, and that of its fruit one part should be offered, and the rest consumed in the temple of the idol; this is stated in the regulations concerning the asherah. In the same manner, they made it a rule, that the first-fruit of every fruit tree should be partly offered as a sacrifice and partly consumed in the idol's temple. It was also a widespread belief that if the first-fruit of any tree was not treated in this manner, the tree would dry up, its fruit would be cast off, its increase would be diminished, or some disease would come over it—just as they spread the belief that every child, that was not passed through the fire, must die. People in their anxiety for their property obeyed also this precept unhesitatingly. The Law, in opposition to this doctrine, commanded us to burn the produce of fruit trees the first three years; for some trees bear fruit after one year, while some begin to yield fruit after two, and others after three years. The law is based upon the nature of trees grown in an ordinary way, namely, in one of the three well-known methods: planting, propagation, and inoculation (neti'ah, habrakah, and harcabah). . . .

It is further mentioned in the *Nabatean Agriculture* that the ancient idolaters caused certain things named in that work to rot, waited till the sun stood in a certain degree (of the ecliptic), and then they performed many acts of sorcery. They believed that that substance should be kept ready by everyone, and when a fruit tree is planted, a portion of that rotten substance should be scattered round the tree or under it; the tree would then grow quicker and produce more fruit than is generally the case. They say that this process is very extraordinary; it acts like a talisman, and is more efficient than any kind of sorcery in accelerating the productiveness of fruit trees. I have already shown and explained to you how the Law opposes all kinds of sorcery. The Law, therefore, prohibits us to use the fruit yielded by a tree in the first three years after it has been planted, so that there should be no opportunity for accelerating, according to their imagination, the productiveness of any tree. After three years most fruit trees in Palestine yield fruit by the ordinary course of nature, without the application of those magical performances, which were very general in those days. Note this remarkable fact.

Another belief which was very common in those days, and survived the Sabeans, is this: when a tree is grafted into another in the time of a certain conjunction of sun and moon and is fumigated with certain substances while a formula is uttered, that tree will produce a thing that will be found exceedingly useful. More general than anything mentioned by the heathen writers was the ceremony of grafting an olive branch upon a citron tree, as described in the beginning of the *Nabatean Agriculture*. I am of opinion that the book of medicines which Hezekiah [king of Judea, d. c. 686 BCE] put away (Babylonian Talmud Pesachim 56a) was undoubtedly of this kind. They also said that when one species is grafted upon another, the branch which is to be grafted must be in the hand of a beautiful damsel, while a male person has disgraceful and unnatural sexual intercourse with her; during that intercourse the woman grafts the branch into the tree. There is no doubt that this ceremony was general and that nobody refused to perform it, especially as the pleasure of love was added to the (supposed) future results of the grafting.

The Law, therefore, prohibits us to mix different species together, that is, to graft one tree into another, because we must keep away from the opinions of idolaters and the abominations of their unnatural sexual intercourse. In order to guard against the grafting of trees, we are forbidden to sow any two kinds of seed together or near each other. When you study the traditional explanation of this precept, you will find that the prohibition of grafting, the principal element in this commandment, holds good for all countries, and is punishable by forty stripes, but the sowing of seeds—one near the other—is only prohibited in Palestine. In the *Nabatean Agriculture* it is further distinctly stated that it was the custom of the people in those days to sow barley and stones of grapes together, in the belief that the vineyard could only prosper in this way. Therefore the Law prohibits us to use seed that has grown in a vineyard, and commands us to burn both the barley and the produce of the vineyard.

For the practices of the heathen, which they considered as of a magic and talismanic character, even if not containing any idolatrous element, are prohibited, as we have stated above in reference to the dictum of our sages, "We must not hang upon a tree the fetus of an animal belonging to the sanctuary." The Law prohibits all heathen customs, called by our sages "the ways of the Amorite," because they are connected with idolatry. On considering the customs of the heathen in their worship, you will find that in certain kinds of worship they turn toward stars, in others to the two great luminaries; frequently they choose the rise of signs in the zodiac for sowing and fumigating; and as to the circuits made by those who plant or sow, some complete five circles, corresponding to the five planets, with the exclusion of the two luminaries; others go seven times round, according to the number of the planets, when including sun and moon. They believe that all these practices are magic charms of great efficiency in agriculture. Thus those practices lead to the worship of stars; and therefore all practices of those nations have been prohibited, in the words, "You shall not walk in the manners of the nation which I cast out before you" (Leviticus 20:23). Those practices which were more general and common, or were distinctly connected with idolatry, are particularly pointed out as prohibited, for example, eating the fruit of a tree during the first three years, intermixing of species and the mixed species sown in a vineyard. . . .

Questions: What is Maimonides' attitude toward women? What does Maimonides use as the basis of his argument? What does Maimonides consider the major danger of sorcery?

45. WEATHER WELL AND MAGIC RING: CHRÉTIEN DE TROYES

Relatively little is known of Chrétien de Troyes (c. 1160–c. 1191). He was a French poet who worked with Welsh and other Celtic folkloric mythologies and was central to the development of the distinctively medieval genre of romance. Chrétien served in the court of Marie de Champagne (1145–1198)—foremost patron of chivalric literature—between 1160 and 1181; there he developed the legendary character Lancelot. His "proto-novels" were very popular in their own time, as evidenced by the high survival rate of the texts.

Yvain is a story about a knight of King Arthur's Round Table who seeks to prove his prowess as a warrior, and, as is typical of romance, marvelous and magical rituals, objects, and substances figure in the plot. For example, Morgan le Fey, the famous fairy queen, makes an appearance. Also consistent with the genre, magic is amoral and often employed to virtuous ends.

Source: trans. William Wistar Comfort, Chrétien de Troyes, *Arthurian Romances*, Everyman's Library 698 (New York: E.P. Dutton & Co, 1913), pp. 185–86, 192–95.

Yvain

[Calogrenant tells Yvain how he can test his mettle.] Says he, " . . . Close by here you can easily find a path which will lead you thither. If you would go right, follow the straight path; otherwise you may easily go astray among the many other paths. You shall see the spring which boils, though the water is colder than marble. It is shadowed by the fairest tree that ever nature formed, for its foliage is evergreen regardless of the winter's cold, and an iron basin is hanging there by a chain long enough to reach the spring. And beside the spring you shall find a massive stone, as you shall see, but whose nature I cannot explain, never having seen its like. On the other side a chapel stands—small, but very beautiful. If you will take the water in the basin and spill it upon the stone, you shall see such a storm come up that not a beast will remain within this wood; every doe, stag, deer, boar, and bird will issue forth. For you shall see such lightning-bolts descend, such blowing of gales and crashing of trees, such torrents fall, such thunder and lightning, that, if you can escape from them without trouble and mischance, you will be more fortunate than ever any knight was yet."

I left the fellow then, after he had pointed out the way. It must have been after nine o'clock and might have been drawing on toward noon when I espied the tree and the chapel. I can truly say that this tree was the finest pine that ever grew on earth. I do not believe that it ever rained so hard that a drop of water could penetrate it but would rather drip from the outer branches. From the tree I saw the basin hanging, of the finest gold that was ever for sale in any fair. As for the spring, you may take my word that it was boiling like hot water. The stone was of emerald, with holes in it like a cask, and there were four rubies underneath— more radiant and red than is the morning sun when it rises in the east.

Now not one word will I say which is not true. I wished to see the marvel- ous appearing of the tempest and the storm, but therein I was not wise, for I would gladly have repented, if I could, when I had sprinkled the perforated stone with the water from the basin. But I fear I poured too much, for straight- way I saw the heavens so break loose that from more than fourteen directions the lightning blinded my eyes, and all at once the clouds let fall snow and rain and hail. The storm was so fierce and terrible that a hundred times I thought I should be killed by the bolts which fell about me and by the trees, which were rent apart. Know that I was in great distress until the uproar was appeased. But God gave me such comfort that the storm did not continue long, and all the winds died down again. The winds dared not blow against God's will. And when I saw the air, clear and serene, I was filled with joy again. For I have observed that joy quickly causes trouble to be forgot. As soon as the storm was completely past, I saw so many birds gathered in the pine tree (if anyone will believe my words) that not a branch or twig was to be seen which was not entirely covered with birds. The tree was all the more lovely then, for all the birds sang in harmony, yet the note of each was different, so that I never heard one singing another's note. . . .

[After Yvain raises the storm, he finds himself threatened by King Escla- dos, guardian of the stone. The two fight. Yvain wounds Esclados and barely manages to escape the pursuing band of the king's warriors by slipping into a small enclosure just past the castle gate. One of the castle's serving maids approaches Yvain.]

"Surely, sir knight," she says, "I fear you have come in an evil hour. If you are seen here you will be all cut to pieces. For my lord is mortally wounded, and I know it is you who have been the death of him. My lady is in such a state of grief, and her people about her are crying so that they are ready to die with rage, and, moreover, they know you to be inside. . . . I know full well what your name is, and I recognized you at once; your name is my lord Yvain. You may be sure and certain that if you take my advice you will never be caught or treated ill. Please take this little ring of mine, which you will return when I shall have delivered you."

Then she handed him the little ring and told him that its effect was like that of the bark which covers the wood so that it cannot be seen, but it must be worn so that the stone is within the palm. Then he who wears the ring upon his finger need have no concern for anything; for no one, however sharp his eyes may be, will be able to see him any more than the wood which is covered by the outside bark. All this was pleasing to my lord Yvain. And when she had told him this, she led him to a seat upon a couch covered with a quilt so rich that the duke of Austria had none such, and she told him that if he cared for something to eat she would fetch it for him, and he replied that he would gladly do so. Running quickly into the chamber, she presently returned bringing a roasted fowl and a cake, a cloth, a full pot of good grape-wine covered with a white drinking-cup; all this she offered to him to eat. And he, who stood in need of food, very gladly ate and drank.

By the time he had finished his meal the knights were astir inside looking for him and eager to avenge their lord, who was already stretched upon his bier. Then the damsel said to Yvain, "Friend, do you hear them all seeking you? There is a great noise and uproar brewing. But whoever may come or go, do not stir for any noise of theirs, for they can never discover you if you do not move from this couch. Presently you will see this room all full of ill-disposed and hostile people, who will think to find you here, and I have no doubt that they will bring the body here before interment, and they will begin to search for you under the seats and the beds. It will be amusing for a man who is not afraid when he sees people searching so fruitlessly, for they will all be so blind, so undone, and so misguided that they will be beside themselves with rage. I cannot tell you more just now, for I dare no longer tarry here. But I may thank God for giving me the chance and the opportunity to do some service to please you, as I yearned to do."

Then she turned away, and when she was gone all the crowd with one accord had come from both sides to the gates armed with clubs and swords. There was a mighty crowd and press of hostile people surging about, . . . but none of them had sharp enough eyes to see my lord Yvain, whom they would gladly have killed, and he saw them beside themselves with rage and fury, as they said, "How can this be? For there is no door or window here through which anything could escape, unless it be a bird, a squirrel, or marmot, or some other even smaller animal; for the windows are barred, and the gates were closed as soon as my lord passed through. The body is in here, dead or alive, since there is no sign of it outside there; we can see more than half of the saddle in here, but of him we see nothing, except the spurs which fell down severed from his feet. Now let us cease this idle talk, and search in all these corners, for he is surely in here still, or else we are all enchanted or the evil spirits have filched him away from us."

Thus they all, aflame with rage, sought him about the room, beating upon the walls, and beds, and seats. But the couch upon which he lay was spared and missed the blows so that he was not struck or touched. But all about they thrashed enough and raised an uproar in the room with their clubs, like a blind man who pounds as he goes about his search. While they were poking about under the beds and the stools, there entered the queen, one of the most beautiful ladies that any earthly creature ever saw. Word or mention was never made of such a fair Christian dame, and yet she was so crazed with grief that she was on the point of taking her life. . . .

The procession passed, but in the middle of the room a great crowd gathered about the [funeral] bier, for the fresh warm blood trickled out again from the dead man's wound, and this betokened certainly that the man was still surely present who had fought the battle and had killed and defeated him. Then they sought and searched everywhere, and turned and stirred up everything, until they were all in a sweat with the trouble and the press which had been caused by the sight of the trickling crimson blood. Then my lord Yvain was well struck and beaten where he lay, but not for that did he stir at all. And the people became more and more distraught because of the wounds which burst open, and they marveled why they bled, without knowing whose fault it was.

And each one to his neighbor said, "The murderer is among us here, and yet we do not see him, which is passing strange and mysterious."

At this the lady showed such grief that she made an attempt upon her life, and cried as if beside herself, "Ah God, then will the murderer not be found, the traitor who took my good lord's life? Good? Aye, the best of the good, indeed! True God, yours will be the fault if you do let him thus escape. No other man than you should I blame for it who hides him from my sight. Such a wonder was never seen, nor such injustice, as you do to me in not allowing me even to see the man who must be so close to me. When I cannot see him, I may well say that some demon or spirit has interposed himself between us, so that I am under a spell."

Question: Is there magic in this story, and if so, by what definition is it magic?

46. NORSE MAGIC: *SAGA OF THE VOLSUNGS*

The Volsung saga is an Icelandic, Old Norse heroic tale about the origins and decline of the royal clan of the Volsungs. Snorri Sturluson (1179–1241), an Icelandic poet and historian, recorded the story around 1220, but the material dates to events that took place centuries before. Versions of the stories in the saga exist in earlier works, some of which appear in the Poetic Edda, *a collection of Norse poetry.*

In the saga, there is no notion that shape-shifting, werewolves, sorcery, and anthropomorphized dragons are demonic in the Christian sense. Authors who recorded this tale, passed down from their ancestors, often painted the dragon-slayer as a second Saint Michael, himself a slayer of dragons. The world Sturluson creates in his version of the saga, however, is unapologetically pagan.

Source: trans. William Morris and Eirikr Magnusson, *The Story of the Volsungs* (London: Walter Scott Press, 1888), pp. 6–8, 12–15, 17–18, 20–22, 46–48, 59–60, 62–63, 65, 67–68; rev. Martha Rampton.

3. There was a king called Siggeir who ruled over Gothland [island off Sweden]—a mighty king ruling over many folk; he went to meet Volsung, the king of Hunland, and asked him for the hand of Signy, his daughter, and the king and his sons looked favorably on the proposal. Signy was loath, yet she deferred to her father in this as in all other things that concerned her; so the king, after much consideration, gave her to King Siggeir, and they were betrothed. For the feast and the wedding, King Siggeir was to come to the house of King Volsung. The king prepared a feast according to his best ability, and when all things were ready, the king's guests came on the appointed day, including King Siggeir, and many a man of great account had come with Siggeir.

The tale goes that great fires were made at each end of the hall, and the great tree [an oak called Branstock] stood in the middle. Folk say that one evening as the men sat by the fires, a certain person came into the hall unlike any they had ever seen. He was dressed such that over him was a spotted cloak, and he was barefoot and had linen breeches knit tight, even to the bone, and a slouched hat upon his head. He had a sword in his hand and he went up to the Branstock. Huge he was, and seeming-ancient, and one-eyed [the man was Odin, god of wisdom]. So he drew his sword and smote it into the tree trunk so that it sank in up to the hilt, and all held back from greeting the man. Then he spoke and said, "Whoever draws this sword from this stock shall have it as a gift from me and shall find that never will he carry a better sword in his hand than is this."

Therewith out went the old man from the hall, and none knew who he was or where he went. Now men stood up, and none wanted to be the last to lay hand to the sword, for they deemed that he would have the best of it who could first touch the weapon. So all the noblest came forward first, and then the others, one after other, but none could pull it out; for it would not come away however hard they tugged at it. But then up came Sigmund, King Volsung's son, and sets hand to the sword and pulled it from the stock, even as if it lay loose before him. So good that weapon seemed to all that none thought he had seen such a sword before. And Siggeir wanted to buy it from Sigmund at three times its weight in gold, but Sigmund said, "You could have taken the sword no less than I from where it stood if it had been your lot to bear it, but now, since it has first of all fallen into my hand, never shall you have it, though you offer all the gold you have."

King Siggeir grew angry at these words and felt that Sigmund had answered him scornfully, but because he was a wary man and double-dealing, he made as if he heeded this matter little; yet that same evening he thought how he might retaliate, as we shall see.

[King Siggeir marries Signy, Volsung's daughter, and invites his in-laws, to visit him at Gothland where his army attacks the party and kills King Volsung and seizes his ten sons.]

5. Now all [Volsung's] sons were taken, and laid in bonds, and led away, and . . . a mighty beam was brought and set on the feet of those ten brothers in a certain place in the wild woods, and there they sat daylong until night, but at midnight, as they sat in the stocks, there came on them a she-wolf from the woods. She was old and both great and evil of aspect, and the first thing she did was to bite one of those brothers till he died, and then she ate him up withal and went on her way. But the next morning Signy sent a man to her brothers, one whom she most trusted, to learn of the tidings, and when he came back he told her that one of them was dead, and great and grievous she deemed it if they should all have the same fate, and yet she could not help them.

Soon, as the tale goes, nine nights in all came the she-wolf at midnight and each night slew and ate up one of the brothers until all were dead, save Sigmund only. So now, before the tenth night came, Signy sent her trusted man to Sigmund, her brother, and gave him honey, bidding him to put it all over Sigmund's face and set a little bit of it in his mouth. So he went to Sigmund and did as he was bidden and then came home again. And so the next night came the she-wolf, according to her wont, planning to slay Sigmund and eat him even as she had eaten his brothers, but then she sniffed the air around him, inasmuch as he was anointed with the honey, and licked his face all over with her tongue and then thrusts her tongue into his mouth. No fear he had, but caught the she-wolf's tongue between his teeth, and so hard she started back and pulled herself away so mightily, setting her feet against the stocks, that they were broken asunder, but Sigmund held so fast that the tongue came away by the roots, and she had her ruin. Some men say that this same she-wolf was the mother of King Siggeir, who had turned herself into this likeness by troll's lore and witchcraft.

6. Now whereas the stocks were broken and Sigmund was loosed, he dwelt in the woods and hid there, but Signy sent yet again to learn of the tidings—whether Sigmund was alive or not. But when those who were sent

came to Sigmund, he told them all that had happened and how things had gone between him and the wolf; so they went home and told Signy the tidings. But she went and found her brother, and they decided to make a house underground in the wild woods, and so things went on a while. . . .

7. So one night as Signy sat in her bower, there came to her a witch-wife exceedingly cunning, and Signy talked with her, "Desirous am I," said she, "that we should change shapes with each other." She said, "Let it be as you wish." And so by her wiles she brought it about that they changed appearances, and now the witch-wife took Signy's place, according to the scheme, and went to bed with King Siggeir that night, and he thought Signy was beside him. But the tale tells of Signy, that she went to the earth-house of her brother and prayed him give her harbor for the night, "For I have gone astray abroad in the woods and don't know where I am going." So he said she could stay and that he would not refuse harbor to one lone woman, thinking that she would not pay back his good hospitality by revealing his hiding place. So she came into the house, and they sat down to meat, and his eyes were often on her, and a goodly and fair woman she seemed to him. But when they were full, then he said to her that he was right desirous that they should have but one bed that night. She agreed, and so for three nights together they shared a bed. Thereafter she returned home and found the witch-wife and bade her change appearances again, and she did so. Now as time wore on, Signy brought forth a man-child, who was named Sinfjotli, and when he grew up he was both big and strong, and fair of face, and much like unto the kin of the Volsungs. . . .

8. The tale goes that Sigmund thought Sinfjotli was too young to help him avenge the death of his father and brothers and would first of all harden him with manly deeds; so in summer they travel wide through the woods and slayed men for their wealth. . . . Now one time as they went abroad in the woods to get wealth, they found a certain house and two men with great gold rings were asleep therein. Now these two were spellbound skin-changers, and wolf-skins were hanging up over them in the house, and every tenth day they came out of those skins, and they were kings' sons. So Sigmund and Sinfjotli put on the wolf-skins, and they were not able to get them off, but they still had the faculties of men. They howled as wolves howl, but both knew the meaning of that howling; they went out in the wild wood, and each went his way. They agreed that they would each be able to risk the onset of seven men, but no more, and that he who was first to be set on should howl wolfish wise. . . . [They roam the woods, killing men. The two argue, and Sigmund wounds Sinfjotli.] Thereafter they went home to their earth-house and abode there till the time came for them to put off the wolf shapes; then they burnt the skins up with fire and prayed that no more hurt might come to anyone because of them. But in that uncouth guise they had accomplished many famous deeds in the kingdom and lordship of King Siggeir. . . .

[As the saga continues, Sinfjotli is poisoned, Sigmund sires a child named Sigund and dies in battle, and a man named Regin becomes Sigund's foster father.]

14. Regin told a tale of his brothers and the gold called Andvari's Hoard, "The tale begins," said Regin. "Hreidmar was my father's name—a mighty and wealthy man—and his first son was named Fafnir, his second Otter, and I was the third . . . But Fafnir was by far the greatest and greediest and would have all things called his."

"Now," said Regin, "there was a dwarf called Andvari who lived in a waterfall, which was called Andvari's Waterfall, and in the guise of a pike he got meat for himself; for many fish there were in the waterfall. Now Otter, my brother [who often took the shape of an otter] was accustomed to enter into the Waterfall and bring fish aland and lay them one by one on the bank. And so it befell that [the gods] Odin, Loki, and Hoenir, as they went their ways, came to Andvari's waterfall, and Otter had taken a salmon, eaten it and was slumbering upon the riverbank. Then Loki took a stone and cast it at Otter [who was at that point in the guise of an otter] so that he was killed thereby. The gods were well content with their prey, and fell to flaying off the otter's skin, and in the evening, they came to Hreidmar's house and showed him what they had taken. Thereon Hreidmar [knowing it was his son] laid hands on them and doomed them to such ransom; they had to fill the otter skin with gold and cover it on the outside with red gold. So they sent Loki to gather gold together for them . . ."

[Loki sought out Andvari's Waterfall, where Andvari had a stash of gold.] "So Loki beheld the gold of Andvari, and when Andvari had given up the gold, he had but one ring left, and that also Loki took from him; then the dwarf went into a hollow of the rocks and cried out that that gold-ring, yea and all the gold, should be the bane of every man who should own it thereafter. Now the gods rode with the treasure to Hreidmar, and filled the otter-skin, and set it on its feet . . ."

"Thereafter," said Regin, "Fafnir slew his father and murdered him [for the gold], nor got I any of the treasure, and so evil he grew that he fell to lying around and begrudged any share in the wealth to any man and so became the worst of all worms and ever now lies brooding upon that treasure . . ."

18. Now Sigurd and Regin rode up the heath along that same way wherein Fafnir was wont to creep when he went to the water, and folk say that thirty fathoms was the height of that cliff along which he lay when he drank of the water below. Then Sigurd spoke, "Why did you say, Regin, that this dragon was no greater than any other dragon worm; I think the track of him is marvelous great?" Then said Regin, "Make a hole and sit down in it, and when the worm comes to the water, smite him in the heart, and so do him to death and win great fame thereby." But Sigurd said, "What will happen to me if

I sit in the blood of the worm?" Said Regin, "What is the use of counseling you if you are still afraid of everything? Little are you like your kin in stoutness of heart."

Then Sigurd rode right over the heath, but Regin left—very much afraid. But Sigurd fell to digging a pit, and while he was at that work, there came to him an old man [Odin] with a long beard who asked what he was doing, and Sigurd told him. Then the old man answered and said, "You have had bad advice; rather dig many pits and let the blood run therein, but sit down in one of them, and so thrust the worm's heart through." And then he vanished away, and Sigurd made the pits even as it was shown to him. Now crept the worm down to his place of watering, and the earth shook all about him, and he snorted forth venom all the way before him as he went, but Sigurd neither trembled nor dreaded his roaring. So when the worm crept over the pits, Sigurd thrust his sword under his left shoulder so that it sank in up to the hilt; then up leapt Sigurd from the pit and drew the sword back again, and his arm was all bloody up to the very shoulder. Now when that mighty worm was aware that he had his death-wound, he lashed out head and tail so that all things that were before him were broken to pieces. So when Fafnir had his death-wound, he asked "Who are you? And who is your father? And who are your kin that you were so hardy as to bear weapons against me?" . . .

"I am Sigurd, the son of Sigmund," answered the hero. . . .

"Ride to my lair then," said Fafnir, "and you shall find gold enough to suffice you for all your days; yet that gold shall be your bane and the bane of everyone who owns it." . . . And therewithal Fafnir died.

19. . . . Then Sigurd went his way and roasted Fafnir's heart on a rod, and when the blood bubbled out, he laid his finger on it to test if it were fully done, and then he set his finger in his mouth, and lo, when the heart-blood of the worm touched his tongue, straightway he understood the speech of birds and heard how the woodpeckers chattered in the brush beside him. . . . Then Sigurd ate some of Fafnir's heart, and the remnant he kept. Then he leapt on his horse and rode along the trail of the worm, Fafnir, right unto his hiding place, and he found it open and beheld that all the doors and the beams of the house were wrought of iron, and it was dug down deep into the earth. There found Sigurd gold exceeding plenteous and the sword called Rotti, and he took the Helm of Awe, and the Gold Byrny, and many things fair and good.

Questions: How does the attitude toward shape-shifting in the saga compare with the view of shape-shifting in the early Christian tradition? What is the implicit definition of "magic" in the context of the saga? What is the relationship between the gods and humans? What role do women play in the saga?

47. MAGIC AS A CAUTIONARY TALE:
CAESARIUS OF HEISTERBACH

Caesarius of Heisterbach (c. 1180–c. 1240) was a prior in the Cistercian Abbey of Heisterbach near Oberdollendorf in the German Rhineland. He is best known for his Dialogue on Miracles, *which comprises 746 stories written in the form of dialogues between a monk and his novice. The work was widely distributed as a reference book for preachers needing material for sermons. Magic and demons make brief appearances in the dialogues' cautionary tales. His miracle stories cover myriad topics, but Caesarius is not concerned about magic, except inasmuch as it helps him prove a point about other themes important to him, such as pride. His Devil is more like the pitiable demons of the early Middle Ages than the Devil of Thomas Aquinas (1225–1274).*

Source: trans. Henry von Essen Scott and Charles Cooke Swinton Bland, Caesarius of Heisterbach, *The Dialogue on Miracles*, Broadway Medieval Library, 2 vols. (London: George Routledge & Sons, Ltd., 1929), vol. 1, pp. 318–20, 327, 366–68; vol. 2, pp. 180–81.

Book 5

4. . . . . There were in Toledo many scholars from different countries studying the art of necromancy, and among them some young men from Swabia and Bavaria. They, hearing from their master certain stupendous and incredible statements, and determined to search out the truth, said to him, "Master, we beg you to give us ocular demonstration of what you have been telling us so that we may gain some result of our studies."

He tried to put them off, but failed owing to the persistence of their national character, and so at the proper hour, he took them into a field, drew a circle round them, and warned them, under the penalty of death, to remain within the circle and not to give anything to any who might ask or take anything from any who might offer. Then he withdrew a little way from them and called the demons by his incantations. Immediately they showed themselves under the appearance of well-armed soldiers practicing their military games around the youths. At one time they would pretend to fall, at another they would stretch out their lances and swords against them, trying in every way to induce them to leave the circle. When they found that this was of no avail, they changed themselves into very beautiful girls and danced about them, inviting the young men with every kind of alluring movement. One of them, more beautiful than the rest, chose out one of the scholars, and as often as she danced up to him, held out a gold ring inflaming him to love both by inward suggestion and by the outward motion of the body. When she had done this over and over again, the youth was at last overcome and put his finger outside the circle to receive the ring, and immediately she drew him out by that finger and disappeared with him.

As soon as the quarry was caught, the whole assembly of fiends became a whirling mist. The scholars raised an outcry, the master ran up, and they all complained to him of the loss of their companion. He answered, "It is not my fault; you urged me to this. I told you what would happen; you will never see him again." They at once rejoined, "Unless you get him back for us, we will kill you." Then afraid for his life; for he knew what madmen Bavarians are, he answered, "I will try if there may be any hope for him." Then he summoned the chief of the band of demons, reminded him of all his faithful service, and told him that this would be a great blow to his teaching and that he himself would be killed by his pupils if the youth were not restored. The Devil was moved with compassion and replied, "Tomorrow I will hold a council in such a place for your sake; you must be present, and if you can in any way get him back by the vote of the meeting, I shall be pleased."

Why should I say more? The council of the fiends met at the command of the chief, and the master made his complaint of the violence done to his disciple. The adversary replied, "Sir, I have done him neither wrong nor violence, he was disobedient to his master; he did not keep the law of the circle." While they thus disputed, the leader spoke to a certain demon, his coadjutor as to the decision they were to give. "Oliver, you were always a good counsellor; you are never a respecter of persons in defiance of justice; solve the question of this dispute." The other replied, "I decide that the youth should be restored to his master," and turning at once to the adversary he said, "You must give him back because you were too importunate." The others gave assent to this decision, and at the command of the judge, the scholar was at once brought back from hell and restored to his master, the council was broken up, and the master returned to his disciples rejoicing in the booty he had recovered. . . .

NOVICE: If we may judge from what is said of this Oliver, it would seem that all demons are not equally malicious.

MONK: In those, who in heaven cherished the most intense pride and envy against the creator, there flourishes even now the bitterest eagerness to do harm. It is said that some simply consented to join the others, who with Lucifer rebelled against God, and while these fell with the rest, yet they are less evil, and do men less harm. . . .

7. The following story was told me by a worthy citizen, who assured me that it actually happened in his own time at Mainz, if my memory serves me. A priest was going round his church and sprinkling the people with holy water, and

when he came to the door of the church, he met there, striding haughtily, in came a matron dressed out with all kinds of adornments, as gay as a peacock, and on her skirts, which she was dragging far behind her, he saw a number of demons sitting. They were as small as dormice and as black as Ethiopians, grinning and clapping their hands and leaping hither and thither like fish enclosed in a net; for in truth feminine extravagance is a net of the Devil. Now when he saw this chariot of demons he bade the woman wait outside, called the congregation to come to the door and adjured the devils not to move. She stood there in terror while he prayed that the people might have grace to see the vision, and because he was a good and upright man, his prayer was granted. When the woman realized that the extravagance of her dress had thus made her an object of mockery to demons, she went home and changed her dress, and thus, that vision became an occasion of humility both to her and all the other women.

36. A demon once took the form of a respectable young man and went to a knight and offered himself as a servant. The latter being much taken both with his appearance and manner of speech, gladly accepted the offer, and forthwith the demon began his service so diligently and respectfully, so faithfully and willingly that the knight was pleased beyond all expectation. Never did he mount his horse nor descend from it but he found his servant always ready to hold the stirrup on bended knee, and always and in all things he showed himself full of discretion, foresight and cheerfulness.

One day they were riding together and had come to the bank of a great river, when the knight, looking back, saw a number of his mortal enemies in pursuit and said to his servant, "We are dead men. See, my enemies are hastening after me; the river bars the way before us, and there is no way of escape. They will either kill me or take me prisoner." The other answered, "Sir, have no fear; I know well a ford of this river; only follow me, and we shall easily escape." The knight objected that no man had ever forded that river at that point, but nevertheless in the hope of escape he followed his servant, and came safe to the other side. As soon as they were safely across, the knight's enemies reached the bank, and said in wonder, "Whoever heard of a ford on this river? None but the Devil could have carried him across," and they went home in fear.

Later it happened that the knight's wife fell sick with a mortal illness, and when all the skill of the physicians proved useless, the demon said to his master, "If my lady would allow herself to be anointed with the milk of a lioness, she would be cured at once." When the knight said, "Where can such milk be got? " He replied, "I will get it." He went away and came back in an hour bringing with him a vessel full of milk. The lady was anointed with this and immediately grew better and soon recovered all her former strength. Then the knight asked the servant where he had got the milk so quickly, and he said, . . . "Do not trouble yourself about that, for I am just your serving man."

The knight persisted, and at last the servant confessed, "I am a demon, one of those who fell with Lucifer." Then his master, more astounded than ever said, "If you are a devil by nature, how do you come to serve a man so faithfully?" The demon answered, "It is my greatest consolation to be with the sons of men." Then said the knight, "But I do not dare to use your service any longer," and he replied, "Be quite sure of this that, if you keep me, no harm shall ever come to you through me or because of me." "No, I do not dare," said the other," but anything that you like to ask as a reward, I will gladly give you, even to the half of my property. Never did man serve man so well and faithfully; it was by your providing that I escaped death at the river, and it was through you that my wife recovered her health." Then the demon said, "Since I may no longer be with you, I ask nothing for my service except only five gold pieces." When he had received these, he gave them back to the knight with these words, "I beg that with this money you will buy a bell, and hang it over the roof of that poor forsaken church that at least by it the faithful may be invited to the divine office each Sunday." And he saw the demon no more.

Book 10

11. . . . [A pious knight named Albert Scothart], before taking the vows, was so vigorous a soldier and so famous in war that almost all the nobles of our land rivaled one another in sending him gifts, such as warhorses and costly garments, so as to win his friendship. One day as a girl of twelve years old, the daughter of a knight, sitting in a church was being exorcised by monks, breaking out into a laugh she cried, "See, here comes my friend, here comes my friend." . . . Now he was dressed in slashed scarlet and coming up to her he said, "Am I your friend?" To which the Devil replied by the mouth of the girl, "Yes, my best friend, for you do everything I want." . . . When the Devil said, "If you want me to go with you, let me enter into your body." The knight replied, "You shall certainly not enter into me." And the Devil said, "Let me sit on your saddle." And when the knight refused the Devil begged for a place on some part of the horse or the bridle, but to all the knight said "no."

Again, the Devil said to him, "I cannot run afoot. If you wish me to go with you, give me at least some place near your person." Now the knight, feeling pity for the girl possessed of the Devil, said to him, "If you will leave her, I will allow you one opening in my coat on condition that you in no wise harm me and only stay with me while I am on my way to the tournament. When I give you the order, you will go of your own free will and without dispute." And the Devil took an oath and said, "I will not harm you, but advance you." And going out of the girl he leapt into the opening of the knight's coat, passing with marvelous speed.

From that hour, such glory came to the knight in the tournaments that he overthrew whom he would with his lance and at will took captives. Wherever he went, the Devil went too, and they talked with one another. When the knight prayed too long in church, the other would say, "Now you are mumbling overmuch." When he sprinkled himself with holy water, again the Devil would say, "Mind you touch me not." And the knight said to him, "If a single drop touches you, I shall be sorry." At the time when the cross was being preached and the knight entered a church to take it, the Devil strove to draw him back saying, "What are you doing here?" The knight replied, "I propose to serve God and to renounce you. Therefore, flee from me." When the knight said that, Satan answered, "What have I done to displease you? I have never hurt, but enriched you. Through me you have become exceedingly famous. Yet I cannot remain with you without your consent, for so I promised." Then said the knight: "Behold, I now take the cross, and I adjure you in the name of the crucified to leave me and never to return." And the Devil left him.

Questions: What point is Caesarius making in each of the miracle stories above, and how does his use of demons and the Devil help him make the point? How much of a threat do the devils pose to the other characters in the vignette? Why are some demons more menacing than others?

48. A SAINTLY DOG AND THE CHANGELINGS

In the early thirteenth century, several mendicant religious orders of friars were founded. The mendicants differed from older monastic establishments in that the brothers were itinerant and not bound to one community. They traveled and lived primarily in urban areas and adopted a lifestyle of exacting poverty. Their calling was to minister to the poor and, through preaching and evangelism, to impress upon a growing wealthy urban population a return to apostolic purity in worship, practice, and belief.

Étienne de Bourbon (c. 1180–1261) was a Dominican friar who promoted the crusades and virulently opposed heresy. Shortly after 1235, Étienne was recruited by the Inquisition, and he was very active for many years as a preacher and inquisitor throughout France. He is best known for his preacher's manual, Of the Seven Gifts of the Holy Spirit, *which was unfinished when he died. Many of the events described in the text are drawn from Étienne's years of practical experience or from stories related to him.*

One such story of Saint Guinefort opens a window onto peasant life, Christian devotion, and magic. Sorcery enters the account when the mothers suspect that their children are changelings, a common motif in folklore and folk religion. A changeling baby was believed to be a fairy (or demon) child who was left in place of a human infant stolen by the fairies. If a child was born weak or sickly, a mother often suspected her infant had been taken and substituted with the changeling.

Source: trans. G.G. Coulton, *Life in the Middle Ages*, vol. 1 (New York, The Macmillan Company, 1930), pp. 92–94.

Dishonorable to God are all superstitions which attribute divine honors to the demons or to any other creatures, as idolatry does, and as those wretched witches do who seek health by adorning elder trees or making offerings to them, in contempt of the churches and the relics of saints. Some misguided rustics carry their children to trees or to ant hills or to other places for health's sake. So they did lately in the diocese of Lyons, where I preached against witchcraft and heard confessions. Many women confessed they had taken their children to Saint Guinefort; whereof I enquired, supposing him to be some true saint, and at last I heard that he was a certain greyhound who came to his death in the following way.

In the diocese of Lyons, near the nuns' town called Villeneuve, on the lands of the lord de Villars, was a certain castle where the lord had one little boy by his wife. One day he and his lady and the nurse had gone out, leaving the child alone in his cradle, and a vast serpent glided into the house. The hound, seeing this, followed the snake in all haste even beneath the cradle which they overturned in their struggles, for the dog gnawed upon the serpent which strove to defend itself and bit him in turn. Yet at length the dog slew it and cast it far from the child, after which he stood then by the bloody cradle and the bloodstained earth with his own head and jaws all bloody, for the serpent had dealt roughly with him. Hereupon the nurse came in, and at this sight, believing that the hound had slain and devoured the child, she cried aloud in lamentation; hearing which the mother hastened to the spot, and saw, and believed and cried likewise. The knight also came and believed the same; wherefore, drawing his sword, he slew the hound. Then, coming to the child, they found him unhurt and softly sleeping, and seeking further, they found the dead serpent all torn to pieces by the hound's teeth. Wherefore, recognizing the truth, and grieving that they had so unjustly slain this hound which had done them so great a kindness, they put him into a well right by the castle gate, and placed an immense heap of stones over him, and planted trees by the spot as a memorial of his deed.

But God so willed that this castle should be destroyed and the land made desert and left without inhabitants. Wherefore the country folk, hearing of that dog's prowess and how he lost his guiltless life for a deed that deserved so great a reward, flocked to that place and honored the hound as a martyr, praying to him for their sicknesses and necessities. This all came to pass at the instigation of the Devil, who oftentimes deluded them there, that he might thus lead men into error. More especially the women who had weak or sickly children were wont to bring them to that spot, and they used to take an old woman from a town that lay a league distant, who would teach them the due rites of offering to the demons and calling upon their name, and would guide them to that place. When they were come thither, they offered salt with other oblations, and hung the child's clothes upon the bushes around. They then thrust a needle into the wood which grew over the spot and thrust the naked child through a hole between two tree-trunks—the mother standing on one side to hold him and casting him nine times into the hands of the hag who stood on the other side. They called with demoniacal invocations upon the hobgoblins which haunted that forest of Rimita, and beseeched them to take the child (who, as they said, belonged to the fiends) and bring back their own child whom the fiends had carried off—fat and feeling well and safe and sound.

After this these murderous mothers took the child, and they laid him naked at the foot of the tree upon the straw of his cradle, and, taking two candles an inch long, they lit them at both ends from a fire which they had brought thither, and fixed them upon the trunk overhead. Then they would withdraw so far that the candles might burn out and they themselves might neither see nor hear the wailing babe. And thus, these white-hot candles would often burn the children alive, as we found there in certain cases. Moreover, one woman told me how, when she had called upon the hobgoblins and was withdrawing from the spot, she saw a wolf come forth from the forest towards the child, whom he would have devoured (or a devil in wolf's form, as she said), if her motherly love had not driven her to prevent him. After the candles had burned down, if, returning to the child, the mother found her son still living, then she would take him to a nearby stream of rushing water called Chalaronne, wherein nine times she plunged that child, who indeed must have had the toughest of bowels to live through this ordeal, or at least not to die soon afterwards. Wherefore we went to that place and called together the folk of that country and preached against this custom. We caused the dead hound to be dug up and the grove to be cut down and burned together with the dog's bones, and we persuaded the lords of that country to issue an edict threatening confiscation of property and public sale against all who should thenceforth resort to that same place for this purpose.

Questions: From Étienne's point of view, which of the villagers' behaviors and beliefs are objectionable? How might the concept of changelings help a peasant mother cope when her newborn is sickly and likely to die? If a child dies during the rigors of the changeling ritual, what assumption does the mother make about the child?

49. *PICATRIX*: ARABIC MAGIC

Picatrix, meaning "the goal of the wise," was one of the most famous and influential handbooks of astral magic of the late Middle Ages and Renaissance and a mainstay of Hermetic literature. The identity of the author/compiler is in dispute, as is the date of composition; most estimates place the text in the mid-eleventh century. Picatrix *originated as an esoteric Arabic work written in Moorish-controlled Spain and was translated into Castilian Spanish c. 1256 (and shortly after into Latin) when Alfonso X (the Wise) of Castile (1221–1284) took an interest in it. "Picatrix" sometimes refers to the author of the compilation as well as the compilation itself. The author/compiler of this somewhat unwieldy handbook of talismanic and celestial magic claims to have synthesized 224 older works on astrology, drawing from Indian, Persian, Arab, and Hellenistic sources.*

Picatrix was revered for its philosophical, theological, poetic, and practical dimensions. Part of the allure was, and is, its reconciliation of metaphysical and otherworldly systems: the entire universe is one of divine origins and suffused with soul, which is superior to matter. Stars are composed of the purest spiritual essence, and their numinous energy can be harnessed through talismans and brought to earth to work upon matter. Everything that exists or happens on earth has a relationship to the heavens. Picatrix's cosmological program strips magic of it diabolical agency. Those who consulted it would likely have interpreted the talismans as benign or sublime natural magic, yet even to own a copy of this occult text was forbidden by the Inquisition and very dangerous.

Source: trans. Hashem Atallah, *Picatrix (Ghayat Al-Hakim)*, vol. 1 ed. William Kiesel (Seattle: Ouroboros Press, 2002), pp. 11–12, 19, 29, 44–45, 67–68, 128–29, 132, 133, 139, 143.

Book 1

2. You may know that this conclusion is what is termed as magic. Magic is, in fact, everything that absolutely fascinates minds and attracts souls by means of words and deeds. This fascination and attraction are demonstrated by exclamation, following, listening, and approval. They are difficult for the mind to perceive, and their causes are veiled from the simpleton. That is because it is a divine force associated with advanced reasons for the purpose of understanding it. What I am working on is a vague discipline. Its subject is a spirit within a spirit that includes analysis and imagination. A talisman is a spirit within a body, while chemistry is a body within a body. In summary, the causes of magic are beyond the understanding of the majority and it is difficult to invent.

The fact about a talisman is that its name is reversed (The letters of the word talisman in Arabic are "*talsam*," and when this combination is reversed, it becomes "*maslat*," which means domination, control); it is domination because its essence is coercion and control. It functions according to the purpose it was composed for: overpowering and coercing by using numerical ratios and placing astrological secrets in certain bodies at appropriate times and by using incenses that are powerful and capable of bringing out the spirit of that talisman. . . .

I would like to go back to our topic to state that magic is limited to two branches: theoretical and practical. The science of magic deals with knowing the positions of fixed planets, the location of their pictures, the manner by which they cast their light on orbiting planets, and the astrological ratios. These are the elements to be known in order to achieve what you are looking for. Under the science of magic, all options and talismans were dealt with and discussed by our forbearers. You may know that he who chooses to do this, will have delved in magic. This is necessary. The best art of the scientific magic is speech. . . .

4. Then when the people needed to make talismans, they found that they must know the planets' direct ratios, affecting their spreading functions, which are the essence of making talismans. . . . What determines whether work is good or bad depends on whether the overlooking planets are bad luck or good luck planets. If the ascendant was in a straight-ascending constellation, but a bad luck planet was looking over it, or there was bad luck in it, that will damage the work and make it very difficult. But if it was in a curved-ascending constellation, and a good luck planet was looking over it, or if there is good luck in it, that will make work easy. Similarly, if the daytime and night time constellations ascend in a different form; that is if the daytime constellations ascend at night and the night time constellations at daytime and the good luck planets are looking over them, work will progress, but if the bad luck constellations are looking over, it will become more evil. . . .

5. Another condition is to isolate yourself from human beings, to shelter yourself from the sunrise and the sunlight, and not to be visited by anybody except those who have good intentions, trustworthy, not belittling or scorning the ugly, astounding, and forceful effects of the astrological spiritual powers. Be aware of that. You may review what Tabit ibn Qurra [c. 836–901] wrote in his *Treatise on Talismans*, "The noblest science of stars is the science of talismans." He claims that there is no life in the body that does not have a spirit. He means that talismans made in the wrong manner and for the wrong purpose will not be compatible with the radiating spirit of the planets. Accordingly, they are similar to dead bodies that have no spirits in them. However, if the spirits of the celestial bodies agree, by virtue of their configuration and make-up, with such arrangements that lead to the sought objective, then they will be similar to living bodies that can do strange things. . . .

The people who specialize in this field agree on the necessity of associating the words used in making talismans for special purposes, appealing to have those effects accepted. In this regard, the philosopher in *Timaeus* [Plato, c. 428/427-348/347 BCE], indicates that talking to talismans represents the relationship of the soul to the body; it moves the spiritual powers, especially when the speaker talks with a sound intention. This is the noble element with which all talismans can be made. This means that what you say must agree with the meaning of the spoken words inasmuch as the talisman maker gathers of his conscious and mental strength. . . .

Book 2

1. . . . Going back to our objective, I would like to say that no one can find out how the higher world affects the lower world without having full knowledge of the different branches of philosophy; I mean the mathematical, physical, and metaphysical arts. He who falls short in acquiring these sciences will not be able to fulfill his real goal because the primary perquisites of knowledge are taken from these three branches of philosophy. As for the mathematical art, without numbers, the movements of the higher bodies and the methods by which geometry is obtained cannot be learned. Furthermore, mathematical survey is a prerequisite for learning the geometry of the celestial bodies; without it, star observation or their measurements, which are primarily derived from the proofs of mathematical survey, will be impossible to learn. Moreover, the art of matching, by which similarity and difference can be recognized, is necessary for learning the similarities between celestial and earthly bodies and which of the high bodies' behavior is similar to which of those on earth. How can anyone match between things that are similar if he does not command that knowledge? . . .

10. Images on Stones

The images of the ☉ carved on a pure red segment of onyx portray the ☉ as a king sitting on a chair with a crown on his head, holding the figure of a crow in his hands and under his feet are the following letters: o | ♋. The holder of this segment will triumph over all kings. This was presented in *The Interpretation of Spiritual Talismans* by Picatrix. He claims that the ☉ will be at its highest rank.

Some of these figures are presented in Aristotle's [384–322 BCE] advice to Alexander. He says that whoever carves an image of a lion, with this figure: △ on a segment of onyx, while the ascendant is ♌ and the ☉, cleared of all *nuhus*, . . . will never be defeated. Moreover, he will fulfill all his wishes and will never have frightening dreams. Additionally, if you carve a picture of a woman sitting on a carriage pulled by four horses with a mirror in her right hand, a whip in her left hand, seven candles on her head and a pool inside the onyx stone, if you carve these images when the ☉ is at its highest rank, you will gain the respect and fear of everyone you come across or meet. . . .

Hermes [mythical Hellenistic sage] mentions in his book, *Al-Haditus*, that whoever carves on a stone called *samalinun*—a yellow stone with black spots, green marks, light and shiny—a figure of a fly in the hour of the ☉ and its ascendant and holds onto it, he will not be burned by fire even if he gets into it. He claims that this stone is available in Persia. . . .

Moreover, carve a picture of a woman with a wrapped rope in her hand. Her body is striped with fuzz-like stripes. She holds in the other hand a fruit that looks like an apple with which she stamps wax to cure children from their disease and all other ailments. This is to be done in the hour when ♀ is ascendant.

Furthermore, carve a picture of the head of a zebra with the head of a fly on it on a granite stone. The head should be a little oversized. This ought be done in the hour and ♀ is ascendant. The stone is used to stamp wax for increased production. This has been successfully experimented in labyrinths.

Mercury

The Interpretation of Spiritual Talismans states that for releasing prisoners and the like, carve on a stone of crystallite the picture of a man sitting on a chair with a rooster on his head. His legs are those of an eagle, a torch in his hand and the following symbols are under his feet: ⊥∘T∘T. This is to be done in the hour and honor of ☿. . . .

You may also carve in any of its stones the picture of a rabbit in the ascendant of ♎ and while ♄ is 13° from ♊ and the ☉ 5° from ♋. Draw around it these symbols: ᴎᓎᱮᓎᒯᴎᒲᵖ; then mount the stone on a ring and wear it. The woman with whom you have a sexual relationship will not get pregnant from you.

II. . . . Many people do not appreciate the time it takes the astrologer to study and research this science. Since we know that this time is beyond the limits of the celestial sphere itself, how can we expect it to be within the capabilities of the astrologer? If he reaches the right conclusion, he will not be commended, but, if he fails, he will be insulted. Therefore, you should not reveal this secret to the public. The wise achieved these spiritual arts only through hard work, long tiring effort and sharp intellect. . . .

Questions: What is "magic," according to Picatrix? *Why should philosophers take pains to hide the knowledge of astrological magic from "simpletons"? What factors make the use or effectiveness of talismans challenging? What is the relationship among soul, body, and talismans? What are the general kinds of concerns that the talismans address? What type of people or class of society made talismans?*

50. ASTRONOMY: NATURAL MAGIC OR NECROMANCY?

The authorship of The Mirror of Astronomy *is uncertain, but most scholars attribute the treatise to Albert the Great (c. 1200–1280). One goal of the text is to defend astronomy systematically as a branch of learning compatible with Christian theology. This project spoke to contemporary disagreement over whether natural philosophy and learned magic were demonic necromancy in disguise.*

A decade or so after The Mirror of Astronomy was written, the controversy escalated to the point that the University of Paris issued the Condemnations of 1277, which contained 219 propositions forbidding astrology as a prognostic tool. The impetus behind the condemnations was, to a large extent, a reaction against the recent influx of Aristotelian philosophy into European universities. There was some unease that Aristotle, a pagan, had an inappropriate sway over Christian thinkers. The author of The Mirror hoped to reconcile God's omniscience with the influence of the stars on the terrestrial region. He argued that God transmitted his celestial energy through the nine upper spheres of creation down to the sublunar realm. Note the familiar notion that the moon represents the division between the higher and lower realms and that humans live out their lives in the murky atmosphere of the tenth sphere. For the author, the zodiac can predict physical conditions and actions but does not affect the soul. The Mirror of Astrology was widely influential and became the standard reference book in the debate about astrology from the thirteenth to fifteenth centuries.

Source: trans. Paola Zambelli, *The* Speculum astronomiae *and Its Enigma: Astrology, Theology and Science in Albert Magnus and His Contemporaries,* Boston Studies in the Philosophy of Science, vol. 135 (Dordrecht: Kluwer Academic Publishers, 1992), pp. 209, 219, 223, 229, 231, 241, 243, 247, 257, 259, 261, 263, 265, 267, 269, 271, 273.

Proem

On account of certain books, which lack the essentials of science (and) which, since they are hostile to the true wisdom (that is, our Lord Jesus Christ who is the image of the father and his wisdom, by whom he the father made the secular world) are rightly suspect by the lovers of the Catholic Faith, it has pleased some great men to accuse some other books which are perhaps innocent. For, since many of the previously mentioned books, by pretending to be concerned with astrology disguise necromancy, they cause noble books written on the same (subject, astrology) to be contaminated in the eyes of good men, and render them offensive and abominable. Therefore, a certain man zealous for faith and philosophy, (putting) each in its proper place, of course, has applied his mind towards making a list of both types of books, showing their number, titles, *incipits* [first few words of a text] and the contents of each in general, and who their authors were, so that the permitted ones might be separated from the illicit ones, and he undertook to speak according to the will of God.

1. There are two great wisdoms and each is defined by the name of astronomy. The first of these deals with (1) the science of the configuration of the first heaven; and with the nature of its motion about the poles of the equator of day (and night), and with the heavens placed beneath it, which are placed on other

poles away from the first. These are the heavens of the fixed and wandering stars, whose configuration is like the configuration of spheres enclosing one another. It also deals (2) with the science of drawing circles on them (the heavens). . . .

[T]he more useful books of astronomy concerning motion [are] found in the Latin language; for the *Perspectiva* of Aristotle does not descend to the (subjects) mentioned above. And these are the books, which if they are removed from the sight of men wanting (to study them), a great and truly noble part of philosophy will be buried at least for a certain time, that is, until it would rise again due to a sounder attitude; for, as Thebit, the son of Chora [Arab astronomer], says, "There is no light in geometry when astronomy has been removed." And the readers of the aforementioned books already know that not even a single word is found in them that might be or might seem to be against the honor of the Catholic faith; nor, perhaps, is it fair that those who have never touched these (books), should presume to judge them.

4. This wisdom, then, is divided into two parts. The first (part) is introductory and is concerned with the principles of (astrological) judgments. But the second part is fulfilled in the exercise of making judgments, and this (second part) is further divided into four sections. The first is concerned with revolutions (of the years); the second with nativities [birthdays], the third with interrogations, (and) the fourth with choosing favorable hours—to which that section which deals with images is subjoined, of which it is said, "The most sublime part of astronomy is the science of images." But those cursed necromantic books on images, illusions and characters, rings and sigils [seals] are associated with this part (of the science) because they (the necromancers) borrow certain astronomical observations for themselves for the purpose of simulation in order to render themselves (as) slightly credible. By the will of God, I will disclose their poison in what follows, but for now let me return to the introductory part and the other (sections) in (their) order, as promised.

7. . . . The second part, however, concerning the revolution of the years of the world consists (1) in the knowledge of the signifier at the hour of the entrance of the sun into the first minute of the sign of Aries; (this signifier) is called the Lord of the Year; (that is, the disposer by the command of God). And (2) from the knowledge of the (Lord of the Year) and the aspect of the planets to it, (and) also from the impediment and the (good) fortune of each one (of the planets), together with the knowledge of the lots and their latitude amongst the twelve signs and their rising and setting, (and) also their direct and retrograde motion. (All this) indicates what God, glorious and sublime, will produce in a given year, using the stars as if they were instruments, on the rich men of some climes and on the whole of their common populace with respect to the high or low price of grain, war or peace, earthquake and floods, falling stars and terrible prodigies, and other events which happen in this world; (3) as well as what may

come to pass due to the effects of the fixed stars in the revolution of the year of the world; and what the ascending and descending (lunar) nodes and the stars which are called comets may signify. . . .

11. As I have said, the science of images is added to the part on elections, not any of them (the images) whatsoever, however, but only the astronomical ones, since images are made in three ways. One way is abominable—(that) which requires suffumigations [applying fumes] and invocation, such as the images of Toz the Greek and Germath the Babylonian, which have stations for the worship of Venus, (and) the images of Balenuz and Hermes, which are exorcized by using the 54 names of the angels, who are said to be subservient to the images of the moon in its orbit, (but) perhaps are instead the names of demons, and seven names are incised on them in the correct order to affect a good thing and in inverse order for a thing one wants to be repelled. They are also suffumigated with the wood of aloe, saffron, and balsam for a good purpose; and with galbanum, red sandalwood and resin for an evil purpose.

The spirit is certainly not compelled (to act) because of these (names and fumigations), but when God permits it on account of our own sins, they (the spirits) show themselves as (if they were) compelled to act, in order to deceive men. This is the worst (kind of) idolatry, which, in order to render itself credible to some extent, observes the 28 mansions of the moon and the hours of day and night along with certain names (given) to these days, hours and mansions themselves. May this method be far from us, for far be it that we show that (sort of) honor to the creature which is due (solely) to the creator.

There is another method (of making images) that is somewhat less unsuitable—(but it is nevertheless detestable), which is effected by means of inscribing characters which are to be exorcized by certain names, such as the four rings of Solomon, and the nine candles and three figures of the spirits (who are called the princes of the four regions of the world), and the Almandal of Solomon, and the sigil for those possessed by demons. Further (there are) the seven names from the book of Muhameth, and the other fifteen from the same, and, in addition, (there are) the names from the *Liber institutionis* (*The Book of Instruction*) which is said to be by Raziel [the Angel of Mysteries], namely of the earth, the sea, the air and the fire, of the winds, and of the cardines of the world, (and) also of the signs and the planets and of their angels, according to which each thing takes a different name in the triplicites [three signs of the same element] of the day and the night. May this method also be far from us; for it is suspected that something lies under the names of the unknown language that might be against the honor of the Catholic faith.

These are the two sorts of necromantic images, which (as I have said) have presumed to usurp the noble name of astronomy for themselves, and a long time ago I inspected many of these books, but since I shrank with horror from them, I do not have perfect memory regarding their number, titles, *incipits* or contents or their authors. In fact, my spirit was never tranquil when dealing with these (matters); all the same, I wanted to observe them well while passing over them so that, at least, I might not be ignorant of how to ridicule their wretched believers. . . . The third type is (that) of astronomical images, which eliminates this filth [of necromancy], does not have suffumigations or invocations and does not allow exorcisms or the inscription of characters, but obtains (its) virtue solely from the celestial figure. . . .

13. . . . I turn now to nativities, which seems to be the section that offends free will more severely than the other parts, so (much so) that it even seems that (the two) might destroy each other mutually, nor do they seem to be compatible in any respect, especially as far as that part which pertains to the character of the soul is concerned. For, with regard to the knowledge of the length of the native's [the person whose horoscope is being considered] life by means of the degree of the *hylech* [giver of life] and the planet which is the *alchochoden* [dignified essence of the *hylech*], it has already been said that the judgment cannot be made about how long he (the native) ought to live by necessity, but about the time beyond which his life is not [to] be extended naturally, for the days of a man can be shortened, but not increased. . . . [The knowledge learned from the stars provides information so that a person can prepare for what is about to befall.]

14. I pass on to interrogations . . . concerning future possibilities, [some of which] have greater uncertainty than others; such as, those which concern things which are completely subjected to free will. For some things are possible and future, which, nonetheless, no one's will can impede, such as a question concerning the high or low price of grain in the coming year (although this can be known more certainly from the revolution of the year, or a question about) whether someone might acquire wealth from his profession or from business, or whether a certain man might acquire this or that kingdom, and so on in this manner. Because such events do happen to a man due to the significa-tion of his own nativity [horoscope], because when he asked (questions about himself, he) was moved by heaven according to a radical intention, (namely, that) due to his nativity, he has already come to the good or evil which his nativity signified. For the concern of a man at the hour of the interrogation, will be in accordance with the situation of the (zodiacal) circle (of his nativ-ity); and the circle at that hour is in accordance with his (own) intention. . . . [I]n those things which God operates by means of the heavens; the indication of heaven is nothing other than divine providence. In those things, indeed, which we initiate, nothing prevents (the fact) that there is also not a cause in heaven, but a signification. For of the two sides of a dilemma from which man can choose one or the other, God knew from eternity which of these he (the man) would choose. . . .

15. . . . But all philosophers are in agreement on this point, (namely,) that when we know the hour of the impregnation of some woman, we may know, by means of that hour, what might happen with regard to the fetus until (the time when) it is quickened or what (will happen) until it is delivered from the uterus, and, perhaps, what (will happen), until its death. For astrologers have not judged (these things) by means of nativities, only because the exact hour of conception can rarely be verified. . . . Why, therefore, when the wife of a king or prince or magnate exists in the optimum conditions, do we not choose for her husband the hour for getting a child from her, if the creator of all generation allows, so that good things might come to him when he is born, which the astrologer could predict as (being) about to happen from the series of books of nativities? . . . And if we know in addition to this that they ought to be struck by the aspect of both malefic (planets), that is, Saturn or Mars, because Saturn fixes medicine and Mars draws it to the blood. . . .

Again, in the profession of surgery, why shall I not take care not to make an incision in a limb when the moon is in a sign which has significance over that limb? For at that time, the limb is very rheumatic and pain provokes rheum. And I have the courage to say that I myself have seen, as it were, an infinite number of inconveniences happen as a result of this. I have seen a man who was an expert in astronomy and medicine, who due to the threat of angina, bled himself from (his) arm while the moon was in Gemini, which has significance for the arms, and without any apparent illness, except for a moderate inflammation of the arm, he died seven days later. I also knew a certain patient who was suffering from an ulcer near the head of his gut (and) was cut open by some miserable surgeon who was completely ignorant of both professions (namely, medicine and of the stars) while the moon was in Scorpio (which has significance over those parts) and without the cutting of a vein or some other reasonable cause, he was found dead in the arms of the men who were holding him within that very hour, and (his death) was attributed to the operations of heaven, since it did not seem to have occurred due to any cause that kills suddenly, such as obstructions in the ventricles of the brain or a lesion or failure of the air passages. . . .

17. Concerning those books, however, which are (truly) necromantic, without the prejudice of a better opinion, it seems that they ought to be put aside rather than destroyed. For perhaps the time is already at hand, when, for certain reasons about which I am now silent, it will be useful on occasion to have inspected them, but, nevertheless, their inspectors should be wary of using them. Moreover, there are certain experimental books whose names are coterminous with necromancy, such as (those which treat) geomancy, hydromancy, aerimancy, pyromancy, chiromancy [divination by sixteen geometric figures, water, atmosphere, fire, and palm reading], which really do not deserve to be called

sciences, but "garamancies." Of course, hydromancy (dealing with the washing of the interiors of animals and of inspecting their fibers) and pyromancy (dealing with the figure of a fire, by which the holocaust is consumed) undoubtedly do not exclude the appearance of idolatry.

I find nothing like this, however, in geomancy, since it relies on Saturn and the lord of the hour, which are put down as its root, and it rejoices to be based on the ratio of number, and there are many who bear testimony in its favor. But aerimancy is not like this; as it is frivolous even though it presumes to boast of the ratio of number. I really do not want to make a precipitous determination about chiromancy at the moment, perhaps because it is a part of physiognomy, which seems to be collected from the significations of the profession of the stars over the body and over the soul, while it makes conjectures about the character of the mind from the exterior figure of the body; not because the one might be the cause of the other, but because both are found to be caused by the same thing.

Questions: According to the Proem, what is the purpose of The Mirror of Astrology? *How does the author distinguish "true wisdom" of the stars from necromantic astrology? Are suffumigations and incantations effective in bringing forth demons? How does the author reconcile astrological predictions and free will? Why are astrological predictions based on a person's date of birth (nativity) a particularly sensitive subject?*

51. *THE GOLDEN LEGEND:* SAINTS AND DEVILS

The Golden Legend *is a compilation of the* vitae *of over 200 Christian saints that Jacobus de Voragine, the archbishop of Genoa (c. 1228–1298), collected. The text was a veritable best seller from its creation in about 1275 to the mid-sixteenth century, by which time it had been translated into virtually every European language. More than a thousand copies of the book are extant in various editions. The work was popular because of its simplicity, accessibility, and versatility; it was mined for private and public spiritual readings, sermons, and iconography. The sources for the saints commemorated in the seven volumes range from the earliest* vitae *of the church to medieval oral legends.*

Although magic and sorcery are rarely plot elements, a devil of some sort makes an appearance as an adversary of the saint in nearly every story in The Golden Legend. *The devils resemble the antagonists in earlier hagiography in that they are usually pitiful and inept creatures—impotent against the power of the cross. They form a vivid contrast to the insidious and dangerous nature of the Devil that was emerging at the time. The following tale is set in the reign of the Roman emperor, Diocletian [244–311].*

Source: trans. Frederick Startridge Ellis and William Caxton, Jacobus de Voragine, *The Golden Legend or Lives of the Saints*, ed. Frederick Startridge Ellis, vol. 5 (Philadelphia: Temple Classics, 1900), pp. 166–72; rev. Martha Rampton.

Volume 5. . . . Justina the virgin was of the city of Antioch and daughter of a priest of the idols. Every day she sat at a window listening to a [Christian] priest who read the Gospel, by whom, at the last, she was converted. And when her mother told her father just before he went to sleep, Jesus Christ appeared to him [in a dream] with his angels, saying, "Come to me; I shall give to you the kingdom of heaven." And when he awoke, they were baptized along with their daughter. And this virgin was strongly grieved and vexed by [a local magician named] Cyprian, but at last she converted him to the faith of Jesus Christ.

Cyprian from his childhood had been an enchanter; for from the time that he was seven years old he was consecrated by his parents to the Devil. And he used the craft of necromancy and made women turn into mares and beasts, as they seemed, and many other similar things. And he longed for the love of Justina, and burnt with desire for her, and resorted to his magic art that he might have her for himself or for a man named Acladius, who also burnt in love for her. Then he called upon a devil to the end that he might have Justina with the demon's help. And when the devil came he said to Cyprian, "Why have you called me?" And Cyprian said to him, "I love a virgin; can you not do something so that I may have my pleasure with her?" And the devil answered, "I was able to cast man out of paradise, persuade Cain to slay his brother, make the Jews slay Christ, and have troubled men; do you think I cannot cause a maid to come to you so that you can use her at your pleasure? Take this ointment and anoint her house with it, and I shall come and kindle her heart for your love, and I shall compel her to assent to you." And the next night, the devil went and moved her heart to unlawful love. And when she felt it, she devoutly put herself in God's hand and fortified herself with the sign of the cross, and the devil, afraid of the sign of the cross, fled away from her, and came again to Cyprian and stood before him. And Cyprian said to him, "Why have you not brought me this virgin?" And the devil said, "I saw in her a sign [of the cross] which frightened me so that all my strength failed me."

Then Cyprian left him and called another devil stronger than the first. And he said, "I have heard your commandment and have seen his powerlessness, but I shall amend it and accomplish your will." Then the devil went to her and endeavored to move her heart in love and inflame her courage in dishonest things. And she recommended herself to God devoutly, and put from herself that temptation by the sign of the cross and blew on the devil and threw him away from her. And he fled all confused and came to Cyprian, and Cyprian said to him, "Where is the maid that I sent you for?" And the devil said, "I acknowledge that I am overcome and am rebutted, and I shall say how; for I saw in her a sign horrible, and lost all my power."

Then Cyprian left him, and blamed him and called for the prince of the devils. And when he came he said, "Why is your strength so little, which is overcome by a maid?" Then the prince said to him, "I shall go and vex her with great fevers, and I shall inflame more ardently her heart, and I shall arouse and imbue her body with so ardent desire for you that she shall be frantic, and I shall offer to her so many things that I shall bring her to you at midnight." Then the Devil transfigured himself into the likeness of a maid and came to this holy virgin, and said, "I have come to you to live with you in chastity, and I ask that you say what reward we shall have [if we keep ourselves pure]." And the virgin answered, "The reward is great, and the labor is small." And the Devil said to her, "What is it then that God commanded when he said, 'Grow, and multiply, and replenish the earth?' Then, fair sister, if we abide in virginity we shall make the word of God vain and be also despising and disobedient for which we shall fall into a grievous judgment, where we shall have no hope of reward but shall run in great torment and pain." Then by the enticement of the Devil the heart of the virgin was smitten with evil thoughts and was greatly inflamed in desire for the sin of the flesh so that she would have relented, but then the virgin came to herself and considered who it was who spoke to her. And anon she blessed [her companion] with the sign of the cross and blew against the Devil, and he vanished away and melted like wax, and she was delivered from all temptation. . . .

And when the Devil saw that he profited nothing, he transfigured himself into the form of Justina in order to defame her. And to mock Cyprian, he approached saying that he was bringing Justina. Then the Devil came to Cyprian in the likeness of Justina and would have kissed him as if she had languished for his love. And when Cyprian saw him and supposed that it was Justina, he was full of joy, and said, "You are welcome, Justina, the fairest of all women." And when Cyprian called out the name Justina, the Devil could not suffer the name, but as soon as he heard it he vanished away as a fume or smoke. And when Cyprian saw himself deceived, he was heavy and sorrowful and was then more burning and desirous in the love of Justina. . . .

Then the Devil, being vanquished in all things, returned to Cyprian . . . and Cyprian said, "Tell me, I pray you, how it is that Justina has all this great might and strength." And the Devil said, "If you will swear to me that you will not depart from me nor forsake me, I shall show you her strength and her victory." Cyprian said, "By what oath shall I swear?" And the Devil said, "Swear by my great strength that you shall never depart from me." And Cyprian said, "I swear to you by your great strength that I shall never depart from you." Then the Devil said to him, weeping, "This maid makes the sign of the cross, and then we devils wax feeble and lose all our might and strength and flee from her as wax flees from the face of the fire." And Cyprian said then to him, "The crucified God is then greater than you?" And the Devil said, "Yea, certainly he is greater than all others. And all whom we deceive, he judges to be tormented with fire inextinguishable." And Cyprian said, "Then ought I to befriend him that was crucified, lest I fall here-after into such pains?" To which the Devil said, "You have sworn by the might and virtue of my strengths, which no man may forswear, that you shall never depart from me." To this Cyprian said, "I despise you, and forsake you and all your power, and renounce you and all your devils, and garnish and mark myself with the sign of the cross." And soon the Devil departed all confused.

Then Cyprian went to the bishop, and when the bishop saw him he thought that he had come to find fault with Christians, and the bishop said to him, "Let it suffice unto you, Cyprian . . . that nothing you do can prevail against the church of God, for the virtue of Jesus Christ is joined thereto and is not overcome. And Cyprian said, "I am certain that the virtue of our Lord Jesus Christ is not overcome," and then he recounted all that had happened and asked the bishop to baptize him. And after that, he profited much, as well in wisdom as in life. And when the bishop was dead, Cyprian was ordained bishop and placed the blessed virgin Justina with many virgins in a monastery and made her abbess over many holy virgins. Saint Cyprian then sent letters to martyrs and comforted them in their martyrdom.

The ruler of that country heard of the fame and renown of Cyprian and Justina, and he ordered them to present themselves before him and demanded that they sacrifice to pagan idols. And when he saw that they held stead-fastly to the faith of Jesus Christ, he commanded that they should be put in a caldron full of wax, pitch, and grease, burning and boiling. And all this refreshed them marvelously and did not cause them grief or pain. And the priest of the idols said to the provost of that place, "Command me, sire, to stand near the caldron by the fire, and I shall overcome all their virtue." And then he came before the caldron and said, "Great is the god Hercules and Jupiter, the father of gods." And at that point the great fire jumped from under the caldron and burnt and consumed him. Then Cyprian and Justina were taken out of the caldron and sentence was passed, and they were both beheaded together. Their bodies were thrown to hounds and lay exposed for seven days, and after they were taken up and transported to Rome, and it is said that now they rest at Placentia. And they suffered death in the seventh kalends of October, about the year of our Lord two hundred and eighty, under Diocletian.

Questions: What is the hierarchy among evil spirits? What powers do humans have over devils? Describe the tone of the descriptions of relationships between humans and devils. What moral do you think Jacobus de Voragine was hoping his readers would take away from this vignette?

52. HERESY VERSUS SORCERY

The Inquisition developed in the early thirteenth century in order to counter heresy, which refers to beliefs that were contrary to Catholic doctrine. The inquisitorial process involved bishops and other clerics questioning people in local populations about their views on established dogma.

Source: trans. Martha Rampton, from Joseph Hansen, *Quellen und Untersuchungen zur Geschichte des Hexenwahns und der Hexenverfolgung im Mittelalter* (Hildesheim: Georg Olms, 1963), p. 1.

Papal Decree, Pope Alexander IV

. . . It is the case that those charged with the affairs of the faith, which is the highest privilege, ought not interfere or hinder other business. That is, the inquisitors themselves commissioned by the see; ought not intervene in cases of divination or sorcery unless they savor of manifest heresy. Nor should they punish those who are engaged in these things, but leave them to other judges to decide how the offender should be corrected.

Question: How might "divination or sorcery" rise to the level of "manifest heresy"?

53. A NEW KIND OF DEVIL: THOMAS AQUINAS

Saint Thomas Aquinas (1225–1274) was an Italian Dominican friar and the most influential philosopher and theologian of his era. A doctor of the church, Aquinas was instrumental in promoting the concept of natural law and developing the scholastic method of inquiry. Given Aquinas's meticulous examination of all aspects of theology, it is not surprising that magic, the nature of evil, and demonology came under scrutiny, and given Aquinas's unparalleled reputation as a seminal thinker on faith and reason, it is equally unsurprising that his methodical appraisal of Satan and Satan's relationship to the world found fertile ground in medieval universities and became the standard for many centuries (although his works were controversial when he first wrote them). Aquinas's Satan differs from the patristic "Devil" in that he is more cunning, devious, menacing, powerful, and his knowledge increases over the eons. Whereas demons of the early medieval world were relatively ineffectual and, for the most part, kept at bay by the sign of the cross, in scholastic theology Satan poses a grim threat to individual salvation and stages his assault by permeating the patterns of everyday life. The Thomist Satan has more freedom to tempt humans and more ability to manipulate natural active forces in order to create real effects in the material world. For instance, whereas in the ninth century Agobard of Lyon (see doc. 29) held that control of the weather was God's prerogative and impossible to demons, in Aquinas's discussion of Job, he argues that demons can cause storms by stirring up air masses.

234

At Aquinas's hand, those alienated from grace—Satan and his host of demons—were systematized into a tightly organized, highly efficient hierarchical structure with Lucifer as its despotic chief. The competition was God and his angels; the strategy was to damn as many souls as possible in order to thwart the salvific plan. Aquinas fully developed the notion of "the pact with the Devil." His understanding of magic was deeply informed by Scripture and the works of the church fathers; in that vein, he condemned traditional magical practices such as astrology, divination, and superstitious folk observances, but he never made the leap from Satan as the prince of darkness to a fully fleshed-out model of witchcraft.

Aquinas's dialectical method in the Summa Theologica *is first to list a series of "objections," which are the opinions of others on a given topic that he plans to refute. Then he cites his authorities with a paragraph beginning "On the contrary," next comes his own conclusions beginning with, "I answer that." He ends each section with "reply to objections." For the articles below, all the stages of the argument have been omitted except "I answer that."*

Sources: trans. English Dominican Fathers, Thomas Aquinas, *Summa Theologica*, 3 vols. (New York: Benziger Bros. Inc., 1947/1948), vol. 1, pp. 318, 320, 538, 556–58; vol. 2, pp. 1592–93, 1603, 1609, 2080–81; vol. 3, p. 2780; trans. English Dominican Fathers, Thomas Aquinas, *Summa Contra Gentiles*, bk. 3 (London: Burns, Oates & Washbourne Ltd., 1928), pp. 76, 78–79.

Summa Theologica

First Part, Question 63, Article 8. The sin of the highest angel [Satan] was the cause of the others sinning, not as compelling them, but as inducing them by a kind of exhortation. A token thereof appears in this: that all the demons are subjects of that highest one as is evident from our Lord's words, "Go, you cursed, into everlasting fire, which was prepared for the Devil and his angels" (Matthew 25:41). For the order of divine justice exacts that whosoever consents to another's evil suggestion shall be subjected to him in his punishment; according to Peter, "By whom a man is overcome, of the same also he is the slave" (2 Peter 2:19).

Question 64, Article 1. The knowledge of truth is twofold: one which comes of nature and one which comes of grace. The knowledge which comes of grace is likewise twofold: the first is purely speculative, as when divine secrets are imparted to an individual; the other is effective and produces love for God, knowledge of whom properly belongs to the gift of wisdom.

Of these three kinds of knowledge the first was neither taken away nor lessened in the demons. For it follows from the very nature of the angel, who, according to his nature, is an intellect or mind—since on account of the simplicity of his substance, nothing can be withdrawn from his nature—so to punish him by subtracting from his natural powers is like a man is punished by being deprived of a hand or a foot or of something else. Therefore Dionysius the Areopagite [fl. early first century] says that the natural gifts remain entire in them (*On the Divine Names* 4). Consequently [demons'] natural knowledge was not diminished. The second kind of knowledge, however, which comes of grace and consists in speculation, has not been utterly taken away from them but lessened; because, of these divine secrets only so much is revealed to them as is necessary, and that is done either by means of the angels, or "through some temporal workings of divine power," as Augustine says [*On Christian Doctrine* 9.21; see doc. 15], but not in the same degree as to the holy angels, to whom many more things are revealed and more fully, in the Word [Jesus] himself. But of the third knowledge, as likewise of charity, they are utterly deprived.

Question 109, Article 2. Since action follows the nature of a thing, where natures are subordinate, actions also must be subordinate to each other. Thus it is in corporeal things, for as the inferior bodies by natural order are below the heavenly bodies, their actions and movements are subject to the actions and movements of the heavenly bodies. Now it is plain from what we have said that the demons are by natural order subject to others, and hence their actions are subject to the action of those above them, and this is what we mean by precedence—that the action of the subject should be under the action of the prelate. So the very natural disposition of the demons requires that there should be authority among them. This agrees too with divine wisdom, which leaves nothing inordinate, which "reaches from end to end mightily, and orders all things sweetly" (Wisdom 8:1).

Question 114, Article 1. Two things may be considered in the assault of the demons, the assault itself, and the ordering thereof. The assault itself is due to the malice of the demons, who through envy endeavor to hinder man's progress and, through pride, usurp a semblance of divine power by deputing certain ministers to assail man, as the angels of God in their various offices minister to man's salvation. But the ordering of the assault is from God, who knows how to make orderly use of evil by ordering it to good. On the other hand, in regard to the angels, both their guardianship and the ordering thereof are to be referred to God as their first author.

Article 2. Various beings are said to tempt in various ways. For man is said to tempt, sometimes indeed merely for the sake of knowing something, and for this reason, it is a sin to tempt God; for man, being uncertain as it were, presumes to make an experiment of God's power. Sometimes too he tempts in order to help, sometimes in order to hurt. The Devil, however, always tempts in order to hurt by urging man into sin. In this sense it is said to be his proper [natural] office to tempt; for though at times man tempts thus; he does this as minister of the Devil. God is said to tempt that he may know in the same sense as that is said to know which makes others to know. Hence it is written, "The Lord your God tries you, that it may appear whether you love him" (Deuteronomy 13:3).

The flesh and the world are said to tempt as the instruments or matter of temptations; inasmuch as one can know what sort of man someone is, according as he follows or resists the desires of the flesh and according as he despises worldly advantages and adversity—of which things the Devil also makes use in tempting.

Article 3. One thing can be the cause of another in two ways: directly and indirectly. Indirectly as when an agent is the cause of a disposition to a certain effect, it is said to be the occasional and indirect cause of that effect. For instance, we might say that he who dries the wood is the cause of the wood burning. In this way we must admit that the Devil is the cause of all our sins, because he it was who instigated the first man to sin, from whose sin there resulted a proneness to sin in the whole human race, and in this sense we must take the words of John of Damascus [c. 676–749] and Dionysius.

Article 4. As is clear from what has been said above, if we take a miracle in the strict sense, the demons cannot work miracles, nor can any creature but God alone, since in the strict sense a miracle is something done outside the order of the entire created nature, under which order every power of a creature is contained. But sometimes miracle may be taken in a wide sense—for whatever exceeds the human power and experience. And thus demons can work miracles, that is, things which rouse man's astonishment by reason of their being beyond his power and outside his sphere of knowledge. For even a man, by doing what is beyond the power and knowledge of another, leads another to marvel at what he has done, so that in a way, he seems to the other to have worked a miracle.

It is to be noted, however, that although these works of demons which appear marvelous to us are not real miracles; they are sometimes nevertheless something real. Thus the magicians of Pharaoh by the demons' power produced real serpents and frogs [see doc. 1]. And "When fire came down from heaven and at one blow consumed Job's servants and sheep, when the storm struck down his house and with it his children, these were the work of Satan, not phantoms," as Augustine says [*City of God* 22.19; see doc. 15].

Second Part of the Second Part, Question 92, Article 2. As stated above, sins against religion consist in going beyond the mean of virtue in respect of certain circumstances. . . . Accordingly the species of superstition are differentiated, first on the part of the mode, secondly on the part of the object. For the divine worship may be given either to whom it ought to be given, namely, to the true God, but "in an undue mode," and this is the first species of superstition; or to whom it ought not to be given, namely, to any creature whatsoever, and this is another genus of superstition [which is] divided into many species in respect of the various ends of divine worship. For the end of divine worship is in the first place to give reverence to God, and in this respect the first species of this genus is "idolatry," which unduly gives divine honor to a creature. The second end of religion is that man may be taught by God whom he worships, and to this must be referred "divinatory" superstition, which consults the demons through compacts made with them, whether tacit or explicit. Thirdly, the end of divine worship is a certain direction of human acts according to the precepts of God—the object of that worship—and to this must be referred the superstition of certain "observances."

Augustine alludes to these three where he says, "Anything invented by man for making and worshipping idols is superstitious," and this refers to the first species. Then he goes on to say, "Or any agreement or covenant made with the demons for the purpose of consultation and of compact by tokens," which refers to the second species. And a little further on he adds, "To this kind belong all sorts of amulets and such like," and this refers to the third species [*On Christian Doctrine* 2.20; see doc. 16].

Question 95, Article 4. All divination by invoking demons is unlawful for two reasons. The first is gathered from the principle of divination, which is a compact made expressly with a demon by the very fact of invoking him. This is altogether unlawful, wherefore it is written against certain persons, "You have said, 'We have entered into a league with death, and we have made a covenant with hell'" (Isaiah 28:15). And still more grievous would it be if sacrifice were offered or reverence paid to the demon invoked. The second reason is gathered from the result. For the demon who intends man's perdition endeavors, by his answers—even though he sometimes tells the truth—to accustom men to believe him and so to lead him on to something prejudicial to the salvation of mankind. Hence Athanasius [c. 296–373], commenting on the words of Luke 4:35, . . . "[F]or it is wicked, while we have the divine Scriptures, to seek knowledge from the demons" [Luke 4:35].

Question 96, Article 1. The magic art is both unlawful and futile. It is unlawful because the means it employs for acquiring knowledge have not in themselves the power to cause science [knowledge], consisting as they do in gazing certain shapes, and muttering certain strange words, and so forth. Wherefore this art does not make use of these things as causes, but as signs—not however as signs instituted by God, as are the sacramental signs. It follows, therefore, that they are empty signs and consequently a kind of "agreement or covenant made with the demons for the purpose of consultation and of compact by tokens" (Augustine, *On Christian Doctrine* 2.20). Wherefore the magic art is to be absolutely repudiated and avoided by Christians, even as other arts of vain and noxious superstition, as Augustine declares.

This art is also useless for the acquisition of science. For since it is not intended by means of this art to acquire science in a manner connatural to man, namely, by discovery and instruction, the consequence is that this effect is expected either from God or from the demons. Now it is certain that some have received wisdom and science infused into them by God, as related of Solomon (1 Kings 3:12; 2 Chronicles 1:11). Moreover, our Lord said to his disciples, "I will give you a mouth and wisdom, which all your adversaries shall not be able to resist and gainsay" (Luke 21:15). However, this gift is not granted to all or in connection with any particular observance, but according to the will of the Holy Ghost, as stated in 1 Corinthians 12:8, "To one indeed by the spirit is given the word of wisdom, to another the word of knowledge, according to the same spirit." And afterwards it is said, "All these things one and the same spirit works, dividing to everyone according as his will" (1 Corinthians 12:11). On the other hand, it does not belong to the demons to enlighten the intellect [as stated in the First Part]. Now the acquisition of knowledge and wisdom is effected by the enlightening of the intellect; wherefore never did anyone acquire knowledge by means of the demons. . . . The demons may, however, be able by speaking to men to express in words certain teachings of the sciences, but this is not what is sought by means of magic.

Third Part, Question 8, Article 7. As was said above, the head not only influences the members interiorly, but also governs them exteriorly, directing their actions to an end. Hence it may be said that anyone is the head of a multitude, either as regards both, that is, by interior influence and exterior governance, and thus Christ is the head of the church, as was stated, or as regards exterior governance, and thus every prince or prelate is head of the multitude subject to him. And in this way the Devil is head of all the wicked. For, as is written, "He is king over all the children of pride" (Job 41:34). Now it belongs to a governor to lead those whom he governs to their end. But the end of the Devil is the aversion of the rational creature from God; hence from the beginning he has endeavored to lead man from obeying the divine precept. But aversion from God has the nature of an end, inasmuch as it is sought for under the appearance of liberty, according to Jeremiah 2:20: "Of old time you have broken my yoke, you have burst my bands, and you said, 'I will not serve.'" Hence, inasmuch as some are brought to this end by sinning, they fall under the rule and government of the Devil, and therefore he is called their head.

Article 8. As was said above, in the head are found three things: order, perfection, and the power of influencing. But as regards the order of the body, Antichrist is not said to be the head of the wicked as if his sin had preceded, as the sin of the Devil preceded. So likewise, he is not called the head of the wicked from the power of influencing, although he will pervert some in his day by exterior persuasion; nevertheless those who were before him were not beguiled into wickedness by him nor have imitated his wickedness. Hence he cannot be called the head of all the wicked in this way, but of some. Therefore it remains to be said that he is the head of all the wicked by reason of the perfection of his wickedness. Hence, on 2 Thessalonians 2:4: "Showing himself as if he were God," a gloss says, "As in Christ dwelt the fullness of the godhead, so in Antichrist the fullness of all wickedness." Not indeed as if his humanity were assumed by the Devil into unity of person, as the humanity of Christ by the son of God; but that the Devil by suggestion infuses his wickedness more copiously into him than into all others. And in this way, all the wicked who have gone before are signs of Antichrist, according to 2 Thessalonians 2:7, "For the mystery of iniquity already works."

Supplement, Question 58, Article 2. Some have asserted that witchcraft is nothing in the world but an imagining of men who ascribe to spells those natural effects, the causes of which are hidden. But this is contrary to the authority of holy men who state that the demons have power over men's bodies and imaginations when God allows them; wherefore by their means, sorcerers can work certain signs. Now this opinion grows from the root of unbelief or incredulity, because [those who hold that witchcraft is not real] believe that demons exist only in the imagination of the common people—who ascribe to the demon the terrors which a man conjures from his thoughts—and that, owing to a vivid imagination, certain shapes such as a man has in his thoughts become apparent to the senses and then he believes that he sees the demons. But such assertions are rejected by the true faith; whereby we believe that angels fell from heaven, and that the demons exist, and that by reason of their subtle nature they are able to do many things which we cannot, and those who induce them to do such things are called wizards.

Wherefore others have maintained that witchcraft can set up an impediment to carnal copulation, but that no such impediment is perpetual; hence, it does not void the marriage contract, and they say that the laws asserting this have been revoked. But this is contrary to actual facts and to the new legislation which agrees with the old. We must therefore draw a distinction, for the inability to copulate caused by witchcraft is either perpetual and then it voids marriage, or it is not perpetual and then it does not void marriage. And in order to put this to practical proof the church has fixed the space of three years in the same way as we have stated with regard to frigidity. There is, however this difference between a spell and frigidity: that a person who is impotent through frigidity is equally impotent in relation to one as to another, and consequently when the marriage is dissolved; he is not permitted to marry another woman. Whereas through witchcraft a man may be rendered impotent in relation to one woman and not to another—and consequently, when the church adjudges the marriage to be dissolved—each party is permitted to seek another partner in marriage.

Summa Contra Gentiles

That the intellectual substance whose assistance is employed in the magic arts is not evil in its nature.

It is impossible that there be natural malice in the intellectual substances whose assistance is employed in the practice of the magic arts. For if a thing tends to something by its nature, it tends thereto not accidentally but per se, as a heavy body tends downwards. Now if these intellectual substances are evil essentially, they tend to evil naturally, and consequently, not accidentally but per se. But this is impossible, for we have proved that all things tend per se to be good, and nothing tends to evil except accidentally. Therefore, these intellectual substances are not naturally evil.

Again, everything that exists must be either cause or caused, otherwise there would be no order between it and other things. Hence the substances in question are either causes only, or are also caused. If they be causes, since evil cannot cause a thing save accidentally, as proved above, and since whatever is accidental must be traced to something per se; it follows that there must be in them something preceding their malice, whereby they are causes. Now in each thing it is the nature and essence that comes first. Therefore, these substances are not evil by nature. . . .

This is confirmed by the authority of Scripture. For it is said, "Every creature of God is good" (1 Timothy 4:4), and "God saw all things that he had made, and they were very good" (Genesis 1:31). Hereby also we refute the error of the Manicheans [third century Persian religion] who held that these intellectual substances, whom we are wont to call demons or devils, are naturally evil.

We also exclude the error described by Porphyry [philosopher, c. 233–c. 305 CE] in his letter to Anebontes, where he says, "Some are of the opinion that there is a genus of spirits, whose specialty it is to grant the prayers of magicians: spirits naturally deceitful, appearing under all kinds of forms, pretending to be gods, or demons or souls of the departed. It is they who cause all these effects that seem either good or evil. As to those that are really good they give no assistance, in fact they know nothing about them. But they counsel evil and impugn and sometimes hinder those who are intent on leading a virtuous life, they are full of presumption and arrogance, they delight in vanities and are fascinated by flattery." These words of Porphyry indicate clearly enough the malice of the demons, whose assistance the magic arts employ. In this alone are his words reprehensible that he states this malice to be natural to the demons.

Questions: What is the relationship between Satan and Antichrist? What are Aquinas's major sources in the reading above? What is the hierarchical structure within the demonological scheme? According to Aquinas, what aspects of their angelic nature did demons, including Satan, retain after their fall from grace? How does Aquinas reconcile God's omnipotence, nature, and what appears to be evil in the demons? Is traffic with demons possible without a pact?

CHAPTER FIVE

THE FOURTEENTH AND FIFTEENTH CENTURIES: DIABOLISM

Figure 5.1 Albrecht Dürer's (1471–1528) engraving, *Witch Riding Backward on a Goat* (c. 1500), represents the stereotype of an old hag flying to a witches' sabbath. Three of the *putti* hold paraphilia that the witch will need to work her sinister magic: an alchemist's cauldron, a thorn, and a potted plant. The "D" in Dürer's signature monogram is backwards, perhaps to reflect the out-of-kilter world of satanic witchcraft.

New concepts about the nature of magic emerged in the fourteenth and fifteenth centuries, but they did not drive out older traditions. Quotidian spells for worldly success and love charms had changed little since Late Antiquity. Even as re-evaluations of demonology were coalescing in the works of the scholastic schoolmen, other writers continued to produce romance stories celebrating the world of magic and marvels. The Italian Renaissance spurred an increased interest in Neoplatonic theurgy, and occult books on natural magic flourished, although writing or owning them was risky.

Before the mid-thirteenth century, the premise behind the relationship between humans and evil spirits is best characterized as "demonism." Increasingly, due in large part to the growing influence of scholasticism among the intelligentsia in ecclesiastic and university circles, the perception of that same interaction between people and fallen angels metamorphosed into "diabolism," because Satan had taken center stage over all other demons. However, the construct of the devil as the commander-in-chief of an army of demons may not have led to the witch-hunts if other dynamics had not been in place in the late Middle Ages.

Medieval jurisprudence is integral to any discussion of magic and witchcraft. Canon, or church law, incipient in the primitive church, expanded in the fourth century as a result of local synods and ecumenical councils. The prescripts that emerged from those early medieval assemblies were collected and organized by, among others, Burchard of Worms (see doc. 39), and jurists continued the work of systemization that found expression in Gratian's [fl. mid-twelfth century] authoritative corpus of canon law, the *Decretum*. Along with church law, continental Christians were governed by a mélange of local secular law codes and Roman legal collections, such as the *Corpus Juris Civilis* that the Roman emperor Justinian (482–565) commissioned. This tangle of competing and overlapping legal systems did not include encompass the concept of criminal law whereby "the state" could initiate a law suit. Rather, as in modern civil cases, individuals accused each other of offences and brought their neighbors to court; however, there were disincentives and stiff penalties for false accusation, so trials were not undertaken lightly. As jurisprudence evolved, these accusatorial legal practices were augmented by inquisitorial processes; meaning that courts—church or secular—could instigate proceedings against a suspected malefactor.

By his papal bull entitled *Ad abolendam*, Pope Lucius III (c. 1100–1185) created the office of the Inquisition, a series of ecclesiastical tribunals charged with suppressing heresy. Local bishops were instructed to carry out interrogative surveys in their own dioceses twice a year to ferret out unorthodoxy. The methods of this "episcopal inquisition" were not centralized, so bishops' investigative practices varied from one diocese to another. This approach to squelching heresy proved to be ineffectual because, first, bishops were often willing to interpret minor irregularities as local folk practices or "innocent" superstitions, and they often turned a blind eye to them. Second, although the Holy See provided some guidelines, there was not a uniform understanding of what constituted heresy. Pope Gregory IX (c. 1145–1241) formalized procedures and instigated the "papal inquisition" in 1231. His goal was to correct those whose beliefs deviated from Catholic doctrine. The Franciscan and Dominican orders of friars emerged in the thirteenth century, and because friars were itinerant and university-trained in theology and law, it was natural that the papacy would employ them as inquisitors. Pope Innocent III (1161–1216) had already enlisted the friars in his crusade against a heretical movement in France (1209–1229).

About the same time as the Inquisition was formed, at the Fourth Lateran Council (1215), Innocent III forbade priestly participation in trials by ordeal. This was a prosecutorial method of determining guilt by testing the accused, on whose behalf God would intervene if the person was innocent. An example a person drawing a piece of metal out of a cauldron of boiling water. If the burned hand was healed after three days, the accused was judged not guilty. Trials by ordeal were possible only with the cooperation of the clergy, whose presence and blessings were essential to the process. Canon lawyers objected to the ordeals on the grounds that they "tested God." That left courts in need of some method of judging the guilt or innocence of a suspect when there was no definitive evidence and no confession; torture was that method.

In 1252, Pope Innocent IV (c. 1195–1254) issued the bull *Ad exstirpanda*, which stipulated the use of torture as an acceptable method to obtain evidence. Specific procedures were mandated for torture; the interrogator was to "stop short of danger to life or limb," and shedding blood or causing a miscarriage were forbidden. Torture could only be performed once and for a limited duration. Further, a confession obtained under torture did not serve as conclusive evidence. Other corroborating proof was necessary, and the accused had to sign a confession out of sight of the instruments of torture. The hope was that miscreants would confess, renounce their heretical views, and accept penance. It was also expected that guilty persons would name accomplices who shared in their heretical beliefs and concomitant deeds.

In addition to being a sin, under Roman law public heresy was a crime against the state. If those found culpable persisted in the "most severe heresy," they were excommunicated and "relaxed" to the secular arm, at which time either a second trial took place or the condemned heretics were burned at the stake on the recommendation of the inquisitional judges. The clergy were forbidden to kill, so the church itself could not administer punishment. The situation in England was somewhat different. Canon law did not allow for judicial torture, and as a result the Inquisition was not operative in the British Isles and confessions of heresy were less frequent.

Until the late Middle Ages, the Inquisition was focused on heresy and relatively disinterested in sorcery. It was Pope John XXII (c. 1249–1334) who formulated a correlation between the two and brought witchcraft under the jurisdiction of the Inquisition; however, the witch-hunts that resulted from this conflation did not begin in earnest until the end of the fifteenth century. In 1487, Pope Innocent VIII (1432–1492) empowered two Dominican friars, Heinrich Kramer (c. 1430–1505) and Jacob Sprenger (c. 1438–1495), to carry out inquests and bring "heretics" to trial for acts of sorcery. Soon after, Kramer wrote the influential manual *Malleus Maleficarum*, which laid out methods for finding, trying, and punishing those guilty of heretical sorcery—that is, witches.

54. A PRIEST DUPES HIS FRIEND WITH A PROMISE OF MAGIC IN *THE DECAMERON*

Giovanni Boccaccio's (1313–1375) Decameron *is a collection of a hundred short stories told over a period of ten days by a fictional group of ten young women and men who have retired to a secluded villa outside Florence to escape the bubonic plague. The narrative frames consist of love stories, practical jokes, tragedies, criticism of the clergy, human foibles, human virtue, betrayal, comeuppance, and fortune's role in people's lives.*

In the novellas, magic never becomes a theme, and although sorcery features in several of the stories, it is included as an amusing touch that supports plot lines. The book opens up the world of fourteenth-century Italian culture, where common sorcery was taken lightly and viewed as the domain of the uneducated. This is interesting because Boccaccio produced his work at the same time that magic of any kind, carried out by a person on any rung of the socio-economic scale, was increasingly a clerical concern.

Source: trans. John Payne, *The Decameron of Giovanni Boccaccio* (New York: Walter J. Black, 1931), pp. 458–60; rev. Martha Rampton.

The Ninth Day, the Tenth Story

[Dioneo begins his story,] . . . "I will, therefore, tell you a story not overly long, whereby you may apprehend how diligently it behooves us to observe the conditions imposed by those who use enchantment and how one mistake can mar everything done by the magician.

A year or two ago there was at Barletta a priest called Dom Gianni di Barolo, who, because he made little money from his parish, took to eking out his livelihood by hawking merchandise hither and thither, buying and selling in the fairs of Apulia with the help of a mare. In the course of his travels he developed a close friendship with one who called himself Pietro da Tresanti and plied the same trade with the aid of an ass. In token of friendship and affection, he called him

Gossip Pietro, after the Apulian fashion, and whenever Pietro visited Barletta, Don Gianni invited him to his parsonage and there lodged him and entertained him to the best of his power. Pietro, on his part, was very poor and had but a sorry little house at Tresanti, which scarce sufficed for himself, his young and buxom wife, and his ass. Yet, as often as Dom Gianni came to Tresanti, Pietro brought him to his home and entertained him as best he could in return for the hospitality received from him at Barletta. Nevertheless, in the matter of lodging, having but one sorry little bed in which he slept with his handsome wife, he could not entertain Dom Gianni as he would like, and it was necessary for the priest to bed down in the stable on a truss of straw with his own mare and Pietro's ass.

The wife, knowing the hospitality which the priest offered her husband at Barletta, had more than once offered to sleep with her neighbor, Zita Caraprese by name, daughter of Giudice Leo, so that the priest could sleep in the bed with her husband. But Dom Gianni would never hear of it, and once, among other times, he said to her, 'Gossip Gemmata, fret not for me; I fare very well, for at times [by use of sorcery] I cause this mare of mine to become a handsome wench and couch with her, and after, when I wish, I change her into a mare again; wherefore I do not want to part from her.'

The young woman marveled, but believed his tale and told her husband, saying, 'If he is so much your friend as you say, why do you not make him teach you his charm so you can turn me into a mare and use me to carry your wares when you go out buying and selling? Then you would have use of an ass and a mare. In that way we would gain two for one, and when we were back at home, you could make me a woman again, as I am.'

Pietro, who was somewhat dull of wit, believed what she said, and falling in with her counsel, began, as best he knew, to importune Dom Gianni to teach him the trick. The latter did his best to cure Pietro of that folly, but availing not, he said, 'See here, since you will have it so, we will arise tomorrow morning before day, as usual, and I will show you how it is done. To tell you the truth, the hardest part of the matter is putting on the tail, as you shall see.'

Accordingly, when day drew near, Goodman Pietro and Gossip Gemmata, who had scarce slept that night, with such impatience did they await the accomplishment of the matter, arose and called Dom Gianni, who, arising in his shirt, came to Pietro's little chamber and said to him, 'I know no one in the world except you for whom I would do this; wherefore since it pleases you, I will do it, but you must do as I bid you if you want the thing to succeed.' They answered that they would do what he said; whereupon, taking the light, he put it into Pietro's hand and said to him, 'Mark what I do and keep well in mind what I say. Above all, have a care or else you will spoil everything. Whatever you hear or see, say not a single word, and pray God that the tail will stick fast.' Pietro took the light, promising to do exactly as he said, whereupon Dom Gianni let Gemmata strip as naked as she was born and caused her to stand on all fours, mare-fashion, enjoining her, likewise, not to utter a word or else the spell could be ruined. Then, passing his hand over her face and her head, he proceeded to say, 'Be this a fine mare's head,' and touching her hair, said, 'Be this a fine mare's mane'; after that he touched her arms, saying, 'Be these fine mare's legs and feet,' and coming presently to her breast and finding it round and firm, a certain part of Dom Gianni awoke and stood up on end, whereupon he said, 'Be this a fine mare's chest.' And he did likewise with her back and belly and buttocks and thighs and legs. Ultimately, nothing remained but to do the tail; he pulled up his shirt and taking the dibble [garden tool] used for planting, he thrust it hastily into the furrow made therefore and said, 'And be this a fine mare's tail.'

Pietro, who had watched everything intently, seeing this last proceeding and thinking it was poorly done, said, 'Ho there, Dom Gianni, I won't have a tail there; I won't have a tail there!' The radical moisture, wherewith all plants are watered, was by this time come, and Dom Gianni drew it out, saying, 'Alas, Gossip Pietro, what have you done? Did I not tell you not to say a word whatever you saw? The mare was all made; but you have marred everything by talking; nor is there any means of doing it over again.' Pietro said, 'By Mary, I did not want that tail there. Why did you not say to me, "Do you want this tail here?" Because it seems you were setting it too low.' 'Because,' answered Dom Gianni, 'this being your first time watching the spell, you did not know as well as I where the tail should go.' The young woman, hearing all this, stood up and said to her husband, in all good faith, 'Dolt that you are, why have you ruined your affairs and mine? What mare have you ever seen without a tail? So God help me, you are poor, but it would serve you right were you much poorer.' Then, because of the words that Pietro had spoken there was no longer any means of making a mare of the young woman, so she donned her clothes, woebegone and disconsolate, and Pietro, continuing to ply his old trade with an ass, as he was used to, went in company with Dom Gianni to the Bitonto fair and never again asked such a favor from him."

Questions: Is it important to the author whether the priest is actually a magician? What point is Boccaccio making about Pietro and his wife and about the use of magic?

55. *SIR GAWAIN AND THE GREEN KNIGHT*

Sir Gawain and the Green Knight *is an anonymous chivalric romance in alliterative verse from the late Middle Ages written in Middle English. It survives in one copy, which was nearly lost in a fire in 1731. The story draws on Celtic themes and is set in King Arthur's court at Christmas time. Consistent with the romance genre, it contains many folkloric elements that might, in another context, be called magical. The color green has special significance, with connotations of pagan sacred space, yet there is no implication of demonism in this tale.*

Source: trans. K.G.T. Webster and W.A. Neilson, *Sir Gawain and the Green Knight, Piers the Ploughman,* The Riverside Literature Series (Boston: Houghton Mifflin Company, 1917), pp. 3–8.

Sir Gawain and the Green Knight

Part 2.3. This king [Arthur] lay royally at Camelot at Christmas tide with many fine lords, the best of men, all the rich brethren of the Round Table, with rich revel and careless mirth. There many heroes jousted at times, jousted full gaily; then returned these gentle knights to the court to make carols [dancing and singing]. For there the feast was held a full fifteen days with all the meat and the mirth that men could devise. Such a merry tumult, glorious to hear—joyful din by day, dancing at night. . . .

7. . . . [At the New Year's feast] there was no lack of opportunity for the people to take their food. Suddenly, a noise was heard, for scarcely had the music ceased a moment and the first course been properly served in the court, then there burst in at the hall door an awesome being, in height one of the tallest men in the world; from the neck to the waist so square and so thick was he, and his loins and his limbs so long and so great, that half giant I believed him to have been. . . .

8. All green was this man and his clothing; a straight coat was tight to his sides; a fair mantle above, adorned within; the lining showed, with costly trimming of shining white fur, and such his hood also that was caught back from his locks and lay on his shoulders; the hem well stretched; hose of the same green, that clung to his calf and clean spurs under, of bright gold upon silk bands richly barred and shoes on his shanks as the hero wears. And all his clothing verily was clean verdure, both the bars of his belt and the other beauteous stones that were set in fine array about him and his saddle, worked in silk. It would be too difficult to tell the half of the trifles that were embroidered there with birds and flies, with gay gauds of the pendants of the poitrel [breastplate], the proud crupper [strap buckled to the back of the saddle], the bits,—and all the metal was enameled; the stirrups that he stood on were colored the same, and his saddle bow [curved portion of the saddle behind the rider] likewise, and his fine reins that glimmered and glinted all of green stones. The horse that he rode was of the same color too, a green horse—great and thick—a steed stiff to guide, in gay embroidered bridle, and one right dear to his master.

10. He had neither helmet, nor hauberk [coat of mail], nor gorget [a steel or leather collar], armor nor breastplate, nor shaft, nor shield to guard or to smite,

but in his one hand he had a holly twig, that is greenest when groves are bare, and an ax in his other, a huge and prodigious one, a weapon merciless almost beyond description. The head had the vast length of an aleyard [a yard-long glass of beer], the blade all of green steel and of beaten gold; the bit was brightly burnished with a broad edge as well shaped for cutting as sharp razors. The stern warrior gripped it by the steel of its stout staff, which was wound with iron to the end of the wood and all engraved with green in beauteous work. A lace was lapped about it that was fastened at the head and tied up along the haft, with many precious tassels attached on rich embroidered buttons of the bright green. This hero entered the hall, riding straight to the high dais, fearless of mischief. He greeted no one, but looked loftily about, and the first word that he uttered was, "Where is the governor of this company? Gladly I would see that hero and speak with him." He cast his eye on the knights and rode fiercely up and down, stopped and pondered who there was the most renowned.

11. All gazed fixedly on the man, for everybody marveled what it might mean that a knight and a horse could have such a color: as green grown as the grass, and greener, it seemed, shining brighter than green enamel on gold. All were amazed who stood there and stalked nearer to him, with all the wonder in the world as to what he would do; for many marvels had they seen, but never such before. Therefore the folks deemed it a phantom or fairy, and for that reason many a noble warrior was slow to answer, and all were astonished at his voice and sat stone still in a deep silence through the rich hall. Their voices sank as though they had suddenly fallen asleep. I deem, however, that it was not all for fear, but somewhat for courtesy. But now let him to whom all defer undertake the man.

12. Then Arthur, before the high dais, beheld that adventure and saluted the stranger properly, for never was he afraid, and said, "Sir, welcome indeed to this place. I am called Arthur, the head of this hostel. Light courteously down and tarry, I pray you, and what you wish we shall provide."

"Nay, so help me he that sits on high," said the hero. "To dwell for a time in this house was not my errand, but because the fame of this people is lifted up so high and your town and your men are held the best—the stoutest in steel gear on steeds to ride, the weightiest and the worthiest of the world's kind and proved opponents in other proper sports, and here courtesy is known, as I have heard tell,—it is this that has enticed me hither certainly at this time. You may be sure by this branch that I bear here that I pass in peace and seek no quarrel, for if I had set out with a company in fighting fashion, I have a hauberk at home and a helmet both, a shield and a sharp spear shining bright, and other weapons I expect to wield often, but since I wished no war, my clothes are softer. Now if you be as bold as all men tell, you will grant me graciously the game that I ask." Arthur knew how to answer and said, "Sir courteous knight, if it is battle that you crave, you shalt not fail to have a fight here."

13. "Nay, I demand no fight; in faith I tell you there are but beardless children about on this bench. If I were clasped in fetters on a high steed, there is no man here to match me; their might is so weak. Therefore I crave in this court a Christmas game, for it is Yule and New Year, and here are many gallants. If there be a man in this house who holds himself so hardy—is so bold in his blood, so rash in his head—that he dares take one strike at me in exchange for one I take at him, I shall give him as my gift this rich gisarme [long-shafted ax], this weapon, that is heavy enough, to handle as he likes, and I shall abide the first blow as bare as I sit. If any warrior be man enough to try what I propose, let him leap lightly to me and take this weapon—I quit-claim it forever, let him keep it as his own—and I shall stand him a stroke firmly on this floor. At another time, by our Lady Virgin Mary, you will grant me the boon of dealing him a blow; I will give him a respite of twelve months and a day. Now hie, and let us see quickly if any herein dare say yes."

14. If he had astonished them at first, stiller then were all the retainers in the hall, the high and the low. The warrior on his steed settled himself in his saddle and fiercely he reeled about his red eyes, bent his thick brows—shining green— and waved his beard awaiting who would rise. When none would answer him he coughed aloud, stretched himself haughtily and began to speak, "What! Is this Arthur's house," said the hero, "that is famous through so many realms? Where is now your pride and your conquests, your fierceness, and your wrath and your great words? Now is the revel and the renown of the Round Table overcome by the word of a single man; for all tremble for dread without a blow shown." With this he laughed so loud that King Arthur grieved; the blood shot for shame into his fair face. He waxed as angry as the wind, and so did all that were there. The king so keen of mood then stood near that proud man.

15. "Sir," said he, "by heaven your asking is foolish, and as you have demanded folly, it behooves you to find it. I know no man that is aghast at your great words. Give me now this gisarme, for God's sake, and I will grant your boon that you have bidden." Quickly he leaped to him and caught at his hand, and the other alighted fiercely on foot. Now Arthur had his ax, and griped the haft; he whirled it sternly about as if he meant to strike with it. The bold stranger stood upright before him, higher than any in the house by a head and more; with stern cheer he stood there, stroked his beard, and with cool countenance drew down his coat, no more afraid or dismayed for Arthur's great strokes than if someone had brought him a drink of wine upon the bench. Gawain, who sat by the queen, turned to the king, "I beseech now with all courtesy that this affair might be mine."

16. "Would you, worthy lord," said Gawain to the king, "bid me step from this bench and stand by you there, that I without rudeness might leave this table and that my liege lady would not think it ill. I would come to your help before your rich court, for methinks it is obviously unseemly that such a request

is made in your hall, even though you yourself are willing to take it upon you, while so many bold ones sit about you on the bench. I reckon that none under heaven are higher of spirit, nor more mighty on the field where swords are raised. I am the weakest, I know, and feeblest of wit, and to tell the truth there would be the least lost if I lose my life. I am only to be praised because you are my uncle; no other nobility than your blood have I in my body. And since this adventure is so foolish, it belongs not to you. I have asked it of you first; give it to me. Let this great court decide if I have not spoken well." The heroes took counsel together, and they all gave the same advice—to free the crowned king and give the game to Gawain.

17. Then the king commanded Gawain to rise from the table, and he right quickly stood up and made himself ready, kneeled down before the king and took the weapon, and Arthur lovingly gave it to him, lifted up his hand, and gave him God's blessing, and gladly bade him be hardy both of heart and of hand. "Take care, cousin," said the king, "that you give him a cut, and if you handle him properly, I readily believe that you shall endure the blow which he shall give after." Gawain went to the man with gisarme in hand and he boldly awaited him—shrinking never a whit. Then Sir Gawain spoke to the knight in green, "Let us rehearse our agreement before we go farther. First, I ask you, hero, what you are called, that you tell me it truly, so that I may believe it." "In good faith," said the knight, "Gawain am I called, who gives you this buffet, whatever befalls after, and at this time in twelve months I am to take from you a blow with whatever weapon you will, and from no other man alive." The other answered again, "Sir Gawain, as I live, I am heartily glad that you shall give this blow."

18. "By God," said the green knight, "Sir Gawain, it delights me that I am to get at your fist what I have requested here, and you have readily and truly rehearsed the whole of the covenant that I asked of the king, save that you shall assure me, sir, by your troth, that you will seek me yourself whereever you think I may be found upon the earth and fetch for yourself such wages as you deal me today before this rich company." "Where should I seek you?" said Gawain. "Where is your place? I know not where you live—by him that made me—nor do I know you, knight, your court nor your name. But tell me truly the way to your place and how you are called, and I will use all my wit to find my way there, and that I swear to you, for a fact, and by my sure pledge." "New Year will suffice for that; no more is needed now," said the man in green to Gawain the courteous. "To tell the truth, after I have received your tap and you have smitten me well, I shall promptly inform you of my house and my home and my own name. Then you may inquire about my journey and keep your promise, and if I don't answer, then you are the better for it, for you may linger at ease in your land and seek no further. Now pick up your grim tool and let us see how you knock." "Gladly, sir, certainly," said Gawain as he stroked his ax.

19. The green knight on the ground prepared himself properly. With the head a little bowed he disclosed the flesh. His long, lovely locks he laid over his crown and let the naked nape of his neck show for the blow. Gawain gripped his ax and gathered it on high; the left foot he set before on the ground and let the ax light smartly down on the naked flesh so that the sharp edge severed the giant's bones, and sank through the clear flesh, and sheared it in twain, till the edge of the brown steel bit into the ground. The fair head fell from the neck to the earth, and many pushed it with their feet where it rolled forth. The blood burst from the body and glistened green. Yet never faltered nor fell the hero for all that, but stoutly he started up with firm steps and fiercely he rushed forth where the heroes stood, caught his lovely head, and lifted it up straightaway. Then he turned to his steed, seized the bridle, stepped into the stirrup, and strode aloft, holding the head in his hand by the hair. And soberly the man sat in his saddle as if no mishap had ailed him, though he was headless on the spot. He turned his trunk about—that ugly body that bled. Many of them thought that he had lost his reason.

20. For he held the head straight up in his hand, turned the face toward the highest on the dais, and it lifted up the eyelids, and looked straight out, and spoke thus with his mouth. "Look Gawain, that you be ready to go as you have promised and seek loyally, hero, till you find me, as you have promised in this hall in the hearing of these knights. To the green chapel go you; I charge you to receive such a blow as you have dealt. You deserve to be promptly paid on New Year's morn.

Many men know me as the knight of the green chapel; therefore, if you strive to find me, you shall never fail. And so come, or it behooves you to be called recreant." With a wild rush he turned the reins and flew out at the hall door—his head in his hand—so that the fire of the flint flew from the foal's hoofs. To what country he vanished, no one there knew—no more than they knew from whence he had come. The king and Gawain roared with laughter at that green man, but this adventure was reckoned a marvel among men.

Questions: Is the green knight a positive character or an antagonist? Are the marvelous elements in the story magical according to the understanding of magic at the time? Given early medieval proscriptions about pagan practices, what is the significance of the colour green? Why is the story set in King Arthur's court?

56. KEY TO OCCULT MYSTERIES OF SOLOMON

The Key of Solomon is a Renaissance grimoire, or practical handbook of magic, that contains instructions on how to summon angels, spirits, and demons in order to compel them to do the will of the practitioner or "exorcist." Many grimoires attributed to the biblical King Solomon, the wise, were written in the early modern period.

The origins and provenance of The Key of Solomon *are as mysterious as the content itself. The archetype was probably a late medieval Latin or Italian manuscript, and there are numerous versions of the text with minor or significant alterations in Latin and Hebrew from the sixteenth to the eighteen centuries. Interest in books of the occult such as* The Key of Solomon *developed in the context of Renaissance erudition and fascination with the Jewish mystical tradition and the esoteric teaching contained in the Kabbalah.*

According to the introduction, Solomon wrote the book for his son, Roboam, who hid it in his father's sepulcher. Centuries later, The Key *was found by a group of philosophers from Babylon, but they could not decipher the writing. However, after entreating God for understanding, the angel of the Lord appeared, agreeing to unlock the wisdom of the book if the philosophers promised to keep it from the wicked and unworthy. They agreed and placed a spell on* The Key *so that those without wisdom and purity of spirit or who might take the name of God in vain, would be unable to apply the magic contained therein.*

Source: trans. S. Liddell MacGregor Mathers, *The Key of Solomon* (London: George Redway, 1889), pp. 9–11, 13–19, 22, 24–26, 28–29, 31, 36, 38, 46, 49, 56.

The Key of Solomon

Book 1

1. Solomon, the son of David, king of Israel, has said that the beginning of our key is to fear God, to adore him, to honor him with contrition of heart, to invoke him in all matters which we wish to undertake, and to operate with very great devotion, for thus God will lead us in the right way. When, therefore, you shall wish to acquire the knowledge of magical arts and sciences, it is necessary to have prepared the [astrological] order of hours and of days and of the position of the moon, without the operation of which you can affect nothing. But if you observe them with diligence you may easily and thoroughly arrive at the effect and end that you desire to attain.

2. . . . . It is, therefore, advisable to know that the hours of the day and of the night together are twenty-four in number and that each hour is governed by one of the seven planets in regular order, commencing at the highest and descending to the lowest [which is the moon]. . . . Note that each experiment or magical operation should be performed under the planet, and usually in the hour, which refers to the same. For example, in the days and hours of Saturn you can perform experiments to summon the souls from Hades, but only of those who have died a natural death. Similarly on these days and hours you can operate to bring either good or bad fortune to buildings; to have familiar spirits attend you in sleep; to cause good or ill success in business, possessions, goods, seeds,

fruits, and similar things; in order to acquire learning; to bring destruction and to give death; and to sow hatred and discord. . . .

Verily, since no experiments for converse with spirits can be done without a circle being prepared, whatsoever experiments therefore you wish to undertake for conversing with spirits, you must learn to construct a certain particular circle—that being done, surround that circle with the circle of [the magic] art for better caution and efficacy.

3. . . . Before commencing operations, both the master and his disciple must abstain, with great and thorough continence during the space of nine days, from sensual pleasures and from vain and foolish conversation. . . . Six of these nine days having expired, he must recite frequently the prayer and confession as will be told him, and on the seventh day, the master being alone, let him enter into a secret place, let him take off his clothes and bathe himself from head to foot in consecrated and exorcised water, saying devoutly and humbly the prayer, "O Lord ADONAI." . . .

The prayer being finished, let the master quit the water, and put upon his flesh raiment of white linen, clean and unsoiled, and then let him go with his disciples to a secret place and command them to strip themselves naked. And they having taken off their clothes, let him take exorcised water and pour it upon their heads so that it flows down to their feet and bathes them completely, and while pouring this water upon them let the master say, "Be you regenerate, renewed, washed, and pure." . . . This being done, the disciples must clothe themselves, putting upon their flesh, like their master, raiment of white linen— clean and unsoiled. And the three last days the master and his disciples should fast, observing solemnities and prayers . . .

Note that the three last days should be calm weather, without wind and without clouds rushing hither and thither over the face of the sky. . . . Let the master alone say the confession [to God of his sins and shortcomings]. The which being finished, the master in sign of penitence, will kiss the disciples on the forehead, and each of them will kiss the other. Afterwards let the master extend his hands over the disciples, and in sign of absolution, absolve and bless them; which being done he will distribute to each of his disciples the instruments necessary for magical art, which he is to carry into the circle.

The first disciple will bear the censer, the perfumes, and the spices. The second disciple will bear the book, papers, pens, ink, and any stinking or impure materials. The third will carry the knife, and the sickle of magical art, the lantern, and the candles. The fourth, the Psalms, and the rest of the instruments. The fifth, the crucible or chafing dish, and the charcoal or fuel, but it is necessary for the master himself to carry in his hand the staff, and the wand or rod. The necessary things being thus attended to, the master will go with his disciples unto the assigned place where they have proposed to construct the circle for the magical arts and experiments [procedures], repeating on the way the prayers and orations . . . .

When the master will have arrived at the place appointed together with his disciples, he having lighted the flame of the fire and having exorcised it afresh . . . shall light the candle and place it in the lantern, which one of the disciples is to always hold in his hand to provide light for the master at his work. Now the master of the art, every time that he has occasion for some particular purpose to speak with the spirits, must endeavor to form certain circles which shall differ somewhat, and which have some particular reference to the particular experiment under consideration. Now, in order to succeed in forming such a circle concerning magical art, for the greater assurance and efficacy you shall construct it in the following manner. . . . You shall circumscribe around these circles two squares, the angles of which shall be turned toward the four quarters of the earth, and the space between the lines of the outer and inner square shall be half a foot. The extreme angles of the outer square shall be made the centers of four circles, the measure or diameter of which shall be one foot. All these are to be drawn with the knife or consecrated instrument of art, and within these four circles you must write four names of God the most holy one [while reciting Psalms]. . . .

That being finished, and the fumigations being performed, . . . the master should reassemble his disciples, encourage them, reassure them, fortify them, and conduct them into the parts of the circle of art where he must place them in the four quarters of the earth, encourage them, and exhort them to fear nothing and to keep in the places assigned to them. Also, the disciple who is placed toward the east should have a pen, ink, paper, silk, and white cotton, all clean and suitable for the work. Furthermore, each of the companions should have a new sword drawn in his hand (besides the consecrated sword of magical art), and he should keep his hand resting upon the hilt of the sword, and he should on no pretext quit the place assigned to him, nor move from it.

After this the master should quit the circle, light the fuel in the earthen pots and place upon them the censers in the four quarters of the earth, and he should have in his hand the consecrated taper of wax, and he should light it and place it in a hidden and secret place prepared for it. Let him after this re-enter and close the circle [and say the following prayer] . . . "O Lord God, all powerful and all merciful, you who desire not the death of a sinner, but rather that he may turn from his wickedness and live, give and grant unto us your grace, by blessing and consecrating this earth and this circle, which is here marked out with the most powerful and holy names of God. And you, I conjure, O earth, by the most holy name of ASHER EHEIEH entering within this circle, composed and made with mine hand. And may God, even ADONAI, bless this place with all the virtues of heaven, so that no obscene or unclean spirit may have the power to enter into this circle or to annoy any person who is therein; through the Lord God ADONAI, who lives eternally unto the ages of the ages. Amen. . . .

Let the master now arise and place upon his head a crown made of paper (or any other appropriate substance), on which there must be written . . . these four names: AGLA, AGLAI, AGLATA, AGLATAI. These names are to be placed in the front, behind, and on either side of the head. Furthermore, the master ought to have with him in the circle those pentacles or medals which are necessary to his purpose, which are described hereinafter, and which should be constructed according to the rules given in the chapter on pentacles. They should be described [written] on virgin paper with a pen and ink, blood, or colors, prepared according to the manner which we shall hereafter show in the chapters on these subjects. It will be sufficient to take only those pentacles which are actually required; they should be sewed to the front of the linen robe on the chest with the consecrated needle of the art and with a thread which has been woven by a young girl.

After this, let the master turn himself toward the eastern quarter (unless directed to the contrary, or unless he should be wishing to call spirits which belong to another quarter of the universe) and pronounce with a loud voice the conjuration contained in this chapter. And if the spirits be disobedient and do not then make their appearance, he must arise and take the exorcised knife of art by which he has constructed the circle and raise it toward the sky as if he wished to beat or strike the air, and conjure the spirits. Let him then lay his right hand and the knife upon the pentacles or medals, constructed of and written upon virgin paper, which are fastened to or sewn upon his breast, and let him repeat the following conjuration upon his knees. . . . "[O Lord,] I beseech you to have the kindness to be favorable unto us, your splendor, your magnificence, and your holiness, and by your holy, terrible, and ineffable name IAH, at which the whole world does tremble, and by the fear with which all creatures obey you. Grant, O Lord, that we may become responsive unto your grace, so that through it we may have a full confidence in and knowledge of you, and that the spirits may discover themselves here in our presence, and that those which are gentle and peaceable may come unto us, so that they may be obedient unto your commands." . . .

After having said all these words devoutly, let the master arise, and place his hands upon the pentacles, and let one of the companions hold the book open before the master, who, raising his eyes to heaven and turning unto the four quarters of the universe, shall say, "O Lord, be you unto me a tower of strength against the appearance and assault of the evil spirits." . . .

That being said and done, you shall see [the spirits] draw near and approach from all parts. But if they are hindered, detained, or occupied in some way, and so that they cannot come, or if they are unwilling to come, then, the suffumigations and [vapors from the censers] being performed anew, and (the disciples) having anew, by especial order, touched their swords, and the master having encouraged his disciples, he shall reform the circle with the knife of art, and, raising the said knife toward the sky, he shall, as it were, strike the air with it. After this he shall lay his hand upon the pentacles, and having bent his knees before the most high, he shall repeat with humility the following confession, which his disciples shall also do, and they shall recite it in a low and humble voice, so that they can scarcely be heard [confession follows, then prayer].

5. . . . Let the exorcist lay his hand upon the pentacles while one of the disciples holds open before him the book wherein are written the prayers and conjurations proper for conquering, subduing, and reproving the spirits. Then the master, turning toward each quarter of the earth, and raising his eyes to heaven, shall say, "O Lord, be you unto me a strong tower of refuge, from the sight and assaults of the evil spirits." . . . After this he shall see the spirits come from every side. But in case they are occupied in some other place, or they cannot come, or that they are unwilling to come, then let him commence afresh to invoke them after the following manner, and let the exorcist be assured that even were they bound with chains of iron and with fire, they could not refrain from coming to accomplish his will.

"O you spirits, . . . I conjure you, and I command you absolutely, O demons, in whatsoever part of the universe you may be, by the virtue of all these holy names: ADONAI, YAH, HOA, EL, ELOHA [etc.] and by all the holy names of God which have been written with blood in the sign of an eternal alliance."

6. If [the spirits] then immediately appear, it is well; if not, let the master uncover the consecrated pentacles which he should have made to constrain and command the spirits and which he should wear fastened round his neck, holding the medals (or pentacles) in his left hand, and the consecrated knife in his right; and encouraging his companions, he shall say with a loud voice, . . . "Here again I conjure you and most urgently command you; I force, constrain, and exhort you to the utmost, by the most mighty and powerful name of God EL, strong and wonderful, and by God the just and upright; I exorcise you and command you that you in no way delay, but that you come immediately and upon the instant hither before us, without noise, deformity, or hideousness, but with all manner of gentleness and mildness. . . . Otherwise, if you contravene and resist us by your disobedience unto the virtue and power of this name YIAI, we curse you even unto the depth of the great abyss, into which we shall cast, hurl, and bind you. If you show yourselves rebellious against the secret of secrets, and against the mystery of mysteries. AMEN, AMEN. FIAT, FIAT. . . .

[There follow further conjurations if the demons still refuse to appear.] Then it is certain that they will come, even if they are bound with chains of fire, unless prevented by affairs of the very greatest importance, but in this latter case they will send ambassadors and messengers by whom you shall easily and surely learn what occupies the spirits and what they are about. But if they appear not yet in answer to the above conjuration, and are still disobedient, then let the master of the art or exorciser arise and exhort his companions to be of good cheer, [and let them beseech the aid of angels]. . . .

7. . . . These things being thus done and performed, you shall see the spirits come from all sides in great haste with their princes and superiors. . . . Then the exorcist, or master of the art, at the arrival of the king, whom he shall see crowned with a diadem, should uncover the holy pentacles and medals which he wears upon his breast covered with a cloth of silk or of fine twined linen, and show them to him, saying, "Behold the signs and holy names by and before whose power every knee should bow, of all that is in heaven, upon earth, or in hell. Humble yourselves, therefore, under the mighty hand of God. Then will the king bow the knee before you, and will say, "What do you wish, and why have you caused us to come hither from the infernal abodes?" . . . He should then cover the pentacles, and he will see wonderful things, which it is impossible to relate, touching worldly matters and all sciences. This being finished, let the master uncover the pentacles, and demand all that he shall wish from the king of the spirits, and if there are one or two spirits only, it will be the same. And having obtained all his desire, he shall thus license them to depart.

You should further make a book of virgin paper and therein write the foregoing conjurations, and constrain the demons to swear upon the same book that they will come whenever they are called and present themselves before you whenever you shall wish to consult them. Afterwards you can cover this book with sacred sigils [symbols] on a plate of silver and therein write or engrave the holy pentacles. You may open this book either on Sundays or on Thursdays, rather at night than by day, and the spirits will come.

10. [To render oneself invisible], make a small image of yellow wax in the form of a man in the month of January and in the day and hour of Saturn, and at that time write with a needle above the crown of its head and upon its skull which you have adroitly raised. . . . After that you shall replace the skull in proper position. You shall then write upon a small strip of the skin of a frog or toad which you have killed, [magic] words and characters. You shall then go and suspend the said figure by one of your hairs from the vault of a cavern at the hour of midnight, and perfuming it with the proper incense you shall say, "METATRON, MELEKH, BEROTH, NOTH, VENIBBETH, MACH, and all you, I conjure you O figure of wax, by the living god, that by the virtue of these characters and words, you render me invisible, wherever I may take you with me. Amen."

And after having perfumed it anew, you shall bury it in the same place in a small deal [wooden] box, and every time you wish to pass or enter into any place without being seen, you shall say these words, carrying the aforesaid figure in your left pocket, "Come unto me and never quit me wherever I shall go." Afterwards you shall take it carefully back to the before-mentioned place and cover it with earth until you need it again.

13. [How to make a magic carpet] . . . Make a carpet of white and new wool, and when the moon is at her full, in the sign of Capricorn and in the hour of the sun, you shall go into the country away from any habitation of man in a place free from all impurity, and you shall spread out your carpet so that one of its points is toward the east and another toward the west, and having made a circle around it and enclosing it, you shall remain within upon the point toward the east, and holding your wand in the air for every operation, you shall call upon Michael, toward the north upon Raphael, toward the west upon Gabriel, and toward the south upon Uriel [all archangels]. After this you shall return to the point of the east and devoutly invoke the great name AGLA, and take this point of the carpet in your left hand; turning then toward the north you shall do the same, and continuing so to the other points of the carpet, you shall raise them so that they do not touch the ground, and holding them up thus, and turning anew toward the east, you shall say [a prayer] with great veneration . . .

18. The medals or pentacles, which we make for the purpose of striking terror into the spirits and reducing them to obedience, have besides this wonderful and excellent virtue. If you invoke the spirits by virtue of these pentacles, they will obey you without repugnance, and having considered them they will be struck with astonishment and will fear them, and you shall see them so surprised by fear and terror that none of them will be sufficiently bold to wish to oppose your will. They are also of great virtue and efficacy against all perils of earth, of air, of water, and of fire, against poison which has been drunk, against all kinds of infirmities and necessities, against binding, sortilege, and sorcery, against all terror and fear, and wherever you shall find yourself, if armed with them, you will be in safety all the days of your life. . . . These pentacles are usually made of the metal the most suitable to the nature of the planet, and then there is no occasion to observe the rule of particular colors. They should be engraved with the instrument of art in the days and hours proper to the planet. . . . They may also be made with exorcised virgin paper, writing thereon with the colors adopted for each planet, referring to the rules already laid down in the proper chapters, and according to the planet with which the pentacle is in sympathy. Wherefore unto Saturn the color of black is appropriated; Jupiter rules over celestial blue, Mars over red, the sun over gold, or the color of yellow or citron, Venus over green; Mercury over mixed colors, the moon over silver, or the color of argentine earth. . . .

Questions: Describe the condition of the exorcist necessary for the efficacy of the magic transactions. What role does God play in the "art"? In order for the "experiments" to work, what items must be present, and where must the practitioners stand? What is the power relationship between the magician and the spirits? What are the nature and importance of names in the text? What aspects of the text hint that this sort of art was carried out only by the educated? Do the exorcists view themselves as practicing magic?

57. CLERICAL MAGIC: A HANDBOOK

Richard Kieckhefer's work on the "clerical underworld" of late medieval society has done much to bring to light the ubiquity of magic in European culture. The fifteenth-century Munich Handbook *is an example of a type of material easily accessible to the clergy in the Middle Ages. We cannot be sure how widespread such books were because the spells ("conjurations" or "experiments") in them were forbidden, and the books were routinely burned. There are, however, frequent references to magic handbooks in the writings of those who opposed or destroyed them. The* Munich Handbook *was written in Germany and escaped detection, in part, because the first two identifying folios of the work are missing, which obscured the nature of the manuscript.*

Often those who worked the experiments in the necromantic handbooks were monks or nuns and clergy of the lower orders, but in some cases priests, bishops, and even popes were implicated. Although many experiments depend on the good graces of God and his angels, the spells are explicitly necromantic and efficacious only with the cooperation of demons ensnared by the precision of the practitioners' craft. The experiments are all self-serving, petty, and opportunistic—worked for entertainment, personal gain, revenge, or sexual assault. The numbering of the readings is out of order here, as in the original document.

Source: trans. Richard Kieckhefer, *Forbidden Rites: A Necromancer's Manual of the Fifteenth Century* (University Park: Pennsylvania State University Press, 1997), pp. 51–53, 59–63, 82–85, 104–5.

A Necromancer's Handbook

7. Here follows another experiment for invoking spirits so that a man can make a fine and well-fortified castle appear, or for summoning countless legions of armed men, which can easily be done and among other things is deemed most beautiful.

First, go out on the tenth (day of) the moon, under a clear sky, outside of town to some remote and secret place, taking milk and honey with you, some of which you must sprinkle in the air. And with bare feet and head, kneeling, read this while facing west: "O Usyr, Salaul, Silitor, Demor, Zanno, Syrtroy, Risbel, Cutroy, Lytay, Onor, Moloy, Pumotor, Tami, Oor, and Ym, squire spirits, whose function it is to bear arms and deceive human senses wherever you wish, I, so-and-so, conjure and exorcize and invoke you . . . that, indissolubly bound to my power, you should come to me without delay, in a form that will not frighten me, subject and prepared to do and reveal for me all that I wish, and to do this willingly, by all things that are in heaven and on earth." Having read this once facing west, do so again facing south, east, and north.

And from far off you will see a band of armed men coming toward you, who will send ahead a squire to say that those you summoned are coming to you. You should tell him, "Go to them and tell them to come to me in such a state that they frighten no one, but I may abide safely with them." When you have said this, he will return at once to them.

After a short interval, they will come to you. When you see them, show them at once this circle, which has great power to terrify those fifteen demons; they will see it and say, "Ask whatever you wish in safety, and it will all come to pass for you through us." You should then tell them to consecrate their circle so that whenever you gaze on it and invoke them they must come to you quickly and do that which is natural to them, namely make fortifications and castles and moats and a multitude of armed men appear. They will say they are willing to do so. You should extend a book to them, and you will see one of them place his hand on the book and speak certain words, which you will not understand. When this is done, they will restore it to you.

Then they will ask you to permit them to leave, because they cannot depart from you except with permission. You should say to them, "Make a castle here so that I may see your power." Immediately they will make a castle around you, with many other things, and you will see yourself in the middle of the castle, and a great multitude of knights will be present. But these fifteen will not be able to depart from you. After the space of an hour they will ask you that they may depart, and you should say, "Be ready whenever I gaze on this circle and invoke you to return at once." They will swear to come immediately. Then tell them to depart wherever they wish. And the entire spectacle will be destroyed, and no one will remain there. . . .

Once when I (wished to test) this art I exercised it with the emperor, when many nobles were accompanying him on a hunting expedition through some dark forest. This is how I proceeded. First I gazed at the circle, calling the aforesaid demons with a clear voice. And at once a handsome knight came to me, whom no one but I could see, and who said to me, "I am one of the spirits you have invoked; I am named Salaul, and the others have sent me. Command what you will, and it will be done." I said to him, "I want you to have a legion of armed men appear, whom the emperor and his companions will take to be rebels." He said, "It is done." And then all the counts and the emperor himself turned and looked to the north, and from far off they saw coming to them an innumerable multitude of knights and soldiers. One of them dismounted, and before an hour's time came to the emperor and said, trembling, "Lord emperor, behold, an innumerable horde is coming toward us, swearing to put us and all your counts to death and to kill you pitilessly." On hearing this, the emperor and the counts did not know what to do. Meanwhile, the spirits approached.

Seeing and hearing them and their terrifying weapons, they began to flee, but the others followed them, shooting arrows, and cried with one voice, "You cannot escape your death today!" Then I said, "O Salaul, make a wondrous castle before the emperor and his men, so that the emperor and the others can enter it." And it was done. A perfectly safe castle was made for the counts, with towers and moat and the drawbridge down. It seemed excellently constructed and filled with mercenaries, who were crying out, "O lord emperor, enter quickly with your companions!" They entered, and it seemed that servants and many friends of the emperor were in it; he supposed he had come upon people who would defend him manfully. When they had entered, they raised the drawbridge and began to defend themselves. Then the spirits with their war machines attacked the castle with wondrous power, so that the emperor and the others feared all the more. Then Salaul said to me, "We do not have the power to remain here longer than a quarter of the day, so we must now withdraw." Then the castle disappeared, and the attackers, and everything else. The emperor and the others then looked around and found themselves in some marsh, which left them greatly astonished. I said to them, "This episode has been quite an adventure!" And after this experiment I made a dinner for them.

Remember that this art cannot last longer than a quarter of a day, unless it lasts one quarter one time (and is then renewed for another quarter day), etc.

11. I shall treat also of the art of invisibility, unknown in these days to nearly all. When you wish to become invisible and insensible to all beings, both rational and otherwise, first, under a waxing moon on a Wednesday, in the first hour of the day, having remained chaste for three days beforehand, and with cut hair and beard, and dressed in white, in a secret place outside of town, under a clear sky, on level ground, trace a circle such as appears here, with a magnificent sword, writing these names and everything shown along with them.

When this is done, place the sword toward the west, on (the name) Firiel. And while you have it placed there, have a vessel in which there is fire with frankincense, myrrh and other incense, and with the smoke from these go about the circle, suffumigating it, beginning and ending with (the name) Firiel. When you have done this, take blessed water and sprinkle yourself and the circle, saying, "*Asperges me, Domine, ysopo* [Sprinkle me Lord with hyssop]" (Psalm 49:9 Vulgate). . . . When you have done this, kneel facing the east, and in a strong voice say, "I, so-and-so, conjure you, O Fyriel, Mememil, Berith, (and) Taraor, powerful, magnificent, illustrious spirits, in whom I place all my trust, by the one, inseparable and undivided Trinity . . . that all four of you should come here with utmost humility, bound, constrained, and sworn to carry out my command, whatever I ask of you. Come without delay. . . ."

When you have said this invocation four times—once toward Firiel, once toward Melemil and toward Berith and Tarator—four spirits will at once be present in the circle, saying to you, "Tell us what you wish, and we will obey you completely." You will say to them, "I wish a cloak of invisibility, which should be thin and incorruptible, so that when I wear it no one can see me or sense my presence." When you have said this, one will withdraw, and within an hour will bring forth a cloak, which you asked them to bring you. . . . On the third day, return there with the cloak, and you will find your [white] garment, which you will take. Be sure to remember; if on the third day you do not return, or you do not take the garment left there, on the fourth day you will find nothing, but in seven days you will die. . . .

10. When you wish to infuse a spirit into a dead person, so that he appears alive as he was previously, this is the procedure to follow. First have a ring made of gold. Around the outside these names should be carved: Brimer, Suburith, Tranauit; on the inside, these names: Lyrath, Beryen, Damayn. When the names have been carved, on a Sunday before sunrise, go to running water and place the ring in it, and let it remain there for five days.

On the sixth day, take it out and take it to a tomb, and place it inside, so that it remains there on Friday and Saturday. On Sunday, before sunrise, go outside of town under a clear sky, in a remote and secret place, and make a circle with a sword, and on it write with the sword the names and figures that appear here.

When this has been inscribed, enter into it (the circle) as is designated, and place the sword beneath your knees, and, facing south, recite this conjuration: "I conjure you, all the demons inscribed on this ring"—which you should have in your hand—"by the father and the son and the Holy Spirit, and by almighty God, maker of heaven and earth . . . [you] should proceed hither in benign form, so that I will not fear, and should consecrate this ring in such a way that it may possess this power, namely that whenever I place it on the finger of a dead person, one of you will enter him, and he will appear alive as before, in the same likeness and form. . . ."

When you have said this once, six spirits will at once appear at the circle, requesting the ring, which you will give them. When you have given it, they will depart, and you likewise should leave the circle, taking the sword with you, and not destroying the circle.

On the sixth day, return with the sword, and say, facing south, "I conjure you, O Brimer, Suburith, (etc.) . . . that you should come to me now without delay, bearing the consecrated ring, so that when I place it on the finger or in the hand of a living person he will fall to the ground as if dead, and when I take it away he will return to his former state, and when I place it on a dead person, as aforesaid, a spirit will enter him and he will appear alive as before. . . ." [The demons will bring the ring;] keep this ring with you, wrapped in a sheet of white cloth. When you wish to cause someone to appear dead, so that he will seem to everyone devoid of life, place this ring on his finger, and he will appear to be a corpse; and when you remove it, he will return to his former state. And when you wish a corpse to appear animated, place the ring as aforesaid, or bind it to a hand or foot and within an hour it will arise in the form to which it is previously accustomed, and will speak before all with a living voice, and will be able to display this quality for six days. . . .

The circle given above has many powers, of which I shall mention three known to me. If you draw it on a Friday with the feather of a hoopoe and with its blood on a freshly prepared sheet of parchment and touch a person with it, you will be loved by that person above all others forever. And if you place that circle, written as aforesaid, on the head of a sick person without his knowledge, if he is to die he will say that he can by no means recover, and if he is to recover he will see that he is altogether freed. And if you carry this circle, written in like manner, on your person, no dog will be able to bark at you. And I have experienced these effects; I do not mention those I have not experienced.

3. When you wish to have the love of whatever woman you wish, whether she is near or far, whether noble or common, on whatever day or night you wish, whether for the furtherance of friendship or to its hindrance, first you must have a totally white dove and a parchment made from a female dog that is in heat, from whom it is most easily to be had. And you should know that this kind of parchment is most powerful for gaining the love of a woman. You should also have a quill from an eagle. In a secret place, take the dove and with your teeth bite into it near the heart, so that the heart comes out, and with the eagle's quill write on the parchment with the (dove's) blood the name of her whom you wish, and draw the image of a naked woman as best you can, saying, "I draw so-and-so, [name], daughter of so-and-so, whom I wish to have, in the name of these six hot spirits, namely Tubal, Satan, Reuces, Cupido, Afalion, Duliatus, that she may love me above all others living in the world." . . .

Then write on her right arm "Satan," and on her left arm "Reuces." When these (names) have been written, say, "As you, Satan, and you, Reuces, are inscribed on this image made in the name of so-and-so, may you so afflict her arms without delay so that she can do nothing but desire to embrace me."

When you have this, write your own name near the heart of the image, saying, "As I am on the heart of this image, may so-and-so, [name], thus have me in her heart day and night."

When you have done this, write on the genitals of the image the name "Cupid," saying, "As you, Cupid, are on the genitals of this image, may you thus remain always on the genitals of so-and-so, arousing her so that she despises all men of this world and desires me alone, and may the fire of love for me torment and inflame her." . . .

When you have said this, take the image with both hands, kneel, and say, "I have drawn the heart and mind of so-and-so with this image, and with powerful invocation I arouse her to love, desire, and yearn for me, and to have me in mind all night in her sleep, through our Lord Jesus Christ, who lives and reigns and commands forever."

When you have said this, take myrrh and saffron, kindle a fire, and fumigate the image, saying this conjuration: "I conjure all you demons inscribed on this image, by your lords to whom you are bound in obedience—Sobedon, Badalam and Berith—that you should inflame so-and-so, whose image is designed in this name, to love of me, so that day and night she may think of me, (and) may hope for me, until she fulfills my will with ardor. And as you are inscribed and fixed on this image, may you thus dwell in her until I do with her whatever I wish."

When you have said this conjuration three times, and made the fumigation, take a hair from the tail of a horse and suspend the parchment with this hair, so that it moves in the air, and let it hang. On that day, or the next, or some other, or whenever you can, go to that woman, and without doubt she will be very glad to see you, and will say she cannot live without you. And this will occur immediately, and she will do your heart's desire, and will love you above all things for all eternity. . . . If you cannot approach her, whether from fear or because of distance or any obstacle, you can still have her brought by the aforesaid demons, who are so effective that if you were in the east, within an hour they could carry her without danger from the west, and likewise they could return her, without exposure.

The image having been made as has been said, and suspended on a particular day, at any hour of the day, you may blow on it so that it moves with your breath, and likewise on the second and third day. On the night of the third day, or on the day itself, either alone or with three faithful companions, take the image and hang it around your neck with the (horse's) hair, and have it lie on your chest. And take a sword and make with it a circle on the ground. When you have made the circle, stand inside it and summon your companions (if you have any), who should do nothing but stand in the circle and watch the spectacle—but it is better if you do not have them. Take an iron stylus and trace [a band with names in it] round the circle, as is shown here, preserving constant silence. . . .

When you have said this three times, gazing at a ring, you will hear a voice, saying, "Behold, we are here!" Immediately you will see six handsome and gentle young men, saying to you with one voice, "We are here, ready and willing to obey your command. Tell us what you wish, and at once we will do it." You should say, "Go to so-and-so and bring her to me without delay." When you have said this, they will at once depart, and within an hour they will bring her without harm.

You should know that none of these (six) can enter the circle, but they will bring her to it and she will stretch out her hand to you, and you will draw her in. She will be a bit astonished, but quite willing to remain with you. I should inform you that it is better to make the circle as large as possible, because in it you can make a circle (sic), and in it you can stretch out more effectively. For if anything of yours (any part of your body?) should go outside the circle, it would be bad for you. When the woman has come, all the spirits will vanish.

You can keep the woman in the circle as long as you please. For when the woman has entered the circle, you should say to the spirits, "Let one of you go to the place from which you brought so-and-so and remain there in (her) form while I have her here." When you have said this, they will all depart in silence. On the day or night and month and year when it pleases you to have her return home, say, "O you spirits, who brought so-and-so here, take her and carry her to her home. And whenever I wish her back, be compliant in carrying her here. Go, therefore, by the wondrous powers which you ineffably exercise." When you have said this three times, five spirits will come and carry her off in your sight.

When she enters the circle and you greet her, remember to touch her with the image that you have around your neck, and on this account she will love you for all eternity and will not care to see anyone but you. While you are with the woman, the image which you should keep around your neck will always be invisible to the woman herself, and when she leaves you should take it from your neck and lay it aside carefully in some sort of vessel. When it is thus laid aside, erase the entire circle, and you may depart safely. And when you wish to have (her) again come to you, do as is said above.

And note that this experiment is most effective and is not at all dangerous. By this experiment alone, Solomon had whatever women he wished. And let this suffice on the subject of obtaining women. And it should be carried out with the greatest solemnity.

23. Have a mirror made of pure steel, measuring one palm around, with a handle for holding it, and have it bright and shiny like a sword. And have it made in the name of Floron, and around the rim of the mirror, on the part that is not polished, have these ten names (Latranoy Iszarin, Bicol, Danmals, Gro, Zara, Ralkal, Sigtonia, Samah and Meneglasar) inscribed with ten characters with the name of the aforesaid spirit (Floron) written in the middle. After it has been made, it should be anointed with pure and bright balsam, and fumigated with aloes, ambergris, myrrh and white frankincense.

When this has been done, the master of this work should sit and have his mirror held with both hands by a virgin boy before his chest. The master himself should be bathed and dressed in clean garments. Before he begins to exercise this work he should sprinkle in the air honey, milk and wine, mixed together in equal proportions, while saying, "O Floron, respond quickly in the mirror, as you are accustomed to appear." . . . [Conjuration follows to be read before the mirror, and a mounted knight will appear who will tell the future.]

Questions: To achieve invisibility it is important to remain chaste for three days; what is the significance of the number three? What is the role of the moon in the conjuration for invisibility? What threat do the spirits/demons pose to the necromancer, and how can he protect himself? What is a likely reason that necromancers are virtually always men? In the conjurations above, the necromancers invoke God and demons; what theology underlies the procedures, and what separates the necromancers from witches? How are prophecy by the finger nail of a virgin boy (see doc. 41) and prophecy by a mirror similar?

58. A WARNING TO THE PEOPLE OF SIENA TO EXPUNGE WITCHES FROM THE CITY

Bernardino of Siena (1380–1444) was a Franciscan friar and preacher known as "the Apostle of Italy." He took it as his mission to reinvigorate the Catholic Church and in so doing played a major role in the religious revivals of the late Middle Ages. The friar was an indefatigable preacher; for over thirty years he traveled on foot the length and breadth of Italy, from city to city, warning his audiences of the evils of gambling, luxurious living, sodomy, usury, and witchcraft. His fiery and castigating sermons filled piazzas and cathedrals, attracted crowds from distant villages, and lasted three or four hours at a time; he often spoke up to fifty consecutive days in one location. According to his biographer, Barnaby of Sienna (fl. 1450), once Bernardino even took direct action by gathering and burning books and other magic paraphernalia. On another occasion he led an agitated crowd to a spring to destroy a structure where some citizens carried out "illicit" rites. Cities vied for this demagogue because of his zeal for moral cleansing and his success at orchestrating large public peace-making rituals.

One of the reasons Bernardino may have been so effective is that he drew upon the perceptions of magic and witchcraft his audiences already held. In the sermon below, the preacher condemns traditional sorcery, but new themes appear in his harangue against magic.

Source: trans. Helen Josephine Robins, Saint Bernardino of Siena, *Sermons*, ed. Nazareno Orlandi (Siena: Tipografia Sociale, 1920), pp. 163–68; rev. Martha Rampton.

Sermon 26. The Scourges of God

Would God it will not befall that a fearful judgment shall overtake you because of your sin; for I know well that you have blasphemed and that daily you do blaspheme God and the saints. Your land will be laid waste, and fire will light upon this, your city of Siena, and your country will fall under the rule of the enemy and will be sacked of all the good things found therein. . . .

2. Another sin which derives from pride is the sin of using charms and divinations. Because of this, God many times sends his scourges into cities. I know well that I spoke of this before, and I said so much about it that those who heard and those who comprehended must have been possessed with fear; for I spoke so plainly and clearly that I believe there remained nothing to be said in regard to it. Some of you here do magic by palm reading, others with letters, others with charms, others with sorceries, others with divinations; and there are those who have gone to the enchanter and to the diviner if they have been robbed of five pence. Do you know what you have done? You have caused men to renounce God, and you have caused the Devil to be adored. Ay me, ay me! The lord of heaven and earth has been debased. And to think that the Devil is adored through such great iniquity. You may say, "I do not understand the matter; for I find diviners have told me the truth." And I say to you in reply that you do not perceive how you have been deceived, and that one thing has been presented to you for another. Alas! You who are so blinded. Have you never comprehended the Devil's snares and deceits, how he has always deceived us and has exerted himself to do so? Go look at the beginning of Genesis, when Satan commenced to tempt and to deceive Eve and Adam, how persuading them to break the commandment of God, he said, "You shall be as gods, and you shall know good and evil" [Genesis 3:5] if you eat the fruit of this particular tree. So that thereby he made them fall.

You who have recourse to casting lots [similar to rolling dice], how great an evil you do, and how many there are who have trusted in them and followed you! Oh how well the casting of lots teaches you the truth! And have they never told you anything by which you can perceive that they lie? Yet even given their falsehood, you have never been willing to forsake them? Woe unto you! You who have recourse to the charm of "the three good friars," how great an evil you do! You who have recourse to the charm of the "misshapen cripple" [two healing charms], to you, and to him or to her who says that she is bewitched, and who makes you believe that she is bewitched; to all these I say, take heed, for the first to feel the strokes from the scourges of God will be those who have trusted in these enchantments and followed them, and next vengeance will overtake those who have not brought them to justice. Have you never noted in the Old Testament how God condemned this solely because it was displeasing to God? And this he made plain and clear. Know that she or he who says that she has power to break a charm knows as well, be assured, how to work one. When such as these say that they wish to cure anyone, do you know what you should do? There is nothing better to do than to cry, "To the fire, to the fire!" Woe is me! Do you not know what was done at Rome while I preached there? I wish I could make the same thing happen here. Come; let us offer a little incense here at Siena to the Lord God. I wish to relate what happened at Rome.

3. I preached of these charms and of witches and of sorceries, and it seemed to them as if I dreamed up all of which I spoke. Finally it came into my mind to say that whoever knows a man or a woman who does sorceries, if he does not accuse them, he is guilty of the same sin. And after I had preached, a multitude of witches and enchanters were accused. And because of the very great number of those accused, the guardian of the monastery came to me and said to me, "Don't you know that one and all are going to the flames?" I asked him, "What then? What is this, what is this? A great number of men and women has been accused." Finally, seeing how the matter stood, he took counsel with the pope, and it was determined that the most important of these women should be taken into custody; that is to say those who had done the worst. And there was taken among others one who confessed, without being put to torture, that she had killed thirty children or thereabouts, by sucking their blood; and she said also that she had let sixty go free; and she said that every time she let one of them go free she must sacrifice a limb to the Devil. And she used to offer the limb of an animal, and she had continued for a long time doing this. And yet she confessed even more, saying that she had killed her own little son and had made a powder of him, which she gave people to eat in these practices of hers. And because it seemed beyond belief that any creature could have done so many wicked things, they wished to prove whether this was indeed true.

Finally it was asked of her whom she had killed. She told who they were, and whose children they were, and in what way and when she had killed them. And they sought the proof from the father of those children who had been killed. Did you have a little son, who began to pine away, and then died? Finally, since he replied that this was so, and all agreed as to the day and the hour and the manner in which this had come to pass, it was shown to be nor more nor less than as she said. And she told how she used to go before dawn up into the Piazza of Saint Peter, and there she had certain jars of unguents made of herbs, which were gathered on the feast of Saint John and on the feast of the Ascension.

Do you know this? Do you comprehend me? Are you really present? Are there here perchance some of those cursed ones who are in league with the Devil? Finally these unguents came into my hands, and when I put them to my nose, they stank with so foul a stench that they seemed truly to be of the Devil, and that is because they were. It is said that with these unguents witches anoint themselves, and when they are anointed in this way they seem to be cats. But this is not so; for their bodies do not change into another form, but it seems to them that they do. At length the witch was condemned to be burned at the stake, and was burned so that nothing of her remained but her ashes.

4. There was also another one taken who confessed that she had done similar deeds, and she was also condemned to be burned, but she died in another manner. For she was not strangled before she was put upon pyre, and the fire

was kindled while she was alive, and nothing was seen of her thereafter her except her ashes. And what was done with these witches, the same should be done wherever one of them is found. And therefore I would give you this caution, and I warn you that wherever a witch may be, and whoever may know of one, or know her—within or outside the city—should straightway accuse her before the inquisitor, whether in the city or in the confines outside the walls, accuse her, every witch, every wizard, every sorcerer or sorceress or worker of charms and spells.

Do what I tell you in order that you are not called upon to answer for it on the day of judgment, having been able to prevent so great an evil, which might have been prevented if you had accused her. Again I say to you another thing, that if any man or woman is accused of such things and if any person goes to the aid of such a one, the curse of God will light upon his house, and he will suffer for it by losing his goods, and in his body, and afterwards also his soul. Fye! Answer me. Does it indeed seem to you that one who, when she was alive, killed twenty or thirty little children in such a fashion has done so well that when at length they are accused before the rulers you should go to their aid and beg mercy for them? If it had befallen you that she killed one of your little children, how then would the matter seem to you? From your own feelings take thought for another. Think of another and greater fact; do you not think that such enchanters, every time they have worked any charms or spells whatsoever, by so doing have denied God? How great a sin does this seem to you, to deny God, eh?

Questions: What elements in Bernardino's sermon are familiar aspects of the magic arts, and which are new? What role does gender play in Bernardino's perception of witches? Does Bernardino's audience, in general, appear to agree with his assessment of the "problem" in Siena? According to Bernardino, what is the major reason people should turn in witches?

59. TRIAL OF JOAN OF ARC

Joan of (or Jeanne d') Arc (c. 1412–1431), also called the Maid of Orléans, is likely the best-known woman of the Middle Ages. At a young age, Joan, a French peasant born in Lorraine, began to receive messages from the Archangel Michael and Saints Margaret and Catherine indicating that she would someday save France. At the time the French and English were fighting the Hundred Years' War (1337–1453), and France was on the defensive. Joan traveled to the town of Chinon, where she sought out Charles (later VII, r. 1422–1461), the uncrowned heir to the French throne, and emboldened him to claim his crown, lead his people, and drive the English from the continent. Charles followed Joan's advice, and from that point the tides of war turned in favor of the French. Many attributed the military victories to Joan, who wore soldiers' apparel and assisted on the battlefield. People, including soldiers, were inspired by a widely known legend that a maiden from Lorraine would bring deliverance to her people.

On 23 May 1430, the Burgundian allies of the English captured Joan at Compiègne and put her on trial. The case was momentous because of the political/military events involving English, French, and Burgundian court factions and the involvement of the Inquisition, the pope, and the University of Paris. On 30 May 1431, Joan was burned at the stake as a heretic.

Source: trans. T. Douglas Murray, *Jeanne D'Arc, Maid of Orléans: Deliverer of France: Being the Story of Her Life, Her Achievements, and Her Death as Attested on Oath and Set Forth in the Original Documents* (London: William Heinemann, 1903), pp. 20–21, 40–42, 66–67, 84, 87–88, 93, 111, 117, 119–21, 123–24, 129, 139–40, 142–45, 341–44, 348, 350, 352–53, 357–58, 361–64.

Third Public Examination: 24 February

QUESTION: What have you to say about a certain tree which is near to your village?

"Not far from Domrémy [in Lorraine] there is a tree that they call 'The Ladies' Tree.' Others call it 'The Fairies' Tree.' Nearby, there is a spring where people sick of the fever come to drink, as I have heard, and to seek water to restore their health. I have seen them myself come thus; but I do not know if they were healed. I have heard that the sick, once cured, come to this tree to walk about. It is a beautiful tree, a beech, from which comes the beau-may [flower]. It belongs to the Seigneur Pierre de Bourlement, knight. I have sometimes been to play with the young girls to make garlands for Our [Virgin] Lady of Domrémy. Often I have heard the old folk—they are not of my lineage—say that the fairies haunt this tree. I have also heard one of my godmothers named Joan, wife of the Marie Aubery of Domrémy, say that she has seen fairies there; whether it be true, I do not know. As for me, I never saw them that I know of. If I saw them anywhere else, I do not know. I have seen the young girls putting garlands on the branches of this tree, and I myself have sometimes put them there with my companions; sometimes we took these garlands away; sometimes we left them. Ever since I knew that it was necessary for me to come into France, I have given myself up as little as possible to these games and distractions. Since I was grown up, I do not remember having danced there. I may have danced there formerly with the other children. I have sung there more than danced.

There is also a wood called the Oak-Wood, which can be seen from my father's door; it is not more than half a league away. I do not know and have never heard if the fairies appear there, but my brother told me that it is said in the neighborhood, 'Jeannette received her mission at the Fairies' Tree.' It is not the case, and I told him the contrary. When I came before the king, several people asked me if there were not in my country a wood, called the Oak-Wood, because there were prophecies, which said that from the neighborhood of this wood would come a maid who should do marvelous things. I put no faith in that." . . .

Fifth Public Examination: 1 March

QUESTION: Did Saint Catherine and Saint Margaret speak to you under the tree of which mention has been made?
"I know nothing of it."

QUESTION: Did they speak to you at the spring which is near the tree?
"Yes, I have heard them there, but what they said then I do not know."

QUESTION: What did they promise you, there or elsewhere?
"They have never promised me anything, except by God's leave."

QUESTION: But still, what promises have they made to you? . . .

QUESTION: What have you done with your mandrake [a plant associated with sorcery]?
"I never have had one. But I have heard that there is one near our home, though I have never seen it. I have heard it is a dangerous and evil thing to keep. I do not know for what it is (used)."

QUESTION: Where is this mandrake of which you have heard?
"I have heard that it is in the earth near the tree of which I spoke before, but I do not know the place. Above this mandrake there was, it is said, a hazel tree."

QUESTION: What have you heard said was the use of this mandrake?
"To make money come, but I do not believe it. My voices [visions] never spoke to me of that." . . .

Third Private Examination: 12 March

. . . In order to give all security to this matter and by an excess of precaution, we have, by the advice of the masters, decided to write about it to the chief inquisitor requesting him to come himself without delay to Rouen or specially to appoint a deputy to whom, for the deduction and completion of the process, he might wish to give full powers. The said inquisitor has received our letter and acceding with kindness to our request. . . .

Seventh Private Examination: 15 March

. . . "When Saint Michael came to me, he said to me, 'Saint Catherine and Saint Margaret will come to you; follow their counsel; they have been chosen to guide you and counsel you in all that you have to do; believe what they shall tell you; it is the order of our Lord.'"

QUESTION: If the Devil were to put himself in the form or likeness of an angel, how would you know if it were a good or an evil angel? . . .

Eighth Private Examination: 17 March

QUESTION: Did your godmother, who saw the fairies, pass as a wise woman?
"She was held and considered a good and honest woman, neither divineress nor sorceress." . . .

QUESTION: Before today, did you believe fairies were evil spirits?'
"I know nothing about it." . . .

Ninth Private Examination: 17 March

QUESTION: Do you know nothing of those who came in the air with the fairies?
"I have never done or known anything about them, but I have heard of them and that they came on Thursdays; but I do not believe it; I think it is sorcery." . . .

Act of Accusation Prepared by the Promoter, the 70 Articles [of Joan's errors]: 27 March

Article 1: And first, according to divine law, as according to canon and civil law, it is to you, the bishop, as Judge Ordinary, and to you, the deputy, as Inquisitor of the Faith, to drive away, destroy, and cut out from the roots in your diocese and in all the kingdom of France, heresies, witchcrafts, superstitions, and other crimes of that nature. It is to you to punish, to correct, and to amend heretics and all those who publish, say, profess, or in any other manner act against our Catholic faith, to wit: sorcerers, diviners, invokes of demons, those who think ill of the faith, all criminals of this kind, their abettors and accomplices. [It is to you to] apprehend [heretics] in your diocese or in your jurisdiction, not only for the misdeeds they may have committed there, but even for the part of their misdeeds that they may have committed elsewhere, saving, in this respect, the power and duty of the other judges competent to pursue them in their respective dioceses, limits, and jurisdictions. And your power as to this exists against all lay persons, whatever be their estate, sex, quality, and pre-eminence. . . .

Article 2: The accused, not only this year, but from her infancy, and not only in your diocese, bishop, and your jurisdiction, deputy, but also in many other places of this kingdom, has done, composed, contrived, and ordained a number of sacrileges and superstitions. She made herself a diviner; she caused herself to be adored and venerated, she has invoked demons, and evil spirits; consulted them; associated with them; has made and has with them compacts, treaties, and conventions; has made use of them; has furnished to others—acting in the same manner—aid, succor, and favor; and has, in much, led them on to act like herself; she has said, affirmed, and maintained that to act thus, to use witchcraft, divinations, and superstitions, was not a sin or a forbidden thing, but, on the contrary, a thing lawful to be praised and worthy of approval. Also she has led into these errors and evil doings a very great number of persons of diverse estates, of both sexes, and has imprinted on their hearts the most fatal errors. Joan has been taken and arrested within the limits of your diocese of Beauvais, in the very act of perpetrating all these misdoings.

QUESTION: What have you to say to this article?
"I deny ever having used witchcraft, superstitious works, or divinations. As to allowing myself to be adored, if any kissed my hands and my garments, it was not my doing or by my wish. I sought to protect myself from it and to prevent it as much as I was able. And as for the rest of the article, I deny it."

Article 3: The accused had fallen into many diverse and detestable errors which reek of heresy. She has said, vociferated, uttered, published, and inculcated within the hearts of the simple, false and lying propositions allied to heresy. . . .

QUESTION: What have you to say to this Article?
"I deny it, and on the contrary affirm that I have always upheld the church so far as it lay in my power."

Article 5: Near the village of Domrémy there is a great tree, big and ancient; it is called the "Charmed Tree of the Fairy of Bourlement." Nearby is a spring; round this tree and this spring lived, it is said, evil spirits called fairies, with whom those who use witchcraft are accustomed to come and dance at night. . . .

Article 6: Accustomed to frequent this tree and this spring, above all by night, sometimes also by day, but at the times when the church celebrates the divine office, Joan, in order to find herself more alone, danced roundelays around this tree and this spring; from time to time she hung from its branches garlands of herbs and flowers woven by her own hands, accompanying her dances with songs mingled with invocations, sorceries, and other witchcrafts. The garlands, thus left overnight, on the following morning were not to be found.

QUESTION: What have you to say to this article?
"I refer for a part to my previous answers; the rest I deny."

Article 17: When Joan found herself in the presence of Charles, thus attired and armed, she promised him these three things among others: that she would raise the siege of Orléans, that she would have him consecrated at Rheims, that she would avenge him on his enemies, who, all of them English or Burgundians, should be, thanks to her, killed or driven out of the kingdom. Many times and in many places did she repeat publicly the same boasts, and to give them greater weight, then and often afterwards, she did use divinations and by these means unveiled the morals, the entire life, the most secret acts, of persons who came before her, whom she had never before seen or known; she boasted of knowing all by revelation. . . .

Article 23: The tenor of the letter contained in the preceding article proves well that Joan had been the sport of evil spirits, and that she often consulted them to know what she ought to do, or at least that, to seduce the people, she imagined these inventions by lying or wickedness.

QUESTION: What have you to say to this article?
"I deny ever having done anything under the inspiration of evil spirits."

Article 33: Joan had presumptuously and audaciously boasted, and does still boast, of knowing the future and of having foreseen the past, of knowing things that are in the present, but hidden or unknown, all which, an attribute of the deity, she claims for herself, a simple and ignorant creature.

QUESTION: What have you to say on this article?
"It is in our Lord's power to give revelations to whom he pleases." . . .

Article 49: On the foundation of this fancy alone Joan has venerated spirits of this kind, kissing the ground on the which she said they had walked, bending the knee before them, embracing them, kissing them, paying all sorts of adoration to them, giving them thanks with clasped hands, taking the greatest familiarities with them; when she did not know if they were good or evil spirits, and when, by reason of all the circumstances revealed above, these spirits should have been rather considered by her as evil. This worship, this veneration, is idolatry; it is a compact with demons. . . .

Article 51: Joan has not feared to proclaim that Saint Michael, the archangel of God, did come to her with a great multitude of angels in the house of a woman where she had stopped at Chinon, that he walked with her, holding her by the hand, that they together mounted the stairs of the castle and together gained the chamber of the king. . . .

Article 59: At St. Denis in France, Joan did offer and cause to be placed in the church, in the most prominent place, the armor she wore when she was wounded while attacking the town of Paris; she desired that this armor should be honored as relics. In this same town, she did cause to be lighted candles for the melted wax to fall on the heads of little children saying that this would bring them happiness, and making by such witchcrafts, many divinations.

QUESTION: What have you to say on this article?"
"As to my armor, I have answered; as to the candles lighted and melted, I deny it."

Article 62: Joan has labored to scandalize the people, to induce them to believe in her talk, taking to herself the authority of God and his angels. . . .

Article 66: Of many of the deeds and words that have just been noticed, some are opposed to the divine law, to Gospel law, to canon law, to civil law, and to the rules of general councils; others are witchcrafts, divination, or superstitions; others breathe heresy and errors in faith; others are attempts against peace and tend to the effusion of human blood; others constitute blasphemies against God and the saints and are wounding to pious ears. In all this, the accused, by her audacious temerity, at the instigation of the Devil, has offended God and sinned against holy church; she has been a cause of scandal; she is on all these points notoriously defamed. She should be punished and corrected by you.

QUESTION: What have you to say to this article?
"I am a good Christian; for all with which you charge me I refer to our Lord."

Public Admonition by the Judges: 2 May

. . . Before we [judges] come to a final decision, many honest men, conscientious and wise, have thought it would be well to seek by all means to instruct her on the points in which she seems to be lacking and to reinstate her in the way and knowledge of the truth. This result we have always desired, and we ardently desire it still. For we ought all to bend ourselves thereto, we who live in the church and in the ministration of holy things, we ought to strive to show to this woman, with all gentleness, that she is, by her words and by her actions, outside the faith, the truth, and religion, and to warn her charitably to think of her salvation. . . .

Admonition: 9 May

. . . We, the judges, being in the great tower of the castle of Rouen, assisted by the reverend fathers, doctors, and masters . . . did cause Joan to be brought before us. We did require and warn her to speak the truth to us on diverse and numerous points on which she has hitherto refused to reply or has replied untruthfully, the which are established in the highest degree by information, proofs, and grave presumptions. A great number of these points was read and shown to her. Then she was told that if she would not tell the truth, she would immediately be put to the torture, the instruments of which were here, in this same tower, under her eyes. There also were present the executioners, who by our order, had made all the necessary preparations for torturing her in order to bring her back by this means into the way and knowledge of the truth and thus to procure for her salvation both of body and soul, which she does expose to such grave peril by her lying inventions.

To which Joan replied in this manner.

"Truly if you were to tear me limb from limb and separate soul from body, I will tell you nothing more, and if I were to say anything else, I should always afterward declare that you made me say it by force." . . .

We, the judges, after having gathered the opinion of each, taking into consideration the answers made by Joan at the sitting on Wednesday last, taking into consideration also the disposition of her mind, her will so energetically manifested, and all the other circumstances of the case, decide that it is neither profitable nor expedient to submit her to the torture. . . .

Deliberations: 19 May

. . . We [bishops] did decide to send the assertions in question to our mother the University of Paris and principally to the faculties of theology and of decrees and to beseech the deliberation of the doctors and masters of the said university. . . . We decided that Joan should be again warned to return into the way of truth and salvation of soul and body. . . . We [judges] decided that we will, after this last monition, pronounce the closing of the process and give a day for the announcement of the sentence.

Final Session: 23 May

. . . "Therefore, if such things [visions] have appeared to you, do not believe them. The belief which you may have had in such illusions, put it away from you. Believe rather in the words and opinions of the University of Paris and other doctors, who, knowing the law of God and holy Scripture, decide that no faith should be placed in such apparitions, nor should faith be placed in any extraordinary apparitions, in any novelty, which is not supported by holy Scripture, by a sign, or by a miracle.

You have very lightly believed in such things, you who have not turned to God in earnest prayer that he would grant you certainty you who, to enlighten yourself, have not applied to a prelate or a learned ecclesiastic. This you ought to have done; it was your duty, considering your estate and the simplicity of your knowledge. . . .

The Sentence: 24 May

In the name of the Lord, amen. All the pastors of the church who have it in their hearts to watch faithfully over their flock, should, when the perfidious sower of errors [Satan] works by his machinations and deceits to infest the flock of Christ, strive with great care to resist his pernicious efforts with the greatest vigilance and the most lively solicitude, and above all in these perilous times, when so many false prophets are come into the world with their sects of error and perdition, according to the prediction thereof made by the Apostle [Paul]. Their diverse and strange doctrines might cause the faithful in Christ to stray if holy mother church, with the aid of wholesome doctrine and canonical sanction, did not study with great zeal to refute their inventions and errors. . . .

Final Adjudication: 29 May

. . . Joan should be considered a heretic; the sentence declaring her to be so, once given by us, the judges, she should be abandoned to the secular authority, which should be prayed to act toward her with gentleness. . . .

Sentence of Death: Final Sentence
Given before the People, 30 May

. . . At all times when the poisoned virus of heresy attaches itself with persistence to a member of the church and transforms him into a member of Satan, extreme care should be taken to watch that the horrible contagion of this pernicious leprosy does not gain other parts of the mystic body of Christ. The decisions of the holy fathers have willed that hardened heretics should be separated from the midst of the just, so that to the great peril of others this homicidal viper should not be warmed in the bosom of pious mother church. . . . We decree that you are a relapsed heretic, by our present sentence which, seated in tribunal, we utter and pronounce in this writing. We denounce you as a rotten member—and that you may not vitiate others—as cast out from the unity of the church, separate from her body, abandoned to the secular power as, indeed, by these present, we do cast you off, separate and abandon you, praying this same secular power, so far as concerns death and the mutilation of the limbs, to moderate its judgment toward you, and, if true signs of penitence should appear in you, (to permit) that the sacrament of penance be administered to you.

Here follows the sentence of excommunication . . . that you have been, on the subject of your pretended divine revelations and apparitions, lying, seducing, pernicious, presumptuous, lightly believing, rash, superstitious, a divineress and blasphemer toward God and the saints. [You have been] a despiser of God himself in his sacraments [and] a prevaricator of the divine law, of sacred doctrine, and of ecclesiastical sanctions. [You have been] seditious, cruel, apostate, schismatic, erring on many points of our faith, and in all these ways rashly guilty toward God and holy church. And also, because that often, very often, not only by us on our part but by doctors and masters—learned and expert, full of zeal for the salvation of your soul—you have been duly and sufficiently warned to amend, to correct yourself, and to submit to the disposal, decision, and correction of holy mother church, which you have not willed and have always obstinately refused to do, having even expressly and many times refused to submit yourself, to our lord, the pope, and to the general council. For these causes, as hardened and obstinate in your crimes, excesses, and errors, we declare you rightly excommunicate and heretic. . . .

Questions: Was Joan considered a "witch"? How did the judges define "heresy"? Why did the judges think it was important for the sake both of Joan and fellow Christians that she be killed? Which court issued the death sentence: church or state? Why were the inquisitors interested in the tree and well near Joan's childhood home? Why were the judges troubled by the "voices" of Archangel Michael and Saints Margaret and Catherine that spoke to Joan?

60. WITCH BELIEFS COALESCE: *FORMICARIUS*

Johann Nider (c. 1380–1438) was a Dominican friar and professor of theology in Vienna. A celebrated scholar, preacher, and inquisitor, he was invited in 1431 to participate in the important general reform Council of Basel (1431–1449). In 1437 Nider published Formicarius, *a treatise consisting of five books, of which the fifth is entitled "witches and their deceptions." *Formicarius *was only the second book published on witchcraft to that point. It is a seminal text for understanding the origins of witch beliefs and the early stages of the witch-hunts.* Formicarius *was instrumental in articulating the concept of "the witch" that was coalescing at the time, and Nider was the first ecclesiastical authority to attribute the crime of witchcraft specifically to women. The book circulated*

widely and served as source material for numerous subsequent treatises on witchcraft. It sur-
vives in over twenty-five manuscripts, and seven editions were printed from the 1470s to 1692.

The title of the work means "ant colony," from Proverbs (6:6), and is a metaphor for a
rightly structured society. Formicarius *takes the form of a dialogue between a theologian*
and a doubter, a conceit that allows Nider to relate incidents from his personal experience
or those his colleagues had related to him. As Nider hoped, these stories provided clergy-
men with ready-made exempla *frequently used in sermons. Although* Formicarius *is*
best known as a manual on witchcraft, the author's intent was to promote overall church
reform—a project that he felt was impeded by the existence of heretics and witches in
league with the forces of evil.

Sources: Book 5.3: George L. Burr, Johannes Nider, *Formicarius*, in *The Witch Persecutions*, Translations and Reprints from the Original Sources of European History, vol. 3 (Philadelphia: University
of Pennsylvania, 1907), pp. 6–7; Books 5.6 and 10: G.G. Coulton, *Life in the Middle Ages*, vol. 1 (New
York, The Macmillan Company, 1930), pp. 210–11, 213–15.

Book 5.3

[Master:] I will relate to you some examples which I have gained in part from
the teachers of our faculty, in part from the experience of a certain upright
secular judge, worthy of all faith, who, from the torture and confession of
witches and from his experiences in public and private, has learned many things
of this sort—a man with whom I have often discussed this subject broadly and
deeply—to wit, Peter [of Gruyères, d. 1406], a citizen of Bern, in the diocese of
Lausanne, who has burned many witches of both sexes and has driven others out
of the territory of the Bernese. I have moreover conferred with one Benedict,
a monk of the Benedictine order, who, although now a very devout cleric in
a reformed monastery at Vienna, was a decade ago, while still in the world, a
necromancer, juggler, buffoon, and strolling player, well-known as an expert
among the secular nobility. I have likewise heard certain of the following things
from the Inquisitor of Heretical Pravity [the Inquistion] at Autun, who was a
devoted reformer of our order in the convent at Lyons and has convicted many
of witchcraft in the diocese of Autun.

(After relating two or three anecdotes derived from these sources, the theologian closes his answer with the following.)

The same procedure was more clearly described by another young man
arrested and burned as a witch, although, as I believe, truly penitent, who had
earlier, together with his wife, a witch invincible to persuasion, escaped the
clutches of the aforesaid judge, Peter. The aforesaid youth, being again indicted
at Bern with his wife and placed in a different prison from hers, declared, "If
I can obtain absolution for my sins, I will freely lay bare all I know about witchcraft, for I see that I have death to expect." And when he had been assured by

the scholars that if he should truly repent he would certainly be able to gain absolution for his sins, then he gladly offered himself to death and disclosed the methods of the primeval infection.

"The ceremony," he said, "of my seduction was as follows. First, on a Sunday, before the holy water is consecrated, the future disciple with his masters must go into the church and there in their presence must renounce Christ and his faith, baptism, and the church universal. Then he must do homage to the *magisterulus*, that is, to the little master (for so, and not otherwise, they call the Devil). Afterward he drinks from the aforesaid flask [filled with liquid made from murdered infants], and, this done, he forthwith feels himself to conceive and hold within himself an image of our art and the chief rites of this sect. After this fashion was I seduced, and my wife also, whom I believe of so great pertinacity that she will endure the flames rather than confess the least whit of the truth. But, alas, we are both guilty. What the young man had said was found in all respects the truth. For, after confession, the young man was seen to die in great contrition. His wife, however, though convicted by the testimony of witnesses, would not confess the truth even under the torture or in death; but, when the fire was prepared for her by the executioner, uttered in most evil words a curse upon him, and so was burned.

Book 5.6

Master: Hear, therefore, what befell a certain woman whom I saw at Regensburg in the days of this present Council of Basel (after 1431), and whom I helped to examine. She was an unmarried girl, nor had she ever a husband, nor was she suspected of incontinence, but she had often changed her abode from city to city, from house to house, and this had gone on for very many years. Then, at the age of about fifty-three she came to Regensburg, where she uttered certain very incautious words concerning the Rule of the Faith, on which account she was accused before the vicar of the bishop of Regensburg, who clapped her into prison. Meanwhile there came the lord John de Polomar, archdeacon of Barcelona [fl. 1430], as envoy of the said General Council [at Basel] in the matter of the Bohemian (rebellion), a man full of all devotion and singularly learned both in canon and in civil law. I was his companion and colleague in those days upon the same mission. Therefore we were called in to the examination of the said woman, wherein she was daily proved and found to be in many errors; yet she seemed to have no hurt in her brain that would cause defect of reason, for she answered very astutely to each objection made against her, and, when we questioned her, she answered with great deliberation and caution to avoid contradicting herself. For she said that she had had a spirit of God, or divine revelations; she refused obedience to the pope in matters which he had ill disposed; she affirmed herself more blessed than the chiefs of the apostles had been in this present life; she believed herself inerrant or impeccable; and, in short, she asserted both in word and by signs of her head that she was the mother of the whole church of Christ, which was represented at this Council of Basel.

I therefore, and many who were present, strove by persuasive words from holy Scripture to get these wayward thoughts out of the woman's head, but there we profited nothing; for she answered boldly that she knew she was in no error with regard to the aforesaid matters, but rather that her examiners erred, and thus she showed herself ready to go through fire in defense of her own truth. When we saw this, the above-mentioned archdeacon said unto the doctors both of divinity and of other faculties, whereof there were many present, "You shall see that vexation alone shall make her understand (Isaiah 28:19); wherefore it is necessary that she be racked by the torture of public justice, somewhat slowly in proportion as her sex may be able to endure it, but you" (this he said secretly to me and to my companion in the [Dominican] Order, a certain very devout and learned lector) "show in this woman's sight that you will not be present at her torture, and, if you please, absent yourselves in order that her goodwill towards you may the more endure, and thus, when she has been humbled by torture, you will then be the better fitted to convert her."

So we did, and all things were done as I have described. And they asked of her, while she was being tortured, from whom she had learned her errors and whether she had any disciple or accomplice therein; for on these points she had never before given anything but denial, saying that no man had taught her these errors, nor had she taught any woman, but that she had believed them silently in her own heart, taught (as she said) by an angel or by the spirit of God. Therefore, having been tortured for a little while, she added nothing new, confessed no man's guilt but her own, and abode constantly by her assertions. And I think she spoke truth; yet she was much humbled by the vexation [anguish] of her limbs; wherefore she was brought back to her prison tower and, at the archdeacon's bidding, my companion and I visited the wretched woman that same evening. She could scarce stir for pain, but when she saw us she broke into loud lamentations, and told us in good faith how grievously she had been hurt. So we, considering that she had been humbled and that she had a good opinion of us, told her many stories to show how many eminent and learned men had been deceived by incautious revelations and misled by the angel, Satan, and we adduced many citations from holy Scripture to show how frail is the female sex when unaided.

Then, by Christ's grace, she began to change her mind for the better and to promise that she would follow me and my companion in all things. Therefore she believed herself to have been deceived, and of her own accord she made sacramental confession to me of all that she had done from her youth up and showed herself ready to revoke her error publicly and to repent. Thus on the third day after, before the whole city of Regensburg, while many wept for joy and compassion, she performed all that I have said.

10. Pupil: In your opinion, have some good men been deceived by sorceresses or witches in our own day?

Master: In what here follows, I suspend my judgment; I will tell you what is repeated by public rumor and report. We have in our days the distinguished professor of divinity, brother Heinrich Kaltyseren, Inquisitor of Heretical Pravity. Last year, while he was exercising his inquisitorial office in the city of Cologne, as he himself told me, he found in the neighborhood a certain maiden who always went about in man's dress and bore arms and dissolute garments like one of the nobles' retainers. She danced in dances with men and was so given to feasting and drink that she seemed altogether to overpass the bounds of her sex, which she did not conceal. And because at that time, (as, alas! even today) the see of Trier was sorely troubled by two rivals contending for the bishopric, she boasted that she could and would set one party upon the throne, even as Maid Joan, of whom I shall presently speak, had done shortly before with Charles, king of France, by confirming him in his kingdom. Indeed, this woman claimed to be that same Joan, raised up by God [see doc. 59].

One day therefore, when she had come into Cologne with the young count of Württemberg, who protected and favored her, and there, in the sight of the nobles, had performed wonders which seemed due to the magic arts, she was at last diligently scrutinized and publicly cited by the aforesaid inquisitor, in order that she might be examined. For she was said to have cut a napkin in pieces and suddenly to have restored it whole in the sight of the people, to have thrown a glass against the wall and broken it and to have repaired it in a moment, and to have shown many such idle devices. But the wretched woman would not obey the commands of the church; the count protected her from arrest and brought her secretly out of Cologne; thus she did indeed escape from the inquisitor's hands but not from the sentence of excommunication. Thus bound under curse, she quitted Germany for France, where she married a certain knight to protect herself against ecclesiastical interdict and the sword. Then a certain priest, or rather pimp, seduced this witch with talk of love so that she stole away with him at length and went to Metz, where she lived as his concubine and showed all men openly by what spirit she was led. . . .

Pupil: I cannot sufficiently marvel how the frail sex can dare to rush into such presumptuous things.

Master: These things are marvelous to simple folk like you, but they are not rare in the eyes of wise men. For there are three things in nature, which, if they transgress the limits of their own condition, whether by diminution or by excess, attain to the highest pinnacle whether of goodness or of evil. These are, the tongue, the ecclesiastic, and the woman; all these are commonly best of all, so long as they are guided by a good spirit, but worst of all if guided by an evil spirit.

Questions: What does a person gain by confession and contrition when found guilty of witchcraft? For Nider, is the gender of a witch an important issue? Explain. Taking into account the above segments of Formicarius *as a whole, how central is the Devil to witchcraft?*

61. THE ORDINAL OF ALCHEMY

Alchemy was a proto-science embedded within an ancient philosophic tradition that was practiced in Egypt, Asia, and the Islamic world for centuries before it found its way into Europe in the twelfth century through translations of Arabic texts. The basic premise is that the creation of a "philosopher's stone" would facilitate the transmutation of "base metals" like lead into "noble metals," specifically silver and gold. The correctly performed alchemical process could also produce both "panacea," a cure-all, and a potion called the "elixir of life"—"white drops" of liquid gold that granted eternal life or perpetual youth. The desired alchemical results depended on a rigid process that required arcane erudition, secrecy, expensive paraphernalia, and a practitioner of great virtue and spiritual purity.

Thomas Norton (c. 1433–c. 1513) was a poet, alchemist, and courtier under Henry VI (r. 1422–61, 1470–71) and Edward IV (r. 1461–70, 1471–83) of England. His how-to book, The Ordinal of Alchemy, *written in verse, was well respected and widely circulated. Although alchemy was generally revered and practiced in universities and courts, the esoteric and ritualistic nature of the art was, to some extent, dependent on astrology and therefore dangerously similar to necromantic magic.*

Source: trans. into prose by Arthur Edward Waite, *The Chemical Treatise of Thomas Norton, The Englishman, Called Believe-Me, or The Ordinal of Alchemy.* The Hermetic Museum, vol. 2 (London: James Eliott and Co., 1893), pp. 4–5, 12–13, 16–17, 22–26, 41–42, 64.

Preface Second

. . . If you enquire into the motives of men, you will find many who are induced to give their minds to the study of alchemy only by the desire of gain and riches, and such men are found even among cardinals of highest rank, archbishops, and bishops of lofty order, abbots and religious priors, also among hermits, monks, and common priests, and among kings, princes, and lords of high degree.

For men of all classes desire to partake of our good things. . . . The goldsmiths are consumed with the desire of knowing—though them we may excuse since they have daily before their eyes that which they long to possess. But we may wonder that weavers, freemasons, tailors, cobblers, and needy priests join in the general search after the philosopher's stone, and that even painters and glaziers cannot restrain themselves from it. Nay, tinkers presumptuously aspire to exalt themselves by its means, though they should be content with the color with which glass is stained. Many of these workmen, however, have been deceived by giving credulous heed to impostors who helped them to convert their gold into smoke, and though they are grieved and disappointed at the loss, they yet buoy themselves up with sanguine thoughts and hope that they will after all reach the goal; alas, too many have I known, who, after amusing themselves with delusive hopes through a long life, have at last died in squalid poverty. For them it would have been better if they had stayed their hands at once, seeing that they met with nothing but disappointment and vexation of spirit. For, surely, he who is not very learned will do well to think twice before he meddles with this art. Believe me, it is by no means a light matter to know all the secrets connected with the science. Nay, it is a profound philosophy, a subtle science, and a sacred alchemy. . . .

1. . . . But even if this art could, on account of its effects, be justly denied a claim to sanctity, it would still be sacred on account of its nature and essence. For as, on the one hand, no one can discover it except by the grace of God, so it is also holy because it is a divine labor and work to change vile copper into the finest silver and gold. For no one could discover a method of producing such effects by his own thought, seeing that the substances are diverse, and man cannot separate that which God has joined together. Nor could the course of nature be quickened unless God himself had granted the aid of this mighty science to those whom he loves. Therefore, the ancient sages have well called alchemy a sacred science, and no one should be so presumptuous as to cast away the blessed gift of God. For let us only consider that God has hidden this knowledge from great and learned doctors, and out of his mercy has revealed it to men of low degree, who are faithful lovers of truth and lowly of heart, and as there are only seven planets among the vast multitude of the stars of heaven, so among millions of millions of men hardly seven attain to this knowledge. . . .

Nevertheless, we have known one metal to be transmuted into another of a different kind by means of the cognate nature of their substances; so, for instance, iron has been changed into bronze. But nothing can produce real silver or gold except the medicine of the philosophers. Hence the falsehoods affected by the multipliers are eschewed and shunned by all true sages. But all honor and reverence is due to the genuine art of sacred alchemy, which is concerned with the precious medicine that has virtue to produce pure gold and silver. . . .

This science derives its name from a certain King Alchymus of illustrious memory, who, being a generous and noble-hearted prince, first set himself to study this art. He ceased not to question nature by day and by night, and at last extorted from her a blessed answer. King Hermes [Trismegistus, legendary] also did a similar thing, being deeply versed in every kind of learning. His *Quadri-partite* deals with the four great branches of natural science: astrology, medicine, alchemy, and natural magic. . . .

2. . . . Again, let me tell you a little more about the sorrows and troubles of the alchemist, which may considerably moderate your desire to acquire the practice of this art. At first it is most difficult, as the sages say, to find out among so many impostors, the man who has a perfect understanding of our science. And when you have found a truly learned master, you have not yet by any means left all your trouble far behind you. If your mind is devoted to virtue, the Devil will do his utmost to frustrate your search by one or the other of three stumbling blocks, namely, haste, despair, or deception. For he is afraid of the good works which you may do if you succeed in mastering this secret. The first danger lies in undue haste, which destroys and mars the work of many.

All authors who have written about this art agree in saying, like the author of the little book of *The Philosopher's Feast*, that undue haste is of the Devil. Hence he will the soonest make an end who tarries a little at the beginning, and those who act otherwise will discover to their cost the truth of the proverb which says, "The greater haste we make, the less will be our speed." For he who is in a hurry will complete his work neither in a month, nor yet in a year, and in this art it will always be true that the man who is in a hurry will never be without matter of complaint. Rest assured also that haste will precipitate you from the pinnacle of truth. It is the Devil's subtlest device to ensnare us; for this haste is an *ignis-fatuus* [deceptive hope] by which he causes us to wander from the right path. . . .

I will say no more about hurry, but blessed is he who possesses patience. If the enemy does not prevail against you by hurry, he will assault you with despondency and will be constantly putting into your minds discouraging thoughts about how those who seek this art are many while they are few that find it, and how those who fail are often wiser men than yourself. He will then ask you what hope there can be of your attaining the grand *arcanum* [mystery]; moreover, he will vex you with doubts: whether your master is himself possessed of the secret which he professes to impart to you, or whether he is not concealing from you the best part of that which he knows. The Evil One [Satan] will endeavor to fill your mind with these doubts, in order to turn you from your purpose by diffidence and despondency. Nor will anything avail against his assaults except the calm confidence inspired by virtue, and the sound conclusions of reason. . . .

The third enemy against whom you must guard is deceit, and this one is perhaps more dangerous than the other two. . . . For when I had all my experiments in proper train, some thievish servants ran away with my materials and utensils, and left me nothing but the empty laboratory, and when I calculated the cost, time, and labor of beginning the work all over again, I had almost in the bitterness of my heart resolved to bid an everlasting farewell to this art of alchemy. For it will hardly be believed how completely I had been stripped of all that I possessed, although ten trustworthy persons still survive to attest the fact. Indeed, the blow was so great that it could hardly have been inflicted on me by human agency alone, without the instigation and cooperation of the Devil. I also made an elixir of life, of which a merchant's wife bereft me, and I procured a quintessence, with many other precious preparations, but of all these things I was robbed. . . .

5. . . . But, as far as this art is concerned, we must regard as the mistress of all sciences, the science of natural magic. Now, when the four elements have been wisely combined, and each thing ordered in its own proper degree, then we shall behold in the various stages of coction [advancement], a constantly shifting succession of colors until perfection is attained. For the substance is wrought upon from within by the natural warmth, which is found to exist intellectually in our substance, though it can be neither seen, nor felt, nor handled. Its operation is known only to a few. When this inward natural heat is stirred up by the influence of outward artificial heat, nature, having once been roused into activity, will go on to operate and produce the various changes which the substance has to undergo, and this is one cause, as the sages will tell you, why so many colors are seen in our work. . . .

6. . . . The fifth rule is well known to the learned. There should exist a certain harmony between the celestial spheres and our work. Nothing on earth is so simple or so easily influenced as the elements of our stone, and when they are being prepared they obey their own proper constellations, as the needle yields to the influence of the magnet. Let this amicable concord prevail, then, in a direct and fiery ascendant, and let your happy and favorable ascendant be in fortunate aspect with his Lord. The work should be sheltered from all adverse and evil influences; if these cannot be set aside, let them have a trine [one third of a circle] aspect. When you prepare the white tincture, let the moon be fortunate, as also the Lord of the Fourth House, which is the Treasure of Hidden Things, according to the old sages. The Sixth House must be favorable for the servants.

Preserve your work from all great impediments, and see that it be not affected by the adverse constellation of your nativity. The virtue of the mover of the orb is the formal influence; the virtue of the eighth sphere is instrumental to it; the virtue of the planet is proper and special; and that of the elements is material and embodies the working of the other agents. The first resembles the genius of the operator; the second is analogous to his hands; the third corresponds to his instruments; and the fourth answers to the substance which is prepared. Let the things on earth correspond to things in heaven, and you will obtain the elixir, and become a great master. Do not trust to geomancy [divination by geometric figures], which is a superstitious art; nor to all astrologers, because this science is secret, like that of alchemy. Necromancy God forbids and the church condemns; therefore, if you wish for success, let your hands be pure from all superstitious practices. Necromancy is of the Devil and a lying art. God will bless you if you give yourself wholly to the study of our own blessed art. In the next chapter I will speak about the regulation of the fire.

Questions: Why does Norton consider alchemy a sacred science? With what other categories of knowledge does Norton classify alchemy? Why and in what manner does the Devil seek to hamper the work of the alchemist? What is the relationship between alchemy and philosophy and between alchemy and astrology? Is there anything in the excerpts above that indicate that Norton was conflicted about his art in terms of the Catholic Church's stand on magic?

62. NATURAL MAGIC AND RENAISSANCE HUMANISM: ORATION ON THE DIGNITY OF MAN

Giovanni Pico della Mirandola (1463–1494) was a philosopher, humanist, and perhaps the most influential Renaissance magus (wise man). He studied in the vital scholarly centers of his day. The Oration on the Dignity of Man *is the preface to a treatise in which Pico lays out the concept of the syncretism among various religious and mystical traditions from classical thought, Jewish mysticism, Christian and Islamic theology, and contemporary Neoplatonic theories of natural philosophy. The* Oration *is sometimes called the manifesto of the Renaissance. The thesis of the work is that since human beings were created last and had no fixed place in the chain of being, God placed them at the center of the world with independent will to determine their own destinies. It is a paean to the human potential for spiritual, moral, and intellectual grandeur and a masterpiece of humanist thinking.*

Pico places magic within his continuum of systems of knowledge, but he is clear that there are two doctrines commonly called "magic": demonic and natural. Although Pico felt that any genuine philosopher would know the difference, there were many, he feared, who did not.

Source: trans. Charles Glenn Wallis, Pico della Mirandola, On the Dignity of Man (Indianapolis: Hackett Publishing Company, 1998), pp. 26–29.

. . . I have proposed theorems about magic, too, wherein I have signified that magic is twofold. The first sort is put together by the work and authorship of demons, and is a thing, as God is true, execrable and monstrous. The other sort is, when well explored, nothing but the absolute consummation of the philosophy of nature. When the Greeks mention these, they call the first sort [*goetia*], not dignifying it in any way by the name magic. They call the second sort by its proper and peculiar name [*mageia*], the perfect and highest wisdom, as it were. Porphyry [philosopher, c. 233–c. 305] says that in the language of the Persians, magician means the same thing as interpreter and lover of divine things means in our language. Now there is a great, or rather, fathers, there is the greatest disparity and unlikeness between these arts. Not only the Christian religion, but all laws, every well-ordered state, condemns and curses the first. All wise men, all nations studious of things heavenly and divine, approve and embrace the second.

The first is the most fraudulent of arts; the second is firm, faithful, and solid. Whoever cultivated the first always dissimulated it, because it would be in ignominy and disgrace of the author. From the second comes the highest splendor and glory of letters, desired in ancient times and almost always since then. No man who was a philosopher and desirous of learning good arts has ever been studious of the first. Pythagoras, Empedocles, Democritus, Plato [ancient Greek philosophers], traveled across seas to learn the second. When they came back, they preached it and held it chief among their esoteric doctrines. The first can be proved by no arguments nor certain founders; the second, [is] honored, as it were, by most illustrious parents. . . . I find three among the moderns who have caught the scent of it, Alchindus the Arab [unknown], Roger Bacon [c. 1220–92], and William of Paris (of Auvergne) [c. 1190–1249]. Plotinus [204–270] too mentions it, where he shows that the magician is the minister and not the maker of nature. That most wise man proves and asserts this second magic, so abhorring the other that, invited to the rites of evil demons, he replied that it was more fitting for them to come to him than for him to go to them, and rightly so. For as the first magic makes man subject to and delivered over to the powers of wickedness, so the second makes him their prince and lord. Finally, the first cannot claim for itself the name of either art or science.

The second is full of the deepest mysteries and includes the most profound and hidden contemplation of things, and finally, the knowledge of all nature. The second, among the virtues sown by the kindness of God and planted in the world, as if calling them out from darkness into light, does not so much make wonders as carefully serve nature which makes them. Having carefully investigated the harmony of the universe, which the Greeks very expressively call [sympathy], and having looked closely into the knowledge that natures have of each other, this second magic, applying to each thing its innate charms, which are called by magicians [*iugges*], as if it were itself the maker, discloses in public the wonders lying hidden in the recesses of the world, in the bosom of nature, in the storerooms and secrets of God. And as the farmer marries elm to vine, so the magician marries earth to heaven, that is, lower things to the qualities and virtues of higher things. Hence the first magic appears as monstrous and harmful as the second, divine and salutary. And especially because the first magic delivers man over to the enemies of God, calls him away from God, this second magic arouses that admiration at the works of God which so prepares that charity, faith, and hope most surely follow. For nothing impels more toward religion and the worship of God than assiduous contemplation of the wonders of God. When we shall have well explored these wonders by means of this natural magic we are speaking of, we shall be inspired more ardently to the worship and love of the maker, and shall be driven to sing: "The heavens are full, all the earth is full of the majesty of your glory" [Isaiah 6:3].

And this is enough about magic, about which I have said these things because I know there are many people who, as dogs always bark at strangers, so also often condemn and hate what they do not understand.

Questions: Why does Pico condemn goeteia? *What is the nature of* mageia, *and why does Pico praise it so? From which socio-economic level was the intended audience for Pico's* Oration *likely to have been drawn? Why were Italian Renaissance thinkers so fascinated with magic?*

63. POPE INNOCENT VIII EMPOWERS THE INQUISITORS

The Hammer of Witches (Malleus Maleficarum) *is an extensive treatise on the theory, activities, detection, prosecution, and punishment of witches, written by Heinrich Kramer and [c. 1430–1505] (ostensibly by) Jacob Sprenger [c. 1438–1495], two German Dominican friars. The work was controversial in its time, but it was widely disseminated and consulted throughout the era of the witch-hunts.*

*Kramer was a self-styled magistrate with a deep commitment to eradicating what he saw as the growing pestilence of witchcraft in Christendom. Without a formal commission, he began prosecuting alleged witches in Tyrol, but the local bishop of Innsbruck expelled him for usurping episcopal prerogatives. After this incident, Kramer solicited Sprenger, dean of the faculty of theology at the University of Cologne and inquisitor for the provinces of Mainz, Trier, and Cologne, to join his crusade, and in 1484 the two friars acquired a papal bull (*Summis desiderantes affectibus: *"desiring with the greatest ardor") that reaffirmed the entitlement of the Inquisition, generally, and authorized Kramer and Sprenger, specifically, to apprehend and try witches in the areas under their jurisdiction. Three years later, when the* Malleus Maleficarum *was published, the papal bull was included as the preface to the work, giving the false impression that Innocent VIII (1432–1492) had fully endorsed the contents of the treatise.*

Source: trans. Montague Summers, *Malleus Maleficarum* (New York: Benjamin Blom, 1928), pp. xliii–xlv.

Summis desiderantes affectibus

Innocent, bishop, servant of the servants of God, for an eternal remembrance.

Desiring with the most heartfelt anxiety, even as our apostleship requires, that the Catholic faith should, especially in this our day, increase and flourish everywhere and that all heretical depravity should be driven far from the frontiers and boundaries of the faithful, we very gladly proclaim and even restate those particular means and methods whereby our pious desire may obtain its wished effect, since when all errors are uprooted by our diligent avocation as by the hoe of a provident husbandman, a zeal for, and the regular observance of, our holy faith will be all the more strongly impressed upon the hearts of the faithful.

It has indeed lately come to our ears, not without afflicting us with bitter sorrow, that in some parts of northern Germany, as well as in the provinces, townships, territories, districts, and dioceses of Mainz, Cologne, Trier, Salzburg, and Bremen, many persons of both sexes, unmindful of their own salvation and straying from the Catholic faith, have abandoned themselves to devils, *incubi*, and *succubi,* and by their incantations, spells, conjurations, and other accursed charms and crafts, enormities, and horrid offences, have slain infants yet in the mother's womb (as also the offspring of cattle) have blasted the produce of the earth, the grapes of the vine, the fruits of trees, nay, men and women, beasts of burden, herd-beasts, as well as animals of other kinds, vineyards, orchards, meadows, pasture-land, corn, wheat, and all other cereals; these wretches furthermore afflict and torment men and women, beasts of burden, herd-beasts, as well as animals of other kinds, with terrible and piteous pains and sore diseases, both internal and external; they hinder men from performing the sexual act and women from conceiving, whence husbands cannot know their wives nor wives receive their husbands; over and above this, they blasphemously renounce that faith which is theirs by the sacrament of baptism and, at the instigation of the enemy of mankind, they do not shrink from committing and perpetrating the foulest abominations and filthiest excesses to the deadly peril of their own souls, whereby they outrage the divine majesty and are a cause of scandal and danger to very many.

Our dear sons, Heinrich Kramer and Jacob Sprenger, professors of theology of the Order of Friars Preachers, have been by letters apostolic delegated as inquisitors of these heretical depravities, and still are inquisitors—the first in the aforesaid parts of Northern Germany—wherein are included those aforesaid townships, districts, dioceses, and other specified localities, and the second in certain territories which lie along the borders of the Rhi. Nevertheless not a few clerics and lay folk of those countries, seeking too curiously to know more than concerns them, since in the aforesaid delegatory letters there is no express and specific mention by name of these provinces, townships, dioceses, and districts, and further since the two delegates themselves and the abominations they are to encounter are not designated in detailed and particular fashion, these persons are not ashamed to contend with the most unblushing effrontery that these enormities are not practiced in those provinces. Consequently [they claim that] the aforesaid inquisitors have no legal right to exercise their powers of inquisition in the provinces, townships, dioceses, districts, and territories, which have been rehearsed, and that the inquisitors may not proceed to punish, imprison, and penalize criminals convicted of the heinous offences and many wickednesses which have been set forth. Accordingly, in the aforesaid provinces, townships, dioceses, and districts, the abominations and enormities in question remain unpunished not without open danger to the souls of many and peril of eternal damnation.

Wherefore we, as is our duty, are wholly desirous of removing all hindrances and obstacles by which the good work of the inquisitors may be impeded, also of applying potent remedies to prevent the disease of heresy and other turpitudes diffusing their poison to the destruction of many innocent souls, since our zeal for the faith especially incites us, lest that the provinces, townships, dioceses, districts, and territories of Germany, which we have specified, be deprived of the benefits of the Holy Office thereto assigned. By the tenor of these presents in virtue of our apostolic authority we decree and enjoin that the aforesaid inquisitors be empowered to proceed to the just correction, imprisonment, and punishment of any persons, without let or hindrance, in every way as if the provinces, townships, dioceses, districts, territories, yea, even the persons and their crimes in this kind were named and particularly designated in our letters. Moreover, for greater surety we extend these letters deputing this authority to cover all the aforesaid provinces, townships, dioceses, districts, and territories, persons, and crimes newly rehearsed, and we grant permission to the aforesaid inquisitors, to one separately or to both, as also to our dear son John Gremper, priest of the diocese of Constance, master of arts, their notary, or to any other public notary, who shall be by them, or by one of them, temporarily delegated to those provinces, townships, dioceses, districts, and aforesaid territories, to proceed, according to the regulations of the Inquisition, against any persons of whatsoever rank and high estate, correcting, mulcting, imprisoning, punishing, as their crimes merit, those whom they have found guilty, the penalty being adapted to the offence.

Moreover, they shall enjoy a full and perfect faculty of expounding and preaching the word of God to the faithful, so often as opportunity may offer and it may seem good to them, in each and every parish church of the said provinces, and they shall freely and lawfully perform any rites or execute any business which may appear advisable in the aforesaid cases. By our supreme authority we grant them anew full and complete faculties. At the same time by letters apostolic we require our venerable brother, the bishop of Strasburg

[Albrecht von Bayern, 1440–1506] that he himself shall announce, or by some other or others cause to be announced, the burden of our bull, which he shall solemnly publish when and so often as he deems it necessary, or when he shall be requested so to do by the inquisitors or by one of them. Nor shall he suffer them in disobedience to the tenor of these presents to be molested or hindered by any authority whatsoever, but he shall threaten all who endeavor to hinder or harass the inquisitors, all who oppose them, all rebels, of whatsoever rank, estate, position, preeminence, dignity, or any condition they may be, or whatsoever privilege of exemption they may claim, with excommunication, suspension, interdict, and yet more terrible penalties, censures, and punishment, as may seem good to him, and that without any right of appeal. If he will he may by our authority aggravate and renew these penalties as often as he deems fit, calling in, if so please him, the help of the secular arm. . . . But if any dare to [impede the inquisitors' work], which God forbid, let him know that upon him will fall the wrath of almighty God, and of the blessed apostles Peter and Paul.

Questions: What are the pope's major concerns with the incidences of witchcraft? What is the essential message of the Summis desiderantes affectibus? *What are the areas of Europe to which the bull applies?*

64. THE WITCH HAMMER

The Malleus Maleficarum (Hammer of Witches) *is a comprehensive text on witchcraft and witch-hunting written by Heinrich Kramer and (and putatively) Jacob Sprenger, two German Dominican Friars (see doc. 63). The tome struck a chord in the legal profession in both ecclesiastical and secular sectors, initially in Germany, but it spread rapidly across the continent. The* Malleus *was published fifteen times between 1486 and 1520, with nineteen more editions between 1574 and 1669 during the height of the witch persecutions—an impressive number, given the infancy of printing technology.*

The Malleus *is divided into three parts. The first lays out theological arguments based on Scripture, the opinions of the church fathers, and ecclesiastical law supporting the reality of witches and the magic they manipulate under the direction and control of the Devil and with God's permission. The second part details the activities of witches, their superhuman powers, spells, methods of recruitment, and so forth, and provides remedies for those afflicted by witches' work. The third portion painstakingly outlines procedures for the trial, torture, and execution of witches.*

The work systematized centuries of discussion on magic, heresy, and the nature of witchcraft and served as a pan-European handbook for detecting and dealing with sorcery. The treatise reflected, confirmed, and prorogated the perception that women are more given to maleficium *than men. For the first time, in the* Malleus *the default gender of "the witch" is female.*

Historians have speculated that the Malleus *did not represent the consensus of churchmen of the time on witchcraft, as was once thought and as the published version of the* Malleus *might imply. First, there was nothing like a full collaboration between Kramer and Sprenger; rather the latter only agreed to lend his name as co-author at Kramer's request, who was looking to give his* magnum opus *prestige. In 1490, the Catholic Church denounced the* Malleus Maleficarum, *and in 1538, the Spanish Inquisition warned inquisitors to approach the claims of and evidence used in the* Malleus *with skepticism. Sprenger himself turned against Kramer and used his position at the University of Cologne to impede his colleague's work. The theology faculty as a whole condemned the book for distortion and errors of established Catholic doctrine. Some scholars hold that a letter of approbation that was appended to the* Malleus *represents a minority view of the faculty or is an outright forgery.*

Source: trans. Montague Summers, *Malleus Maleficarum* (New York: Benjamin Blom, 1928), pp. 41–45, 99–102, 140–43, 147–49, 173–75, 216–17, 227–30, 264–66.

Malleus Maleficarum

Part 1

Question 6. There is also, concerning witches who copulate with devils, much difficulty in considering the methods by which such abominations are consummated. On the part of the Devil: first, of what element the body is made that he assumes; second, whether the act is always accompanied by the injection of semen received from another; third, as to time and place, whether he commits this act more frequently at one time than at another; fourth, whether the act is invisible to any who may be standing by. And on the part of the women: first, it has to be inquired whether only they who were themselves conceived in this filthy manner are often visited by devils; or second, whether it is those who were offered to devils by midwives at the time of their birth; and third, whether the actual venereal delectation of such is of a weaker sort. . . . Therefore, let us now chiefly consider women: and first, why this kind of perfidy is found more in so fragile a sex than in men. And our inquiry will first be general, as to the general conditions of women. Second, particular as to which sort of women are found to be given to superstition and witchcraft; and third, specifically with regard to midwives, who surpass all others in wickedness.

Why Superstition Is Chiefly Found in Women.

As for the first question, why a greater number of witches is found in the fragile feminine sex than among men, it is indeed a fact that it is idle to contradict, since it is accredited by actual experience, apart from the verbal testimony of credible witnesses. . . . What else is woman but a foe to friendship, an inescapable punishment, a necessary evil, a natural temptation, a desirable calamity, a domestic danger, a delectable detriment, an evil of nature, painted with fair colors! Therefore if it be a sin to divorce her when she ought to be kept, it is indeed a necessary torture; for either we commit adultery by divorcing her, or we must endure daily strife. . . . And the tears of woman are a deception, for they may spring from true grief, or they may be a snare. When a woman thinks alone, she thinks evil. . . . Wherefore in many vituperations that we read against women, the word woman is used to mean the lust of the flesh. As it is said, "I have found a woman more bitter than death" [Ecclesiastes 7:26] and a good woman subject to carnal lust.

Others again have propounded other reasons why there are more superstitious women found than men. And the first is that they are more credulous, and since the chief aim of the Devil is to corrupt faith, therefore he rather attacks them. See Ecclesiasticus 19: "He that is quick to believe is light-minded, and shall be diminished." The second reason is that women are naturally more impressionable and more ready to receive the influence of a disembodied spirit and that when they use this quality well they are very good, but when they use it ill they are very evil.

The third reason is that they have slippery tongues and are unable to conceal from fellow-women those things which by evil arts they know, and since they are weak, they find an easy and secret manner of vindicating themselves by witchcraft. . . . There are also others who bring forward yet other reasons, of which preachers should be very careful how they make use. For it is true that in the Old Testament the Scriptures have much that is evil to say about women, and this because of the first temptress, Eve, and her imitators; yet afterward in the New Testament we find a change of name, as from Eva to Ave (as Saint Jerome says, c. 340–420), and the whole sin of Eve taken away by the benediction of Mary. Therefore, preachers should always say as much praise of them as possible.

But because in these times this perfidy is more often found in women than in men, as we learn by actual experience, if anyone is curious as to the reason, we may add to what has already been said: that since they are feebler both in mind and body, it is not surprising that they should come more under the spell of witchcraft. For as regards intellect or the understanding of spiritual things, they seem to be of a different nature from men—a fact which is vouched for by the logic of the authorities, backed by various examples from the Scriptures. . . . Proverbs 11: as it were describing a woman, says, "As a jewel of gold in a swine's snout, so is a fair woman which is without discretion."

But the natural reason is that she is more carnal than a man, as is clear from her many carnal abominations. And it should be noted that there was a defect in the formation of the first woman, since she was formed from a bent rib, that is, a rib of the breast, which is bent as it were in a contrary direction to a man. And since through this defect she is an imperfect animal, she always deceives. . . . And as to her other mental quality, that is, her natural will, when she hates someone whom she formerly loved, then she seethes with anger and impatience in her whole soul, just as the tides of the sea are always heaving and boiling. Many authorities allude to this cause. Ecclesiasticus [cf. 25:15–16]: "There is no wrath above the wrath of a woman." . . .

Part 2

QUESTION I

2. The method by which they profess their sacrilege through an open pact of fidelity to devils varies according to the several practices to which different witches are addicted. And to understand this it first must be noted that there are, as was shown in the first part of this treatise, three kinds of witches; namely, those who injure but cannot cure; those who cure but, through some strange pact with the Devil, cannot injure; and those who both injure and cure. And among those who injure, one class in particular stands out, which can perform every sort of witchcraft and spell, comprehending all that all the others individually can do. Wherefore, if we describe the method of profession in their case, it will suffice also for all the other kinds. And this class is made up of those who, against every instinct of human or animal nature, are in the habit of eating and devouring the children of their own species.

And this is the most powerful class of witches, who practice innumerable other harms also. For they raise hailstorms and hurtful tempests and lightning, cause sterility in men and animals, offer to devils or otherwise kill the children whom they do not devour. But these are only the children who have not been reborn by baptism at the font, for they cannot devour those who have been baptized, nor any without God's permission. They can also, before the eyes of their parents and when no one is in sight, throw into the water children walking by the waterside. They make horses go mad under their riders; they can transport themselves from place to place through the air either in body or in imagination; they can affect judges and magistrates so that they cannot hurt them; they can cause themselves and others to keep silence under torture; they can bring about a great trembling in the hands and horror in the minds of those who would arrest them; they can show to others occult things and certain future events by the information of devils, though this may sometimes have a natural cause (see the question: "Whether devils can foretell the future," in the *Second Book of Sentences*) [see doc. 40]; they can see absent things as if they were present; they can turn the minds of men to inordinate love or hatred; they can at times strike whom they will with lightning and even kill some men and animals; they can make of no effect the generative desires and even the power of copulation, cause abortion, kill infants in the mother's womb by a mere exterior touch; they can at times bewitch men and animals with a mere look, without touching them, and cause death; they dedicate their own children to devils; and in short, as has been said, they can cause all the plagues which other witches can only cause in part, that is, when the justice of God permits such things to be. All these things this most powerful of all classes of witches can do, but they cannot undo them.

But it is common to all of them to practice carnal copulation with devils; therefore, if we show the method used by this chief class in their profession of their sacrilege, anyone may easily understand the method of the other classes. There were such witches lately, thirty years ago, in the district of Savoy, towards the state of Berne, as [Johannes] Nider [1380–1438] tells in his *Formicarius* [see doc. 60]. And there are now some in the country of Lombardy, in the domains of the duke of Austria, where the Inquisitor of Como, as we told in the former part, caused forty-one witches to be burned in one year; and he was fifty-five years old, and still continues to labor in the Inquisition.

Now the method of profession is twofold. One is a solemn ceremony, like a solemn vow. The other is private, and can be made to the Devil at any hour alone. The first method is when witches meet together in the conclave on a set day, and the Devil appears to them in the assumed body of a man and urges them to keep faith with him, promising them worldly prosperity and length of life; and they recommend a novice to his acceptance. And the Devil asks whether she will abjure the faith and forsake the holy Christian religion and the worship of the "anomalous woman" (for so they call the most blessed Virgin Mary) and never venerate the sacraments. And if he finds the novice or disciple willing, then the Devil stretches out his hand, and so does the novice, and she swears with upraised hand to keep that covenant. And when this is done, the Devil at once adds that this is not enough, and when the disciple asks what more must be done, the Devil demands the following oath of homage to himself: that she give herself to him, body and soul, forever, and do her utmost to bring others of both sexes into his power. He adds, finally, that she is to make certain unguents from the bones and limbs of children, especially those who have been baptized, by all which means she will be able to fulfill all her wishes with his help.

We inquisitors had credible experience of this method in the town of Breisach in the diocese of Basel, receiving full information from a young girl witch who had been converted, whose aunt also had been burned in the diocese of Strasburg. And she added that she had become a witch by the method in which her aunt had first tried to seduce her.

For one day her aunt ordered her to go upstairs with her, and at her command, to go into a room where she found fifteen young men clothed in green garments after the manner of German knights. And her aunt said to her, "Choose whom you wish from these young men, and I will give him to you, and he will take you for his wife." And when she said she did not wish for any of them, she was sorely beaten and at last consented and was initiated according to the aforesaid ceremony. She said also that she was often transported by night with her aunt over vast distances, even from Strasburg to Cologne.

This is she who occasioned our inquiry in the first part [of this handbook] into the question whether witches are truly and bodily transported by devils from place to place, and this was on account of the words of the *Canon episcopi* [see doc. 35], which seem to imply that they are only so carried in imagination; whereas they are at times actually and bodily transported.

For when she was asked whether it was only in imagination and phantastically that they so rode, through an illusion of devils, she answered that they did so in both ways according to the truth which we shall declare later of the manner in which they are transferred from place to place. She said also that the greatest injuries were inflicted by midwives, because they were under an obligation to kill or offer to devils as many children as possible; and that she had been severely beaten by her aunt because she had opened a secret pot and found the heads of a great many children. And much more she told us, having first, as was proper, taken an oath to speak the truth.

And her account of the method of professing the Devil's faith undoubtedly agrees with what has been written by that most eminent doctor, Johannes Nider, who even in our times has written very illuminatingly, and it may be especially remarked that he tells of the following which he had from an inquisitor of the diocese of Edua, who held many inquisitions on witches in that diocese and caused many to be burned.

For he says that this inquisitor told him that in the duchy of Lausanne, certain witches had cooked and eaten their own children, and that the following was the method in which they became initiated into such practices. The witches met together and, by their art, summoned a devil in the form of a man, to whom the novice was compelled to swear to deny the Christian religion, never to adore the Eucharist, and to tread the cross underfoot whenever she could do so secretly.

Here is another example from the same source. There was lately a general report, brought to the notice of Peter the judge in Boltingen, that thirteen infants had been devoured in the state of Berne, and the public justice exacted full vengeance on the murderers. And when Peter asked one of the captive witches in what manner they ate children, she replied, "This is the manner of it. We set our snares chiefly for unbaptized children, and even for those that have been baptized, especially when they have not been protected by the sign of the cross and prayers," (Reader, notice that, at the Devil's command, they take the unbaptized chiefly, in order that they may not be baptized) "and with our spells we kill them in their cradles or even when they are sleeping by their parents' side, in such a way that they afterward are thought to have been overlain or to have died some other natural death. Then we secretly take them from their graves and cook them in a cauldron until the whole flesh comes away from the bones to make a soup which may easily be drunk. Of the more solid matter we make an unguent which is of virtue to help us in our arts and pleasures and our transportations, and with the liquid we fill a flask or skin, whoever drinks from which, with the addition of a few other ceremonies, immediately acquires much knowledge and becomes a leader in our sect." . . .

Now there are certain points to be noted concerning the homage which the Devil exacts, as, namely, for what reason and in what different ways he does this. It is obvious that his principal motive is to offer the greater offence to the divine majesty by usurping to himself a creature dedicated to God, and thus more certainly to ensure his disciple's future damnation, which is his chief object. Nevertheless, it is often found by us that he has received such homage for a fixed term of years at the time of the profession of perfidy, and sometimes he exacts the profession only, postponing the homage to a later day.

And let us declare that the profession consists in a total or partial abnegation of the faith: total, as has been said before, when the faith is entirely abjured; partial, when the original pact makes it incumbent on the witch to observe certain ceremonies in opposition to the decrees of the church, such as fasting on Sundays, eating meat on Fridays, concealing certain crimes at confession, or some such profane thing. But let us declare that homage consists in the surrender of body and soul. . . .

Part 2

QUESTION I

13. We must not omit to mention the injuries done to children by witch midwives, first by killing them, and secondly by blasphemously offering them to devils. . . . For in the diocese of Basel at the town of Dann, a witch who was burned confessed that she had killed more than forty children by sticking a needle through the crowns of their heads into their brains, as they came out from the womb. Finally, another woman in the diocese of Strasburg confessed that she had killed more children than she could count. And she was caught in this way. She had been called from one town to another to act as midwife to a certain woman, and, having performed her office, was going back home. But as she went out of the town gate, the arm of a newly born child fell out of the

cloak she had wrapped around her, in whose folds the arm had been concealed. This was seen by those who were sitting in the gateway, and when she had gone on, they picked up from the ground what they took to be a piece of meat, but when they looked more closely and saw that it was not a piece of meat, but recognized it by its fingers as a child's arm; they reported it to the magistrates, and it was found that a child had died before baptism, lacking an arm. So the witch was taken and questioned and confessed the crime and that she had, as has been said, killed more children than she could count.

Now the reason for such practices is as follows. It is to be presumed that witches are compelled to do such things at the command of evil spirits and sometimes against their own wills. For the Devil knows that, because of the pain of loss, or original sin, such children are debarred from entering the kingdom of heaven. And by this means the last judgment is delayed when the devils will be condemned to eternal torture, since the number of the elect is more slowly completed, on the fulfillment of which the world will be consumed. And also, as has already been shown, witches are taught by the Devil to concoct from the limbs of such children an unguent which is very useful for their spells.

But in order to bring so great a sin into utter detestation, we must not pass over in silence the following horrible crime. For when they do not kill the child, they blasphemously offer it to the Devil in this manner. As soon as the child is born, the midwife, if the mother herself is not a witch, carries it out of the room on the pretext of warming it, raises it up, and offers it to the prince of devils, that is Lucifer, and to all the devils. And this is done by the kitchen fire.

A certain man relates that he noticed that his wife, when her time came to give birth, against the usual custom of women in childbirth, did not allow any woman to approach the bed except her own daughter, who acted as midwife. Wishing to know the reason for this, he hid himself in the house and saw the whole order of the sacrilege and dedication to the Devil, as it has been described. He saw also, as it seemed to him, that without any human support, but by the power of the Devil, the child was climbing up the chain by which the cooking-pots were suspended. In great consternation, both at the terrible words of the invocation of the devils and at the other iniquitous ceremonies, he strongly insisted that the child should be baptized immediately.

While it [the child] was being carried to the next village, where there was a church, and when they had to cross a bridge over a certain river, he drew his sword and ran at his daughter, who was carrying the child, saying in the hearing of two others who were with them, "You shall not carry the child over the bridge; for either it must cross the bridge by itself, or you shall be drowned in the river." The daughter was terrified and, together with the other women in company, asked him if he were in his right mind (for he had hidden what had happened from all the others except the two men who were with him). Then he answered, "You vile drab; by your magic arts you made the child climb the chain in the kitchen; now make it cross the bridge with no one carrying it, or I shall drown you in the river." And so, being compelled, she put the child down on the bridge and invoked the Devil by her art; and suddenly the child was seen on the other side of the bridge. And when the child had been baptized and he had returned home, since he now had witnesses to convict his daughter of witchcraft (for he could not prove the former crime of the oblation to the Devil, inasmuch as he had been the only witness of the sacrilegious ritual), he accused both daughter and mother before the judge after their period of purgation; and they were both burned, and the crime of midwives of making that sacrilegious offering was discovered.

But here the doubt arises: to what end or purpose is the sacrilegious offering of children, and how does it benefit the devils? . . . They entice young virgins and boys into their power; for though they might solicit such by means of evil and corrupt men, yet they rather deceive them by magic mirrors and reflections seen in witches' finger-nails and lure them on in the belief that they love chastity, whereas they hate it. For the Devil hates above all the blessed Virgin, because she bruised his head [Genesis 3:15]. Just so in this oblation of children they deceive the minds of witches into the vice of infidelity under the appearance of a virtuous act. And the third reason is that the perfidy of witches may grow, to the Devils' own gain, when they have witches dedicated to them from their very cradles. . . . From this it follows that a child who has been offered to the Devil in sign of subjection and homage to him cannot possibly be dedicated by Catholics to a holy life, in worthy and fruitful service to God for the benefit of himself and others. . . . In the same way, when a witch offers a child to the devils, she commends it body and soul to him as its beginning and its end in eternal damnation; wherefore not without some miracle can the child be set free from the payment of so great a debt. . . .

15. That devils and their disciples can, by witchcraft, cause lightning, and hailstorms, and tempests, and that the devils have power from God to do this, and their disciples do so with God's permission, is proved by holy Scripture in Job 1 and 2. For the Devil received power from God and immediately caused it to happen that the Sabeans [ancient peoples of Yemen] took away from Job fifty yoke of oxen and five hundred asses . . . and finally the Devil smote the body of the holy man with the most terrible sores and caused his wife and his three friends to vex him grievously.

Saint Thomas Aquinas [1225–1274] in his commentary on Job says as follows. It must be confessed that, with God's permission, the devils can disturb the air, raise up winds, and make the fire fall from heaven [see doc. 53]. For although, in the matter of taking various shapes, corporeal nature is not at the command of any angel, either good or bad, but only at that of God the creator, yet in the matter of local motion corporeal nature has to obey the spiritual nature. And this truth is clearly exemplified in man himself; for at the mere command of the will, which exists subjectively in the soul, the limbs are moved to perform that which they have been willed to do. Therefore whatever can be accomplished by mere local motion, this not only good, but bad, spirits can, by their natural power, accomplish, unless God should forbid it. But winds and rain and other similar disturbances of the air can be caused by the mere movement of vapors released from the earth or the water; therefore the natural power of devils is sufficient to cause such things. So says Saint Thomas.

For God in his justice, using the devils as his agents of punishment, inflicts the evils which come to us who live in this world. Therefore, with reference to that in the Psalms, "He called a famine on the land, and wasted all their substance of bread" [Psalm 105:16]. The gloss says, "God allowed this evil to be caused by the bad angels, who are in charge of such matters, and by famine is meant the angel in charge of famine."

We refer the reader also to what has been written above on the question as to whether witches must always have the Devil's help to aid them in their works and concerning the three kinds of harm which the devils at times inflict without the agency of a witch. But the devils are more eager to injure men with the help of a witch, since in this way God is the more offended and greater power is given to them to torment and punish. . . .

A story is told in the *Formicarius* [see doc. 60] of a certain man who had been arrested and was asked by the judge how they went about to raise up hailstorms and tempests and whether it was easy for them to do so. He answered, "We can easily cause hailstorms, but we cannot do all the harm that we wish because of the guardianship of good angels." And he added, "We can only injure those who are deprived of God's help, but we cannot hurt those who make the sign of the cross. And this is how we got to work. First we use certain words in the fields to implore the chief of the devils to send one of his servants to strike the man whom we name. Then, when the Devil has come, we sacrifice to him a black cock at two cross-roads, throwing it up into the air, and when the Devil has received this, he performs our wish and stirs up the air, but not always in the places which we have named, and, according to the permission of the living God, sends down hailstorms and lightning.

In the same work we hear of a certain leader or heresiarch of witches named Staufer, who lived in Berne and the adjacent country and used publicly to boast that whenever he liked, he could change himself into a mouse in the sight of his rivals and slip through the hands of his deadly enemies and that he had often escaped from the hands of his mortal foes in this manner. But when the divine justice wished to put an end to his wickedness, some of his enemies lay in wait for him cautiously and saw him sitting in a basket near a window and suddenly pierced him through with swords and spears, so that he miserably died for his crimes. Yet he left behind him a disciple, named Hoppo, who had for his master that Stadlin whom we have mentioned before in the sixth chapter [see doc. 79].

These two could, whenever they pleased, cause the third part of the manure or straw or corn to pass invisibly from a neighbor's field to their own; they could raise the most violent hailstorms and destructive winds and lightning, could cast into the water in the sight of their parents children walking by the water-side when there was no one else in sight, could cause barrenness in men and animals, could reveal hidden things to others, could in many ways injure men in their affairs or their bodies, could at times kill whom they would by lightning, and could cause many other plagues when and where the justice of God permitted such things to be done.

It is better to add an instance which came within our own experience. For in the diocese of Constance, twenty-eight German miles from the town of Regensburg in the direction of Salzburg, a violent hailstorm destroyed all the fruit, crops, and vineyards in a belt one mile wide, so that the vines hardly bore fruit for three years. This was brought to the notice of the Inquisition, since the people clamored for an inquiry to be held—many of the townsmen . . . being of the opinion that it was caused by witchcraft. Accordingly it was agreed after fifteen days of formal deliberation that it was a case of witchcraft for us to consider, and among a large number of suspects, we particularly examined two women, one named Agnes, a bath-woman, and the other Anna von Mindelheim. These two were taken and shut up separately in different prisons, neither of them knowing in the least what had happened to the other. On the following day the bath-woman was very gently questioned [tortured] in the presence of a notary by the chief magistrate, a justice named Gelre—very zealous for the faith, and by the other magistrates with him, and although she was undoubtedly well provided with that evil gift of silence which is the constant bane of judges, and at the first trial affirmed that she was innocent of any crime against man or woman; yet, in the divine mercy that so great a crime should not pass unpunished, suddenly, when she had been freed from her chains, although it was in the torture chamber, she fully laid bare all the crimes which she had committed. For when she was questioned by the notary of the Inquisition upon the accusations which had been brought against her of harm done to men and cattle, by reason of which she had been gravely suspected of being a witch, although there had been no witness to prove that she had abjured the faith or performed coitus with an *incubus* devil (for she had been most secret); nevertheless, after she had confessed to the harm which she had caused to animals and men; she acknowledged also all that she was asked concerning the abjuration of the faith and copulation committed with an *incubus* devil, saying that for more than eighteen years she had given her body to an *incubus* devil, with a complete abnegation of the faith.

After this she was asked whether she knew anything about the hailstorm which we have mentioned and answered that she did. And, being asked how and in what way, she answered, "I was in my house, and at midday a familiar [devil in the form of an animal] came to me and told me to go with a little water onto the field or plain of Kuppel (for so is it named). And when I asked what he wanted to do with the water, he said that he wanted to make it rain. So I went out at the town gate, and found the Devil standing under a tree." The judge asked her, under which tree; and she said, "Under that one opposite that tower," pointing it out. Asked what she did under the tree, she said, "The Devil told me to dig a hole and pour the water into it." Asked whether they sat down together, she said, "I sat down, but the Devil stood up." Then she was asked with what words and in what manner she had stirred the water, and she answered, "I stirred it with my finger and called on the name of the Devil himself and all the other devils." Again the judge asked what was done with the water, and she answered, "It disappeared, and the Devil took it up into the air." Then she was asked if she had any associate, and answered, "Under another tree opposite I had a companion (naming the other captured witch, Anna von Mindelheim), but I do not know what she did." Finally, the bath-woman was asked how long it was between the taking up of the water and the hailstorm, and she answered, "There was just sufficient interval of time to allow me to get back to my house."

But (and this is remarkable) when on the next day the other witch had at first been exposed to the very gentlest questions, being suspended hardly clear of the ground by her thumbs, after she had been set quite free, she disclosed the whole matter without the slightest discrepancy from what the other had told. . . . Accordingly, on the third day they were burned. And the bath-woman was contrite and confessed, and commended herself to God, saying that she would die with a willing heart if she could escape the tortures of the Devil and held in her hand a cross which she kissed. . . .

QUESTION 2

4. In what has already been written it has clearly enough been shown the remedies which are available for the relief of those who are deluded by an [illusion] and think that they have lost their virile member [penis] or have been metamorphosed into animals. For since such men are entirely destitute of divine grace, according to the essential condition of those who are so bewitched, it is not possible to apply a healing salve while the weapon still remains in the wound. Therefore before all things they must be reconciled to God by a good confession. Again, as was shown in the seventh chapter of the "first question" of the

second part [of this text], such members are never actually taken away from the body, but are only hidden by an [illusion] from the senses of sight and touch. It is clear, too, that those who live in grace are not so easily deluded in this way, either actively or passively, in such a manner, that is, that they seem to lose their members, or that those of others should appear to them to be missing. Therefore the remedy as well as the disease is explained in that chapter, namely, that they should as far as possible come to an amicable agreement with the witch herself.

As to those who think that they have been changed into beasts, it must be known that this kind of witchcraft is more practiced in eastern countries than in the west; that is to say, in the east witches more often bewitch other people in this way, but it appears that the witches so transform themselves more frequently in our part of the world; namely, when they change themselves, in full sight, into the shapes of animals. . . .

But in the east, the following remedy is used for such delusions. For we have learned much of this matter from the Knights of the Order of Saint John of Jerusalem in Rhodes, and especially this case which happened in the city of Salamis in the kingdom of Cyprus. For that is a seaport, and once when a vessel was being laden with merchandise suitable for a ship which is sailing into foreign parts, and all her company were providing themselves with victuals, one of them, a strong young man, went to the house of a woman standing outside the city on the seashore and asked her if she had any eggs to sell. The woman, seeing that he was a strong young man and a merchant far away from his own country, thought that on that account the people of the city would feel less suspicion if he were to be lost, and said to him, "Wait a little, and I will get you all that you want." And when she went in and shut the door and kept him waiting, the young man outside began to call out to her to hurry, lest he should miss the ship. Then the woman brought some eggs and gave them to the young man, and told him to hurry back to the ship in case he should miss it. So he hastened back to the ship, which was anchored by the shore, and before going on board, since the full company of his companions was not yet returned, he decided to eat the eggs there and refresh himself. And behold! an hour later he was made dumb as if he had no power of speech, and, as he afterwards said, he wondered what could have happened to him but was unable to find out. Yet when he wished to go on board, he was driven off with sticks by those who yet remained ashore and who all cried out: "Look what this ass is doing! Curse the beast; you are not coming on board."

The young man being thus driven away and understanding from their words that they thought he was an ass, reflected and began to suspect that he had been bewitched by the woman, especially since he could utter no word, although he understood all that was said. And when, on again trying to board the ship, he was driven off with heavier blows, he was in bitterness of heart compelled to remain and watch the ship sail away. And so, as he ran here and there, since everybody thought he was an ass, he was necessarily treated as such. At last, under compulsion, he went back to the woman's house, and to keep himself alive, served her at her pleasure for three years, doing no work but to bring to the house such necessities as wood and corn and to carry away what had to be carried away like a beast of burden; the only consolation that was left to him being that, although everyone else took him for an ass, the witches themselves, severally and in company, who frequented the house, recognized him as a man, and he could talk and behave with them as a man should. . . .

After three years had passed in this way, in the fourth year it happened that the young man went one morning into the city with the woman following a long way behind, and he passed by a church where holy mass was being celebrated and heard the sacred-bell ring at the elevation of the host (for in that kingdom the mass is celebrated according to the Latin, and not according to the Greek rite). And he turned towards the church, and, not daring to enter for fear of being driven off with blows, knelt down outside by bending the knees of his hind legs, and lifted his forelegs, that is, his hands, joined together over his ass's head, as it was thought to be, and looked upon the elevation of the sacrament. And when some Genoese merchants saw this prodigy, they followed the ass in astonishment, discussing this marvel among themselves, and behold, the witch came and belabored the ass with her stick. And because, as we have said, this sort of witchcraft is better known in those parts, at the instance of the merchants the ass and the witch were taken before the judge, where, being questioned and tortured, she confessed her crime and promised to restore the young man to his true shape if she might be allowed to return to her house. So she was dismissed and went back to her house where the young man was restored to his former shape. And being again arrested, she paid the debt which her crimes merited. And the young man returned joyfully to his own country.

Part 3

QUESTION I, HEAD 2

Question 9. . . . If the accused says that she is innocent and falsely accused and that she wishes to see and hear her accusers, then it is a sign that she is asking to defend herself. But it is an open question whether the judge is bound to make the deponents known to her and bring them to confront her face to face. For here let the judge take note that he is not bound either to publish the names of the deponents or to bring them before the accused unless they themselves should freely and willingly offer to come before the accused and lay their depositions in her presence. And it is by reason of the danger incurred by the deponents that the judge is not bound to do this. For although different popes have had different opinions on this matter, none of them has ever said that in such a case the judge is bound to make known to the accused the names of the informers or accusers (but here we are not dealing with the case of an accuser). On the contrary, some have thought that in no case ought he to do so, while others have thought that he should in certain circumstances.

But, finally, Boniface VIII [c. 675–754] decreed as follows, "If in a case of heresy it appears to the bishop or inquisitor that grave danger would be incurred by the witnesses of informers, on account of the powers of the persons against whom they lay their depositions, should their names be published, he shall not publish them. But if there is no danger, their names shall be published just as in other cases. . . . So that any such judge, even if he be secular, has the authority of the pope, and not only of the emperor.

Also a careful judge will take notice of the powers of the accused persons; for these are of three kinds, namely, the power of birth and family, the power of riches, and the power of malice. And the last of these is more to be feared than the other two since it threatens more danger to the witnesses if their names are made known to the accused. . . . Further, let the judge take notice that, as he acts in this matter with the authority of the supreme pontiff [pope] and the permission of the Ordinary [court], both he himself and all who are associated with him at the depositions, or afterward at the pronouncing of the sentence, must keep the names of the witnesses secret, under pain of excommunication. And it is in the power of the bishop thus to punish him or them if they do otherwise. Therefore he should very implicitly warn them not to reveal the name from the very beginning of the process. . . . It is further to be noted that just as it is a punishable offence to publish the names of witnesses indiscreetly, so also it is to conceal them without good reason from, for instance, such people as have a right to know them, such as the lawyers and assessors whose opinion is to be sought in proceeding to the sentence. In the same way the names must not be concealed when it is possible to publish them without risk of any danger to the witnesses. . . .

Question 15. The judge should act as follows in the continuation of the torture. First he should bear in mind that, just as the same medicine is not applicable to all the members, but there are various and distinct salves for each member, so not all heretics or those accused of heresy are to be subjected to the same method of questioning, examination and torture as to the charges laid against them; but various and different means are to be employed according to their various natures and persons. . . . For if the sons of darkness were to become accustomed to one general rule they would provide means of evading it as a well-known snare set for their destruction.

If he wishes to find out whether she is endowed with a witch's power of preserving silence, let him take note whether she is able to shed tears when standing in his presence, or when being tortured. For we are taught both by the words of worthy men of old and by our own experience that this is a most certain sign, and it has been found that even if she be urged and exhorted by solemn conjurations to shed tears, if she be a witch she will not be able to weep; although she will assume a tearful aspect and smear her cheeks and eyes with spittle to make it appear that she is weeping; wherefore she must be closely watched by the attendants.

In passing sentence the judge or priest may use some such method as the following in conjuring her to true tears if she be innocent, or in restraining false tears. Let him place his hand on the head of the accused and say, "I conjure you by the bitter tears shed on the cross by our savior the Lord Jesus Christ for the salvation of the world, and by the burning tears poured in the evening hour over his wounds by the most glorious Virgin Mary, his mother, and by all the tears which have been shed here in this world by the saints and elect of God, from whose eyes he has now wiped away all tears, that if you be innocent you do now shed tears, but if you be guilty that you shall by no means do so. In the name of the father, and of the son, and of the holy ghost, amen."

And it is found by experience that the more they are conjured, the less are they able to weep, however hard they may try to do so or smear their cheeks with spittle. Nevertheless it is possible that afterward, in the absence of the judge and not at the time or in the place of torture, they may be able to weep in the presence of their gaolers. And as for the reason for a witch's inability to weep, it can be said that the grace of tears is one of the chief gifts allowed to the penitent; for Saint Bernard of Clairvaux [1090–1153] tells us that the tears of the humble can penetrate to heaven and conquer the unconquerable. Therefore there can be no doubt that they are displeasing to the Devil and that he uses all his endeavor to restrain them, to prevent a witch from finally attaining to penitence.

But it may be objected that it might suit with the Devil's cunning, with God's permission, to allow even a witch to weep, since tearful grieving, weaving, and deceiving are said to be proper to women. We may answer that in this case, since the judgments of God are a mystery, if there is no other way of convicting the accused, by legitimate witnesses or the evidence of the fact, and if she is not under a strong or grave suspicion, she is to be discharged. . . . A second precaution is to be observed, not only at this point but during the whole process, by the judge and all his assessors; namely, that they must not allow themselves to be touched physically by the witch, especially in any contract of their bare arms or hands, but they must always carry about them some salt consecrated on Palm Sunday and some blessed herbs. For these can be enclosed together in blessed wax and worn round the neck, . . . and that these have a wonderful protective virtue is known not only from the testimony of witches, but from the use and practice of the church, which exorcizes and blesses such objects for this very purpose, as is shown in the ceremony of exorcism when it is said, "For the banishing of all the power of the Devil," etc. But let it not be thought that physical contact of the joints or limbs is the only thing to be guarded against; for sometimes, with God's permission, they are able, with the help of the Devil, to bewitch the judge by the mere sound of the words which they utter, especially at the time when they are exposed to torture.

And we know from experience that some witches, when detained in prison, have importunately begged their gaolers to grant them this one thing, that they should be allowed to look at the judge before he looks at them, and by so getting the first sight of the judge they have been able so to alter the minds of the judge or his assessors that they have lost all their anger against them and have not presumed to molest them in any way, but have allowed them to go free. He who knows and has experienced it gives this true testimony, and would that they were not able to effect such things! . . .

And if it can conveniently be done, the witch should be led backward into the presence of the judge and his assessors. And not only at the present point, but in all that has preceded or shall follow it, let him cross himself and approach her manfully, and with God's help the power of that old serpent will be broken. And no one need think that it is superstitious to lead her in backwards; for, as we have often said, the canonists [lawyers] allow even more than this to be done for the protections against witchcraft and always say that it is lawful to oppose vanity with vanity.

The third precaution to be observed in this tenth action is that the hair should be shaved from every part of her body. The reason for this is the same as that for stripping her of her clothes, which we have already mentioned; for in order to preserve their power of silence they are in the habit of hiding some superstitious object in their clothes or in their hair, or even in the most secret parts of their bodies which must not be named. . . .

This can be made clear from the example of a certain witch in the town of Hagenau, whom we have mentioned in the second part of this work. She used to obtain this gift of silence in the following manner. She killed a newly-born first-born male child who had not been baptized, and having roasted it in an oven together with other matters which it is not expedient to mention, ground it to powder and ashes, and if any witch or criminal carried about him some of this substance, he would in no way be able to confess his crimes. . . . It may proceed from some instrument of witchcraft carried about the person, as has been said, either in the clothes or in the hairs of the body. And thirdly, even if the prisoner has no such object secreted about her person, they are sometimes endowed with this power by other witches, however far they may be removed from them. For a certain witch at Issbrug used to boast that if she had no more than a thread from the garments of any prisoner, she could so work that however much that prisoner were tortured, even to death, she would be unable to confess anything. So the answer to this objection is clear.

But what is to be said of a case that happened in the diocese of Regensberg? Certain heretics were convicted by their own confession, not only as impenitent, but as open advocates of that perfidy, and when they were condemned to death it happened that they remained unharmed in the fire. At length their sentence was altered to death by drowning, but this was no more effective. All were astonished, and some even began to say that their heresy must be true, and the bishop, in great anxiety for his flock, ordered a three day fast. When this had been devoutly fulfilled, it came to the knowledge of someone that those heretics had a magic charm sewed between the skin and the flesh under one arm, and when this was found and removed, they were delivered to the flames and immediately burned. Some say that a certain necromancer learned this secret during a consultation with the Devil and betrayed it; but however it became known, it is probable that the Devil, who is always scheming for the subversion of faith, was in some way compelled by divine power to reveal the matter. . . .

Now in the parts of Germany such shaving, especially of the secret parts, is not generally considered delicate, and therefore we inquisitors do not use it, but we cause the hair of their head to be cut off, and placing a morsel of blessed wax in a cup of holy water and invoking the most holy Trinity, we give it them to drink three times on a fasting stomach, and by the grace of God we have by this means caused many to break their silence. But in other countries the inquisitors order the witch to be shaved all over her body. . . . But it may be asked whether, in a time of need, when all other means of breaking a witch's silence have failed, it would be lawful to ask the advice in this matter of sorceresses who are able to cure those who are bewitched. We answer that, whatever may have been done in that matter at Regensburg, it is our earnest admonition in the Lord that no one, no matter how great may be the need, should consult with sorceresses on behalf of the state, and this because of the great offence which is thereby caused to the divine majesty, when there are so many other means open to us which we may use either in their own proper form or in some equivalent form, so that the truth will be had from their own mouths and they can be consigned to the flames. Or failing this, God will in the meantime provide some other death for the witch. . . .

HEAD 3

Question 33. The fourteenth method of finally concluding a process on behalf of the faith is used when the person accused of heresy, after a careful discussion of the circumstances of the process with reference to the informant in consultation with learned lawyers, is found to be accused of that heresy only by another witch who has been or is to be burned. And this can happen in thirteen ways in thirteen cases. For a person so accused is either found innocent and is to be freely discharged; or she is found to be generally defamed for that heresy; or it is found that, in addition to her defamation, she is to be to some degree exposed to torture; or she is found to be strongly suspected of heresy; or she is found to be at the same time defamed and suspected; and so on up to thirteen different cases. . . .

The first case is when she is accused only by a witch in custody and is not convicted either by her own confession nor by legitimate witnesses and there are no other indications found by reason of which she can truly be regarded as suspect. In such a case she is to be entirely absolved, even by the secular judge himself who has either burned the deponent or is about to burn her either on his own authority or on that commissioned to him by the bishop and judge of the Ordinary, and she shall be absolved in the manner explained in the twentieth question. . . .

The third case, then, happens when the person so accused is not convicted by her own confession, not by the evidence of the facts, nor by credible witnesses, nor are there any other indications as to any fact in which she had ever been marked by the other inhabitants of that town or village, except her general reputation among them. But the general report has become intensified by the detention of that witch in custody, as that it is said that she had been her companion in everything and had participated in her crimes. But even so, the accused firmly denies all this, and nothing of it is known to other inhabitants, or of anything to save good behavior on her part, though her companionship with the witch is admitted.

In such a case the following is the procedure. First they are to be brought face to face and their mutual answers and recriminations noted, to see whether there is any inconsistency in their words by reason of which the judge can decide from her admissions and denials whether he ought to expose her to torture; and if so, he can proceed as in the third manner of pronouncing a sentence, explained in the twenty-second Question, submitting her to light tortures, at the same time exercising every possible precaution, as we explained at length towards the beginning of this Third Part, to find out whether she is innocent or guilty.

The fourth case is when a person accused in this manner is found to be lightly suspected, either because of her own confession or because of the depositions of the other witch in custody. There are some who include among those who should be thus lightly suspected those who go and consult witches for any purpose, or have procured for themselves a lover by stirring up hatred between married folk, or have consorted with witches in order to obtain some temporal advantage. But such are to be excommunicated as followers of heretics, according to the canon *excommunicamus*, where it says: "Similarly we judge those to be heretics who believe in their errors." For the effect is presumed from the facts. Therefore it seems that such are to be more severely sentenced and punished than those who are under a light suspicion of heresy and are to be judged from light conjectures. For example, if they had performed services for witches or carried their letters to them, they need not on that account believe in their errors, yet they have not laid information against them, and they have received wages. . . .

The judge must take into consideration the household and family of each witch who has been burned or is detained; for these are generally found to be infected. For witches are instructed by devils to offer to them even their own children; therefore there can be no doubt that such children are instructed in all manner of crimes, as is shown in the First Part of this work. Again, in a case of simple heresy it happens that, on account of the familiarity between heretics who are akin to each other, when one is convicted of heresy it follows that his kindred also are strongly suspected; and the same is true of the heresy of witches. . . .

Questions: How interested are the authors in the heresy, per se, of witches? What do Kramer and Sprenger see as the major danger witches pose? Why do Kramer and Sprenger target midwives? How are "witches" different from the practitioners of magic of the earlier Middle Ages? What are the differences between the legal procedures Kramer and Sprenger recommend and those employed in the trial of Joan of Arc (see doc. 59), and what might account for the differences? What is the connection between magic and sexuality?

CHAPTER SIX

THE SIXTEENTH AND SEVENTEENTH CENTURIES: THE FULL FURY OF THE WITCH-HUNTS

A 2

Figure 6.1 Here a priest pronounces the Benedictine formula of exorcism, "Step back Satan," as his assistant holds down a woman possessed of a devil. The rite is successful, as evidenced by the demon escaping from the victim's mouth. This woodcut is from the 1598 edition of Pierre Boaistuau's (c. 1517–1566) *Histoires prodigieuses et mémorables extraictes de plusieurs fameux autheurs Grec and Latins, sacrez and prophanes.* The work is a compilation of natural wonders, monstrocities, oddities, and legends and was immensely popular in the sixteenth and seventeenth centuries.

The zeitgeist that prevailed among Christians during the Twelfth-Century Renaissance had changed by the late Middle Ages. Cities had grown, and with them emerged a class of burghers who drove economic development, serfs formerly bound to the land had become free tenant farmers, the renaissance of classical learning that Italy spearheaded expanded across Europe, and the New World had been reached—opening up unfathomable possibilities for people of all ranks. And yet there were reasons for Christians to be disappointed. In 1291, the last crusader stronghold at Acre fell to the Muslims. The failure of the crusades was a shock and a sorrow to Christians who had dutifully answered the church's call to arms and spent two centuries in a struggle to reclaim the Holy Land.

In addition, from 1315 to 1322, European populations suffered several years of disastrous weather followed by famine, inflation, starvation, and elevated levels of crime. The first wave of the bubonic plague reached western Europe in 1347, killing approximately a third of the population, and the epidemic recurred periodically until the early eighteenth century. Military conflicts became increasingly frequent, of longer duration, more professionalized, and deadlier. The aristocracy of France and England fought the Hundred Years' War (1337–1453) over questions of legitimate succession, and the French population of all classes suffered the obscenities of warfare. Amid all these disasters, the Roman Catholic clergy, shepherds of the people, were in many cases not accessible—literally or spiritually, either because so many had died in the plague administering to the sick, or because of the corruption rampant throughout the church, which was obvious to all. From 1378 to 1417 there was a schism in the papacy, and at one point three men simultaneously claimed to be the legitimate pope, which damaged the reputation of the office.

Uncertainty and insecurity in the late Middle Ages and early modern era drove a lay piety movement whereby laymen and laywomen sought religious fulfillment outside the institutionalized church. Movements that the papacy considered heretical proliferated—from large regional heresies, to night-walkers in a small and rural pocket of Italy; to the idiosyncratic views of isolated heresiarchs such as one Menocchio (1532–1599), who was executed for his cosmological beliefs involving cheese and worms.

Most Christians were not involved in heretical activity, but they were led to ask why things had gone so amiss in their generation, and one answer was that demons were maneuvering within their communities—a conclusion easily deduced as preachers warned their audiences that the evils besetting them stemmed from their own sins and those of their neighbors. By 1500, witchcraft was roundly believed to be one of the worst expressions of heresy, and the construct of "the witch" had coalesced as an individual who made a pact with Satan to sow destruction wherever possible in a worldwide conspiracy to destroy Christendom.

Once all the factors had come together—the judicial apparatus, the conflation of heresy and sorcery, a general fear that there was a cancer in the belly of the times, and the church's endorsement of witch prosecutions—the hunts began in earnest. Treatises on witch-hunting like the *Malleus Maleficarum* were plentiful; the *Malleus* is the best known of this sort of literature, but it was only one of many. The *Malleus* did not circulate in England because some of its recommendations on torture and punishment were impermissible within the legal system; other treatises, however, were written for witch-hunting in the British Isles. During the period from about 1450 to 1650, between 80,000 and 100,000 people were executed for witchcraft across England and western Europe.

In 1517, the Protestant Reformation began in Germany and spread quickly to other regions, but the Reformation had little impact on the dynamics of witch-hunting. Both Catholics and Protestants subscribed to the same demonology based on the same biblical and patristic authorities. Nevertheless, each was firmly convinced that their counter-religionists were heretical, and the leap from heretic to witch was a short one. Protestants' antipathy for Catholic "papists" often found voice in accusations of witchcraft.

The reasons a witch-hunt began, persisted, and ended in a given locality are many and multifaceted. Scholars have warned against generalizations in reference to the early modern witch-hunts and many prefer to focus on micro-histories or in-depth regional studies. Some witch-hunts were small and ended after a handful of people were executed, and sometimes witch-hunts became panics claiming hundreds of lives and depopulating villages to the point that the trials ended only when the members of the tribunals themselves were accusing each other of the crime.

Four of the principal reasons for the ubiquity of witch-hunts in Europe were the witch-hunting manuals, torture, leading questions, and naming names. Because the profile of "the witch" was articulated in treatises on witchcraft, the jurists who carried out investigations had it clearly in their heads what they were looking for: people who flew to large diabolical gatherings in the woods called sabbaths, kept animal familiars, killed and cooked babies, had sexual relations with devils, renounced baptism, worshipped Satan, and practiced *maleficium*. When a person accused of heretical witchcraft was tortured, the interrogator asked leading questions from the manuals, to which the accused often responded in whatever way would please the interrogator and stop the pain. The inquisitors were horrified when trial records from across the continent included the same kinds of minute details, and they were convinced that a world-wide conspiracy had been uncovered. Even when "witches" confessed and repented, the interrogation was not over; the court expected them to identify other witches—usually acquaintances they had seen at the satanic sabbaths.

Sorcery, spells, curses, cures, and charms were features of everyday life in European medieval and early modern cultures. People blamed neighbors for everything from spoiled crops to stillbirths. The accusations of magic among the common people generally had little to do with heresy; it was *maleficium* that average people understood and feared. But when a complaint of simple sorcery went to court, the officials tended to see it through the lens of scholastic diabolism. In this way, accusations of village-level sorcery could escalate into full blown witch-hunts.

Most of those who fueled the judicial machine during the witch-hunts were educated men, but not all educated people endorsed the trials; there were many skeptics who objected to various aspects of the process. The witch trials began to peter out in the mid-seventeenth century and were essentially over by the early eighteenth century. Why the trials ended is as puzzling as why they began and why they took the form they did. Skepticism about the validity of the trial process, especially the use of torture, grew, and many doctors, lawyers, magistrates, and intellectuals held that, although witches did exist and presented a hazard, there was no reliable mechanism for detecting them. Others objected to the inhumanity of the trial system that preyed upon the ignorant and dispossessed. Laws began to change, and more than the Devil's mark was required to initiate litigation. However, it is worth noting that popular witch beliefs changed little in the early modern era. Ordinary people sustained the hunts, to some degree, by turning in their neighbors for *maleficium* and often pressing for prosecution when law courts failed to act.

The intellectual and scientific revolutions of the Enlightenment were a factor in shifting beliefs about magic and witchcraft. The educated elite effectively dismantled scholasticism and rejected slavish adherence to inherited wisdom from biblical and patristic texts. Copernicus's heliocentric universe operated on fixed, orderly, and natural laws, which left little room for magic or miracle. In the end there is no simple understanding as to why Europeans began killing witches and why they stopped.

65. DEFENDING THE HARVEST: THE CULT OF THE *BENANDANTI*

In the city of Cividale in 1575, a series of trials for heresy began that involved men and women living in the Friuli region in northeastern Italy. The transcripts prepared by the Holy Office of the Inquisition provide evidence of a sect called the benandanti, *or "good walkers," with seemingly ancient roots in German, Italian, and Slavic peasant agrarian cultures. These were men and women whose spirits left their bodies at night to travel through the sky and fight against malevolent witches* (malandanti). *The fertility of the fields for the coming season was dependent on the* benandanti's *success in these nocturnal struggles.*

The text sheds light on the intersection and symbiosis of ecclesiastical and popular perceptions of "witches" in the early modern period. Note how and why the testimony of the accused transmuted over the course of the trials. The investigation into the activities of the benandanti *ended finally in 1705.*

Source: Carlo Ginzburg, *The Night Battles: Witchcraft and Agrarian Cults in the Sixteenth and Seventeenth Centuries*, trans. John and Anne Tedeschi (Baltimore: The Johns Hopkins University Press 1992), pp. 147–48, 150, 153–63, 165–66.

Trial of Paolo Gasparutto, [March] 1575

[Bartolomeo Sgabarizza, rector of the parish church of Brazzano gave testimony]: "I heard that in Brazzano a child, the son of M. Piero Rotaro, was sick from an unknown ailment, and that to learn about this ailment, a certain Madonna Aquilina had been consulted who was reputed to know if a person was bewitched. . . . I begged M. Piero to summon the aforesaid Paolo and to inquire diligently of him what might serve in the present case. And he promptly had Paolo come and when he·was there he questioned him on the doorstep of his shop. Since I was passing by I went up to them and asked, 'What are you two discussing here?' And M. Piero replied that they were talking about his little boy and was asking Paolo if there was any way to heal him. And I turned to Paolo and inquired, well, what was his opinion about these spells, and he replied that this little boy had been possessed by witches, but at the time of the witchery the vagabonds were about and they snatched him from the witches' hands, and if they had not done so he would have died. At this point I interrupted, saying, 'Do you by any chance have some way to cure this child?' And he said that he did not have anything else besides what he had already taught M. Piero, namely to weigh him for three Thursdays, and that if the child gained in weight the second Thursday he would be cured [and the witch would die], but if he decreased, he would die.

Since I wanted to learn more I asked him how and when they did such things. He told me that on Thursdays during the Ember Days of the year [seasonal days for fasting and prayer] they were forced to go with these witches to many places, such as Cormons, in front of the church at Iassico, and even into the countryside about Verona. When I asked him what they did in these places, he said that they fought, played, leaped about and rode various animals, and did different things among themselves. The women beat the men who were with them with sorghum stalks, while the men only had bunches of fennel, and for this reason he begged me not to sow sorghum in my field, and whenever he finds any growing he pulls it up, and he curses whoever plants it. And when I said that I wanted to sow it, he began to swear. Because this all seemed very strange to me, I came to Cividale to talk with you sir, or with the father inquisitor. And since I chanced upon this Paolo here in Cividale, I brought him to the father inquisitor in San Francesco, to whom he admitted all these things, and also, as he had told me before, that when the witches, warlocks, and vagabonds return from these games all hot and tired and pass in front of houses where they find clear, clean water in pails, they drink it, if not they also go into the cellars and overturn all the wine [or the witches urinate in it], and he urged me always to keep clean water in the house. When I said that I did not believe these stories, he invited me to accompany him and he would show them to me. And he told me all the above things in the presence of M. Piero (Rotaro) and repeated them before the father inquisitor." . . .

Questioned again he said, "After the father inquisitor and I had promised to go with him so that we might get him to talk, he said that he would go twice before Easter, and even if the father inquisitor was in Cividale and I in Brazzano, he would arrange it for us to be together, and having promised, one was then obliged to go. Once we were there we were to say nothing, even if we were to see certain wild dancing, otherwise we would be compelled to remain there, and he also told me that he had been badly beaten by the witches for having spoken about these things, and some of these who are good, called vagabonds, and in their own words *benandanti*, prevent evil, and some of them commit it. . . ."

[April 1575]

. . . [A second witness questioned] said, "The above-named Paolo said that when they go to these games, some may travel on horseback, others on a hare or a cat, on one animal or another, but he would not name the men and women who attended."

He stated, questioned again, "He (Paolo) told me that when he goes to these games his body stayed in bed and the spirit went forth and that, while he was out, if someone approached the bed where the body lay and called to it, it would not answer, nor could he get it to move even if he should try for a hundred years, but if he did not look at it and called it, it would respond at once, and when they err or speak with someone, their bodies are beaten, and they are found all black and blue, and he has been beaten and mistreated because he spoke with others. He told me that he would be mistreated for fifteen days for having told me these things, and if I did not believe him that I should promise to go with him, and I would see them for myself."

He also stated: "He said that for any who wait twenty-four hours before returning and who might say or do something, the spirit would remain separated from the body, and after it was buried the spirit would wander forever and be called *malandante*. . . . This Paolo told me that these *malandanti* eat children." . . .

[Trial of Battista Moduco, June 1580]

. . . Questioned, [Moduco] replied, "I have not known anyone who is a heretic, nor had any dealings with them."

Questioned, he replied, "Of witches I do not know if there are any, and of *benandanti* I do not know of any others besides myself." . . .

Questioned, he replied, "I am a *benandante* because I go with the others to fight four times a year, that is during the Ember Days, at night; I go invisibly in spirit and the body remains behind; we go forth in the service of Christ, and the witches of the Devil; we fight each other, we with bundles of fennel and they with sorghum stalks. And if we are the victors, that year there is abundance, but if we lose there is famine."

Questioned: How long have you been involved in this, and are you now? He replied,

"It is eight years and more that I have not participated. One enters at the age of twenty and is freed at forty if he so wishes."

Questioned: How does one enter this company of the *benandanti*? He replied, "All those who have been born with the caul [thin, translucent birth membrane remaining on the head] belong to it, and when they reach the age of twenty they are summoned by means of a drum the same as soldiers, and they are obliged to respond."

Questioned: How can it be that we know so many gentlemen who are born with the caul and nevertheless are not vagabonds? He replied, "I am saying everybody born with the caul must go." Cautioned to tell the truth about the way one entered in this profession, he replied, "Nothing else happens, except that the spirit leaves the body and goes wandering."

Questioned: Who is it that comes to summon you, God, or an angel, a man, or a devil? He replied, "He is a man just like us, who is placed above us all and beats a drum and calls us."

Questioned: Are there many of you who go? He replied, "We are a great multitude, and at times we are five thousand and more."

Questioned: Do you know one another? He replied, "Some who belong to the village know one another, and others do not."

Questioned: Who placed that being above you? He replied, "I do not know, but we believe he is sent by God, because we fight for the faith of Christ." . . .

Questioned, he replied, "Our standard bearer carries a banner of white silk stuff gilded with a lion."

Questioned, he replied, "The banner of the witches is of red silk with four black Devils, gilded."

Questioned, he replied, "The captain of the witches had a black beard; he is big and tall—of the German nation." . . .

Questioned, he replied, "We all go on foot, and we *benandanti* fight with bundles of fennel, and the witches with stalks of sorghum."

Questioned: Do you eat fennel and garlic? He replied, "Yes, father we do, because they serve against the witches."

Questioned, he replied, "There are no women among us, but it is true that there are women *benandanti*, and women go against women."

Questioned, he replied: "In the fighting that we do, one time we fight over the wheat and all the other grains, another time over the livestock, and at other times over the vineyards. And so, on four occasions we fight over all the fruits of the earth and for those things won by the *benandanti* that year there is abundance."

Questioned, he replied: "I cannot say the names of my companions because I would be beaten by the entire company."

Questioned: Tell me the names of your enemies, of the witches, that is. He replied, "Sir, I cannot do it."

Questioned: If you say that you fight for God, I want you to tell me the names of these witches. He replied, "I cannot name nor accuse anyone, whether he be friend or foe."

Repeatedly admonished and asked to give the names of the witches, he replied, "I cannot say them."

Questioned: For what reason can't you tell me this? He replied, "Because we have a life-long edict not to reveal secrets about one side or the other."

Questioned, he replied, "This commandment was made by the captains of each side, whom we are obliged to obey."

Questioned: This is just a dodge; since you assert that you are no longer one of them, you cannot be obliged to obey them. So, tell me who these witches are. He replied,

"The woman who used to be the wife of Paulo Tirlicher of Mersio in Slavonia near Santo Leonardo, and another named Piero di Cecho of Zuz from Prestento, thirty-six years of age."

Questioned, he replied: "This woman has dried up the milk of animals, putting some things over the covers and roofs of houses, such as certain pieces of wood tied with ropes, and I think that if she isn't dead she could still be found today."

Having heard these things, the reverend father inquisitor dismissed [Moduco] so that he might reconsider, etc.

[Re-questioning of Paolo Gasparutto, June 1580]

. . . Questioned: Have you thought better about speaking the truth than before? He replied, "Yes father, and I will tell it rightly." . . .

Questioned: What did you have to do to enter this company, and what age were you? He replied "I was twenty-eight, and when I entered it was because I was summoned by the captain of the *benandanti* of Verona."

Questioned: What time of the year were you called? He replied, "During the Ember Days of Saint Matthias."

Questioned: Why didn't you tell me this yesterday? He replied, "Because I was afraid of the witches, who would have attacked me in bed and killed me."

Questioned: The first time that you went did you know that you were going with *benandanti*? He replied, "Yes, father, because I had been warned first by a *benandante* of Vicenza, Battista Vicentino by name."

Questioned about his family name, he replied, "I don't know it." . . .

Questioned: What did he say when he came to warn you? He replied, "He told me that the captain of the *benandanti* was summoning me to come out and fight for the crops. And I answered him, 'I do want to come, for the sake of the crops.'"

Questioned: When he spoke to you were you awake or asleep? He replied, "When Battista appeared before me I was sleeping."

Questioned: If you were asleep, how did you answer him and how did you hear his voice? He replied, "My spirit replied to him." . . .

Questioned: Before you were called, that is the day before by this Battista, had you known this Battista? He replied, "No, father, but they know who is a *benandante*."

Questioned: How do they know who is a *benandante*? He replied, "The captain of the *benandanti* knows it."

Questioned: How many are in your company? He replied, "We are only six." . . .

[Re-questioning of Paolo Gasparutto, September 1580]

. . . Questioned: When did this angel appear before you? He replied: "At night, in my house, perhaps during the fourth hour of the night, at first sleep."

Questioned: How did it appear? He replied, "An angel appeared before me all made of gold, like those on altars, and he called me, and my spirit went out."

Questioned, he said, "He called me by name, saying, 'Paolo, I will send you forth as a *benandante*, and you will have to fight for the crops.'"

Questioned, he said, "I answered him, 'I will go, I am obedient.'"

Questioned: What did he promise you: women, food, dancing, and what else? He said, "He did not promise me anything, but those others do dance and leap about, and I saw them because we fought them."

Questioned: Where did your spirit go when the angel summoned you? He replied, "It came out because in the body it cannot speak."

Questioned: Who told you that your spirit had to come out if it was to speak to the angel? He replied, "The angel himself told me."

Questioned: How many times have you seen this angel? He replied, "Every time that I went out, because he always came with me."

Questioned: When he appears before you or takes his leave, does this angel frighten you? He replied, "He never frightens us, but when the company breaks up, he gives a benediction."

Questioned: Doesn't this angel ask to be adored? He replied, "Yes, we adore him just as we adore our Lord Jesus Christ in church, and it isn't many angels but one only who leads the company."

Questioned: When he appears before you, does he show himself seated? He replied, "We all appear at once and he stays in person by our flag."

It was asked of him, does this angel conduct you where that other one is seated on that beautiful throne? He replied, "But he is not of our company; God forbid that we should get involved with that false enemy!" Then he added, "It is the witches that have the beautiful thrones." It was asked of him: Did you ever see witches by that beautiful throne? He replied, gesturing with his arms, "No, sir, we did nothing but fight!"

Questioned: Which is the more beautiful angel, yours or the one on the beautiful throne? He replied, "Didn't I tell you that I have not seen those thrones?"

Adding: "Our angel is beautiful and white; theirs is black and is the Devil."

Questioned: Who was the first *benandante* sent by the angel to call you? He replied, "It was Battista of Vicenza, as I stated on another occasion." . . .

After hearing the above, the reverend father inquisitor ordered that the aforesaid Paolo be returned to his cell.

[Re-questioning of Battista Moduco, October 1580]

. . . Questioned, he said, "The witches do reverence and pray to their masters, who go about with great solemnity in black dress and with chains around their necks and who insist on being kneeled to."

It was asked of him: Do you *benandanti* kneel before your captain? he replied, "No, sir, we only pay our respects to him with our caps, like soldiers to their captain."

It was asked of him: After they have knelt, do the witches play other games? He replied, "Sir, this I have not seen because they go hither and yon."

It was asked of him: When did you see the witches kneel down and where? He replied, "In the field of Mazzone after we had fought when they were setting out in every direction."

It was asked of him: How could you make yourself believe that these were God's works? Men do not have the power either to render themselves invisible or to lead the spirit away, nor are God's works carried out in secrecy. He replied, "That one begged me so much, saying: 'Dear Battista, get up,' and it seemed as if I was both sleeping and not sleeping. Since he was older than me, I allowed myself to be persuaded, thinking it was proper."

Questioned, he said, "Yes sir, now I do believe that this was a diabolical work, after that other one told me of that angel of his, which I mentioned before. . . . I wish I had a *scudo* [a coin] for every time we drank in the wine cellars entering through the cracks and getting on the casks. We drank with a pipe, as did the witches." . . .

[Re-questioning of Paolo Gasparutto, October 1580]

. . . Questioned, he replied, "I believe that the apparition of that angel was really the Devil tempting me, since you have told me that he can transform himself into an angel."

Questioned, he replied, "About a year before the angel appeared to me, my mother gave me the caul in which I had been born, saying that she had it baptized with me, and had nine masses said over it, and had it blessed with certain prayers and scriptural readings, and she told me that I was born a *benandante*, and that when I grew up I would go forth at night, and that I must wear it on my person, and that I would go with the *benandanti* to fight the witches." . . .

[Moduco and Gasparutto Summoned to Hear Their Sentences, November 1581]

. . . In the name of Christ, amen. We, brother Felice da Montefalco, doctor in sacred theology and inquisitor general against heretical pravity for the entire patriarchate of Aquileia and diocese of Concordia, especially delegated by the Holy Apostolic see.

Since you, Battista Moduco, public crier in the city of Cividale, diocese of Aquileia, was denounced to us by individuals worthy of belief as a suspect of heretical pravity, and that you had been so infected for many years, to the great detriment of your soul . . . after having diligently discussed the merit of the trial, as indicated above, we have ascertained that in following our frequent instructions and those of other virtuous men, you have returned, adhering to a healthier opinion, to the bosom of holy mother church and to its unity, salubriously fleeing the aforesaid heresies and detesting the errors and acknowledging the irrefutable truth of the faith of the holy church, impressing it within the very viscera of your body. Consequently we have admitted you (and we admit you) as a warning to publicly abjure the aforementioned heresies and any other, according to the following formula. After the abjuration we shall absolve you from the sentence of greater excommunication by which you became bound after your fall into heresy, and in reconciling you to holy mother church, we restore the sacraments to you, provided that with a true heart and unfeigned faith you return to the unity of the church, just as we believe and hope you have done.

. . . I [Battista Moduco] promise to believe with my heart and confess with my tongue that holy, catholic and apostolic faith which, holy mother church believes, confesses, proclaims and observes. Consequently, I abjure, revoke, detest and disown every heresy of whatever kind it might be, and sect raised up against the holy, Roman and apostolic church. . . . If I learn that someone is infected with heresy or belongs to the witches, or to the witches and *benandanti*, I will reveal this information to you the father inquisitor or to your successors. . . .

[Sentence] First: We condemn to a term of six months in a prison which we shall assign to you, which you will not leave without our express permission, obtaining in writing. Second: on every Friday of the Ember Days you will fast and beseech God to forgive you the sins which you committed on those days, and you will observe this for two continuous years. Third: three times a year, at the Resurrection, at the Assumption of the Blessed Virgin Mary in the month of August and at the Nativity of our Lord, for five years you will confess your sins and receive the most sacred sacrament of the Eucharist, bringing or sending an attestation from your priest to the Holy Office that this was fulfilled. Fourth: you are and will be obliged to send to the Holy Office of the Inquisition all the wrapping or cauls in which your children were or will be born, without burning these cauls by fire. Moreover, as salutary penance on individual holy days for a period of three years you will recite the Rosary, praying to God to forgive the sins and errors you have committed.

[Both Battista Moduco and Paolo Gasparutto were given similar sentences and both pleaded that the prison sentence be remitted so they could care for their families; the prison sentences were remitted.]

Questions: What aspect of the men's testimony do the inquisitors find the most trou-bling? Why do the inquisitors continue to ask the defendants the same questions? Why do Moduco and Gasparutto differ on the number of benandanti who fight? Why do the inquisitors want to know the names of others at the battles? Why does Moduco change his mind about the nature of the angel? Why are the two men given such mild sentences when all over Europe people were being tortured and burned for similar activities? Do you get the sense that the court was coercive?

66. IN PRAISE OF NATURAL MAGIC: CORNELIUS AGRIPPA

Heinrich Cornelius Agrippa (1486–1535) was born in Nettesheim, Germany. He gradu-ated from the University of Cologne and then moved to Paris where he joined a secret society dedicated to examination of the occult. In 1509, Agrippa returned to Germany and studied under the humanist Abbot Johannes Trithemius (1462–1516), to whom he dedicated On the Occult Philosophy. *Agrippa was influenced by the major writings of his day, including those of Giovanni Pico della Mirandola (see doc. 62), the legendary Hermes Trismegistus, and the Jewish mystical works of the Kabbalah tradition. Trithemius, concerned for Agrippa's safety in the current environment of the witch-hunts, urged his former pupil to keep his books on natural philosophy secret. Trithemius's advice proved prophetic when Agrippa clashed with the Inquisition over his defense of a woman accused of witchcraft and the Dominican inquisitor Conrad Köllin of Ulm denounced his work as heretical. That condemnation led to the retraction appended to book 3, in which Agrippa states that magicians are idolatrous creatures of the Devil destined for hell.*

Source: trans. Willis F. Whitehead, Henry Cornelius Agrippa, *Three Books of Occult Philosophy or Magic*, bk. 1 (Chicago: Hahn & Whitehead, 1898), pp. 25–26, 28–30, 34–35, 89,124–25, 127–28, 141–42, 150–51, 157–58, 184–85.

Cornelius Agrippa to the Reader

I do not doubt that the title of our book of *Occult Philosophy*, or of magic, may by the rarity of it, allure many to read it, among whom, some of a disordered judgment and some that are perverse, will come to hear what I can say, who, by their rash ignorance, may take the name of magic in the worse sense and, though scarce having seen the title, cry out that I teach forbidden arts, sow the seed of heresies, offend the pious, and scandalize excellent wits—that I am a sorcerer, and superstitious, and devilish, and that indeed a magician. I answer them that a magician does not, among learned men, signify a sorcerer or one that is superstitious or devilish but rather a wise man, a priest, a prophet, and that the Sibyls [Roman prophetesses] were magicianesses, and therefore prophesied most clearly of Christ and that magicians, as wise men, who, by the wonderful secrets of the world, knew Christ, the author of the world, to be born, and they came first of all to worship him, and that the name of magic was received by philosophers, commended by divines, and it is not unacceptable to the gospel. I believe that the supercilious censors will object to the Sibyls, holy magicians, and the gospel itself sooner than receive the name of magic into favor. So conscientious are they that neither Apollo nor all the Muses [nine daughters of Zeus], nor an angel from heaven can redeem me from their curse. Therefore I advise those people not to read our writings, nor understand them, nor remember them. . . . But you who come without prejudice to read it, if you have so much discretion of prudence as bees have in gathering honey, read securely and believe that you shall receive no little profit and much pleasure. . . .

I confess that magic teaches many superfluous things and curious prodigies for ostentation; leave them as empty things, yet be not ignorant of their causes.

But those things which are for the profit of men, for the turning away of evil events, for the destroying of sorceries, for the curing of diseases, for the exterminating of phantasms, for the preserving of life, honor, or fortune may be done without offense to God or injury to religion, because they are, as profitable and necessary. . . .

Letter from Agrippa to John Trithemius

Heinrich Cornelius Agrippa of Nettesheim sends greeting: When I was of late, most reverend father, for a while conversant with you in your monastery of Herbipolis, we conferred together of diverse things concerning chemistry, magic, and the Kabbala, and of other things, which as yet lie hidden in secret sciences and arts; and then there was one great question among the rest, "Why magic, whereas it was accounted by all ancient philosophers to be the chief science, and by the ancient wise men and priests was always held in great veneration, came at last, after the beginning of the Catholic church, to be always odious to and suspected by the holy fathers, and then exploded by divines, and condemned by sacred canons, and, moreover, by all laws and ordinances forbidden?" Now, the cause, as I conceive, is no other than this. Because, by a certain fatal depravation of times and men, many false philosophers crept in under the name of magicians, heaping together, through various sorts of errors and factions of false religions, many cursed superstitions and dangerous rites, and many wicked sacrileges, even to the perfection of nature; and the same set forth in many wicked and unlawful books, to which they have by stealth prefixed the most honest name and title of magic, hoping, by this sacred title, to gain credit to their cursed and detestable fooleries. Hence it is that this name of magic, formerly so honorable, is now become most odious to good and honest men and accounted a capital crime if any one dare profess that he is a magician, either in doctrine or works, unless, by chance, some certain old doting woman, dwelling in the country, would be believed to be skillful and have a divine power, . . . Hence those things that Lucan relates of Thessala [Erictho; see doc. 5], and Homer of the omnipotence of Circe [see doc. 3]. Whereof many others, I confess, also have a fallacious opinion and a superstitious diligence and pernicious labor; for when they cannot come under a wicked art yet they presume they may be able to cloak themselves under that venerable title of magic. . . .

[Modern writers] promise to treat of magic but do nothing but relate irrational tales and superstitions unworthy of honest men. Hence my spirit was moved, and, by reason partly of admiration and partly of indignation, I was willing to play the philosopher . . . [and] I have at last composed three compendious books of magic, and titled them *Of Occult Philosophy*. . . .

Book 1

2. Magic is a faculty of wonderful virtue, full of most high mysteries, containing the most profound contemplation of most secret things together with the nature, power, quality, substance, and virtues thereof, as also the knowledge of the whole of nature. . . . All regulative philosophy is divided into natural, mathematical and theological. Natural philosophy teaches the nature of those things which are in the world—searching and inquiring into their causes, effects, times, places, fashions, events, their whole and parts. Also "The number and the nature of those things called elements—water, fire, earth, air—brings forth; from whence the heavens their beginnings had; whence tide, whence rainbow, in gay colors clad" [Source unknown]. . . .

22. . . . The several signs, also, of the zodiac take care of [humans' bodies]. So Aries governs the head and face; Taurus, the neck; Gemini, the arms and shoulders; Cancer, the breast, lungs, stomach; Libra, the kidneys, and arms; Leo, the heart, stomach, liver and back; Virgo, the bowels and bottom of the stomach [and so forth] . . . thighs and buttocks; Scorpio, the secrets; Sagittarius, the thighs and groins; [and so forth]. Whence it is, if a medicine be applied to the one it helps the other; [for example], as by the warming of the feet, the pain of the belly ceases. . . .

40. We have spoken concerning the virtues and wonderful efficacy of natural things. It remains now that we understand a thing of great wonderment, and it is a binding of men into love or hatred, sickness or health, or such like. Also the binding of thieves and robbers, that they cannot steal in any place; the binding of merchants, that they cannot buy or sell in any place; the binding of an army, that they cannot pass over any bound; the binding of ships, that no winds, though never so strong, shall be able to carry them out of the haven . . . the binding of dogs, that they cannot bark; the binding of birds and wild beasts, that they shall not be able to fly or run away. And such like as these, which are scarce credible, yet often known by experience. Now, there are such kind of bindings as these made by sorceries, collieries [salves], unguents, and love potions, by binding to or hanging up of things, by rings, by charms, by strong imaginations and passions, by images and characters, by enchantments and imprecations, by lights, by numbers, by sounds, by words, and names, invocations, and sacrifices, by swearing, conjuring, consecrations, devotions, and by diverse superstitions, and observations, and such like.

42. Now I will show you what some of the sorceries are, that by the example of these there may be a way opened for the consideration of the whole subject of them. Of these, therefore, the first is the catamenia [menstrual blood], which, how much power it has in sorcery, we will now consider. . . . They report, that if catamenious persons [menstruating women] shall walk, being nude, about the

standing corn, they make all cankers, worms, beetles, flies, and all hurtful things, to fall off from the corn, but they must take heed that they do it before sunrise or else they will make the corn wither. Also, they say, they are able to expel hail, tempests, and lightning, more of which Pliny the Elder [Roman author, 23–79 CE] makes mention of. Know this, that [catamenious women] are a greater poison if they happen in the decrease of the moon, and yet much greater if they happen between the decrease and change of the moon, but if they happen in the eclipse of the moon or the sun, they are an incurable poison. But they are of greatest force of all when they happen in the first early years, even in the years of virginity, for if they do but touch the posts of the house, there can no mischief take effect in [the house]. Also, they say, that the threads of any garment touched therewith cannot be burnt, and if they be cast into the fire it will spread no further. . . .

47. Rings, also, which were always much esteemed by the ancients, when they are opportunely made, do in like manner impress their virtue upon us inasmuch as they do affect the spirit of him who carries them with gladness or sadness, and render him courteous or terrible, bold or fearful, amiable or hateful; inasmuch as they do fortify us against sickness, poisons, enemies, evil spirits, and all manner of hurtful things, or, at least, will not suffer us to be kept under them. Now, the manner of making these kinds of magical rings is this. When any star ascends fortunately, with the fortunate aspect or conjunction of the moon, we must take a stone and herb that is under that star and make a ring of the metal that is suitable to this star and in it fasten the stone, putting the herb or root under it—not omitting the inscriptions of images, names, and characters, as also the proper suffumigations [exposure to smoke or fumes] but we shall speak more of these in another place, where we shall treat of images and characters.

So we read in Philostratus Jarchus [Greek author, fl. 230 CE] that a wise prince of the Indies bestowed seven rings made after this manner (marked with the virtues and names of the seven planets) to Apollonius [c. 15–c. 100]; of which he wore one every day of the week, distinguishing them in their order according to the names of the days, as set forth by astrologers. That is, Sunday, the ring marked with the virtues and inscribed with the name and seal of the sun, that planet which rules over Sunday and from which the day takes its name; Monday, the ring of the virtues, seal and name of the moon, [and so forth] . . . It is said, that Apollonius, by the benefit of these seven magical rings, lived more than one hundred and thirty years, and that he always retained the beauty and vigor of his youth. In like manner Moses, the lawgiver and ruler of the Hebrews, being skilled in the magic of the Egyptians, is said by Josephus [Jewish scholar, c. 38–100] to have made rings of love and oblivion. . . .

50. Fascination [evil eye] is a binding which comes from the spirit of the witch, through the eyes of him that is bewitched, and enters his heart. Now the instrument of fascination is the spirit, that is to say, a certain pure, lucid, subtle vapor generated of the purer blood by the heat of the heart. This always sends forth, through the eyes, rays like to itself. Those rays, being sent forth do carry with them a spiritual vapor, and that vapor a blood (as it appears in swollen and red eyes), whose rays, being sent forth to the eyes of him that looks upon them, carry the vapor of the corrupt blood together with itself; by the contagion of which it infects the eyes of the beholder with the like disease. So the eye, being opened and intent upon any one with a strong imagination, darts its beams (which are the vehicle of the spirit) into the eyes of him who is opposite to him, which tender spirit strikes the eyes of him that is bewitched, being stirred up from the heart of him that strikes, and possesses the breast of him that is stricken, wounds his heart and infects his spirit . . . as if it were with a dart or stroke, penetrating the whole body, whence then the spirit and amorous blood, being thus wounded, are carried forth upon the lover and enchanter, no otherwise than the blood and spirit of the vengeance of him that is slain are upon him that slays him. . . .

52. . . . The signs [of the zodiac] and the faces of signs have their figures and shapes, which, he that would know, must seek them out in books of astrology. Lastly, upon these figures and gestures, both physiognomy [divination by examination of the face or body] and metoposcopy [divination by examination of the forehead], arts of divination, do depend; also chiromancy [palm reading], foretelling future events, not as causes but as signs, through like effects, caused by the same cause. And although these diverse kinds of divinations may seem to be done by inferior and weak signs, yet the judgments of them are not to be slighted or condemned when prognostication is made by them, not out of superstition but by reason of the harmonic correspondence of all the parts of the body. Whosoever, therefore, does the more exactly imitate the celestial bodies, either in nature, study, action, motion, gesture, countenance, passions of the mind, and opportunity of the season, is so much the more like the heavenly bodies and can receive larger gifts from them.

59. There is also a certain kind of divination by dreams which is confirmed by the traditions of philosophers, the authorities of divines, the examples of histories, and by daily experience. . . . I call that a true dream which is caused by the celestial influences in the fantastic spirit, mind or body, being all well-disposed. The rule of interpreting these is found among astrologers, in that part which is written concerning questions; but yet that is not sufficient. . . . Now, dreams are more efficacious when the moon overruns that sign which was in the ninth number of the nativity, or revolution of that year, for in the ninth sign from the sign of perfection. For it is a most true and certain divination,

neither does it proceed from nature or human arts, but from purified minds, by divine inspiration. . . .

Questions: For Agrippa, what is the difference between natural philosophy and demonic magic? What is Agrippa's view of women in relation to magic and natural philosophy? What elements of Agrippa's natural philosophy had already been condemned as magical by earlier Christian thinkers such as Augustine? Why did Agrippa write his books on magic? What elements of Agrippa's thinking likely drew the denunciation of inquisitors?

67. MARTIN LUTHER'S DEVIL

Martin Luther (1483–1546) was a German friar, priest, professor of theology, and the father of the Protestant Reformation. Luther rejected several aspects of Catholic theology, but he and his co-religionists subscribed to witch beliefs as articulated throughout the Christian tradition, and their demonology was essentially Thomist (see doc. 53). Satan was a threatening adversary of God, who, although bested by Christ's incarnation, labored endlessly to ensnare humankind and could be silenced only by faith. Luther was very much a man of his time in terms of his belief in witches and their malevolence, but witchcraft per se plays a minor role in his numerous works. The Devil, on the other hand, is a persistent theme; he is the archenemy—omnipresent and menacing. Luther's relationship with Satan, however, was complex in that it was experiential rather than simply theoretical. The two interacted on a familiar basis that had elements of intimacy.

The two selections below are from Luther's theological writing, "Commentary on the Epistle to the Galatians," and Table Talk, *which is an anthology of Luther's informal conversations recorded by those who shared his meals, as collected by Johannes Mathesius (1504–1565) and published in 1566. In* Table Talk, *Luther speaks informally, and a different side of the man emerges from the one we see in his theological works.*

Sources: trans. Theodore Graebner, *A Commentary on St. Paul's Epistle to the Galatians*, 2nd ed. (Grand Rapids, MI: Zondervan Publishing House, 1939), pp. 87–88, 228–29; trans. William Hazlitt, *The Table Talk of Martin Luther* (London: H.G. Bohn, 1857), pp. 251–68, 274; rev. Martha Rampton.

"Commentary on the Epistle to the Galatians"

Chapter 3

Verse 1. Paul calls the Galatians foolish and bewitched. In the fifth chapter he mentions sorcery among the works of the flesh, declaring that witchcraft and sorcery are real manifestations and legitimate activities of the Devil. We are all exposed to the influence of the Devil, because he is the prince and god of the world in which we live.

Satan is clever. He does not only bewitch men in a crude manner, but also in a more artful fashion. He bedevils the minds of men with hideous fallacies. Not only is he able to deceive the self-assured, but even those who profess the true Christian faith. There is not one among us who is not at times seduced by Satan into false beliefs. This accounts for the many new battles we have to wage nowadays. But the attacks of the old serpent are not without profit to us, for they confirm our doctrine and strengthen our faith in Christ. Many a time we were wrestled down in these conflicts with Satan, but Christ has always triumphed and always will triumph. Do not think that the Galatians were the only ones to be bewitched by the Devil? Let us realize that we too may be seduced by Satan.

Verse 1. In this sentence Paul excuses the Galatians, while he blames the false apostles for the apostasy of the Galatians, as if he were saying, "I know your defection was not willful. The Devil sent the false apostles to you, and they tallied you into believing that you are justified by the law of Moses. With this our epistle we endeavor to undo the damage which the false apostles have inflicted upon you." Like Paul, we struggle with the word of God against the fanatical Anabaptists of our day, and our efforts are not entirely in vain. The trouble is there are many who refuse to be instructed. They will not listen to reason; they will not listen to the Scriptures because they are bewitched by the tricky Devil, who can make a lie look like the truth. Since the Devil has this uncanny ability to make us believe a lie until we would swear a thousand times it was the truth, we must not be proud, but walk in fear and humility and call upon the Lord Jesus to save us from temptation.

Although I am a doctor of divinity and have preached Christ and fought his battles for a long time, I know from personal experience how difficult it is to hold fast to the truth. I cannot always shake off Satan. I cannot always apprehend Christ as the Scriptures portray him. Sometimes the Devil distorts Christ to my vision. But thanks be to God, who keeps us in his word, in faith, and in prayer. The spiritual witchery of the Devil creates in the heart a wrong idea of Christ. Those who share the opinion that a person is justified by the works of the law of Moses, are simply bewitched. Their belief goes against faith and Christ.

Chapter 5

Verses 19, 20. "Now the works of the flesh are manifest, which are these: adultery, fornication, uncleanness, lasciviousness, idolatry, witchcraft . . ."

Idolatry: The best religion, the most fervent devotion without Christ is plain idolatry. It has been considered a holy act when the monks in their cells meditate upon God and his works and in a religious frenzy kneel down to pray and to weep for joy. Yet Paul calls it simply idolatry. Every religion which worships God in ignorance or neglect of his word and will is idolatry. They may think about God, Christ, and heavenly things, but they do it after their own fashion and not after the word of God. They have an idea that their clothing, their mode of living, and their conduct are holy and pleasing to Christ. They not only expect to pacify Christ by the strictness of their life, but also expect to be rewarded by him for their good deeds. Hence their best "spiritual" thoughts are wicked thoughts. Any worship of God, any religion without Christ is idolatry. In Christ alone is God well pleased. I have said before that the works of the flesh are manifest. But idolatry puts on such a good front and acts so spiritual that the sham of it is recognized only by true believers.

Witchcraft: This sin was very common before the light of the gospel appeared. When I was a child there were many witches and sorcerers around who "bewitched" cattle and people, particularly children, and did much harm. But now that the gospel is here you do not hear so much about it because the gospel drives the Devil away. Now he bewitches people in a worse way with spiritual sorcery. . . .

The Table Talk of Martin Luther

581. 25 August 1538, the conversation fell upon witches, who spoil milk, eggs, and butter in farmyards. Dr. Luther said, "I should have no compassion on these witches; I would burn all of them. We read in the old law, that the priests threw the first stone at such malefactors. 'Tis said this stolen butter turns rancid and falls to the ground when any one goes to eat it. He who attempts to counteract and chastise these witches is himself corporeally plagued and tormented by their master, the Devil. Sundry schoolmasters and ministers have often experienced this. Our ordinary sins offend and anger God. What, then, must be his wrath against witchcraft, which we may justly designate high treason against divine majesty—a revolt against the infinite power of God. The jurisconsults who have so learnedly and pertinently treated of rebellion, affirm that the subject who rebels against his sovereign is worthy of death. Does not witchcraft, then, merit death, which is a revolt of the creature against the creator, a denial to God of the authority it accords to the demon?"

582. Dr. Luther discoursed at length concerning witchcraft and charms. He said that his mother had had to undergo infinite annoyance from one of her neighbors, who was a witch and whom she was fain to conciliate with all sorts of attentions; for this witch could throw a charm upon children which made them cry themselves to death. A pastor having punished her for some knavery, she cast a spell upon him by means of some earth upon which he had walked and which she bewitched. The poor man hereupon fell sick of a malady, which no remedy could remove, and shortly after died.

583. It was asked: "Can good Christians and God-fearing people also undergo witchcraft?" Luther replied, "Yes, for our bodies are always exposed to the attacks of Satan. The maladies I suffer are not natural, but devil's spells."

584. "When I was young, someone told me this story. Satan had, in vain, set all his craft and subtlety at work to separate a married pair that lived together in perfect harmony and love. At last, having concealed a razor under each of their pillows, he visited the husband, disguised as an old woman, and told him that his wife had formed the project of killing him; he next told the same thing to the wife. The husband, finding the razor under his wife's pillow, became furious with anger at her supposed wickedness and cut her throat. So powerful is Satan in his malice."

585. Luther, taking up a caterpillar, said: "'Tis an emblem of the Devil in its crawling walk and bears his colours in its changing hue."

589. He who will have for his master and king, Jesus Christ, the son of the Virgin, who took upon himself our flesh and our blood, will have the Devil for his enemy. It is very certain that, as to all persons who have hanged themselves or killed themselves in any other way, 'tis the Devil who has put the cord round their necks or the knife to their throats.

590. A man had a habit, whenever he fell, of saying, "Devil take me." He was advised to discontinue this evil custom, lest someday the Devil should take him at his word. He promised to vent his impatience by some other phrase, but one day, having stumbled, he called upon the Devil in the way I have mentioned and was killed upon the spot, falling on a sharp-pointed piece of wood.

591. A pastor, near Torgau, came to Luther and complained that the Devil tormented him without intermission. The doctor replied, "He plagues and harasses me too, but I resist him with the arms of faith." I know of one person at Magdeburg who put Satan to the rout by spitting at him. But this example is not to be lightly followed, for the Devil is a presumptuous spirit and not disposed to yield. We run great risk when, with him, we attempt more than we can do. One man, who relied implicitly on his baptism, when the Devil presented himself to him, his head furnished with horns, tore off one of the horns. But another man, of less faith, who attempted the same thing, was killed by the Devil.

593. The Devil cannot but be our enemy, since we are against him with God's word, wherewith we destroy his kingdom. He is a prince and god of the world and has a greater power than all the kings, potentates, and princes upon earth; wherefore he would be revenged of us and assaults us without ceasing, as we both see and feel. We have against the Devil a great advantage—powerful, wicked, and cunning as he is—he cannot hurt us since 'tis not against him we have sinned, but against God. Therefore we have nothing to do with that archenemy, but we confess and say, "Against thee, Lord, have we sinned." . . .

597. I maintain that Satan produces all the maladies which afflict mankind, for he is the prince of death. Saint Peter speaks of Christ as healing all that are oppressed of the Devil. He not only cured those who were possessed, but he restored sight to the blind, hearing to the deaf, speech to the dumb, strength to

the paralytic; therefore I think all grave infirmities are blows and strokes of the Devil, which he employs as an assassin uses the sword or other weapon. So God employs natural means to maintain the health and life of man, such as sleep, meat, drink, etc. The Devil has other means of injury; he poisons the air, etc. . . .

598. Satan plagues and torments people in all manner of ways. Some he affrights in their sleep with heavy dreams and visions so that the whole body sweats in anguish of heart. Some he leads, sleeping, out of their beds and chambers up into high dangerous places so that if, by the loving angels who are about them, they were not preserved, he would throw them down and cause their death. . . .

608. Witchcraft is the Devil's own proper work, wherewith, when God permits, he not only hurts people, but often makes away with them; for in this world we are as guests and strangers, body and soul cast under the Devil; he is god of this world, and all things are under his power, whereby, we are preserved in temporal life, as are meat, drink, air, etc. The Devil is so crafty a spirit, that he can ape and deceive our senses. He can cause one to think he sees something, which he sees not, that he hears thunder or a trumpet, which he hears not. . . .

610. When I could not be rid of the Devil with sentences out of the holy Scripture, I made him often fly with jeering words; sometimes I said unto him, "Saint Satan! If Christ's blood, which was shed for my sins, be not sufficient, then I desire that you would pray to God for me. When he finds me idle, with nothing in hand, he is very busy, and before I am aware, he wrings from me a bitter sweat, but when I offer him the pointed spear, God's word, he flies, yet before he goes, he makes a grievous hurricane. When I began to write against the pope, and the gospel was going on, the Devil set himself strongly to work, rumbling and raging about, for he would willingly have preserved purgatory at Magdeburg. There was a citizen, whose child died, for whom he refused to have [Catholic] vigils and masses sung. The Devil played his tricks, came every night about twelve o'clock into the chamber where the boy died and made a whining like a young child. The good citizen being therewith full of sorrow, knew not what course to take. The popish priests said, "Now you see how it goes when vigils are not solemnized. Whereupon the citizen sent to me, desiring my advice, (for the sermon I had lately preached on this text, "They have Moses and the prophets," had been printed, and been read by him), and I wrote to him from Wittenberg and advised him not to suffer any vigils at all to be held, for he might be fully assured that these were merely pranks of the Devil; whereupon, the children and servants in the house jeered the Devil, and said, "What do you think you're doing, Satan? Avoid, your cursed spirit, get you gone to the place where you ought to be, to the pit of hell." When the Devil marked their contempt, he left off his game, and came there no more. He is a proud spirit, and cannot endure scorn.

620. God gives to the Devil and to witches power over human creatures in two ways; first, over the ungodly when he will punish them by reason of their sins; secondly, over the just and godly when he intends to try whether they will be constant in the faith and remain in his obedience. Without God's will and our own consent, the Devil cannot hurt us; for God says, "Who so touches you, touches the apple of my eye" [Zechariah 2.8]. And Christ said, "There cannot fall a hair from your head, without your heavenly father's notice" [Matthew 10:29–31].

625. The Devil gives heaven to people before they sin, but after they sin, brings their consciences into despair. Christ deals quite contrary, for he gives heaven after sins committed and makes consciences joyful. Last night as I waked out of my sleep, the Devil came and said, "God is far from you and does not hear your prayers." Whereupon I said, "Very well, I will call and cry the louder. I will place before my sight the world's unthankfulness and the ungodly doings of kings, potentates, and princes; I will also think upon the raging heretics; all these will inflame my praying."

628. At Mohlburg, in Thuringia, not far from Erfurt, there was a musician who gained his living by playing at merry-makings. This man came to the minister of his parish and complained that he was every day assailed by the Devil, who threatened to carry him off because he had played at an unlawful marriage. The minister consoled him, prayed for him, recited to him numerous passages of Scripture directed against the Devil, and, with some other pious men, watched over the unfortunate man, day and night, fastening the doors and windows, so that he might not be carried off. At length the musician said, "I feel that Satan cannot harm my soul, but he will assuredly remove my body," and that very night, at eight o'clock, though the watch was doubled, the Devil came in the shape of a furious wind, broke the windows, and carried off the musician, whose body was found next morning, stiff and black, stuck on a nut-tree. 'Tis a most sure and certain story," added Luther.

630. Men are possessed by the Devil two ways: corporally and spiritually. Those whom he possesses corporally, as mad people, he has permission from God to vex and agitate, but he has no power over their souls. The impious, who persecute the divine doctrine and treat the truth as a lie and who, unhappily, are very numerous in our time, these the Devil possesses spiritually. They cannot be delivered but remain, horrible to relate, his prisoners, as in the time of Jesus Christ were Annas, Caiaphas [both Jewish high priests who tried Jesus], and all the other impious Jews whom Jesus himself could not deliver, and as, now-a-days, are the pope, his cardinals, bishops, tyrants, and partisans.

Questions: What is the source of Luther's anxiety about the "law" of the Old Testament? What is Luther's objection to monks worshipping the Christian God? What is the difference between the "bewitching" of cattle or children and spiritual sorcery? Does Luther equate witchcraft and heresy? How powerful is Luther's Devil? What can humans do to protect themselves from his assaults? Characterize Luther's relationship with the Devil. In what ways does Luther's thinking about Satan depart from Catholic theology of the same period?

68. PAPISTS, POPEDOM, AND WITCHERY: JOHN CALVIN

John (or Jean) Calvin (1509–1564) was an eloquent and forceful voice of the Protestant Reformation. He broke with the Roman Catholic Church around 1530 over a number of theological differences and his self-proclaimed prophetic calling to reform Christianity. Due to the Protestant persecutions in France, Calvin was compelled to flee his homeland for Switzerland, and there, in Basel, he published the first edition of the Institutes of the Christian Religion *(1536), an exhaustive textbook on the Protestant faith which Calvin revised throughout his life, the definitive edition being published in 1559. By 1541 Calvin was established in Geneva, where he created his model society in which church and state worked closely together to maintain conformity to Calvinist religious, social, and political ideals. During his time in Geneva, Calvin wrote and preached over 2,000 sermons, including the following sermon on Deuteronomy 18:10–15.*

Calvin's demonology was firmly grounded in Old Testament theology and was consistent with traditional Christian thinking on magic and sorcery. He interpreted passages on diabolism and witchcraft literally and similar to Catholic exegetes of the time. All the same, in his sermons he pejoratively refers to "poperie" and "popedom" to characterize Catholicism and goes so far as to label all Catholics sorcerers, wizards, and witches. As far as Calvin's own Protestant society goes, the Consistory, a morals court that he established in Geneva, was comparatively lenient on those accused of sorcery, especially people tried for superstitious healing. Even cases of maleficium *were treated with some skepticism.*

Sources: trans. John Allen, John Calvin, *Institutes of the Christian Religion*, vol. 1, 7th ed. (Philadelphia: Presbyterian Board of Publication, 1936), pp. 20, 26–28; trans. Arthur Golding, John Calvin, *The Sermons of M. John Calvin upon the Fifth Book of Moses called Deuteronomie* (London: Henry Middleton, 1583; rpt. The Banner of Trust Facsimile Reprint, 1987), pp. 668–71; rev. Martha Rampton.

Dedication: To his most Christian majesty, Francis I, king of the French [r. 1515–1547], and his sovereign, John Calvin wishes peace and salvation in Christ.

. . . [Our Catholic adversaries] requiring miracles of us is altogether unreasonable; . . . It is the characteristic of sound doctrine, given by Christ, that [miracles] tend to promote, not the glory of men, but the glory of God. Christ having laid down this proof of a doctrine, it is wrong to esteem those as miracles which are directed to any other end than the glorification of the name of God alone. And we should remember that Satan has his wonders, which, though they are juggling tricks rather than real miracles, are such as to delude the ignorant and inexperienced. Magicians and enchanters have always been famous for miracles; idolatry has been supported by astonishing miracles; and yet we do not admit them as proofs of the legitimacy of the superstition of magicians or idolaters. With this battering-ram the simplicity of the people was exploited by the Donatists [a Christian sect of the fourth and fifth centuries], who abounded in miracles. We therefore give the same answer now to our adversaries as Augustine gave to the Donatists, that our Lord has cautioned us against these miracle-mongers by his prediction and that there should arise false prophets, who, by various signs and lying wonders, "should deceive (if possible) the very elect" [Matthew 24:24]. And Paul has told us that the kingdom of Antichrist would be "with all power, and signs, and lying wonders" [2 Thessalonians 2:9]. But these miracles (they say) are wrought, not by idols, or sorcerers, or false prophets, but by saints; as if we were ignorant that it is a stratagem of Satan to "transform" himself "into an angel of light" [2 Corinthians 11:14]. . . . We are by no means without miracles, and such as are certain, and not trivial, but those under which [Catholics] shelter themselves are mere illusions of Satan, seducing the people from the true worship of God to vanity.

Sermon on Deuteronomy

The 109 Sermon which is the Third upon the Eighteenth Chapter

 . . . Notwithstanding that this evil was practiced among the Jews—that they sacrificed their children to Moloch [Leviticus 18:21]—the heathen had yet another way of transgressing by making their children go through the fire, of which Moses speaks in the same passage. They considered it a kind of purging or cleansing when they used such ceremonies, and there remain remnants of it in popedom, in their bonfires on Midsummer Night. It is a type of purging to take the air of that holy fire (as they esteemed it), which is in fact witchery. But our lord considers such superstitions as enchantments. Likewise the papists have their holy water, and what else is that than a kind of cleansing they invented to set against the blood of our lord Jesus Christ and against baptism, which is the true sign of Christ? Then let us mark well that our lord condemns all manner of purging or cleansing that the papists invent, when, in fact, they cannot be cleansed by any other means than that which God has ordained, which is by the sacrifice of our Lord Jesus Christ commemorated in the sacraments as attested in Scripture. . . . Concerning astrology, if men hold themselves within those bounds [marking time by observing the heavens], no evil will come of it, but if they range outside of these limits and fall to inventing occult meanings for the ordinary course of nature, then it is devilish superstition and what men call judicial astrology. . . .

[Deuteronomy makes mention of] enchanters, sorcerers, calkers, workers with familiars, and those who ask counsel from the dead. As concerning enchanters, I am not referring to those jugglers who blear men's eyes with sleight of hand and make men believe they see things which they do not; rather I refer to the Devil who has such dominion over the unbelievers, that although a thing is not done in fact; yet the illusion is such as makes men believe they see that which they do not see. And so it is a kind of enchantment, that is to say of devilish illusion, when a man shall be made to think that one is transformed into a wolf, or that he sees the shape of a thing that has no substance or truth.

Now it is asked whether such illusions can be created or not. And why not? We have an example in Pharaoh's sorcerers, who made frogs come up as well as Moses did [Exodus 8:7; see doc. 1]; this is not because the Devil has anything in his own power; for we must not imagine that he can fight against God and impose his own will. We know he is under God's hand and can do nothing without leave or license. The Devil may well attempt much, but yet he cannot stir one finger as you would say. . . . But yet for all that, it is abominable before God, and so are soothsayers. It is a question as to whether it is possible for man to foretell things; for it is God's prerogative to foreknow things to come; how then can such a power belong to the Devil? It is true (as says the prophet Isaiah) [Isaiah 41:22–24] that idols can foresee nothing. And as for Satan, he is always the father of lies and deceives all who ask counsel of him. Yet notwithstanding, God does now and then suffer Satan to tell of things to come, and this is for the hardening of those who will not obey the truth (as we have seen by example in the thirteenth chapter) and it has been treated of partly already. Yet notwithstanding it is true also that soothsayers lie most commonly, and by that means our lord deludes those who do not obey the truth to seek the counsel of Satan after that fashion. And besides, let us not think it strange that enchanters, soothsayers, and such others do now and then tell of things to come. For it is God's just sufferance that they should more deeply be plunged into error. For since they are willingly deceived, God lets them be so that they may perish. . . .

Also in Deuteronomy mention is made of workers with familiars, in regard to which Satan's illusions are horrible. But what? Such people have existed in all ages, and we see a notable example of it in King Saul when he went to the Witch of Endor [see doc. 2]. He, as king, had forbidden all enchantments and all manner of damnable crafts, and he had behaved virtuously in executing God's law. And yet in the end, he became so wretched that he fell to running after a witch [1 Samuel 28]. And why did he despise God? Whereupon in the end he fell into despair and gave himself over altogether to Satan, which he showed full well. For if you look carefully into the matter, you shall find that Satan's illusions get the upper hand of men when their wits are amazed by sorrow and gnaw them inwardly, and for that, instead of receiving some comfort from God's word, they are overwhelmed with such anguish that they fall into utter despair. When does Satan meet a man in some bodily shape and tangle him in his snares? When a man is in some grief of mind, or in some hatred against his neighbor, or when a woman spites her husband. Well then, although such considerations bear sway, God still gives Satan the bridle to reign over men until they reach such extremities that they fall to chawing upon the bit and become so willful in their sorrow that they fall into despair and will no more admit any comfort, but refuse all remembrance of God and wish that his name were buried. For then is the gate open to Satan, and he enters to work his illusion, which a man is not able to withstand. Of this we have a fair warning in Saul. . . .

Finally Deuteronomy makes mention of those who seek counsel from the dead. For it is not our Lord's will that we should have anything to do with the dead. Therefore they who use such conjurations go about to pervert the whole order of nature. For let men do what they can, yet they cannot bring the living and the dead together, but the Devil steps in and pretends to be the dead person being sought, so outwardly it seems like the dead man himself has appeared (as discussed above), whereas in fact, it is the Devil that works such illusions. And therefore let us note well that, seeing our lord has forbidden us to have anything to do with the dead, we cannot be deceived so long as we keep within our bounds and do not attempt anything which we see is outside the order he has set. And thereby we also see that all the things that have been said about the coming-up again of dead men's ghosts have been but slights of Satan, and when men have been beguiled by these illusions, it was as if they had willfully yielded themselves slaves to Satan. And yet communication with the dead is considered a great devotion in poperie, and it is for this reason that [Catholics] make pilgrimages and have masses sung. Yea and their feast of All Souls, which is kept each year, is due to a revelation or dream of some devout monk that had an idle head. He heard the crying of dead men's souls and thereupon the papists concluded that a solemn feast was to be kept for the dead, and such and such things were to be done for them. In short, these services for the dead that have been invented in the popedom are nothing else but mere witchery, even such as God dislikes and utterly abhors. And all those who participate in the devotion and pray for the dead are witches and sorcerers, for they believe in Satan's enchantments in defiance of God.

And now let us note that these enchantments are not small and tolerable faults; but it is said expressly "that they be abominable before God, and that the people of Canaan were to be rooted out for such crimes and misdeeds" [Deuteronomy 18:12]. Whereby we see that although other vices were to be pardoned, yet sorcery ought to be punished and utterly routed out. Therefore if we will be taken for God's people, let us see that we understand what this word "abomination" means, namely that we must be very wary of sorceries, enchantments, and other such things. And indeed we see how such things have always been disliked, even among the heathen. However much witch-craft had reigned, yet was it a great thing for a heathen man to have asked, "Should this be done?" For every man would have said, "Why should it?" It is a monster; it is a shameful and cursed thing. In this way even the heathen spoke of it. For it was God's will that hatred of sorcery should be so ingrained in men's hearts that it was reproved even without the doctrine of the law [of Moses]. It is true that in poperie all [Catholics] are witches in their idolatries, for in the fifteenth chapter of the first book of Samuel, God couples those two sins together.

Yea and I have told you already that the service of the dead is a kind of witchcraft. Yet [Roman Catholics] claim to abhor the term and condemn the practice. And why? Because God has allowed [service of the dead] to make [papists] the more inexcusable. So then let us note, that it is not for us to suffer either enchanters or witches among us. And if these are forbidden; we must understand that all other kinds of wizardry are deadly crimes before God. And if judges and magistrates do their duties, it is certain that they will no more tolerate them than they do murderers. . . . Why? It is the overthrowing of God's service and a perverting of the order of nature. Is it not worth punishment and punishment again if the order of nature should be confounded between men and brute beasts? Is there any reason in so doing? And surely when men begin with such enchantments it is certain that they fall into a deeper and more dreadful dungeon than if they give over their bodies to the lusts of the brute beasts. And yet we see the selfsame illusions to be wrought by Satan upon all witches and sorcerers. And what is the original cause thereof, but that they turned away from God's truth? Even if the only wrong committed was in attributing God's power to Satan, it is a matter that cannot be born. If, for example, there were something concealed from me, and I wished to know it, yea, but God did not want to reveal it, so should I say "That is no matter, I will find it out by some means or other regardless of God's wishes? Yea I will have understanding of it by a devilish illusion." Is this not making war against God if this is allowed? So if we will be taken for Christians, witchcrafts, enchantments, and such things must not be born among us even more so than robberies and murders. . . .

Questions: How does Calvin distinguish the miracles of magicians and the miracles of saints? Why and under what circumstances does God give Satan free rein over human beings? On what grounds does Calvin conclude that all Catholics are given to wizardry? When are humans most susceptible to Satan's snares? Which biblical motifs are present in the sermon on Deuteronomy that appear again and again in texts about magic?

69. A VOICE OF SKEPTICISM FROM THE MEDICAL PROFESSION: JOHANN WEYER

The Dutch physician Johann Weyer's (1515–1588) On the Illusions of the Demons and on Spells and Poisons *was the first systematic refutation of many of the premises that supported the witch trials. Although Weyer did not doubt the existence or capabilities of demons, he rejected as "fantastical" those elements of witchcraft, such as flight and sexual congress with demons that were not observable in the natural order. Weyer's skepticism was fed by his profession as a doctor and, in some respects, an association with Heinrich Cornelius Agrippa (see doc. 66), his friend and mentor. In 1548, Weyer was asked his professional advice, as a physician, about a witchcraft court case involving a fortune teller. His recommendations characterize the intellectual restraint with which he approached wonders, magic, and witches. This caution informs his book, which initiated a European debate about the veracity of aspects of witchcraft. The work went through several Latin, German, and French editions, and for the next two centuries virtually every author who wrote about witches cited Weyer. Predictably,* On the Illusions *found both advocates and detractors. As a result of the book, some jurists were more likely to consult physicians to determine whether a given defendant was too "melancholic," mentally deranged, or senile to stand trial. In the final analysis, Weyer's witchcraft beliefs were not fundamentally different from those whom he ridiculed, and because of the book's detailed descriptions of the deceits of demons, the treatise was often used to bolster the arguments of men and women who promoted the witch-hunts and preached to the dangers of human involvement in magic and satanic witchcraft.*

Source: trans. John Shea, *On Witchcraft: An Abridged Translation of Johann Weyer's* De praestigiis daemonum, ed. Benjamin G. Kohn and H.C. Erik Middleport (Asheville, NC: Pegasus Press, 1998), 72–74, 122, 124, 173–75, 177–80, 268–75, 289.

On the Illusions of the Demons and on Spells and Poisons

Book 2

17. Many priests and monks also find their place here in the family of those who are swollen with a familiar "Pythian" [divining] spirit. . . . With lying tongue they convince such a person that the disease has come about from witchcraft or enchantment. Moreover, these Pythian prophets often have the unspeakable effrontery to use their notorious art to point out the "enchantress" or "witch" by "signs" (please God!). They often thus brand some respectable, guiltless, and pious matron; and never will the mark heal, either for her or for her descendants, even far into the future. These prophets think that they are not busy enough with their fallacious discussions of disease unless they also overwhelm the innocent by means of false charges, stir up hatreds of more than vatinian [immense]

344

intensity among this over-credulous race of men, make whole neighborhoods resound with lawsuits, rend friendships asunder, dissolve the blood-bonds of unity, stir men to fighting, attend to the jails (see that they are filled); and finally, in various ways, contrive the murder of those who desire to vindicate or help the innocent woman branded as the cause of this imaginary "evil-doing" or else contrive the murder of the woman herself, who is either killed by others or punished by an ill-trained magistrate.

If I say that I am a living witness of these things, I shall certainly not be lying, even if Codrus and members of his sect burst with indignation. And so these men "of the church"—perfect slaves to their training—greatly assist their champion Beelzebub [another name for Satan] (as he discovers, to his vaunting delight), usually under the mantle of religion. In their quest for money or their itching desire for undeserved esteem they thus prostitute and surrender their souls and the souls of others to demons; by their belief in such enchantments in the case of naturally caused diseases, they risk life and health and besmirch medicine, which is at once the most ancient of the arts and the most useful and necessary. . . .

In a well-known town of Gilders where I once practiced medicine on public commission, [a] fellow went to a convent of strictly cloistered maidens and persuaded one of their number, who had been in somewhat poor health, that her troubles stemmed from witchery; he added that these troubles could not be resolved unless the sacrifice of the mass were celebrated on her belly. Later the superior of the convent (who was addressed by the title "Mother"), a woman deserving of respect by reason of her birth, her age, and her righteousness, often complained that it was only after permission had been granted and the mass had been completed that the young woman first began to be vexed by witchery, having previously been troubled (slightly) by some natural malady. . . .

Book 3

20. . . . It is demonstrated beyond all doubt that the lying of demons with women is nonsense and purely imaginary. The vanity and falsity of this sexual congress will be shown by clear "eye-witness" testimony and irrefutable proof, if the maiden who is disturbed by this bewitching of her depraved imagination and who is suffering these illusions—the maiden who is thought to have been corrupted by intercourse with a demon (such as the nun that I know of in Holland who was consigned to the flames on the basis of her own confession of filthy relations with a demon)—be examined visually and manually by a skilled midwife or by some other trained woman. She will be found to be still protected by this "girdle of virginity," namely, the hymen, provided that she has not lain with a man on some other occasion. Indeed, I wish to show that, contrary to the opinion of many who argue otherwise, all virgins have been endowed with this membrane from the beginning by God the creator. . . .

Let it be enough to have indicated—or rather, clearly displayed—the plain reasons by which the falsity of the *incubus* and *succubus* is exposed, . . . Now if someone who is deceived by the narrow aperture of the hymen should suggest that the Devil, as a creature of many forms, could enjoy sexual relations with a virgin, I would respond by asking him to explain to me how the womb can bring forth monstrous objects as a result of such congress if that defense of maidenhood is intact—objects as large, hard uneven, rough, and sharp as were brought to "birth" (as I shall show a little later) by a certain Magdalena, who was taken prisoner in Constance because of her lying with a demon. If indeed, after procreating these strange and unnatural objects, the girl had been examined visually and manually in professional fashion by persons familiar with the parts of the uterus, it would have been clearly established that the deception was brought about in the first instance by an illusion impressed upon the imagination during the (supposed) act of intercourse, and that then the birth pangs were set in motion by the spirit, and a mass of strange, incomprehensible, lifeless objects were displayed by the arch-schemer as the offspring of that coition, so that the imaginary sexual congress might be judged real.

Book 4

14. Although everyone will cry out in one voice that this amazing spectacle [a knife in a woman's body] was truly produced, without any trickery on the part of the Devil, and that it admits of no gloss or explanation, I shall not be reluctant to give my own opinion on the subject with some simple words of explanation. With God's help, and for his glory, and in despite of the demon and his deluded crowd of followers, I shall strive to demonstrate as briefly as possible that the knife had not been in the girl's body but that a demon's trickery and illusions had clouded the eyes of all, and the girl had been possessed by a demonic spirit. And yet I am well aware that many will howl out their opposition in stentorian tones.

First of all, it should have been observed that this simple girl had been worn down by a long fever—a quatran fever (as I gather from its duration) produced from an excess of heavy, bitter, melancholic humor [bodily fluid] putrefied within the body. Melancholic humor often obstructs the spleen and produces swelling, hardness, and abscess therein, in which case a quatran fever occasionally leaves such a "progeny" behind, even after it has passed. Upon this foundation—female sex, youthful age, wearing effect of a lengthy illness—the demon built and constructed the rest of his work with eager and untiring zeal. He gains credibility far more easily with women than with males of mature age and good health. To support his work, he adopted the humor most suitable for his activities—namely the melancholic humor; far from being cleansed of these biles, the girl's brain and body were burdened all the more. The Devil takes great delight in immersing himself in this humor, as being the proper moisture for himself and his activities by virtue of its analogous properties; with its assistance he induces wondrous phantasms and rare imaginings. I have demonstrated this point so clearly in the previous book that I think there is no need for repetition.

Now, to continue this act of the tragedy, the demon rose early in the morning and took advantage of the maiden's solitude while no others were present who might perhaps have impeded his efforts by their lively faith. He first assumed the features of the old woman who inquired about the girl's health, so that later, when the girl became crazed by the belief that a knife was buried in her body, she might more easily be led to suspect that a *lamia* [witch] had done this deed by using charms. For it is the principal aim of that bloodthirsty scoundrel to promote strife and devise slaughter (especially of the innocent) and to inculcate a false belief that runs contrary to the true worship of God. To implant it more deeply in her mind that the knife had been transferred from her lap into her side by an old *lamia* in league with the Devil, he then appeared to her in the form of a black dog, which she later adjudged, after she had partly recovered, to have been a demon.

Approaching her at the beginning of the possession, the demon thus induced a sensation of catarrh, or of cold humor dripping down from her head to her back, so that after she was restored to her senses, she might believe that the knife had been conveyed into her body at the very moment when she experienced this feeling of cold. Soon afterwards, he entered into her and so disturbed her organs of sensation that for three days she appeared as though dead. Meanwhile, he confirmed her imaginary impressions with so strong a conviction about the knife's being implanted in her side that she could not persuade herself that it had not really happened thus. The old scheming physician had known in advance that, following the lengthy fever, remains of the malignant moisture had gathered in that part of her body—remains which were liable to decay and likely to produce an ulcer, or which he (as spirit) might be able to move and prod towards putrefaction. Or else he had known that he could even summon from her head the chill humor suitable for a collecting of matter like this.

I have seen such an abscess produced among the abdominal muscles on the left side as a result of the trickling of humor following a long fever. I saw it in the case of the elector of happy memory Master Anton, archbishop of Cologne; may the one and only father of mercies remember him graciously in the resurrection of the just. Now the demon contrived the girl's ulcer, in a suitable place and in a suitable moisture, in order that when it was opened he might display the point of the knife and provide an occasion for surgery. While he thus presented the form of a knifepoint, or the true tip of a knife brought from elsewhere, with the remainder of its length being covered over by dense air, he blinded the eyes of the girl and her parents and the onlookers and the surgeon. This he can do easily with the aid of air or that of an impaired visual spirit or humor. In this way Satan took a knife from the refuse somewhere, where it had been gathering rust, and he put it down on top of the ulcer. There he displayed the point, but he covered over the remaining portion of the knife by means of tricks and illusions. The surgeon drew it forth with his instruments while the Devil held it back a little to make it seem as though it was being pulled out; but it came not from inside the body—for it was in no way lodged therein—but rather from the surface of the body. There it lay hidden in shadows during the precise moment when the point was seen and when the surgeon pulled, but certainly not before that. . . .

20. I think that a demon dulls the senses and blinds the eyes of those persons who think that their testicles or all of their sexual organs are removed by a charm; they seem to be bereft of the organs for a while and then to be made whole again. In these cases, the nerves of the testes and pudenda can be drawn back to their point of origin by the power and skill of Satan. We often see this also in incurable diseases, and Hippocrates says [Greek physician, c. 460 –c. 370 BCE] that it is a bad sign. "The retraction of the testicles and sexual organs indicates violent pain and mortal danger. For the vital faculty is in abeyance and the nerves are drawn back to their point of origin" (*Prognostica* 2.10). But when a demon is at work, loss of life need not be feared and the underlying natural cause is not permanent. The demon deludes the victim temporarily "bewitching" him, or deceives him by a false retraction of the nerves. Afterwards, when he has driven those who are so afflicted to seek forbidden counsels, and when he has made them guilty of impiety, he freely and willingly ceases from his activity, although he pretends to be compelled, so that he can strengthen people's attachment to superstition and ensnare others more tightly in the same superstitious beliefs. If these members were truly removed, when was this done and by what means? Surely it could not have taken place unfelt, without bloodshed and without impairment or injury to the affected parts, and then have been healed in an instant. And even if we, should grant this, though it be impossible, whence comes the restoration I ask, if the organs have been torn totally away from the body and if, deprived of nourishment and vital warmth, they have been dead for so long a time and subject to decay? Surely it is not possible for Satan and his angels to create new organs, or to restore life at will to parts that have been totally removed and deprived of living strength, and to fasten them on again as though with glue, or by their own demonic power attach them in their natural place, as we believe unhesitatingly that Malchus' ear was restored by Christ after it had been cut off by Peter (John 18:10). In no way could these things be done, because, as we have heard before, the demons can create nothing at all, and we have explained what is inimitable for him. . . .

As for the fact that some men are thought to be bound by enchantment and rendered totally impotent, as though they had been emasculated, this can result naturally from various causes when the sexual organs are impaired or impeded either by nature or by accident. (They can also be damaged by the administering of a drug.) Consequently, the theologians have proposed the law "Concerning frigid individuals and victims of witchcraft who are incapable of sexual functions" [Gregory XI, c. 1329–1378, *Decretalia* 4.15]. This flaw should therefore not always be ascribed to enchantment nor should an innocent person at once be put under a burden of suspicion. However, just as I certainly admit that the genitals can be rendered unsuitable for intercourse by a demon, so do I resolutely deny that this can be done by the ill will and the vapid imprecations of a vile old woman—although she herself, under the false persuasion of the demon, may sometimes believe otherwise. The demon is also responsible for the fact that the same man can be permitted to have intercourse on many occasions with one particular woman and his organs are left free to function, but with another woman he is inhibited and his sexual organs are impeded. The demon requires the help of no second party in this activity. So, too, in Italy, and especially at Rome, the most notorious and disgusting prostitutes believe that they also render a man impotent if they secretly remove the front band of his underclothes and tie knots in it. By returning it they claim to free the man again from his impotence. The same effect is supposedly achieved by knotting or unknotting a wolf's penis in the name of some victim. Likewise, when a groom is lying in the bedchamber with his bride, if some ill-wisher merely knocks upon the door and calls out (the groom's name) while implanting a knife in the door, and the groom responds, and if the malefactor breaks off the tip of the knife and leaves it in the wood and silently departs, they say that the groom will not be able to perform the sexual act during that night. But this is nonsense. . . .

Book 6

8. Since the so-called *lamiae* are indeed poor women—usually old women—melancholic by nature, feeble-minded, easily given to despondency, and with little trust in God, the Devil all the more gladly attaches himself to them, as being suitable instruments for him, and he insinuates his way into their bodies all the more easily, in order to confound their minds with various images. Bewitched by these illusory images, they believe and confess that they have done that which it was quite impossible for them to have done—because if one assesses the whole matter with clearer mental vision, on the basis of what can be done and is done by the demon, and what is supposed to be done by men with the demon's help and with the instruments that he supplies, one will find that everything is really contrived and perpetrated by the demon. And so I would hardly dare to include those women among the heretics, since no one deserves the name of heretic unless he is warned once or twice and still constantly and stubbornly persists in his fanatical beliefs; heresy is not an error

of the mind but a stubbornness of the will. Therefore, if these women—their minds totally corrupted by Satan and distracted by false imaginings—do nothing more in actual deed against another person, they should be examined and given a sounder instruction in the chief doctrines of our Christian faith, so that they might repent and—as a result of this saving instruction—strive with all their might to do (with God's grace) that which they promised to do when they first took up this religion (in baptism) and renounced Satan (although at his hidden and deceptive prompting they carelessly deviated from this promise, even as we know that our first parent Eve also went astray).

Why will the faithful minister of Jesus Christ be less effective here, with his countering arguments, than the demon has been? He will search out the sheep that has become lost by following Satan, and he will lead it back to the fold of Christ. If she has wandered astray because of false beliefs, a careful test—by an examination of the articles of faith—will reveal the fact readily. It will be clearly seen whether she struggles stubbornly against sounder doctrine (and thus deserves the brand of heresy) or whether she changes her mind and wakes from the lethargy of error and mental impairment, longing with all her heart to be accepted again as a member of the church and begging that prayers be said on her behalf. In the case of these old women—weak of faith and mind because of their sex and their age—Christians should not be so quick on the basis of false and malicious accusations to throw them into those noisome, filthy, prisons unfit for keeping men in custody—the horrid lodgings of evil demons who torment their captives. Christians should not strip themselves of every human emotion (as is done in many places, with less wisdom than severity) and hand these women over for the torture chamber (as though locking them up in the bull of Phalaris [tyrant of Syracuse who roasted enemies in a bronze bull]), where they will be tormented most cruelly by the executioner with the most savage tortures.

Apart from the pain of excessive torture unfairly inflicted, we should also note that the legal profession has established a great distinction between imprisonment and custody. In no way do the lawyers intend that the custody of a person who is later to be put to death should be a punishment; and yet they have perceived that a dreadful punishment is imposed by the horror of prison—even upon innocent persons who have sometimes been undeservedly thrown into jail. But just as considerations of fairness and compassion have fallen into neglect and contempt, so, too, the name and practice of custody has all but disappeared among many peoples. And so it happens that these poor creatures of God are frightened by long solitude, filthy cells, grim darkness, and various demonic specters. Already somewhat impaired of mind by the Devil's constant promptings, charms, and illusions, and now harassed anew by varied torments, they are cruelly subjected to questioning [torture] and they choose to exchange their wretched life for a swift death; they freely confess to any crime proposed to them rather than be thrust headlong back into the same dungeons and tortures within the stinking prisons.

In this way it came to pass that not so very long ago a poor old woman was driven by torture to confess—as she was just about to be offered to Vulcan's flames—that she had caused the incredible severity of the previous winter (1565), and the extreme cold, and the lasting ice. And although nothing in the whole world could be sillier than all of this, there was no shortage of solemn individuals who believed these things to be truer than truth itself—as I was told in writing by Anton Hovaeus, the abbot of Echternach [d. 1568], a man renowned for his learning, piety, and excellent reputation.

So that nothing might be overlooked in bringing this violent and tragic drama to a fitting conclusion, the bloodthirsty examiners are usually called in, and by their potions (which must be concocted precisely of those substances which bring drunkenness or madness) they trick the women into confessing to unheard of outrages and to things which do not exist in reality. How then can one look for truth—so necessary to a criminal process—from these women whose minds have been impaired by the powers of such potions?

11. Now to clarify by example a matter that is obscure in itself and wrapped in darkness, I have chosen to give at this point the confessions of two poor women who were imprisoned and put to death by burning a few years ago in an imperial city. I requested these confessions, and they were communicated to me from the judicial registers with the permission of the consul. And to these two I have added a third.

First of all, one woman confessed that she had deserted almighty God and joined herself to the Devil by means of *maleficium* and that her lover was named Bernard. She claimed that she once gave an apple to a matron called A, thus causing the woman to have six miscarriages. She also confessed that she had used *maleficium* to murder the daughter of a man named B, by means of a draught of beer, and that she had likewise used *maleficium* to injure the wife of C, who is consequently now confined to bed as though suffering from some disease. Because of this confession, the magistrate decreed that the poor woman should be consigned to the flames, and this decision was certainly not unwarranted if it had truly been demonstrated that she had perpetrated those crimes.

But now I ask that we examine this confession with respect to three of the statements. As for the fact that she confessed to deserting God and adhering to the demon, this will not be actionable in a civil court. For who of us is there who does not do the same?—since indeed everyone who sins is a slave to sin (John 8:34) . . . But admonished, we are able to come to our senses and there is room for repentance. And so if this woman has been shown the error of her ways and had been given better instruction, what would have prevented her, too, from being restored to her right senses? . . .

As for the woman saying that she experienced sexual relations with the demon Bernard, it is clear from what has been said in early passages that this is totally fantastical and imaginary. This phantasm is there expressly done away with, and on this account, at least, less credence should have been accorded to her confession, and it should be thought of as erroneous and as proceeding from a wandering mind. Who else but the demon himself, I ask you, gave the name of Bernard to this suitor of hers? He suggested it to her corrupt sense of hearing or to her imagination so that by giving out a name in common use among Christians he might seduce the poor wavering woman into trusting him more and might bind her to himself. And the death penalty should not have been imposed on account of this satanic illusion and the woman's mental impairment.

Nor could a fetus have been killed by means of the apple unless there had been some poison added—which should have been carefully investigated, just as they should have investigated whether that poison had the peculiar ability to kill the fetus without harming the mother and whether this single poison, administered only once, could expel fetuses so many times in different years; the magistrate should not have relied solely upon her invalid confession. That which happens by God's will and by God's hidden plan, or that which is permitted to the Devil by God, is often suggested by the demon to a woman's defective brain—as though it has all been done by her. And yet anyone who carefully weighs the individual details on the scale of reason will find that she is wholly innocent of this crime.

The very same must be said of the daughter of A, who was a victim of *maleficium*, being carried off by a draught of beer. A more alert investigation was required, including a consultation with doctors known for their understanding of such matters, in order to find out what had been put into the beer that had the destructive power to kill. A no less diligent inquiry should have been made as to what means or instruments she had used to inflict disease upon the wife of B. People should not have listened so readily to the common and despicable cry of enchantment and *maleficium*. In fact, when these deranged and unstable old women say that they produce misfortune of every sort by simple incantations, I would not hesitate to assert under oath that this misfortune occurs at the perverse prompting of a demon, that the women are bearing false witness against themselves, and that they are as innocent as anyone else of truly bringing on such disease. Let those who sometimes pronounce such rash and ill-considered sentences reflect, therefore, upon the crime that they themselves are committing.

Now let us hear, and briefly investigate, the published confession of the second woman who was sentenced to death by burning in that same city. She confessed that six years previously she was so despondent that she was contemplating suicide one morning, when a tall and rather handsome man approached her, clad all in black and wearing a black cloak. He consoled her in her grief, and among other things bade her not to be downcast but confident. He promised his support and said that he would always see to her needs and provide her with money in abundance, if only she in turn would pledge herself to follow his advice and his wishes. The man then displayed for her a great heap of gold. She agreed to his plan, renouncing almighty God, Mary the mother of Jesus Christ, and all the saints. Then he removed the chrism from her forehead and promised that he would share her bed forever, saying that his name was Alexander. She further confessed that her lover had sexual relations with her four times in her bed at home and also that she used enchantment to take away the good fortune of A, a brewer of beer, by slipping a small amount of common resin into the vessel used for boiling the beer. Similarly, she deprived the wife of the carter B of her health by means of enchantment, because she had refused to give her a certain gift. And by means of *maleficium*, she crippled the child of C and made him ill.

Certainly these outrages deserve to be punished if they are true. And yet you see that this mentally unstable woman virtually put her neck in the noose, and that she entered into a contract that was either imaginary or surely of little moment (as I have demonstrated abundantly in book three) with a fantastical lover who appeared to her clad in that imaginary form, although he was merely a spirit devoid of color and clothing. By trickery, he exhibited the appearance of gold (whereby he deceived her) and not gold itself—just as the intercourse that he had with her was illusory. . . .

The woman's denial of Christ and the saints, made under the terms of the fraudulent contract, will also bear little significance. In fact, if she had been admonished and given sounder instruction, and if she had come to recognize these wiles of the Devil, repenting and confessing her error, she should have been received again into the bosom of the church. Though of sound mind and body, and though forewarned by Christ, Peter denied Christ three times, going against the testimony of his heart; he even added an oath thereto . . . .

There should also have been a more careful investigation as to whether a small amount of resin slipped into the cooking vessel would have the power to spoil the beer. All those who use true reason to examine and understand the wellsprings of nature will affirm that there must have been another cause of the spoilage of the beer. Nor could the wife of the carter have been deprived of her health, or the boy crippled, through enchantment, unless poisoning were also involved—and of this there is no mention.

The third confession goes as follows. In Rotterdam and Schiedam, two maritime towns in Holland, fishing is the principal livelihood. When inhabitants of these towns had sailed out to fish for herring and the men of Rotterdam were bringing in their ships laden down with a great quantity of fish, the men of Schiedam pulled their nets in full of stones. This unexpected misfortune was at once attributed to *maleficium*, and they laid hold of a woman who admitted without hesitation that the misfortune had come about by means of her evil-doing arts. She said that while they were waiting in readiness to catch the fish, she flew through a hole in the windowpane (she showed it to them and it was scarcely big enough to put a finger through) and plunged into the sea in a mussel shell (it is called *mossels* by our countrymen), passing through the water until she came to where the herring were; there she drove the herring away by enchantment and substituted the stones. Sentence was passed at once and she was consigned to the flames to be consumed.

In the case of this confession, the following question should have been weighed: Can it happen in nature that by any activity whatsoever of the Devil—acting as he pleases and with all his might—a fully grown human being can be passed through a narrow crack in a windowpane not even the size of a finger? We are speaking not of an airy creature made only of spirit or one fashioned from a substance that can be drawn out fine or melted, but of a human being compounded of solid bones, gripping cartilage, firm tendons, ligaments, nerves, and membranes, as well as muscular flesh. Even if such a creature could have been resolved into blasts of wind, their force in bursting through must still have shattered the glass. Similarly we must apply the norm of reason to the question of how a woman of advanced years with so great a load of stones could plow through the changing turbulent sea in a mussel-shell. And she did not even have any need for passage in the shell, since she had just flown swiftly through a narrow hole in a windowpane. And so, in truth, this whole confession is foolish, futile, inconsistent, absurd, and full of lies. Anyone who is not altogether devoid of intelligence will be able to determine that the poor woman was raving or driven by melancholia or else led on by a depraved imagination or possessed by a demon who controlled her tongue or spoke out from within her.

Let these judges make up all the explanations that they wish; they will never convince me by any line of reasoning that so bloodthirsty a sentence can rightly be pronounced in a matter that is either not understood or located in a sphere outside of reason and the nature of things. And why should I not sooner and more readily believe that with God's permission (to punish men for their unbelief or to test the faithful, if there be any present) the Devil (who could do such things) conveyed those stones in order to deceive the people—which is his special goal? Why, I say, should I not believe this rather than admit that these deeds were done by a poor woman who had no such powers at all? If the cry goes up that she acted with the demon's support, this, too, I stoutly deny. If the Devil willed it and attempted it a thousand times over, he could in no way cause a woman to pass through a tiny crack—and yet this is what she said happened. If I make my point that this is pure raving nonsense and falsehood, gentlemen of the senate, what credence shall then be given to other nursery tales of this sort?

In the same way, an infinite number of confessions might be recounted from the public documents of the magistrates. But if one weighs them carefully, he will find a labyrinth of impossibility, if I may use the term, inconsistency, vanity, diversity, and lies disguised and covered over by truth. In short, he will find pure fables.

21. In the case of evil-doers of either sex (the females are called *le strige* in Italian), whose accursed incantations had done no harm to humankind or to the lives of beasts, the custom at Bologna was to strip them to the waist and lead them from the ancient palace riding backwards upon an ass, their bound hands holding the ass's tail, while the executioner's assistant walked slowly before them. Upon their head was placed a paper mitre showing pictures of frightful demons who stirred the fires of hell with their tongs. As the evildoers were conducted about in this solemn procession, the accompanying torturer beat them severely about the chest and back with birch rods. When they had come from the public square to the cemetery of the Dominican church (which was a famous burial place for people of German descent) the prisoners were taken down from the ass and led by the executioner to an upper room, the balcony of which faced the cemetery. The balcony is protected by a loosely wrought iron grating and is said to have been designed for the punishment of heretics by the monks of that monastery—the inquisitors "of heretical perversions." The prisoners were then helmeted and seated upon an official chair which moved on four wheels; they were pushed out onto the balcony three times, where they remained for a quarter of an hour while the crowd watching from without mocked, shouted, and threw stones, but usually to no avail, because of the iron bars of the grating. Finally the prisoners were released; having been punished in proportion to their offense, they were sent into exile.

This moderation on the part of the magistrate at Bologna—which still savored somewhat of the wisdom of ancient Italy—is infinitely to be preferred to the tyranny of some other magistrates who rush all too quickly to the sacrificial fire, from which they appear to derive as much enjoyment as the demons do from the shedding of innocent blood. "Oh benighted minds of men, benighted hearts!" (Sextus Propertius [Roman poet, c. 50–c. 16 BCE], *Elegiae* 1.2).

Questions: Why does Weyer write with a tone of personal indignation? Why does he dedicate several chapters in his work to subjects dealing with sexual congress of various types? On what grounds does Weyer refute that the knife was actually in the girl's side in 4.14 above? What is Weyer referring to when he claims that the Devil can create the illusion that a man has lost his testicles so that he will "seek forbidden counsels"? Is Weyer's opinion of women consistent with those of his contemporaries who fully supported the witch trials?

70. WITCH PERSECUTIONS IN TRIER

By the mid-sixteenth century, the profile of "the diabolical witch" was firmly established. Popular fear of those who trafficked with demons and brought misfortune on their neighbors had essentially fused with the learned ecclesiastical understanding of witchcraft as a heretical conspiracy headed by Satan to undermine Christianity. One of the areas where the trials raged most fiercely was in the jurisdiction of the elector-archbishop of Trier in western Germany, which was experiencing drought and a severe economic downturn between 1581 and 1593. The following reading comes from a clergyman named Linden, who witnessed the events in Trier and wrote about them years later.

Source: George L. Burr, *The Witch Persecutions,* Translations and Reprints from The Original Sources of European History, vol. 3 (Philadelphia: University of Pennsylvania, 1907), pp. 13–14.

Inasmuch as it was popularly believed that the continued sterility of many years was caused by witches through the malice of the Devil, the whole country rose up to exterminate the witches. This movement was promoted by many in office, who hoped wealth from the persecution. And so, from court to court throughout the towns and villages of all the diocese scurried special accusers, inquisitors, notaries, jurors, judges, constables, dragging to trial and torture human beings of both sexes and burning them in great numbers. Scarcely any of those who were accused escaped punishment. Nor were there spared, even the leading men in the city of Trier. For the judge, with two burghomasters, several councilors and associate judges, canons [priests who live together in religious communities] of sundry collegiate churches, parish-priests, rural deans, were swept away in this ruin. So far, at length, did the madness of the furious populace and of the courts go in this thirst for blood and booty that there was scarcely anybody who was not besmirched by some suspicion of this crime.

Meanwhile notaries, copyists, and innkeepers grew rich. The executioner rode a blooded horse, like a noble of the court, and went clad in gold and silver; his wife vied with noble dames in the richness of her array. The children of those convicted and punished were sent into exile; their goods were confiscated; plowman and vintner failed—hence came sterility. A direr pestilence or a more ruthless invader could hardly have ravaged the territory of Trier than this inquisition and persecution without bounds. Many were the reasons for doubting that all were truly guilty. This persecution lasted for several years, and some of those who presided over the administration of justice gloried in the multitude of the stakes, at each of which a human being had been given to the flames.

At last, though the flames were still unsated, the people grew impoverished, rules were made and enforced restricting the fees and costs of examinations and examiners, and suddenly, as when in war funds fail, the zeal of the persecutors died out.

Questions: In what ways did people profit economically from the witch persecutions? Were the persecutions enacted on a population in which the majority opposed the procedures but kept silent out of fear, or did most condone the trials?

71. CHARMS, TRICKS, AND DAY-TO-DAY SORCERY

The following excerpts are from two sources. One is Reginald Scot's (c. 1538–1599) Discoverie of Witchcraft, *an exposé of witch beliefs as they developed in early modern Europe. Scot exposes popular charms, legerdemain, and common sorcery as irrational and clerical magic as misguided and un-Christian. Scot argues against punishing simple people who are deluded by foolish superstitions and manipulated by the legal apparatus of the Catholic Church. His work was controversial—copied both by those who refuted and those who supported his analysis. Due to the encyclopedic nature of* Discoverie of Witchcraft, *a myriad of charms and tricks have been preserved that shed light on popular magical beliefs and behaviors.*

Alexander Roberts's (fl. early seventeenth century) Treatise of Witchcraft *is a legal document written from the elite point of view. The majority of the text is a rehearsal of what had become the traditional understanding of diabolical magic and witchcraft based on commonly used biblical explanations as to why one ought not suffer a witch to live (Exodus 22:18). The true value of the work rests in the detailed description of the evidence given against Mary Smith and the purported mischief she wrought against her neighbors. The accusations against Mary exemplify village-level tensions in tightly knit communities that sometimes expressed themselves through dread of malicious sorcery, which was quite unrelated to concern for heresy.*

Sources: Reginald Scot, *The Discoverie of Witchcraft* (London: Elliot Stock, 1886; rpt. of 1584 first ed.), pp. 186–87, 198–201, 215; rev. Martha Rampton.

Discoverie of Witchcraft

Book 12

9. A charm against shot, . . . A holy garment, called a waistcoat, was much used by our forefathers as a holy relic, etc., as given by the pope—or some such arch-conjuror—who promised thereby all manner of immunity to the wearer thereof; insomuch as he could not be hurt with any shot or other violence. And otherwise, that woman that would wear it should have quick deliverance. The composition [of the charm] was in this order following. On Christmas day at night, a thread must be spun of flax by a little virgin girl in the name of the Devil, and it must be woven by her and also wrought with the needle. In the

breast or forepart of the waistcoat must be made with needle work two heads; on the head at the right side must be a hat and a long beard; the left head must have on a crown, and it must be so horrible that it may resemble Beelzebub [another name for Satan], and on each side of the waistcoat must be made a cross.

This is as true a copy of the holy writing that was brought down from heaven by an angel to Saint Leo III [d. 816], pope of Rome, and the angel did bid him take it to king Charles [Charlemagne, 742–814], when he went to the Battle at Roncesvalles [778]. And these effects are, the angel said, that whatever man or woman bears this writing with devotion and says verily their Paternosters, three Aves [Maria], and one Creed, shall not that day be overcome by his enemies—either bodily or ghostly; neither shall be robbed or slain of thieves, pestilence, thunder, or lightening; neither shall be hurt with fire or water, nor bothered with spirits; neither shall have displeasure of lords or ladies; he shall not be condemned with false witness, nor taken with fairies, or any manner of aches [pain], nor yet with the falling evil [epilepsy].

Also, if a woman be in travail [in childbirth], lay this writing upon her belly; she shall have easy deliverance, and the child will be the right shape and Christian, and the mother purification of Holy Church, and all through virtue of these holy names of †Jesus Christ following. †Jesus, †Christus, †Messiah, †Soter, †Emmanuel, †Sabbaoth, †Adonai, †Unigenitus, †Majestas, †Paracletus, †Salvator noster, †Adanatos, †Gasper, †Melchior, †Balthasar, †Matthew, †Mark, †Luke, †John. The epistle of Saint Savior, which Pope Leo sent to king Charles, saying that whosoever carries the same about him, or in what day so ever he shall read it, or shall see it, he shall not be killed with any iron tool, nor be burned with fire, nor be drowned with water, neither any evil man or other creature may hurt him. . . .

14. A gentlewoman, having sore and blinded eyes [from uncontrollable weeping], made her way to one who promised to help her if she would follow his advice, which was only to wear about her neck a sealed-up scroll into which she must not look. And she, hoping for a cure thereby, received it under that condition and left him weeping and tearful. She continued to bewail the miserable darkness, which she doubted she could endure. But in a short time her eyes were better. But alas, she soon after lost that precious [scroll] and therefore returned to her weeping, and by consequence her eyes became sore again. However, her precious scroll, being found again, her dear friends looked into it, and there was only a posy therein. . . .

A pretty charm for one possessed. The possessed person must crawl upon his or her knees to the church, however far it may be from their lodging, and so must creep without going astray, but follow the common highway. No matter how foul and dirty it might be or whatsoever lie in the way, he must not shun anything whatsoever until he comes to the church, where he must hear mass devotedly, and then recovery will follow.

Another for the same effect. The sick man must fast three days, and then he, with his parents, must come to church, upon an Ember Friday [seasonal days of fasting and prayer] and must hear the mass appointed for that day, and so likewise the Saturday and Sunday following. And the priest must read over the sick man's head that Gospel which is read in September, and in grape harvest after the feast of the Holy Cross, "In the days of the four seasons," in Ember days, then let him write it and carry it about his neck, and he shall be cured.

A charm for the bots [disease caused by botflies in the stomach] in a horse. You must both say and do thus upon the diseased horse three days together before the rising of the sun, "In the name of God the father, the son, and the Holy Ghost, I conjure you, O worm, by God the father, the son, and the Holy Ghost that you neither eat nor drink the flesh, blood, or bones of this horse. You will then be made as patient as Job and as good as Saint John the Baptist when he baptized Christ in the Jordan River. In the name of the father, the son and the Holy Ghost. And then say three Paternosters and three Aves in the right ear of the horse to the glory of the holy trinity. . . .

17. The means how to find out a thief is thus: turn your face to the east, and make a cross upon crystal with olive oil, and under the cross write these two words, "Saint Helena" [d. c. 328]. Then an innocent child ten years of age, born of a chaste virgin in true wedlock and not begotten in a base manner, must take the crystal in his hand, and behind his back, kneeling on your knees, you must devoutly and reverently say this prayer three times, "I beseech you my lady Saint Helena, mother of King Constantine [Roman Emperor, 272–337], who did find the cross whereupon Christ died, by your holy devotion and finding of the cross, and by the same cross, and by the joy which you conceived at the finding thereof, and by the love which you bare to your son Constantine, and by the great goodness which you do always exhibit, that you show me in this crystal, whatsoever I ask or desire to know; amen. And when the child sees the angel in the crystal, demand what you will, and the angel will obey. Take note that this be done just at the sun rising, when the weather is fair and clear.

Book 13

12. Many writers have been abused as well by untrue reports, as by illusion, and practices of confederacy and legerdemain . . . if these things be done for mirth and recreation, and not to the hurt of our neighbor nor to the abusing or profaning of God's name, in my opinion they are neither impious nor altogether unlawful, though herein or hereby a natural thing be made to seem supernatural. Such are the miracles wrought by jugglers, consisting in fine and nimble connivance called legerdemain, as when they seem to cast away, or to deliver to another something that which they retain still in their own hands or

convey otherwise, or seem to eat a knife, or juggling some such other thing, when indeed they hide the same secretly into their bosoms or laps. Another point of juggling is when they appear to thrust a knife through the brains and head of a chicken or hen and seem to cure the same with words, which would live and do well, though never a word were spoken. Some of these toys also consist in arithmetical devises, partly in experiments of natural magic, and partly in private as also in public.

13. By private I mean, when one (by a special plot laid by himself, without any compact made with others) persuades the beholders that he will suddenly and in their presence do some miraculous feat, which he has already accomplished privately. As for example, he will show you a card, or any other like thing, and will say further unto you, "Behold and see what a mark it ha," and then burn it; and nevertheless fetch another like card so marked out of somebody's pocket, or out of some corner where he himself before had placed it, to the wonder and astonishment of simple beholders, which conceive not that kind of illusion, but expect miracles and strange works. . . . If this or the like feat should be done by an old woman, everybody would cry out for fear and faggot to burn the witch.

Alexander Roberts, A Treatise on Witchcraft, A True Narration of Some of the Witchcrafts which Marie, Wife of Henry Smith Glower, did Practice, Of her Contract Verbally Made with the Devil in Solemn Terms, by Whose Means She Hurt Sundry Persons whom She Envied, which is Confirmed by her Own Confession, and from the Public Records of the Examination of Many People upon their Oaths, of Her Death, and Execution for the Same, which was on the Twelfth Day of January Last.

HER WICKED PRACTICE AGAINST JOHN ORKTON

The first who tasted of the gall of [Mary Smith's] bitterness was John Orkton, a sailor and a man of strong constitution of body, who about some five years since, returning out of Holland in the Netherlands or low Countries beyond the seas, happened, for some misdemeanors committed by him, to strike the son of this Mary Smith (but in such sort as could not reasonably be offensively taken) who hearing his complaint, came forth into the street, cursing and banning him therefore—as oftentimes she did because she dwelt in the next adjoining house—and wished in a most earnest and bitter manner that his fingers might rot off. Whereupon presently he grew weak, distempered in his stomach and could digest no meat nor other nourishment received, and this decrease or feebleness continued for the space of three quarters of a year; which time expired, the aforementioned pain fell down from the stomach into his hands and feet, so that his fingers did corrupt and were cut off. Also his toes putrefied and were consumed in a very strange and mysterious manner. . . .

His former grief increasing, he sought to obtain help and remedy by surgery, and for this end went to Yarmouth, hoping to be cured by one there who was accomplished and very skillful, but no medicines applied by the rules of art and experience wrought any expected or hoped for effect, for both his hands and feet, which seemed in some measure every evening to be healing, in the morning were found to have gone backward, and grown far worse than before. So the surgeon, perceiving his labor to be wholly frustrated, gave up hope of a cure, and the diseased patient still continued in a most distressed and miserable estate, which brought him to the hellish practices of this malicious woman, who long before openly in the streets, (when as yet the neighbors knew of no such thing) rejoicing at the calamity, said, "Orkton, now lies a rotting." And it is no marvel that she could tell that which she herself had done, and her good master, the Devil, would not suffer to be concealed, and the testimony of her own tongue remained as a record towards her further detection and condemnation. Then Mary sought means of her voluntary accord to be reconciled with the woeful distressed John Orkton, but this was nothing else but to plaster over and disguise her former inhumane and barbarous actions, for no relief at all followed. For oftentimes, as has been proved, . . . devils and witches, his instruments, do cause such diseases, which neither the one, nor the other can remove again. And this is not any vaporous imagination, but a most undoubted truth. For now this poor man continued still in a lamentable estate, grief—and pains increasing, without hope of help, unless God in the abundance of his tender mercies vouchsafes to grant comfort and deliverance.

HER WICKED PRACTICE AGAINST ELIZABETH HANCOCKE

The second person distressed by this witch was Elizabeth Hancocke, then a widow, now wife of James Scot, the manner, occasion, and proceeding of whose dealing against her was thus. She was coming out of the town from the shop of one Simon Brown, a silk merchant to whom, and she had carried home some work, which he gave her. Henry Smith, as she passed by his door, took her by the hand and smilingly said that his duck (meaning his wife, Mary, this woman of whom we now speak) told him that she had stolen Mary's hen; which words Elizabeth then passed over as only spoken in merriment, and she denied the same. In the meantime, as they were interchanging these words, Mary came herself and directly charged Elizabeth with the theft of the hen and wished that the bones thereof might stick in her throat when she should eat the same. Mary was not serious and supposed they might be uttered in jest. Nevertheless, thinking it over, Elizabeth was angry that she was accused of stealing the hen and to be counted one of so evil, and seeing that hen for which she was accused, sitting upon the hatch of Mary's shop door, went to Mary, and moved

with the indignity of that slander and unjust imputation, told her in some passion and angry manner that it was dishonest that Mary had blemished the good
name of her neighbors so unjustly. Whereupon, Mary, breaking forth in some
violence, wished the pox to light upon Elizabeth, and named her Proud Jinny,
proud flirt, and shaking her hand, bade her go in, for she should repent it. And
the same night, within three or four hours after these curses and imprecations
were uttered, Elizabeth was taken and pinched at the heart, and felt a sudden
weakness in all the parts of her body; her appetite diminished to mere nothing
and so continued for the space of three weeks; in which time, when she was
feeling a little better, would come to the door, and lean upon the stall, whom
this Mary Smith seeing, did ever repeat the former curse: "The pox light upon
you, can you yet come to the door?"

And at the end of these three weeks, being but very weak, Elizabeth came
forth as she used to do to take the air, and this mischievous woman most bitterly
cursed her again, whereupon she went into the house, fell into such a torturing
fit and nipping at the heart, that she fainted, hardly recoverable for the space
of half an hour, and so grievously racked and tormented through all parts of
her body, as if the very flesh had been torn from the bones by the violent pain
that she could not stop, but tore the hair from off her head, and became as one
distraught, bereaved of sense, and understanding. And the same night the bed
whereon she lay was so tossed, and lifted up and down, both in her own feeling and in the sight of others, by the space of one hour or more, that she was
exceedingly terrified, and did think oftentimes in her sleep, that she did see this
Mary Smith standing before her.

And this fit continued sixteen hours, during which Edward Drake, her father,
came to the town, touched with grief for this torture of his daughter (as parents hearts are relenting and tender and natural compassion is soon stirred up
in them), took her urine, went to a healer for his advice (which is in no way
justifiable, and argued but a small measure of religion and the knowledge of
God in him) who first told him the cause of his coming, that is, to seek help for
his daughter, and then added, that she was so far gone that if he had stayed but
one day longer the woman who had wronged her [Mary], would have ruined
her heart and so it would become unrecoverable. Thereupon the healer showed
Mary's face in a glass, and further, related the beginning cause of the falling out
which was for a hen, which before this Drake neither knew nor heard of. The
healer then gave his counsel for remedy, which was the matter sought for and
desired, and this was the order. Drake was to make a cake with flour from the
bakers and to mix it, instead of using other liquid, use her own urine, and bake
it on the hearth, whereof the one half was to be applied and laid to the region
of the heart, the other half to the back directly opposite. And further the healer
gave Drake a box of ointment like treacle, which must be spread upon that cake,

and a powder to be cast upon the same, and certain words written on a paper to be laid on likewise with the other, adding this caveat, that if his daughter did not amend within six hours after the taking of these receipts, then there was no health or recovery to be looked for. And further he asked silence to be kept herein, for the woman who had done this [Mary Smith], would know anything.

And being thus furnished with instructions and returning home, as she alighted from his horse to enter into that house where his daughter lay (being the next unto Mary Smith's) she then stood leaning over her shop window, whom he knew to be that person which was showed unto him in the glass, and she cursed him passing by and told his daughter that her father had been with a wizard. And the next day following after they had put in practice the directions given, and Mary affirmed to many of the neighbors, that Drake, the afflicted woman's father, had been to ask counsel and made a Witch Cake, but he would learn how they came to have that knowledge. Yet for the present Elizabeth found help and was freed from the languishing and other pains she had suffered for the space of six weeks.

After this, being married to James Scot, a great cat this witch kept (of whose infernal both purposes and practices we now speak) frequented their house, and upon doing some scratching, her husband moved therewith, thrust it twice through with his sword, which, notwithstanding those wounds, the cat ran away. Then he hit it with all his force upon the head with a great pike staff, yet could not kill her, but she leapt after this upward almost a yard from the boards of that chamber where she now was and crept down, which he seeing this, asked his lad (a boy of fourteen years) to drag her to the muck-hill, but he was not able; and therefore put the cat into a sack, and she still moved and stirred. Whereupon they took her out again and cast her under a pair of stairs, thinking in the morning to get more help and carry her away. But then she could not be found, though all the doors that night were locked.

Not long after, this witch came forth with a birch broom and threatened to lay it upon the head of Elizabeth Scot, and defiled her clothes therewith as she swept the street before her shop door, and that in the sight of her husband, who not permitting this indignity offered to his wife, threatened that if she had any such fits as she endured being a widow before marriage, he would hang her. At this she clapped her hands and said he killed her cat. And within two or three days after this interchange of words between them, his wife was vexed with the like pain and grief at her heart as formerly she had been, and for two days and a night, wherefore her husband went to this wrathful and malicious person, assuring that if his wife did not heal, he would accuse her to the magistrate, and cause the rigor of the law to be executed upon her which is due to such malefactors. These things were done some three years hence. The party troubled yet lives, but in no improved health nor perfect soundness of body.

A third subject whereupon this wrathful woman's anger wrought was Cicely Balye, then servant to Robert Coulton, now wife of William Vaux, who, when she was sweeping the street before her master's door upon a Saturday in the evening, Mary Smith began to pick a quarrel about the manner of sweeping and said to her she was a great fat-tailed sow, but that fatness should shortly be pulled down and abated. And the next night being Sunday immediately following, a cat came to Cicely and sat upon her breast, by which she was grievously tormented and so oppressed that she could not, without great difficulty, draw her breath, and at the same instant did perfectly see the said Mary in the chamber where she lay, who (as she conceived) set that cat upon her, and immediately she after fell sick, languished, and grew exceeding lean. She so continued for the space of half a year together, during the whole time in her master's service. Until departing from him, she dwelt with one Mistress Garoway and then began to be amended in her health and recover from her former pining sickness, for this witch had said that so long as she dwelt near her, she should not be well, but grow from evil to worse.

Thus every light trifle (for what can be less then sweeping of a little dust awry?) can become matter to set on fire a wrathful indignation and inflame it to desired revenge, the Devil being willing to apprehend and take hold on such an occasion so he might do some pleasing office to his bond slave. Mary adored the Devil in a submissive manner, upon her knees, with strange gestures, and uttering many murmuring, broken, and imperfect speeches, as this Cicely did both hear and see, there being no other partition between the chamber where she performed these rites and the house of her master with whom she then dwelt. There was only a thin board with a cranny or rift through which she looked, listened attentively to Mary's words, and beheld diligently her behavior, and might have seen and heard much more, but she was so affrighted, that she hastened down in much fear and distemper.

The fourth damaged by this hag was one Edmund Newton. The discontentment did arise from this ground: because he had bought several Holland cheeses at a bargain and sold them again, and she thought her benefit to be somewhat impaired by this kind of trading. The manner of her dealing with him was in this sort. Whenever he bought cheese, he was grievously afflicted. This happened three times, and at the last, either she or a spirit in her likeness, did appear to him and whisked about his face (as he lay in bed) a wet cloth of very loathsome smell, after which he did see one clothed in russet with a little bush beard, who told him he was sent to look upon his foreleg, and would heal it. But rising to show his leg to the bearded man, he perceived the man had cloven feet, so refused that offer; the bearded man then (these being no vain conceits, or fantasies, but well advised and diligently considered observances) suddenly vanished out of sight. After this Mary Smith sent her imps, a toad, and crabs crawling about the house, which was a shop with a wooden floor where his servants (he being a shoemaker) did work. One of the servants took that toad and put it into the fire, where it made a groaning noise for one quarter of an hour before it was consumed; during which time Mary Smith, who sent it, did endure, (as was reported) torturing pains, testifying the grief she felt by the outcries she made.

The sickness which Edmund Newton first sustained was in the manner of a madness or frenzy, yet with some interposed release from the worst of his affliction, so that for thirteen or fourteen weeks together he would be of perfect memory, other times distracted and deprived of all sense. Also the joints and parts of his body were numbed, besides other pains and grief from which he is not yet freed, but he continued in great weakness, disabled to perform any labor whereby he may get sufficient and competent maintenance. And by the counsel of some, he sent for this woman by whom he was wronged that he might scratch her (for it is believed that this is a reliable method for discovering a sorceress, but it is a foul sin among Christians to think one witchcraft can drive out another), but his nails turned like feathers, having no strength to lay his hands upon her.

And it is not improbable but that Mary Smith had dealt no better with others then these above mentioned. For Mr. Thomas Yonges of London, fishmonger, reported to me that after the demand of a debt due to Mr. John Mason, a silk merchant of the same city, . . . from Henry Smith Glower, Mary's husband, some execrations and curses were wished unto him. Within three or four days (being then gone to Yarmouth in Norfolk upon necessary business) Mason there fell sick and was tortured with exceeding and massacring pain, which by no means (means having used the advice of sundry learned and experienced physicians in Norwich) could in any part be mitigated. He was so extraordinarily vexed for thirteen months that he was constrained to go on crutches, not being able to feed himself, and he was amended not before this mischievous woman was committed to prison, (accused for other wickedness of the like kind) at which time (so near as he could conjecture) he then received some release of his former pains; though at the present time when he made this return, which was at Candlemas last past, had not perfectly recovered his wonted strength. For his left hand remained lame and without use.

But thus much by the way only; I omit how before this accident a great Water Dog [salamander] ran over his bed, the door of the chamber where he lay being shut, no such one known (for careful enquiry was made) either to have been in that house where he lodged, or in the whole town at any time.

I do not insist upon this, because she did not mention him or any others to us, but only those four already expressed, and for the wrongs done to them, she craved mercy at God's hand, as for all her other sins, and in particular for that of witchcraft, renounced the Devil, embraced the mercies of God purchased by the obedience of Jesus Christ, and professed that her hope was only by his suffering and passion to be saved. And all these, that is to say, her former grievous offences committed against God and his people, her defiance of the Devil, and reposing all confidence of salutation in Christ Jesus alone and his merits, she in particular manner confessed openly at the place of execution, in the audience of multitudes of people gathered together (as is usual at such times) to be beholders of her death. And made there also profession of her faith and hope of a better life hereafter and the means whereby she trusted to obtain the same, as before, haths been specified. And being asked if she would be contented to have a Psalm sung, answered willingly that she desired the same and appointed it herself, *The Lamentation of a Sinner*, whose beginning is, "Lord turn not away thy face," and after the ending thereof, thus finished her life. So in the judgment of charity we are to conceive the best and think she rests in peace, notwithstanding her heinous transgressions formerly committed, for there is no malady incurable to the almighty physician. . . .

Questions: Are the charms above magical? What is the agency at work in the expected efficacy of most of the charms? Why is Scot indulgent when it comes to the matter of magical tricks or sleight of hand? What is Scot's opinion of the measures Elizabeth's father takes to heal his daughter? Do the people in Robert's text worry that their neighbors are heretics? Why was blaming misfortune on others by accusing them of witchcraft so appealing and common in early modern Europe?

72. DEMON MANIA IN FRANCE: JEAN BODIN

Jean Bodin (1530–1596) lived in France and served in the Parlement of Paris at a time when the nation was stressed in a variety of ways. The growth of French Protestantism and a series of weak kings resulted in extended periods of instability and civic brutality. Bodin, trained in political philosophy and law, addressed the causes of and solutions to the problems in his world by writing on the theory of sovereignty and demonology. Whereas contemporary theorists subscribed to differing postulates of demonology on the grounds of what they held to be physically possible, for Bodin, demons were not governed by the laws of nature, so there were no natural limits as to what demons and witches could do. His Demon-Mania was an immediate success; eleven editions were published between 1581 and 1616.

Source: trans. Randy A. Scott, Jean Bodin, *On the Demon-Mania of Witches* (Toronto: Centre for Reformation and Renaissance Studies, 2001), pp. 112–24, 126, 128, 203–14, 216–18.

On the Demon-Mania of Witches

Book 2

4. . . . Now Satan wants to tear from the hearts of men all fear of committing offense. And as for the express agreement, it is sometimes made verbally, and without writing. Or sometimes Satan, to be sure of his people, makes them write down their obligation and sign it if they can write, before they can obtain what they ask. Sometimes he makes them sign with their blood, . . . Moreover, it has been verified by many trials that the mutual contract between the Devil and the witch sometimes involves a term of one year, two years, or other periods of time. And one person may ask for the power to cure toothaches and another the quartan fever, or some other illness, on condition that they kill or cause death to others or perform other abominable sacrifices. . . .

As for [the Devil's] marks, they are certainly a sure sign, which judges frequently see unless they are well hidden. I learned from a gentleman of Valois that there are some who have the mark between their lips, others under their eyelids, as Daneau wrote [in *Les sorciers*], others on their backside when they fear discovery and frequently on the right shoulder, and women on the thigh or under the armpit or on the shameful parts.

Aubert de Poitiers, a lawyer of the Parlement, told me that he had been present at the examination of evidence in the trial of a sorcerer Mareschal of Château Thierry, who was found marked on the right shoulder, and the following day the Devil had erased his mark. . . . The one who was condemned by the city provost in 1571, who was called Trois-es-chelles du Maine, having obtained immunity in order to persuade him to reveal his accomplices, when he was led into the assemblies, recognized those whom he had seen at the sabbaths, or by some other mark which they know among themselves. And to verify his statements, he said that they were marked and that one would find the mark by undressing them. In fact, it was found that they bore a mark like the paw or track of a hare, which had no feeling, so that witches do not feel the punctures when they are pierced right to the bone in the location of the mark. But there was such a great number of them, both rich and poor, that they enabled each other to escape. . . .

It is stranger still that most witches are not satisfied to renounce God, but also have themselves re-baptized in the name of the Devil and given another name, which is the reason why witches usually have two names. And it is important to note that it takes only one witch to make five hundred. For to do what is most pleasing to the Devil and have peace with him, when one has given oneself to him, means attracting many subjects. And usually the wife attracts her husband, the mother leads her daughter, and sometimes the whole family carries on for many centuries as it has been proven by countless trials. . . .

Paolo Grillando, an Italian jurisconsult who tried many witches, writes that in the year 1526 near Rome, there was a peasant who saw his wife apply grease to herself at night completely naked, and, then no longer finding her in his house, on the following day he took a cudgel and did not stop beating her until she had confessed the truth and asked for pardon. The husband pardoned her on condition that she would take him to the assembly that she described. The next day, the wife smeared him with the grease she had, and they both found themselves heading to the assembly each one lightly riding on a billy goat. But the wife warned the man to be careful not to say the name of God, unless in mockery, or in blasphemy. For they all agree that the Devil immediately leaves the one he is carrying on the roadways, which clearly shows that the grease the witches apply to themselves does nothing, and that the Devil transports them faster than a bowshot. . . .

Now at the assembly, the wife had him stand a little apart in order to witness the whole mystery until she had done reverence to the head of the assembly, who was pompously dressed as a prince and accompanied by a great multitude of men and women, who all paid homage to the master. And then he observed after the reverences that they did a dance in a circle with their faces turned outward from the circle so that the people, not seeing each other face to face as in ordinary dances, perhaps would not have the opportunity so easily to observe and recognize each other and denounce the others if they were arrested by the officers of justice. When the dance was finished, the tables were set out with many meats. Then the wife made her husband draw near to do reverence to the prince. He then sat down at the table with the others, and finding that the meats were not salted and that there was no salt on the tables, he complained so much that he was brought salt, or what seemed to be, and before having tasted it he exclaimed, "Now praised be God since the salt has come." As soon as he had said, "praised be God," suddenly everything disappeared: people, meats, and tables, and he was left alone, completely naked, very cold, and not knowing where he was. After daybreak he found some shepherds whom he asked where he was, who told him that he was on the hillside of Benevento. This is the finest estate of the pope, beneath a great walnut tree, a hundred miles away from Rome. He was forced to beg food and clothing, and on the eighth day he arrived back at his home very thin and wasted. Then he went and denounced his wife who was arrested, and he denounced others who were burned alive, after confessing the truth. . . .

As for being transported, I have read that it takes place after the ointment is applied, and often without ointment: sometimes on a billy goat, sometimes on a flying horse, sometimes on a broom, sometimes on a pole, other times without any pole or beast. Some go naked—as do most in order to grease themselves, as we have described—others dressed, some at night, others by day. But usually [they go] at night, and most often between Monday and Tuesday night. . . . [In Maine] there were not less than thirty witches who denounced each other through mutual envy. Their confessions agreed about the transporting, the worship of the Devil, the dances and the renunciations of all religion. . . .

[At Poitiers] three sorcerers and a witch were condemned and burned alive after being convicted of having caused the death of many people and animals. They confessed that they did this, moreover, by means of the Devil who furnished them with powders to bury beneath the entrances of stables, sheepfolds and houses, and they declared that three times a year they went to the general assembly, where many witches congregated near a cross at a crossroads, which served as a sign. Also present there was a great black billy goat which spoke like a person to them, and they danced around the goat. Then each kissed his rear while holding a burning candle. After that, the billy goat was consumed in fire and each one took some of the ash to kill a steer or cow of his enemy: for one it was to kill an ewe, for another a horse, for another to induce languor, for another to bring death to people. And finally the Devil said to them with a terrible voice these words, "Take revenge or you will die!" Following that each returned as they had come with the aid of the Devil. It is important to note that they were obliged to go three times a year to make this sacrifice to the Devil, mimicking the sacrifice of the he-goat described by God's law in Leviticus, Chapter 16 [5–28] and the commandment which declared that all males had to appear before God three times a year, at the three solemn feasts [Exodus 23:17]. . . .

I also read the summary of the trial of the witches of Potez, which was communicated to me by Master Adrian de Fer, lieutenant general of Laon, which reported their confession: how they were transported near Longny at the Frenquis mill by pronouncing certain words, which I shall not set down, with a broom or chimney-cleaner, and they found the others who each had a chimney-cleaner in hand, and with them six devils who are named there. And after renouncing God, they kissed the devils in human form, though extremely hideous to behold, and worshiped them; then they danced with their brooms in their hand, and finally the devils copulated with the women. Then they asked for powders to destroy cattle, and it was decreed that they should return there eight days later, which was Monday after sunset, and they were there for about three hours and then taken back.

I had forgotten to mention that each witch must render an account of the evil he did, on pain of being soundly beaten. As for this last point, Bouvin, bailiff of Chateauroux, while deputy for the region of Berry at Blois, told me that he had burned a witch denounced by her daughter whom the mother had taken to the assemblies, and she had presented her to the Devil for instruction. Among other villanies, she confessed that they danced around the billy goat and finally that each gave an account of what he had done since the last assembly and on what he had used the powder. One said that he killed a child, another a horse, another that he made a tree die. And because one was discovered who had done nothing since the last assembly, she got several raps with a cudgel on the soles of the feet, along with mockery and laughter from all the others. And he said that they often had to get new powders. This conforms with what I read in another trial of a witch who confessed that she got no rest unless she did some evil deed every day, even just break a vessel. . . .

But it is important to note that there is no assembly carried on where they do not dance, and, according to the confession of the witches of Longny, while dancing they would cry, "Har, har, Devil, Devil, jump here, jump there, play here, play there." And the others would chant "Sabbath, Sabbath"—that is to say, the feast and day of rest—raising their hands and brooms up high to testify and give a sure witness of gladness and that willingly they serve and worship the Devil, and also to mimic the worship which is due to God. . . . The witches' dances make men frenzied and women abort. . . .

It would be mocking the Gospel story to call into doubt whether the Devil transports witches from one spot to another, since it is stated in the Gospel that Satan transported Jesus Christ to the top of the temple, then onto a mountain. . . .

6. . . . The most difficult thing to believe, and the most wonderful [amazing], is the changing of the human figure into a beast, and even more from one body into another. Nonetheless, the trials conducted of witches and the divine and human histories of all peoples are undeniable proof. We read in the book of the five inquisitors of witches, which I have mentioned quite often, that a witch named Staufer in the territory of Bern, who had many enemies, often escaped suddenly from their midst and could not be killed except in his sleep. He left two disciples, the greatest witches in Germany, Hoppo and Stadlin, who brought tempests, lightening and violent thunderstorms [see doc. 79] . . . [Gilles Garnier from Lyons] on Saint Michael's day, while in the form of a werewolf, seized a young girl of ten or twelve years old near the Serre woods, in a vineyard in the wine region of Chastenoy, a quarter of a league from Dôle. There he killed her with his paw-like hands and his teeth, and ate the flesh of her thighs and arms, and took some to his wife. . . .

This corroborates the trial conducted against the witches of Vernon who usually gathered and assembled in an old ruined chateau in the guise of a great number of cats. There were four or five men who decided to spend the night there, where they were attacked by the multitude of cats. One of the men was killed and the others all scratched up, however they wounded several cats, which were later found changed into women and severely wounded. . . .

[I]n Livonia, every year at the end of the month of December, there is a scoundrel who goes and summons all the witches to be present at a certain place, and if
they fail to do so, the Devil compels them with blows from an iron rod so hard
that the bruises remain. Their captain goes on ahead and thousands follow him
traversing a river, and when they have crossed it they change their shape into
wolves and fall upon men and flocks and inflict enormous damage. Then twelve
days later they return to the same river, and are changed back into men. . . .

Thus it is really quite ridiculous [to deny the reality of lycanthropy]. . . .
Saint John Chrysostom [d. 407 c. 347-407] says that the witch Circe had so
stupefied the companions of Ulysses by bestial pleasures, that they were like
pigs [see doc. 3]. Here it seems that he means only their reason was paralyzed
and deadened and not that their body was changed. However, all those who
have written about lycanthropy, both ancient and modern, are in agreement that
the human form changes while the mind and reason remain intact. . . . But in
whatever way, it is clear that men are sometimes transmuted into beasts while
their human shape and reason remain. Either it is done by the power of God
directly, or he gives this power to Satan the executor of his will. . . .

Book 4

5. . . . [T]here is no penalty cruel enough to punish the evils of witches, since all
their wickedness, blasphemies, and all their designs rise up against the majesty
of God to vex and offend him in a thousand ways. . . . Some people raise objections to burning witches, even witches who have a formal pact with Satan. For
it is principally against those witches that one must seek vengeance with the
greatest diligence and utmost rigor in order to bring an end to the wrath of God
and his vengeance upon us. And especially since those who have written on it
interpret a magic spell as heresy, and nothing more—although true heresy is the
crime of treason against God and punishable by the fire. It is necessary, however,
to note the difference between this crime and simple heresy. For we showed
initially that the first occupation of witches is to deny God and all religion, but
he renounces all religion, either true or superstitious, which can keep men in
the fear of committing offence.

The second crime of witches is, after having renounced God, to curse, blaspheme, and scorn him and any other god or idol which he feared. Now the law
of God declares as follows, "Whoever curses his God shall bear his sin. He who
blasphemes the name of the Lord shall be put to death" [Leviticus 24:16]. . . . For
it seems that God wants to show that those who blaspheme what they think is
God, do blaspheme God, with respect to their intention, which is the foundation
of the hearts and minds of men: like the witches described above who broke the
arms and legs on crucifixes, which they thought were gods. They also offered

toads the host to feed on. One sees then a double outrage of impiety with witches who blaspheme the true God and anything they think has some divinity, so as to uproot all pious conviction and fear of offence. The third crime is even more abominable. Namely, they do homage to the Devil, worship him, offer sacrifice, and the most despicable make a trench and put their face in the ground praying and worshiping him with all their heart. . . . Now witches are not content to worship or only to bow down before Satan, but they offer themselves to Satan, pray to him and invoke him.

The fourth crime is even greater: many witches have been convicted, and have confessed to promising their children to Satan. The fifth is even worse; that is that witches are frequently convicted by their confession of having sacrificed to the Devil their infant children before they are baptized. They raise them in the air and then insert a large pin into their head, which causes them to die and is a crime more bizarre than the one before. In fact Sprenger relates that he had one burned who had killed forty-one of them in this way [see doc. 63]. . . . The seventh and the most common is that witches make an oath and promise the Devil to lure as many as they can into his service, which they customarily do, as we showed earlier. Now the law of God states that that person who is called this way, must stone the one who tried to entice him. . . .

The ninth is that witches are incestuous, which is the crime they have been charged with and convicted of from earliest times. For Satan gives them to understand that there was never a perfect sorcerer or enchanter who was not born from father and daughter, or mother and son. . . . All these impieties are directly against God and his honor, which judges must avenge with the utmost rigor and bring an end to God's wrath against us. As for the other crimes of witches, they concern injuries done to men, which they will avenge whenever they can. Now there is nothing so displeasing to God as to see judges avenge the smallest offences committed against themselves or others but dissemble the horrible blasphemies against the majesty of God, such as those I have cited about witches.

Let us continue then with the other crimes. The tenth is that witches make a profession of killing people, and worse, of murdering little children then boiling them to render their humors and flesh drinkable, which Sprenger says he learned from their confessions, . . . The thirteenth crime of witches is to kill livestock, something which is customary. . . . The fourteenth is common, and recognized by law, namely, killing crops and causing famine and sterility in an entire region. The fifteenth is that witches have carnal copulation with the Devil (and very often near their husbands, as I remarked earlier), a wickedness they all confess to. . . .

Not only does God show the magnitude of the crime, but also his will that swift and true justice be done regarding it, and particularly the law calls for the death sentence so that the penalty is not reduced for the female sex, as it is done for all other crimes in legal parlance. . . . And as for court sorcerers, since this vermin approaches as near to princes as it can, not only now but from earliest times, in order to ruin the whole state, they lure princes into it, who then later lure their subjects. The law here is noteworthy. For it is stated that if there is a sorcerer who follows the court, or magician, or soothsayer, or augurer or one interpreting dreams by divining art, of whatever rank and however great a lord he might be, he shall be exposed to torments and tortured without making allowances for his rank. This law should be engraved in gold letters on the doors of princes, for they have no more dangerous plague in their following. . . . And since the crime is more detestable, the penalty must be more severe. That is to say, stoning where the penalty is practiced, or burning which is the normal penalty observed from earliest times throughout Christendom.

If with the crime of witchcraft it is established, either by confession or by witnesses or by factual evidence, that the witch caused someone's death, the crime is even greater, especially if it is a child. And even should it happen that the spell cast by the witch to bring about the death of his enemy made another person die, nevertheless, it is punishable by death. If she caused someone's death while trying to make him fall in love, she also deserves death, even though she may not be a witch, as the law says. But with one who is not a witch, the penalty ought to be lightened. . . . And for the same reason the proof of household witnesses is admissible for things done secretly in the home, which otherwise would not be admissible.

Now the wickedness of witches is usually done at night, in a deserted place, away from people, and by means one could never suppose or think of. It is sufficient, therefore, to have strong presumptions to impose corporal punishment in such a revolting case, and up to but not including bodily death. That is to say, beatings, amputations, brandings, life imprisonment, fines, confiscations, and other such penalties except banishment, unless the witch is confined to a particular place. For it is a normal thing with witches to move from one place to another when they have been discovered, carrying the plague elsewhere. And if they are obliged not to move from a place, they no longer dare to do anything, realizing they are watched and suspected.

As for life imprisonment, although it is forbidden in ordinary law, canon law, however, has made more provision for it, especially in the present case. For there is nothing that witches fear more than prison, and it is one of the best ways to make them confess the truth and bring them to repentance. But one must not separate them from other prisoners who are not witches. For it has been found by experience that when they are alone the Devil makes them persist in their wickedness and sometimes helps them to end their lives. If then a witch is seized in possession of toads, lizards, communion wafers, or other strange bones and ointments, and if she is rumored to be a witch, such presumptions are very strong and compelling. Or if in the past she was brought before the courts and never cleared, it is an extremely compelling presumption, or if she has been seen coming out of the stable or sheepfold of her enemy, and then later the livestock of the sheepfold dies. Or if those whom she threatened have died afterward or fallen into a languor, especially if there were several of them, it is a most powerful presumption. Because of these presumptions, even though there was no other proof from confession or witnesses, one must however pronounce sentence according to the above-mentioned penalties, up to and excluding death. . . .

When there is factual evidence one must impose capital punishment, for example, if the one accused of witchcraft was found in possession of human members, especially of little children, one must not hesitate to pronounce the death sentence. For there is concrete factual evidence. If the one accused of witchcraft, in order to cure someone invokes the Devil openly, or with his face to the ground prays to his "little master," as they say, there is concrete factual evidence. One must not have misgivings about imposing the death penalty, as did Mr. Jean Martin who condemned to the flames a witch from Sainte Preuve, who was accused of making the mason of Sainte Preuve stooped and impotent. She had him take a bath, and gave him three lizards wrapped in a handkerchief, enjoining him to throw them into the bath and to utter, "Go in the name of the Devil." For the invocation of the Devil is a hateful idolatry, and this point alone was enough to convict her even though she did not confess anything, and there was no proof of her having made the mason impotent. For many remove the charm and the illness given by other witches. One must also proceed against them if one sees that the remedies they apply are not natural or fitting (such as the three lizards, which were never found afterward in the bath, or for example the witch of Angers, whom we have mentioned, who to effect a cure used cat's brain, which is a strong poison, and crows' heads and other filth) and with other presumptions and information, one must impose corporal punishment.

If it happens that a witch invokes or calls on the Devil, one must without doubt pronounce sentence of death, for the reasons stated above, and not only of death, but one must condemn such monsters to be burned alive, according to the general custom observed from earliest times in all Christendom. The judge must never deviate or depart from this custom and general law or reduce the penalty unless there is an important and compelling reason. For the law states that it is one and the same to reduce or remit the penalty at all. And moreover, the law deems guilty a judge who remits or reduces the penalty of the law. . . . Indeed it goes even further. For it brands a judge with infamy for this reason. And that poses no problem in terms of law. Furthermore, the law requires that one punish with confiscation anyone who remits or reduces the prescribed penalty— and sometimes with exile and other penalties according to the difference in the cases, including punishing the judges with the same penalties that the guilty and convicted person would be punished with, as the law states. . . . As much may be said of those who send witches away acquitted (even though they are guilty) and give as their only excuse that they cannot believe what is said about them; they deserve death. For it calls into doubt the law of God, and all human laws and histories, and countless executions carried out against this for two or three thousand years, and grants impunity to all witches. If someone tells me that all sentences in this realm are discretionary, I grant it, unless the death penalty is restricted by decree or by custom. Now according to very ancient custom, witches in all of Europe are condemned to be burned alive.

We have spoken chiefly about witches who have a sworn compact and a formal partnership with the Devil. But there are other kinds of witches whom we have treated at length in the second book, who are not so loathsome, but who still have partnership with the Devil in diabolical acts, such as those who tie codpieces [a spell causing impotence], which is an abominable wickedness. And although there are some who do it without having a formal agreement or partnership with the Devil, nonetheless the act in itself is diabolical and deserves capital punishment. For one who practices it cannot deny that he is a transgressor of the law of God and of nature, preventing the consequence of marriage ordained by the law of God. . . . As for the other kinds of sorceries, which are performed to learn future events, . . . all those who have been involved in it and have been convicted for the first time must be sentenced to fines and reparations, then on the second time to the lash and branded, and the third time hanged.

There are also those who profess to cure by removing a spell, as they claim, or by diabolical means drive off a storm, and prevent rains and hail. The law does not demand that they be punished, but I maintain that such doctors ought to be questioned and examined to learn whether they are witches, and until proof is found, they must be forbidden on pain of corporal punishments to dabble with medicines, and a close eye kept on them.

With respect to chiromancy which is practiced by those who meddle in fortune telling by hand lines [palm reading], I recommend that they who make it their occupation, as some do, on the first occasion be forbidden to practice it ever again, upon suitable penalty. The books of chiromancy and geomancy, furthermore, which are sold everywhere should be burned, and printers and booksellers prohibited to print or display any for sale, with penalty for those who have been discovered with any in their possession to be exacted the first time by fines, and the second by public amends. And so that no one plead ignorance, it would certainly be necessary to specify the authors in detail and to enjoin all judges to burn on the spot any books of magic which have been found by inspecting inventories. . . .

With regard to natural astrology and its knowledge, since, through it are known the marvels of God, the courses of the celestial lamps, the years, and the seasons—plus the fact that it is necessary for doctors and for the use of meteoric instruments, it must not be mixed with the others. But one must prevent the abuses of those who profess to divine the situation and the life of people, which brings with it a distrust of God and impiety. This is why the finest science in the world has been maligned, so that the words, "*astrologus*," "*mathematicus*" and "*chaldeus* [Chaldean]" in laws are often taken to mean "sorcerers." But excellent sciences must not be rejected because of their abuse. Otherwise one would have to condemn all the arts and sciences in the world. . . . One must pay careful heed to the distinctions between spells, in order to weigh their heinousness and gravity, distinguishing between witches who have a formal agreement with the Devil and those who employ ligatures and other arts of sorcery. For there are some things which cannot be suppressed or punished by magistrates, such as the superstition of many people about not walking through the fields, which the pagans feared, as they feared bleeding from the left nostril, or meeting a pregnant woman before dining. But it is a much greater superstition to carry rolls of paper hung around the neck, or the consecrated host in one's pocket. This is what Judge Gentil did, who was found in possession of a host by the executioner who hanged him at Montfaucon. . . .

It has been found in countless trials that witches very often are priests, or they have secret dealings with priests. And by money or by favors they are induced to say masses for witches, and they accommodate them with hosts, or they consecrate blank parchment, or they place rings, inscribed blades or other such things on the altar, or beneath the altar cloths as has often been discovered. Not long ago a curate was caught in the act, and he escaped since he had a good protector, who had given him a ring to place beneath the altar cloths when he said his mass.

After the priests and ministers of God, the magistrates who are guardians and depositories of justice must be investigated, and if necessary, punished should any be found. For if there is a magistrate involved he will always let witches escape and will maintain in this way the reign of Satan. And the first presumption [evidence] against the magistrate who is a witch is when he makes a joke of such witchcraft. For under the pretense of laughter he brews his fatal poison. . . .

And as for those who did not renounce God, but who made use of characters, circles, and invocations, which they found written in some forbidden books, and though the "familiar spirit," as they say, did not come, one must distinguish the rank of the persons. If it is an ignorant joker who does not think that such familiar spirits are devils, he must be punished by stiff fines. . . . And if the person who made such an invocation is an educated man and of sound judgment, he merits death. For it cannot be denied in this case that he knowingly invoked Satan. And if the one who is sentenced to make amends for such wickedness is stubborn, and he refuses to obey justice, he must be sentenced to death. . . .

It is not within the power of princes to pardon a crime that the law of God punishes with death, such as the crimes of witchcraft. Moreover, princes do a great offence to God to pardon such horrible wickedness committed directly against his majesty, since the smallest prince avenges his injuries with capital punishment. So those who let witches escape or who do not carry out their punishment with utmost rigor, can be assured that they will be abandoned by God to the mercy of witches. And the country which tolerates them will be struck by plagues, famines, and wars—but those who take vengeance against them will be blessed by God, and will bring an end to his wrath. This is why one who is charged and accused of being a witch must never be simply let off and acquitted, unless the calumny of the accuser or informer is clearer than the sun. Since the proof of such wickedness is so hidden and so difficult, no one would ever be accused or punished out of a million witches if parties were governed, as in an ordinary trial, by a lack of proof. . . .

Questions: What practices does Bodin discuss that amount to binding spells? How does Bodin's discussion of the responsibility of judges and princes explain how convictions for witchcraft could escalate? What, for Bodin, is the greatest sin one commits when one becomes a witch? Is there a sense in the reading that witchcraft is gendered? Is there any magic that is acceptable to Bodin?

73. MECHANICS OF TORTURE: DR. FIAN AND SUZANNE GAUDRY

In 1252, Pope Innocent IV (d. 1254) issued the bull Ad exstirpanda, *which stipulated the use of torture as an acceptable investigatory aid to obtain evidence in trials for heresy and witchcraft. However, the restrained circumstances under which the Inquisition speci- fied that torture could legitimately be applied were ignored as the witch trials progressed, or, as in the case of Dr. Fian (d. 1591) from Scotland, were irrelevant because he was tried by a civil court in a Protestant country. Of particular interest in the trial processes recorded below are the role of torture, leading questions, confessions, and the insistence that the accused name other witches. In addition to the methods of torture used on Dr. Fian and Suzanne Gaudry (d. 1652), another common application was the* strappado, *whereby the accused's hands were tied behind the back, and the person was suspended by a rope attached to the wrists, which resulted in the dislocation of the shoulders. Often weights were attached to the feet to increase the pain.*

"A True Discourse of the Damnable Life of Doctor Fian" forms a portion of "News from Scotland," a pamphlet distributed at the time of Dr. Fian's trial in 1591. The original account of the trial of Suzanne Gaudry is found in the archives of Lille, France, although the trial took place in Rieux.

Sources: ed. David Webster, "A True Discourse of the Damnable Life of Doctor Fian and Sundry Other Witches, Lately Taken in Scotland," in *A Collection of Rare and Curious Tracts on Witchcraft and the Second Sight with an Original Essay on Witchcraft* (Edinburgh: Thomas Webster, 1820), pp. 26–34; rev. Martha Rampton; the Gaudry trial: trans. Martha Rampton, J. Français, *L'Eglise et la Sorcelleri, e* Librairie Critique (Paris: Émile Nourry, 1910), pp. 236–50.

Declaring the Damnable Life of Doctor Fian, a Notable Sorcerer, Who was Burned at Edinburgh

As touching the aforesaid Doctor Fian, alias John Cunningham, the examination of his acts since his apprehension, revealed the great subtlety of the Devil. Doctor Fian was identified by the witch, Gilly Duncane, when she was interrogated. She confessed he was the witches' register and that there was not one man allowed to come to the Devil's readings but only he. The said doctor was taken and imprisoned, and subjected to the accustomed pain provided for those offences, such as was inflicted upon the other witches also apprehended with Doctor Fian [see doc. 74].

First, by thrawing [cinching] his head with a rope, whereat he would confess nothing. Secondly, he was persuaded to freely confess his guilt, but that would prevail as little. Lastly, he was put to the most severe and cruel pain in the world, called the boots [wooden or iron castings fitted around the ankles and feet]. After he had received three strokes [which tightened the boots], being asked if he would confess his damnable acts and wicked life, his tongue would not serve him to speak, in respect whereof the rest of the witches agreed to search his tongue, under which was found two pins thrust up to the heads of the pins. The witches said, "Now is the charm revealed, and those charmed pins were the cause he could not confess anything." Then was he immediately released from the boots, brought before the king, his confession was taken, and his own signature was willingly set thereunto, which reads as follows:

First, that at the general meetings of those witches, he was always present, that he was clerk to all those that were in subjection to the Devil's service, bearing the name of witches, that always he did take their oaths. . . .

Item, he confessed that by his witchcraft he did bewitch a gentleman dwelling near to the Saltpans, where the said doctor taught school, only because the gentleman was enamored of a gentlewoman whom he loved himself. By means of his sorcery, witchcraft, and devilish practices, he caused the said gentleman to fall into lunacy and madness every twenty-three hours and to remain such for one whole hour together. . . .

Item, . . . It happened, this gentlewoman, being unmarried, had a brother who went to school with the said doctor. Doctor Fian called the scholar to him and asked if he slept in the same room as his sister, and the student answered that he did. Knowing this, the doctor thought to carry out his purpose, and therefore secretly promised to teach the student without stripes [teachers regularly hit their students], if he would bring him three hairs of his sister's privates, at such time as he should see the best occasion for it; which the youth promised faithfully to perform and vowed speedily to put it in practice. He took a piece of conjured paper from his master to wrap the hairs in when he had gotten them; and thereupon the boy set about nightly to carry out his master's request, especially when his sister was asleep. But God, who knows the secret of all hearts, and reveals all wicked and ungodly practices, would not suffer the intents of this devilish doctor to achieve his purpose. . . . The girl's mother, being very sharp, did vehemently suspect Doctor Fian's intention, by reason that she was a witch herself, and therefore was very eager to know her son's intent, and so she beat him with many stripes, whereby he told her the truth.

The mother, therefore, being well practiced in witchcraft, did think it most convenient to best the doctor in his own art, and thereupon took the paper from the boy wherein he would have put the same hairs, and went to a young heifer which never had borne a calf nor mated with a bull, and with a pair of sheers clipped off three hairs from the udder of the cow and wrapped them in the same paper, which she again delivered to the boy. She told him to give the same to his said master, Doctor Fian, which he immediately did. The school master received the hairs, and thinking them indeed to be the maid's hairs, went straight and worked his sorcery upon them. . . . But the doctor had no sooner finished than the heifer cow, whose hairs they were indeed, came unto the door of the church where the school master was, entered, and made towards the school master, leaping and dancing, and following him out of the church and wherever he went, to the great admiration of all the townsmen of Saltpans, and many others who did behold the same.

The report of this made all men imagine that he worked with the assistance of the Devil, and thereupon the name of the said Doctor Fian (who was but a young man), began to grow common among the people of Scotland, and he was secretly thought to be a notable conjurer.

All of this, although in the beginning he denied, and would not confess, yet having felt the pain of the boots (and the charmed pins stuck in his mouth as said above), he confessed all the aforesaid to be most true, without producing any witnesses to justify the same, and thereupon before the king's majesty he wrote down his confession with his own hand, which for truth remaineds upon record in Scotland.

After the depositions and examinations of the said Doctor Fian, alias Cunningham, were taken, as already said, with his own hand willingly set thereunto, he was led by the master of the prison to a ward and committed to a chamber by himself. There, forsaking his wicked ways, acknowledging his most ungodly life, showing that he had too much followed the allurements and

EUROPEAN MAGIC AND WITCHCRAFT: A READER

enticements of Satan, and willingly practiced his art by conjuring, witchcraft, enchantment, sorcery, and such like, he renounced the Devil and all his wicked works, vowed to lead the life of a Christian, and seemed newly devoted to God.

The day after, in an interview, he granted that the Devil had appeared unto him in the night before, appareled all in black with a white wand in his hand, and that the Devil demanded him to continue his faithful service, according to his first oath and promise made to that effect. Whom (as he then said), he utterly renounced him to his face, and said unto him in this manner, "Flee, Satan, flee, for I have listened too much to you, and by the same you have undone me, in respect whereof I utterly forsake you." To which the Devil answered, "Once you die you shall be mine." And with that (as he said), the Devil broke the white wand and immediately vanished forth from his sight.

Thus all the day this Doctor Fian continued very solitary and seemed to have a care of his own soul, and would call upon God, showing himself penitent for his wicked life; nevertheless, the same night he found such means that he stole the key of the prison door and chamber in which he was, which in the night he opened and fled away to the Saltpans, where he was always resident and first apprehended. When the king's majesty heard of this sudden departure, he caused diligent inquiry to be made for the doctor's apprehension, and to make this happen, he sent public proclamations into all parts of his land. Because of the hot and hard pursuit, Doctor Fian was again taken and brought to prison; and then being called before the king's highness, he was reexamined regarding his escape and all that had happened before. But this doctor, notwithstanding that his own confession remained in record under his own hand writing, and the same thereunto fixed in the presence of the king's majesty and sundry of his council, yet did he utterly deny the same.

Thereupon the king's majesty, perceiving his stubborn willfulness, conceived and imagined that in the time of his absence he had entered into new confer- ence and league with the Devil, his master, and that he had been again newly marked, but the mark could not in any way be found; yet though others tried to make him confess, they could not, and he was commanded to have a most extreme torment, which was done in this manner following. His nails upon all his fingers were riven and pulled off with an instrument called in Scottish a Turkas, which in England we call a pair of pincers, and under every nail there was thrust in through needles up to the heads. At all which torments notwith- standing the doctor never shook any whit; neither would he then confess it despite all the tortures inflicted upon him.

Then was he with all convenient speed, by commandment, conveyed again to the torment of the boots, wherein he continued a long time, and did abide so many blows in them, that his legs were crushed and beaten together as small as might be, and the bones and flesh so bruised, that the blood and marrow

spouted forth in great abundance, whereby they were made unserviceable forever. And notwithstanding all these grievous pains and cruel torments, he would
not confess anything. So deeply had the Devil entered into his heart, that he
utterly denied that which he confessed and would say nothing thereunto but
this, that what he had done and said before, was only done and said for fear of
pains which he had endured.

Upon great consideration, therefore, . . . the said Doctor Fian was soon after
arraigned, condemned, and adjudged by the law to die and then to be burned
according to the law of that land. Whereupon he was put into a cart, and being
first strangled [being strangled before burning was a mercy], he was immediately
put into a great fire, having been made ready for that purpose, and was there
burned in the Castle Hill of Edinburgh, on a Saturday in the end of January
last past, 1591.

The Trial of Suzanne Gaudry

At Ronchain, 28 May 1652

Interrogation of the person of Suzanne Gaudry, prisoner at the court de
Rieux.

Asked about her age, where she is from, and who her father and mother are.

—She says her name is Suzanne Gaudry, daughter of Jean Gaudry and of
Marguerite Gerné, both natives of Rieux, but she was born in Esgavans near
Odenarde where her father fled [with the family] due to the wars, that she was
born on the day they made bonfires for the peace treaty between France and
Spain, without being able to say any more about her age.

Asked why she had been brought here.

—Answers that it is for the salvation of her soul.

Questioned why she had left the area of Rieux for about a year and a half.

—Says that she was afraid of being taken prisoner for the crime of witchcraft.

Inquired as to how long she had been in subjugation to the Devil.

—Says that about twenty-five or twenty-six years ago she was his lover and
that he called himself Petit-Grignon, and he was fitted out with black breeches,
that he gave her the name Magin, that she gave him a pin with which he gave
her his mark on her left shoulder, that he had a small, flat hat; also says that he
had sexual relations with her two or three times only.

Asked how many times she attended the nocturnal dance.

—Responds that she found herself there around a dozen times, having first
renounced God, the chrism, and baptism, that the dance took place at the small
marsh of Rieux; she saw that there were different kinds of dances there. The
first time she did not recognize anyone there because she was half blind. The
other times she saw and recognized Noëlle and Pasquette Gerné, Noëlle, wife of

Nochin Quinchou, and Pasquette, wife of Paul Doris, Marie Nourette, widow. Not having recognized any others because the young people were separated from the older people. She then said that when the dance was large the table was similarly large.

Questioned what was on the table.

—Says that there were no salt or napkins, unsure why they were not there because she never ate there. That her lover took her there and back.

Asked if her lover had ever given her some powder.

—Responds that he offered it but that she never wanted to take it, [the Devil] says that it was for doing whatever she wanted, that the powder was gray, that her lover told her that she could deliver someone a good blow and that it would especially help her steal from Elisabeth Dehau, which she did not want to do, although her lover pressed the issue because Elisabeth had disturbed her grain by knocking it around with a stick.

Questioned how and in what manner they danced.

—Says they were ordinarily dances, saw that there was a guitarist and some whistlers who were men she did not recognize, that they played for around an hour and then everyone fell down in a faint, exhausted.

Questioned what they did after the dance.

—Says that they made a circle, that there was a king with a long black beard dressed in black, a red hat, that he made all obey him, and that after the dance (word missing from text) everyone disappeared. (Brought out a rosary with an image of Our Lady of Hal whom she invoked).

Questioned how long it had been since she saw Grignon, her lover.

—Says that it has been three or four days ago.

Questioned if she had abused the holy sacrament.

—Says never and that she always swallowed it. Then says that her lover asked her for it many times but that she never wanted to give it to him.

After many admonitions, she signed this mark, X [Suzanne Gaudry].

Second Interrogation, 29 May 1652

In the presence of the above-named jurists, this prisoner was led back into the chamber to hear the facts and charges against her and asked if what she declared and confessed yesterday is true.

—Responds that if this [information] was asked in order to put her in prison, that it is not true; then says after having kept quiet said that it is true. . . .

Questioned how many times she was at the carol and the nocturnal dance and whom she recognized there.

—Responds that she was there eleven or twelve times, that she went on foot with her lover where the third time she saw and recognized Pasquette and Noëlle

Gerné, Marie Homitte, but she never spoke to them because people did not speak to one another. And that that sabbath was held at the small pond of Rieux.

Questioned how long since she saw her lover and if she did not also see Marie Hourie and her daughter Marie at the dance.

—Says that it was a long time ago, about two years and that she did not see Marie Hourie nor her daughter there, since she said it, after having asked for some time to think, said it was indeed five days or three weeks, having renounced completely the demons of hell and the one who deceived her.

Asked what they did at the dance and what happened after.

—Says that right after the dance they collected themselves and approached the leader who had a long black beard dressed also in black and with a red hat, that someone gave them some powder for doing what they wanted, but that she did not want to take any.

Charged with having taken some and having used it evilly.

—Says, after having insisted that she did not want any powder, that she took some and that her lover encouraged her to do evil, but she did not want to do it.

Questioned whether if she did not obey his commands, did he hit or menace her and what she did with the powder?

—Answers that she was never beaten; invoked the name of the Virgin and that she threw away the powder that she had, and vowed that she did not want to do evil things.

Pressed to say what she did with this powder. And didn't she fear her lover too much to have thrown it away?

—Says, after having been pressed on this point, that she had destroyed some herbs from her garden at the end of the summer, five or six years ago, she threw it there because she did not know what to do with it. . . .

Charged again with having done magic with this powder, pressed to say the truth.

—Responds that she did not kill anyone nor any beast; later she says that she had killed a red horse of Philippe Cornié with the powder about two or three years ago, that she had put it where he would pass on the road near to her house. . . .

Asked how and in what way they danced in the carol.

—Says that they dance in a circle, holding each other's hands, each with their lover at their side, she says that they never speak with one another and if someone spoke that she did not hear it because she is hard of hearing. There was a guitarist and a whistler that she did not recognize, later she says that these were devils who played. . . .

After being admonished to examine her conscience, was returned to prison after she signed this mark, X [Suzanne Gaudry].

Deliberation at the Court of Mons, 3 June 1652

[The only malicious deed to which Susan Gaudry confessed is having killed an animal of Philippe Cornié by magic]; but there is no evidence except a previous statement. Because of this before going forward it is necessary to learn more about it, to examine, and to probe the mark and hear Philippe Cornié on the death of the horse and when and in what fashion it died. . . .

Deliberation at the Court of Mons, 13 June 1652

[The court] reviewed the present criminal trial of Suzanne Gaudry and along with it, the trial of Antoinette Lescouffre, also a prisoner at the same court. It seemed to the court that it was necessary to probe the places where the prisoners are said to have received the mark of the Devil and, after that they should be interrogated and examined seriously on their confessions and denials so that this [case] be definitively in order. . . .

Deliberation at the Court of Mons, 22 June 1652

The trials of Antoinette Lescouffre and Suzanne Gaudry having been recommended to the undersigned lawyers of the court of Mons. The lawyers were told by the peasants who took the accused to prison that they persuaded them to confess, and if they did confess, they would be allowed to go free. For this reason it seemed that the confessions were not so spontaneous.

They advised that the office, to effectively discharge its duty would do well to follow up the two preceding resolutions by probing the place of the marks that they had indicated and if found that they are ordinary marks of the Devil, they can proceed with their examination, then follow up their first confessions, and if they deny, the court can proceed to the torture, given that they come from a parentage of witches and that they have always been suspected, that they fled the crime (to avoid the judgment of witchcraft) and that by their confession have confirmed [their guilt] notwithstanding that since then they have wanted to revoke and vacillate.

Third Interrogation, 27 June 1652

Suzanne Gaudry, on 27 June, in the presence of the above-named jurists. This prisoner was led into the room for examination to determine if what she said and confessed during her imprisonment at the beginning was true.

—Responds no and what she said had been by force.

. . . Pressed to tell the truth otherwise they would apply torture to her, reminding her that her aunt had been burned for the same subject.

—Responds that she was never a witch.

Asked how long she had been in subjugation to the Devil and pressed that she must renounce the Devil and the one that misled her.

—Says that she was never a witch, that she had not been with the Devil, so she did not want to renounce the Devil saying that he did not mislead her and on the question of having confessed that she was at the carol, says that she said it but that it was not true and that she was not a witch.

Charged with having confessed to killing a horse by using powder that the Devil had given her.

—Responds that she had said that because she was pressed by inquisitors that she must have done some.

She was put in the hands of the officer in charge of torture, throwing herself to her knees, trying to make herself cry, uttering many exclamations, without being able to get out a single tear. Saying at each moment that she is not a witch.

(Torture)

The same day in the place of the torture. This prisoner, before being strapped down, was admonished to maintain her first confessions and to renounce her lover.

—Says that all that she had said was a lie and that she never had a lover; she feels herself being strapped down and says that she is not a witch and tried to cry.

Questioned why she had fled the village of Rieux.

—Says that she did not want to say, that God and the Virgin Mary forbid her; that she is not a witch. And at this it was asked why she confessed to being one and says that she was forced to say it.

Told that she was not forced, on the contrary, without any menace she declared herself to be a witch.

—Says that she had confessed and that she was not a witch, and was a little stretched [on the rack] screams without ceasing that she is not a witch, calls the name of Jesus and of Our Lady of Grace. Not wanting to say anything else.

Asked if she had not confessed to being a witch for twenty-six years.

—Says that she had said that, that she denies it, crying Jesus-Maria, that she is not a witch.

Asked if she had killed a horse of Philippe Cornié like she confessed.

—Responds no, crying out Jesus-Marie, that she is not a witch.

The mark having been probed by the officer present, in the presence of the doctor called Bouchain, it was judged by the aforementioned doctor and officer that it was truly the mark of the Devil. Being more strongly stretched on the rack, was pressed to maintain her confessions.

—Says that it is true that she is a witch and that she would maintain what she had said. Asked how long she was in subjugation to the Devil.

—Responds that it was twenty years ago that the Devil appeared to her when she was in her square [near her lodgings] in the form of a man dressed in a small cow-hide [vest] and short black trousers.

Questioned what her lover called himself.

—Says that she had said Petit-Grignon, then pulled from the rack, and upon interrogation says she was never a witch and that she did not want to say anything.

Asked if her lover had carnal copulation with her and how many times.

—At this she did not respond to anything, acted sick, they could no longer get a word from her.

Everyone present remarked that as soon as she began to confess, she asked who was alongside her touching her, without, however, there being anyone there. And it was noticed that as soon as she said this, she no longer wanted to confess anything, and for that reason she was returned to prison.

Verdict, 9 July 1652

Given the questions, responses and investigations made on the charges against Suzanne Gaudry, together with her confessions, it appears that she has always been known to be stained by the crime of witchcraft, and that from fear of being arrested by the law she fled and took refuge in this city of Valenciennes, seeing that her relatives were also marred by the same crime and were executed, seeing by her own confessions that she made a pact with the Devil, received from him a mark, which is in the report of Mr. Michel de Roux and judged by the doctor of Ronchain and officials of the *haultes oeuvres* [torturers] of Cambrai, after having proved that the mark was not natural but of the Devil, and under oath they swore that this was true, she renounced God, the chrism and baptism and she had carnal relations and enjoyed it. Also that she went to the place of the carol and nocturnal dances. These are the crimes of divine lèse-majesté. For expiation of which the advice of the undersigned of the court of Rieux can legitimately condemn the aforementioned Suzanne Gaudry to a final torture, tying her to the gallows and strangling her until she is dead, to burn her body and bury it nearby in the woods. . . .

Questions: What are the similarities and differences in the two trials recorded above? Why did both prisoners retract confessions they had formerly given? Why did Suzanne Gaudry first confess to being a witch? What is the significance of the information that some of Suzanne's relatives were suspected witches? What is the significance of the fact that Suzanne tried to cry but could not shed a tear? What are some of the contradictions in Suzanne's testimony? Why did her interrogators insist that Suzanne hold to her incriminating but not her exculpatory confessions?

74. KING JAMES AND THE WITCHES OF
NORTH BERWICK: "NEWS FROM SCOTLAND"

King James VI ruled Scotland from 1567 to 1625 and became king of England as James I in 1603. Although staunchly Protestant, his views on witchcraft differed little from those of his Catholic contemporaries. He began to take a special interest in sorcery when two storms at sea adversely affected him: one prevented his Danish bride from joining him at the appointed time, and the second almost claimed his life. The king personally attended the trials that took place in 1590 (the first major witch trials in Scotland under the Witchcraft Act of 1563) and witnessed the torture of those thought to be responsible for the storms and the attempt on his life. The North Berwick affair occupied James for nine months, and after that he continued to take a keen interest in witchcraft, which he considered a great peril to himself, specifically, and to the body politic in general. He went on to write a full treatise on the dangers of witchcraft (see doc. 76). The following account was most likely written contemporary to the events it chronicles by James Carmichael, the minister of Haddington in Lincolnshire, and distributed in pamphlet form.

Source: author unknown (possibly James Carmichael, the minister of Haddington), "News from Scotland," in *A Collection of Rare and Curious Tracts on Witchcraft and the Second Sight* (Edinburgh: Thomas Webster, 1820), pp. xv–xvi, 17–26; rev. Martha Rampton.

To the Reader: Because of the manifold untruths which are spread abroad concerning the detestable actions and apprehension of those witches, . . . I have undertaken to produce this short treatise, which is the true discourse of all that happened, as well as what was pretended by those wicked and detestable witches against the king's majesty, and also by what means they did the same. . . . All the examinations (gentle reader) I have here published faithfully as they were taken and uttered in the presence of the king's majesty, praying you to accept their veracity because it is so true that it cannot be reproved. . . . God, by his omnipotent power, has at all times, and daily does, take such care and is so vigilant for the well-being and preservation of his own, that he frustrates the wicked practices and evil intents of all who, by any means whatsoever, seek indirectly to conspire contrary to his holy will. . . .

Within the town of Tranent in the kingdom of Scotland, there dwells one David Seaton, who being deputy bailiff in the said town, had a maid called Gilly Duncan, who used secretly to leave her master's house every other night. This Gilly Duncan helped all those troubled or grieved with any kind of sickness or infirmity, and in a short space of time did perform many matters most miraculously. These things, because she began to do them suddenly, having never done anything like it before, made her master and others distrustful, and they wondered how. So the said David Seaton greatly suspected that his maid did not do those things by natural and lawful methods, but rather supposed them to be done by some extraordinary and unlawful means.

Whereupon her master began to grow very inquisitive and asked her which way and by what means she was able to perform matters of so great an importance; whereat she gave him no answer. Nevertheless, her master with the intent that he might the better try and find out the truth of the same, did with the help of others, torment her with the torture of the pilliwinkes [thumbscrews] upon her fingers, which is a grievous torture, and binding or cinching her head with a cord or rope, which is a most cruel torment also, yet she would not confess anything; whereupon they, suspecting that she had been marked by the Devil (as commonly witches are), made diligent search about her and found the enemy's mark to be in the fore part of her throat; which being found, she confessed that all her doings were done by the wicked allurements and enticements of the Devil, and that she did them by witchcraft. After this her confession, she was committed to prison, where she continued a season, and immediately she accused [several] persons to be notorious witches and caused them to be apprehended, one after another . . . [Among them were Dr. Fian (see doc. 73) and Agnes Sampson].

Agnes Sampson, which was the elder witch, was taken and brought to Holyroodhouse House before the king's majesty and various other of the nobility of Scotland, where she was intensively examined, but all the persuasions which the king's majesty used on her, with the rest of his counsel, did not provoke or induce her to confess anything, but she stood stiffly in the denial of all that was laid to her charge. Whereupon they caused her to be conveyed away unto prison, there to receive such torture as has been lately provided for witches in that country. By due examination of witchcraft and witches in Scotland, it has lately been found that the Devil generally licks them with his tongue in some private part of their body before he receives them to be his servants. In this way he marks them with a private mark, which has often given the witches away so that they confess. The mark commonly is given them under the hair in some part of their body, so that whereby it may not easily be found out or seen, although they be searched. And generally so long as the mark is not seen to those who search them, the parties which have the mark will never confess anything. Therefore by special commandment this Agnes Sampson had all her hair shaven off in each part of her body and her head rung with a rope according to the custom of that country, being a pain most grievous, which they continued almost an hour. During that time she would not confess anything until the Devil's mark was found upon her privates, then she immediately confessed whatsoever was demanded of her, verifying that those persons aforesaid were notorious witches.

Item, the said Agnes Sampson was after brought again before the king's majesty and his counsel, and being examined about the meeting and detestable dealings of those witches, she confessed that upon the night of All Hallows Eve last she was accompanied with the persons aforesaid and with a great many other witches to the number of two hundred, and that all together they went to sea, each one in a strainer or a sieve . . . with flagons of wine, making merry and drinking all the way to the church of North Berwick in Lothian. And that after they had landed, they took hands on the land and danced a reel or a short dance, singing all with one voice, "Commer goe ye before, commer goe ye, Gif ye will not goe before, commer let me." At that time she confessed that this Gilly Duncan did go before them playing this reel upon a small trumpet, called a Jew's trumpet, until they entered into the church of North Berwick.

These greatly astonished the king, and he sent for Gilly Duncan, who upon the same trumpet did play the said dance before the king's majesty, who in respect of the strangeness of these matters, took great interest in being present at their examinations.

Item, the said Agnes Sampson confessed that the Devil was at North Berwick church waiting for them in the habit or likeness of a man, and seeing that they tarried over long, he at their coming commanded them all to pay penance. That is they should kiss his buttocks in sign of duty to him; which being put over the pulpit bare, everyone did as he had enjoined them. And having made his ungodly exhortations, wherein he did greatly inveigh against the king of Scotland, he received their oaths for their good and true service towards him, and departed. Which done, they returned to sea, and so home again. At which time the witches demanded of the Devil why he did bear such hatred to the king? Who answered, by reason the king is the greatest enemy he has in the world. All their confessions and depositions are still extant upon record.

Item, the said Agnes Sampson confessed before the king's majesty sundry things, which were so miraculous and strange that his majesty said they were all extreme liars; whereat she answered that she would not wish his majesty to suppose her words to be false, but rather to believe them, in that she would prove such matters unto him such as his majesty would be in no doubt. And thereupon taking his majesty a little aside, she declared unto him the very words which passed between the king's majesty and his queen at Oslo in Norway the first night of their marriage. At this the king's majesty wondered greatly and swore by the living God that he believed all the devils in hell could not have discovered the same, acknowledging her words to be most true, he therefore gave all the more credence to the rest that was before declared.

Touching this Agnes Sampson, she is the only woman who, by the Devil's persuasion, could have intended and put into execution the attempted death of the king's majesty in the following way. She confessed that she took a black toad, and did hang the same up by the heels three days, and collected and gathered the venom it dropped and fell from it in an oyster shell, and kept the same venom close covered until she should obtain any part or piece of used linen cloth that the king has soiled—such as a shirt, handkerchief, napkin, or any other thing. . . . [She was not able to obtain any of the king's effects.] And the said Agnes Sampson, by her depositions since her apprehension, said that if she had obtained any one piece of linen cloth which the king had worn and dirtied, she would have bewitched him to death and put him to such extraordinary pain as if he had been lying upon sharp thorns and ends of needles. Moreover she confessed, that at the time when his majesty was in Denmark, she being accompanied by the parties before specially named, took a cat and christened it, and afterward bound to each part of that cat the chief part of a dead man and several joints of his body, and that the following night the said cat was conveyed into the middle of the sea by all the witches, sailing in their screens and sieves, as is recorded above, and so they left the said cat right before the town of Leith in Scotland. This done, there did arise such a tempest in the sea as a greater has not been seen; which tempest was the cause of the perishing of a boat or vessel coming over from the town of Brunt Island to the town of Leith, in which were sundry jewels and rich gifts, which should have been presented to the, now, queen of Scotland at her majesty's coming to Leith.

Again it is confessed that the said christened cat was the cause that the king's majesty's ship leaving from Denmark had a contrary wind from the rest of the ships then being in his company, which thing was most strange and true as the king's majesty acknowledged. For when the rest of the ships had a fair and good wind, then was the wind contrary and altogether against his majesty, and further, the said witch declared, that his majesty would have never come safely from the sea if his faith had not prevailed above their intentions. Moreover, the said witches, being asked how the Devil would use them when he was in their company, confessed that when the Devil did receive them for his servants, and they had vowed themselves unto him, then he would carnally use them, albeit to their little pleasure, in respect to his colder nature [his penis was ice cold] and would do the like at sundry other times.

Questions: Why did Gilly Duncan give up the names of other "witches"? What elements of witchcraft in this document are familiar from earlier treatises on witchcraft? Which elements of witchcraft are new in this text? How does the author flatter King James?

75. SKEPTICISM AND A FORCED RECANTATION

Cornelius Loos (1546–1595), born in Holland, was a professor of theology at the University of Trier during the height of the witch trials. He wrote On True and False Magic *(1592), a tract opposing not just the legal procedures used in the witch trials but also the demonological basis of witchcraft itself, denying the physical existence of demons. The manuscript was seized before it could be printed, and Loos was imprisoned. In 1593, before an assembly of churchmen, he was coerced into recanting the assertions he made in his book. The recantation was later (1599–1600) incorporated into* Six Books of Magical Investigations, *a work by a Jesuit priest, Martin Del Rio (1551–1608), a staunch demonologist and advocate of the extermination of witches.*

Source: George L. Burr, *The Witch Persecutions,* Translations and Reprints from the Original Sources of European History, vol. 3 (Philadelphia: University of Pennsylvania Press, 1907), pp. 14–18.

And, finally, as I [Martin Del Rio] have made mention of Losæus Callidius [Cornelius Loos], who tried by a thousand arts to make public the book which he had written in defense of the witches (and some fear that even yet some evil demon may bring this about), I have brought forth an antidote, the recantation signed by him. Its authentic and so-called original copy is in the possession of a devout and most honorable man, Joannes Baxius, J. U. Lie. (whose energy and zeal against this nefarious heresy, God will someday reward), from whom I have received the following transcript, certified by a notary:

I, Cornelius Losæus Callidius, born at the town of Gouda in Holland, but now (on account of a certain treatise *On True and False Witchcraft,* rashly and presumptuously written without the knowledge and permission of the superiors of this place, shown by me to others, and then sent to be printed at Cologne) arrested and imprisoned in the imperial monastery of St. Maximin, near Trier, by order of the most reverend and most illustrious lord, the papal nuncio, Octavius, bishop of Tricarico; whereas I am informed of a surety that in the aforesaid book and also in certain letters of mine on the same subject sent clandestinely to the clergy and town council of Trier, and to others (for the purpose of hindering the execution of justice against the witches, male and female), are contained many articles which are not only erroneous and scandalous, but also suspected of heresy and smacking of the crime of treason, as being seditious and foolhardy, against the common opinion of decisions and bulls of theological teachers and the decisions and bulls of the supreme pontiffs, and contrary to the practice and to the statutes and laws of the magistrates and judges, not only of this archdiocese of Trier, but of other provinces and principalities, I do therefore revoke, condemn, reject, and repudiate the said articles, in the order in which they are here subjoined.

1. In the first place, I revoke, condemn, reject, and censure the idea (which both in words and writing I have often and before many persons pertinaciously asserted and which I wished to be the head and front of this my disputation) that the things which are written about the bodily transportation or translation of witches, male and female, are altogether fanciful and must be reckoned the empty superstition; (and this I recant) both because it smacks of rank heresy and because this opinion partakes of sedition and hence savors of the crime of treason.

2. For (and this in the second place I recant), in the letters which I have clandestinely sent to sundry persons, I have pertinaciously, without solid reasons, alleged against the magistracy that the (aerial) flight of witches is false and imaginary, asserting, moreover, that the wretched creatures are compelled by the severity of the torture to confess things which they have never done, and that by cruel butchery innocent blood is shed, and by a new alchemy gold and silver coined from human blood.

3. By these and by other things of the same sort, partly in private conversations among the people, partly in sundry letters addressed to both the magistracies, I have accused of tyranny, to their subjects the superiors and the judges.

4. And consequently, inasmuch as the most reverend and most illustrious archbishop and prince-elector of Trier not only permits witches, male and female, to be subjected in his diocese to deserved punishment, but has also ordained laws regulating the method and costs of judicial procedure against witches, I have with heedless temerity tacitly insinuated the charge of tyranny against the aforesaid elector of Trier.

5. I revoke and condemn, moreover, the following conclusions of mine, to wit, that there are no witches who renounce God, pay worship to the Devil, bring storms by the Devil's aid, and do other like things, but that all these things are dreams.

6. Also, that magic (*magia*) ought not to be called witchcraft (*maleficium*), nor magicians (*magi*) witches (*malefici*), and that the passage of holy Scripture, "Thou shalt not suffer a witch to live" (*Maleficos non patieris vivere*) [Exodus 22:18] is to be understood of those who by a natural use of natural poisons inflict death.

7. That no compact does or can exist between the Devil and a human being.

8. That devils do not assume bodies.

9. That the life of Hilarion [the hermit saint of Gaza and Cyprus, c. 291–371] written by Saint Jerome [c. 347–420] is not authentic.

10. That there is no sexual intercourse between the Devil and human beings.

11. That neither devils nor witches can raise tempests, rainstorms, hailstorms, and the like, and that the things said about these are mere dreams.

12. That spirit and form apart from matter cannot be seen by man.

13. That it is rash to assert that whatever devils can do, witches also can do through their aid.

14. That the opinion that a superior demon can cast out an inferior is erroneous and derogatory to Christ.

15. That the popes in their bulls do not say that magicians and witches perpetrate such things (as are mentioned above).

16. That the Roman pontiffs granted the power to proceed against witches, lest if they should refuse they might be unjustly accused of magic, just as some of their predecessors had been justly accused of it.

These assertions, all and singular, with many calumnies, falsehoods, and sycophancies toward the magistracy, both secular and ecclesiastical, spitefully, immodestly, and falsely poured forth, without cause, with which my writings on magic teem, I hereby expressly and deliberately condemn, revoke, and reject, earnestly beseeching the pardon of God and of my superiors for what I have done and solemnly promising that in future I will neither in word nor in writing, by myself or through others, in whatsoever place it may befall me to be, teach, promulgate, defend, or assert any of these things. If I shall do to the contrary, I subject myself thenceforward, as if it were now, to all the penalties of the law against relapsed heretics, recusants, seditious offenders, traitors, backbiters, and sycophants, who have been openly convicted, and also to those ordained against perjurers. I submit myself also to arbitrary correction, whether by the archbishop of Trier or by any other magistrates under whom it may befall me to dwell and who may be certified of my relapse and of my broken faith, that they may punish me according to my deserts, in honor and reputation, property and person.

In testimony of all which I have, with my own hand, signed this my recantation of the aforesaid articles, in presence of notary and witnesses. . . .

Here you have the recantation in full. And yet afterwards again at Brussels, while serving as curate in the church of Notre Dame de la Chapelle, he was accused of relapse, and was released only after a long imprisonment, and being again brought into suspicion (whence you may understand the pertinacity of his madness) escaped a third indictment through a premature death; but (much the pity!) left behind not a few partisans, men so imperfectly versed in medicine and sound theology as to share this stupid error. Would that they might be wise and seriously realize at last how rash and noxious it is to prefer the ravings of a single heretic, [Johann] Weyer [see doc. 69] to the judgment of the church!

Questions: What evidence do we have from the reading above that opposition to the witch trials was not isolated to a few people? What does the reading imply about the position of some popes on witchcraft? Summarize Cornelius Loos's beliefs about witches.

76. KING JAMES I OF ENGLAND: TREATISE ON DEMONS AND WITCHCRAFT

Being the son of Mary, queen of Scots (1542–1587), James VI (b. 1566) inherited the throne of Scotland (r. 1567–1625) and became James I of England when the two kingdoms united in 1603. After his experience with the Berwick witches (see doc. 74), James became obsessed with witchcraft and fashioned himself the "faithful and true" apocalyptic warrior on a white horse come to defend the "king of kings and lord of lords" (Revelation 19:11–16) from the evils of diabolism. He set it as his personal crusade to fight Satan, the chief adversary in the last days (Revelation 12:12), which James felt had arrived. The king wrote Demonology *as a declaration of his intention to ferret out and punish witches in his realms, and at the same time he pushed through Parliament a comprehensive and draconian statute against any practice of magic.* Demonology *owes much to continental witchcraft theorists, but some of the themes are unique to James. Among the most important theses of the work is that all types of magic, whether learned or popular, amount to the same crime and merit the same punishment.*

James's treatise is in the form of a dialogue between Philomathes, who asks questions, and Epistemon, who answers them. In the excerpts below, Philomathes' questions are generally omitted because they are essentially repeated in Epistemon's responses.

Source: James I of England, *Daemonologie, in Form of a Dialogue, Divided into Three Bookes* (Edinburgh: Robert Walde-grave, 1597), preface, pp. 1–2, 5, 8–14, 66–69, 73–76, 80–81; rev. Martha Rampton.

The Preface: To the Reader

The fearful abounding at this time in this country of these detestable slaves of the Devil, the witches or enchanters, has moved me (beloved reader) to dispatch this following treatise of mine, not in any wise (as I protest) to serve for a show of my learning and ingenuity, but only (moved of conscience) to try thereby, so far as I can, to resolve the doubting hearts of many, both that such assaults of Satan are most certainly practiced and that the instruments thereof [witches] merit most severely to be punished. [This I assert] against the damnable opinions of, principally two in our age; the one called Scot, an Englishmen [Reginald Scot, c. 1538–1599], is not ashamed in public print to deny that there can be such a thing as witchcraft and so maintains the old error of the Sadducees [ancient Jewish sect or party]. The other called Wierus [Johann Weyer; (see doc. 69)], a German physician, sets out a public apology for all these craft-folks, whereby, procuring for their impunity, he plainly betrays himself to have been one of that profession. . . .

First Book

1. Epistemon: . . . [M]y first proposition is that there can be such a thing as witchcraft and witches. There are many more places in the Scriptures than [the case of the pythoness who, through circles and conjurations, sought to summon the dead Samuel, [1 Samuel 28; see doc. 2] (as I said before). As first in the law of God, it is plainly prohibited ["Thou shalt not suffer a witch to live" (Exodus 22:18)]. But certain it is that the law of God speaks nothing in vain, neither does it lay curses or enjoin punishments upon shadows condemning them to be ill, which do not exist in essence or being, as we call it. Secondly it is plain where wicked Pharaoh's wise men imitated a number of Moses' miracles to harden

the tyrant's heart thereby [Exodus 7–8; see doc. 1]. Thirdly, said not Samuel to Saul, "Disobedience is as the sin of witchcraft [1 Samuel 15]? To compare to a thing that does not exist is too absurd. Fourthly, was not Simon Magus a man of that craft? [Acts 8; see doc. 6] . . .

3. Epistemon: This word "magic" in the Persian tongue imports as much as to be a contemplator or interpreter of divine and heavenly sciences, which being first used among the Chaldeans—through their ignorance of the true divinity— was esteemed and reputed among them as a principal virtue and therefore was named unjustly in an honorable style, which name the Greeks imitated, and they generally imported all these kinds of unlawful arts. And this word "necromancy" is a Greek word compounded of νεκρός [*nekros*] and μαντεία [*manteia*], which is to say, prophecy by the dead. This last name is given to this black and unlawful science by the figure synecdoche, because it is a principal part of that art to serve themselves with dead carcasses in their divinations.

Surely the difference ordinary people put between them is very agreeable, and in a manner true; for they say that the witches are servants only and slaves to the Devil, but the necromancers are his masters and commanders. Yes, they may be, but it is only *secundum quid* [a simplistic view], for it is not by any power that they can have over him, but *ex pacto* [from the pact] whereby he obliges himself in some trifles to them so that he may, on the other part, obtain the fruition of their bodies and souls, which is the only thing he hunts for.

. . . There are two sorts of folks that may be enticed to this art, to wit, learned or unlearned. So are there two means which are the first temptations and feeders of their curiosity, thereby to make them give themselves over to their inquisitiveness, which I call the Devil's school and his rudiments. The learned have their curiosity wakened up and fed by that which I call their school: this is astrology. For diverse men, having attained to a great perfection in learning and yet remaining unaware (alas) of the spirit of regeneration and the fruits thereof— finding all natural things common to the stupid pedants as to themselves—they try to garner a greater name by not only knowing the course of things heavenly, but likewise to claim to the knowledge of things to come. Which, on the face of it appears lawful to them. In this respect, the basis of astrology seems to proceed from natural causes only. They are so allured thereby, that finding their practice to prove true in many things, they study to know the cause thereof, and so mounting from degree to degree, upon the slippery and uncertain scale of curiosity, they are at last enticed to the point that lawful arts or sciences fail to satisfy their restless minds, so they seek to that black and unlawful science of magic. Finding at the first that such various forms of circles and conjurations, rightly joined, will raise various forms of spirits, resolves them of their doubts. And attributing the doing thereof to the power inherent in the circles with many words of God wrapped in, they blindly glory of themselves, as if they had by their cleverness made a conquest of Pluto's dominion and become emperors over the Stygian habitat [underworld]. Where, in the meantime (miserable wretches) they have become in very deed, bond slaves to their mortal enemy. And their knowledge, for all that they presume thereof, has not increased, except in knowing evil and the horrors of hell for punishment, as Adam's was by eating of the forbidden tree (Genesis 3:6).

4. Epistemon: The Devil's rudiments, I call first, in general, all that which is called by the average person the power of word, herb, and stone, which is used by unlawful charms without natural causes. As likewise are all kind of practices, charms, or other like extraordinary actions which cannot abide the true touch of natural reason. I mean either by such kind of charms as commonly wives use for healing of [bewitched goats], for preserving them from evil eyes, and by knitting rune-trees [wands inscribed with arcane markings] or sundry kinds of herbs to the hair or tails of the goats. [Other charms are] curing the worm [illness] by stemming of blood, by healing of horse-crooks, by turning of the riddle [like a Ouija board], or doing of such like innumerable things by words, without applying anything appropriate to the part offended, as doctors do. [They also interfere with married couples who would naturally want sexual relations with each other] (by knitting so many knots upon a point at the time of their marriage) and such like things, which men do to practice their mischief. For unlearned men (being naturally curious and lacking the true knowledge of God) find these practices to prove true, as sundry of them will work by the power of the Devil for deceiving men, and not by any inherent power in these vain words and charms. . . .

There are two things which the learned have observed from the beginning in the science of the heavenly creatures, the planets, stars, and such like. The one is their course and ordinary motions, which for that cause is called astronomy, which word is a compound of νομος [nomos] and αστερων [asteron], that is to say "the law of the stars." And this art indeed is one of the categories of mathematics and, not only lawful, but most necessary and commendable. The other is called astrology, being compounded of αστερων and λογος, which is to say "the word and preaching of the stars," which is divided in two parts. The first consists of knowing thereby the powers of simples [simple medicines] and sicknesses, the course of the seasons, and the weather, being ruled by their influence, which is a kind of astrology, although it is not of itself a part of mathematics, yet it is not unlawful, being moderately used, but perhaps not so necessary and commendable as mathematics.

The second part is to trust so much to the influence of the stars, as thereby to foretell what commonwealths shall flourish or decay, what persons shall be fortunate or unfortunate, what side shall win in any battle, what man shall obtain victory at singular combat, what way and of what age shall men die, what horse shall win at match running, and diverse such like incredible things wherein Cardanus Cornelius Agrippa [see doc. 66] and diverse others have, more from curiosity than usefulness, written at large. Of this root last spoken of spring innumerable branches, such as knowledge by the nativities, chiromancy, geomancy, hydromancy, arithmancy, physiognomy [divination by the horoscope, palm reading, characteristics of the earth, water, numerology, and lines in the face] and a thousand others which were much practiced and held in great reverence by the pagans of old.

And this last part of astrology whereof I have spoken, which is the root of their branches, was called by them *pars fortuna* (fortune telling). This part is now utterly unlawful to be trusted in or practiced among Christians having no grounding in natural reason, and it is this which I called the Devil's school. . . .

Third Book

3. Epistemon: That abominable kind of devil abusing men or women was called of old *incubi* and *succubae*, according to the difference of the sexes that they conversed with. By two means this great kind of abuse might possibly be performed. The one is when the a devil, only as a spirit who has stolen the sperm of a dead body, abuses women in such a way, and they do not clearly see any shape or feel anything except the sensation in that part where they are being abused—as we read of a monastery of nuns who were burnt for being abused that way. The other means is when a devil borrows and inhabits a dead body and so is visible, and it seems to the one being abused that a man has sexual relations with her naturally. But it is to be noted that in whatsoever way he uses it, that sperm seems intolerably cold to the person abused. For if he steals it from a live person, it cannot be so quickly carried because it will lose both the strength and heat along the way, which it could never have had for lack of agitation, which in the time of procreation is the cause of these strength and heat. And if the spirit is occupying a dead body, the sperm it expels must likewise be cold by the participation with the qualities of the dead body out of which it comes. And whereas you inquire if these spirits be divided in sexes or not, I think the rules of philosophy may easily convince a man to the contrary. For it is a sure principle of philosophy that nothing can be divided into sexes except such living bodies as must have a natural seed to generate. But we know spirits have no seed proper to themselves, nor can they procreate.

These tales [of monsters born of *succubae*] are nothing but fables. For spirits have no semen of their own; . . . Indeed, it is possible for the craft of the Devil to make a woman's belly swell after he has abused her, which he may do either by stirring up her own humor [bodily fluids] or by herbs, as we see beggars daily do. And when the time of her delivery should come to make her labor in great anguish, as is natural, the Devil may subtly slip into the midwives' hands, sticks, stones, or some monstrous child brought from some other place. But this is more reported and guessed at by others, and not believed by me.

5. Epistemon: That fourth kind of spirits, which by the pagans was called Diana and her wandering court, and amongst us was called the fairies, or our good neighbors (as I told you), was one of the sorts of illusions that was rife in the time of the papistry [Catholicism]. For although it was odious to prophesy by the Devil, yet those whom these kind of spirits carried away were thought to be happiest and to have the best life. To speak of the many vain prattles founded upon that illusion: how there was a king and queen of fairies of such a jolly court and train, how they had a tithe and duty, as it were, of all goods, how they naturally rode and went, ate and drank, and did all other actions like natural men and women, I think it is like Virgil's Elysian Fields [resting place for heroic souls], not anything that ought to be believed by Christians, except in general. As I spoke many times before, the Devil deluded the senses of sundry simple creatures in making them believe that they saw and heard such things that were not real.

Philomathes: But how can it be, then, that sundry witches have gone to death with that confession, that they have been transported with the fairy to such a hill, which opening, they went in and there saw a fairy queen, who, being now lighter, gave them a stone that had sundry virtues, which at sundry times has been produced in judgment?

Epistemon: I say that, even as I said before of that imaginary rising of the spirit forth from the body, may not the Devil produce in their fantasy—their senses being dulled and, as it were, asleep—such hills and houses within them, such glistering courts and trains, and whatsoever such like he pleases to delude them, and in the meantime their bodies—being senseless—convey in their hand any stone or such like thing, which he makes them to imagine to have received in such a place? . . .

Philomathes: I would know now whether [fairies] may only appear to witches, or if they may also appear to any other.

Epistemon: They may do to both, to the innocent sort—either to scare them or to seem to be better than unclean spirits—and to the witches, to be a cover of safety for them so that ignorant magistrates may not punish them for it, as I told even now. But the first sort being troubled with them ought to be pitied, so ought the other sort (who may be discerned by their taking upon themselves to prophesy). That sort, I say, ought as severely to be punished as any other witches, and rather the more, because they deceive by their work.

Philomathes: And what makes the spirits have so different names from others.

Epistemon: Even the knavery of that same Devil; who deludes the necromancers with innumerable feigned names for him and his angels, especially making Satan, Beelzebub, and Lucifer to be three different spirits, where we find diverse names given to the prince of all the rebelling angels by the Scripture. By Christ, the prince of all the devils is called, Beelzebub, as I alleged when I spoke against the power of any heretics to cast out devils. . . .

6. Epistemon: . . . There are two good helps that may be used for [a witch's] trial. The one is the finding of their Devil's mark and trying the insensibility thereof. The other is their floating on the water, for, as in a secret murder if the dead carcass be at any time thereafter handled by the murderer, it will gush out blood, as if the blood were crying to the heaven for revenge of the murderer, God having appointed that secret supernatural sign for trial of that secret unnatural crime [see doc. 45]. So it appears that God has appointed (for a supernatural sign of the monstrous impiety of the witches) that the water shall refuse to receive in her bosom those who have shaken off the sacred water of baptism and willfully refused the benefit thereof. Their eyes are not even able to shed tears (threaten and torture them as you please) before they repent (God not permitting them to hide their obstinacy in so horrible a crime). Albeit the women especially are able otherwise to shed tears at every light occasion when they will, yea although it is deceptive like crocodile tears.

Questions: Why does King James think that Johann Weyer is a witch? James grounds his theories in biblical texts; which of them are traditional explanations that authors of the period used to argue that witchcraft was a sin? What is the difference between astronomy and astrology? When is astrology acceptable? Does James believe that generation is possible between a human and a demon? Diana is a persistent figure in the history of magic (see docs. 7 and 35), but what is her role in this document? If a "witch" is cast into the water, what will be the result? Why?

77. A MIDSUMMER NIGHT'S DREAM

William Shakespeare (1564–1616) wrote A Midsummer Night's Dream *sometime between 1590 and 1596, a few years before the production of* Macbeth *(see doc. 78), but in* A Midsummer Night's Dream *the nature of magic is very different; the fairies are delightful, the enchanted forest is whimsical, and potions and love spells are harmless. Puck, whose name is a derivation of hobgoblin, evil spirit, and witch's familiar, plays a major role in the play as a protagonist. He keeps company with Hecate and traffics with the goddess Diana, both of whom were traditionally powerful demons associated with sorcery, night flight, and wayward women.* A Midsummer Night's Dream *follows the tradition of romances like "Lanval" (see doc. 42) more than it does* Macbeth, *(see doc. 78), where magic is sinister and destructive and the witches who manipulate the occult are hideous denizens of the outdoors. When one keeps in mind the fact that* A Midsummer Night's Dream *was written in a period when thousands of people were being persecuted for taking to the forests at night to dance with demons and fairies and indulge in the same mischief to which Puck happily confesses, the light-hearted dependence on magic in the plot may be seen as puzzling.*

Source: William Shakespeare, *A Midsummer's Night Dream*, ed. Arthur Rackham (New York: Double-day, Page & Co., 1908), pp. 32, 34, 37–38, 40, 42, 44, 59–61, 65, 84–85, 96, 133.

A Midsummer's Night Dream

[The play is set in an enchanted wood on a moonlit night. When the scene opens, the fairy king, Oberon, and his queen, Titania, are having a tiff over possession of one of Titania's changelings, which is the offspring of a fairy, elf, or troll who has been left in the place of a human baby stolen from its family [see doc. 48]. Oberon, angry with his wife, decides to punish her and calls on Robin Puck Goodfellow, the woodland sprite and consummate trickster. Oberon asks Puck to concoct a magical liquid from the flower called "love-in-idleness," which when applied to the eyes of a person sleeping, causes that person to fall in love with the first creature he or she encounters on waking].

Act 2, Scene 1

OBERON [speaking to Puck]: That very time I saw . . . Cupid's fiery shaft
Quench'd in the chaste beams of the watery moon,
And the imperial votaress passed on,
In maiden meditation, fancy-free.
Yet mark'd I where the bolt of Cupid fell:
It fell upon a little western flower,
Before milk-white, now purple with love's wound,
And maidens call it "love-in-idleness."
Fetch me that flower; the herb I shew'd thee once:
The juice of it on sleeping eyelids laid
Will make or man or woman madly dote
Upon the next live creature that it sees.
Fetch me this herb; and be thou here again
Ere the leviathan can swim a league.

PUCK: I'll put a girdle round about the earth
In forty minutes. (Exit)

OBERON: Having once this juice,
I'll watch Titania when she is asleep,
And drop the liquor of it in her eyes.
The next thing then she waking looks upon,
Be it on lion, bear, or wolf, or bull,
On meddling monkey, or on busy ape,
She shall pursue it with the soul of love:

And ere I take this charm from off her sight,
As I can take it with another herb,
I'll make her render up her [changeling] to me. . . .

(Enter Puck)

SCENE 2

OBERON: Hast thou the flower there? Welcome, wanderer.

PUCK: Ay, there it is.

OBERON: I pray thee, give it me.
I know a bank where the wild thyme blows,
Where oxlips and the nodding violet grows,
Quite over-canopied with luscious woodbine,
With sweet musk-roses and with eglantine:
There sleeps Titania sometime of the night,
Lull'd in these flowers with dances and delight;
And there the snake throws her enamell'd skin,
Weed wide enough to wrap a fairy in:
And with the juice of this I'll streak her eyes,
And make her full of hateful fantasies.
Take thou some of it, and seek through this grove: . . .

PUCK: Fear not, my lord, your servant shall do so. (Exit)

Act 2

SCENE 2: ANOTHER PART OF THE WOOD. ENTER TITANIA, WITH HER TRAIN.

TITANIA: Come, now a roundel and a fairy song;
. . . Sing in our sweet lullaby;
Lulla, lulla, lullaby, lulla, lulla, lullaby:
Never harm,
Nor spell nor charm,
Come our lovely lady nigh;
So, good night, with lullaby. . . .

A FAIRY: Hence, away! Now all is well:
One aloof stand sentinel.

(Exit Fairies. Titania sleeps. Enter Oberon and squeezes
the juice of the flower on Titania's eyelids.)

401

OBERON: What thou seest when thou dost wake,
Do it for thy true-love take,
Love and languish for his sake:
Be it ounce, or cat, or bear,
Pard [panther], or boar with bristled hair,
In thy eye that shall appear
When thou wakest, it is thy dear:
Wake when some vile thing is near. (Exit)

[A man named Bottom who has the hideous head of
an ass wanders into the grove where Titania is sleeping.]

Act 3

SCENE 1: (TITANIA AWAKING FROM HER NAP)

TITANIA: What angel wakes me from my flowery bed?

BOTTOM: (Sings) The finch, the sparrow and the lark,
The plain-song cuckoo grey, . . .

TITANIA: I pray thee, gentle mortal, sing again:
Mine ear is much enamour'd of thy note;
So is mine eye enthralled to thy shape;
And thy fair virtue's force perforce doth move me
On the first view to say, to swear, I love thee.

BOTTOM: Methinks, mistress, you should have little reason
for that: and yet, to say the truth, reason and
love keep little company together now-a-days; the
more the pity that some honest neighbours will not
make them friends. Nay, I can gleek [joke] upon occasion.

TITANIA: Thou art as wise as thou art beautiful.

BOTTOM: Not so, neither: but if I had wit enough to get out
of this wood, I have enough to serve mine own turn.

TITANIA: Out of this wood do not desire to go:
Thou shalt remain here, whether thou wilt or no.
I am a spirit of no common rate;
The summer still doth tend upon my state;
And I do love thee: therefore, go with me;
I'll give thee fairies to attend on thee,
And they shall fetch thee jewels from the deep,
And sing while thou on pressed flowers dost sleep:

And I will purge thy mortal grossness so
That thou shalt like an airy spirit go. . . .

SCENE 2: ANOTHER PART OF THE WOOD. ENTER OBERON.

OBERON: I wonder if Titania be awaked;
Then, what it was that next came in her eye,
Which she must dote on in extremity.

(Enter Puck)

Here comes my messenger.
How now, mad spirit!
What night-rule now about this haunted grove?

PUCK: My mistress with a monster is in love. . . .

   [Oberon is pleased with the effect the potion has had on his queen,
     but Puck reminds him that their antics in the woods cannot
       last much longer because day is breaking.]

PUCK: My fairy lord, . . . night's swift dragons cut the clouds full fast,
And yonder shines Aurora's harbinger;
At whose approach, ghosts, wandering here and there,
Troop home to churchyards: damned spirits all,
That in crossways and floods have burial,
Already to their wormy beds are gone;
For fear lest day should look their shames upon,
They willfully themselves exile from light
And must for aye consort with block-brow'd night.

OBERON: But we are spirits of another sort . . . .

Act 4

SCENE I

OBERON: . . . I will release the fairy queen.
Be as thou wast wont to be;
See as thou wast wont to see:
Dian's bud o'er Cupid's flower
Hath such force and blessed power.
Now, my Titania; wake you, my sweet queen.

TITANIA: My Oberon! what visions I have seen!
Methough I was enamour'd of an ass.

Act 5

SCENE I: (ENTER PUCK)

PUCK: If we shadows have offended,
Think but this, and all is mended,
That you have but slumber'd here
While these visions did appear.
And this weak and idle theme,
No more yielding but a dream . . .

Questions: What does Oberon mean when he says "We are spirits of another sort?" (3.2).
What is the tone of the play? What role might Puck's final speech in the play accomplish?
What potential "problem" does his speech address?

78. SHAKESPEARE'S WITCHES: *MACBETH*

Many scholars consider Macbeth Shakespeare's (1564–1616) most pessimistic play, given
how malicious forces conspire against Macbeth and his kingdom as the witches' prophecies
and conjuring drive the plot. The "weird sisters" are painted with great precision, reflect-
ing the contemporary concept of the old, vile witch—a depraved and heinous hag able to
prophesy through perverse rituals and apparitions. It is likely that Shakespeare was drawing
on a triad of supernatural beings that in earlier literature were clairvoyant goddesses honored
for their ability to see into the future. Hecate (see doc. 8), the three-faced goddess of the clas-
sical era, also makes an appearance as the airy mistress of witches, spirits, and the moon.

Macbeth was commissioned by the King's Men of the court of James I, whose views on magic
were well known; James wrote Demonology denouncing witchcraft and, in effect, launched a
witch-hunt in Scotland in 1590 (see docs. 74, 76). Shakespeare may well have portrayed the weird
sisters as stereotypical witches, in part to suit the proclivities of his patron, the king.

Source: William Shakespeare, *Macbeth*, ed. Richard Grant White, Riverside Literature Series, vol. 106
(Boston: Houghton, Mifflin & Company, 1897), pp. 7, 11–14, 60–61, 63–69.

MACBETH

Act 1

SCENE 1: A DESERT PLACE. THUNDER AND LIGHTNING. ENTER THREE WITCHES.

FIRST WITCH: When shall we three meet again?
In thunder, lightning, or in rain?

SECOND WITCH: When the hurlyburly's done,
When the battle's lost and won.

THIRD WITCH: That will be ere the set of sun.

FIRST WITCH: Where the place?

SECOND WITCH: Upon the heath.

THIRD WITCH: There to meet with Macbeth.

FIRST WITCH: I come, Graymalkin!

SECOND WITCH: Paddock calls.

THIRD WITCH: Anon.

ALL: Fair is foul, and foul is fair;
Hover through the fog and filthy air.

> [Two nobles, Macbeth and Banquo, having come
> from success in battle, encounter the witches as they
> cross the moor.]

SCENE 3: THUNDER. ENTER THE THREE WITCHES.

FIRST WITCH: Where hast thou been, sister?

SECOND WITCH: Killing swine.

THIRD WITCH: Sister, where thou?

FIRST WITCH: A sailor's wife had chestnuts in her lap,
And munch'd, and munch'd, and munch'd: —
'Give me,' quoth I:
'Aroint thee, witch!' the rump-fed ronyon cries.
Her husband's to Aleppo gone, master o' the Tiger:
But in a sieve I'll thither sail,
And, like a rat without a tail,
I'll do, I'll do, and I'll do. . . .

THIRD WITCH: A drum, a drum!
Macbeth doth come.

ALL: The weird sisters, hand in hand,
Posters of the sea and land,
Thus do go about, about:
Thrice to thine and thrice to mine

And thrice again, to make up nine.
Peace! the charm's wound up.

(Enter Macbeth and Banquo)

MACBETH: So foul and fair a day I have not seen.

BANQUO: How far is't call'd to Forres? What are these
So wither'd and so wild in their attire,
That look not like the inhabitants o' th' earth,
And yet are on't? Live you? or are you aught
That man may question? You seem to understand me,
By each at once her chappy finger laying
Upon her skinny lips: you should be women,
And yet your beards forbid me to interpret
That you are so.

MACBETH: Speak, if you can: what are you?

FIRST WITCH: All hail, Macbeth! hail to thee, thane of Glamis!

SECOND WITCH: All hail, Macbeth! hail to thee, thane of Cawdor!

THIRD WITCH: All hail, Macbeth, thou shalt be king hereafter!

BANQUO: Good sir, why do you start; and seem to fear
Things that do sound so fair? (to the witches) I' the name of truth,
Are ye fantastical, or that indeed
Which outwardly ye show? My noble partner
You greet with present grace and great prediction
Of noble having and of royal hope,
That he seems rapt withal: to me you speak not.
If you can look into the seeds of time,
And say which grain will grow and which will not,
Speak then to me, who neither beg nor fear
Your favours nor your hate.

FIRST WITCH: Hail!

SECOND WITCH: Hail!

THIRD WITCH: Hail!

FIRST WITCH: Lesser than Macbeth, and greater.

SECOND WITCH: Not so happy, yet much happier.

THIRD WITCH: Thou shalt get kings, though thou be none:
So all hail, Macbeth and Banquo!

FIRST WITCH: Banquo and Macbeth, all hail!

MACBETH: Stay, you imperfect speakers, tell me more:
By Sinel's death I know I am thane of Glamis;
But how of Cawdor? the thane of Cawdor lives,
A prosperous gentleman; and to be king
Stands not within the prospect of belief,
No more than to be Cawdor. Say from whence
You owe this strange intelligence? or why
Upon this blasted heath you stop our way
With such prophetic greeting? Speak, I charge you.

(Witches vanish)

BANQUO: The earth hath bubbles, as the water has,
And these are of them. Whither are they vanish'd?

MACBETH: Into the air; and what seem'd corporal melted
As breath into the wind. Would they had stay'd!

BANQUO: Were such things here as we do speak about?
Or have we eaten on the insane root
That takes the reason prisoner? . . .

[Soon Macbeth is named thane of Cawdor, and after that he kills
the king and is himself crowned. Fearful of the witches' prophecy that Banquo's heirs will seize the throne, Macbeth hires a group of mercenaries to kill
Banquo, but his son escapes.]

Act 3

SCENE 5: A HEATH. THUNDER. ENTER THE THREE WITCHES MEETING HECATE.

FIRST WITCH: Why, how now, Hecate! you look angerly.

HECATE: Have I not reason, beldams as you are,
Saucy and overbold? How did you dare
To trade and traffic with Macbeth
In riddles and affairs of death;
And I, the mistress of your charms,
The close contriver of all harms,
Was never call'd to bear my part,
Or show the glory of our art?
And, which is worse, all you have done
Hath been but for a wayward son,

Spiteful and wrathful, who, as others do,
Loves for his own ends, not for you.
But make amends now: get you gone,
And at the pit of Acheron
Meet me i' the morning: thither he
Will come to know his destiny:
Your vessels and your spells provide,
Your charms and everything beside.
I am for the air; this night I'll spend
Unto a dismal and a fatal end:
Great business must be wrought ere noon:
Upon the corner of the moon
There hangs a vapourous drop profound;
I'll catch it ere it come to ground:
And that distill'd by magic sleights
Shall raise such artificial sprites
As by the strength of their illusion
Shall draw him on to his confusion:
He shall spurn fate, scorn death, and bear
His hopes 'bove wisdom, grace and fear:
And you all know, security
Is mortals' chiefest enemy.

                (Music and a song within: 'Come away, come away,')

Hark! I am call'd; my little spirit, see,
Sits in a foggy cloud, and stays for me.

                                       (Exit)

FIRST WITCH: Come, let's make haste; she'll soon be back again.

        [Macbeth's kingship incites increasing resistance from his nobles, who are led by Macduff. Frightened, Macbeth visits the witches in their cavern to hear the future prophesied, as Hecate had predicted he would.]

Act 4

SCENE 1: A CAVERN. IN THE MIDDLE, A BOILING CAULDRON. THUNDER. ENTER THE THREE WITCHES.

FIRST WITCH: Thrice the brinded cat hath mew'd.

SECOND WITCH: Thrice and once the hedge-pig whined.

THIRD WITCH: Harpier cries 'Tis time, 'tis time.

FIRST WITCH: Round about the cauldron go;
In the poison'd entrails throw.
Toad, that under cold stone
Days and nights has thirty-one
Swelter'd venom sleeping got,
Boil thou first i' th' charmed pot.

ALL: Double, double toil and trouble;
Fire burn, and cauldron bubble.

SECOND WITCH: Fillet of a fenny snake,
In the cauldron boil and bake;
Eye of newt and toe of frog,
Wool of bat and tongue of dog,
Adder's fork and blind-worm's sting,
Lizard's leg and owlet's wing,
For a charm of powerful trouble,
Like a hell-broth boil and bubble.

ALL: Double, double toil and trouble;
Fire burn and cauldron bubble.

THIRD WITCH: Scale of dragon, tooth of wolf,
Witches' mummy, maw and gulf
Of the ravin'd salt-sea shark,
Root of hemlock digg'd i' th' dark,
Liver of blaspheming Jew,
Gall of goat, and slips of yew
Silver'd in the moon's eclipse,
Nose of Turk and Tartar's lips,
Finger of birth-strangled babe
Ditch-deliver'd by a drab,
Make the gruel thick and slab:
Add thereto a tiger's chaudron,
For the ingredients of our cauldron.

ALL: Double, double toil and trouble;
Fire burn and cauldron bubble.

SECOND WITCH: Cool it with a baboon's blood,
Then the charm is firm and good.

(Enter Hecate to the other three witches)

HECATE: O well done! I commend your pains;
And every one shall share i' th' gains;

And now about the cauldron sing,
Live elves and fairies in a ring,
Enchanting all that you put in.

(Hecate retires)

SECOND WITCH: By the pricking of my thumbs,
Something wicked this way comes.
Open, locks,
Whoever knocks!

(Enter Macbeth)

MACBETH: How now, you secret, black, and midnight hags!
What is't you do?

ALL: A deed without a name.

MACBETH: I conjure you, by that which you profess,
Howe'er you come to know it, answer me. . . .

FIRST WITCH: Speak.

SECOND WITCH: Demand.

THIRD WITCH: We'll answer.

FIRST WITCH: Say, if thou'dst rather hear it from our mouths,
Or from our masters?

MACBETH: Call 'em; let me see 'em.

FIRST WITCH: Pour in sow's blood, that hath eaten
Her nine farrow; grease that's sweaten
From the murderer's gibbet throw
Into the flame.

ALL: Come, high or low;
Thyself and office deftly show!

(Thunder. First Apparition: an armed head)

MACBETH: Tell me, thou unknown power—

FIRST WITCH: He knows thy thought:
Hear his speech, but say thou nought.

FIRST APPARITION: Macbeth! Macbeth! Macbeth! beware Macduff;
Beware the thane of Fife. Dismiss me. Enough. (descends)

MACBETH: Whate'er thou art, for thy good caution, thanks;
Thou hast harp'd my fear aright: but one
word more, —

FIRST WITCH: He will not be commanded: here's another,
More potent than the first.

> (Thunder. Second Apparition: a bloody child)

SECOND APPARITION: Macbeth! Macbeth! Macbeth!

MACBETH: Had I three ears, I'd hear thee.

SECOND APPARITION: Be bloody, bold, and resolute; laugh to scorn
The power of man, for none of woman born
Shall harm Macbeth.

MACBETH: Then live, Macduff: what need I fear of thee?
But yet I'll make assurance double sure,
And take a bond of fate: thou shalt not live;
That I may tell pale-hearted fear it lies,
And sleep in spite of thunder.

> (Thunder. Third Apparition: a child crowned, with a tree in his hand)

What is this
That rises like the issue of a king,
And wears upon his baby-brow the round
And top of sovereignty?

ALL: Listen, but speak not to't.

THIRD APPARITION: Be lion-mettled, proud; and take no care
Who chafes, who frets, or where conspirers are:
Macbeth shall never vanquish'd be until
Great Birnam wood to high Dunsinane hill
Shall come against him.

MACBETH: That will never be
Who can impress the forest, bid the tree
Unfix his earth-bound root? Sweet bodements! good!
Rebellion's head, rise never till the wood
Of Birnam rise, and our high-placed Macbeth
Shall live the lease of nature, pay his breath
To time and mortal custom. Yet my heart
Throbs to know one thing: tell me, if your art

Can tell so much: shall Banquo's issue ever
Reign in this kingdom?

ALL: Seek to know no more.

MACBETH: I will be satisfied: deny me this,
And an eternal curse fall on you! Let me know.
Why sinks that cauldron? and what noise is this?

(Hautboys [instruments similar to the modern oboe])

FIRST WITCH: Show!

SECOND WITCH: Show!

THIRD WITCH: Show!

ALL: Show his eyes, and grieve his heart;
Come like shadows, so depart!

(A show of eight kings, the last with a glass in his hand;
Ghost of Banquo following)

MACBETH: Thou art too like the spirit of Banquo: down!
Thy crown does sear mine eyeballs. And thy hair,
Thou other gold-bound brow, is like the first.
A third is like the former. Filthy hags!
Why do you show me this? A fourth! Start, eyes!
What, will the line stretch out to the crack of doom?
Another yet! A seventh! I'll see no more:
And yet the eighth appears, who bears a glass
Which shows me many more; and some I see
That twofold balls and treble scepters carry:
Horrible sight! Now, I see, 'tis true;
For the blood-bolter'd Banquo smiles upon me,
And points at them for his.

(Apparitions vanish)

What, is this so?

FIRST WITCH: Ay, sir, all this is so: but why
Stands Macbeth thus amazedly?
Come, sisters, cheer we up his sprites,
And show the best of our delights:
I'll charm the air to give a sound,

While you perform your antic round:
That this great king may kindly say,
Our duties did his welcome pay.

(Music. The witches dance and then vanish, with Hecate)

MACBETH: Where are they? Gone? Let this pernicious hour
Stand aye accursed in the calendar!
Come in, without there!

[The witches' prophecies prove true. The soldiers of the
opposing army advance shielding themselves with boughs cut
from Birnam Wood, and Macbeth is killed by Macduff who was "not of
woman born," but taken by caesarian section.]

*Questions: How do the "weird sisters" conduct their divination? Is their method particular
to women? Why is Hecate in the play? What is her role? Which elements of the witches'
brew are stereotypes in the early seventeenth century?*

79. A JACOBEAN COMEDY

*The Witch is a tragicomedy written by Thomas Middleton (1580–1627) around 1610.
The play was well known in theatrical circles (even though it did not have a long run)
because the King's Men acting company performed it at the popular Blackfriars Theatre
in London and Middleton was a revered playwright in his own time. In* The Witch, *
Middleton pulls in virtually every contemporary stereotype of witches and witchcraft;
for example, the names and personalities of the male witches are the same as those
identified in Jean Bodin's treatise,* Demon-Mania *(see doc. 72). The plot rests on
characters that reflect the very long shadow of particular personas associated with magic
since the classical period. Hecate is one of those personalities, but she is portrayed quite
differently in* The Witch *than she is in* Macbeth *(see doc. 78). Almost certainly
Middleton meant the representation of the witches to be farcical and likely employed
the motif because the inclusion of witches in shows of the time was a crowd-pleaser. All
the same, the traits of the witches upon which the play draws were taken seriously by
most of the population.*

Source: Thomas Middleton, *The Witch*, ed. Elizabeth Shafer (London: A & C Black Limited, 1944),
pp. 12–24, 55–59.

The Witch

[The play opens with Sebastian, who was reported to have been killed in battle.
His fiancé Isabella subsequently becomes engaged to the nobleman, Antonio.

Sebastian unexpectedly returns home from battle and is desperate to regain Isabella's hand. He determines to acquire a love charm from Hecate, leader of the local brood of witches.]

Act 1

SCENE 2 [WITCHES' FOREST HAUNT]

HECATE: Titty and Tiffin, Suckin and Pidgen, Liard and Robin, white spirits, black spirits, grey spirits, red spirits, Devil-toad, Devil-ram, Devil-cat and Devil dam [mother]. Why Hoppo and Stadlin, Hellwain and Puckle.

STADLIN: (Within) Here, sweating at the vessel.

HECATE: Boil it well.

HOPPO: (Within) It gallops now.

HECATE: Are the flames blue enough? Or shall I use a little seeton [wisps of thread] more?

STADLIN: (Within) The nips of fairies upon maids' white hips are not more perfect azure.

HECATE: Tend it carefully. Send Stadlin to me with a brazen dish that I may fall to work upon these serpents and squeeze 'em ready for the second hour. Why when?

STADLIN: Here's Stadlin and the dish.

HECATE: There, take this unbaptized brat, (gives Stadlin a dead baby) boil it well, preserve the fat; you know 'tis precious to transfer our 'nointed flesh into the air in moonlight nights, o'er steeple tops, mountains and pine trees, that, like pricks or stops [dots] seem to our height—high towers and roofs of princes like wrinkles in the earth. Whole provinces appear to our sight then even leek [like] a russet mole upon some lady's cheek. When hundred leagues in the air we feast and sing, dance, kiss, and coll [embrace]; use everything. What young man can we wish to pleasure us. But we enjoy him in an *incubus*? Thou know'st it Stadlin?

STADLIN: Usually that's done.

HECATE: Last night thou got'st the mayor of Whelplie's son. I knew him by his black cloak lined with yellow; I think thou'st spoiled the youth; he's but seventeen; I'll have him the next mounting. Away, in! Go feed the vessel for the second hour.

STADLIN: Where be the magical herbs?

HECATE: They're down his throat; his mouth crammed full, his ears and nostrils stuffed. . . .

STADLIN: Then there's all Hecate.

HECATE: Is the heart of wax stuck full of magic needles?

STADLIN: 'Tis done Hecate.

HECATE: And is the farmer's picture and his wife's laid down to th'fire yet?

STADLIN: They're a-roasting both, too.

HECATE: Good. (Exit Stadlin) Then their marrows are a-melting subtly, and three months' sickness sucks up life in'em. They denied me often flour, barm [beer] and milk, goose grease and tar, when I ne'er hurt their charmings [churning butter], their brew-locks, nor their batches, nor forespoke any of their breedings. Now I'll be meet with 'em. Seven of their younger pigs I've bewitched already, of the last litter, nine ducklings, thirteen goslings, and a hog fell lame last Sunday after evensong too, and mark how their sheep prosper or what sop [milk] each milch-kine [milk cow] gives to th' pail. I'll send those snakes; shall milk 'em all beforehand. The dewed-skirted dairy wenches shall stroke dry dugs for this and go home cursing. I'll mar their syllabubs [curdled milk] and frothy feastings under cows' bellies with the parish youths. Where's Firestone? Our son Firestone!

FIRESTONE: Here am I mother.

HECATE: Take in this brazen dish full of dear ware. Thou shalt have all when I die, and that will be even just at twelve o'clock at night come three year.

FIRESTONE: And may you not have one o'clock into th' dozen, mother?

HECATE: No.

FIRESTONE: Your spirits are then more unconscionable than bakers; you'll have lived then, mother, six-score year to the hundred. And methinks after six-score years the Devil might give you a cast [chance], for he's a fruiterer too and has been from the beginning; the first apple that e'er was eaten came through his fingers. The costermonger's [vendor of fruit and vegetables], then, I hold to be the ancientest trade, though some would have the tailor pricked down before him.

HECATE: Go, and take heed you shed not by the way. The hour must have her portion, 'tis dear syrup; each charmed drop is able to confound [kill] a family consisting of nineteen or one-and-twenty feeders.

FIRESTONE: (Aside) Marry, here's stuff indeed! Dear syrup call you it? A little thing would make me give you a wip on't in a posset [hot drink of curdled milk] and cut you three years shorter.

HECATE: Thou'rt now about some villainy?

FIRESTONE: Not I forsooth. (Aside) Truly the Devil's in her, I think. How one villain smells out another straight! There's no knavery but is nosed like a dog and can smell out a dog's meaning. (To Hecate) Mother I pray give me leave to ramble abroad tonight with the Nightmare, for I have a great mind to overlay a fat parson's daughter.

HECATE: And who shall lie with me then?

FIRESTONE: The great cat for one night mother. 'Tis but a night; make shift with him for once.

HECATE: You're a kind son! But 'tis the nature of you all, I see that. You had rather hunt after strange women still than lie with your own mothers. Get thee gone. Sweat thy six ounces out about the vessel and thou shalt play at midnight. The Nightmare shall call thee when it walks.

FIRESTONE: Thanks, most sweet mother. (Exit)
(Enter Sebastian [who is seeking out a love charm to make Antonio impotent])

HECATE: Urchins, elves, hags, satyrs, pans, fauns, Silens, Kit-with-the-candlestick, tritons, centaurs, dwarves, imps, the Spoorn, the Mare, the Man i'th'oak, the Hell-wain, the Fire-drake, the Puckle. A ab hur hus [various goblins].

SEBASTIAN: (Aside) Heaven knows with what unwillingness and hate I enter this damned place. But such extremes of wrongs in love fight 'gainst religious knowledge, that were I led by this disease to deaths as numberless as creatures that must die, I could not shun the way. I know what 'tis to pity madmen now. They're wretched things that ever were created if they be of woman's making and her faithless vows. I fear [Isabelle and Antonio] are now a-kissing. What's o'clock? 'Tis now but supper-time, but night will come, and all new-married couples make short suppers. (To Hecate) Whate'er thou art, I have no spare time to fear thee; my horrors are so strong and great already that thou seem'st nothing. Up and laze not. Hadst thou my business, thou couldst ne'er sit so; 'Twould firk [jerk] thee into air a thousand mile beyond thy ointments. I would I were read so much in thy black power as mine own griefs. I'm in great need of help; wilt give me any?

HECATE: Thy boldness takes me bravely. We're all sworn to sweat for such a spirit. See, I regard thee; I rise and bid thee welcome. What's thy wish now?

SEBASTIAN: Oh my heart swells with't. I must take breath first.

HECATE: Is't to confound some enemy on the seas? It may be done tonight. Stadlin's within; she raises all your sudden, ruinous storms that shipwreck barks [boats] and tears up growing oaks, flies over houses and takes *Anno Domini* [plaque with the year the house was built] out of a rich man's chimney—a sweet place for't! He would be hanged ere he would set his own years there; they must be chambered in a five-pound picture, a green silk curtain drawn before the eyes on't, his rotten diseased years. Or dost thou envy the fat prosperity of any neighbor? I'll call forth Hoppo and her incantation can straight destroy the young of all his cattle, blast vineyards, orchards, meadows, or in one night transport his dung, hay, corn, by ricks—whole stacks, into thine own ground.

SEBASTIAN: This would come most richly now to many a country grazier, but my envy lies not so low as cattle, corn, or vines; 'twill trouble your best powers to give me ease.

HECATE: It is to starve up generation? To strike a barrenness in man or woman?

SEBASTIAN: Hah!

HECATE: Hah? Did you feel me there? I knew your grief.

SEBASTIAN: Can there be such things done?

HECATE: Are these the skins of serpents? These of snakes?

SEBASTIAN: I see they are. (Hecate gives them to Sebastian.)

HECATE: So sure into what house these are conveyed; knit with these charmed and retentive knots; neither the man begets nor woman breeds, no, nor performs the least desires of wedlock, being then a mutual duty. I could give thee *chiroconita, adincatida, archimadon, marmaritin, calicia* [all poisons], which I could sort to villainous barren ends. But this leads the same way. More I could instance, as the same needles thrust into their pillows that sows and socks up dead men in their sheets, a privy gristle [phallus] of a man that hangs after sunset. Good, excellent! Yet all's there sir.

SEBASTIAN: You could not do a man that special kindness, to part 'em utterly now? Could you do that?

HECATE: No, time must do't. We cannot disjoin wedlock; 'tis of heaven's fastening. Well may we raise jars, jealousies, strifes and heart-burning disagreements like a thick scurf o'er life, as did our master upon that patient miracle [the biblical Job], but [marriage] itself our power cannot disjoint.

SEBASTIAN: I depart happy in what I have then, being constrained to this. (Aside) And grant, you greater powers that dispose men, that I may never need this hag again! (Exit)

HECATE: I know he loves me not, nor there's no hope on't; 'Tis for the love of mischief I do this, and that we're sworn to, the first oath we take.

(Enter Firestone)

FIRESTONE: Oh mother, mother!

HECATE: What's the news with thee now?

FIRESTONE: There's the bravest young gentleman within and the fineliest drunk; I thought he would have fallen into the vessel. He stumbled at a pipkin [pot] of child's grease, reeled against Stadlin, overthrew her and, in the tumbling-cast, struck up old Puckle's heels with her clothes over her ears.

HECATE: Hoyday!

FIRESTONE: I was fain to throw the cat upon her to save her honesty [modesty], and all little enough. I cried out still "I pray to be covered!" See where he come now mother.

(Enter Almachildes [Looking for a love charm in order to seduce a woman.])

ALMACHILDES: Call you these witches? They be tumblers, methinks, very flat tumblers.

HECATE: 'Tis Almachildes—fresh blood stirs in me—the man that I have lusted to enjoy. I have had him thrice in *incubus* already.

ALMACHILDES: Is your name Goody Hag?

HECATE: 'Tis anything. Call me the horrid'st and unhallowed'st things that life and nature trembles at; for thee I'll be the same. Thou com'st for a love-charm now?

ALMACHILDES: Why thou'rt a witch I think.

HECATE: Thou shalt have choice of twenty, wet or dry.

ALMACHILDES: Nay, let's have dry ones.

HECATE: If thou wilt use't by way of cup and potion; I'll give thee a remora shall bewitch her straight.

ALMACHILDES: A remora? What's that?

HECATE: A little suck-stone; some call it a sea-lamprey, a small fish.

ALMACHILDES: And must't be buttered?

HECATE: The bones of a green frog too, wondrous precious, the flesh consumed by pismires [ants].

ALMACHILDES: Pismires? Give me a chamber pot!

FIRESTONE: (Aside) You shall see him go nigh to be so unmannerly; he'll make water before my mother anon.

ALMACHILDES: And now you talk of frogs; I have somewhat here; I come not empty pocketed from a banquet. I learned that of my haberdasher's wife. Look Goody Witch, there's a toad in marchpane for you. (Gives it to Hecate)

HECATE: Oh sir, you've fitted me.

ALMACHILDES: And here's a spawn or two of the same paddock-brood [frogs] too for your son. (Gives it to Firestone)

FIRESTONE: I thank your worship sir. How comes your handkercher so sweetly thus berayed? Sure 'tis wet sucket sir.

ALMACHILDES: 'Tis nothing but the syrup the toad spit. Take all I prithee.

HECATE: This was kindly done sir, and you shall sup with me tonight for this.

ALMACHILDES: How? Sup with thee? Dost think I'll eat fried rats and pickled spiders?

HECATE: No; I can command, sir, the best meat i'th' whole province for my friends, and reverently served in too.

ALMACHILDES: How?

HECATE: In good fashion.

ALMACHILDES: Let me but see that, and I'll sup with you.
(She conjures and enter Malkin, a spirit like a cat playing on a fiddle, and spirits with meat)

The cat and fiddle? An excellent ordinary [pub]. You had a devil once in a fox-skin.

HECATE: Oh I have him still. Come walk with me sir. (Exit, all but Firestone)

FIRESTONE: How apt and ready is a drunkard now to reel to the Devil! Well I'll even in and see how he eats, and I'll be hanged if I be not the fatter of the twain with laughing at him. (Exit)
[Hecate's charm works, and as a result, Antonio is unable to consummate his marriage with Isabella; all he can think to do is drink chicken broth—a cure for impotence.]

Act 3

SCENE 3: (ENTER HECATE, WITCHES: STADLIN, PUCKLE, HOPPO, HELLWAIN, AND FIRESTONE IN THE BACKGROUND CARRYING EGGS AND HERBS)

HECATE: The moon's a gallant; see how brisk she rides.

STADLIN: Here's a rich evening, Hecate.

HECATE: Ay, is't not, wenches, to take a journey of five thousand mile?

HOPPO: Ours will be more tonight.

HECATE: Oh 'twill be precious. Heard you the owl yet?

STADLIN: Briefly in the copse as we came through now.

HECATE: 'Tis high time for us then.

STADLIN: There was a bat hung at my lips three times as we came through the woods, and drank her fill, old Puckle saw her.

HECATE: You are fortunate still; the very screech-owl lights upon your shoulder and wooes you like a pigeon. Are you furnished? Have you your ointments?

STADLIN: All.

HECATE: Prepare to flight then. I'll overtake you swiftly.

STADLIN: Hie [hasten] thee Hecate. We shall be up betimes.

HECATE: I'll reach you quickly. (Exit all witches except Hecate)

FIRESTONE: [Aside] They're all going a-birding tonight. They talk of fowls i'th' air that fly by day; I am sure they'll be a company of foul sluts there tonight. If we have not morality after it, I'll be hanged, for they are able to putrefy it, to infect a whole region. She spies me now.

HECATE: What, Firestone, our sweet son?

FIRESTONE: [Aside] A little sweeter than some of you or a dunghill were too good for me.

HECATE: How much hast here?

FIRESTONE: Nineteen, and all brave plump ones, besides six lizard's and three serpentine eggs.

HECATE: Dear and sweet boy; what herbs hast thou?

FIRESTONE: I have some marmartin and mandrake.

HECATE: *Marmaritin* and *mandragora* thou wouldst say. Here's *panax* too; I thank thee.

FIRESTONE: My pan aches I am sure with kneeling down to cut 'em.

HECATE: And *selago*, hedge-hyssop too. How near he goes my cuttings! Were they all cropped by moonlight?

FIRESTONE: Every blade of 'em, or I am a moon-calf [idiot] mother.

HECATE: Hie thee home with 'em. Look well to the house tonight; I am for aloft.

FIRESTONE: (Aside) Aloft, quoth you? I would you would break your neck once that I might have all [my inheritance] quickly! (Music) (To Hecate) Hark, hark, mother! They are above the steeple already, flying over your head with a noise of musicians.

HECATE: They are there indeed. Help, help me; I'm too late else.

(VOICES OF WITCHES IN THE AIR): Come away, come away; Hecate, Hecate, come away.

HECATE: I come, I come, I come, I come, with all the speed I may, with all the speed I may. Where's Stadlin?

STADLIN: (In the air) Here.

HECATE: Where's Puckle?

PUCKLE: (In the air) Here. And Hoppo too and Hellwain too; we lack but you, we lack but you. Come away; make up the count.

HECATE: I will but 'noint and then I mount. (Voices of witches above) There's one comes down to fetch his dues.

MALKIN: [A spirit like a cat descends] A kiss, a coll [hug], a sip of blood, and why thou stay'st so long; I muse, I muse since the air's so sweet and good.

HECATE: Oh art thou come? What news, what news?

MALKIN: All goes still to our delight; either come or else refuse, refuse.

HECATE: Now I am furnished for the flight.

FIRESTONE: Hark, hark! The cat sings a brave treble in her own language.

HECATE: (Going up with Malkin) Now I go; now I fly, Malkin my sweet spirit and I. Oh what a dainty pleasure 'tis to ride in the air when the moon shines fair

and sing and dance and toy [pet] and kiss. Over woods, high rocks and mountains, over seas, our mistress' fountains, over steeples, towers and turrets. We fly
by night, 'mongst troops of spirits. No ring of bells to our ears sounds; no howls
of wolves, no yelps of hounds. No, not the noise of water's breach or cannon's
throat our height can reach.

VOICES [Above]: No ring of bells to our ears sounds, no howls of wolves, no
yelps of hounds; no, not the noise of water's breach or cannon's throat our height
can reach.

FIRESTONE: Well mother, I thank your kindness; you must be a gambolling i'th' air
and leave me to walk here like a fool and a mortal. (Exit)
      [The tragicomedy ends with Hecate's coven dancing merrily, unmolested.
All the spells and potions are effective, and none of the characters suffer any
                                    censure for using the witches' services.]

*Questions: What elements are present in the play that are also outlined in the treatises
on witch-hunting? What is the tone of the play in regard to the witches? How has the
perception of Hecate changed over time? Has the role of the moon in magic, as represented
in the play, been consistent throughout western history?*

80. THE *WITCHES' SABBATH*

Jan Ziarnko (c. 1575–c. 1630) was a Polish printmaker. His Witches' Sabbath *was
produced as a visual aid for the second edition of Pierre de Lancre's* On the Inconstancy
of Witches *(1612). Lancre (1553–1631) was a judge in Bordeaux, France, who in 1609
zealously oversaw a massive witch-hunt in the Basque region of Labourd in response to
King Henry IV's (r. 1589–1610) request that he put an end to witchcraft in the province.
In four months, Lancre sentenced nearly seventy people to death.*

*Ziarnko's tableau synthesizes the components of the fully developed witch theory as
it had emerged by the seventeenth century. Writers and artists often seem voyeuristic in
their fixation over minute details of witch gatherings: where do they eat, is there salt at
the table, does Satan sit on a throne, do they kiss Satan's posterior? This interest, however, was as much theological as it was puerile or pedantic. Because the black mass was
the inverse of the Catholic mass it mimicked, some clerics held that the most important
elements of their own religious ceremonies could be best understood by detecting which of
them Satan thought were significant enough to ridicule.*

*The image is poster-sized and represents the various elements of a full-blown sabbath.
An alphabetic key (not represented here) at the bottom of the drawing allowed the reader
to locate each of the chilling events taking place in the illustration.*

Source: Jan Ziarnko, *Description et figure de sabbat*, in Pierre de Lancre, *Tableau de l'inconstance des mauvais anges et démons*, 2nd ed. (Paris, 1613), facing p. 118 (British Library [719.i.ll]).

Question: What elements of the mature witchcraft theory are portrayed in the illustration?

81. PERSECUTION OF THE BURGOMASTER OF BAMBERG

In 1628 Johannes Junius (b. 1573), Burgomaster (mayor) of Bamberg in Germany, was arrested, tried, tortured, and burned at the stake for witchcraft. In most respects the case is typical of German witchcraft trials at the peak of the witch-hunts of the seventeenth century. But what is unusual is that there survives a letter the accused wrote to his daughter from prison. Rarely are we able to learn about the experiences of those charged with the crime of witchcraft apart from what the biased prosecutors record in trial transcripts.

Source: trans. George L. Burr, "The Witch Persecution at Bamberg," in *The Witch Persecutions*, Original Sources of European History, vol. 3 (Philadelphia: University of Pennsylvania, 1907), pp. 23–28.

Trial Transcripts

. . . On Wednesday, 28 June 1628, was examined without torture Johannes Junius, Burgomaster at Bamberg on the charge of witchcraft: how and in what fashion he had fallen into that vice. Is fifty-five years old and was born at Nie-derwaysich in the Wetterau. Says he is wholly innocent, knows nothing of the crime, has never in his life renounced God, says that he is wronged before God and the world, would like to hear of a single human being who has seen him at such gatherings (as the witch sabbaths).

Confrontation of Dr. Georg Adam Haan. Tells him to his face he will stake his life on it that he saw him, Junius, a year and a half ago at a witch gathering in the electoral council room where they ate and drank. Accused denies the same wholly.

Confronted with Hopffens Elsse. Tells him likewise that he was on Haupts-moor at a witch dance, but first the holy wafer was desecrated. Junius denies. Hereupon he was told that his accomplices had confessed against him and was given time for thought.

On Friday, 30 June 1628, the aforesaid Junius was again, without torture, exhorted to confess, but again confessed nothing, whereupon, . . . since he would confess nothing, he was put to the torture, and first the thumbscrews were applied. Says he has never denied God his savior nor suffered himself to be oth-erwise baptized; will again stake his life on it; feels no pain in the thumbscrews.

Leg-screws. Will confess absolutely nothing (and) knows nothing about it. He has never renounced God; will never do such a thing; has never been guilty of this vice; feels likewise no pain. Is stripped and examined; on his right side is found a bluish mark, like a clover leaf, is thrice pricked therein, but feels no pain and no blood flows out.

Strappado [see doc. 73]. He has never renounced God; God will not forsake him; if he were such a wretch he would not let himself be so tortured; God must show some token of his innocence. He knows nothing about witchcraft. . . .

On 5 July, the above named Junius is without torture, but with urgent persuasions, exhorted to confess and at last begins and confesses. When in the year 1624 his lawsuit at Rothweil cost him some six hundred florins, he had gone out, in the month of August, into his orchard at Friedrichsbronnen, and, as he sat there in thought, there had come him a woman like a grass maid, who had asked him why he sat there so sorrowful; he had answered that he was not despondent, but she had led him by seductive speeches to yield him to her will. . . . And thereafter this wench had changed into the form of a goat, which bleated and said, "Now you see with whom you have had to do. You must be mine or I will forthwith break your neck." Thereupon he had been frightened, and trembled all over for fear. Then the transformed spirit had seized him by the throat and demanded that he should renounce God Almighty, where-upon Junius said, "God forbid," and thereupon the spirit vanquished through the power of these words. Yet it came straightway back, brought more people with it, and persistently demanded of him that he renounce God in heaven and all the heavenly host, by which terrible threatening he was obliged to speak this formula: "I renounce God in heaven and his host and will henceforward recognize the Devil as my God."

After the renunciation, he was so far persuaded by those present and by the evil spirit that he suffered himself to be otherwise baptized in the evil spirit's name. [Christiana] Morhauptin had given him a ducat as dower gold [wedding payment], which afterward became only a potsherd. He was then named Krix. His paramour he had to call Vixen. Those present had congratulated him in Beelzebub's [another name for Satan] name and said that they were now all alike. At this baptism of his there were among others the aforesaid Christiana Morhauptin, the young Geiserlin, Paul Glaser, (and others). After this they had dispersed. At this time his paramour had promised to provide him with money and from time to time to take him to other witch gatherings. . . . Whenever he wished to ride forth (to the witch sabbath) a black dog had come before his bed, which said to him that he must go with him, whereupon he had seated himself upon the dog and the dog had raised himself in the Devil's name and so had fared forth. About two years ago he was taken to the electoral council room, at the left hand as one goes in. Above at a table were seated the chancellor, the burgomaster Neydekher, Dr. George Haan, (and many others). Since his eyes were not good, he could not recognize more persons.

More time for consideration was now given him. On 7 July, the aforesaid Junius was again examined to know what further had occurred to him to con-fess. He confesses that about two months ago, on the day after an execution was held, he was at a witch dance at the Black Cross where Beelzebub had shown himself to them all and said expressly to their faces that they must all be burned together on this spot and had ridiculed and taunted those present. . . .

Of crimes. His paramour had immediately after his seduction demanded that he should make away with his younger son, Hans Georg, and had given him for this purpose a gray powder; this, however, being too hard for him, he had made away with his horse, a brown, instead. His paramour had also often spurred him on to kill his daughter, . . . and because he would not do this, he had been maltreated with blows by the evil spirit.

Once at the suggestion of his paramour he had taken the holy wafer out of his mouth and given it to her. . . .

A week before his arrest as he was going to Saint Martin's church, the Devil met him on the way in the form of a goat, and told him that he would soon be imprisoned, but that he should not trouble himself; he would soon set him free.

Besides this, by his soul's salvation, he knew nothing further; but what he had spoken was the pure truth; on that he would stake his life.

On 6 August 1628, there was read to the aforesaid Junius this his confession, which he then wholly ratified and confirmed and was willing to stake his life upon it. And afterward he voluntarily confirmed the same before the court.

[Junius's letter to His Daughter, 24 July 1628]

Many hundred thousand goodnights, dearly beloved daughter, Veronica. Innocent have I come into prison; innocent have I been tortured; innocent must I die. For whoever comes into the witch prison must become a witch or be tortured until he invents something out of his head and—God pity him—bethinks him of something. I will tell you how it has gone with me. When I was the first time put to the torture, Dr. Braun, Dr. Kötzendörffer, and two strange doctors were there. Then Dr. Braun asks me, "Kinsman, how come you here?" I answer, "Through falsehood, through misfortune." "Hear, you," he says, "you are a witch; will you confess it voluntarily? If not, we'll bring in witnesses and the executioner for you." I said "I am no witch; I have a pure conscience in the matter; if there are a thousand witnesses, I am not anxious, but I'll gladly hear the witnesses." Now the chancellor's son was set before me . . . and afterward Hoppfen Elss. She had seen me dance on Hauptsmoor. . . . I answered, "I have never renounced God and will never do it; God graciously keep me from it. I'll rather bear whatever I must." And then came also—God in highest heaven have mercy—the executioner and put the thumbscrews on me: both hands bound together so that the blood ran out at the nails and everywhere, so that for four weeks I could not use my hands, as you can see from the writing. . . . Thereafter they first stripped me, bound my hands behind me, and drew me up in the torture [*strappado*]. Then I thought heaven and earth were at an end; eight times did they draw me up and let me fall again, so that I suffered terrible agony. . . .

And this happened on Friday, 30 June, and with God's help I had to bear the torture. . . . When at last the executioner led me back into the prison, he said to me: "Sir, I beg you, for God's sake confess something, whether it be true or not. Invent something, for you cannot endure the torture which you will be put to, and even if you bear it all, yet you will not escape, not even if you were an earl, but one torture will follow after another until you say you are a witch. Not before that," he said, "will they let you go, as you may see by all their trials, for one is just like another." . . .

And so I begged, since I was in wretched plight, to be given one day for thought and a priest. The priest was refused me, but the time for thought was given. Now, my dear child, see in what hazard I stood and still stand. I must say that I am a witch, though I am not, must now renounce God, though I have never done it

THE FULL FURY OF THE WITCH-HUNTS

before. Day and night I was deeply troubled, but at last there came to me a new idea. I would not be anxious, but, since I had been given no priest with whom I could take counsel, I would myself think of something and say it. It were surely better that I just say it with mouth and words, even though I had not really done it, and afterwards I would confess it to the priest and let those answer for it who compel me to do it. . . . And so I made my confession, as follows, but it was all a lie. Now follows, dear child, what I confessed in order to escape the great anguish and bitter torture, which it was impossible for me longer to bear.

(Here follows his confession, substantially as it is given in the minutes of his trial, but he adds:)

Then I had to tell what people I had seen (at the witch sabbath). I said that I had not recognized them. "You old rascal, I must set the executioner at you. Say, was not the chancellor there?" So I said, "Yes." "Who besides?" I had not recognized anybody. So he said, "Take one street after another; begin at the market; go out on one street and back on the next." I had to name several persons there. Then came the long street. I knew nobody. Had to name eight persons there. Then the Zinkenwert, one person more. Then over the upper bridge to the Georgthor, on both sides. Knew nobody again. Did I know nobody in the castle? Whoever it might be, I should speak without fear. And thus continuously they asked me on all the streets, though I could not and would not say more. So they gave me to the executioner, told him to strip me, shave me all over, and put me to the torture. "The rascal knows one on the marketplace, is with him daily, and yet won't name him." By that they meant Dietmeyer, so I had to name him too.

Then I had to tell what crimes I had committed. I said nothing. . . . "Draw the rascal up!" So I said that I was to kill my children, but I had killed a horse instead. It did not help. I had also taken a sacred wafer and had desecrated it. When I had said this, they left me in peace.

Now, dear child, here you have all my confession, for which I must die. And they are sheer lies and made-up things, so help me God. For all this I was forced to say through fear of the torture, which was threatened beyond what I had already endured. For they never leave off with the torture till one confesses something; be he never so good, he must be a witch. Nobody escapes, though he were an earl. . . .

Dear child, keep this letter secret so that people do not find it, else I shall be tortured most piteously and the jailers will be beheaded. So strictly is it forbidden. . . .

Dear child, pay this man a dollar. . . . I have taken several days to write this: my hands are both lame. I am in a sad plight. . . . Good night, for your father Johannes Junius will never see you more.

(And on the margin of the letter he adds:)

Dear child, six have confessed against me at once: the chancellor, his son, Neudecker, Zaner, Hoffmaisters, Ursel, and Hoppfen Els—all false, through compulsion, as they have all told me, and begged my forgiveness in God's name before they were executed. . . . They know nothing but good of me. They were forced to say it, just as I myself was. . . .

Questions: Why does the transcript mention that Junius felt no pain when the thumb-screws and leg screws were applied? Why were the judges not satisfied with a full confession from Junius? Why was Junius's social class mentioned in the transcript? What aspects of Junius's confession and the trial process are typical of the witch trials of the period? Why did Junius write to his daughter, and can we trust that his letter was truthful?

82. THE WITCHES OF WÜRZBURG

The atmosphere in which the persecution of witches took place in the city of Würzburg and environs in the 1620s can best be described as a panic. The accusations, arrests, trials, and executions were particularly relentless, following a pattern of extremism that surfaced periodically in southern Germany in the sixteenth and seventeenth centuries. The pervading tension is conveyed in the following letter, which the chancellor of the prince-bishop of Würzburg wrote to a friend in 1629.

Source: George L. Burr, *The Witch Persecutions*, Translations and Reprints from the Original Sources of European History, vol. 3 (Philadelphia: University of Pennsylvania, 1907), pp. 28–29.

As to the affair of the witches, which your grace thinks brought to an end before this, it has started up afresh, and no words can do justice to it. Ah, the woe and the misery of it—there are still four hundred in the city, high and low, of every rank and sex, nay, even clerics, so strongly accused that they may be arrested at any hour. It is true that of the people of my gracious prince here, some out of all offices and faculties must be executed: clerics, electoral councilors and doctors, city officials, court assessors, several of whom your grace knows. There are law students to be arrested. The prince-bishop has over forty students who are soon to be pastors; among them thirteen or fourteen are said to be witches. A few days ago a dean was arrested; two others who were summoned have fled. The notary of our church consistory, a very learned man, was yesterday arrested and put to the torture. In a word, a third part of the city is surely involved. The richest, most attractive, most prominent, of the clergy are already executed. A week ago a maiden of nineteen was executed, of whom it is everywhere said that she was the fairest in the whole city and was held by everybody a girl of singular modesty and purity. She will be followed by seven or eight others of the best and most attractive persons. . . . And thus many are put to death for renouncing God and being at the witch dances, against whom nobody has ever else spoken a word.

To conclude this wretched matter, there are children of three and four years, to the number of three hundred, who are said to have had intercourse with the Devil. I have seen put to death children of seven, promising students of ten, twelve, fourteen, and fifteen. Of the nobles—but I cannot and must not write more of this misery. There are persons of yet higher rank, whom you know, and would marvel to hear of, nay, would scarcely believe it; let justice be done. . . .

P.S. Though there are many wonderful and terrible things happening, it is beyond doubt that, at a place called the Fraw-Rengberg, the Devil in person, with eight thousand of his followers, held an assembly and celebrated mass before them all, administering to his audience (that is, the witches) turnip-rinds and parings in place of the holy Eucharist. There took place not only foul but most horrible and hideous blasphemies, whereof I shudder to write. It is also true that they all vowed not to be enrolled in the book of life [Revelation 3:5–22:19], but all agreed to be inscribed by a notary who is well known to me and my colleagues. We hope, too, that the book in which they are enrolled will yet be found, and there is no little search being made for it.

Questions: What is the emotional tone of the reading? What are the class, gender, and socio-economic levels represented by those accused of witchcraft in the reading? Does the author believe in the reality of witches and their maleficium?

83. WITCH PANIC IN BONN

Pastor Duren of the village of Alfter, near Bonn in Germany, wrote to Count Werner von Salm describing the state of affairs in his city. It has been suggested that this letter from Pastor Duren may be a forgery because the manuscript source is not extant and it reads very much like the letter the chancellor of the prince-bishop of Würzburg wrote to a friend (see doc. 82). Whereas the details in the Würzburg letter have external verification, the same is not true of the letter from Bonn in that the events described are not recorded in another source. Nevertheless, the Bonn letter is worth reading because it did circulate and was considered legitimate by contemporaries, which means it has a semblance of verisimilitude, even if the events it describes were more like those in Würzburg.

Source: trans. George L. Burr, *The Witch Persecutions*, Translations and Reprints from the Original Sources of European History, vol. 3 (Philadelphia: University of Pennsylvania Press, 1907), pp. 18–19.

Those burned are mostly male witches of the sort described. There must be half the city implicated; for already professors, law students, pastors, canons, vicars, and monks have here been arrested and burned. His princely grace has seventy wards who are to become pastors, one of whom, eminent as a musician, was yesterday arrested; two others were sought for, but have fled. The chancellor and his wife and the private secretary's wife are already executed. On the eve of Our Lady's Day [Feast of the Annunciation, 25 March], there was executed here a maiden of nineteen who bore the name of being the fairest and the most blameless of all the city, and who from her childhood had been brought up by the bishop himself. A canon of the cathedral, named Rotenhahn, I saw beheaded and burned. Children of three or four years have devils for their paramours. Students and boys of noble birth, of nine, ten, eleven, twelve, thirteen, fourteen years, have here been burned. In fine, things are in such a pitiful state that one does not know with what people one may talk and associate.

Question: What atypical elements are found in the description of events in the Bonn letter?

84. IN DEFENSE OF THE ACCUSED

The Jesuit priest Friedrich Spee (1591–1635) had the unhappy task of being confessor to condemned witches during the frenzy of the persecutions in Würzburg in the 1620s, during the course of which he became aware first-hand of what he considered the brutality, illogic, and court abuses visited on those arrested for witchcraft. Spee was one of the first to voice opposition to the torture of witches (and torture in general, which he called a demonic invention). He pointed out that confessions gained under torture were contaminated. He also objected to the practice of forcing the accused to provide names of other "witches" (see doc. 81). Spee did not deny the reality of witchcraft, nor did he advocate elimination of witch prosecutions. Rather, he sought procedural reform.

Because of the danger of questioning the judicial machine when it came to witch trials, Spee's tract, Precautions for Prosecutors, *was published anonymously in 1631, and possibly by someone other than Spee. It met fertile ground and was quickly translated into German. Decades later, the philosopher Gottfried Wilhelm Leibniz (1646–1716) revealed the authorship of the text.*

Source: trans. George L. Burr, *The Witch Persecutions*, Translations and Reprints from the Original Sources of European History, vol. 3 (Philadelphia: University of Pennsylvania Press, 1907), pp. 30–35.

Precautions for Prosecutors

1. Incredible among us Germans and especially (I blush to say it) among Catholics, are the popular superstition, envy, calumnies, backbitings, insinuations, and the like, which, being neither punished by the magistrates nor refuted by the pulpit, first stir up suspicion of witchcraft. All the divine judgments which God

has threatened in holy writ are now ascribed to witches. No longer do God or nature do aught, but witches everything.

2. Hence it comes that all at once everybody is clamoring that the magistrates proceed against the witches—those witches whom only their own clamor has made seem so many.

3. Princes, therefore, bid their judges and counselors to begin proceedings against the witches.

4. These at first do not know where to begin, since they have no testimony or proofs, and since their conscience clearly tells them that they ought not to proceed in this rashly.

5. Meanwhile they are a second time and a third admonished to proceed. The multitude clamors that there is something suspicious in this delay; and the same suspicion is, by one busybody or another, instilled into the ear of the princes.

6. To offend these, however, and not to defer at once to their wishes, is in Germany a serious matter. Most men, and even clergymen, approve with zeal whatever is but pleasing to the princes, not heeding by whom these (however good by nature) are often instigated.

7. At last, therefore, the judges yield to their wishes, and in some way contrive at length a starting point for the trials.

8. Or, if they still hold out and dread to touch the ticklish matter, there is sent to them a commissioner [inquisitor] specially deputed for this. And, even if he brings to his task something of inexperience or of haste, as is wont to happen in things human, this takes on in this field another color and name, and is counted only zeal for justice. This zeal for justice is no whit diminished by the prospect of gain, especially in the case of a commissioner of slender means and avaricious, with a large family, when there is granted him as salary so many dollars per head for each witch burned, besides the fees and assessments which he is allowed to extort at will from the peasants.

9. If now some utterance of a demoniac or some malign and idle rumor then current (for proof of the scandal is never asked) points especially to some poor and helpless Gaia [generic woman, like Jane Doe], she is the first to suffer.

10. And yet, lest it appear that she is indicted on the basis of rumor alone without other proofs, as the phrase goes, lo a certain presumption is at once obtained against her by posing the following dilemma: either Gaia has led a bad and improper life, or she has led a good proper one. If a bad one, then, say they, the proof is cogent against her; for from malice to malice the presumption is strong. If, however, she has led a good one, this also is none the less a proof; for thus, they say, are witches wont to cloak themselves and try to seem especially proper.

11. Therefore it is ordered that Gaia be hauled away to prison. And lo now a new proof is gained against her by this other dilemma. Either she then shows

fear or she does not show it. If she does show it (hearing forsooth of the grievous tortures wont to be used in this matter), this is of itself a proof; for conscience, they say, accuses her. If she does not show it (trusting indeed in her innocence), this too is a proof; for it is most characteristic of witches, they say, to pretend themselves peculiarly innocent and wear a bold front.

12. Lest, however, further proofs against her should be lacking, the inquisitor has his own creatures, often depraved and notorious, who question into all her past life. This, of course, cannot be done without coming upon some saying or doing of hers which evil-minded men can easily twist or distort into ground for suspicion of witchcraft. If, too, there are any who have borne her ill will, these, having now a fine opportunity to do her harm, bring against her such charges as it may please them to devise, and on every side there is a clamor that the evidence is heavy against her.

14. And so, as soon as possible, she is hurried to the torture, if indeed she be not subjected to it on the very day of her arrest, as often happens.

15. For in these trials there is granted to nobody an advocate or any means of fair defense, for the cry is that the crime is an excepted one [regular procedures are abated], and whoever ventures to defend the prisoner is brought into suspicion of the crime—as are all those who dare to utter a protest in these cases and to urge the judges to caution; for they are forthwith dubbed patrons of the witches. Thus all mouths are closed and all pens blunted, lest they speak or write.

16. In general, however, that it may not seem that no opportunity of defense has been given to Gaia, she is brought out and the proofs are first read before her and examined—if examine it can be called.

17. But, even though she then denies these and satisfactorily makes answer to each, this is neither paid attention to nor even noted down; all the proofs retain their force and value, however perfect her answer to them. She is only ordered back into prison, there to bethink herself more carefully whether she will persist in her obstinacy—for, since she has denied her guilt, she is obstinate.

19. Before she is tortured, however, she is led aside by the executioner, and, lest she may by magical means have fortified herself against pain, she is searched, her whole body being shaved, although up to this time nothing of the sort was ever found.

22. She is, however, tortured with the torture of the first degree, that is, the less severe. This is to be understood thus: that, although in itself it is exceeding severe, yet, compared with others to follow, it is lighter. Wherefore, if she confesses, they say and noise it abroad that she has confessed without torture.

23. Now, what prince or other dignitary who hears this can doubt that she is most certainly guilty who thus voluntarily without torture confesses her guilt?

24. Without any scruples, therefore, after this confession she is executed. Yet she would have been executed, nevertheless, even though she had not confessed;

for, when once a beginning has been made with the torture, the die is already cast—she cannot escape, she must die.

25. . . . If she does not confess, the torture is repeated twice, thrice, four times; anything one pleases is permissible, for in an excepted crime there is no limit of duration or severity or repetition of the tortures. As to this, think the judges, no sin is possible which can be brought up before the tribunal of conscience.

26. If now Gaia, no matter how many times tortured, has not yet broken silence, if she contorts her features under the pain, if she loses consciousness, or the like, then they cry that she is laughing or has bewitched herself into taciturnity, and hence deserves to be burned alive, as lately has been done to some who though several times tortured would not confess.

27. And then they say—even clergymen and confessors—that she died obstinate and impenitent, that she would not be converted or desert her paramour [Satan], but kept rather her faith with him.

28. If, however, it chances that under so many tortures one dies, they say that her neck has been broken by the Devil.

29. Wherefore unjustly, the corpse is dragged out by the executioner and buried under the gallows.

30. But if, on the other hand, Gaia does not die and some exceptionally scrupulous judge hesitates to torture her further without fresh proofs or to burn her without a confession, she is kept in prison and more harshly fettered, and there lies for perhaps an entire year to rot until she is subdued.

31. For it is never possible to clear herself by withstanding and thus to wash away the aspersion of crime, as is the intention of the laws. It would be a disgrace to her examiners if when, once arrested, she should thus go free. Guilty must she be, by fair means or foul, whom they have once but thrown into bonds.

32. Meanwhile, both then and earlier, they send to her ignorant and headstrong priests, more importunate than the executioners themselves. It is the business of these to harass in every way the wretched creature to such a degree that, whether truly or not, she will at last confess herself guilty; unless she does so, they declare, she simply cannot be saved, nor share in the sacraments.

35. Some, however, to leave no stone unturned, order Gaia to be exorcised and transferred to a new place, and then to be tortured again, in the hope that by this exorcism and change of place the bewitchment of taciturnity may perhaps be broken. But, if not even this succeeds, then at last they commit her alive to the flames. Now, in heaven's name, I would like to know, since both she who confesses and she who does not, perish alike, what way of escape is there for any, however innocent? O unhappy Gaia, why have you rashly hoped; why have you not, at first entering prison, declared yourself guilty; why, O foolish woman and mad, will you die so many times when you might die but once?

Follow my counsel, and before all pain declare yourself guilty and die. You will not escape; for this were a disgrace to the zeal of Germany.

36. If, now, any, under stress of pain, has once falsely declared herself guilty, her wretched plight beggars description. For not only is there in general no door for her escape, but she is also compelled to accuse others, of whom she knows no ill, and whose names are often suggested to her by her examiners or by the executioner, or of whom she has heard as suspected or accused or already once arrested and released. These in their turn are forced to accuse others, and these still others, and so it goes on; who can help seeing that it must go on without end?

38. And so at last those are brought into question who at the outset most loudly clamored for the constant feeding of the flames; for they rashly failed to foresee that their turn, too, must inevitably come—and by a just verdict of heaven, since with their pestilent tongues they created us so many witches and sent so many innocent to the flames.

46. From all which there follows this corollary, worthy to be noted in red ink: that, if only the trials be steadily pushed on with, there is nobody in our day, of whatsoever sex, fortune, rank, or dignity, who is safe, if he has but an enemy and slanderer to bring him into suspicion of witchcraft. . . .

Questions: Was Gaia tried in a secular or church court? To what aspects of the judicial treatment of witches did Spee particularly object? Was Spee a skeptic as to the reality of witchcraft? What was Spee's warning to those responsible for the miscarriage of justice in regard to witch trials?

85. THE DEMONIC POSSESSION OF THE NUNS OF LOUDUN

The trial and execution of a priest in the French town of Loudun in the mid-seventeenth century drew a great deal of attention in its own time and has continued to do so ever since. Urbain Grandier (c. 1590–1634), who was politically controversial with a reputation for licentiousness, was accused of witchcraft and enabling the demonic possession of the nuns of a convent of the order of Saint Ursula. Spirit possession of nuns was not infrequent in Europe between 1435 and 1690, and exorcism in general was proliferating. Loudun was fractured by conflicts between French Protestants (Huguenots) and the Catholic faction, and a severe outbreak of the bubonic plague in the summer of 1632 claimed the lives of nearly a fourth of the population. All in all, tensions in the city ran high. The case of the devils of Loudun was particularly well known because it drew the attention of the royal court of Louis XIII (r. 1610–1643) and, largely for that reason, became a cause célèbre across France. The following text survives in two copies. Its author is Monsieur des Niau, counselor at la Flèche and eyewitness to several of the events. Niau firmly believed in demonic possession and in Grandier's culpability.

Source: trans. Edmund Goldsmid, Monsieur des Niau, *The History of the Devils of Loudun, the Alleged Possession of the Ursuline Nuns, and the Trial and Execution of Urbain Grandier, Told by an Eye-Witness*, 3 vols., Collectanea adamantea 21 (Edinburgh: Privately Printed, 1887), vol. 1, pp. 21, 38–43; vol. 2, pp. 5–21, 24–29, 31–48, vol. 3, pp. 5–17.

Volume 1

At the beginning of the seventeenth century, the curate of Loudun was Urbain Grandier. To those talents, which lead to success in this world, this man united a corruption of morals which dishonored his character. His conduct had made him many enemies. These were not merely rivals, but husbands and fathers, some of high position, who were outraged at the dishonor he brought on their families. . . .

[When the confessor of the Ursuline convent died, Grandier put himself forward to become spiritual advisor to the nuns, but the mother superior emphatically objected, and Canon Mignon was appointed. Grandier took this as a grave insult and openly expressed his irritation.]

[After this], extraordinary symptoms began to declare themselves within the convent, but they were hushed up as far as possible and not allowed to be known outside the walls. To do otherwise would have been to give the new institution a severe blow and to risk ruining it at its birth. This the nuns and their confessor understood. It was therefore decided to work in the greatest secrecy and to cure, or at least mitigate, the evil. . . . As usually happens, the extraordinary phenomena displayed in the persons of the nuns were taken for the effects of sexual disease. But soon suspicions arose that they proceeded from supernatural causes, and at last they perceived what God intended everyone to see. Thus, the nuns, after having employed the physicians of the body, apothecaries, and medical men, were obliged to have recourse to the physicians of the soul and to call in both lay and clerical doctors, their confessor no longer being equal to the immensity of the labor. For they were seventeen in number, and everyone was found to be either fully possessed, or partially under the influence of the evil one. . . .

It became necessary to have recourse to exorcisms. This word alone is for some people a subject of ridicule, as if it had been clearly proved that religion is mere folly and the faith of the church a fable. True Christians must despise these grinning impostors. Exorcisms, then, were employed. The demon, forced to manifest himself, yielded his name. He began by giving these girls the most horrible convulsions; he went so far as to raise from the earth the body of the mother superior, who was being exorcised, and to reply to secret thoughts, which were manifested neither in words nor by any exterior signs. Questioned according to the form prescribed by the ritual as to why he had entered the body of the nun, he replied it was from hatred. But when, being questioned as to the name of the magician, he answered that it was Urbain Grandier; profound astonishment seized Canon Mignon and his assistants. They had indeed looked upon Grandier as a scandalous priest; but never had they imagined that he was guilty of magic. They were therefore not satisfied with one single questioning; they repeated the interrogatory several times and always received the same reply.

Volume 2

The declaration of the evil spirit could not fail to make a great commotion and to have results, which required precautions to be taken at once. Canon Mignon, like a wise man, put himself in communication with the department of justice and informed the magistrates of what was passing at the convent on 11 October 1632. Grandier, prepared for all contingencies, had already taken his measures. Many of the magistrates belonged to the new religion [Calvinism] and were favorable to him, looking upon him as a secret adherent; they served him as he expected. . . . Excitement rose in the public mind, a thousand arguments on this or that side permeated the town, and a thousand quarrels took place on all sides. This excitement, however, and these disputes settled nothing, and the exorcisms, which continued, had no better result. . . .

Until now, the court had taken no notice of the affair, but the noise it had made in the world since the first days of October 1632 had reached the queen's [Anne of Austria, 1601–1666] ears. She requested information, and the Abbé Marescot, one of her chaplains, was sent to examine the matter and report to her. . . . The king had resolved to raze the castles and fortresses existing in the heart of the kingdom and commissioned M. de Laubardemont to see to the demolition of [the castle] of Loudun. He arrived and saw what a ferment the town was in, the animosity that reigned there, and the kind of man who caused the commotion. The complaints of those who were victims of the debaucheries, of the pride, or of the vengeance of the curate, touched him, and it seemed to him important to put an end to the scandal. On his return, he informed the king and the cardinal-minister [Cardinal Richelieu, 1585–1642] of the facts. Louis XIII, naturally pious and just, perceived the greatness of the evil, and deemed it his duty to put a stop to it. He appointed M. de Laubardemont to investigate the matter without appeal with orders to choose in the neighboring jurisdictions the most straightforward and learned judges. The commission is dated 30 November 1633.

Nothing less was needed to bring to justice a man upheld by a seditious and enterprising party and so well versed in the details of chicanery—an art always shameful in any man, but especially to an ecclesiastic. The king issued at the same time two decrees to arrest and imprison Grandier and his accomplices. . . .

[T]he commissioner commenced his investigation and proceeded to hear witnesses on 17 December 1633. . . . The evidence of the nuns was also heard, and that of lay persons of both sexes, among others, of two women, the one of whom confessed having had criminal relations with Grandier and that he had offered to make her Princess of Magicians, while the second confirmed the evidence of the first.

As regards the nuns, they deposed that Grandier had introduced himself into the convent by day and night for four months without anyone knowing how he got in, that he presented himself to them while standing at divine service and tempted them to indecent actions both by word and deed, that they were often struck by invisible persons, that the marks of the blows were so visible that the doctors and surgeons had easily found them, and that the beginning of all these troubles was signaled by the apparition of Prior Moussaut, their first confessor. The mother superior and seven or eight other nuns, when confronted with Grandier, identified him, although it was ascertained that they had never seen him save by magic and that he had never had anything to do with their affairs. The two women formerly mentioned and the two priests maintained the truth of their evidence. In a word, besides the nuns and six lay women, "sixty witnesses deposed to adulteries, incest, sacrileges, and other crimes, committed by the accused, even in the most secret places of his church, as in the vestry, where the holy host was kept, on all days and at all hours." . . .

[Monsieur de Laubardemont] considered it necessary to examine the nuns carefully; for this purpose, with the consent of the bishop, he sequestrated them in different convents and interrogated them so severely that one might have thought that they themselves were the magicians. "He saw them all, the one after the other, for several days and listened to their conversations to observe their mode of thought. He enquired minutely into their lives, their morals, their behavior, not only secular but religious. His depositions, or notes, which represented the evidence of twenty girls, including a few who were not nuns, filled fifty rolls of official paper and were the admiration of all judges—so great was the prudence and care they demonstrated." On the other hand, the bishop of Poitiers, after having sent several doctors of theology to examine the victims, came to Loudun in person and exorcised them himself, or had them exorcised by others in his presence, for two months and a half. Never was work done with such care and attention. All precognitions over, the commissioner began to confront the accused with the witnesses, and the latter maintained, face to face with Grandier, the evidence they had given against him. . . .

If, as calumny asserts, the only thing sought was the death of Grandier, here were sufficient proofs to burn him, if only for abusing the privileges of his ministry and of his church or for the sacrileges he had committed therein. But justice is not satisfied with punishing one kind of crime when she finds traces of another still more serious. It was moreover a Christian duty to assist the views of God, who permitted so strange an event to confound the calumnies of the Protestants and to prove the "possession" of the nuns and the magic exercised by the accused. To this the commissioners and the other judges applied themselves.

Thus, as it was a matter rather of religion than of jurisprudence, they resolved to begin by prayer to God, who is the father of all light, rightly considering that all France was watching the trial with eager eyes, that it was shrouded in a thick veil of obscurity, and that their verdict would entail important consequences. They therefore prepared to receive divine assistance and grace by frequent confessions and by often receiving the holy sacrament. Then they decreed a general procession to implore celestial aid in so difficult a matter, and, to excite the devotion of the masses by their example, they went in a body, during the whole of the trial, to visit the churches of the city, set aside by the bishop for forty hour services, and reached each in time for the elevation of the host. Thence the exorcists went to the church fixed upon for the exorcisms, and the judges proceeded to the tribunal to continue the case; in the evening all returned to church for evensong.

The examination lasted forty days, during which demons gave them the clearest proofs of their presence in the bodies of the persons exorcised, and every day added new evidence against Grandier and yet never said anything against him which did not turn out strictly true. These assertions merit distinct proof, which will be found interesting. As regards the presence of devils in the possessed, the church teaches us in its ritual that there are four principal signs by which it can be undoubtedly recognized. These signs are the speaking or understanding of a language unknown to the person possessed, the revelation of the future or of events happening far away, the exhibition of strength beyond the years and nature of the actor, and floating in the air for a few moments. . . . Now, they are all to be found in the nuns of Loudun and in such numbers that we can only mention the principal cases.

Acquaintance with unknown tongues first showed itself in the mother superior. At the beginning she answered in Latin the questions of the ritual proposed to her in that language. Later, she and the others answered in any language [that the exorcists] thought proper to question in. M. de Launay de Razilli, who had lived in America, attested that during a visit to Loudun he had spoken to them in the language of a certain savage tribe of that country and that they had answered quite correctly and had revealed to him events that had taken place there. Some gentlemen of Normandy certified in writing that they had questioned Sister

Clara de Sazilli in Turkish, Spanish, and Italian, and that her answers were correct. M. de Nismes, Doctor of the Sorbonne and one of the chaplains of the Cardinal de Lyon, having questioned them in Greek and German, was satisfied with their replies in both languages. . . .

As to the revelation of hidden matters or of events passing afar off, proofs are still more abundant. We will only select a few of the most remarkable. . . . M. Chiron, prior of Maillezais, desiring to strengthen his belief in demoniacal possession, begged M. de Morans to allow him to whisper to a third party the sign he required, and he thereon whispered to M. de Fernaison, canon and provost of the same church, that he wished the nun to fetch a missal then lying near the door and to pat her finger on the introit of the mass of the holy Virgin, beginning, "*Salve, sancta parens*" [Hail holy mother]. M. de Morans, who had heard nothing, ordered Sister Clara, who was likewise ignorant of what had been said, to obey the intentions of M. Chiron. This young girl then fell into strange convulsions, blaspheming, rolling on the ground, exposing her most secret parts in the most indecent manner without a blush and with foul and lascivious expressions and actions until she caused all who looked on to hide their eyes with shame. Though she had never seen the prior, she called him by his name and said he should be her lover. It was only after many repeated commands and an hour's struggling that she took up the missal, saying, "I will pray." Then, turning her eyes in another direction, she placed her finger on the capital "S" at the beginning of the introit aforesaid, of which facts reports were drawn up. . . .

Chevalier de Meré, who was present, asked the devil on what day he had last confessed. The devil answered Friday. The chevalier acknowledged this to be correct; whereupon Sister Clara withdrew. But as he wished to try the devil again, he begged the exorcist to make her return and whispered some words to the marquis and the monk for the nun to repeat. The exorcist refused, as the words were indecent. He changed them, therefore, into "*pater et filius et spiritus sanctus*" [father and son and holy spirit]. He whispered these words so low that the exorcist could hardly hear them. The nun, who was in another room, came at the command of the father, and addressing the chevalier, first said the indecent words the monk had refused and then repeated several times "*Gloria patri et filio et spiritui sancto*" [glory to the father the son and the holy spirit]. . . .

"When it rained," says Father Surin, "the devil used to place the mother superior under the water spout. As I knew this to be a habit of his, I commanded him mentally to bring her to me; whereupon she used to come and ask me: 'What do you want.'" Another thing which struck the exorcists, was the instantaneous answers they gave to the most difficult questions of theology, as to grace, the vision of God, angels, the incarnation and similar subjects, always in the very terms used in the schools.

The corporal effect of possession is a proof which strikes the coarsest minds. It has this other advantage, that an example convinces a whole assembly. Now the nuns of Loudun gave these proofs daily. When the exorcist gave some order to the devil, the nuns suddenly passed from a state of quiet into the most terrible convulsions and without the slightest increase of pulsation. They struck their chests and backs with their heads, as if they had had their necks broken, and with inconceivable rapidity; they twisted their arms at the joints of the shoulder, the elbow, and the wrist two or three times round; lying on their stomachs they joined their palms of their hands to the soles of their feet; their faces became so frightful one could not bear to look at them; their eyes remained open without winking; their tongues issued suddenly from their mouths, horribly swollen, black, hard, and covered with pimples, and yet while in this state they spoke distinctly; they threw themselves back till their heads touched their feet and walked in this position with wonderful rapidity and for a long time. They uttered cries so horrible and so loud that nothing like it was ever heard before; they made use of expressions so indecent as to shame the most debauched of men. Their acts, both in exposing themselves and inviting lewd behavior from those present, would have astonished the inmates of the lowest brothel in the country; they uttered maledictions against the three divine persons of the trinity—oaths and blasphemous expressions so execrable, so unheard of, that they could not have suggested themselves to the human mind. They used to watch without rest and fast five or six days at a time or be tortured twice a day, as we have described, during several hours without their health suffering; on the contrary, those that were somewhat delicate appeared healthier than before their possession.

The devil sometimes made them fall suddenly asleep; they fell to the ground and became so heavy that the strongest man had great trouble in even moving their heads. Françoise Filestreau, although her mouth was closed, one could hear within her body different voices speaking at the same time, quarrelling and discussing who should make her speak. Lastly, one often saw Elizabeth Blanchard in her convulsions with her feet in the air and her head on the ground, leaning against a chair or a windowsill without other support. The mother superior, from the beginning, was carried off her feet and remained suspended in the air at the height of 24 inches. . . . Both she and other nuns lying flat, without moving foot, hand, or body, were suddenly lifted to their feet like statues. In another exorcism the mother superior was suspended in the air, only touching the ground with her elbow. Others, when comatose, became supple like a thin piece of lead so that their bodies could be bent in every direction, forward, backward, or sideways, until their heads touched the ground, and they remained thus so long as their position was not altered by others. . . .

But sometime before the death of Grandier, [the mother superior] had a still stranger experience. In a few words this is what happened. In an exorcism the devil promised Father Lactance, as a sign of his exit, that he would make three wounds on the left side of the mother superior. He described their appearance and stated the day and hour when they would appear. He said he would come out from within without affecting the nun's health and forbade that any remedy should be applied as the wounds would leave no mark. On the day named, the exorcism took place, and many doctors had come from the neighboring towns to be present at this event. . . . M. de Laubardemont asked the doctors to tie her, but they begged him to let them first see the convulsions they had heard spoken of. He granted this, and during the convulsions the mother superior suddenly came to herself with a sigh, pressed her right hand to her left side and withdrew it covered with blood. She was again examined, and the doctors with the whole assembly saw three bloody wounds of the size stated by the devil; the chemise [undergarment], the stays [corset], and the dress were pierced in three places, the largest hole looking as if a pistol bullet had passed through. The nun was thereupon entirely stripped, but no instrument of any description was found upon her. A report was immediately drawn up, and monsieur, brother of the king, who witnessed the facts with all the nobles of his court, attested the document. [Doctors of the Sorbonne confirmed that this was a case of possession.]

Volume 3

On Friday, 23 June 1634, about three o'clock in the afternoon, the bishop of Poitiers and M. de Laubardemont being present, Grandier was brought from his prison to the church of St. Croix in his parish to be present at the exorcisms. All the possessed were there likewise. And as the accused and his partisans declared that the possessions were mere impostures, he was ordered to be himself the exorcist, and the stole was presented to him. He could not refuse; and therefore, taking the stole and the ritual [book], he received the pastoral benediction, and after the *Veni Creator* [Come Creator Spirit] had been sung, commenced the exorcism in the usual form. But where he should haughtily have given commands to the demon, instead of saying "*Impero*. I command," he said, "*Cogor vos*," that is, "I am constrained by you." The bishop sharply reprimanded him, and as he had said that some of the possessed understood Latin, he was allowed to interrogate in Greek. At the same time, the demon cried out by the mouth of Sister Clara, "Eh! speak Greek, or any language you like, I will answer." At these words, he became confused, and could not say anything more.

To behave thus or to acknowledge the truth of the accusation is one and the same thing, but other circumstances strengthened this certainty. Any man whose own writing testifies against him is lost. Now this is what Grandier experienced. The devils, in several instances, confessed four pacts he had entered into. This word, "pact," is somewhat equivocal. It may mean either the document by which a man gives himself to the Devil or the physical symbols, whose application will produce some particular effects in consequence of the pact. Here is an example of each case. Grandier's pact, or magical characters, whereby he gave himself to Beelzebub, was as follows,

> My lord and master, Lucifer, I recognize you as my god, and promise to serve you all my life. I renounce every other god, Jesus Christ and all other saints, the catholic, apostolic and Roman church, its sacraments, with all prayers that may be said for me, and I promise to do all the evil I can. I renounce the holy oil and the water of baptism, together with all the merits of Jesus Christ and his saints, and should I fail to serve and adore you and do homage to you thrice daily, I abandon to you my life as your due.

These characters were recognized as being in Grandier's own hand. Now here is a specimen of the other kind of pact or magical charm. It was composed of the flesh of a child's heart, extracted in an assembly of magicians held at Orléans in 1631, of the ashes of a holy wafer that had been burnt, and of something else which the least straight-laced decency forbids me to name.

A most convincing proof of Grandier's guilt is that one of the devils declared he had marked him in two parts of his body. His eyes were bandaged, and he was examined by eight doctors who reported they had found two marks in each place, that they had inserted a needle to the depth of an inch without the criminal having felt it, and that no blood had been drawn. Now this is a most decisive test. For however deeply a needle be buried in such marks no pain is caused, and no blood can be extracted when they are magical signs. But if the devils, overcome by the exorcisms, at times gave evidence against the criminal, at others they seemed to conspire to blacken him still more under the sem-blance of an apparent justification. Thus several of the possessed spoke in his favor, and some even went so far as to confess that they had calumniated him. Indeed, the mother superior herself, one day when M. de Laubardemont was in the convent, stripped herself to her shift, and, with a rope round her neck and a candle in her hand, stood for two hours in the middle of the yard, although it was raining heavily, and when the door of the room in which M. de Lau-bardemont was seated, was opened, she threw herself on her knees before him, declaring she repented of the crime she had committed in accusing Grandier, who was innocent. She then withdrew and fastened the rope to a tree in the garden, attempting to hang herself but was prevented by the other nuns. When the devil played these kind of tricks, they forced him to retract by calling on him to take Jesus Christ present in the Eucharist as witness of the truth of his statement, which he never dared to do. . . .

The trial being completed and the magician duly convicted, there only remained to sentence the evildoer. The commissioners assembled at the Carmelite Convent, and it was noticed that there was not the slightest difference of opinion among all the fourteen judges . . . No one among the Catholics, or, indeed, among all honest men, failed to applaud the sentence on Grandier. It was as follows.

> We have declared and declare the said Urbain Grandier attainted and convicted of the crimes of magic, maleficence, and possession occurring through his act in the persons of certain nuns of this town of Loudun and other women together with other crimes resulting therefrom. For reparation whereof we have condemned, and do condemn, the said Grandier to make '*amende honorable*' bareheaded, a rope round his neck, holding in his hand a burning torch of the weight of two pounds, before the principal gate of Saint Pierre du Marché, and before that of Saint Ursula of the said town, and there, on his knees, to ask pardon of God, the king, and justice and that done, to be led to the public square of Sainte Croix, to be there tied to a stake, which for that purpose shall be erected in the said square, and his body to be there burnt with the pacts and magical inscriptions now in custody of the court together with the manuscript book written by him against the celibacy of priests, and his ashes to be scattered to the wind. We have declared all his property forfeited and confiscated to the crown, less a sum of 150 livres, which shall be expended in the purchase of a copper plate, on which shall be engraved the present sentence, and the same shall be placed in a prominent position in the said Church of Sainte Ursula, there to be preserved for ever. And before this present sentence shall be carried out, we order that the said Grandier shall be put to the question ordinary and extraordinary [torture], to discover his accomplices. Pronounced at Loudun on the said Grandier, and executed 18 August 1634.

In execution of this sentence, he was taken to the Court of Justice of Loudun. His sentence having been read to him, he earnestly begged M. de Laubardemont and the other commissioners to mitigate the rigor of their sentence. M. de Laubardemont replied that the only means of inducing the judges to moderate the penalties was to declare at once his accomplices, and by some act of repentance for his past crimes, to implore divine mercy. The only answer he gave was that he had no accomplices, which was false; for there is no magician but must be accompanied by others. For the last forty days the commissioner had placed at his side two monks to convert him. But all was in vain. Nothing could touch this hardened sinner. It is true, however, that the conversion of a magician is so rare an occurrence that it must be placed in the rank of miracles. "I am not astonished," says one who was present, "at his impenitence, nor at his refusing to acknowledge himself guilty of magic, both under torture and at his execution, for it is known that magicians promise the Devil never to confess this crime, and he in return hardens their hearts so that they go to their death stupid and altogether insensible to their misfortunes." Before being put to the torture, the prisoner was addressed by Father Lactance, a man of great faith, chosen by the bishop of Poitiers to exorcise the instruments of torture, as is always done in the case of magicians, in order to induce him to repent. Every one shed tears except the prisoner. M. de Laubardemont also spoke to him, together with the Lieutenant Criminel of Orléans, but, notwithstanding their efforts, they made no impression. This determined M. de Laubardemont to try the effects of torture. The boots [instrument to crush feet or legs] were applied, and the judge repeated his questions as to his accomplices. He always replied that he was no magician, though he had committed greater crimes than that. Questioned as to what crimes, he replied, crimes of human frailty and added that were he guilty of magic, he would be less ashamed of that than of his other crimes. This speech was ridiculous, especially in the mouth of a priest, who must know better than a layman that of all crimes the greatest is that of sorcery.

Torture drew from him nothing but cries, or rather sighs from the depth of his bosom, unaccompanied by tears, though the exorcist had abjured him, according to the ritual, to weep if he were innocent, but if guilty to remain tearless. Though he was very thirsty, he several times refused to drink holy water when presented to him. At length, pressed to drink, he took a few drops, with glaring eyes and a horrible look on his face. Never in the greatest agony of torture did he mention the name of Jesus Christ or of the Holy Virgin, save when repeating words he was ordered to speak, and then only in so cold a manner and with such constraint that he horrified the assistants. He never cast his eyes on the image of Christ nor on that of the Virgin, which were opposite to him, and they were offered to him in vain, whereupon the judges remonstrated with him. They were still more scandalized when they tried to make him say the prayer which every good Christian addresses to his guardian angel, especially in great extremities, and he said he did not know it. Such was his conduct under torture; in such a crisis every feeling of religion would be awakened in an ordinary man.

His legs were then washed and placed near the fire to restore circulation; he then began to talk to the guards, joking and laughing, and would have gone on had they allowed him. He spoke neither of receiving the sacrament of penitence nor of imploring God's pardon. They had given him for a confessor Father Archangel, who asked him if he did not wish to confess. He replied that he had done so the previous Tuesday, after which he sat down and dined with the same appetite as usual, drank three or four glasses of wine, and spoke of all kinds of things except of God. Instead of listening to what was said to him for the good of his soul, he made speeches he had prepared beforehand as if he were preaching. They consisted in complaints as to the pain in his legs and of a feeling of chilliness about his head, in asking for something to drink or to eat, and in begging that he might not be burnt alive.

When he was carried to the courthouse, where the holy fathers began to prepare him for death, he pushed back with his hand a crucifix that was presented to him and muttered between his teeth some words which were not heard. His guards, witnessing this action, were scandalized and told the monk not to offer him the crucifix again since he rejected it. He recommended himself to no one's prayers, neither before nor during the execution of the sentence. Only, as he passed through the streets, turning his head on one side and the other to see the people, it was noticed that he said twice, with an appearance of vanity, "Pray God for me" and that those to whom he spoke were Huguenots, among whom was an apostate. . . .

Having reached the place of execution, the fathers redoubled their charitable solicitude and pressed him most earnestly to be converted to God at that moment, offered him the crucifix, and placed it over his mouth and on his chest; he never deigned to look at it, and once or twice even turned away; he shook his head when holy water was offered him. He seemed eager to end his days and in haste to have the fire lighted, either because he expected not to feel it, or because he feared he might be weak enough to name his accomplices; or perhaps, as is believed, in fear lest pain should extract from him a renunciation of his master, Lucifer. For the Devil, to whom magicians give themselves body and soul, so thoroughly masters their minds that they fear him only and expect and hope for nothing save from him. Therefore did Grandier protest, placing his hand on his heart that he would say no more than he had already said. At last, seeing them set fire to the faggots, he feared they did not intend to keep their promise to him, but wished to burn him alive and uttered loud complaints. The executioner then advanced, as is always done, to strangle him, but the flames suddenly sprang up with such violence that the rope caught fire, and he fell alive among the burning faggots. Just before this a strange event happened. In the midst of this mass of people, notwithstanding the noise of so many voices and the efforts of the archers who shook their halberts [combined spear and battle-ax] in the air to frighten them, a flight of pigeons flew round and round the stake. Grandier's partisans, impudent to the end, said that these innocent birds came, in default of men, as witnesses of his innocence; others thought very differently and said that it was a troop of demons who came, as sometimes happens on the death of great magicians, to assist at that of Grandier, whose scandalous impenitence certainly deserved to be honored in this manner. His friends, however, called this hardness of heart constancy and had his ashes collected as if they were relics. . . .

Questions: What role did Calvinism play in the events of Loudun? What in particular convinced Monsieur des Niau that the nuns were, beyond doubt, possessed? Not everyone was as certain as the author that the nuns were controlled by demons; what were the counterarguments? What role did torture play in the proceedings?

86. ENGLAND'S WITCH FINDER GENERAL

Matthew Hopkins (c. 1620–1647) was a self-styled professional witch-hunter in Essex, England. He called himself "Witch Finder General," although no official body approved the appellation. Hopkins and his company of witch-hunters were responsible for the convictions of over half of the nearly 500 people hanged for witchcraft in England from the fifteenth to the eighteenth centuries.

The Discovery of Witches is particularly valuable because there are relatively few treatises on witch-hunts and trials from England. The methods of torture and capital punishment that Hopkins describes are different from those used in Europe because continental processes of interrogation and execution were forbidden under English Common Law.

Many opposed Hopkins's methods, and The Discovery of Witches is a response to those critics. The book is organized around "queries"—objections others have made to Hopkins, and "answers"—Hopkin's defense of his practices. He refers to himself in the third person, or as "Witch Finder," "the discoverer," or "Witch Catcher."

Source: Matthew Hopkins, *The Discovery of Witches*, in Montague Summers, *The Discovery of Witches: A Study of Master Matthew Hopkins Commonly Call'd Witch Finder Generall* (London: Cayme Press, 1928), pp. 49–59, 61–62; rev. Martha Rampton.

QUERY 3. From whence came his skill [to find witches]? Was it from his profound learning or from much reading of learned authors concerning that subject?

ANSWER. From neither, but from experience, which might not be respected, yet it is the surest and safest way to judge.

QUERY 4. I pray where was this experience gained? And why gained by him and not by others?

ANSWER. The discoverer never traveled far for it, but in March, 1644, he had some seven or eight of that horrid sect of witches living in the town where he lived, a town in Essex called Manningtree. There many other witches of adjacent other towns had their meeting every six weeks in the night (being always on Friday night) close by his house, and they had several solemn sacrifices there offered to the Devil. This discoverer heard one of the witches speaking to her imps [evil spirits in the form of animals] one night, and she bid them to go suckle from another witch, who was thereupon apprehended and searched by women who had for many years known the Devil's marks. She was found to have three teats, which honest women have not. So upon command of the justice they were to keep her from sleep two or three nights, expecting in that time to see her [animal] familiars. On the fourth night she called the imps in by their names, and told them what shapes they would assume a quarter of an hour before they came in. There were ten of us in the room.

The first imp called was Holt, who came in like a white kitling [kitten]. 2) Jarmara came in like a fat spaniel without any legs at all. She said she kept him fat and clapped her hand on her belly and said he sucked good blood from her body. 3) Third was Vinegar Tom, who was like a long-legged Greyhound with a head like an Ox, a long tail and broad eyes, who, when this discoverer spoke to him and bade him go to the place provided for him and his angels, immediately transformed himself into the shape of a child of four years old without a head, gave half a dozen turns around the house, and vanished at the door. 4) Sack and Sugar were next, like a black rabbit. 5) Newes was in the shape of a polecat.

All these imps vanished away in a little time. Immediately after this witch confessed, she named several other witches (from whom she got her imps) and told where their marks were, the number of their marks, imps, and imps' names, which were Elemanzer, Pyewacket, Peckin the Crown, Grizzel, Greedigut, etc., which no mortal could invent. And upon their searching the witches, the marks were found, the same number, and in the same place as had been reported. These other witches confessed to having imps (though they knew not what the first witch told us before) and so exposed one another, all of whom joined together in the like damnable practice. In our Hundred [administrative division of a county] in Essex, twenty-nine witches were condemned at once. Four of the witches were brought twenty-five miles to be hanged for sending the Devil like a bear to kill this discoverer in his garden. So by seeing many paps [teats from which imps suckled], and observing hundreds of witches, he gained this experience, and any man can find witches as well as he and his company if they had the same skill and experience.

QUERY 6. It is impossible for any man or woman to judge rightly on Devil's marks because they are so near to natural excrescences [a distinct outgrowth], and those who find them cannot give oath that they were drawn by evil spirits unless they have already used unlawful types of torture, which makes the accused person say anything to ease the pain and have some quiet, as who would not do? I want to know how and when he discovers the Devil's mark from natural skin imperfection, and so be satisfied in that.

ANSWER: The reasons he can recognize the Devil's mark and judges them to differ from natural marks are three. 1) He judges by the unusualness of the place where he finds the teats in or on their bodies, being far distant from any usual place from whence such natural marks proceed. For instance, a witch could plead the marks found are hemorrhoids if I find them on the bottom of the back-bone, but the marks are not near that vein. Others claim their marks to be from childbearing, when it may be they are in a part of the body contrary to where childbearing marks would be. 2) Devil's marks are most commonly insensible and feel neither pin nor needle thrust through them. 3) The frequent variations and mutations of these marks into several forms, confirms the matter. If a witch hears a month or two before that the Witch Finder (as they call him) is coming, they put out their imps to others to suckle them, even to their own young and tender children; then when the women are searched, they are found to have dry skins and the teats are close to the flesh and barely noticeable. If you watch the witch for twenty-four hours with a diligent eye, so that none of her spirits come in any visible shape to suck her, the next day the woman's teats have extended out to their former size, full of corruption ready to burst. And leave the witch alone one quarter of an hour, and she will have drawn her imps close again; it is proven. Now as for the answer to their tortures, that will be addressed in its due place.

QUERY 7. How can it possibly be that the Devil, being a spirit and wanting no nutriment or substance, should desire to suck any blood? And indeed as he is a spirit he cannot draw any such excrescences, having neither flesh nor bone, nor can be felt.

ANSWER: He seeks not their blood, as if he could not subsist without that nourishment, but he often goes to them and gets it, the more to bring about the witch's damnation and to put her in mind of her covenant and pact with him. And as he is a spirit and prince of the air, he appears to them in any shape whatsoever. The shape is occasioned by the Devil through joining of condensed thickened air together, and many times he does assume shapes of many creatures. But he cannot create anything; that is only proper to God. But in this case of the drawing out of these teats, he does really enter into a body, real, corporeal, substantial, and he forces that body to his desired ends and uses the organs of that body to speak in order to make his compact with the witches, be the creature cat, rat, mouse, etc.

QUERY 8. When these paps are fully discovered, the Witch Finder does not consider that sufficient to convict the witches, but they must be tortured and kept from sleep two or three nights to distract them and make them say anything; which is a way to tame a wild colt, or hawk, etc.

ANSWER: In the infancy of this discovery, watching [sleep deprivation] was not only thought fitting, but recommended in Essex and Suffolk by the magistrates, with this intention only, because the witches being kept awake would be more inclined to call their imps in open view the sooner to suckle them. . . .

QUERY 9. Besides that unreasonable watching, they were extraordinarily forced to walk till their feet were blistered, and forced, through the cruelty, to confess, etc.

ANSWER: . . . They were walked only to keep them awake, and the reason was this. When they did sit in a chair, if they wanted to lie on a couch, then the watchers [custodians] just asked them to sit up and walk about, for indeed when they were allowed to lie down, immediately comes their familiars into the room, and they scare the watchers and hearten the witch. Though contrary to our procedures, many rustic people have heard witches confess, and have misused, spoiled, and abused them. Many witches have suffered at the hands of their neighbors, but it could never be proved against this discoverer that he had a hand in it or consented to it. As for the method of torture, it has been unused by him and others ever since the time the witches were kept from sleep and the judges disallowed both watching and walking.

QUERY 10. But there has been an abominable, inhumane, and unmerciful trial of these poor creatures by tying them, and heaving them into the water—a trial not allowable by law or conscience, and I would like to know the reasons for that.

ANSWER: It is not denied that many witches who had paps were swam [thrown into a body of water] and floated; others that had no paps were tried and sunk, but mark the reasons. 1) For first the Devil's policy is great in persuading many to come of their own accord to be tried, persuading them that their marks are so hidden they shall not be found out, so that some have come ten or twelve miles to be searched of their own accord and hanged for their labor (as one Meggs a Baker did, who lived within seven miles of Norwich and was hanged at Norwich Assizes for witchcraft). Then when they find that the Devil tells them false, they reflect on him, and he, (as forty have confessed) advised them to be swam and tells them they shall sink and be cleared that way. When they are tried that way and float, they see the Devil deceives them again and have so been detected due to his treachery. 2) Whether a witch floated or sunk was never brought in against any of them at their trials as any evidence. 3) King James in his *Demonology* [see doc. 76] says that it is a certain rule that witches deny their baptism when they covenant with the Devil, water being the sole element thereof, and so when they are heaved into the water, the water refuses to receive them into her into bosom, (they being such miscreants to deny their baptism) and suffers them to float, as the froth on the sea, which the water will not receive but casts up and down till it comes to the earthy element, the shore, and there disappears. . . .

QUERY 11. Oh! but if this torturing Witch Catcher can by all or any of these means, wring out a word or two of confession from any of these stupefied, ignorant, unintelligible, poor silly creatures, (though none hear the confession but himself) he will egg her on and put her in fear to confess, telling her else she shall be hanged, but if she does, he will set her at liberty. And so he puts a word into her mouth, and makes such a silly creature confess she knows not what.

ANSWER: He is of a better conscience, and for your better understanding of him, he does thus justify himself to all and declares what confessions (though made by a witch against herself) he does not allow, and does altogether account of no validity, or worthy of credence, and ever did so discount it, and ever likewise shall. 1) He utterly denies that confession of a witch is of any validity when it is drawn from her by any torture or violence whatsoever. . . . 2) He utterly denies that confession of a witch drawn from her by flattery is valid, for example: if you will confess you shall go home; you shall not go to the goal, nor be hanged, etc. 3) He utterly denies that confession of a witch is reliable when she confesses any improbable or impossible feat, such as flying in the air, riding on a broom, etc. 4) He utterly denies a confession of a witch when he interrogates her and words are put into her mouth . . . [as in the following example]. "You have four imps have you not?" She answers affirmatively, "Yes." "Did they not suck you?" "Yes," says she. "Are not their names so, and so?" "Yes," says she. "Did not you send such an imp to kill my child?" "Yes," says she. . . .

ANSWER TO QUERY 12: When a witch is first found with teats, then sequester her from her house, which is only to keep her old associates from her, and so by good counsel she is brought into a sad condition by understanding of the horribleness of her sin and the judgments threatened against her. And knowing the Devil's malice and subtle circumventions, she is brought to remorse and sorrow for complying with Satan so long and disobeying God's sacred commands. She does then desire to unfold her mind with much bitterness, and then without any of the before mentioned tortures or questions put to her, does of her own accord declare what was the occasion of the Devil's appearing to her and tells whether ignorance, pride, anger, malice, etc., was predominant over her. . . .

QUERY 14. All that the Witch Finder does is to fleece the country of their money, and therefore rides and goes to towns to have employment and promises them fair promises, and he may do nothing for it, but he convinces many men that they have so many wizards and so many witches in their town, and so heartens them on to listen to him.

ANSWER: You do him a great deal of wrong in each of these accusations. For, first, he never went to any town or place, but that the people of the town rode, wrote, or sent often for him, and were (for ought he knew) glad of him. 2)

He is a man that does disclaim that ever he detected a witch, or said, "Thou art a witch," until she had been searched and given her own confessions. 3) Lastly, judge how he fleeces the country and enriches himself by considering the vast sum he takes of every town. He demands but twenty shillings a town and does sometimes ride twenty miles for that and has no more for all his charges thither and back again (and it may be he stays a week there) and finds there three or four witches, or if it be but one—still cheap enough. And this is the great sum he takes to maintain his company with three horses.

Questions: What tone does Hopkins express in the reading? Does it appear that Hopkins is generally accepted as a valid witch finder based on his treatise? Why do those who are guilty of witchcraft float when they are "swam," and those who are innocent sink? How do the methods of interrogation and torture in England differ from those on the continent, and how are they similar?

SOURCES

Cornelius Agrippa. *Three Books of Occult Philosophy or Magic.* Trans. Willis F. Whitehead. Chicago: Hahn & Whitehead, 1898.

Apuleius. *The Golden Ass: Being the Metamorphoses of Lucius Apuleius.* Trans. William Adlington. New York: Liveright Publishing Corp., 1927.

Thomas Aquinas. *Summa Contra Gentiles.* Trans. the English Dominican Fathers. London: Burns, Oates & Washbourne, Ltd., 1928.

Thomas Aquinas. *Summa Theologica.* Trans. the English Dominican Fathers. Benzinger Bros., 1947.

Athanasius of Alexandra. *Life of Saint Anthony from Nicene and Post-Nicene Fathers,* second series, Vol. 4, *St. Athanasius: Selected Works and Letters.* Trans. H. Ellershaw. Grand Raids: Wm. B. Eerdmans Publishing Co., 1891.

Saint Bernardino of Siena. *Sermons.* Ed. Nazareno Orlandi. Trans. Helen Josephine Robins. Rev. by Martha Rampton. Siena: Tipografia Sociale, 1920.

Franz Beyerle, ed. *Die Gesetze der Langobaren.* Trans. Martha Rampton. Weimar: H. Böhlaus Nachf, 1947.

Burchard of Worms. *Decretum.* Patrologiae cursus complectus. Series Latina, vol. 140. Ed. J.P. Migne. Paris, 1841–1865.

Samuel Butler, trans. *The Odyssey of Homer.* Toronto: D. Van Nostrand Company, Inc., 1944.

Allen Cabaniss, *Charlemagne's Cousins: Contemporay Lives of Adalard and Wala.* Syracuse, New York: Syracuse University Press, 1967. Reprinted by permission of the publisher.

Caesarius of Heisterback. *Dialogue on Miracles*, 2 vols. Trans. H von E. Scott and C.C. Swinton Bland. London: George Routledge & Sons, Ltd., 1929.

John Calvin. *Institutes of the Christian Religion.* 2 vols., 6th Edition. Trans. John Allen. Philadelphia: Presbyterian Board of Publication, 1813.

Richard Challoner, trans. *Douay-Rheims Bible.* Baltimore: John Murphy Co., 1899.

Chretien de Troys. *Four Arthurian Romances.* Trans. William Wistar Comfort. New York: E.P. Dutton & Co., 1913.

John Chrysostom. "On Christian Doctrine," in *Augustine, Saint, Bishop of Hippo.* Trans. Philip Schaff. Grand Rapids: W.R. Eerdmans Pub. Co., 1886–1889.

Oswald Cockayne, *Leechdoms, Wortcunning, and Starcraft of Early England.* Roll Series, vol. 35. London: Longman, Green, Longman, Roberts, and Green, 1864–6.

Marcus Dods, trans. *The Works of Aurelius Augustine, Bishop, The City of God,* 2 vols. Edinburg: T. & T. Clark, 1872.

Marcus Dods, trans. *The Writings of Justin Martyr and Athenagoras,* Ante-Nicene Christian Library, vol. 2. Edinburg: T. and T. Clark, 1874.

T. Douglas Murray, trans. *Jeanne D'Arc, Maid of Orléans: Deliverer of France: Being the Story of Her Life, Her Achievements, and Her Death as Attested on Oath and Set Forth in the Original Documents*. London: William Heinemann, 1903.

P.E. Dutton, trans. "Agobard of Lyons and the Popular Belief in Weather Magic," in *Carolingian Civilization: A Reader*, 2nd Edition. Ed. P.E. Dutton. Toronto: University of Toronto Press, © 2009. Reprinted with permission of the publisher. Pp. 220-223.

K.A. Eckhardt, MGH, ed. *Leges* 4.1. Trans. Martha Rampton. Hanover: Brepols, 1962.

Formicarius. *The Witch Persecutions*. Translations and Reprints from the Original Sources of European History, vol. 3. Ed. George L. Burr and Johannes Nider. Philadelphia: University of Pennsylvania, 1907.

J. Français. *L'Eglise et la Socellerie*. Trans. Martha Rampton. Paris: Émile Nourry, 1910.

CURSE TABLES AND BINDING SPELLS FROM THE ANCIENT WORLD by John G. Gager (1999). © 1992 by John G. Gager. By permission of Oxford University Press USA.

Ginzburg, Carlo. With a New Preface. Translated by John and Anne C. Tedeschi. *The Night Battles: Witchcraft and Agrarian Cults in the Sixteenth and Seventeenth Centuries*. pp. 147-148, 150, 153-163, 165-166. English translation copyright © 1983 Routledge & Kegan Paul plc. Edition with new preface © 2013 The Johns Hopkins University Press. Reprinted with permission of Johns Hopkins University Press.

Theodore Graebner, trans. *A Commentary on St. Paul's Epistle to the Galatians*. Grand Rapids, 1992.

Gregory of Tours. *History of the Franks*. Trans. Ernest Brehaut. New York: Columbia University Press, 1916.

Lesslie Hall, trans. *Beowulf: An Anglo-Saxon Epic Poem*. Boston, New York, Chicago: D.C. Heath & Co., 1892.

Joseph Hansen. *Quellen un Untersuchungen zur Geschicte des Hexenwahns und der Hexenverfolgung im Mittelalter*. Trans. Martha Rampton. Hildesheim: George Olsm, 1963.

William Hazlitt, trans. *The Table Talk of Martin Luther*. Rev. by Martha Rampton. London: H.G. Bohn, 1857.

Matthew Hopkins. "The Discovery of Witches," in *The Discovery of Witches: A Study of Master Matthew Hopkins Commonly Called Witch Finder Generall*. Ed. Montague Summers. Rev. by Martha Rampton. London: Cayme Press, 1928.

Jacobus de Voragine. *The Golden Legend or Lives of the Saints*, vol. 5. Ed. Frederick Startridge Ellis. Trans. William Caxton. Rev. by Martha Rampton. Philadelphia: Temple Classics, 1900.

James I of England. "Daemonologie," in *Form of a Dialogue, Divided into Three Bookes*. Edinburgh: Robert Walde-Grave, 1597.

John of Salisbury. *Frrivolities of Courtiers and Footprints of Philosophers: Being a Translation of the First, Second, and Third Books and Selections from the Seventh and Eighth Books of the* Policraticus *of John of Salisbury.* Trans. Joseph B. Pike. Minneapolis: University of Minnesota Press, 1938.

POPULAR RELIGION IN LATE SAXON ENGLAND: ELF CHARMS IN CONTEXT by Karen Louise Jolly. Copyright © 1996 by the University of North Carolina Press. Used by permission of the publisher. www.uncpress.unc.edu.

Richard Kieckhefer, trans. *Forbidden Rights: A Necromancer's Manual of the Fifteenth Century.* University Park: Pennsylvania State University Press, 1997. Reprinted with permission of the publisher.

William Kiesel, ed. *Picatrix (Ghayat Al-Hakim).* Trans. Hashem Atallah. Seattle: Ouroboros Press, 2002.

Benjamin G. Kohl and H.C. Erik Midelfort, eds. *Witchcraft: An Abridged Translation of Johann Weyer's* De prestigiis daemonum. Trans. John Shea. Asheville: Pegasus Press, 1988.

S. Liddell MacGregor Mathers, trans. *The Key of Solomon.* Rev. by Martha Rampton. London: George Redway, 1889.

Moses Maimonides. *Guide for the Perplexed*, 2nd Edition. Trans. Michael Friedlander. New York: Routledge & Kegan Paul Ltd., 1904.

Ruth Majercik, trans. *The Chaldean Oracles: Text, Translation and Commentary.* Leiden: The Prometheus Trust, 1989.

Eugene Mason, trans. *Medieval Romances from the Lays of Marie de France.* London: J.M. Dent & Sons, Ltd., 1911.

Hrabanus Maurus. "On the Magic Arts," in *Patrologiae cursus completus*, Latin series, Vol. 100, cols. 1095-1097. Ed. Jacques-Paul Migne. Trans. Martha Rampton.

"Radegund, Queen of the Franks and Abess of Poitiers (ca. 524-587)," in *Sainted Women of the Dark Ages*, Jo Ann McNamara, Gordon Whatley, Eds., pp. 60-105. Copyright, 1992, Duke University Press. All rights reserved. Republished by permission of the copyright holder. www.dukeupress.edu.

John T. McNeil and Helena M. Gamer, trans. *Medieval Handbooks of Penance.* New York: Columbia University Press, 1938.

Thomas Middleton. *The Witch.* Ed. Elizabeth Shafer. London: A & C Black Limited, 1944.

Pico Della Mirandola. *On the Dignity of Man and Other Works.* Ed. Charles Glenn Wallis. Indianapolis: The Bobbs-Merrill Company, Inc., 1965. Reprinted with permission of Hackett Publishing Company, all rights reserved. Pp. 26-29.

William Morris and Eirikr Magnusson, trans. *The Story of the Volsungs.* London: Walter Scott Press, 1888.

Mary M. Mueller, trans. *Saint Caesarius of Arles, Sermons*, Vol. 1. New York: Father of the Church, Inc., 1956.

D.C. Munro, trans. *Laws of Charles the Great*, Translations and Reprints from the Original Sources of European History, Vol. 6.5. Philadelphia: The University of Pennsylvania, 1899.

Monsieur des Niau. *The History of the Devils of Loudun, The Alleged Possession of the Ursuline Nuns, and The Trial and Execution of Urbain Grandier, Told By an Eye-Witness*, collectanea adamantea 21. Trans. Edmund Goldsmid. Edinburgh: Privately printed, 1887.

A.D. Nock, trans. "Some Latin Spells," in *Folk-Lore* 85. 1920.

Robert O'Brien, trans. *The Sentences of Peter Lombard.*, vol. 2. Rev. by Martha Rampton. Toronto: Pontifical Institute of Medieval Studies, 2007-2010.

John Payne, trans. *The Decameron of Giovanni Boccaccio*. Rev. by Martha Rampton. New York: Walter J. Black, Inc., 1903.

B.P. Pratten, Marcus Dods, and Thomas Smith, trans. "The Clementine Recognitions," in *Translations of the Writings of the Christian Fathers*, vol. 3. Edinburg: T. and T. Clark, 1871.

Regino of Prum. *De Dynodallibus causis et desciplinis ecclesiasticis* 2.371. Ed. F.G.A. Wasserschleben. Trans. Martha Rampton. Leipzig: Engelmann, 1840. Reprint, Graz: Akademishe Druck-u. Verlagsanstalt, 1964.

Timothy Reuter, trans. *The Annals of Fulda*. Manchester: Manchester University Press, 1992. Reprinted with permission of the publisher.

Edward Ridley, trans. *The Pharsalia of Lucan*, second edition. Rev. by Martha Rampton. New York: Longmans, Green, and Co., 1905.

Alexander Roberts. *A Treatise of Witchcraft*. Rev. by Martha Rampton. London: Samuel Man, 1616.

Alexander Roberts, trans. "Sulpitius Severus on the Life of St. Martin," in *The Works of Sulpitius Severus, A Select Library of Nicene and Post-Nicene Fathers of the Christian Church*, second series, Vol. 11. New York: The Christian Literature Company; Oxford and London: Parker & Company, 1894.

Reginald Scot. *The Discoverie of Witchcraft*. Rev. by Martha Rampton. London: Elliot Stock, 1886; rpt. 1584 First Edition.

Randy A. Scott and Jean Bodin, trans. *On the Demon-Mania of Witches*. Toronto: Centre for Reformation and Renaissance Studies, 2001.

S.P. Scott, trans. *The Visigothic Code (Forum Judicum)*. Boston: The Boston Book Company, 1910.

A.M. Sellar, trans. *Bede's Ecclesiastical History of England*. London: George Bell and Sons, 1907.

Seneca. *Two Tragedies of Seneca: Medea and the Daughters of Troy*. Trans. Ella Isabel Harris. Boston: Houghton Mifflin and Co., 1899.

William Shakespeare. *Macbeth*, Riverside Literature Series, vol. 106. Ed. Richard Grant White. Boston: Houghton, Mifflin and Co., 1897.

Shakespeare. *A Midsummer's Night Dream*. New York: Doubleday, Page & Co., 1908.

Walter W. Skeat, ed. *Aelfric's Lives of the Saints*, Early English Texts Society, 2 vols. Trans. Ms Cunning and Ms Wilkinson. London: Trubner, 1881-1900.

Rachel Stone and Charles West, trans. *The Divorce of King Lothar and Queen Theutberga: Hincmar of Rheims's* De divortio. Manchester: Manchester University Press, 2016.

Montague Summers, trans. *The Geography of Witchcraft, History of Civilization.* New York: Alfred A. Knopf, Inc., 1927.

Montague Summers, trans. *Malleus Maleficarum.* New York: Benjamin Blom, Inc., 1928.

Arthur Edward Waite, trans. *The Chemical Treatise of Thomas Norton, The Englishman, Called Believe-Me, or The Ordinal of Alchemy.* The Hermetic Museum, vol. 2. London: James Elliot and Co., 1893.

K.G.T. Webster and W.A. Neilson, trans. *Two Middle English Poems.* Boston: Houghton Mifflin Company, 1916.

Albert Weminghoff, ed. *Monumenta Germaniae Historica. Conilia Aevi Karolini 1.2.* Trans. Martha Rampton. Hannover: Hahnsche Buchhandlung, 1979.

Newport D. J. White, trans. *St. Patrick: His Writings and Life*, Translations of Christian Literature, series 5, Lives of the Celtic Saints, Society for Promoting Christian Knowledge. London: Richard Clay & Sons, Limited; New York: The McMillian Company, 1920.

Paola Zabelli, trans. *The Speculum astronomiae and its Enigma: Astrology, Theology, and Science in Albert Magnus and his Contemporaries.* Boston Studies in the Philosophy of Science, vol. 135. Dordrecht: Kluwer Academic Publishers, 1992.

"News From Scotland," in *A Collection of Rare and Curious Tracts on Witchcraft and the Second Sight.* Edinburg: Thomas Webster, 1820.

The Sermons of M. John Calvin upon the Fifth Book of Moses called Deuteronomy. London: Henry Middleton, 1583. The Banner of Trust Facsimile Reprint, 1987, revised.

FIGURES

Figure 1.1: Image copyright © Metropolitan Museum of Art. Image source: Art Resource, NY.

Figure 1.2: CURSE TABLES AND BINDNG SPELLS FROM THE ANCIENT WORLD by John G. Gager (1999): Fig. 10 (p. 72). © 1992 by John G. Gager. By permission of Oxford University Press USA.

Figure 2.1: © Trustees of the British Museum.

Figure 3.1: Utrecht University Library, Ms. 32, fol. 22r.

Figure 4.1: © Museum of Cultural History, University of Oslo, Norway/ Ove Holst. CC-BY-SA 4.0

Figure 5.1: bpk Bildagentur/Staatlich Museen/Joerg P. Anders/Art Resource, NY.

Figure 6.1: Woodcut by Pierre Boaistuau, *Histoires prodigieuses et memorables extraictes de plusieurs fameux autheurs Grec et Latins, sacrez et prophanes,* vol. 1. Paris, 1598. Houghton Library at Harvard University.

Figure 6.2: Jean Berjon., "Description et Figure du Sabbat des Sorciers," in Pierre de Lancre, *Tableau de l'inconstance des mauvais anges et demons, ou il est amplement traicté des sorciers & de la sorcellerie.* Paris, 1612. Used by permission of the Folger Shakespeare Library, CC–BY-SA 4.0 International.

INDEX OF TOPICS

Topics are listed by document number. The index is intended to be used in tandem with the Table of Contents. The topics "demon," "devil," "Devil/Satan," "magic/magician," and "witch/witchcraft" are common to almost all of the readings and are not listed in the index below.

READINGS IN MEDIEVAL CIVILIZATIONS AND CULTURES
Series Editor: Paul Edward Dutton

"Readings in Medieval Civilizations and Cultures is in my opinion
the most useful series being published today."
—William C. Jordan, Princeton University